THE PICTURE PERFECT ENCYCLOPEDIA OF

COOKING

Nearly 2000 recipes and full-color illustrations

An Easy to use, Illustrated Guide to Creative Cooking
with 78 pictorial step-by-step guides to gourmet dishes

CULINARY GUILD PRESS

TABLE OF CONTENTS

AN EDITOR'S NOTE TO THE HOME CHEF:

You will find The Picture Perfect Encyclopedia of Cooking delightfully easy to use in the preparation of some extraordinary and pleasing foods.

The book constitutes a gourmet cooking guide that will teach you secrets and techniques of professional chefs. With it you can produce hundreds of original as well as traditional recipes for every occasion. The array of recipes includes a world-wide selection of ethnic dishes as well as foods common to the North American household.

You will be particularly pleased with the 78 "Look 'n Cook" illustrated, step-by-step guides to specific and complex dishes. These guides teach basic culinary skills and will direct you with ease through difficult or unusual recipes and cooking techniques. Each illustration relates to an essential step in the preparation and cooking method and is clearly explained in the accompanying text. The guides will make it possible for you to create gourmet dishes on your first attempt.

You will find in these pages recipes that are simple and easy to prepare and others that require considerably more time and skill and are more complex in their preparation.

Each recipe is coded with three symbols to indicate the ease of preparation, the relative time required, and the relative costs involved.

A single gold coin indicates an inexpensive dish; two coins a more costly recipe.

One blue star marks a simple recipe to follow; two stars indicate a more complex dish to prepare.

A single red hourglass indicates less than one hour preparation time; two hourglasses, one to three hours; and three hourglasses indicate more than three hours of preparation needed for the dish.

Soups

Clear soups, like consommé, are light on the palate and ideal for formal dinner parties. Hearty soups—broths, purées and brews packed with chunks of meat, fish, rice, pasta or vegetables—can easily be meals in themselves. Creamy soups, thickened by the addition of cream, egg yolk or flour, demand greater care in their making

Stocks

A full-bodied flavorsome stock is the basis of so many good dishes but especially of soups — even packet and canned soups can be pepped up and enriched by stock — sauces, gravies and many casserole dishes.

Most of us use ready-made stock preparations like the cubes just to save time, but they are often highly seasoned and very salty, so exercise care when adding seasonings. But if you take the trouble to make your own stock, you'll get a lot more satisfaction from a dish — and a tastier one as well.

There's an economic stock, largely using whatever is on hand, a white or chicken base for light-colored soups and sauces, a brown base for consommé, dark soups, sauces and gravy, and a fish base.

A really concentrated bone stock sets as a firm gelatin when cold, and slow and lengthy cooking is the only way to concentrate the flavors.

Unlike soups to which almost anything can be added, stock must be clear — vital when making consomme or aspic (savory gelatin) — so avoid using starchy foods like rice and potatoes, or thickened liquids, which will turn it cloudy; and leave out strongly-flavored vegetables like turnip and cabbage, as well as mutton bones, which will give a bitter taste.

Make as large a pan of stock as possible (a pressure cooker will save time and fuel) and, if not using at once, keep stock in the refrigerator for a couple of days — otherwise boil up daily. Fish stock, however, should always be used the same day.

Household Stock

2 lbs. raw or cooked beef bones
1 onion
1 carrot
1 branch celery (optional)
8½ cups cold water
1 bouquet garni
1 teaspoon salt
6 peppercorns

1 Wash the bones. Peel, wash and roughly chop the onion and carrot; wash and chop the celery.

2 Put the bones in a large stewpan, add the water, bring to a boil and remove any scum that rises to the surface.

3 Add the chopped vegetables, bouquet garni and seasonings to the pan. Reduce the heat and simmer, with the pan lid on, for about 4 hours.

4 Strain the stock and then let cool. When cold remove the fat from the surface.

Makes about 6¼ cups

Tip: additions to this stock can include tomato paste, meat trimmings and leftovers (but not liver), bacon rinds and cooked ham bones.

Brown Stock

2 lbs. raw beef marrow bones or knuckle of veal bones
1 lb. lean stewing beef
2 onions
2 carrots
1 branch celery
8½ cups cold water
1 bouquet garni
1 teaspoon salt
6 peppercorns

1 Wash the bones and meat and dry on absorbent paper. Cut the meat into about 1-inch cubes.

2 Peel, wash and chop the onions and carrots; wash and chop the celery.

3 Put the chopped bones, cubes of beef and the chopped onion in a roasting pan and bake in a moderate oven 350°F. until well browned.

4 Strain off any fat in the pan, then transfer the bones, beef and onion to a large stewpan. Add the water, sliced carrots and celery, bouquet garni and seasonings. Bring to a boil, remove any scum, reduce the heat, cover the pan, and simmer 5 hours.

5 Strain the stock and then let cool. When cold remove the fat from the surface

Makes about 6¼ cups.

White Stock

2 lbs. raw knuckle of veal, (chopped), or stewing veal
10 cups cold water
½ teaspoon lemon juice
1 onion
1 carrot
1 bouquet garni
1 teaspoon salt
6 peppercorns

1 Wash the veal bones, then put them in a large stewpan with the water and lemon juice. Bring to a boil and skim off any scum that rises to the surface.

2 Meanwhile, peel, wash and slice the onion and carrot.

3 Add the sliced vegetables, bouquet garni, salt and peppercorns to the pan of bones, bring back to a boil, then reduce the heat and simmer, with the lid on, for about 5 hours.

4 Strain the stock and then let cool. When cold remove the fat from the surface.

Makes about 6¼ cups

Chicken Stock

1-2 raw or cooked chicken carcasses and bones
½ lb. chicken giblets, excluding the liver
8½ cups cold water
2 onions
2 carrots
1 bouquet garni
1 teaspoon salt
6 peppercorns

1 Wash the chicken carcasses, bones and giblets. Put them in a large stewpan, add the water, bring to a boil and remove any scum that rises to the surface.

2 Meanwhile, peel, wash and slice the onions and carrots.

3 Add the sliced vegetables and seasonings to the pan, bring back to a boil, then reduce the heat and simmer, with the lid on, for about 3 hours.

4 Strain the stock and then let cool. When cold remove the fat from the surface.

Makes about 6¼ cups

Variation: to make turkey or game stock, substitute the appropriate carcasses, giblets and feet, if used, for the chicken ingredients.

Fish Stock

2 lbs. fresh fish heads, or fish bones and trimmings
1 carrot (optional)
1 onion
6 cups cold water, or half water and half dry white wine
1 teaspoon salt
4 peppercorns
1 bouquet garni

1 Wash the fish heads or bones and trimmings well. Peel and cut up the carrot, if used, and the onion.

2 Put the fish pieces in a large pan, add the water, bring to a boil and skim the surface. Add the vegetables, salt, peppercorns and bouquet garni to the pan, bring back to a boil and cover. Reduce the heat and simmer slowly for about 40 minutes when the stock should be reduced.

3 Strain the stock through clean cheesecloth or a fine strainer, cover and cool; refrigerate until required.

Makes about 4½ cups

Tip: fish stock should always be used the same day it is made.

Stock, other than fish, can be frozen up to 6 months. Strain it, cool and skim off any fat. Boiling stock down to one-third its volume concentrates it, and it can then be frozen as single cubes in ice trays and diluted with water for use.

Bouquet Garni

Many recipes call for the use of a bouquet garni, the French name for a small bunch of herbs, either fresh or dried, which is used to flavor dishes. The traditional bouquet garni is made up of a bay leaf, a sprig or two of parsley and thyme, and a few peppercorns, all tied in a small piece of cheesecloth.

It doesn't matter too much which herbs are used so long as they are aromatic, so you can experiment with different mixtures, incorporating herbs like chervil, basil, rosemary and tarragon.

Ready-made bouquet garnis in cheesecloth or paper sachets are available, but the paper ones tend to disintegrate with long cooking.

Hearty Soups

Mulligatawny

Created in the days of the British in India, this soup is basically a rich meat stock flavored with curry, and can be made with any meat.

1 lb. lean breast of lamb
1 large onion
1 medium carrot
1 small green tart apple
2 tablespoons oil
1 tablespoon curry powder
salt and pepper
2 tablespoons flour
6 cups brown stock
¾ cup milk
1 teaspoon cornstarch
1 tablespoon cold water
1 teaspoon lemon juice

1 Wipe and trim lamb of excess fat; cut into ½-inch wide strips. Peel and slice the onion and carrot; peel, core and slice the apple.

2 Heat the oil in a large pan. When hot, brown the lamb all over. Take out and add the sliced vegetables and apple and cook, stirring, for about 5 minutes. Stir in the curry powder and cook for a further 2 minutes, then blend in the flour. Add the stock, bring to a boil and return the meat to the pan. Cover and simmer gently for about 1½ hours.

3 Take out the meat and any bones. Rub the liquid through a strainer or purée in a blender. Return the purée to a clean pan. Stir in the milk and reheat but do not boil. Blend the cornstarch with the cold water, stir into the soup and heat nearly to boiling point till thick. Check the seasoning and serve.

Serves 6

3

Beef and Carrot Soup

1 small onion
1 lb. carrots
1 medium potato
3 tablespoons butter
½ teaspoon salt
freshly ground black pepper
½ teaspoon sugar
3 cups brown stock
1 tablespoon chopped parsley
1 teaspoon chopped chervil or
  marjoram

1 Peel and chop the onion; peel and dice the carrots and potato.

2 Melt the butter in a heavy saucepan and add the carrots, onion and potato. Add the salt, pepper and sugar. Cover the pan and cook over low heat for 15 minutes.

3 Add the stock and bring to a boil. Lower the heat, cover the pan and cook for a further 15 minutes. Rub the soup through a strainer or purée in a blender.

4 Reheat until hot, then serve, sprinkling on the chopped herbs.

Serves 4

Fresh Pea Soup

1 head (Boston) lettuce
½ cup butter
1 lb. shelled fresh peas
½ teaspoon salt
1 teaspoon sugar
4 cups chicken stock
freshly ground black pepper

1 Wash the lettuce, drain well, tear the leaves into pieces.

2 Heat the butter in a saucepan, add the lettuce pieces, shelled peas, salt and sugar. Cover the pan, reduce the heat and let the vegetables cook gently over low heat for about 10 minutes. Stir in the stock,

cover and simmer 10 minutes more or until the peas are tender.

3 Purée the soup by rubbing through a strainer or purée in a blender. Return the pea purée to a clean saucepan, add black pepper to taste and heat again until just simmering. Serve at once.

Serves 4

Minestrone

1 carrot
4 potatoes
1 small white cabbage
½ bunch celery
1 cup shelled fresh peas
5 tomatoes
1 clove garlic
4 slices bacon
2 onions
2 tablespoons oil
8½ cups white or brown stock
2-3 tablespoons chopped mixed
  herbs
salt and pepper
¼ cup macaroni
grated Parmesan cheese

1 Peel and dice the carrots and potatoes; trim and cut up the cabbage and celery in small pieces. Wash them well. Skin the tomatoes, then cut them in half and scoop out the seeds. Cut the tomato pulp into small cubes. Peel and crush the garlic. Cut the bacon into strips. Peel and chop the onions.

2 Heat the oil in a large pan and when hot sauté the bacon, onion, carrots, cabbage, celery and tomatoes. Add the stock with the crushed garlic, chopped mixed herbs and salt and pepper to taste. Cover and cook for 1 hour over low heat. Then add the diced potato and the peas and continue cooking for a further 15 minutes.

3 During this time, cook the macaroni in a pan of boiling salted water for about 15 minutes or until just tender. Drain and set aside.

4 When the soup is cooked, add the macaroni and serve immediately with grated Parmesan cheese separately.

Serves 6

Italian Egg Soup

Zuppa Pavese is the Italian name for this very nourishing soup. Instead of poaching the eggs in the stock as we do here, the eggs may be broken into the individual bowls and the boiling stock then poured on. However, the eggs tend not to be cooked sufficiently this way. It is such a substantial soup that only a light main course should follow.

2 cups brown stock
2 cups chicken stock
4 slices sandwich bread
8 very fresh eggs
2 tablespoons oil
¼ cup grated Parmesan cheese
2 tablespoons chopped mixed
  herbs

1 Mix the 2 stocks together in a large pan and put over low heat. Cut the slices of bread into small cubes.

2 Break the eggs, one by one, into a saucer and slide them carefully down the side of the pan into the stock. Draw the white back onto the yolk with a fork to get neat, poached eggs.

3 While the eggs are poaching, heat the oil in a skillet and fry the cubes of bread in it. Then drain them.

4 Put 2 poached eggs into each soup bowl. Pour in the stock and divide the cubes of bread, the Parmesan and the mixed herbs between each; serve.

Serves 4

Minestrone is one of Italy's best known soups and easily a meal in itself. Regional variations are many, ranging from the addition of fresh basil and pork to substituting a goat's milk cheese for Parmesan

Look 'n Cook Farmhouse Soup

1 Ingredients: leeks, carrots, turnips, celery, peas, beans, bacon, potatoes, cabbage, butter **2** Peel the carrots and turnips, trim the leeks and dice **3** Soften the vegetables in the butter **4** Moisten with water or stock. Add the bacon and shredded cabbage; season with salt and pepper and bring to a boil **5** String and

chop the beans **6** Peel and dice the potatoes; place in a bowl of cold water to remove excess starch **7** Drain the potatoes, then add all the vegetables to the pan

8 Take out the bacon and dice; put in tureen **9** Serve the soup, with the croûtons and grated cheese separately

Farmhouse Soup

2 carrots
2 turnips
whites of 2 leeks
2 branches celery
$\frac{1}{2}$ green cabbage
$\frac{1}{4}$ cup butter
1 lb. bacon, thickly sliced
9 cups white or chicken stock
salt and pepper
1$\frac{1}{4}$ cups string beans
2 potatoes
1$\frac{1}{4}$ cups shelled peas
$\frac{3}{4}$ cup grated Gruyère cheese

1 Peel the carrots and turnips, and wash them. Wash the whites of the leeks and the celery. Cut them all into small cubes. Wash and cut the cabbage into thin strips.

2 Melt the butter in a large pan. Put in the prepared vegetables and soften on low heat for 10 minutes; stirring from time to time.

3 Wash the bacon in cold water, then put it into a saucepan. Cover with cold water, bring to a boil and simmer for 10 minutes on low heat. Then drain and rinse in cold water.

4 Add the stock to the vegetables, then add the bacon, cabbage and salt and pepper. Bring to a boil, then reduce the heat, cover and simmer very gently for about 1$\frac{1}{4}$ hours.

5 Remove the 'strings' from the beans, wash them and cut into pieces about 1$\frac{1}{2}$ inches in length. Peel the potatoes. Wash and cut them into tiny cubes. Cover with water and let soak.

6 About 20 minutes before the end of the cooking time, drain the potatoes. Add them to the soup with the peas and the green beans. Leave to finish cooking.

7 Heat a soup tureen. Put the grated Gruyère cheese into a bowl. Drain the bacon, cut into cubes and put into the tureen. Pour on the rest of the soup. Serve the soup with croûtons and the Gruyère cheese served separately.

Serves 4

Rose-colored Cauliflower Soup

1 small cauliflower
3 potatoes
small bunch of chervil
5$\frac{1}{2}$ cups salted water
2 tablespoons tomato paste
salt and pepper
4 tablespoons rice flour
2$\frac{1}{4}$ cups milk
2 tablespoons butter

1 Wash the cauliflower and divide it into small florets. Peel and dice the potatoes.

2 Bring the salted water to a boil. Add the cauliflower and diced potatoes to the water and boil gently for 30 minutes. Cool a little, then rub through a strainer or purée in a blender.

3 Return the purée to the pan and heat, mixing in the tomato paste and seasoning with salt and pepper.

4 Mix the rice flour to a smooth paste with a little of the milk and then mix in the rest. Add to the soup. Cook for 10 minutes more over low heat, stirring constantly. Wash, dry and chop the chervil.

5 Put the butter in a heated tureen, pour on the soup, sprinkle on the chervil and serve.

Serves 6

Rose-colored Cauliflower Soup

8

Belgian Leek Soup — nourishing and one of the simplest soups

Belgian Leek Soup

3 tablespoons butter
½ lb. leeks, or 4 onions
1 lb. potatoes
6 cups beef stock
1 teaspoon salt

½ cup light cream or milk
4-6 slices toasted French bread

1 Trim and wash the leeks well, then slice or peel and slice the onions. Peel and dice the potatoes.

2 Heat the butter in a large pan, add the prepared leeks or onions, and sauté gently for 3 minutes. Add the diced potatoes, beef stock and salt, and bring to a boil. Cover with a lid, reduce the heat and simmer for 40 minutes, stirring occasionally.

3 When ready to serve, stir in the cream or milk. Place a slice of toasted bread in each soup bowl and pour on the hot soup.

Serves 4–6

9

Normandy Soup

giblets of 2 chickens
½ cup butter
salt and pepper
8½ cups white or chicken stock
1 small bouquet garni
½ lb. green beans
2 zucchini
4 small carrots
2 turnips
3 potatoes
1 small branch celery
white part of 2 leeks
1 onion
2 tomatoes
few lettuce leaves
1 cup light cream

1 Put the washed giblets into cold water, bring to a boil and drain. Heat 4 tablespoons butter in a stewpan and lightly fry the giblets in it. Add the salt, pepper, stock and bouquet garni. Bring to a boil, cover with the lid, reduce the heat and simmer for 20 minutes.

2 During this time, remove the 'strings' from the beans and cut them into small pieces. Peel the zucchini, the carrots, the turnips and the potatoes, and dice them. Wash the celery and chop it into tiny slices. Wash and slice the white part of the leeks. Peel and chop the onion.

3 Skin and quarter the tomatoes, remove seeds, then cut the pulp into small pieces. Wash and dry the lettuce and shred.

4 Melt the rest of the butter in a saucepan and cook all the vegetables in it until they begin to color. When the giblets have cooked for 20 minutes, add the vegetables to them and continue simmering for a further hour. Then heat the soup tureen.

5 Remove the bouquet garni. Put the cream into the hot tureen, whisk in the soup and serve.

Serves 6

Tip: During the winter months the green beans can be replaced by soaked, dried navy beans and the zucchini left out, or frozen vegetables can be used.

Portuguese Lobster Soup

2 large onions
2 large carrots
3 medium potatoes
3 cloves garlic
4 cups water
1 cup dry white wine
1 teaspoon salt
12 peppercorns
2-lb. live lobster
2 tablespoons oil
1 cup tomato paste
¾ cup long grain rice
1 tablespoon finely chopped
  parsley
½ teaspoon ground coriander
freshly ground pepper
2 tablespoons brandy

1 Peel and finely chop the onions and carrots; peel and dice the potatoes; peel and crush the garlic cloves.

2 Put the water, white wine, half the chopped onions and carrots, the potatoes, salt and peppercorns in a large saucepan and bring to a boil. Reduce the heat and simmer for 30 minutes. Then put in the lobster and simmer again for about 30 minutes or until the lobster is cooked.

3 Heat the oil in another large saucepan until hot; add the remaining chopped onions and carrots and fry until lightly browned. Stir in the tomato paste and take the pan off the heat.

4 Take out the cooked lobster, strain the cooking liquor and reserve. Split the lobster in half lengthwise, crack the claws and take out the meat from the tail shell and the claws; cut it into ½-inch pieces. Break the lobster shell into pieces (use either a hammer or nut crackers), put them into a pan with the reserved cooking liquor and simmer for 20 minutes.

5 Strain the liquor again and stir into the tomato mixture. Add the raw rice, parsley, coriander, pepper and garlic and simmer for 30 minutes. Stir in the lobster meat pieces and brandy and simmer for another 5 minutes. Check the seasoning and serve at once.

Serves 8–10

Traditional Meatball Soup

6 cups brown stock
¼ lb. ground beef
½ teaspoon salt
freshly ground pepper
3 tablespoons finely chopped
  parsley
2 tablespoons oil
1 teaspoon paprika
½ cup long grain rice
2 cloves garlic
3 tablespoons vinegar

1 Put the stock into a large pan and bring to simmering point. Mix the beef with the salt, pepper and 2 tablespoons of the chopped parsley. Form into small balls about 1 inch in diameter.

2 Add the meatballs to the stock and simmer 15 minutes.

3 Heat the oil in a small pan, stir in the paprika and cook for 2 minutes. Stir this into the soup.

4 Add the rice to the soup, cover the pan and simmer 15 minutes or until the rice is tender. Stir in the rest of the parsley, garlic and vinegar. Serve at once.

Serves 6

Normandy Soup—a hearty broth flavored with chicken

Look 'n Cook French Onion Soup

1 Ingredients: onions, butter, flour, stock, wine, bread, eggs, cheese, salt and pepper 2 Peel and chop onions 3 Brown onions in half the butter 4 Stir in the flour till it browns 5 Add liquid, garlic, salt and pepper, then simmer 6 Toast the slices of bread 7 Poach the eggs and set aside in a bowl of warm water

12

till required **8** When the soup is cooked, divide among individual flameproof bowls **9** Place a poached egg in each soup bowl **10** Butter the toasted slices of bread and sprinkle with grated cheese **11** Put a slice of bread in each bowl **12** Brown the cheese under a hot broiler

French Onion Soup

½ lb. onions
1 clove garlic
⅓ cup butter
2 tablespoons flour
3¼ cups stock
1 cup dry white wine
salt and pepper
4 large slices white bread
scant 1 cup grated cheese
¼ cup white vinegar
4 eggs

1 Peel and chop the onions. Peel and crush the garlic.

2 Melt half the butter in a sauté pan. Add the onions and cook them. When they are golden, add the flour and stir with a wooden spoon until the flour browns.

3 Add the stock and the wine, mixing in well. Add the crushed garlic. Cook for about 40 minutes. Adjust the seasoning without stinting on the pepper.

4 Meanwhile, cut the bread into rounds. Toast them or dry in a low oven.

5 Boil some water in a saucepan. Add the vinegar. Break the eggs one by one into a cup, put each carefully into the pan and let them poach just enough to allow them to be removed without breaking. Keep them warm in a dish containing warm water.

6 When the soup is ready, divide it among flameproof bowls.

7 Place a poached egg in each dish. Butter the slices of bread and sprinkle with grated cheese. Put a slice of bread in each bowl and brown quickly under a hot broiler (the eggs must not continue to cook). Serve piping hot.

Serves 4

Tip: This is a good dish for a small dinner party; if preferred, the poached eggs can be omitted from the soup.

French Onion Soup

Red Pepper and Tomato Soup

1 onion
2 medium red peppers
1 large tomato
1 large leek
4 tablespoons butter
1 tablespoon finely chopped parsley
4½ cups chicken stock
salt and pepper
¼ cup flour

1 Peel and chop the onion. Cut the red pepper in half, remove the seeds and white membrane and chop. Skin and cut the tomato in half, scoop out the seeds and chop the pulp roughly. Trim the outer leaves of the leek and cut off the root; cut in half, wash well, then slice thinly.

2 Heat half the butter in a large pan, put in the onions, red pepper and leek and cook gently until the onions are soft and translucent. Add the chopped tomato and parsley and cook for about 2 minutes.

3 Pour in the stock, add salt and pepper, bring to a boil, cover the pan, reduce the heat and simmer for about 15 minutes or until the vegetables are tender.

4 Soften the remaining butter and, using a fork, blend with the flour to make kneaded butter, then stir this into the soup. Bring to a boil, stirring until the soup thickens. Serve at once.

Serves 6

This classic country hotpot of meat and vegetables in broth hails from France where it is called pot-au-feu. *A two-in-one dish — serve the broth first, with toast, then follow with the beef and vegetables. Turn page for the recipe and step-by-step guide for Hotpot Soup plus a variation using four different meats*

Look 'n Cook Hotpot Soup

1 Tie the beef with string so it holds its shape during cooking 2 Put the beef and bones in a large pot with the water 3 Peel and quarter the carrots and turnips; halve the leeks and celery 4 Add the vegetables, bouquet garni and seasonings and cook 5 and 6 Wrap up the marrowbone, add to pot and cook

Hotpot Soup (Pot-au-feu)

4½ lbs. stewing beef, in one piece
1-2 beef bones
13 cups water
1 bouquet garni
1½ lbs. carrots
1 lb. turnips
1½ lbs. leeks
1 bunch celery
2 large onions
2 cloves garlic
4 cloves
1 large marrowbone, about 4
   inches long

1 Tie the meat with thin string so it holds its shape during cooking. Place it in a large pot together with the beef bones. Add all the water except for ¼ cup and bring slowly to a boil with the lid off.

2 Meanwhile, if using fresh herbs for the bouquet garni, tie them together. Peel the onions and garlic; stud the onion with the cloves.

3 Peel and quarter the carrots lengthwise; peel and quarter the turnips. Trim and cut away the roots of the leeks, then cut in half and wash in several changes of water, fanning out the green stems, so all the dirt is removed. Trim the root end of the celery and discard the green leaves; then quarter and tie the pieces together with the leeks.

4 When the surface of the liquid is covered with scum, take the pot off the heat; pour in the reserved water and skim at once. Return the pot to the heat, cover with a lid and simmer slowly for 1 hour. Then add the prepared vegetables, bouquet garni, garlic, onions, salt and pepper, and cook slowly for a further 1¾ hours.

5 Wrap the marrowbone in cheesecloth and tie with string; this will stop the marrow from slipping out of the bone. Put the wrapped bone in the pot 15 minutes before the end of cooking.

6 When the meat is cooked, take it out of the pot, remove the string, slice and place on a heated serving dish. Drain the vegetables, discarding the bouquet garni, and arrange around the meat; keep hot.

7 Slice the bread and toast on both sides. Meanwhile, lift out and unwrap the marrowbone, scoop out the marrow, then spread on the hot toast.

8 Serve the broth separately with the toast, followed by the platter of meat and vegetables. Traditional accompaniments include dill pickles, pickled onions, mustard and horseradish sauce.

Serves 6–8

Four-meat Hotpot Soup

3 lbs. stewing beef
1 lb. salt pork
1 Cornish hen with liver
1 knuckle of veal, with meat on
21 cups water
coarse salt
pepper
1½ lbs. carrots
4 onions
3 cloves garlic
4 cloves
1½ lbs. leeks
1 celeriac root
1-2 bulbs of fennel
1 bouquet garni

For the forcemeat roll:
½ lb. salt pork
1 shallot
3 cloves garlic
4 cups fresh white breadcrumbs
¼ cup brown stock
1 egg

1 Wipe the various meats and derind the salt pork. Tie the beef with string. Split the hen in half and wash the liver. Put the water in a large pot, add a good handful of coarse salt and some pepper; put in the beef, bring to a boil, with the lid off, remove the scum from the surface, cover, reduce the heat and simmer for 1 hour.

2 Meanwhile, peel the carrots, onions and garlic; stud the onions with the cloves. Trim and wash the leeks, celeriac root and fennel; cut them in quarters.

3 When the beef has cooked for 1 hour, add the knuckle of veal, the hen and salt pork. Bring to a boil again, skim the surface, cover and reduce the heat and cook for 1 hour longer.

4 Meanwhile, prepare the forcemeat roll. Cut the salt pork into tiny pieces; peel and finely chop the shallot and remaining garlic. Chop the liver. Put all the forcemeat ingredients in a mixing bowl, moisten with the stock and mix together well. Season well with salt and pepper.

5 Sprinkle a piece of cheesecloth with a little flour. Place the forcemeat in the center, fold over the cloth and mold into a sausage shape. Tie the ends with string.

6 After 2 hours of cooking, put the forcemeat roll into the pot together with the prepared vegetables, garlic and bouquet garni and simmer for 1 hour longer.

7 Wrap the marrowbones in cheesecloth and tie securely; put in the pot about 15 minutes before the end of cooking.

8 Serve the Four-meat Hotpot as for Hotpot Soup (see previous page), with the broth served separately, the meats carved into portions on one platter, with the toasted slices of bread, and the vegetables on another with slices of forcemeat around them.

Serves 6–8

Four-meat Hotpot Soup — a satisfying dish for family appetites

Cockie-Leekie

3 leeks
1 branch celery
1 carrot
2 lbs. chicken
6¼ cups chicken stock
2 tablespoons butter
salt and pepper
2 tablespoons finely chopped
  parsley

1 Trim the outer leaves of the leeks to within 2 inches of the white stems and cut away the roots. Split the leeks in half lengthwise, wash them well, then cut into chunks. Wash and cut the celery into ½-inch lengths; peel and slice the carrot.

2 Wipe the chicken and wash its giblets well. Put both into a large deep pan, add the stock and simmer for 1 hour or until the chicken is tender. Discard the giblets; take out the chicken, remove the skin and take the meat off the bones. Leave the broth to cool, then chill and remove the fat from the surface.

3 Heat the butter in a large pan, put in the leeks, celery and carrot; add salt and pepper to taste. Cover the pan and cook gently until the leeks are soft but not colored (about 10 minutes). Add the chicken broth and the pieces of chicken meat, increase the heat, cover the pan and simmer for about 15 minutes. Serve at once, garnished with chopped parlsey.

Tip: This soup is improved by making the day before and chilling overnight; then remove the fat the next day and complete the recipe.

Serves 6–8

For this traditional Scottish soup, a chicken (cockie) is poached in stock, the meat taken off the bones, returned to the broth with leeks (leekie); celery and carrot may also be added to vary the flavor

Bacon
Crumble crisply-fried slices and sprinkle over soup.

Pasta
Either cook in the soup toward the end of cooking or cook separately and add to the hot soup.

Croûtes
Remove crusts from slices of French bread, spread with butter (flavored if liked) or grated cheese on one side. Bake until crisp and golden.

Croûtons
Remove crusts from slices of bread, cut into $\frac{1}{4}$–$\frac{1}{2}$-inch cubes and either fry in hot butter or oil until golden and crisp, or toast them.

Melba Toast
Remove crusts from $\frac{1}{4}$-inch thick slices of white bread. Toast until a pale brown, then cut through the middle of each to give extra-thin slices. Toast again, white sides up, until golden. Or bake the thinly-cut slices in the bottom of a very slow oven until very crisp and curled; then brown under broiler.

Sippets
Remove crusts from slices of bread, cut into large triangles and bake in a slow oven till dry and very crisp.

Dumplings or Meatballs
Add either plain or flavored ones to the soup toward the end of cooking and simmer for about 20 minutes.

Herbs and Green Stems
Sprinkle over soups finely chopped herbs, green celery leaves, chives or the green stems of scallions, all either snipped with scissors or chopped.

Mushrooms
Thinly slice and gently sauté in butter for 5 minutes until soft but not colored. Sprinkle on just before serving.

Borsch

2 carrots
2 leeks
4 onions
2 cloves
2 cups diced beets
1 white cabbage
2 lbs. beef bottom round
1 marrowbone
1 bouquet garni
1 fennel branch or pinch of ground cumin
$\frac{1}{4}$ cup tomato paste
salt and pepper
1 lb. cooked garlic sausage
5 pickles (dill)
$1\frac{1}{4}$ cups sour cream

1 Scrape the carrots and cut into small rounds. Clean and chop the leeks. Peel the onions, stud 1 whole onion with cloves and cut the other onions into very fine slices. Peel the beets and chop finely. Cut away the core and stalks, then shred the cabbage.

2 Fill a large saucepan two-thirds with water. Boil. Add the meat and the marrowbone, return to a boil and skim off the scum from the surface as it rises. Add the leeks, the carrots, the onions, the bouquet garni, beets, cabbage and fennel or cumin.

3 Thin the tomato paste with a few tablespoons of hot soup. Pour this back into the pan, season with salt and pepper and bring to a boil. Cover, reduce the heat and simmer for $2\frac{1}{2}$ hours. Remove the meat and marrowbone from the pot, then chop the beef finely.

4 Slice the garlic sausage and the pickles. Add the meat, the garlic sausage and the pickles to the soup. Cover and simmer for about 30 minutes. Heat a soup tureen.

5 Lift the bouquet garni and the clove-studded onion out of the soup. Pour the soup into the warmed tureen. Serve the cream in a sauce boat, allowing a generous spoonful per serving.

Serves 4–6

Pirojkis (Pirogis)

For the pastry:
$2\frac{3}{4}$ cups flour
$\frac{2}{3}$ cup butter
2 eggs plus 1 egg yolk, beaten
pinch salt

For the filling:
3 eggs
8 ozs. cream cheese
2 sprigs parsley
salt and pepper
nutmeg
$\frac{1}{2}$ cup butter

1 To make the pastry: put the flour onto a board or into a bowl and make a well in the center. Cut up the butter. Break the eggs and put with the salt and butter into the well. Mix all together to form a firm and elastic dough. Roll this out with a rolling pin several times, folding between rollings.

2 Prepare the filling. Put 2 of the eggs set aside for the filling into a saucepan of cold water. Bring to a boil. Simmer gently for 10 minutes over moderate heat so the shells do not break. Remove from the boiling water and cool in cold water: they will then be easier to shell.

3 Put the cream cheese into a bowl. Wash and chop the parsley. Add, with the salt, pepper and a little grated nutmeg, to the cream cheese.

4 Put the hard-boiled eggs through a grinder and add to the cream cheese. Blend well together to form a smooth, even mixture. Put the butter in a bowl and cream well before blending with cream cheese-egg mixture.

5 Dust the board or the table work surface with flour. Roll out the pastry to a thickness of about $\frac{1}{8}$

Clear Soups

Consommé is probably the best known clear soup. Prime quality beef, herbs and vegetables are simmered in a well-flavored brown stock, and the addition of egg whites — sometimes crushed eggshells are used as well — help to clarify the liquid. The mixture is then strained, with the crust that has formed on top during the cooking acting as a filter.

To be sure of making a sparkling clear soup, which all consommés must be, all utensils and ingredients — especially the stock — must be completely free from grease.

You can serve consommé hot or cold (in which case it is lightly jellied and usually chopped), and plain or varied by adding different garnishes. A consommé, in fact, takes its name from the garnish, and this should always be cooked or prepared separately and added only at the moment of serving. That way nothing can cloud and spoil the appearance of the soup.

Beef Consommé

1 carrot
1 leek, green part only
2 branches celery
4 ripe tomatoes (optional)
2 egg whites
1 lb. prime lean ground beef
few sprigs chervil and tarragon
8½ cups chilled brown stock
¾ cup cold water
peppercorns
1 tablespoon sherry (optional)

1 Remove all fat from the surface of the brown stock and turn into a large pan. Peel the carrot. Wash and dry it, together with the leek, celery and tomatoes, if used. Chop or slice them. Wash, dry and chop the herbs.

2 Mix the vegetables with the egg whites in a large bowl; stir in the beef, tomatoes, chopped herbs and the water.

3 Add the vegetable mixture to the stock, mix together, then bring slowly to a boil, stirring to the bottom of the pan to prevent the mixture from sticking. Keep whisking the mixture until a thick froth starts to form.

4 As soon as the mixture starts to boil, turn down the heat and simmer, covered, for about 1½ hours without stirring. From time to time remove any fat which rises to the surface (there should be hardly any at all).

5 At the end of the cooking time, pour the contents of the pan through a scalded cloth over a strainer, on which the peppercorns have been put, into a bowl underneath. At first hold back the egg white crust with a spoon, then let it slip onto the cloth. Pour the soup through again and over the egg white filter. The consommé should now be completely clear. Reheat, check the seasoning and add the sherry, if liked, to improve the flavor.

Serves 8

Variations:

Consommé Colbert: add ½ cup port to the above quantity of hot soup; add cooked diced carrots and turnips, cooked garden peas, as well as a poached egg per serving.

Consommé Julienne: add cooked matchstick-thin strips of vegetables (carrot, turnip, celery) to the hot soup.

Consommé à la Brunoise: add a mixture of cooked small diced carrots, green beans or celery to the hot soup. Substitute chicken stock for the brown stock if liked.

Consommé à la Madrilène: substitute chicken stock for brown stock; blanch a few tarragon leaves in boiling water for 2 minutes, then add to the hot soup. Float a thin slice of lemon in each bowl.

Consommé au Riz: add a small quantity of cooked long grain rice to the hot soup.

Consommé au Vermicelli: add vermicelli or other tiny pasta to the soup while reheating.

Quick Consommé
Heat canned consommé gently in a pan and stir in 1 tablespoon sherry or Madeira or to taste to boost the flavor. Garnish and serve as for homemade consommé.

Watercress Soup

½ bunch watercress
⅛ lb. lean pork
1-2 scallions
2¾ cups chicken stock
½ teaspoon grated fresh gingerroot
½ teaspoon soy sauce
1 teaspoon dry sherry
salt and pepper

1 Wash and dry the watercress. Reserve 4 small top clusters for garnish. Remove the thick stems and cut the rest up roughly. Cut the pork into very small slivers; trim and thinly slice the scallions.

2 Put into a pan the chicken stock, gingerroot, soy sauce, sherry, the pork, sliced scallions and salt and pepper to taste. Remember the stock is already well seasoned.

3 Bring to a boil, cover and simmer for 15 minutes. Add the watercress and simmer the soup for 3 more minutes. Serve at once, garnishing each bowl with a sprig of watercress.

Serves 4

1 Ingredients: chilled brown stock, carrots, celery, green part of 1 leek, tomatoes, chervil and tarragon, eggs, ground beef **2** Carefully remove any fat from the surface of the stock **3** Chop or slice the vegetables and tomatoes; wash and chop the herbs **4** Put the prepared vegetables and herbs into a large bowl together with the ground beef. Add the egg whites only **5** Mix the ingredients together well, adding a little cold water to moisten. Add the vegetable mixture to the stock and heat gently, stirring all the time **6** As soon as it begins to boil, reduce the heat so it is only just simmering. Skim off any fat that rises to the surface — there should be hardly any at all — and cook for 1½ hours without stirring; this will allow a 'crust' to form on top **7** Scald a cloth and place over a large strainer; put the peppercorns on the cloth, then slowly pour the soup over the vegetable/egg white mixture to clarify **8** and **9** Two garnishes for consommé: vermicelli and chopped tomatoes.

Cold Soups

Cold Spanish Soup (Gazpacho)

1 cucumber
salt
1½ cups dry white breadcrumbs
3 tomatoes
1 clove garlic
4 tablespoons olive oil
1 tablespoon lemon juice
2¼ cups cold water
salt and pepper
pinch cayenne pepper
2 mild Spanish onions
1 green pepper
bunch chervil
bunch chives

1 Peel the cucumber with a potato peeler. Dice it. Bring a saucepan of salted water to a boil. Add half the diced cucumber and leave to simmer for 10 minutes. Sprinkle salt over the rest of the cucumber to draw out some of its moisture.

2 Drain the cooked cucumber. Purée in a blender or food mill or rub through a strainer. Put the breadcrumbs into a bowl. Add just enough water to moisten them. Skin the tomatoes, then cut half the tomatoes into small pieces.

3 Peel and chop the garlic and put into a mortar. Add a pinch of salt and pound with the pestle. Add the tomato pieces and breadcrumbs. Pound until the mixture is thoroughly blended. Add the oil a little at a time, mixing all the time. Add the lemon juice and cucumber purée. Dilute with the cold water, stirring all the time. Add salt and pepper to taste and a pinch of cayenne pepper. Mix again, then

chill in the refrigerator for at least 2 hours.

4 Chop the rest of the tomatoes into small cubes. Peel the onions and chop roughly. Wash the green pepper. Dry it and cut in half. Remove the seeds and white membrane, then cut the flesh into small cubes. Rinse the cucumber cubes. Squeeze them gently with your hands to make sure they are well drained. Wash and dry the chervil and the chives. Chop them.

5 Arrange the tomatoes, onions, green pepper and cucumber in 4 separate dishes. Divide the soup into 4 individual bowls. Sprinkle the chervil and chives over them. Serve very chilled.

Serves 4

Tip: Each guest puts a little of all the finely chopped raw vegetables into his soup bowl. It is customary to put an ice cube into each soup bowl at the moment of serving.

Gazpacho or gaspacho (below), is a Spanish salad-soup made with a purée of cucumber, tomatoes, garlic, breadcrumbs, and oil. Served chilled, the soup is garnished with herbs and accompanied by bowls of chopped tomato, green peppers, onion and cucumber.

Vichyssoise

3½ cups chicken stock
½ teaspoon salt
4 medium potatoes
3 medium onions
3 leeks (or 1 extra onion)
½ teaspoon fresh chervil or
  marjoram
2 tablespoons fresh parsley
½ cup heavy cream

1 Put the chicken stock in a large pan and bring to simmering point; add the salt. Peel the potatoes and cut into medium chunks. Peel and chop the onions. Prepare, wash, dry and slice the leeks. Add all these vegetables to the stock, bring to a boil, cover, reduce the heat and simmer for about 20 minutes.

2 Cool a little, then put the soup in a blender and blend until smooth or pass through a food mill or strainer. Chill for at least 2 hours.

3 Wash, dry and finely chop the chervil or marjoram and the parsley. Just before serving add the herbs and cream. If wished, put 2 or 3 overlapping raw onion rings in the center of each soup dish when serving.

Serves 6

To Store Soup
Unthickened soup (no thickener has been added) freezes best and can be frozen in handy quantities for up to 3 months. Cool, then skim off any fat from the surface before freezing a soup; allow about ½ inch headspace for expansion.

Vichyssoise (below) is one of the classic French soups. Traditionally garnished with snipped chives, try finely chopped parsley or a few raw onion rings instead

Avocado Soup

2 large plus 1 small avocados
½ teaspoon salt
pinch white pepper
1 cup heavy cream
3½ cups chicken stock
3 tablespoons dry sherry

1 Peel the 2 large avocados, remove the pits and cut the flesh into small pieces. Put It into a blender with salt, pepper and half the cream and blend until smooth or work through a strainer. Then add the remaining cream and blend again until mixed.

2 Heat the chicken stock until it is warm but not hot. Pour in the avocado cream mixture. Taste and adjust the seasoning. Chill this in the refrigerator for 1 hour.

3 Stir in the sherry. Peel the small avocado, remove the pit and cut the flesh into thin slices. Add to the soup and serve.

Serves 4–6

Tip: Do not make this soup too early in the day. Avocado discolors when exposed to the air so put into a covered container when chilling. A little lemon juice brushed over the flesh helps to prevent discoloration.

Watercress and Potato Soup

1 bunch watercress
2 tablespoons butter
1 onion
1 branch celery
2 medium potatoes
2¾ cups chicken stock
1 tablespoon lemon juice
½ teaspoon salt
freshly ground black pepper
½ cup heavy cream

1 Wash the watercress and reserve some of the leaves for decoration. Chop the remainder and the stems into small pieces.

2 Melt the butter in a saucepan. Peel the onion and chop it finely. Clean the celery and chop it. Peel the potatoes and cut into cubes. Add the onion and celery to the pan and cook for 3 minutes.

3 Add the potatoes, stock, chopped watercress, lemon juice, salt and pepper. Cover and simmer for 30 minutes. Remove from the heat and cool a little.

4 Work through a strainer or purée in a blender. Then strain the soup into a container with a lid. Taste and adjust seasoning if necessary. Cover and chill for 2 hours. Just before serving stir in the cream and the reserved watercress.

Serves 4

Cream of Lettuce Soup

3 heads lettuce
2 tablespoons butter
1½ teaspoons salt
freshly ground black pepper
3½ cups water
½ cup heavy cream
juice ½ lemon
6 scallions

1 Cut the lettuce into quarters, remove the cores and wash the leaves. Cook in boiling, salted water for 10 minutes. Drain and then chop roughly.

2 Melt the butter in a saucepan, add the chopped lettuce, put on the lid, then tip it a little and cook slowly for 5 minutes. Season the lettuce with salt and pepper, add the water and bring to a boil. Cover, lower the heat and simmer for 1 hour. Cool a little.

3 Pour the soup into a blender and blend until smooth, or rub through a strainer. Taste and adjust the seasoning.

4 Chill the soup very well and, just before serving, stir in first the cream and then the lemon juice.

5 Trim the scallions, leaving about 1 inch of the green part still on them. With a pair of kitchen scissors or a sharp knife, cut this

Avocados, combined with sherry and cream, make an excellent soup

green part downward, into as many thin strips as possible. Put 1 onion in the center of each bowl of soup so that the thin strips float.

6 Serve very cold.

Serves 6

Chilled Cucumber and Tomato Soup

6⅓ cups chicken stock
⅓ cup long grain rice
4 very ripe tomatoes
½ cucumber
½ cup heavy cream
small bunch chervil
pinch cayenne pepper
salt and pepper

1 Bring the stock to a boil in a saucepan. Wash the rice and add to the vigorously boiling stock; cook 20 minutes.

2 Wash and skin the tomatoes; quarter and squeeze gently to extract the water and seeds. Add tomatoes to the stock after the rice has cooked for 20 minutes. Let cook 30 minutes longer.

3 Remove the end of the cucumber. Cut in two, lengthwise; take out seeds with a small spoon. Cut in thin strips.

4 When cooked, purée the soup in a blender or rub through a strainer. Stiffly whip and fold in cream. Add cayenne pepper. Mix well together. Taste and adjust the seasoning; cool.

5 When cold, add the cucumber strips. Stir. Chill in refrigerator for at least 3 hours. About 5 minutes before serving, wash, dry and chop the chervil. Ladle the chilled soup into individual bowls. Sprinkle on the chervil and serve.

Serves 4

Chilled Cucumber and Tomato Soup, garnished with strips of cucumber

Borsch, Chilled

2 cups diced beets (7-8 medium-
  size beets)
2½ cups beet liquid
1 cup beef stock
1 tablespoon grated onion
1 tablespoon lemon juice
½ teaspoon salt

For the garnish:
sliced hard-boiled eggs (½ egg per
  person)
peeled, sliced cucumber
sour cream

1 Scrub beets and cut stems no
shorter than 1 inch from the top so
that the beets won't bleed.

2 In water to cover boil beets until
tender (approximately 45 minutes).
Eggs may be boiled in the same pan
and removed after 20 minutes.

3 Save the beet water. Drain beets
and place them in cold water. Slip
off skins.

4 Add 2½ cups beet water to the
beef stock.

5 Blend 1 cup beets with 1 cup
beef-beet liquid. Repeat with other
cup of beets.

6 Stir blended beets and remaining
liquid together. Add onion, lemon
juice and salt.

7 Chill at least 2 hours. Stir and
garnish before serving.

Serves 4

Minted Pea Soup, Chilled

2 cups chicken stock
1 cup water
¼ cup mint (3 large sprigs)
3 cups peas (fresh)
¼ cup diced onion
½ cup heavy cream
salt to taste

For the garnish:
whipped cream and fresh mint
  leaves

1 Bring chicken stock, water and
mint to a boil.

2 Drop peas and onions into rapidly boiling stock.

3 Cover and cook peas at a slow
boil until tender (no longer than 12
minutes).

4 Cool and work through a food
mill, using the finest disc. (Note: a
blender will not do in this case. The
outer skins of some peas are tough
and won't blend well.)

5 Stir the cream into the purée.

6 Salt to taste.

7 Chill the soup in a pitcher.

8 If the soup separates, simply stir
it well before pouring into chilled
bowls.

9 Top with whipped cream and a
small mint leaf sprig.

Serves 4

Fruit Soup, Chilled

½ cup raisins
½ cup prunes, cooked, pitted and
  chopped
½ cup dried apricots, chopped
1 cup dry red wine
2 cups cold water
1-lb. can tart pitted cherries with
  juice
2 tart cooking apples, peeled and
  diced
1 cinnamon stick
⅓ cup sugar
½ teaspoon grated orange or lemon
  rind
2 tablespoons cornstarch
½ cup cold water
sugar to taste

For the garnish:
½ cup heavy cream, whipped with 1
  teaspoon confectioners' sugar

1 Soak dried fruit in red wine and
water for 1 hour.

2 Place all fruit in large heavy
saucepan with the liquid.

3 Add cinnamon stick and sugar
and boil 15 minutes (or until apples
are soft but not mushy).

4 Mix cornstarch with ½ cup cold
water and add this mixture to soup.

5 If soup is too tart, add more
sugar. Add grated orange or lemon
rind.

6 Cook soup 2 minutes at slow
boil.

7 Chill soup thoroughly. (May be
put in freezer until chilled only.)

8 Serve in chilled glass bowls or
compôtes with dollops of whipped
cream and a sprinkle of nutmeg,
cinnamon, and grated orange or
lemon rind.

Serves 6–8

Granville Soup
(with Blueberries)

2 cups white wine
2 slices lemon
2 cups water
½ cup sugar
¼ teaspoon salt
⅓ cup tapioca
2 cinnamon sticks
½ cup raspberry and ½ cup currant
  jelly
1 cup grape juice
2 cups fresh blueberries

1 Combine all except blueberries
and leave to stand about 5 minutes.

2 Bring to a boil and stir often.

3 Cover and very gently simmer
about 15-20 minutes, then remove
from heat. Stir in blueberries and
chill well.

4 Remove lemon slice and cinnamon stick.

5 Serve in soup dishes with unsalted unwhipped heavy cream
floating on top.

Serves 6

Creamy Soups

All creamy soups have a smooth, velvety texture achieved by thickening them with cream or egg yolks, flour or some kind of cereal. They can be made with stock or milk or combinations of both.

Green vegetables are popular choices for cream soups; they are usually cooked in milk, then strained and blended and then thickened.

If both egg yolks and cream are used for thickening a soup, the extra velvety consistency achieved is called a *velouté*.

Bisque is a term applied to shellfish soups only. Often a bisque is enriched by the addition of a special butter made with the lobster roe, and in some cases the shells themselves are pounded and incorporated as well to give an extra fishy flavor.

To Thicken Soups

If using cream: put in a bowl, blend in a little of the hot but not boiling soup, then stir back into the pan of soup and reheat but do not boil.

If using egg yolk: blend with a little cold milk or cream in a bowl, mix in a little of the hot soup, then strain back into the pan of soup; reheat very gently but do not boil or else the egg will curdle (if the soup already contains flour/cereal, curdling is less likely to occur).

If using flour or fine cereal: blend with a little cold milk or other liquid in a bowl, mix in a little hot soup, then pour back into the pan, bring to a boil and cook for a few minutes until thickened.

Cream of Spinach Soup

2 lbs. leaf spinach
1 small onion
2 tablespoons butter
4 tablespoons flour
1¼ cups white stock
1¼ cups milk
salt and pepper

1 Wash the spinach well; peel and finely chop the onion. Put the spinach in a large pan with about 2 tablespoons water and cook until tender — about 5 minutes. Drain well and rub through a strainer or work through a food mill; set aside.

2 Heat the butter in a saucepan; put in the onion and cook until soft and transparent. Stir in the flour and blend. Pour in the white stock and milk, a little at a time, stirring continuously until smooth.

3 Stir in the spinach purée, season to taste, cook gently for a few minutes until hot, then serve immediately.

Serves 4–6

Cream of Spinach Soup is a delicious way of serving this underrated vegetable

Cream of Chervil Soup

3 tablespoons butter
5 tablespoons flour
6⅓ cups chicken or white stock
salt and pepper
1 egg yolk
¼ cup heavy cream
2 tablespoons finely chopped
  chervil or parsley

1 Melt the butter in a large sauce-pan. Blend in the flour to make a roux. Pour in the stock a little at a time, and stir continuously over medium heat until the sauce is thick and smooth. Season with salt and pepper to taste.

2 Mix the egg yolk with the cream in a bowl; stir in a little of the hot liquid, then pour into the pan of soup, stirring continuously. Add the chervil, or parsley, reheat gently but do not boil, and serve at once.

Serves 4–6

Cream of Leek and Potato Soup

3 leeks, white part only
2 large potatoes
2 tablespoons butter
8½ cups white stock
salt and pepper
1 egg yolk
½ cup heavy cream
2 handfuls chervil or parsley

1 Wash the leeks well (this is best done by standing them, green stems down, in a jug of cold water so grit and dirt can float out from between the stems). Drain them and cut into thin slices. Peel the potatoes and cut into quarters.

2 In a pan, melt the butter. When hot add the leek slices. Soften them a little in the covered pan, stirring frequently over gentle heat.

3 Take the pan off the heat and pour in the stock. Return to the heat and bring to a boil again. Add salt and pepper. Put in the potato quarters, cover the pan, reduce the heat and simmer about 20 minutes till tender. Then purée in a blender or work through a strainer or food mill.

4 In a bowl blend the cream and egg yolk together, then stir in some of the hot soup. Return this mixture to the soup. Stir and adjust the seasoning, adding plenty of pepper. Heat gently for a few moments but do not boil.

5 Meanwhile, wash and dry the chervil or parsley, then chop it finely.

6 Pour the soup into a heated tureen. Sprinkle with the chopped herbs and serve.

Serves 6

Cream of Chicken Soup

3 tablespoons butter
5 tablespoons flour
3⅔ cups chicken stock
½ cup finely chopped cooked
  chicken
¼ teaspoon salt
freshly ground black pepper

For the thickening:
1 egg yolk
¼ cup heavy cream

1 Melt the butter in a large pan. Stir in the flour to make a roux and cook for about 1 minute without coloring. Then take the pan off the heat and gradually blend in the chicken stock, stirring all the time to make a smooth sauce. Return the pan to the heat and bring to a boil.

2 Reduce the heat, then add the cooked chicken, salt and pepper and cook for 2 minutes.

3 Blend the egg yolk and cream together in a bowl. Stir in a little of the hot soup, then return to the pan and reheat gently, stirring all the time, until thickened. Do not allow the soup to boil after the egg yolk is added. Serve at once.

Serves 4

Cream of Mushroom Soup

1 lb. mushrooms
1 shallot
4 tablespoons butter
2 tablespoons flour
6⅓ cups brown stock
salt and pepper
1 egg yolk
2 tablespoons heavy cream
juice ½ lemon

1 Wipe the mushrooms and slice them finely. Peel and chop the shallot.

2 Heat the butter in a large pan; when hot add the shallot and sauté quickly till golden. Then add the sliced mushrooms and sauté over medium heat for about 4 minutes. Stir in the flour and cook for a further 2 minutes, then blend in the brown stock off the heat. Return the pan to the heat, season with salt and pepper to taste and cook gently for about 10 minutes.

3 To thicken the soup, blend the egg yolk with the cream and the lemon juice, then stir into the hot soup. Reheat very gently but do not boil. Serve at once.

Serves 4–6

Cream of Mushroom Soup — as a variation try stirring in plain yogurt instead of cream

Avgolemono (Greek Egg and Lemon Soup)

7½ cups chicken stock
½ cup long grain rice, vermicelli or
  other pasta
3 eggs
juice 2 small lemons
salt and freshly ground black
  pepper

1 Bring the chicken stock to a boil. Add the rice, vermicelli or pasta and simmer for 15 minutes.

2 Meanwhile, beat the eggs until frothy. Slowly add the lemon juice to the eggs, beating constantly. Add about a quarter of the hot stock, 1 tablespoon at a time, beating all the time. Remove the remaining stock from the heat and stir in the egg mixture.

3 Adjust the seasoning as necessary and serve immediately.

Serves 8

Cream of Carrot Soup

2 medium onions
2 medium potatoes
2 lbs. carrots
2 tablespoons butter
salt and pepper
8½ cups white stock
2 tablespoons raw rice

For the thickening:
1 egg yolk
¼ cup heavy cream

1 Peel and slice the onions. Peel and cut the carrots into strips. Peel and dice the potatoes.

2 Melt half the fat in a large pan. When hot, put in the onions and sauté without coloring over a low heat until soft and translucent.

3 Stir the carrots into the pan. Add the stock and salt to taste, then cover and cook over moderate heat for 30 minutes.

4 Wash the rice under cold running water. Then add the rice and potatoes to the pan and cook for a further 30 minutes. Purée in a blender or work through a strainer or food mill.

5 When the soup is cooked, blend the egg yolk with the cream in a bowl. Season generously with salt and pepper and beat again. Stir in a little of the hot soup; then return the egg yolk mixture to the pan of soup. Reheat gently but do not boil. Serve hot.

Serves 6

Chinese Asparagus Soup

2 onions
2 cups chicken stock
2 tablespoons cornstarch
1 egg
2 tablespoons oil
salt and pepper
1 tablespoon white wine
2 tablespoons cooked tiny peas
3-4 slender, cooked asparagus
  spears per person

1 Peel and chop up the onions so as to obtain the equivalent of 3 tablespoons. Mix 2 tablespoons of cold water with the cornstarch. Break an egg into a bowl and beat until blended.

2 Heat the oil in the saucepan, put in the chopped onions and sauté slowly until lightly browned. Add the chicken stock with salt and pepper, and mix in the cornstarch, stirring all the time.

3 Then add the wine and peas and bring it to a boil. When the soup starts to thicken, slowly add the beaten egg, but keep stirring the whole time. When it thickens, remove from the heat.

4 Cut the asparagus into pieces and place them in bowls or soup plates. Add soup and serve.

Serves 4

Cream of Artichoke Soup

3 shallots
6 globe artichokes
juice of 1 lemon
¼ lb. butter
scant ½ cup flour
4¼ cups milk
salt and pepper
½ cup heavy cream

1 Peel and chop the shallots. Remove the artichoke leaves and hairy choke in the center (see page 58). Trim the artichoke hearts and rub them in the lemon juice to stop them turning black. Cut them into quarters.

2 Gently heat 2 tablespoons butter in a pan. Put in the artichoke hearts and the shallots, cover and cook on low heat for 10 minutes.

3 During this time melt the rest of the butter in another pan. Mix in the flour to make a roux and cook for about 2 minutes, but without letting it brown. Remove the pan from the heat and blend in the milk, little by little, beating continuously with a wooden spoon. When smooth return the pan to the heat and bring to a boil; season with salt and pepper and cook gently for 5 minutes.

4 Pour this white sauce over the artichokes and shallot mixture and simmer 30 minutes. Then remove 2 artichoke hearts and dice them. Purée the rest in a blender or work through a strainer or food mill.

5 Heat a soup tureen. Pour in the cream, add the diced artichoke and pour on the hot soup. Stir well and serve immediately.

Serves 4

Cream of Artichoke soup is an unusual way of serving artichokes

Browned Onion Soup with Madeira

3 medium onions
2 cloves garlic
3 tablespoons butter
2 tablespoons oil
¼ cup flour
½ cup dry white wine
salt and pepper
3 egg yolks
¼ cup Madeira
½ French loaf
cayenne pepper
1 cup grated Cheddar cheese

For the bouquet garni:
sprig parsley
good sprig thyme
bay leaf

1 Wash and dry the parsley. Tie the parsley, thyme and bay leaf together, making sure that the thyme and bay leaf are inside the parsley. Peel the onions and chop them. Peel the garlic.

2 Heat the butter and the oil in a sauté pan. Add the chopped onions and cook them, stirring from time to time with a wooden spoon. When they are golden, add the flour and let it cook while stirring until it too turns brown.

3 Pour in the white wine. Let it reduce (evaporate) by half, then add the stock or water. Add salt and plenty of pepper. Add the bouquet garni. Crush the garlic and add it as well. Bring to a boil, then skim. Cover the soup and allow to simmer for about 45 minutes. About 15 minutes before it is ready, preheat the oven to 400°F. to dry out the bread.

4 Mix yolks with the Madeira. Cut the French loaf into thin slices. Spread them on a baking sheet and dry out in the oven. Take out the bread. Heat the broiler.

5 When the soup is cooked, take it off the heat and discard the bouquet garni. When it has stopped bubbling, pour a little of the soup into the yolk/Madeira mixture, whisking briskly all the time. Then pour it all back into the soup and mix well. Add a hint of cayenne pepper and check the seasoning.

6 Divide the soup among four bowls. Place 2-3 slices of bread in each bowl. Cover the bread with the grated cheese. Stand the bowls in a pan of hot water. Heat on the stove until the water is almost boiling, then brown under the broiler.

7 Serve piping hot as soon as the cheese browns.

Serves 4

Tips: If a soup without onion pieces is preferred, strain it or put through a blender before adding the egg yolks. Don't allow the soup to boil once the egg yolks have been added.

If chopped beet leaves and a potato are added to the onion while frying, the flour would then be unnecessary.

The white wine and Madeira can be replaced with a very full-bodied red wine to produce a 'country' brown soup (gratinée).

Rich Turnip Soup

2 small turnips
4 strips bacon, diced
3 tablespoons butter
¼ lb. sorrel
4¼ cups chicken stock
few sprigs chervil
1 egg yolk
2 tablespoons light cream
salt and pepper

1 Boil 2 small pans of water. Peel and wash the turnips and cut them into cubes. Put the turnips into one pan and the bacon strips into the other. Let each boil for 5 minutes, then drain.

2 Melt the butter in a stewpan. Put the turnips and the bacon into the hot butter and let brown a little on low heat for about 15 minutes.

3 Wash the sorrel and chop it. Add it to the pan and stir in with a wooden spoon, then pour the stock into it and cook for 20 minutes.

4 Wash, dry and chop the chervil. Pour the egg yolk into the soup tureen, add the cream and mix in.

5 When the bacon is cooked, drain. Purée the soup in a blender or work through a strainer or food mill. Taste and adjust the seasoning. Pour the soup into the tureen and beat with a whisk. Add the bacon to the soup and sprinkle it with chervil. Serve very hot.

Serves 4

Bulgarian Beef Soup

½ lb. lean beef
4 large onions
3 tablespoons butter
½ teaspoon cumin seeds
mixed fresh herbs for small bouquet garni
6½ cups brown stock
salt and pepper
3 tablespoons sour cream
1 pint plain yogurt
1 tablespoon paprika
1 tablespoon cornstarch
¼ lb. cooked ham
sprigs parsley

1 Dice the beef finely. Peel the onions and cut into quarters.

2 Melt the butter in a big saucepan. Add the diced beef and onions, and sauté gently for 20 minutes, stirring frequently.

3 Put cumin seeds in a pepper mill and grind them. Wash and dry the herbs for the bouquet garni, and tie them together.

4 When the beef and onions have cooked for 20 minutes, add the brown stock and bouquet garni. Sprinkle with the ground cumin. Add salt and pepper, bearing in mind the seasoning of the stock, and cook for 20 minutes.

5 Put the sour cream into a bowl with the yogurt, paprika and cornstarch. Mix carefully so that lumps do not form, and pour into the soup. Stir with a wooden spoon over low heat.

6 Put the cooked ham through the grinder. Wash and dry the parsley sprigs and chop them finely.

7 Add the ham to the soup and cook a further 2 minutes over low heat.

8 Just before serving, remove the bouquet garni. Taste the soup, and if necessary adjust the seasoning. Pour it into a heated soup tureen, sprinkle with chopped parsley and serve hot.

Serves 6

Bulgarian Beef Soup is a nourishing and spicy meal in itself

Look 'n Cook Jumbo Shrimp Bisque

1 Ingredients for Jumbo Shrimp Bisque **2** For the sauce, make a roux with butter and flour, then blend in milk **3** Soften shrimp and vegetables in oil, add brandy and ignite. Add wine and tomatoes, season and cook **4** Take out shrimp, chop and return to pan **5** Press soup through conical strainer **6** Return to pan, boil, add remaining shrimp; place cream in tureen, pour in boiling soup (see opposite page) and serve

Fish Soups

Shrimp Bisque

4 tablespoons butter
$\frac{1}{4}$ cup flour
$4\frac{1}{4}$ cups milk
salt and pepper
5 tomatoes
1 shallot
1 small onion
1 branch celery
$\frac{1}{2}$ lb. unshelled jumbo shrimp
2 tablespoons oil
1 small bouquet garni
$\frac{1}{4}$ cup brandy
$\frac{1}{2}$ cup dry white wine

To finish:
2 peeled jumbo shrimp
$\frac{1}{2}$ cup heavy cream

1 Melt the butter in a double boiler and blend in the flour to make a roux. Cook for about 1 minute without letting it color. Using a wooden spoon, blend in the milk off the heat, then return to the stove and bring to a boil. Season with salt and pepper and cook for 20 minutes over low heat.

2 Skin the tomatoes and cut them in half. Remove the seeds and chop the pulp roughly. Peel and finely chop the shallot and onion. Wash and finely chop the celery.

3 Wash and dry the shrimp. Remove the heads and tails.

4 Heat the oil in a pan. When hot add the unshelled shrimp, the vegetables (but not the tomatoes) and the bouquet garni. Cook gently for about 10 minutes or until the vegetables are soft.

5 Pour in the brandy, heat for about 1 minute, then ignite. When the flames die down, add the tomatoes and white wine. Add salt and season liberally with pepper, then cook for 20 minutes.

6 Remove the shrimp from the pan. Crush or chop them and put them back into the pan. Add the white sauce, mix and cook slowly for another 15 minutes. Heat a soup tureen.

7 Pour the soup through a fine conical strainer, pressing down well with a wooden spoon, back into the pan. Bring to a boil again, check the seasoning and add the peeled shrimp.

8 Pour the cream into the tureen, add the soup, while stirring vigorously, and serve.

Serves 4

Tip: The shrimp shells are used to add additional flavor to the soup. If unshelled shrimp are not available increase the weight of additional shrimp by about $\frac{1}{4}$ lb.

Cream of Mussel Soup

1¾ pints fresh mussels
2¼ cups dry white wine
2¼ cups water
pepper
1 bouquet garni
4 potatoes
2 carrots
1 onion
2 cloves
1½ lbs. cod fillets

For the thickening:
2 egg yolks
⅞ cup heavy cream
1 tablespoon cornstarch

1 Scrub and wash the mussels in several changes of water to ensure all the sand is removed. Put them in a large pan and add half the white wine and pepper to taste. Bring to a boil on high heat. Shake the pan from time to time until the mussels open.

2 Lift out the mussels, discarding any that stay closed; remove the shells. Pass the cooking juices through a fine piece of cheesecloth. Pour the juices back into the pan. Add the rest of the wine, the water and the bouquet garni. Bring to a boil.

3 Meanwhile, peel the potatoes and cut them into even pieces. Peel the carrots and cut them into thin slices. Peel the onion and stud it with the cloves. Add the carrots and onion only to the pan. Bring to a boil, then reduce the heat, cover and simmer for 20 minutes.

4 After 20 minutes' cooking, add the potatoes to the pan and cook for a further 25 minutes.

5 Put the egg yolks in a bowl, add the cream and cornstarch and mix with a fork.

6 Cut the fillets into small pieces and add to the pan; simmer for 5 minutes. Heat a soup tureen.

7 Pour a little of the hot soup into the egg yolk mixture. Blend well, then return it to the pan. Add the

mussels and reheat the soup gently for 2-3 minutes, without letting it come to a boil.

8 Take out the onion and the bouquet garni. Pour the soup into the tureen and serve hot.

Serves 4

Mock Caviar Soup

2 lbs. cod fillets
2 onions
4 cloves
3 cups fish stock
2¼ cups dry white wine
1 bay leaf
pinch white pepper
½ teaspoon salt

For the thickening:
¼ cup butter
2 egg yolks
2 tablespoons flour
1 cup heavy cream
¼ lb. lumpfish roe

1 Cut the fish fillets into small pieces. Peel the onions and stud 1 of them with the cloves.

2 Pour the stock and white wine into a large saucepan. Add the onions, bay leaf, pepper, salt and pieces of fish. Cover and as soon as it comes to a boil, reduce the heat and simmer for about 30 minutes.

3 Beat the butter to soften it. Then beat in the egg yolks, one at a time, and each time with half of the flour and the cream respectively.

4 Work the soup through a strainer or food mill, pressing the fish with a wooden spoon to extract all the juice. Pour this fish liquid back into the saucepan.

5 Blend a little of the hot fish liquid with the cream mixture in a bowl; then return it to the pan of soup. Reheat gently but do not boil and cook for about 15 minutes.

6 Heat a soup tureen. Pour in the

soup, add the lumpfish roe and stir. Taste and adjust the seasoning and serve at once.

Serves 4

Oyster Bisque

24 fresh large oysters
scant 1 cup water
2 medium onions
¼ cup butter
2 tablespoons flour
2½ cups milk
salt and pepper
¼ teaspoon paprika
2 tablespoons finely chopped
parsley

1 Open the oysters, retain their juice but discard the shells. Soak the oysters in the water and their juice. Peel and finely chop the onions.

2 Heat 3 tablespoons butter in a pan. Add the onions and sauté slowly until they are just beginning to brown. Add the flour and stir with a wooden spoon for 3 minutes. Add one-third of the milk, stir again and cook for 2 minutes.

3 Drain the oysters, keeping the liquid in which they were soaked, and cut them into small pieces.

4 Mix the onion sauce with the rest of the milk and the soaking liquid in a double boiler. Season with salt and pepper to taste.

5 Add the oysters to the pan and leave 20 minutes over low heat, taking care the mixture does not boil. Add the chopped parsley.

6 Just before serving, stir in the rest of the butter and the paprika. Serve at once.

Serves 4

Cream of Mussel Soup — mussels, once considered the 'oysters of the poor,' are now featured in world-famous dishes. They are in season from March to September and should be bought alive. Test for freshness by sliding the two shells against each other — if they move they are probably full of sand or mud, not mussel

Look 'n Cook Bouillabaisse

1 Wash and clean the fish; cut into pieces **2** Skin, seed and chop tomatoes; peel and finely chop onions, garlic and parsley; cut fennel and leeks into matchsticks **3** Sauté vegetables gently in oil **4** Add saffron, tomatoes, garlic and parsley **5** Add fish pieces **6** Strain broth and add to the pan **7** Pound together garlic, saf-

fron and cayenne for rouille **8** Blend in egg yolk and oil **9** Spread croûtes on baking sheet, pour over oil and bake **10** Season broth with salt and pepper as soon as it boils **11** Rub garlic over croûtes **12** Lift pieces of fish onto serving dish **13** Ladle some of the (continued on page 47)

Look 'n Cook Bouillabaisse

13

14

15

Bouillabaisse started as a very simple fish soup made with spiny scorpion fish, olive oil, garlic, onion, leeks and sea water. It then evolved to its present form with the inclusion of many more different rock fish and flavorings, and in particular the special garlic mayonnaise called rouille.

Some rouille sauces can be very fiery, depending on the strength of the cayenne. And the blending of the hot broth with the sauce helps to thicken and bind it.

Sadly, it is difficult to reproduce this delicious dish exactly, away from the Mediterranean, mainly because the local fish are unobtainable, but the recipe here is an excellent alternative.

To be really tasty, Bouillabaisse must combine a wide variety of fish, each kind adding its own particular flavor. So 6 lbs. of fish is the smallest amount to use satisfactorily. The choice of fish is wide, the most popular being eel, bass, cod, halibut, snapper, haddock, together with shellfish like crab, lobster, or jumbo shrimp.

Bourride is another famous Mediterranean soup dish, but the classic recipe doesn't confine its choice of fish to rock sea fish as Bouillabaisse does. Often fatty fish, like sardines, are included and indeed in its earliest form, Bourride was a sardine soup bound with aioli, another kind of garlic mayonnaise.

hot broth over the pieces of fish
14 Pour the remaining broth into a hot soup tureen **15** Serve the platter of fish and shellfish separately from the rouille sauce, broth and croûtes

Bouillabaisse—
Fish Soup Provençale

6 lbs. saltwater fish (use a variety of 6 or more kinds)
8-10 jumbo shrimp, fresh or frozen
few fish bones for stock
4 very ripe large tomatoes
4 large onions
1 carrot
1 bulb garlic (many cloves)
4 large leeks
2 bulbs fennel (not stalks)
1 cup olive oil
1 bouquet garni
pinch saffron
salt and pepper
1 large crusty loaf

For the rouille:
5 cloves garlic
salt
1 egg yolk
pinch cayenne pepper
pinch saffron
1¾ cups olive oil

1 Remove the skin and bones from the fish and wash them well. Roughly chop up the fish bones and wash them.

2 Cut the fish into pieces, making the slices from the more tender and delicate fish larger than the others. Wash them again. Clean the shrimp.

3 Peel, wash and dry the vegetables. Skin, deseed and chop the tomatoes. Peel the onions, carrot and garlic cloves; slice 1 onion and the carrot, then chop the remaining onions finely as well as a few cloves of garlic. Wash, dry and finely chop the parsley. Wash the leeks well, trim them and the fennel, then cut into fine matchsticks.

4 Heat 2-3 tablespoons of oil in a large pan. Sauté the sliced vegetables and chopped garlic in it on a very low heat for 2-3 minutes without letting them color, then add the chopped up fish bones. Cover liberally with cold water and add the bouquet garni. Bring to a boil, then simmer for 20 minutes on

low heat. Skim the fish stock as necessary.

5 Peel 4 or 5 cloves of garlic and crush them.

6 Heat 3 tablespoons of oil in a large heavy pan. Add the chopped onions, fennel and leeks and fry gently for 3 or 4 minutes without letting them color. Then take them off the heat and sprinkle with the saffron. Mix well. Add the tomatoes and garlic and mix again.

7 Add the fish with the shrimp. Mix in carefully and let stand for about 30 minutes.

8 When the fish stock is cooked, pour it through a conical strainer and leave it to cool.

9 Pour the stock over the fish and other ingredients. If the liquid doesn't completely cover them add water to do so. Add salt and pepper, bring to a boil on high heat and simmer for 15 minutes. Check and adjust the seasoning halfway through the cooking.

10 During this time, prepare the rouille. Peel the garlic, chop it up very finely and put it in a mortar with an egg yolk, cayenne pepper, saffron and salt. Pound it well, then little by little incorporate the olive oil by trickling it in as when making mayonnaise, continuously stirring with the pestle instead of a wooden spoon. Then put the mixture in a sauceboat.

11 Cut the bread into slices and place on a baking sheet. Sprinkle with the rest of the olive oil and bake in a hot oven or toast under the broiler. Peel the rest of the garlic cloves. When the croûtes are ready rub them generously with the garlic. Heat a soup tureen.

12 Carefully put the fish and the shrimp onto a large serving dish, pour over them a ladle of stock and keep hot in the oven or under the broiler. Place the toasted croûtes in the hot soup tureen. Strain the stock into it. Serve at once with the rouille.

Serves 6–8

Bourride
(Fish Soup with Garlic Mayonnaise)

2 onions
2 firm, ripe tomatoes
4 cloves garlic
grated rind 1 orange
5 cups water
bunch fresh thyme, 2-3 fennel
  stalks and bay leaf
salt and pepper
pinch saffron
¼ cup olive oil
1¼ cups dry white wine
3 lbs. mixed sea fish (cod,
  haddock, flounder, red mullet)

1¼ cups aioli sauce (see right)
2 egg yolks
toasted croûtes of bread

1 Peel and chop the onions. Wash and chop the tomatoes. Peel and chop the garlic. Wash and dry the herbs. Bring the water to a boil.

2 Put the onions, tomatoes, garlic, grated orange rind and herbs in a large, heavy-based saucepan. Season with salt and pepper and add the saffron.

3 Stir the olive oil, followed by the white wine, into the onion mixture, then mix in the boiling water. Bring back to a boil.

4 Clean and wash the fish and cut into chunks if very large. Add them to the pan of boiling broth and cook for 10 minutes. Then lift the fish out of the pan, using a slotted spoon, and keep hot.

5 Strain the fish broth through a fine strainer; either rub through the vegetables at the same time or purée in a blender and return to the broth; reheat. Heat a soup tureen.

6 Beat the egg yolks and blend with half the aioli in a bowl. Gradually add a ladleful of the boiling broth and blend together; return this mixture to the pot of soup, stir in and reheat gently but do not boil.

7 Put the toasted croûtes of bread in the bottom of a hot soup tureen and pour in the soup. Serve at once, with the dish of fish separately, and accompanied by the rest of the aioli in a sauceboat.

Serves 6

Aioli
(Garlic Mayonnaise)

6 garlic cloves
1 cup olive oil
2 egg yolks
salt and pepper
½ lemon

1 Peel the cloves of garlic, put them in a mortar and pestle and pound, while gradually adding about 1 tablespoon of the oil, until they are reduced to a paste.

2 Add the egg yolks to the garlic paste in the mortar and mix well with a wooden spoon. Then add the remaining oil, little by little, stirring continuously at the same time. Add salt and pepper to taste.

3 When the mayonnaise has thickened, squeeze the juice from the lemon, strain and stir into the mayonnaise. Cover and chill until required.

Makes about 1¼ cups

Bourride

Appetizers

These can be either a single ingredient or two, simply served, like Parma (prosciutto) ham with figs or melon, or several combined together, like Seafood Hors d'Oeuvre or Stuffed Artichokes. Ideally, appetizers should stimulate the appetite, not dull it, so choose ingredients that contrast well in flavor, texture and color, and only serve small portions

Cold Appetizers

Tomatoes Stuffed with Cream and Herbs

4 large round firm tomatoes
bunch mixed fresh herbs (chervil, tarragon, chives, etc.)
2 shallots
1 clove garlic
6 tablespoons heavy cream
salt and pepper
few lettuce leaves

1 Scoop out the tomatoes (see opposite page). Wash, dry and chop the herbs finely. Peel and chop the shallots and garlic.

2 Rinse and dry the tomato shells. Whip the cream until fairly stiff, then fold in the herbs, shallots, garlic, salt and pepper. Fill the tomatoes with this mixture and put a lid on each one. Chill until ready to serve.

3 Wash and dry the lettuce leaves, then arrange on a serving dish. Arrange the stuffed tomatoes on the dish and serve.

Serves 4

Swedish Herring Rissoles

3 medium potatoes
2 onions
2 tablespoons butter
3 fresh herring (skinned and filleted)
salt and pepper
nutmeg
1 cup red currant jelly
½ cup oil

1 Wash the potatoes without peeling them, and cook them in salted boiling water. Peel and finely chop the onions.

2 Melt the butter in a pan, and cook the onions, without letting them color too much, for 7 or 8 minutes. Put them to one side and leave to cool.

Tomatoes Stuffed with Cream and Herbs are simple to prepare and make a light, refreshing start to any meal

3 When the potatoes are cooked, cool them in cold water, then peel them and mash them to a purée.

4 Put the herring fillets through the grinder. Add the onions, potatoes, a little salt, pepper and a little grated nutmeg. Mix well together, then shape into round flat rissoles.

5 Put the red currant jelly and ⅔ cup water in a saucepan and heat slowly.

6 Heat the oil in a skillet. When it is hot, cook the rissoles for about 10 minutes, turning them over once or twice.

7 Heat a serving dish and a sauceboat.

8 Arrange the rissoles on the dish. Pour the hot red currant jelly sauce into the sauceboat and serve very hot.

Serves 4

Tip: The mixture of sweet and savory is typical of Scandinavian cookery. Ascertain the tastes of guests before serving this recipe or leave out the sauce.

Herring in Sherry Pickle

2 salted herring, filleted and skinned
⅓ cup sherry
¼ cup water
3 tablespoons wine vinegar
¼ teaspoon allspice
2 onions, thinly sliced into rings
chopped fresh dill

1 Cover the herring with cold water and leave to soak for 24 hours. Drain, rinse and dry. Place in a non-metallic bowl.

2 Combine the sherry, water, vinegar and allspice. Pour over the herring. Cover with plastic wrap and refrigerate for 24 hours.

3 Serve garnished with the onion rings and dill.

Serves 4

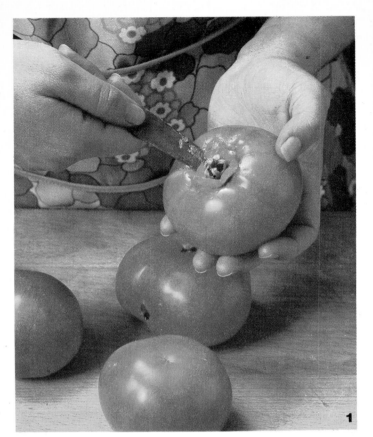

1 and **2** Cut out tomato stalk end, then cut a slice from the other end to give a flat base; use as a lid **3** Using a melon baller or teaspoon, scoop out seeds and core, leaving sides and base intact **4** Sprinkle insides with salt to draw out moisture, turn upside down, drain, dry and then stuff

51

Seafood Hors D'Oeuvre

pinch sea salt
1 onion
bay leaf
bouquet garni
4½ cups mussels
1 can crab
1 small can tomato paste
1 tablespoon brandy
scant 1 cup heavy cream
salt and pepper
1 lb. fresh or frozen shrimp
small bunch parsley

1 Peel the onion and cut in slices.

2 Prepare the cooking liquid (court bouillon): in a large saucepan put 1¼ cups water, the onion, the bay leaf and the bouquet garni; simmer for 20 minutes.

3 Scrape the mussels and wash them in several changes of water. Put the shellfish in the court bouillon and cook gently, stirring now and then, until they open. Discard any which do not open.

4 When the mussels are fully open, lift them out of the saucepan with a skimming ladle. Shell them and put in a dish.

5 Put the liquid through a strainer lined with a fine cloth and set it aside.

6 Open the can of crab, drain it, remove any cartilage and quickly flake the flesh.

7 Open the can of tomato paste. Pour the contents into a bowl. Stir in the brandy, then pour in the cream, stirring constantly, as though thickening mayonnaise. Then add 5 tablespoons of the reserved seafood liquid and mix. Add a little salt and a generous sprinkling of pepper. The sauce should now be well seasoned and very smooth.

8 Divide the mussels, flaked crab and peeled shrimp among 8 individual serving dishes and pour sauce over each.

9 Wash, dry and chop the parsley. Sprinkle some on top of each dish.

10 Refrigerate and serve chilled.

Serves 8

Crunchy Salad Starter

1 small head white cabbage
coarse salt
salt and pepper
⅔ packed cup golden raisins
½ branch celery
2 apples
juice ½ lemon
1 teaspoon prepared mustard
1 tablespoon vinegar
3 tablespoons olive oil
1 cup chopped walnuts

1 Trim the cabbage, pulling off any withered leaves, the hard core and side leaves. Wash the remainder. Dry and shred them finely with a large kitchen knife. Sprinkle with coarse salt and leave for about 30 minutes to draw out excess moisture.

2 Soak the raisins in warm water for 10 minutes.

3 Clean the celery. Wash, dry and dice it. Peel and core the apples, then dice, sprinkle with lemon juice.

4 Drain the shredded cabbage, dry it on absorbent paper and put into a salad bowl with the celery. Mix well.

5 Make a dressing by blending together the mustard, vinegar and oil, season with salt and pepper and stir well. Pour this over the cabbage and celery and mix well but do not crush the ingredients.

6 Drain and dry the raisins and add them to the bowl, together with the nuts and diced apple. Stir again and serve immediately.

Serves 6

Ham Logs

6 thick slices very lean ham
1½ small celery hearts
2 shallots
handful parsley
small bunch chives
juice ½ lemon
3 ozs. cream cheese
1 teaspoon strong mustard
salt
1 teaspoon paprika
pinch cayenne pepper
1 cup chopped walnuts

1 Cut 2 of the slices of ham into fine strips.

2 Clean the celery and chop it as finely as possible. Peel and finely chop the shallots. Wash, dry and chop the parsley and chives.

3 Mash the cheese and beat in the parsley, chives, shallots, 1 tablespoon lemon juice, the mustard, salt, paprika and cayenne pepper.

4 Stir in the chopped ham, celery and nuts. Beat well until the mixture is very smooth and creamy. Spread this mixture on the four remaining ham slices and roll these up to form 'logs.' Serve chilled, on a bed of lettuce and decorated with sliced tomatoes and a few sprigs of parsley.

Serves 4

Seafood Hors d'Oeuvre is a delicious medley of shellfish, brandy and cream

Artichoke Hearts with Cottage Cheese

1½ cups cottage cheese
4 large globe artichokes
large bunch chives, chervil and
  parsley, mixed
salt and pepper
pinch cayenne pepper
few lettuce leaves

For the Blanching Mixture:
juice 3 lemons
1 tablespoon flour
6⅓ cups water

1 Put the cottage cheese in a cloth-lined strainer and leave to drain completely.

2 Prepare the artichoke hearts and blanch (see pages 55-56). Cook them for 40 minutes in the blanching mixture, or till tender, then drain and cool.

3 Wash the herbs; dry them well and chop finely. Put them into a bowl. Add the cottage cheese, salt and pepper, and cayenne, and mix well with a fork; then beat vigorously.

4 Wash and dry the lettuce leaves. Arrange them on a serving dish. Lay the artichoke hearts on the lettuce and pile a pyramid of the cheese mixture on each one. Serve chilled.

Serves 4

Apple Hors d'Oeuvre

1 lemon
1 small celery heart
1 small cucumber
few lettuce leaves
3 tomatoes
few sprigs chives and chervil
¾ cup heavy cream
½ teaspoon paprika
salt and pepper
3 eating apples
12 radishes

1 Squeeze the lemon and reserve the juice. Wash the celery and chop it into fine strips.

2 Peel the cucumber, split it in half lengthwise and remove the seeds. Sprinkle both halves with salt, to remove the excess moisture.

3 Wash and dry the lettuce leaves. Wash and dry the tomatoes and then quarter them. Wash the chives and the chervil; dry and chop them.

4 In a bowl beat together the cream, lemon juice and paprika, and season with salt and pepper.

5 Rinse and dry the cucumber and cut it into small cubes. Peel and core the apples and dice them.

6 Put the cucumber, apples, celery and tomatoes into a dish. Pour the cream sauce over and stir it in.

7 Wash and scrape the radishes. Cut them into flower shapes.

8 Line the sides and bottom of a salad bowl with the lettuce leaves. Arrange the salad in the center. Sprinkle with the chopped chives and chervil, and decorate with the radishes. Serve chilled.

Serves 6

Apple Hors d'Oeuvre is a refreshing starter which sharpens the taste buds

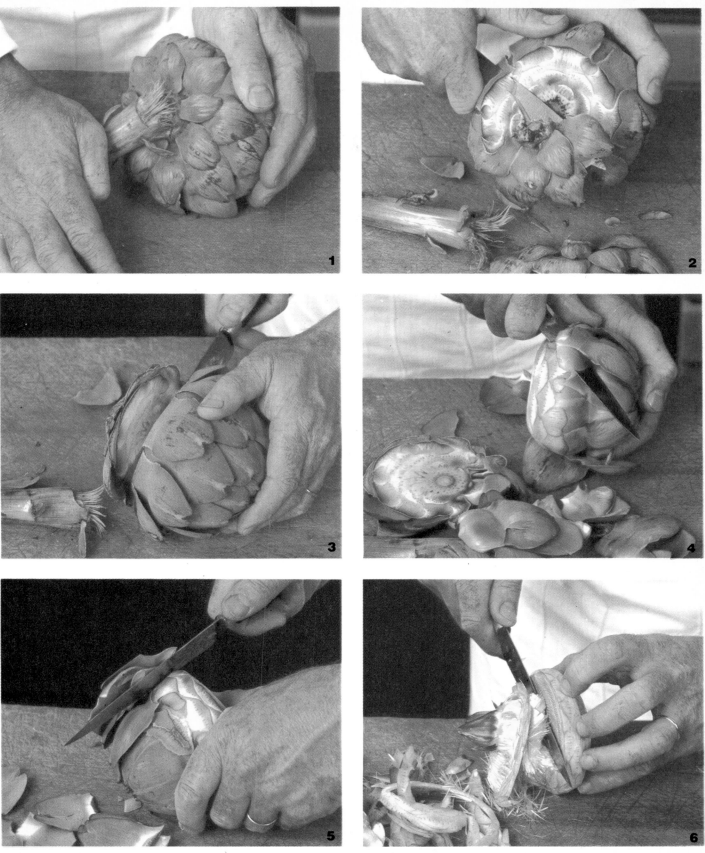

1 Pull away the artichoke stalk **2** and **3** With scissors snip off the tips of the leaves, then cut around and level the base **4** and **5** Cut away remaining leaves to expose the artichoke heart **6** Remove the 'hairy' center (choke) **7** Trim around the heart to neaten **8** and **9** Rub a cut lemon over each heart to

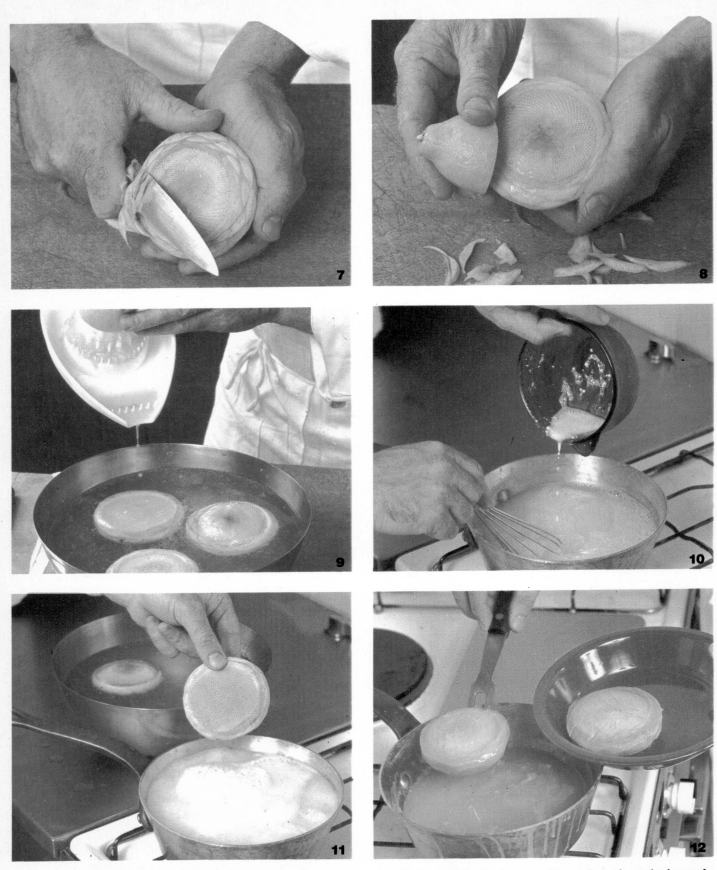

stop it from blackening; place in cold water with some of the lemon juice **10** Mix flour with remaining lemon juice and whisk into boiling salted water **11** and **12**

Cook the artichoke hearts till tender, then drain and chill them until needed

Anchovy and Garlic Stuffed Eggs make an attractive egg starter.

Oyster Cocktails

2 dozen fresh oysters
2 small celery branches
¼ cup tomato catsup
⅓ cup gin
1 tablespoon cream
1 teaspoon lemon juice
salt and pepper
pinch cayenne pepper
bunch chervil
1 teaspoon paprika

1 Open the oysters with an oyster knife and scrape them from the shells. Drain them, keeping the juice. Strain the juice through cheesecloth and put the oysters in a bowl.

2 Wash and dry the celery branches. Chop them finely and add to the oysters.

3 Stir into the oyster liquor the tomato catsup, gin, cream and lemon juice and beat for a moment. Taste and adjust the seasoning. Then add a pinch of cayenne pepper.

4 Pour this sauce over the oysters and celery and mix gently. Spoon the oyster cocktail into 4 glasses or small bowls.

5 Wash, dry and chop the chervil. Sprinkle the chopped chervil over the cocktails together with some paprika. Chill the glasses or bowls in the refrigerator for 1 hour and serve very cold.

Serves 4

Anchovy and Garlic Stuffed Eggs

4 eggs
4 large cloves garlic
3 tablespoons butter
salt and pepper
8 olives
8 anchovy fillets
few lettuce leaves
chopped parsley
4 small tomatoes

1 Put the eggs in a pan of cold water and bring to a boil. Peel the garlic cloves and add to the boiling water. Remove them after 7 minutes, drain and then pound in a mortar.

2 When the water has been boiling for 10 minutes, take out the eggs, cool them in cold water and shell. Cut the shelled hard-boiled eggs in half lengthwise. Leave them to cool.

3 Put the butter in a bowl and work it to a very soft paste with a wooden spoon.

4 Carefully remove the yolks from the eggs, without damaging the whites. Mash and sieve the yolks, and add them to the softened butter. Then add the garlic purée and stir well until smooth. Season.

5 Pile this paste back into the half egg whites. Decorate each with an olive with an anchovy fillet wrapped around it.

6 Arrange the lettuce leaves on a serving platter, place the stuffed eggs on top and sprinkle with the finely-chopped parsley. Slice the tomatoes in half horizontally and use the halves to garnish the platter. Refrigerate and serve cold.

Serves 4

Mussels in Spicy Sauce

1 cup canned or bottled mussels, drained
2 tablespoons mayonnaise
2 teaspoons mustard
1 teaspoon sherry
½ teaspoon lemon juice
2 small bottled or canned pimentos

1 Put the mussels in the serving dish.

2 To the mayonnaise add the mustard, sherry and lemon juice and stir carefully until blended. Cut the pimentos into strips and stir into the sauce.

3 Spoon this sauce over the mussels.

Serves 2

Tip: This is a tasty way of serving mussels when fresh ones are not in season.
   If using fresh, reserve a few shells for decoration.

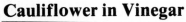

Cauliflower in Vinegar

1 medium cauliflower
salt
1 cup vinegar
1 cup water
1 clove garlic, cut in half
2 teaspoons dried basil
3 tablespoons olive oil
1 tablespoon lime or lemon juice
1 teaspoon chopped parsley
1 teaspoon chopped chives
freshly ground black pepper

1 Wash and trim the cauliflower and divide into florets or sprigs. Add to boiling salted water and cook for 10-15 minutes. Drain.

2 Bring the vinegar, water, garlic and basil to a boil and pour over the cauliflower. Leave until cold, then chill.

3 Mix the oil, lime or lemon juice, parsley, chives, salt and black pepper to make a smooth dressing. Drain the cauliflower, pour on the dressing and serve at once.

Serves 6

Red Peppers and Mushrooms

½ lb. mushrooms
salt and pepper
2 lemons
5 tablespoons olive oil
6 large red peppers
small bunch chervil

1 Clean the mushrooms. Cut the ends off the stalks. Wash the mushrooms quickly but do not leave them underwater longer than necessary. Slice them thinly and season with salt and pepper.

2 Squeeze 1 of the lemons and sprinkle 2 tablespoons of the juice and 2 tablespoons olive oil over the mushrooms. Leave them to marinate.

3 Wash and dry the peppers. Broil them under high heat (the skin should swell and darken) or hold over a flame on a skewer. Then rinse them under cold water and peel them. The darkened outer skin should come off very easily, exposing the soft red flesh underneath.

4 Cut the peppers in half and remove the seeds. Cut the flesh in strips. Season with salt and pepper, and sprinkle on the rest of the lemon juice and oil.

5 Wash the other lemon and quarter it. Wash, dry and chop the chervil.

6 Mix the peppers and mushrooms together in a deep dish. Garnish with the lemon quarters and sprinkle chervil over the top. Chill 1 hour before serving.

Serves 6

Red Herring with Sauerkraut

6 herring fillets (smoked and salted)
3 tablespoons olive oil
2 sweet eating apples
1 lb. sauerkraut
2 mild onions
1 lemon
2 tablespoons heavy cream
1 cup plain yogurt
pepper
bunch parsley

1 Cut the herring fillets into small pieces. Put them on a deep plate and pour the oil over them.

2 Peel, core and dice the apples.

3 Wash the sauerkraut in fresh water. Drain it thoroughly, squeezing with the hands to extract all the water. Put it into a cloth, dry it well, then separate the shreds.

4 Peel the onions. Cut them into rounds, then separate into rings. Squeeze the juice from the lemon.

5 Mix the lemon juice with the cream and yogurt. Add pepper to taste and blend all these ingredients together.

6 Mix the sauerkraut and the diced apple, pour on the lemon-flavored yogurt and stir gently.

7 Wash, dry and chop the parsley.

8 Arrange the sauerkraut and apple salad around the edge of a serving dish.

9 Drain the herring fillets and place them in the center of the dish. Cover them with the onion rings. Sprinkle with chopped parsley and serve very cold.

Serves 6

Tuna Fish with Eggplant in Sweet-sour Sauce (Caponata)

In Sicily this dish is a speciality and is called Caponata; some versions omit the tuna fish.

3 eggplants
1 small branch celery
4¼ cups water
6 canned anchovies, drained
5 large ripe firm tomatoes
1 large onion
1 bunch parsley
½ cup olive oil
salt and pepper
few sprigs thyme
1 bay leaf
1½ tablespoons sugar
2 teaspoons vinegar
1 cup small black olives
3 tablespoons capers
1½ cups canned tuna

1 Peel the eggplants. Cut them into cubes, sprinkle with salt to draw out the excess moisture and any bitterness and leave for about 30 minutes. Wash and trim the celery, and slice thinly.

2 Bring the water to a boil, add salt and put in the celery; simmer for about 8 minutes, then drain and plunge into a pan of cold water; drain again and set aside.

3 Wash the anchovies to remove the excess salt. Separate the fillets and rinse again thoroughly in water. Cut them into small pieces.

4 Skin the tomatoes; quarter them, remove the seeds and chop the flesh. Peel and thinly slice the onion. Wash, dry and chop the parsley.

5 Heat 2 tablespoons oil in a saucepan. When hot, add the onion and cook gently until soft but not browned. Add the tomatoes, season with salt and pepper, add the thyme and bay leaf and cook over very low heat until the mixture is a soft pulp. Remove the thyme and bay leaf and rub the mixture through a conical strainer.

6 Put the tomato purée in a pan.

add the sugar and cook until thickened and lightly browned. Then add the vinegar and cook for a further 3-4 minutes.

7 Meanwhile, drain and dry the eggplant pieces. Heat the rest of the oil in a saucepan, put in the eggplant and cook briskly until lightly browned. Drain off the oil.

8 Remove the pan of tomato sauce from the heat and stir into the eggplants, together with the celery, anchovies, black olives and capers. Correct the seasoning — this dish should be fairly spicy — and mix together.

9 Set the mixture aside to cool, then chill in the refrigerator overnight. Turn the mixture into a salad bowl. Break the tuna fish into regular bite-size pieces and arrange over the top. Chill and serve.

Serves 6

Tuna fish and eggplant in a piquant sauce, a deliciously refreshing dish for a hot summer's day

Smoked Fish Starter

1 head white cabbage (small)
2 marinated herring
½ teaspoon cumin seed
6 tablespoons heavy cream
3 smoked sprats or brisling
  sardines
2 lemons
2 apples
12 thin slices whole wheat bread
¼ cup butter
½ lb. thin slices smoked salmon
6 thin slices smoked eel
coarse salt and pepper

1 Trim, wash and dry the cabbage and shred it finely with a large sharp kitchen knife. Put the shredded cabbage into a bowl, sprinkle lightly with salt and leave to stand while continuing with the preparation.

2 Drain the marinated herring and fillet them. Put the fillets in a blender or through a grinder to make a purée. Add to this half the cumin and 2 tablespoons cream.

3 Wash the smoked sprats

4 Squeeze 1 lemon and reserve juice. Wash and dry the second lemon and cut it in thin rounds, then each round in half.

5 Peel the apples and cut them in quarters, remove the cores and seeds and dice.

6 Butter 9 slices of whole wheat bread and cut them diagonally to make 18 triangles. Arrange the slices of smoked eel on 6 of these triangles, and the slices of smoked salmon on the others. Pipe around a border of mayonnaise if liked.

7 Butter the remainder of the slices of bread with the herring purée, and cut them into triangles. Place 1 fillet on each of the triangles, and a semicircle of lemon on each slice.

8 Drain and dry the cabbage. Add to it the diced apple and the rest of the cumin. Sprinkle with lemon juice and pepper and mix gently.

9 Arrange the cabbage in a heap in the center of a serving dish, and pour on the rest of the cream. Arrange the various fish-covered triangles of bread around the edge of the dish and serve cold.

Serves 6

An eye-catching appetizer, choose several kinds of smoked fish for color and flavor contrast

Vegetables à la Grecque

3 globe artichoke hearts
1 small cauliflower
1 lemon
½ lb. mushrooms
3 carrots
2 bulbs fennel
3 turnips
2 leeks
3 cloves garlic
½ lb. green olives
1 cup olive oil
1 tablespoon tomato paste
1 teaspoon coriander seeds
½ cup wine vinegar
salt and pepper

1 Peel and wash all the vegetables. Break the cauliflower into florets. Squeeze the juice of the lemon.

2 Put the artichoke hearts, the cauliflower florets, the mushrooms (whole small ones, cut in half if large) into water. Add the lemon juice to prevent the vegetables from discoloring.

3 Slice the carrots, fennel, turnips and leeks. Peel and crush the garlic. Pit the olives and wash in cold water.

4 Heat the oil in a pan. When it is hot, add the leeks, then all the other vegetables, stirring all the time to prevent them from sticking.

5 Add the crushed garlic, the tomato paste, the coriander, the vinegar, the water, salt and pepper.

6 Cook for 12–15 minutes, stirring from time to time. The vegetables should stay firm. When cooked, let cool.

Serves 8–10

Artichokes à la Grecque

4 globe artichokes
2 lemons
½ lb. canned tomatoes, drained

6 shallots
½ cup olive oil
6 coriander seeds
1 bouquet garni
½ cup dry white wine
salt and pepper

1 Prepare the artichoke hearts (see page 55). Cut 1 lemon in half. Rub the artichoke hearts with one half. Squeeze the other half, pouring the juice into a bowl. Fill the bowl with water.

2 Cut the hearts into 4 or 6 pieces. Remove all the hairs with a serrated knife. Dip the artichokes into the lemon water.

3 Put the artichokes into a saucepan. Add the lemon water. Bring to a boil and boil for 1 minute. Chop the tomatoes roughly. Peel the shallots and squeeze the last lemon.

4 Warm the oil in a sauté pan. Drain the artichokes and put them into the pan. Add the tomatoes, the shallots, the coriander seeds, the bouquet garni, the lemon juice and the white wine. Add seasoning, cover and cook on low heat for 30 minutes.

5 When the cooking is finished, remove the bouquet garni, put the artichoke pieces into an hors d'oeuvre dish. Leave to cool, then put the dish in the refrigerator.

Serves 4

Vegetables à la Grecque — mixed vegetables served cold in this way make a delicious starter

Look 'n Cook Artichoke Hearts à la Grecque

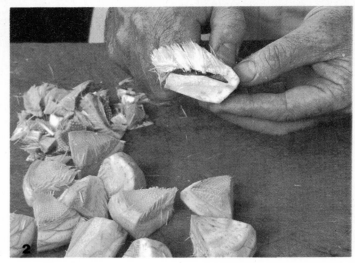

1 Cut the hearts into pieces and put into lemon water
2 Cut away the hairy part **3** Put the hearts into a pan, strain the lemon water over them and boil for 1 minute
4 The ingredients **5** Put all the ingredients into a sauté pan and cook gently **6** The finished dish. Keep in the refrigerator until needed.

Lobster with Avocados

2 lbs. live lobster
sea salt
1 bouquet garni
1 small cucumber
2 avocados
2 tablespoons gin
½ teaspoon Tabasco sauce
salt and pepper
1¼ cups mayonnaise
pinch cayenne pepper
½ teaspoon paprika

1 Wash the lobster.

2 Boil water in a large saucepan with a handful of sea salt and the bouquet garni. Drop the lobster into the boiling water and cook for about 10 minutes.

3 Drain the lobster and let cool.

4 Peel the cucumber and split in two lengthwise. Take out the seeds with a small spoon. Grate the flesh of the cucumber, put it into a bowl and let drain without salting it.

5 Cut the avocados into halves, remove the pits, and, with a melon baller, scoop the flesh into balls.

6 When the lobster are cold, remove the meat from the tails.

7 Put the avocado balls and the lobster tails into a glass serving bowl. Pour over the gin and Tabasco sauce. Season with a little salt and pepper and mix well. Leave to marinate for about 20 minutes.

8 Lay a piece of cheesecloth over a colander. Pour in the cucumber pulp, and press down well to extract as much water as possible. Blend this pulp into the mayonnaise, folding it in gently. Then season with cayenne.

9 Pour the cucumber mayonnaise over the lobster and avocado, mixing well. Sprinkle with paprika and serve very cold.

Serves 4

Crab and Avocado Cocktail

4 eggs
½ lb. crabmeat
1 tablespoon tomato paste
1¼ cups mayonnaise
salt and pepper
3 avocados
paprika

1 Put 6 small glass dishes into the refrigerator.

2 Cook the eggs in boiling water for 10 minutes. Cool them in cold water and then shell them.

3 Flake the crabmeat, removing the cartilage. Add the tomato paste to the mayonnaise. Pass the hard-boiled eggs through a food mill or chop them.

4 Mix together the crabmeat, chopped eggs and the mayonnaise in a bowl. Season.

5 Cut the avocados in half, take out the pits, cut the flesh into large cubes and place them in the chilled dishes. Cover with the crab mixture and sprinkle with paprika. Chill until ready to serve.

Serves 6

Peaches Filled with Crab — a mixture of fruit and fish makes an interesting light first course

Tomatoes Stuffed with Anchovies and Rice

6 firm tomatoes
salt
¾ cup long grain rice
24 canned anchovy fillets
24 black olives
1 small bulb fennel
2 shallots
chopped parsley
1 green pepper
juice of ½ lemon
1¼ cups mayonnaise

1 Scoop out the tomatoes. Wash the rice under running cold water until the water is clear.

2 Bring to a boil a pan of salted water, twice the volume of the rice (i.e. 1¼ cups). Add the rice, simmer for about 12 minutes or until tender, then drain and leave until cold.

3 Put aside 6 anchovy fillets and 6 olives. Chop the rest of the anchovies. Pit the olives and cut into quarters.

4 Trim the fennel, wash, dry and chop. Peel and chop the shallots. Wash, dry and chop the parsley.

Wash and dry the pepper; cut it in half, remove the seeds and white membrane and chop finely.

5 Add the lemon juice to the mayonnaise. Add the cooked rice, chopped anchovies, olives, shallots, fennel, pepper and the parsley to the mayonnaise. Fold carefully together.

6 Rinse and dry the tomatoes. Fill with the rice salad and make a dome on top. Top with an olive and a rolled anchovy fillet. Arrange the stuffed tomatoes on a serving dish and refrigerate for 1 hour before serving.

Serves 6

Peaches Filled with Crab

5 large peaches
¼ lb. crabmeat
½ cup heavy cream
¼ teaspoon lemon juice
2 teaspoons brandy
8 lettuce leaves
large pinch paprika
salt and pepper

1 Peel the peaches: halve them and remove the pits.

2 Drain the crab, and mash the crabmeat together with 1 of the peaches in a basin.

3 Add the cream, lemon juice, brandy, paprika, salt and pepper, and blend all the ingredients together well.

4 Wash the lettuce leaves, and dry them on absorbent paper. Make a bed of the leaves on a flat serving dish, and place a peach half on each of the leaves. Fill each peach half with the crab mixture.

5 Chill the dish for at least 1 hour before serving.

Serves 4

Tomatoes Stuffed with Anchovies and Rice — this simple dish is good for buffet parties

Prepare the fish and make the panada (see page 67).
1 Cook the panada until smooth and thick **2** Sauté the mushrooms, add the shallots and sauté until soft.

Remove **3** Add the cubed fish, cook until golden, then remove **4** Pour in the wine and boil, stirring in all the sediment **5** and **6** Put back the fish, mushrooms and

shallots and stir in the parsley **7** and **8** Blend the fish fillets with 2 egg whites **9** Add the panada, blend and turn into a bowl **10** Stir in the whipped cream **11** and

12 Fold in the fish and mushroom mixture, spoon into a greased terrine and cook

Fish Terrine

⅓ cup butter
3 lbs. firm white fish (e.g. pike, haddock, cod)
3 eggs
1 cup flour
salt and pepper
¾ cup milk
3½ cups button mushrooms
2 shallots
½ cup dry white wine
½ tablespoon chopped parsley
1 pint heavy cream

1 Take the butter out of the refrigerator to soften.

2 Fillet and skin the fish. Put in a basin, cover, and put in the refrigerator.

3 Work 3 tablespoons of the butter in a bowl to soften. Separate the eggs, and beat in the egg yolks and flour to make a stiff paste (panada); add salt and pepper.

4 Bring the milk to a boil in a saucepan, pour onto the panada, little by little, whisking all the time, then turn the mixture into a heavy pan. Cook over low heat, stirring with a wooden spoon all the time, until the mixture comes away cleanly from the sides of the pan. Lightly grease a plate, put the panada on it, cool, then chill in the refrigerator.

5 Peel and wipe the mushrooms. Slice them and sauté in 1½ tablespoons butter. Peel and finely chop the shallots; and add them to the saute pan. Cook very gently for about 3 minutes; season with salt and pepper, then turn the mixture into a bowl.

6 Put the sauté pan back on moderate heat; put in the fish and cook till golden-brown, then turn the fish into the bowl. Place the sauté pan on high heat, add the wine and boil for 2 minutes, stirring and scraping across the bottom of the pan to incorporate all the drippings. Reduce to half the quantity, then return the contents of the bowl to the sauté pan. Sprinkle with chopped pars-ley, add salt and pepper; blend together well and spoon back into the bowl.

7 Season the fish fillets with salt and pepper. Put them in a blender with 2 egg whites and the panada; blend until smooth.

8 Whip the cream until stiff, then stir into the fish mixture and blend again. Turn the mixture into a casserole or bowl. Stir in the mushrooms, shallots and fish.

9 Preheat the oven to 325°F. Lightly butter the terrine with 1½ tablespoons butter; spoon in the mixture and press down well. Cover and seal the terrine, then cook in a pan of water in the oven for about 1½ hours.

10 Cool, then chill until ready to serve.

Serves 10–12

Fish terrine — slicing the terrine into individual portions for serving

All about herbs and their uses

Mint This is a popular herb which is used as a flavoring for boiled new potatoes and peas and as a garnish for fruit and iced drinks. It is probably best known for its use in mint sauce or jelly to accompany roast lamb.

Sorrel The leaves of this herb have a pungent acid flavor and the young ones are used in salads. The older plant can be cooked in the same way as spinach and is used to flavor sauces and soups. Sorrel is also known as dock.

Thyme The excellent flavor of thyme means that it is used extensively in the kitchen and is one of the basic ingredients of a bouquet garni. The leaves contain an oil called thymol which aids the digestion of fatty foods. Thyme can be used with cheese dishes, shellfish and poultry stuffing and as a garnish for vegetables.

Rosemary The leaves are used both fresh and dried and go well with beef, salmon, duck, boiled ham and pork. Rosemary can also be used with sweet dishes such as jellos, fruit salads and biscuits.

Marjoram There are three types of marjoram, sweet marjoram being the one most often used for flavoring. It can be added to soups, stews, cheese and egg dishes, and salads and blends well with other herbs such as thyme.

Fennel This herb is related to dill but is sweeter and more aromatic. The digestive properties of fennel make it a good accompaniment to oily fish dishes, and it is also used to flavor soups, sauces, salads, cakes and pastry.

Sage This is a slightly bitter herb which, because of its strong flavor, should be used carefully. Sage is probably best known for its use with onion in poultry stuffings, but it also gives a good flavor to peas and beans. Chopped fresh leaves can be added to salads, pickles and cheese, and the dried leaves to casseroles and sausage meat.

Bay Leaves These have a strong spicy flavor which goes well with game, meat, fish, poultry, salads, sauces and vegetables. Bay leaves are a basic ingredient of a bouquet garni and can be added to the milk used for custards, molds, and milk puddings and to the stock for boiling fish. Their flavor becomes stronger if they are crushed or dried.

Chives Chive is a member of the leek and onion family and, as would be expected, the flavor is reminiscent of onion. The thin, tubular stalks are a bright green color and so look very attractive chopped into short lengths and sprinkled over soups or mixed into pale dishes such as potato salad and cream cheese.

Dill Dill leaves are blue-green and feathery in appearance and their flavor is similar to aniseed and caraway. They can be chopped and added to salads, green vegetables, soups and stews, but because their flavor soon disappears when they are cooked, they should be added to hot dishes just before serving. Dill adds flavor to pickles and is particularly suited to use with fish dishes.

Basil The large, heart-shaped leaves of basil have a peppery flavor and can be used in combination with other herbs such as rosemary, sage and oregano. The flavor develops with cooking so basil should be used carefully. This herb is particularly effective with vegetables which have little flavor and with chicken, egg and rice dishes.

Mint · Sorrel · Thyme · Rosemary · Marjoram

Fennel · Lemon sage · Bay leaves

Chives · Sage · Dill · Basil

All about Salads

An exotic salad with cheese and fruit

All about Salads

Salads need not only be a mixture of lettuce and tomatoes which are served as an accompaniment to cold meat; they can also be served as hors d'oeuvres or as main meals in themselves. The term 'salad' is now used to encompass a wide range of dishes and foods. Salads can be made with herbs, plants, raw or cooked vegetables, eggs, cheese, meat, fish, fruits, nuts, pasta or rice. The list is seemingly endless.

With the emphasis on healthy, raw and whole foods and the present trend toward a more natural way of eating, salads are becoming ever more popular and original. They are also ideal if you are slimming or diet-conscious, since usually they contain very little carbohydrate or fat and are rich in vitamins and roughage.

Salad Dressings

A perfect salad should be crisp, cool and served in a delicious dressing. Never toss a salad in an acid dressing too long before serving — it will turn soggy. Always toss it at the last moment. The French are masters of the salad dressing. They use only the best olive oil and wine vinegars. A few useful tips to remember when making a French dressing are:

1 Use the best oil if possible—e.g. olive, walnut or peanut oil
2 Never use malt vinegar—it will give your salad a bitter flavor.
3 If you want to use mustard in your dressing, add a wine-flavored type.

There are four types of dressings: the classic French dressing; mayonnaise; creamy white sauce; and blue cheese dressing. Of course, there are many variations on these. Try adding tomato paste, lemon juice, chutneys, herbs and spices, curry powder or Tabasco to mayonnaise for an unusual flavor. French dressings can be more tasty and tangy if you mix in some chopped onions or capers.

Salad Hors d'Oeuvres

Salads are delicious for hors d'oeuvres or appetizers before a main course. They make a light and refreshing start to a meal. Opposite are some ideas for salad starters which will whet your appetite for what is to come. Try them as appetizers or serve them as canapes at a buffet or party. They are all quickly and easily prepared, and can be made in advance and refrigerated until you wish to serve them. The key below will help you to identify them.

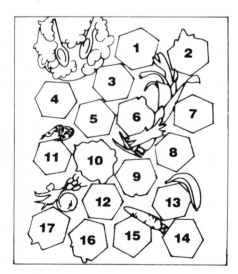

1 Black olives, sliced tomato, halved green grapes and nuts surrounded by orange sections and thinly sliced cucumber, then topped with onion rings.

2 Alternate slices of tomato and hard-boiled egg on a bed of chicory leaves garnished with black and green olives.

3 Chopped beet with scallions on seeded tomato slices arranged like the petals of a flower.

4 Tomato slices and onion rings in a classic French dressing, sprinkled with chopped chives.

5 Sliced tomato, cucumber, hard-boiled eggs and black olives, with onion rings and anchovy strips on a bed of lettuce leaves.

6 Sliced blanched zucchini and sliced tomatoes on a bed of lettuce leaves, generously sprinkled with chopped chives.

7 Seeded segments of tomato with pineapple chunks in an oily dressing to which pineapple juice is added.

8 Lobster chunks in a spicy mayonnaise with sliced bananas and tiny onions, garnished with a sprig of fresh watercress.

9 Hard-boiled eggs, split and filled with chopped red pepper and shrimp in sour cream, then sprinkled with finely grated cheese on a bed of watercress.

10 Shrimp, tomato wedges and black olives heaped on a bed of crisp lettuce leaves.

11 A hollowed-out tomato stuffed with cream cheese, celery seeds and chives surrounded by an attractive border of watercress.

12 Chunks of canned meat with cooked rice, mixed with chopped red and green peppers, onion and hard-boiled eggs.

13 Overlapping thinly sliced tomatoes, dressed with natural yogurt and chopped chives with a cucumber border, and a slice of cucumber in the center.

14 Sliced tomatoes, shrimp, and bean sprouts surrounded by sliced apples which have been sprinkled with lemon juice.

15 Sliced tomatoes and raw mushrooms on a bed of lettuce leaves, sprinkled with chopped chives in a French dressing.

16 Half an avocado on a plain lettuce leaf, filled with chopped ham, onions and red pepper in a vinaigrette dressing.

17 Sliced tomatoes, garnished with Cheddar cheese cubes on a bed of flower-shaped chicory leaves.

Ham and Egg Salad

1 apple
¼ lb. ham cut into ¼-inch cubes
2 boiled new potatoes, cut into ¼-inch cubes
1 tablespoon chopped chives or shallots
½ cup mayonnaise
4 lettuce leaves
4 hard-boiled eggs
1 teaspoon chopped parsley

1 Peel and core the apple. Dice it finely. Combine with the ham, potatoes and chives or shallots. Pour on the mayonnaise, reserving a little for later, and toss.

2 Wash, dry and shred the lettuce. Place a quarter of the lettuce in the bottom of each of 4 glasses. Top with the ham and potato mixture.

3 Cut each egg into 8 wedges and arrange them like the spokes of a wheel on each serving. Dot the yolks with a little mayonnaise and sprinkle with the chopped parsley.

Serves 4

Avocado Starter

2 avocados
1 grapefruit
8 lettuce leaves

For the Dressing:
½ cup mayonnaise
1 tablespoon tomato catsup
2-3 drops Worcestershire sauce
dash Tabasco (optional)
juice half lemon

1 Prepare the dressing by combining the mayonnaise, tomato catsup, Worcestershire sauce, and Tabasco if desired. Add the lemon juice.

2 Peel and pit the avocados and cut them into small pieces.

3 Peel the grapefruit, remove the white skin, and divide into sections. Cut each section into 4 and combine with the avocado.

4 Wash and dry the lettuce. Place one leaf at the bottom of each of 4 glasses. Shred the remaining leaves and place equal amounts in the glasses. Pour in the avocado mixture.

5 Chill for 1 hour before serving.

Serves 4

Ham and Egg Salad is easy to make and attractively served in glasses, garnished with parsley and eggs

Shrimp Starter

2 oranges
8 walnuts, shelled
2 apples, cored
1 branch celery
¾ cup cooked, peeled shrimp (about ¼ lb.)
½ head lettuce
4 slices lemon

72

Shrimp Starter combines juicy apples and oranges with nuts, shrimp and vegetables in a glass, garnished with lemon

Shrimp Salad

Avocado Starter makes a fruity and refreshing start to any meal, and it can easily be prepared the previous day

1 Peel the oranges, remove the white skin and divide into sections. Roughly chop the walnuts and apples and dice the celery. Combine these ingredients in a bowl with the shrimp.

2 Wash and drain the lettuce. Shred it finely and place equal portions in 4 glasses. Pour in the mixture. Chill for 1 hour and garnish with a slice of lemon.

Serves 4

1 lb. cooked, peeled shrimp
½ lb. sliced mushrooms
2 medium tomatoes, each cut into 8 sections
½ lb. cooked asparagus tips
1 cup cooked peas
2 tablespoons olive oil
1 teaspoon white wine vinegar
½ teaspoon salt
¼ teaspoon dried dill
2 hard-boiled eggs

1 Put the shrimp, mushrooms, tomatoes, asparagus and peas into a salad bowl.

2 Mix the oil, wine vinegar, salt and dill together and pour over the salad. Cut each egg into 8 pieces and use as garnish.

Serves 4

Green Olive Salad

12 green stuffed olives, chopped
3 branches celery, chopped
1 onion, finely chopped
3 apples, cored and chopped
¼ cup mayonnaise
¼ cup plain yogurt
1 tablespoon horseradish
1 tablespoon applesauce
1 teaspoon honey
1 teaspoon chopped scallions
2 cups cooked potatoes
6 radishes
few sprigs parsley

1 Make an olive paste by combining the olives with ⅓ of the celery, the onion, half one apple and 1 tablespoon of the mayonnaise. Chill.

2 Mix the yogurt, the rest of the mayonnaise, horseradish, applesauce, honey, and scallions.

3 Season and mix with the remaining celery, potatoes and apples.

4 Serve the salad on lettuce leaves and place the olive paste in the middle, garnished with cut radishes and parsley.

Serves 4

Tuna Olive Salad with Garlic Toast

1 eggplant, peeled and cubed
salt and pepper
2 tablespoons oil
3 tablespoons olive oil
1 tablespoon vinegar
1 clove garlic, crushed
½ teaspoon prepared mustard
8 ozs. tuna
2 branches celery, chopped
8 black olives
loaf French bread

For the Garlic Butter:
¼ cup butter
1 clove garlic, crushed

1 Sprinkle the eggplant with salt and leave for ½ hour. Wash and drain, then fry quickly in the oil. Cool.

2 Preheat the oven to 375 °F.

3 Mix the olive oil, vinegar, garlic, mustard, salt and pepper, and pour over the tuna, celery and eggplant in a bowl. Garnish with black olives. Chill.

4 Slice the bread and toast each piece.

5 Mix the butter with the garlic and brush each piece. Heat in the oven for about 10 minutes, until all the butter is soaked up.

6 Serve the hot garlic toast with the chilled tuna mixture.

Serves 4

Tuna Olive Salad with Garlic Toast (right) and Green Olive Salad (left) are unusual ways of serving olives

Californian Avocado Salad with Olives

few lettuce leaves
3 grapefruit
3 avocados, peeled
½ lb. cooked jumbo shrimp
juice 1 lemon
2 tablespoons brandy
pinch cayenne pepper
dash Tabasco
1 tablespoon catsup
6 stuffed green olives, sliced
1 lemon, sliced

For the Mayonnaise:
1 egg yolk
1 teaspoon prepared mustard
1 tablespoon white wine vinegar
salt and pepper
1 cup olive oil

1 Wash and dry the lettuce leaves.

2 Prepare the mayonnaise. Make sure that the egg yolk is free of all traces of white and place it in a bowl. Add the mustard, a few drops of the vinegar, salt and pepper. Add the oil, a drop at a time at first, beating continually in the same direction. When the mayonnaise thickens, pour in the oil in a thin trickle. Lastly, beat in the rest of the vinegar. Put in a cool place.

3 Cut the grapefruit into halves. Using a grapefruit knife, remove the thin skin separating the sections. Scoop out the flesh and place it in a bowl.

4 Halve the avocados and remove the seeds. Dice. Mix this with the grapefruit pieces. Peel half the shrimp and add them to the mixture. Sprinkle the lemon juice and

---

Californian Avocado Salad with Olives looks delicate but tastes exquisite — it is soaked in Tabasco and brandy

brandy over the top. Season. Add the cayenne pepper, Tabasco and catsup. Carefully fold the mayonnaise into this mixture.

5 Line the base of a shallow serving dish with the lettuce leaves. Spoon the salad into the middle. Garnish with the lemon and the sliced green olives. Chill. Serve surrounded with the remaining shrimp.

Serves 6

Egg and Pepper Salad

2 green peppers
1 red pepper
2 large onions, sliced
3 hard-boiled eggs
6 stuffed green olives

For the Dressing:
1 tablespoon vinegar
2 tablespoons olive oil
½ teaspoon prepared mustard
salt and pepper

For the Mayonnaise:
¼ cup mayonnaise
3 tablespoons heavy cream
1 teaspoon vinegar
1 tablespoon tomato paste
2 teaspoons paprika
pinch salt

1 Seed the peppers and cut them into thickish rings. Place them in salted boiling water and simmer for one minute. Refresh in cold water, drain and dry.

2 Combine all the dressing ingredients and mix well. Toss the vegetables in the dressing.

3 Halve the eggs and place them on top. Garnish with the olives.

4 Whisk together the mayonnaise ingredients and serve with the salad.

Serves 4

Insalata Marinara is tangy and tastes of the sea with chunks of herring, olives and egg in a classic dressing

Insalata Marinara

½ lb. green beans
¼ cucumber
3 tomatoes, skinned and quartered
1 small onion, finely chopped
½ lb. smoked herring, or ½ lb. salmon, well drained
1 hard-boiled egg
8 stuffed green olives
1 teaspoon chopped parsley

For the Dressing:
3 tablespoons oil
1½ tablespoons vinegar
salt and pepper
½ teaspoon French mustard
½ teaspoon powdered sugar
1 clove garlic, crushed

1 Boil the beans for 8 minutes in salted water. Drain, refresh in cold water and allow to cool.

2 Cut the cucumber into slices ½ inch thick, and quarter.

3 Prepare the dressing. Place the oil, vinegar, seasoning and French mustard in a bowl, and whisk together. Add the sugar and crushed garlic and stir well.

4 Place the tomatoes, cucumber, beans and onion in a salad bowl. Pour the dressing over the vegetables and mix thoroughly. Cut the herring into cubes approximately 1 inch in size. If you use salmon, flake it roughly. Add the fish to the vegetables and turn carefully.

5 Shell and quarter the egg. Arrange the pieces on top of the salad with the olives. Chill and serve garnished with the chopped parsley.

Serves 4

Ratatouille Salads

Ratatouille means a mixture of vegetables in French. The basic ingredients, eggplant and zucchini are known as vegetable marrow. Tomatoes, onions and peppers are also traditionally included. For a variation you may add celery, fennel or sliced mushrooms.

It may be served as a hot dish or a cold salad, either on its own or with an assortment of cold meats or fish. Below, we provide a recipe for basic ratatouille. It can be garnished in any number of tasty ways. Try sprinkling it with sliced black olives or pickles. For a complete meal, blend in cooked green noodles and serve with a crisp green salad. Ratatouille also makes a delicious appetizer when served cold on a hot summer's day.

Ratatouille

2 zucchini
2 eggplants
salt and pepper
2 green peppers
1 red pepper
½ cup olive oil
2 medium onions, chopped
2 cloves garlic, chopped
4 tomatoes, skinned, seeded and chopped
pinch thyme
1 bay leaf
½ teaspoon sugar (optional)
¼ cup flour
1 tablespoon vinegar
juice ½ lemon
½ teaspoon basil

Ratatouille is a sautéed dish of vegetables from Provence which can be served hot or cold as a starter or salad

1 Cut the zucchini and eggplants into slices ¾ inch thick. Sprinkle with salt and leave for 30 minutes. Wash, drain and dry.

2 Split the peppers lengthwise. Remove the seeds and cut in thin slices.

3 Heat ½ of the oil in a large pan and sauté the onions for 3 minutes or until tender. Do not allow them to brown.

4 Add the peppers, zucchini and garlic to the pan. Cook for 2 minutes, then add the tomatoes, thyme, bay leaf and sugar (optional). Season and cook for a further 6 minutes.

5 In a separate pan, heat the remaining oil. Coat the eggplant slices in flour. Shake off any excess. If the slices are large, halve or quarter them so that they are equivalent to the zucchini in diameter. Fry for ½ minute on each side or until golden. Remove and drain well.

6 Combine all the vegetables in a casserole dish. Add the vinegar and lemon juice, and mix well. Chill and serve sprinkled with chopped basil.

Serves 6

Ratatouille with Tuna

8 ozs. tuna
juice ½ lemon
6 cups ratatouille

1 Place the tuna fish in the center of a shallow serving dish.

2 Pour on the lemon juice and surround the tuna with the ratatouille. Alternatively, you can flake the fish and blend it with the ratatouille.

Serves 6

Ratatouille with Tuna brings a taste of the Mediterranean to your dinner table — try it as a main meal with green salad

Ratatouille Flan

2 eggs, beaten
1¼ cups milk
1 cup + 2 tablespoons flour
pinch salt
¼ cup olive oil
2 cups ratatouille
¼ cucumber, thinly sliced

1 Preheat the oven to 400°F.

2 Make the batter: beat together the eggs and milk. Beat in the flour and salt, then rest it for a few minutes.

3 Place the oil in a shallow oven-proof dish and put in the oven for about 5 minutes. When the oil is hot, pour half the batter into the dish and cook for 20 minutes.

4 Remove from the oven and add

Ratatouille Flan is really a type of Yorkshire pudding filled with ratatouille layers and served with a crisp salad

the layer of ratatouille and cover with the remaining batter. Reduce the temperature to 375°F. Bake the dish for 20 minutes until risen and golden-brown. Turn out onto a plate, decorate the top with over-lapping cucumber slices and serve with salad.

Serves 4–6

Portofino Fish Salad

¼ cup olive oil
½ onion, chopped
1 clove garlic, crushed
½ lb. mullet or mackerel fillets, cut in small cubes
2 zucchini, sliced
½ red pepper, seeded and thinly sliced
4 new potatoes, cooked and sliced
salt and pepper
pinch rosemary
pinch basil

juice ½ lemon
1¼ cups thin tomato sauce

1 Heat the oil in a skillet. Sauté the onion and garlic for 2-3 minutes until tender, but still crisp.

2 Add the fish and stir-fry for 2 minutes, then add the zucchini, sliced pepper and potatoes. Season with the salt and pepper and herbs.

3 Sauté for 5 minutes, stirring occasionally. Then sprinkle on the lemon juice and arrange on a serving dish. Serve hot or cold with a tomato sauce and salad.

Serves 4

Tip: This dish is a variation on the usual ratatouille. To make it go further, you can add chopped tomatoes and sautéed eggplants. The vegetables should be crisp and firm.

Portofino Fish Salad makes a change from the more traditional ratatouille with its sautéed fish and potatoes

Shrimp Puffs

1 lb. puff pastry, fresh or frozen
  and thawed
1¼ cups peeled, cooked shrimp
1 cup flaked, cooked white fish
scant ½ cup white sauce
1 clove garlic, crushed
pinch chopped parsley
salt and pepper
pinch paprika
oil for deep frying

1 Roll out the pastry ⅛ inch thick and cut out some circles 5 inches in diameter.

2 Mix the shrimp and fish into the white sauce. Stir in the crushed garlic, parsley and seasoning.

3 Place a spoonful of this mixture in the center of each pastry circle. Wet the edges with water and fold over, sealing the edges.

4 Heat the oil to 375°F, and deep-fry the shrimp puffs for 4 minutes until golden-brown.

Serves 4–6

Fruity Avocados

2 oranges
1 grapefruit
6 lettuce leaves
3 avocados, halved and pitted
juice 1 lemon

For the Dressing:
2 tablespoons yogurt
1 tablespoon oil
1 tablespoon lemon juice

1 Peel the oranges and the grapefruit and divide into sections. Then remove the skin from each section.

2 Arrange the lettuce leaves and avocados on a serving dish.

3 Sprinkle the avocados with lemon juice.

4 Fill the avocados with the orange and grapefruit.

5 Mix together the dressing ingredients and serve separately or top each avocado with a spoonful of the dressing.

Serves 6

Taramasalata

6 ozs. smoked cod roe
½ cup olive oil
scant ½ cup heavy cream
1 cup fresh breadcrumbs
1 clove garlic, crushed
juice 1 lemon
salt and pepper
pinch paprika

1 In a bowl, blend the cod roe with the oil until it is smooth.

2 Blend in the cream, then the breadcrumbs and garlic.

3 Lastly add the lemon juice and season to taste.

4 Pile the taramasalata up in a dish and pull a fork around the sides to achieve a 'petalled' effect. Sprinkle with paprika and serve with hot pita bread.

Serves 6

Tip: For a slightly different flavor, you can blend in some cream cheese or sesame oil.

Shrimp Puffs, Taramasalata and Fruity Avocados, served with hot pita bread, all make a tasty Greek start to a meal

Shrimp and Asparagus Salad

1 head lettuce
½ cup long grain rice
½ cup mayonnaise
salt and pepper
pinch paprika
1 lemon
1 tablespoon dry sherry
½ lb. shelled shrimp
½ lb. cooked, drained asparagus
1 red pepper, cut in thin strips
1 tablespoon chopped parsley

1 Wash and drain the lettuce. Arrange the leaves on a serving dish.

2 Cook the rice in boiling salted water until tender. Refresh under cold running water and drain.

3 In a bowl, mix the mayonnaise with the salt and pepper and paprika. Cut the lemon in half and squeeze the juice of one half into the mayonnaise. Put the other half aside for the garnish.

4 Mix in the sherry, the rice and half of the shrimp.

5 Pile the mixture on top of the let-

Shrimp and Asparagus Salad is the ideal choice for a sophisticated dinner party or a cold summer buffet

tuce leaves in the center of the dish. Arrange the remaining shrimp on top.

6 Arrange the asparagus in bundles around the edge to form a border with wedges of lemon in between. Place a thin strip of red pepper around the middle of each asparagus bundle.

7 Sprinkle the shrimp with the chopped parsley and serve.

Serves 4

Riviera Melon Salad

1 cantaloupe
1 head lettuce
2 tablespoons oil
1 small onion, chopped
1 teaspoon curry powder
generous ½ cup mayonnaise

1 teaspoon tomato catsup
juice ½ lemon
¼ lb. cooked, peeled shrimp
¼ lb. crabmeat
salt and pepper
4 whole shrimp
1 lemon, cut in wedges

1 Cut the melon in two, remove the seeds and rind and slice the flesh thinly.

2 Wash, dry and separate the lettuce leaves. Arrange them on a large, flat dish and decorate the border with the melon slices. Chill in the refrigerator.

3 Heat the oil and sauté the onion gently until soft — do not let it brown. Stir in the curry powder and cook for 30 seconds. Then allow to cool.

4 Blend together the onion and mayonnaise in a bowl. Add the tomato catsup and lemon juice. Then stir in the shrimp and crabmeat. Season to taste with salt and pepper.

5 Place a spoonful of the mixture on each lettuce leaf and garnish with the whole shrimp and lemon wedges. Chill for 30 minutes before serving.

Serves 4

'Daisy' Hors d'Oeuvre

2 lbs. firm potatoes, unpeeled
½ cup white wine
1¾ lbs. white fish
4 cups cooked peas
4 hard-boiled eggs, halved
    lengthwise
few lettuce leaves
4 small pickles, quartered
    lengthwise
1 red pepper, sliced

For the Court Bouillon:
6⅓ cups water
1 cup white wine
salt and pepper
bouquet garni
1 onion studded with a clove

For the Sauce:
½ cup olive oil
3 tablespoons vinegar
pinch each chopped parsley and
    chives
4 shallots, chopped
2 cloves garlic, peeled and
    chopped

1 Put the ingredients for the court bouillon in a pan, bring to a boil and boil gently for 30 minutes. Allow to cool.

2 Meanwhile, cook the unpeeled potatoes in boiling salted water. Drain, peel and dice them.

3 Pour the second measure of wine into a small pan. Bring to a boil, pour it over the diced potatoes while they are still warm and stir. Let cool.

4 When the court bouillon is cool, add the fish to it and bring to a boil. Simmer over gentle heat for about 15 minutes. Leave to cool.

5 In a large bowl, mix the cooled potatoes and peas.

6 Prepare the sauce: in another bowl, mix the oil, vinegar, chopped herbs, salt and pepper, shallots and garlic. Beat the sauce lightly, pour it over the potatoes, stir and leave to marinate.

7 Remove the yolks from the eggs and set aside. Cut the whites in half lengthwise again. Rub the yolks through a sieve and form them into a neat round.

8 Drain the fish, remove the bones and skin and flake it.

9 Cover a large round plate with the lettuce leaves and pile the potato and pea mixture in the center. Arrange the fish pieces on the top.

10 On the very top, place the round of egg yolk, to make the center of the 'daisy,' and arrange the lengths of egg white around it, to make the petals of the flower.

11 Decorate the base of the mound with the pickle slices and the edge of the dish with the chopped pepper. Serve chilled.

Serves 8

Tips: A court bouillon is a classic preparation used to cook both small pieces of fish and whole fish. Small pieces should be added to a hot bouillon, but if you are using the whole fish, allow the liquid to cool before adding it to the fish.

Once cooked, the fish can be allowed to cool in the court bouillon and, when completely cold, stored in the refrigerator to be reheated the next day.

You can vary the flavor of the court bouillon by adding carrots, celery, or fennel and by using herbs such as mint.

Spanish Salad

½ head lettuce
4 tomatoes, skinned, quartered
    and seeded
16 anchovy fillets, drained
¼ lb. peeled cooked shrimp
8 stuffed green olives, halved
2 hard-boiled eggs, sliced

For the Dressing:
6 tablespoons oil
2 tablespoons lemon juice
salt and pepper
pinch dry mustard
pinch sugar

1 Wash the lettuce, drain well and tear into small pieces.

2 Place the lettuce in a salad bowl and add the tomatoes, anchovies, shrimp and olives.

3 Mix the ingredients for the dressing together and pour it over the salad. Toss well.

4 Decorate the salad with the sliced hard-boiled eggs.

Serves 4

Scampi Salad Tartlets

dough for 1 large pie crust
1 cup diced cooked potato
½ cup cooked peas
½ cup diced cooked carrot
generous ½ cup mayonnaise
salt and pepper
8 frozen cooked, peeled scampi or
    jumbo shrimp, thawed
8 black olives, halved
1 small pickle, sliced
1 hard-boiled egg, sliced

1 Preheat the oven to 400°F. Roll out the pie crust to ⅛ inch thick. Cut 4 rounds, 4 inches in diameter and use them to line 4 greased tartlet or muffin pans. Prick evenly with a fork and bake them in the preheated oven for 12-15 minutes. Allow to cool.

2 Combine the potato, peas, carrot and mayonnaise in a bowl and check the seasoning. Place the mixture in the cooled tartlets and top each with 2 scampi or shrimp and a few halved olives.

3 Decorate the edge of each tartlet with the slices of pickle. Top each slice of egg with an olive half and arrange the slices around the serving dish.

Serves 4

Scampi Salad Tartlets are delicious little shells filled with shrimp, carrot and peas in a mayonnaise sauce

Exotic Salads

As exotic vegetables and fruits become more widely available, there is a growing tendency to use them in salads. Citrus fruits such as oranges, lemons and limes, and the more unusual avocados, papayas, pineapples and mangoes are now often mixed with salad vegetables and nuts or cheese in a delicious dressing or flavored mayonnaise.

Hawaiian Salad

1 head lettuce
8 radishes
⅔ cup diced ham
¾ cup diced fresh pineapple
1 branch celery, chopped
½ small cucumber, thinly sliced
few sprigs parsley

For the Dressing:
¼ cup pineapple juice
2 tablespoons lemon juice
1 tablespoon sugar
¼ cup oil
pinch salt
pinch paprika

1 Wash the lettuce and radishes. Separate the lettuce leaves and arrange on a serving dish. Slice downward through each radish to make a star-shape on top. Place them in ice water until they open out into flowers.

2 Mix together the dressing ingredients and toss the ham, pineapple and celery in the dressing. Pile on top of the lettuce leaves and decorate with cucumber slices, radishes and parsley.

Serves 4

Ham and Pineapple Salad, mixed with grapes and Gruyère in a fruity mayonnaise, tastes as delicious as it looks

Avocado and Hard Sausage Salad

1 avocado, pitted, peeled and thinly sliced
⅔ cup diced hard cooked sausage
1 cup diced Gruyère cheese
2 branches celery, thinly sliced
1 cup chopped walnuts
1 cup mayonnaise
1 tablespoon lemon juice
2 tablespoons applesauce
salt and pepper
1 tablespoon chopped chives
pinch paprika

1 In a bowl, mix together the sliced avocado, sausage, Gruyère cheese, celery and walnuts. Mix in the mayonnaise, lemon juice and apple purée. Make sure that all the ingredients are coated with the mayonnaise mixture.

2 Season with salt and pepper.

3 Transfer the salad to a serving dish and sprinkle with the chopped

chives and paprika. Or, alternatively, you can serve it in individual bowls as an appetizer.

Serves 4

Ham and Pineapple Salad

⅔ **cup diced ham**
1 cup diced cooked potatoes
1 cup diced Gruyère cheese

Hawaiian Salad combines the fresh, sharp taste of pineapple with ham and celery in a tangy lemon dressing

¼ **lb. seedless grapes, skinned**
½ **cup canned pineapple chunks**
¾ **cup mayonnaise**
2 tablespoons pineapple juice
salt and pepper
2 tablespoons sour cream
3 tablespoons chopped parsley

1 Combine together the ham, cooked potatoes, Gruyère, grapes and pineapple chunks in a bowl.

2 Mix in the mayonnaise and pineapple juice so that all the ingredients are well coated. Season with salt and pepper and stir in the sour cream.

3 Serve in an attractive dish, sprinkled with the chopped parsley.

Serves 4

Tip: As a delicious variation on this salad, why not try adding some sliced bananas or cashew nuts? You can give it a more spicy flavor by mixing in a pinch of curry powder.

Look 'n Cook Cranberry Salad

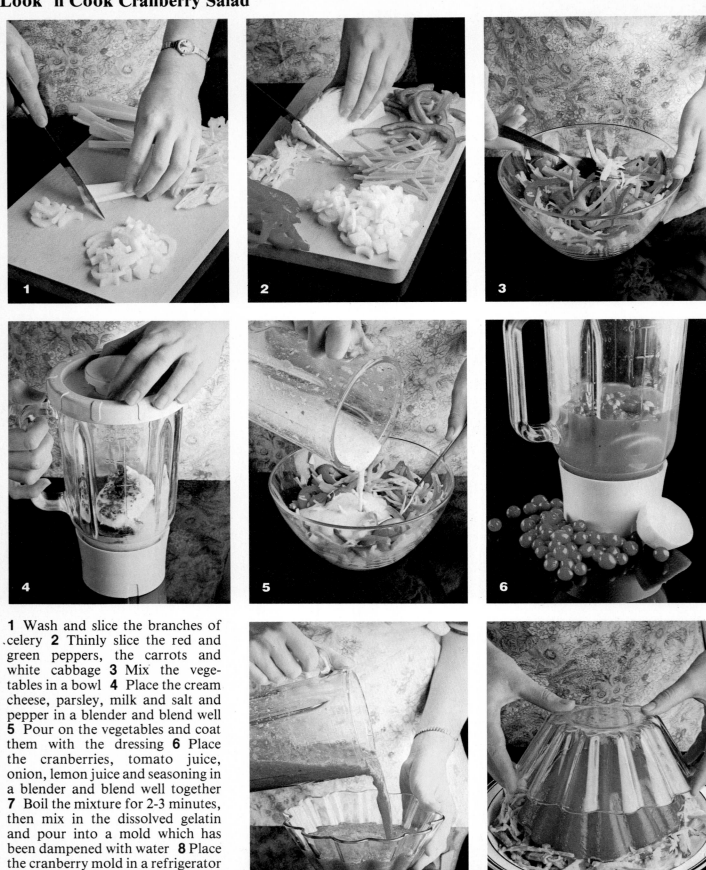

1 Wash and slice the branches of celery 2 Thinly slice the red and green peppers, the carrots and white cabbage 3 Mix the vegetables in a bowl 4 Place the cream cheese, parsley, milk and salt and pepper in a blender and blend well 5 Pour on the vegetables and coat them with the dressing 6 Place the cranberries, tomato juice, onion, lemon juice and seasoning in a blender and blend well together 7 Boil the mixture for 2-3 minutes, then mix in the dissolved gelatin and pour into a mold which has been dampened with water 8 Place the cranberry mold in a refrigerator until set. Turn out, surround with a ring of coleslaw 9 Garnish with cranberries and peppers

Cranberry Salad

2 cups cranberries
1¼ cups tomato juice
juice ½ lemon
1 teaspoon grated onion (optional)
salt and pepper
pinch cinnamon
4 tablespoons gelatin
¼ cup powdered sugar
scant ⅓ cup warm water

For the Coleslaw:
2 branches celery, thinly sliced
½ green pepper, deseeded and
  sliced
½ red pepper, seeded and sliced
1 carrot, cut in thin strips
3 cups shredded white cabbage

For the Dressing:
7 ozs. cream cheese
sprig parsley
scant ⅓ cup milk or light cream
salt and pepper

For the Garnish:
2 rings green pepper
½ cup cranberries

1 Make the coleslaw by mixing all the sliced and shredded vegetables together in a bowl.

2 Make the dressing. Place the cream cheese, parsley, milk or cream and seasoning in a blender and blend well. If you do not have a blender, you can push them through a sieve.

3 Toss the coleslaw vegetables in the dressing until they are well covered and put aside.

4 Place the cranberries, tomato and lemon juice, grated onion, salt, pepper and cinnamon in a blender and blend well.

5 Pour the cranberry mixture into a saucepan and bring to a boil. Boil for 2-3 minutes, then remove from the heat.

6 Mix together the gelatin and sugar and dissolve in the warm water. Stir into the cranberry mixture.

7 Dampen a fluted 2½-cup mold with a little water. Then pour the cranberry mixture into the mold and refrigerate for at least 2 hours until firm and set.

8 Arrange the coleslaw around a serving plate and unmold the cranberry salad into the center.

9 Garnish the top with the rings of green pepper and a few cranberries. Sprinkle the surrounding salad with more of the cranberries.

Serves 4–6

Tip: If you do not have a blender, do not despair — you can still make this delicious recipe. Just rub the ingredients through a nylon strainer using a wooden spoon. The resulting purée will be just as smooth.

Egg and Melon Salad

1 small cabbage
1 firm, ripe papaya or cantaloupe
1 orange
2 carrots, grated
salt and pepper
4 hard-boiled eggs
few sprigs watercress
few leaves chicory
8 radishes

For the Dressing:
1 teaspoon flour
1 tablespoon sugar
salt and pepper
½ teaspoon mustard powder
1 large egg
2 tablespoons vinegar
2 tablespoons water
1 teaspoon butter

1 Prepare the dressing first. Combine the flour, sugar, seasoning and mustard powder in a heavy-based saucepan. Beat the egg and mix it in to form a smooth paste. Add the vinegar, water and butter and stir over low heat until the sauce begins to thicken. Remove from the heat, stir thoroughly and strain if any lumps still remain. Cool in the refrigerator.

2 Chop the cabbage very finely. Cube the papaya or cantaloupe. Peel the orange and cut the segments into pieces. Combine these ingredients with the grated carrot in a mixing bowl. Season.

3 Pour on the cooled dressing and spoon the salad mixture onto a large salad dish.

4 Slice the hard-boiled eggs and arrange them with the watercress and chicory leaves around the salad. Garnish with the radishes cut in a floral pattern and serve.

Serves 4

Salad Ramatuelle

1 head lettuce
1 cup canned bamboo shoots
1 red pepper
6 cups cooked long grain rice
½ cup slivered almonds
3 tablespoons mayonnaise
1 teaspoon prepared mustard
1 teaspoon capers
1 cooked chicken breast, cut in
  strips

1 Wash and dry the lettuce leaves, and tear them into pieces. Drain the bamboo shoots and finely dice the red pepper.

2 Mix the rice and almonds in a salad bowl. Blend the mayonnaise, mustard and capers and add to the rice mixture. Refrigerate for 1 hour to cool.

3 Just before serving add the lettuce, bamboo shoots, red pepper and chicken. Toss and serve.

*Serves 6–8 as starter
  3–4 as a main course*

Egg and Melon Salad makes an unusual and attractive appetizer — you can substitute papayas for an exotic change

Romaine Salad

1 head Romaine lettuce
1 red pepper, seeded
1 green pepper, seeded
1 avocado
1 onion, sliced in rings
1 hard-boiled egg
1 branch celery, diced

For the Dressing:
2 tablespoons olive oil
juice ½ lemon
salt and pepper

1 Wash and dry the lettuce. Tear into pieces. Slice the peppers into rings. Peel the avocado and remove the pit. Quarter lengthwise and slice into segments.

2 Combine the dressing ingredients and mix well.

3 Place the lettuce in the bottom of a salad bowl. Add the peppers and onion in alternate layers, then the avocado and finally the egg. Place the celery on the very top. Chill and serve with the dressing.

Serves 3

Orange and Cabbage Slaw

1½ lbs. cabbage
3 oranges
rind 1 orange, grated
juice ½ orange

For the Dressing:
scant ⅔ cup light cream
1 tablespoon cornstarch
3 tablespoons cold water
½ teaspoon sugar
juice ½ lemon
1 teaspoon vinegar
1 tablespoon oil

Romaine Salad makes a welcome change from the ordinary lettuce — Romaine is crisp like cabbage

1 Make the dressing. Boil the cream. Mix the cornstarch and water to a smooth paste. Add to the cream and simmer for 30 seconds. Remove from the heat and stir in the sugar, lemon juice and vinegar. Slowly add the oil and stir. Strain if necessary to remove any lumps.

2 Shred the cabbage and place in a salad bowl. Break 2 of the oranges into sections, remove any white skin, and dice.

3 Sprinkle the orange rind over the cabbage. Toss well. Add the orange juice, diced orange and dressing a few minutes before serving. Toss and garnish with sections of the remaining orange.

Serves 6

Cheese Salads

Cheese has always been a favorite accompaniment for salads. Its mild but tangy flavor and smooth texture is an excellent complement to crisp, juicy salad vegetables. Mellow, firm English, Dutch and Swiss cheeses may be diced, or cut in strips, to hold their own with crunchy salads. Blue cheeses bring extra flavor to salads and salad dressings. Cream cheese forms an ideal base for mixed salads, or mild dressings that go as well with fruit as with vegetables.

Blue Cheese Salad

1 large head lettuce
3 large tomatoes
3 tablespoons olive oil
1 tablespoon white wine vinegar
salt and pepper
¼ lb. firm blue cheese — Danish Blue, Auvergne Blue, or Stilton

1 Wash the lettuce thoroughly, separating the leaves and discarding any damaged ones.

2 Wash the tomatoes and cut them into ⅜-inch slices.

3 In a bowl, blend the olive oil, vinegar, and a pinch of salt and freshly ground black pepper to taste.

4 Cut the cheese into ¾-inch cubes, and mix them into the salad dressing.

5 Arrange the lettuce and tomato in a salad bowl and pour the cheese dressing over them, tossing the salad lightly so that all the pieces are covered with dressing. Serve with crisp French bread.

Serves 4

Blue Cheese Salad — vinegar, oil and firm blue cheese mixed together and poured over a lettuce and tomato salad

Blue Cheese Salad Dressing

2 ozs. blue cheese — Danish Blue, Roquefort, or Stilton
1¼ cups mayonnaise
¼ cup heavy cream
1 tablespoon chopped fresh parsley and sage
1 clove garlic, crushed
salt and pepper

1 Crumble the blue cheese into small pieces, and stir them into the mayonnaise and the cream.

2 Add the chopped herbs, garlic and salt and pepper to taste. Place all ingredients in a blender and beat until smooth.

3 Serve the Blue Cheese Salad Dressing with a crisp green salad or a potato salad. It may also be poured over hot baked potatoes.

Makes 1⅞ cups

93

Tagliatelle Salad

1 cup green tagliatelle (very
  narrow egg noodles)
1 bunch radishes
4 large tomatoes
12 scallions
2 ozs. Gruyère cheese
½ red pepper, seeded and diced
2 tablespoons olive oil
1 tablespoon lemon juice
1 teaspoon each chopped fresh
  parsley, chives and basil
pinch garlic salt
salt and pepper

1 Boil the tagliatelle noodles in salted water until just tender. Rinse them in cold water, drain and leave to cool.

2 Clean the radishes and remove the leaves from all but 6 (for decoration). Clean and quarter the tomatoes. Wash the scallions and discard the green leaves.

3 Cut the Gruyère cheese into ¾-inch cubes. Mix the cold noodles, radishes, scallions and red pepper.

4 Blend the oil, lemon juice, herbs, garlic salt, and salt and pepper to taste. Pour the dressing over the salad, tossing to ensure that all the ingredients are coated evenly.

5 Arrange the tomato quarters around the salad, decorate with the leafy radishes, and serve.

Serves 4

Dutch Salad

¼ lb. Edam or Gouda cheese
6 crisp white cabbage leaves
6 crisp red cabbage leaves
2 large carrots
½ green pepper, deseeded
2 tablespoons olive oil
1 tablespoon vinegar
1 tablespoon chopped celery leaves
1 teaspoon cumin seeds
salt and pepper

1 Remove any rind from the cheese and cut it into matchstick strips about ¼ inch thick and 1½ inches long.

2 Cut the white and red cabbage leaves, carrots and green pepper into strips of a similar size.

3 Blend together the oil, vinegar, chopped celery leaves, cumin seeds, and salt and pepper to taste. Mix all the ingredients together in a wooden salad bowl and serve with boiled ham or cold meats.

Serves 4

Tagliatelle Salad contains pasta, cheese and lots of salad vegetables and makes a colorful and filling meal

Salade des Fromages

¼ lb. Cheddar cheese
¼ lb. Gruyère cheese
½ lb. ham
4 small pickles
1 head lettuce

For the Dressing:
3 tablespoons olive oil
juice 1 lemon
1 tablespoon light cream
1 teaspoon prepared mustard
salt and pepper
1 tablespoon chopped fresh chives
3 tablespoons grated Parmesan
  cheese

1 Cut the Cheddar cheese and the Gruyère cheese into pieces about ¾ inch across. Cut the ham into cubes of a similar size. Slice the pickles. Wash the lettuce and discard any damaged leaves.

2 Blend all the ingredients for the dressing to form a smooth liquid.

3 Arrange the lettuce leaves in a large salad bowl. Toss the cheese and ham in the salad dressing until well coated. Serve the cheese salad and lettuce separately, or place the cheese salad in the middle of the lettuce.

Serves 4–6

Avocado Creams

2 large ripe avocados
8 ozs. cottage or cream cheese
2 tablespoons mayonnaise
1 tablespoon vinaigrette
juice 1 lemon
salt and pepper
1 tablespoon chopped fresh chives

1 Cut the avocados in half. Discard the pits. Scoop out the pulp, keeping the shells.

2 Place the avocado pulp in a blender with the rest of the ingre-

dients except the chopped chives. Blend until a smooth, thick mixture is formed.

3 Divide the avocado mixture between the four avocado shells. Top each one with a sprinkling of chopped chives. Chill before serving as an hors d'oeuvre.

Serves 4

Pacific Cheese Salad

2 grapefruit
¼ lb. Swiss cheese
12 pearl onions, pickled
12 cocktail cherries
2 tablespoons olive oil
1 tablespoon lemon juice
salt and pepper
6 fresh mint leaves, chopped
1 head lettuce, shredded

1 Cut the grapefruit into halves and remove the fruit, keeping the skins. Remove pith and dice the fruit.

2 Dice the cheese. Mix together the grapefruit, cheese, pickled pearl onions and cocktail cherries.

3 Make a dressing of the oil and lemon juice, seasoned to taste with salt and pepper and blended with the chopped mint.

4 Toss the salad and the dressing together. Divide the salad between the four grapefruit halves. Set each half on a bed of shredded lettuce and serve.

Serves 4

Mandarin Cream Cheese Salad

1 large bunch watercress
1 lb. cottage cheese
1 cup canned mandarin orange
  sections
pinch paprika

1 Wash the watercress thoroughly and discard any thick stalks. Arrange a bed of watercress on each of 4 salad plates.

2 Using a scoop or a soup ladle, place an evenly circular mound of cottage cheese in the middle of each bed of watercress.

3 Drain the juice from the mandarin sections and arrange them in a rosette pattern around each mound of cottage cheese. Dust the cottage cheese with a little paprika, and serve.

Serves 4

Cottage Cheese and Peach Salad

1 cup cottage cheese
¼ cup sour cream
salt and pepper
⅓ cup raisins
½ cup chopped pineapple
1 tablespoon lemon juice
1 head lettuce
4 fresh or canned peach halves
2 carrots, washed and grated

1 Blend together the cottage cheese and the sour cream and season. Stir in the raisins, pineapple, and lemon juice.

2 Wash the lettuce and arrange several leaves on each serving plate. Cut a small slice off the round side of each peach half so that it will stand hollow side upright.

3 Place a peach half in the middle of each serving plate, on the lettuce leaves, and scoop ¼ of the cottage cheese mixture into each peach half.

4 Sprinkle each salad with some grated carrot. Serve.

Serves 4

Fruits de Mer Salad

1 head lettuce
½ lb. cooked white fish
¼ lb. crabmeat
¼ lb. lobster meat or similar
 amount of other shellfish
scant ⅔ cup mayonnaise
1 tablespoon applesauce
1 teaspoon Worcestershire sauce
salt and pepper
12 whole cooked, peeled shrimp

1 Separate the leaves of the lettuce and wash quickly. Drain well, and line a salad bowl.

2 Dice the white fish, crab and lobster, or other shellfish, and place on top of the lettuce.

3 Mix the mayonnaise with the

Fruits de Mer Salad is an infinitely variable dish which you can alter according to the fish that are available

applesauce and Worcestershire sauce. Season.

4 Spoon over the shellfish.

5 Decorate the bowl by arranging the shrimp to curve over the sides.

Serves 4

Avocado and Crab Salad

1 head lettuce
2 avocados
½ lb. crabmeat
2 eating apples
scant ⅔ cup mayonnaise
1 teaspoon tomato catsup
pinch paprika
juice ½ lemon
6 celery leaves

1 Separate the leaves of the lettuce and wash. Drain.

2 Remove the skins of the avo-

cados and cut into segments. Cut the crabmeat into chunks. Peel and dice the apples.

3 Mix the mayonnaise with the tomato catsup, paprika and lemon juice. Toss the salad in the dressing.

4 To serve, line a bowl with the lettuce leaves, garnish with celery leaves and place the salad in the middle.

Serves 4

Quick Fish Salad

Try combining some cooked mussels with cold boiled potatoes cut in slices. Toss in mayonnaise and arrange on a bed of lettuce leaves. Arrange some slices of marinated mushrooms on top. To add color, decorate with radishes or slices of tomatoes.

For that special dinner party, Avocado and Crab Salad — a deliciously delicate mixture with tomato mayonnaise

Chicken Salads

The use of chicken as an ingredient in a mixed salad is often overlooked. The following recipes show just how tasty this delicate meat can be, blended with various dressings and combined with different salad vegetables.

Chicken Salad New York

1 avocado
¼ lb. seedless green grapes
1 head Romaine lettuce
1 head iceberg lettuce
2 branches celery, diced
1 cup thin strips ham, 1½ inches long
1 cup thin strips cooked chicken, 1½ inches long
¼ cup Swiss cheese, cut into thin strips

For the Dressing:
⅓ cup oil
2 tablespoons vinegar
2 tablespoons catsup
2 teaspoons grated onion
1 teaspoon prepared mustard
½ teaspoon salt
¼ teaspoon sugar
dash Tabasco sauce

1 Prepare the dressing. Place all the ingredients in a screw top jar or any watertight container. Cover and shake well. Chill.

2 Peel and halve the avocado. Remove the pit, quarter and slice. Halve the grapes.

3 Wash the lettuce leaves and dry. Tear them into bite-size pieces. Place them in a salad bowl and toss.

4 Arrange the celery, ham, chicken, cheese, avocado and grapes on top of the lettuce.

5 Just before serving toss the salad with the chilled dressing.

Serves 8

Chicken and Cranberry Salad

1 cup jellied cranberry
½ cup sour cream
4 ozs. cream cheese, softened
2 branches celery, diced
½ cup chopped walnuts
1 green pepper, seeded and finely chopped
1⅓ cups diced cooked chicken
1½ cups canned pineapple pieces, drained

1 Spread the jellied cranberry ½ inch thick over the base of a freezing tray. Freeze the jelly for 1 hour or until it has set solid.

2 Blend the sour cream with the cheese. Stir in the celery, walnuts and pepper. Fold in the chicken and pineapple pieces, and season to taste. Chill.

3 Cut the frozen jellied cranberry into small cubes and sprinkle them over the salad before serving.

Serves 4

Chicken Tapenade

1⅓ cups diced cooked chicken
1 head lettuce
4 ozs. anchovy fillets
8 stuffed green olives

For the Dressing:
2 egg yolks
1 teaspoon prepared mustard
salt and pepper
⅔ cup olive oil
juice ½ lemon
2 tablespoons heavy cream

1 small onion, chopped
1 teaspoon capers, chopped

1 First, prepare the dressing. Whisk together the egg yolks (make sure there is no white remaining on the yolk), mustard, salt and pepper in a bowl. Slowly blend in the oil a little at a time until you have a thick creamy mixture of even consistency. Stir in the lemon juice and cream and finally the chopped onion and capers.

2 Toss the diced chicken in the dressing and chill for 30 minutes.

3 Break up the lettuce and wash and dry the leaves. Use as many leaves as necessary to line the base and sides of a salad bowl.

4 Spoon in the chicken and mayonnaise mixture. Decorate with the anchovy fillets by lining them criss-cross over the top of the salad and garnish with the olives. Serve.

Serves 4

Peppers Stuffed with Chicken

2 sweet red peppers, seeded
salt and pepper
2 tablespoons plain yogurt
2 tablespoons canned corn
1⅓ cups diced cooked chicken
few sprigs parsley

1 Halve the peppers and boil them for 5 minutes in salted water. Refresh, dry and allow them to cool.

2 Blend the yogurt with the corn and chicken. Season and spoon into the pepper halves. Garnish with the parsley and serve.

Serves 4

Chicken Tapenade—the chicken is mixed with a creamy dressing and garnished with anchovies and stuffed olives

Mayonnaise Chicken Salad

⅔ cup chicken stock
2 tablespoons gelatin
1¼ cups mayonnaise
2⅔ cups diced cooked chicken
few lettuce leaves
3 ozs. cooked tongue, cut in strips
3 ozs. cooked ham, cut in strips
2 ozs. canned anchovy fillets, drained
4 olives, sliced
1 avocado
juice 1 lemon

1 Place the chicken stock in a pan and bring just to a boil. Remove from the heat, add the gelatin and stir until dissolved. Cool.

2 When the gelatin mixture is cool, blend in the mayonnaise. In a bowl, mix the chicken meat with ¾ of the mayonnaise.

3 Arrange the lettuce leaves in a glass salad bowl and place the chicken and mayonnaise mixture on top. Pour the rest of the mayonnaise over the top and smooth the surface with the blade of a knife.

4 Make a lattice pattern on the mayonnaise with the strips of tongue and ham and with the anchovy fillets. Place olive slices in the spaces of the lattice. Chill.

5 Just before serving, peel and slice the avocado and sprinkle the slices with the lemon juice. Arrange the avocado around the edge of the salad and serve.

Serves 8

Tip: The mayonnaise can be varied by adding a fruit purée, which will taste delicious with cooked meat. Apple would be ideal — for each cup of mayonnaise, add 4 tablespoons of the fruit purée. You could also use crushed pineapple, or a purée of currants or cooked plums. For a lower-calorie meal, the mayonnaise could be replaced by yogurt, to which you could again add a fruit purée.

Chicken and Orange Salad

½ cup long grain rice
1 small onion, chopped
salt and pepper
1⅓ cups diced cooked chicken
2 branches celery, diced
½ green pepper, chopped
4 stuffed olives, chopped
½ cup mayonnaise
2 oranges
few lettuce leaves

1 Cook the rice in boiling salted water until tender. Drain and, while still hot, mix with the onion and seasoning. Cool.

2 Add the chicken, celery, pepper, olives and mayonnaise and toss lightly. Peel the oranges, split them into sections and cut half into small pieces.

3 Add the orange pieces to the salad and mix well. Chill thoroughly.

4 To serve, place the salad on a bed of lettuce and garnish with the rest of the orange sections.

Serves 4

Chicken Noodle Salad

½ lb. cooked chicken meat, cut in ½-inch cubes
1 small onion, finely chopped
1 tablespoon chopped pimento
3 olives, chopped
¾ cup walnuts, chopped
1 tablespoon chopped parsley
juice half lemon
1 teaspoon Worcestershire sauce
salt and pepper
1½ cups noodles
½ cup mayonnaise

1 Combine the chicken, onion, pimento, olives, walnuts, parsley, lemon juice, Worcestershire sauce and seasoning.

2 Cook the noodles in boiling salted water, drain and rinse in cold water.

3 Combine the chicken mixture and the cooked noodles, add the mayonnaise and toss lightly until all the ingredients are well mixed. Chill and serve.

Serves 4

Chicken and Peach Salad

8 fresh or canned peach halves, sliced
4 cold roast chicken breasts, skinned and diced
few lettuce leaves
1 teaspoon chopped parsley

For the Mustard Dressing:
⅔ cup mayonnaise
2 peach halves, chopped
juice 1 lemon
1 teaspoon prepared mustard

1 Mix the sliced peaches and diced chicken in a bowl.

2 Make the dressing: blend the mayonnaise with the chopped peaches, lemon juice and mustard. Toss the chicken mixture in the dressing.

3 Chill the salad for 30 minutes.

4 When ready to serve, arrange the salad in the center of a serving dish on a bed of lettuce leaves. Decorate the top of the salad with the chopped parsley.

Serves 4

Chicken and Peach Salad is a delicious combination of flavors which is topped with a tangy mustard dressing

Ham Espagnole Salad

½ lb. ham
1 onion
4 tomatoes
1 green pepper
2 tablespoons olive oil
1 tablespoon vinegar
2 cloves garlic, crushed
salt and pepper

1 Cut the ham into strips.

2 Slice the onions into rings.

3 Cut the tomatoes in quarters, and the pepper in rings, discarding the seeds.

4 Make a dressing by mixing the oil and vinegar. Add the crushed garlic and season with salt and pepper.

5 Toss the onions, tomatoes, and peppers and ham in the dressing and arrange in a bowl.

6 Serve the new potatoes, tossed in butter, and sprinkled with parsley.

Serves 4

Caesar Salad

1 large head crisp lettuce
½ lb. Canadian bacon
2 tablespoons butter
1 tablespoon oil
2 slices bread, diced
1 raw egg
6 anchovy fillets
3 tablespoons grated Parmesan cheese

For the Dressing:
¼ cup olive oil
2 tablespoons vinegar
salt and pepper
1 teaspoon mild mustard
2 cloves garlic, crushed
2 tablespoons finely chopped parsley

1 Wash the lettuce leaves and shred them. Place in a bowl.

Ham Espagnole Salad makes an ideal start to a meal or it can be served with potatoes as a main meal in itself

2 Cut the bacon into strips and fry them in the butter and oil until crisp. Remove from the pan. Add the diced bread and fry until crisp.

3 Mix the lettuce, bacon, and croutons lightly together in the salad bowl. Break the raw egg over the salad and stir it in.

4 Combine the ingredients for the dressing and toss the salad. Top it with the anchovy fillets and sprinkle on the grated Parmesan cheese.

Serves 4

Chicken and Melon Salad

1 medium-size melon
½ lb. cooked chicken meat
1 green pepper
½ cup walnuts
¼ cup mayonnaise
1 head lettuce, washed and separated
1 tablespoon chopped parsley

1 Cut the melon in half, and remove the seeds. Scoop out with a melon baller, or a teaspoon. Place in a bowl.

2 Dice the chicken.

3 Finely chop the green pepper and walnuts.

4 Place all the ingredients in the bowl. Add the mayonnaise and mix well.

5 Line a shallow dish with lettuce leaves, and place the salad in the middle. Sprinkle with chopped parsley.

Serves 4

Eggplant Ham Salad

1 large eggplant
pinch salt

2 red peppers
2 pickles
¼ cup vinegar
salt and pepper
½ cup flour
¼ cup oil
½ head lettuce, washed and
  separated
1⅓ cups chopped ham
1 tablespoon chopped dill

1 Cut the eggplant into 'chips.' Sprinkle with salt and leave for ½ hour.

2 Dice the peppers and cucumbers and put in a bowl with the vinegar and seasoning.

3 Dry the eggplant 'chips' and roll in flour. Fry in hot oil for 2-3 minutes until crisp. Add to the salad. Leave to cool for a few hours.

4 Serve on a bed of lettuce leaves, with the chopped ham arranged on top. Sprinkle with the dill.

Serves 4

Melon Ball and Prosciutto Salad

1 medium-size melon
1 large grapefruit
½ lb. prosciutto
2 tablespoons oil
1 tablespoon vinegar
salt and pepper
pinch paprika

1 Cut the melon in half, and remove the seeds. Scoop out with a melon baller and place in a bowl.

2 Cut the grapefruit into sections.

3 Cut the prosciutto into thin strips.

4 Make the dressing by mixing the oil, vinegar, salt and pepper, and toss the melon, grapefruit and prosciutto in it.

5 Place in a bowl and sprinkle with the paprika. Chill until served.

Serves 4

Chicken and Melon Salad and Melon Ball and Prosciutto Salad are two tempting salads you can make with melons

Avocado, Egg and Ham Salad

8 hard-boiled eggs
1 avocado
2 tablespoons yogurt
½ teaspoon grated lemon rind
salt and pepper
dash chili sauce
1 head lettuce, washed and
  separated
5 tomatoes, halved
1⅓ cups chopped ham
2 branches celery, chopped
4 sprigs parsley

1 Cut the eggs in half lengthwise and remove the yolks. Mash the yolks thoroughly.

2 Remove the skin and pit from the avocado, mash the avocado and mix with the egg yolks, yogurt, lemon rind, salt, pepper and chili sauce.

3 Put this mixture into a decorator's bag and pipe into the egg whites.

4 Line a shallow dish with the lettuce leaves, and arrange the halved tomatoes, chopped ham and celery on top. Place the eggs on this mixture, and decorate with the sprigs of parsley.

Serves 4

103

Meat and Corn Salad

¼ lb. cooked ham
¼ lb. salami
1 small red pepper
1 small green pepper
3 scallions
1 cup corn, drained
salt and pepper
⅔ cup mayonnaise
few sprigs parsley

1 Cut the ham and salami into ½-inch cubes.

2 Seed the red and green peppers and dice the flesh. Mix them with the meats in a salad bowl.

3 Slice the scallions thinly, including some of the green parts.

4 Mix all the ingredients together in a salad bowl, season, and stir in the mayonnaise until everything is coated. Decorate with the sprigs of parsley.

Serves 4

Farmhouse Salad

1 small red cabbage
salt and pepper
½ lb. salt pork
¼ cup oil
1 tablespoon vinegar
1 teaspoon prepared mustard
½ cup walnuts

1 Cut the cabbage into thin slices. Dust with salt and leave in a bowl for 1 hour. Rinse thoroughly and drain.

2 Meanwhile, cut the salt pork into thin strips. Heat half the oil and fry the pork pieces until golden brown. Drain and allow to cool.

3 Mix together the rest of the oil, vinegar and mustard, and season to taste. Add the dressing to the pork and cabbage and toss the salad to blend well. Add the walnuts just before serving.

Serves 4

Turkey and Cranberry Salad

2 cups cooked turkey
½ cup seedless grapes
1 tablespoon lemon juice
3 branches celery
2 hard-boiled eggs
⅔ cup mayonnaise
⅔ cup cranberry sauce
salt and pepper
pinch dried basil
¼ cup toasted split almonds

1 Dice the turkey meat and mix it with the grapes and lemon juice.

2 Clean and chop the celery. Chop the hard-boiled eggs. Add both to the meat and grapes.

3 Blend together the mayonnaise, cranberry sauce, salt and pepper, and basil. Fold the dressing into the meat mixture. Mix in the nuts and serve.

Serves 6

Carmen Salad

½ cup rice
½ cup peas
2 sweet red peppers
1⅓ cup cooked chicken
3 sprigs fresh tarragon
3 tablespoons olive oil
1 tablespoon vinegar
1 tablespoon lemon juice
1 teaspoon mild mustard
salt and pepper

1 Boil the rice in salted water until just tender. Rinse, drain, and cool.

2 Boil the green peas in a little water until tender. Drain.

3 Holding each red pepper on a fork, turn it over a flame or grill to blister the fine skin. Scrape off the skin. Split the pepper, remove the seeds and dice.

4 Cut the chicken into small chunks. Finely chop the tarragon. Mix the rest of the ingredients to make the dressing.

5 Place the rice, peas, red pepper and chicken in a salad bowl. Toss in the chopped tarragon and dressing. Serve at once.

Serves 4

Lentil and Salami Salad with Artichoke Hearts

1⅓ cups lentils
2 red peppers
½ lb. salami
6 artichoke hearts
¼ cup oil
2 tablespoons wine vinegar
1 teaspoon mild prepared mustard
salt and pepper
2 tablespoons chopped fresh parsley and chervil

1 Boil the lentils according to directions on package (without any salt in the water) until they are tender but not mushy. Drain and cool.

2 Meanwhile, seed the red pepper and cut it into thick strips. Boil the pieces for about 10 minutes until they are soft. Drain and cool.

3 Cut the salami into thin slices. Drain the artichoke hearts. Beat together the oil, vinegar, mustard, salt and pepper to make a dressing.

4 Mix together the lentils and red pepper and toss them lightly in the dressing. Arrange on a large serving platter. Place the artichoke hearts in a row down the middle, and the salami slices around the sides. Sprinkle the whole dish with the chopped fresh herbs.

Serves 6

Salami and Lentil Salad with Artichoke Hearts makes a delicious starter and is easy to prepare well in advance

Asparagus Ham Rolls

2 lbs. fresh asparagus
2 tablespoons butter
salt and pepper
1 tablespoon chopped parsley
2 hard-boiled eggs
6 slices ham
2 tablespoons Parmesan cheese

1 Cook the asparagus spears for 10–12 minutes or until tender in boiling salted water. When they are cooked, remove the white ends. Toss the spears in half the butter seasoned with salt and pepper and allow them to cool.

2 Finely dice the hard-boiled eggs. In a bowl combine the eggs, remaining butter and the chopped parsley. Knead these ingredients together until you have fine crumbs.

3 Spread out the slices of ham and sprinkle each with the Parmesan cheese.

4 Divide the asparagus spears into 7 equal bundles. Reserve one for later and place each of the others on a slice of ham.

5 Roll the ham around the asparagus and place them, seam downward, on a serving dish. Sprinkle on the egg mixture and decorate the dish with the remaining spears. Serve with a crisp green salad and a vinaigrette dressing.

Serves 6

Tip: A delicious alternative to the ham in this recipe is Prosciutto.

Asparagus Ham Rolls make an appetizing and luxurious start to a special dinner or a delicious party snack

Orange Duck Salad

1 head lettuce
3 scallions
1⅓ cups diced cooked duck
1 green pepper, seeded and chopped
1 branch celery, chopped
½ teaspoon finely chopped mint
3 oranges

For the Dressing:
¼ cup olive oil
1 tablespoon vinegar
1 tablespoon orange juice
salt and pepper

1 Remove the heart from the lettuce. Wash and dry both the leaves and the heart. Finely dice the lettuce heart and the scallions.

2 Prepare the dressing. Combine the oil, vinegar and orange juice in

a watertight container. Season and shake well.

3 Place the duck in a bowl. Add the diced lettuce heart, scallions, green pepper and celery to the mixture. Pour on the dressing and toss. Stir in the finely chopped mint and leave for 1 hour.

4 Grate the rind of 2 of the oranges and stir it into the salad mixture.

5 Peel the oranges and remove any excess white skin. Break them into sections. Cut the sections in half and add to the bowl. Chill.

6 Line a salad bowl with the lettuce leaves and spoon in the chilled salad mixture. Serve.

Serves 6

Sweet 'n Sour Turkey Salad

1 head lettuce
1 sweet red pepper
6 radishes
1½ cups rice, cooked
1 tablespoon chopped scallions
1 teaspoon green peppercorns
⅔ cup diced turkey

For the Dressing:
¼ cup canned pineapple pieces, drained
3 tablespoons oil
1 tablespoon vinegar
½ teaspoon Worcestershire sauce
pinch curry powder
salt and pepper

1 Wash and dry the lettuce and break it into small pieces. Seed and finely dice the red pepper. Chop the radishes into small pieces.

2 Prepare the dressing. Chop the pineapple pieces and combine them with the oil, vinegar, Worcestershire sauce, curry powder, salt and pepper. Blend thoroughly or shake well in a watertight container. Chill.

3 Place the rice in a salad bowl. Add the lettuce pieces, red pepper, radishes, scallions, peppercorns and toss. Finally add the turkey meat and pour on the chilled dressing. Toss thoroughly and serve.

Serves 4

Tip: You may substitute any leftover chicken or pork for the turkey in this recipe. For those who like a spicy dressing with more bite, try substituting half the pineapple pieces with 2 tablespoons of chopped mango chutney.

Pork and Shrimp Salad Cantonese

1 cup diced pork, cooked
6 ozs. canned bamboo shoots, drained
1 carrot, cooked
6 ozs. bean sprouts
6 ozs. cooked, peeled shrimp

Sweet 'n Sour Turkey Salad is an oriental dish that uses up turkey and cold rice leftovers in a tasty way

For the Dressing:
1 teaspoon chopped fresh ginger
1 clove garlic, chopped
⅓ cup pineapple juice
¼ cup oil
juice ½ lemon
1 teaspoon soy sauce
salt and pepper

1 Prepare the dressing first. Pound together the ginger and garlic, until they are thoroughly mashed. Combine the pineapple juice, oil, lemon juice, soy sauce, seasoning and the garlic and ginger paste in a bowl. Whisk quickly until all the ingredients are well blended. Strain through a sieve if necessary and chill.

2 Cut the pork into fine strips 2 inches long. Do the same with the bamboo shoots and carrot.

3 Wash and drain the bean sprouts.

4 Combine the pork, shrimp, bamboo shoots, carrot and bean sprouts in a salad bowl. Pour on the dressing, toss and serve.

Serves 4-6

Aspic Salads

Nothing looks as cool or attractive on a summer evening as a brilliantly clear, chilled aspic salad. The great advantage of a salad prepared in this way is that you can use virtually any leftovers from the refrigerator and mold them into a tempting and delicious dish. The best aspics are those made from reduced chicken, beef or veal stocks, but you can use bouillon cubes or canned consommés. Below we give recipes for the quick and easy preparation of an aspic.

Shrimp Aspic

2¼ cups water
1 chicken bouillon cube
5 tarragon leaves
2 celery leaves
4 tablespoons gelatin
salt and pepper
juice 1 lemon
1 carrot
1 turnip
½ cup green beans
½ cup peas
2 hard-boiled eggs
6 lettuce leaves
3 tomatoes
1 radish, sliced
½ lb. cooked, peeled shrimp
8 black olives

Shrimp Aspic—a beautifully colorful dish which is decorated with tomatoes, olives, lettuce and hard-boiled eggs

1 Bring the water to a boil. Crumble the bouillon cube into the water and simmer for 5 minutes. Add 3 of the tarragon leaves and both the celery leaves and boil for 1 minute. Dissolve the gelatin and add it to the stock. Season with the salt and pour in the lemon juice. Simmer for 5 minutes, strain and allow to cool. Do not refrigerate.

2 Meanwhile, peel and dice the carrot and turnip into small cubes. Finely slice the beans. Boil these vegetables and the peas separately in salted water until they are tender.

3 Cut 1 egg into wedges and slice the other. Wash and dry the lettuce leaves and slice the tomatoes.

4 Prepare a 5-cup mold by rinsing it in cold water. Place the mold in a bowl of crushed ice.

5 Pour in ½ the aspic jelly and swirl the mold in one direction in the ice until the inside is covered with a

thin skin of gelatin. When it is set, dip the slices of egg into the remaining aspic and stick them to the side of the mold. Do the same with the sliced radish and a few tarragon leaves, but when you stick them to the mold arrange them around the egg slices to form a floral design.

6 Place the boiled vegetables in a bowl, add the shrimp, season and toss together. Pour the remaining aspic gelatin (it should still be liquid) into the bowl and stir until it is mixed through the vegetables and shrimp. Pour this mixture into the mold. Allow the aspic to set either on the ice or in the refrigerator.

7 Arrange the lettuce leaves on a serving dish. Turn the set aspic onto the bed of lettuce and surround it with the sliced tomatoes, quartered hard-boiled egg and olives before serving.

Serves 6

Tip: For a slightly different flavor you can add other ingredients to this dish. Other seafoods such as minced clams, chopped lobster and tuna fish all blend well with the shrimp.

Vegetables in Aspic makes an impressive and attractive salad for a summer lunch or a dish for a buffet party

Vegetables in Aspic

$\frac{3}{4}$ **cup carrots, peeled**
2 large parsnips, peeled
$\frac{1}{3}$ **cup green beans**
$\frac{1}{3}$ **cup peas**
1 tablespoon gelatin
salt and pepper
3 ozs. canned asparagus tips, drained

1 Dice 1 of the carrots. Cut the remaining carrots and parsnips into small cubes. Cut the French beans into diamond shapes.

2 Boil the carrots, parsnips, beans and peas in salted water, until tender. Drain. Keep the vegetables separate for the moment and allow to cool.

3 Prepare a $3\frac{5}{8}$-cup mold by rinsing it in cold water. Place the mold in a bowl of crushed ice.

4 Make $1\frac{1}{4}$ cups aspic by dissolving in 1 tablespoon gelatin in $\frac{1}{4}$ cup

hot water and adding 1 cup of cold water.

5 Pour $\frac{1}{2}$ the aspic into the mold and immediately start to swirl the bowl in the ice in the same direction all the time. Keep swirling until the aspic coats the inside of the mold and begins to set.

6 Take the carrot slices and asparagus tips and dip them in the remaining aspic. Line the top of the mold with alternate slices of carrot and asparagus.

7 Combine the remaining vegetables in a bowl and gently toss. Check the seasoning. Spoon the vegetables into the mold. Pour on the remaining aspic until the mold is full. Chill until it is firmly set.

8 Turn the aspic salad out onto a plate and serve immediately.

Serves 6

Tip: All sorts of other vegetables may be used in this dish. Choose colorful vegetables such as peppers, beets or tomatoes. Also, you can change the flavor of the aspic by adding a few tablespoons of wine, dry sherry or port or even a liqueur. Always use a dry wine or sherry in a savory aspic mold.

Eggs in Aspic

1 tablespoon gelatin
¼ cup sherry
1¼ cups water
4 hard-boiled eggs
4 tomatoes
1 teaspoon chopped parsley
¼ lb. thin slices ham
sprig rosemary

1 Dissolve the gelatin in the sherry. Bring the water to a boil, then add the gelatin and sherry to the boiling hot water.

2 When the aspic mixture is cool, but still liquid, place 1 tablespoon in the bottoms of 6 oval ⅝-cup molds. Allow to set.

3 Split the hard-boiled eggs and chop the yolk and white of one of the eggs.

4 Skin, seed and chop one of the tomatoes.

5 Sprinkle a little chopped parsley, egg yolk and white, and tomato into each mold. Cut the ham into 6 strips, 2 inches wide. Line each mold with a strip of ham and place a halved egg inside each.

6 Fill up the molds with aspic and pour the remaining aspic into a square mold.

7 Leave in the refrigerator for 2 hours until firm and set. Turn out the aspic eggs onto an attractive serving platter and garnish with the remaining quartered tomatoes and the sprig of rosemary.

8 Cut the aspic in the square dish or mold into small cubes and use as a garnish.

Serves 6

Tip: This dish is ideal for summer parties and buffets. You can decorate the tops of the eggs with chopped herbs, ham or onion as well as eggs and tomatoes. Or, if you feel really extravagant, how about chopped truffles, the most luxurious food of all?

Lamb in Mint Gelatin Mold

1⅔ cups diced cold lamb
1 tablespoon butter
1 cup diced, cooked potatoes
salt and pepper
⅔ cup meat stock
1 tablespoon chopped mint
1 tablespoon sugar
1 tablespoon vinegar
2 tablespoons gelatin

Eggs in Aspic are surrounded by ham, decorated with tomatoes and encased in aspic, topped with parsley

¼ cup water
4 tomatoes, quartered
shredded Romaine lettuce

1 Heat the butter in a skillet and sauté the diced lamb for about 5 minutes. Add the potatoes and toss gently, then remove from the pan and season with salt and pepper.

2 Bring the stock to a boil—it should be clear and transparent.

3 Mix together the mint, sugar and vinegar and add to the boiling stock. Remove from the heat.

4 Blend the gelatin with the cold water and then stir this mixture into the hot stock. Add the meat and potatoes, then pour into a 9-inch ring mold (tube pan).

5 Cool a little, then allow to set for 2 hours in the refrigerator.

6 When set and firm, turn the mint gelatin mold out onto a dish and decorate the center with quartered tomatoes. Arrange the shredded lettuce around the sides of the mold, then serve.

Serves 4

Tip: This dish is an original and tasty way of using up leftover roast lamb which is bound to become a firm favorite with your family. Instead of using fresh mint and making the mint sauce, you can use one of the commercial varieties. It is especially nice if served with a crisp green salad and sautéed potatoes.

Lobster in Aspic

one 2-lb. lobster, live or cooked
4¼ cups court bouillon (fish stock)
4 eggs, separated
8 tablespoons gelatin

Lamb in Mint Jelly Mold is a tasty, attractive way of using up leftover lamb in aspic with a cold salad

½ cup water
¼ lb. minced white fish
1 tablespoon chopped tarragon
7 tomatoes
few tarragon leaves
2 cups diced carrots
2 cups diced turnips
1 cup peas
small bunch chives
½ cup mayonnaise
salt and pepper
few lettuce leaves

1 If the lobster is alive, plunge it into boiling water or the court bouillon (it will die instantly). Cook it for 15 minutes, then leave to cool in the court bouillon until completely cold.

2 Poach two of the egg whites in a pan of simmering water.

3 Soak the gelatin in the cold water and stir well. Place in a bowl with the minced fish, chopped tarragon and 2 uncooked egg whites. Mix briskly, then strain in the warm court bouillon.

4 Mix well, then pour into a saucepan and bring to a boil, stirring constantly. Simmer for 15 minutes until the mixture has coagulated on top.

5 When cooked, pour this gelatin through some damp cheesecloth into a bowl and cool.

6 Place the large mold on top of a bowl of crushed ice.

7 Add some of the fish aspic to the mold and coat the bottom and edges, turning the bowl all the time over the ice.

8 With a knife, remove the skin of 1 tomato and cut into decorative diamond shapes. Do the same with the poached egg whites.

9 Scald the tarragon leaves. Arrange the egg white, tomato, and the tarragon around the inside of the mold in a pattern and fix in place with another layer of aspic. Let set.

10 Shell the lobster, remove the soft skin from the tail and cut the meat into even rounds. Also use the meat in the claws.

11 Arrange the meat in the mold then cover with a layer of aspic and let set. Repeat the layers of lobster and aspic until the mold is full. Place in the refrigerator for 2 hours until set.

12 Meanwhile, cook the carrots, turnips and peas in salted water until cooked.

13 Place them in a bowl with the chives and mayonnaise and mix well.

14 Slice off the tops of the remaining tomatoes and scoop out the pulp. Fill the tomato shells with the mayonnaise mixture.

15 When the aspic mold is set, turn it out onto a serving platter. (Wrap a hot cloth around the mold for a few minutes to unmold.)

16 Decorate with lettuce and surround with the tomatoes.

Serves 6

Look 'n Cook Lobster in Aspic

1 All the ingredients **2** Cook the lobster in a court bouillon of water, carrots, onions with herbs and seasoning. Chop the carrot, and onions and put them in a pot with the fish trimmings. Cover with cold water and simmer **3** Separate the eggs, reserving the yolks. Put the whites in a small dish and poach in simmering water **4** Chop the fillets and tarragon. Add the tarragon leaves, gelatin, 2 egg whites and water. Mix

well **5** Add the fish stock through a strainer **6** Put the mixture into a large saucepan, bring to a boil and simmer **7** Pour the gelatin through a damp cloth. Cool **8** Chill the metal mold in a bowl of ice. Put a little aspic in it and swirl around to coat the mold **9** Cut the poached egg whites and tomato into decorative shapes **10** Arrange in the metal mold **11** Fix in place with more fish aspic **12** Shell the lobster **13** Cut the lobster

into even pieces **14** Arrange the pieces of lobster in the mold **15** Carefully spoon in a little aspic to fix the pieces and allow to set **16** Pour on another layer of aspic and allow to set. Continue with layers of lobster stuck down with a little aspic, followed by a layer of aspic until all the ingredients are used. Put the mold in the refrigerator to set **17** Finely dice the carrots, turnips and chives. Cook the vegetables with the peas for a few minutes, until tender, in boiling salted water. Drain and cool **18** Scoop out the insides of the tomatoes. Discard the seeds and mix the vegetables with the tomato pulp and the mayonnaise, then season. Stuff the tomatoes **19** To unmold the lobster in aspic, either wrap a hot cloth around the mold for a few seconds, or dip the mold in hot water briefly. Turn over on a serving dish, hold the mold and dish firmly and shake the dish once sharply **20** Arrange the stuffed tomatoes alternately with lettuce leaves around the lobster in aspic

Vegetarian Salads

In this section, we give you recipes for delicious, nourishing salads without meat. Although they contain no meat, many have a high protein content derived from nuts, eggs, cheese, lentils, wheat or beans. Do not make the mistake of regarding all vegetarian food as 'rabbit food'—it's not. Just try some of these exciting recipes—at least one of them is bound to become a firm family favorite.

Tabbouleh

2¼ cups water
1¾ cups cracked wheat
1 onion, chopped
juice 1 lemon
¼ cup olive oil
salt and pepper

1 tablespoon chopped parsley
1 tablespoon chopped mint
4 tomatoes, cut in wedges

1 Bring the water to a boil and soak the cracked wheat in it, covered, for about 10 minutes, then drain and refrigerate.

2 Blend together the chopped onion, lemon juice and olive oil. Five minutes before serving the Tabbouleh, season the dressing and stir it into the cracked wheat.

3 Sprinkle with the chopped parsley and mint and arrange the tomato wedges on top. Serve as an appetizer.

Serves 4

Tip: This is a Lebanese salad which can be served as a starter or an accompaniment to kebabs or grilled lamb. The texture should be crunchy but soft. For a slightly different flavor, you can mix some crushed garlic into the dressing. *Never* add the dressing until 5 minutes before serving or the wheat will become soggy.

Tabbouleh, on the left, is shown with its classic accompaniment, fattoush, which is an onion and tomato salad

Curried Spaghetti Salad

1¾ cups cooked spaghetti
3 branches celery, chopped
1¼ cups sliced raw mushrooms
1 tablespoon chopped onion
1 head lettuce

For the Mayonnaise:
⅓ cup mayonnaise
salt and pepper
good pinch curry powder
2 teaspoons mango chutney
1 teaspoon lemon juice
1 tablespoon chopped parsley

1 Mix together the cooked cold spaghetti, celery, mushrooms and onion in a bowl.

2 Prepare the mayonnaise. Mix the mayonnaise, seasoning, curry powder and chutney together in a bowl. Stir in the lemon juice and chopped parsley.

3 Toss the spaghetti mixture in the mayonnaise so that it is evenly coated.

4 Wash and drain the lettuce. Arrange the separated leaves around a serving dish and pile the spaghetti in the center.

Serves 4

Tip: You can use different types of pasta in this salad. Try substituting cooked pasta shells and shapes or macaroni for the spaghetti. A more Italian way to serve this salad is to make a vinaigrette-type dressing with oil, vinegar, garlic and fresh tomato juice. Mix in some catsup, curry powder, mango chutney and sugar. Then toss the spaghetti in this dressing, and serve garnished with chopped herbs such as basil or parsley and sliced red and green peppers. This is a good way of using up cold leftover pasta, and it is also economical.

Mushroom Salad Provençale

1 lb. button mushrooms
2 cloves garlic, crushed
juice and grated rind 1 lemon
2 tablespoons oil
1 tablespoon yogurt
salt and pepper
1 tablespoon chopped parsley

1 Wash and drain the mushrooms. Wipe them dry, then trim the ends from the stalks. Slice the mushrooms thinly and place in a bowl with the garlic.

2 Next make the dressing. Mix the lemon juice and rind, and oil. Stir in the yogurt, salt and pepper.

3 Five minutes before serving, toss the mushrooms in the salad dressing. Sprinkle with the chopped parsley and serve.

Serves 4

Mushroom Salad Provençale will brighten up a summer lunch with its fresh tangy taste of lemons, garlic and yogurt

Leek Salad

8 small leeks
1 teaspoon prepared mustard
salt and pepper
$\frac{1}{4}$ cup oil
1 tablespoon wine vinegar
1 tablespoon light cream
2 teaspoons chopped parsley

1 Trim the green ends of the leeks. Split each leek from the center of the white up into the stem, keeping the leek intact and whole. Wash the leeks thoroughly under running cold water until they are completely clean.

2 Make the leeks into a bundle and tie it securely around the center with string.

3 Fill a pan with water, bring to a boil and add the bundle of leeks to the boiling water. Boil for 5 minutes, then drain and refresh the leeks in ice-cold water. This will restore the vivid green color. Drain again and remove the string.

4 In a bowl, prepare the dressing. Mix together the mustard, salt, pepper and oil. Stir in the vinegar and finally the cream.

5 When the leeks are completely cold, arrange them in a flat serving dish and pour the dressing over the top. Sprinkle them with the chopped parsley, then serve.

Serves 4

Tip: This salad is delicious when served with a new potatoes and watercress salad. If you wish to increase the nutrition content and add some protein, sprinkle in a few chopped nuts or quartered hard-boiled eggs. Other vegetables such as celery, asparagus and fennel can also be cooked.

Diet Salads

A balanced salad makes the perfect meal for dieting. It should be eaten with or include protein in the form of meat, eggs, cheese or fish with an interesting combination of salad and root vegetables and fruit. A little salad dressing will make it delicious, and adds very little in the way of calories.

Eat a light but sensible breakfast of a boiled egg, salads and fruit at lunchtime, and make sure you have a light protein meal in the evening, and you will lose weight gradually.

Eat your meals slowly, savor your food, and include plenty of green vegetables. By the time you have munched your way through plenty of lettuce or cabbage you will feel that you have eaten enough, and will not be tempted to take a second helping. Cut the sugar and starch down, but balance the rest of your diet and you will feel well, healthy, and full of vitality. Aim for slimness, which is compatible with perfect health, and not emaciation. Don't be tempted to diet beyond what is sensible for your build and metabolism, as this will make you feel exhausted and drained of energy.

Greek Onion Salad

8 large onions
1⅓ cups finely chopped ham
1 dill pickle, diced
2 tablespoons corn kernels
salt and pepper
½ cup white wine

½ cup water
juice 1 lemon
⅔ cup light cream
1 teaspoon prepared French mustard
1 tablespoon chopped parsley

1 Remove the outside yellow skin from the onions, but leave them whole. Place them close together in one layer in a large pan and just cover with water. Bring to a boil and cook for 10 minutes.

2 Scoop out the inside of each onion. Chop and blend with the chopped ham and diced pickle. Add the corn and season. Refill the onion cases.

3 Preheat the oven to 375°F.

4 Place the onions in a shallow ovenproof dish. Pour on the white wine mixed with the water, half the lemon juice and 2 tablespoons cream. Bake in the oven for 20 minutes until cooked, but still firm. Cool in the liquid.

5 Make the sauce with the rest of the cream, lemon juice and mustard.

6 When ready to serve, lift the onions onto a dish, pour a little of the sauce on, and serve the remainder separately. Sprinkle the onions with chopped parsley. Serve with a rice salad.

Serves 4

Cauliflower and Cottage Cheese Salad

1 cauliflower
¼ cup oil
2 tablespoons vinegar
1 teaspoon chopped basil
salt and pepper
1½ cups cottage cheese
1 tablespoon chopped chives
½ lettuce
4 tomatoes

1 Wash and trim the cauliflower and divide into sprigs. Boil in salted water until just tender for about 5 minutes. Drain.

2 While hot, pour on a dressing made of the oil, vinegar, basil and salt and pepper. Cool, spooning the liquid over the cauliflower from time to time.

3 Mix the cottage cheese with the chopped chives.

4 When ready to serve, line a shallow dish with the lettuce leaves, arrange the cold cauliflower salad in a circle, and put the cottage cheese in the middle. Decorate with the tomatoes, cut in slices.

Serves 4

Avocado and Chinese Cabbage Salad

1 head Chinese cabbage, or 1 head lettuce
1 avocado
1 grapefruit
2 cups carrots, cut in strips
sprigs of watercress for garnish
1 tablespoon boiled rice (optional)

1 Wash the Chinese cabbage, or lettuce. Drain well and arrange in a bowl.

2 Remove the peel and pit from the avocado and cut into chunks.

3 Peel the grapefruit and cut into cabbage sections.

4 Arrange the avocado, grapefruit and strips of carrots on the Chinese cabbage. Decorate with the watercress, and sprinkle the rice on top. Serve with a bowl of low calorie salad dressing.

Serves 4

Avocado and Chinese Cabbage Salad is an exotic medley of rice, fruit and salad vegetables with a mayonnaise

Salad Antibes

½ head lettuce
⅓ cup cooked green beans
1 small onion, sliced
½ green pepper, sliced
½ sweet red pepper, sliced
1 tomato, quartered
1 hard-boiled egg, quartered
8 black olives

For the Low Calorie Dressing:
⅓ cup lemon juice
⅔ cup water
1 teaspoon sugar
¼ teaspoon salt

1 Combine the dressing ingredients and mix well. Chill.

2 Wash and dry the lettuce. Tear the leaves into pieces and place in a bowl. Cut the beans into pieces 2 inches long.

3 Add the beans, onion and peppers. Toss in the dressing and decorate with the tomato, egg and black olives.

Serves 2

Cucumber and Yogurt Salad

1 large or 2 small cucumbers, peeled and sliced
½ onion, finely chopped
1 cup plain yogurt
½ teaspoon salt
freshly ground black pepper
3 tablespoons finely chopped fresh mint or ½ teaspoon dried mint
1 tablespoon finely chopped basil or ½ teaspoon dried basil

1 Place the cucumber and onion in a bowl. Add the yogurt, salt and pepper and mix well. Chill.

2 Just before serving sprinkle with the mint and basil.

Serves 4

Salad Antibes has the color and exotic flavor of the French Riviera with its olives, peppers and crispy lettuce

Low Calorie Thousand Islands Dressing

¾ cup tarragon vinegar
1¼ cups condensed tomato soup
1 clove garlic, crushed
pinch cayenne pepper
2 tablespoons chopped dill pickle
2 tablespoons finely chopped celery
2 tablespoons finely chopped parsley
1 tablespoon Worcestershire sauce
1 teaspoon paprika
1 teaspoon prepared mustard

1 Combine all the ingredients in a screw top jar or watertight container and shake well. Store in the refrigerator.

Makes 2½ cups

Papaya Citrus Salad

1 papaya
1 orange
1 grapefruit
½ head lettuce
12 olives
1 dill pickle
1 cup plain yogurt
salt

1 Slice the papaya. Peel the orange and grapefruit and separate the sections. Arrange the papaya and fruit on the lettuce leaves. Garnish with the olives and dill pickle.

2 Season the yogurt with a little salt and pour over the salad.

Serves 4

Savory Sauces

An imaginative sauce can transform a simple dish into something special. Once you've mastered the principal basic sauces — béchamel and velouté for white sauces, espagnole for brown sauces, and hollandaise for emulsified sauces — you have the key to countless variations

Basis of a Sauce

The principal elements in a sauce are stock, seasonings and other flavorings, fat and thickening agents. To make a good sauce you must first make a good stock — strongly flavored and concentrated. Never rush a stock — cook it for a long time at simmering point 180°F. to draw out the essential juices and flavor from the meat bones.

Both white and brown stocks are used in sauces, together with concentrated extracts like meat gravies, essences and bouillon cubes. With the basic white or brown sauce made, you can then think about the countless variations possible, for basic sauces are rarely used without adjustment.

These basic sauces (sometimes referred to as 'mother' sauces) are the white béchamel and velouté, and brown espagnole: recipes for all three appear on the following pages. You can save time by making a quantity of very thick basic sauce which can be kept, covered, in a bowl in the refrigerator. Then you can take a spoonful of cold sauce and enrich a gravy or stock in no time at all. And for variations you simply thin down the basic sauce with about ⅔ cup of stock or other liquid, depending on the type of sauce required.

To make a smooth sauce, quite a lot of the fat used (at least 4%) must remain in the sauce. If too much fat is used, however, fatty globules will rise to the surface and spoil both flavor and appearance. You can only skim them off in the event of this happening.

There are various ways to thicken and bind a sauce. Egg yolk, starch (any kind of flour) and sometimes meat juices are the main binding agents used: simply blend the egg yolk or starch with a little of the cold liquid to form a smooth paste, then whisk in a little of the hot liquid, pour back into the pan of liquid, and heat to just below the boiling point, stirring all the time, until the sauce is thick and smooth. If the thickening agent only were added directly to the hot sauce or boiled, the mixture would curdle and look unappetizing.

Arrowroot and cornstarch give better results than ordinary flour in semi- and thick gravies, fruit and sweet-sour sauces. To use, blend the starch with 4 times the amount of cold liquid, then at the last minute stir into the boiling liquid and boil until the sauce clears and thickens. Use at once.

Emulsified sauces like Hollandaise, and its variations such as Béarnaise and mousseline sauces, undergo a different thickening process. Air is beaten into egg yolks, sometimes over heat, so they increase in volume and thicken. In the case of mayonnaise, the thickening is brought about by combining egg yolks, oil and vinegar or lemon juice.

The addition of starch, a white sauce or a gelatinous mixture helps to bind an emulsified sauce together, making separation less likely and the sauce more resistant to heat or refrigeration.

If a sauce has to stand for a while before serving, keep in a double boiler or stainless steel bowl over a pan of hot water so there's no risk of burning or loss of texture and flavor; then place a little butter on top and cover with wax paper to prevent a skin from forming.

And if you want to give a sauce a fillip, any fortified wine (port, Madeira, sherry) can be added at the last moment in the ratio of ¼ cup wine per 2 cups sauce.

If making a béchamel with milk or water instead of stock to serve as a plain white sauce, season with salt, pepper and nutmeg, together with a bouquet garni of 1 bay leaf, celery leaf and thyme and strain before use. If the béchamel is to serve with fish, add the juice of 1 lemon at the last moment.

Thickening Sauces

There are three basic methods of thickening a sauce — by means of a roux, a liaison, and a purée.

Roux

A roux is a paste of flour cooked in butter which can be used to thicken liquids to various consistencies, according to their intended use. The degree to which the roux is cooked determines the flavor and final color of the sauce, and the three stages of cooking a roux are known as white, blond and brown.

White roux: equal quantities of butter and flour are cooked gently together in a pan for about 2 minutes or until the mixture has the appearance of wet sand. It should not be colored. This type of roux is used mainly for thickening béchamel sauces and for any white soups.

Blond roux: the ratio of butter to flour is the same as for a white roux, but the two are cooked together for a slightly longer time until a light-brown, nutty color is obtained. This roux is used for velouté sauces, tomato sauces and soups.

Brown roux: the ratio of butter to flour is increased — the amount of butter is 1¼ times that of the flour — and the two are cooked together for a longer time — about 10-12 minutes or until well browned. The fat used is usually meat drippings, pure vegetable shortening or lard. Since the time taken to brown the roux is so long, the heat beneath the pan must be very low so that the mixture does not burn and become bitter.

In order to shorten this cooking time and to produce the distinctive baked flavor of a brown sauce, the flour can first be toasted in the oven: place it on a baking sheet and cook at 350°F. for about 12 minutes or until golden in color. The flour can then be used for the other kinds of roux and need only be cooked with the butter for about 3-4 minutes.

After the flour and butter have been cooked, the liquid is added by one of two methods. In the first, the cooked roux is taken off the heat and the cold liquid is added gradually, stirring all the time with a wooden spoon, until a smooth sauce is obtained. The pan is then returned to the heat and the sauce heated until thick. Or, you can remove the roux from the heat after cooking, allow it to cool and then add the hot liquid to it beating all the time. The sauce is returned to the heat and cooked until thick. Finally, the sauce can be whisked quickly at the end in order to make sure it is smooth.

Liaison

The two basic liaisons are egg yolks and meat juices; these are ingredients which, when heated gently, coagulate and therefore thicken the sauce into which they have been incorporated. The coagulant is placed in a bowl and blended with a spoonful of cold liquid.

A larger quantity (usually about a cupful) of the warm sauce is then added to the coagulant and the mixture is returned to the main sauce and heated gently until thick. To add the egg yolk or the juice directly to the sauce would only result in a too rapid coagulation and a curdled sauce. Coagulation occurs at about 180°F. and so it is important that the sauce is heated gently — preferably in a bowl over a deep pan of boiling water.

Purée

Another method of thickening a sauce, which reflects new trends in modern cookery, is to add meat, or vegetable purées; these are simply made by mixing in a blender with a little liquid or the food's own cooking juices. In this way, starchy elements can be reduced to a minimum, making purée thickening ideal for weight watchers and dieters in general.

Stuffed Fennel in Mornay Sauce

¼ cup flour
¼ cup butter
8½ cups boiling water
2 tablespoons white vinegar
1½ tablespoons salt
4 large fennel bulbs
1 cup fresh breadcrumbs
2 tablespoons light cream
2 slices cooked ham
¼ lb. smoked bacon
few sprigs parsley
1 clove garlic, peeled and chopped
½ cup grated cheese
1 egg

For the Sauce:
¼ cup flour
2 tablespoons butter
1¼ cups milk
2 tablespoons tomato paste
pinch nutmeg
salt and pepper

1 In a pan, blend the flour with 2 tablespoons of the butter to form a paste and then pour in the boiling water, whisking all the time. Add the vinegar and the salt and bring this mixture to a boil. This forms a white stock in which to cook the fennel bulbs.

Stuffed fennel in mornay sauce, baked in a hot oven till brown and bubbling. Any vegetable can be cooked this way

2 Clean the fennel bulbs and cut away the hard bases but leave them whole. Place the bulbs in the stock and bring to a boil. Simmer for 30 minutes.

3 Place the breadcrumbs in a bowl with the cream and mix well. Chop the ham and bacon; wash, dry and chop the parsley. Add the chopped meats and parsley, the garlic and the egg to the breadcrumbs and mix well.

4 Preheat the oven to 400°F. Drain the fennel. Cut the bulbs in half, fill each half with stuffing and then put the two halves together again. Place the stuffed fennel bulbs in an oven-proof dish.

5 Make the white roux (see page 122) using the flour, butter and milk. Add the tomato paste and nutmeg and season to taste.

6 Coat the fennel bulbs with the sauce and sprinkle them with the grated cheese. Cut the remaining butter into small pieces and dot these over the top. Place the fennel in the preheated oven and bake for 35-40 minutes.

Serves 4

Béchamel Sauce

Béchamel Sauce

The quantity below makes a panada *or thick paste-like mixture which can be stored, covered, in a refrigerator for up to 1 week. For a flowing or pouring sauce, add up to 2 cups liquid — 1¼ cups is usually sufficient; reheat gently, stirring all the time, until smooth.*

**1 small onion, studded with 2
  cloves
2¼ cups milk
¼ cup butter
½ cup flour
salt and pepper
pinch nutmeg
pinch thyme**

1 Place the onion in a saucepan with the milk. Bring it gently to a boil, then remove the pan from the heat and allow to cool. Cover with a lid and leave the milk to steep and absorb the flavor of the onion.

2 Melt the butter in a pan and stir in the flour. Cook the roux over low heat, without letting it color, for about 1 minute, stirring with a wooden spoon. Gradually pour in the milk, stirring continuously until a smooth sauce forms.

3 Add the onion and simmer the sauce for 5 minutes. Remove the onion and add salt, pepper, the nutmeg and thyme.

Makes 2¼ cups

Consistency of Sauces
A useful formula to remember is that the proportion of butter and flour to liquid is 5 percent for a pouring consistency and 10 percent for a coating sauce: that is, 2 tablespoons butter and 4 tablespoons flour to 2½ cups liquid and ¼ cup butter and ½ cup flour to 2¼ cups liquid, respectively.

The liquid used can be milk, cream, stock or water, according to the recipe.

Variations

Anchovy Sauce

1 To 1¼ cups of basic béchamel sauce, add 2 ozs. drained and chopped canned anchovy fillets, 2 tablespoons unsalted butter, 1 teaspoon tomato paste and, for color, a pinch of paprika.

2 Thin the sauce to the required consistency with 1¼ cups stock (use fish stock for fish, and chicken or white stock for meat dishes). Check the seasoning.

Serve with eggs, celery or fish.

Asparagus Sauce

1 To 1¼ cups of basic béchamel sauce, add ¼ cup cooked asparagus, blended with 1¼ cups of the water in which the asparagus was cooked.

2 After the sauce is cooked, remove the pan from the heat and add 4 tablespoons sour cream or plain yogurt to give the sauce a piquant flavor. Check the seasoning.

Serve with chicken, veal or salmon dishes.

Butter Sauce

1 Use the basic béchamel sauce recipe, but replace the milk with water and use butter only. For extra flavor, a chicken bouillon cube can be crumbled into the sauce.

Serve with vegetables and potatoes.

Carrot Sauce

1 To 1¼ cups of basic béchamel sauce, add a purée of ¼ cup cooked carrots, blended with ⅔ cup of their cooking water.

2 Add ¼ cup sour or light cream and reheat. Flavor the sauce with a pinch of paprika, ½ teaspoon honey and 2 tablespoons lemon juice. Check the seasoning.

Serve with boiled beef, chicken or white fish.

Cheese Sauce

1 To 1¼ cups of basic béchamel sauce, add 1¼ cups milk and ½ cup grated cheese (such as Cheddar, Gruyère, Edam or Swiss). If the sauce is to be used for vegetables, such as cauliflower, asparagus, leeks, onions, celery or cabbage, use less milk and make up the liquid content with some of the water in which the vegetables have been cooked. Check the seasoning.

Serve with meat, vegetable, fish and pasta dishes.

Cream Sauce

1 To 1¼ cups of basic béchamel sauce, add 1¼ cups light cream. Blend, bring to a boil and boil for 5 minutes.

2 Add the strained juice of ½ lemon and season with salt and pepper to taste.

Serve with fish, egg and vegetable dishes.

Divine Sauce

1 Boil 2½ cups button mushrooms in the strained juice of 1 lemon and ⅔ cup dry sherry for 2 minutes. Pour this mixture into 1¼ cups of basic béchamel sauce.

2 Finally, add ⅓ cup heavy or light cream, a pinch of paprika and 1 tablespoon catsup or tomato paste. Boil for 8 minutes and season with salt and pepper to taste.

Serve with chicken quenelles.

1 Ingredients for béchamel sauce: butter, flour, milk, nutmeg, and 1 onion studded with cloves **2** Heat the butter gently in a pan until melted **3** Take the pan off the heat and add the flour to make a roux **4** Return to the heat and cook the roux until it bubbles and has the appearance of wet sand. Stir all the time with a wooden spoon **5** Take the pan off the heat again and blend in the milk **6** The sauce is heated again for a few minutes, then seasoned and poured into a sauce boat to serve

Egg Sauce

1 Place 2 egg yolks and ⅔ cup light cream in a bowl and mix together with a whisk. Gradually add 1¼ cups of basic béchamel sauce and return this mixture to the rest of the sauce.

2 Bring to a boil and boil for 5 minutes. Finally, add the strained juice of ½ lemon and season with salt and pepper to taste.

Serve with fish, poultry and vegetables.

Mushroom Sauce

1 Slice 2½ cups white mushrooms. Boil them in the strained juice of ½ lemon and ⅔ cup stock for 3 minutes. Pour this mixture into 1¼ cups of basic béchamel sauce.

2 Season and stir in ⅓ cup light cream.

Serve with chicken, noodles, fish and vegetable dishes.

Mustard Sauce

1 To 1¼ cups of the butter sauce, add, with the pan off the heat, 1 tablespoon of prepared mustard (vary the amount according to taste).

2 Thin the sauce to the required consistency with 1¼ cups chicken or white stock and season with salt and pepper to taste.

Serve with oily fish, pork or grilled duck.

Parsley Sauce

1 To 1¼ cups of basic béchamel sauce, add either 1 tablespoon freshly chopped parsley (never use dried parsley for this sauce) or 2 tablespoons savory butter (see page 145).

2 Thin down the sauce to the required consistency with 1¼ cups chicken or white stock and season with salt and pepper to taste.

Serve with fish and white meat

Soubise Sauce

1 To 1¼ cups of basic béchamel sauce, add ¼ lb. cooked onion, blended with ¾ cup cold milk. If liked, flavor with a pinch of sage.

2 Add ½ cup light cream and boil for 5 minutes. Season with salt and pepper to taste.

Serve with roast or boiled lamb or veal.

Condiments for Sauces

Clearly, one of the most important steps in making sauces is achieving the correct balance of seasoning. The basic ingredient of seasoning is salt.

Salt

Two types of salt are used: table salt and coarse salt which is used to season clear soups or sauces. Table salt is used at the last moment to adjust seasoning. Spice salt is a mixture of salt and spice.

You can make your own spice salt by mixing ¼ lb. salt with 2 tablespoons mixed spice and ½ teaspoon white pepper. Keep the mixture in an airtight container. Salt is used in the ratio of ½ teaspoon salt to 4¼ cups liquid or 2 lbs. solid weight.

Four-spice Mixture

A four-spice mixture can be made by mixing together ½ cup allspice, 1 tablespoon nutmeg, 1 tablespoon clove, 1 tablespoon cinnamon and 1 tablespoon salt. Again, keep the mixture in an airtight container.

Four-herb Mixture

Mix together 1 tablespoon each of the following, in ground form: bay leaf, thyme, rosemary and marjoram. Add 1 tablespoon salt and keep the mixture in an airtight container.

Chili Paste for Curry Sauce

Mix the following ingredients together and combine in a blender: 2 tablespoons fresh green seeded chilies, 2 tablespoons peeled fresh gingerroot, 1 clove fresh peeled garlic, 2 tablespoons chopped onion, ¼ cup olive or peanut oil, 1 tablespoon lemon juice, ¼ cup water.

Spice for Curry

Blend the following ingredients together and mix them with chili paste: ½ teaspoon ground coriander, ½ teaspoon paprika, ½ teaspoon ground cumin, ½ teaspoon ground cloves, ½ teaspoon turmeric, 1 tablespoon cornstarch or arrowroot, 1 teaspoon mustard, and ½ teaspoon ground cardamom.

Brussels Sprouts in Curry Sauce

salt
2¼ lbs. Brussels sprouts
1 tablespoon butter
2 tablespoons flour
2 teaspoons curry powder
1¼ cups milk
pepper

1 Bring salted water to a boil in a saucepan.

2 Meanwhile, prepare and wash the sprouts. Mark a cross in the end of the stalks.

3 Put the sprouts into the boiling water and simmer for 8-10 minutes or until tender.

4 Meanwhile, make a white sauce. Melt the butter in a small pan, stir in the flour and curry powder and cook gently, stirring with a wooden spoon, for 1 minute. Take the pan off the heat and blend in the milk. Return the pan to the heat, bring to a boil and boil for a few minutes, stirring all the time. Keep the sauce hot.

5 When the sprouts are almost cooked, strain off ½ cup of the cooking liquid. Add this to the sauce and stir well. Taste and correct the seasoning.

6 Drain the sprouts well and put them into a heated serving dish. Coat with the curry sauce. Serve hot.

Serves 4

Veal Scallopini
à la Antonia

¼ cup butter
1½ lbs. veal scallopini
1 teaspoon salt
freshly ground black pepper
2 scallions, thinly sliced
3 tomatoes, skinned, seeded and
  cut into strips
1½ cups thinly sliced mushrooms
⅔ cups chicken stock
½ teaspoon dried oregano
⅔ cup béchamel sauce (see
  page 124)
pinch nutmeg
1 tablespoon chopped parsley

1 Melt the butter in a large skillet and fry the escalopes of veal quickly on both sides over high heat. Remove the meat from the pan, season with salt and pepper, and keep warm.

2 Add the sliced onions to the pan and sauté gently for 2 minutes then add the tomatoes and mushrooms and cook for a further 4-5 minutes. Add the stock and oregano, bring to a boil and boil for 5 minutes.

3 Add the béchamel sauce and boil again for 8 minutes to reduce the liquid by half.

4 Check the seasoning and add the nutmeg. Return the veal to the pan and coat it with the sauce until well heated.

5 Transfer the meat and sauce to a warm serving dish and sprinkle with the chopped parsley. Serve with rice and a crisp green salad.

Serves 6

Tip: Instead of using chicken stock, you can add an equal amount of white wine. Also, the béchamel sauce can be replaced by the same amount of light cream or a mixture of cream and sauce.

Brussels sprouts in curry sauce. This creamy béchamel-based sauce turns sprouts into something special

Velouté Sauce

Basic Velouté Sauce

The quantity below makes a panada *or thick paste-like mixture which can be stored, covered, in a refrigerator for up to 1 week. For a flowing or pouring sauce, add up to 1¾ cups liquid — 1¼ cups is usually sufficient; reheat gently, stirring all the time, until smooth.*

¼ cup melted chicken fat
½ cup flour
2¼ cups chicken stock or use a
  vegetable stock with 2 chicken
  bouillon cubes

1 Melt the fat in a heavy pan and cook the flour to a blond roux for 2 minutes or until it looks like wet sand but has a nutty color and flavor.

2 Gradually pour in the cold stock or, alternatively, cool the roux and gradually stir in the boiling stock.

3 Whisk the sauce for a few seconds for smoothness and then simmer for 30 minutes, removing any skin or scum as it rises.

Makes about 2¼ cups

Conil Cucumber Sauce

1 cucumber
1 sweet red pepper
1 medium onion
2 tablespoons white vinegar
salt and pepper
pinch grated nutmeg
juice and rind 1 lemon

2¼ cups velouté sauce
2 egg yolks
½ cup light cream
1 tablespoon chopped chives and
  parsley

1 Peel and seed the cucumber, and dice the pulp neatly. Place in a large mixing bowl. Seed the pepper and chop. Peel and chop the onion, and add with the chopped pepper, the vinegar and the lemon rind and juice to the cucumber. Season.

2 Place the velouté sauce in a saucepan and bring to a boil.

3 Blend the egg yolks and cream in a bowl. Then gradually stir in a little of the sauce, return this mixture to the rest of the sauce, stirring all the time, and simmer for 5 minutes. Add the cucumber mixture and simmer for a further 10 minutes. Season and sprinkle in the herbs.

Serve with boiled meats. Makes 2¼ cups

Curry Sauce

1 Melt 2 tablespoons butter in a saucepan, then stir in 1 teaspoon curry powder and 1 tablespoon coconut. Cook without letting it color for 1 minute, then gradually pour in 1¼ cups basic velouté sauce.

2 Thin with 1¼ cups chicken or white stock. Finally add the strained juice of ½ lemon. Season with salt to taste. The color of the finished sauce should be a very delicate pale yellow.

Serve with eggs, vegetables and chicken.

German Sauce

1 To 1¼ cups of basic velouté sauce, add 2 sliced white button mushrooms, juice of ½ lemon, 1 bouquet garni and 2 branches celery. Thin with up to 1¾ stock to the required pouring consistency.

2 Place 2 egg yolks and ⅔ cup of cold stock in a bowl. Stir well and pour in ⅔ cup of the velouté sauce. Then pour back into the rest of the sauce, while whisking all the time. Simmer for 5 minutes, then remove the bouquet garni.

Serve with fricassée of chicken or veal.

Avocado Sauce

1 Blend or work through a strainer the flesh of 2 ripe avocados, together with the juice of 1 lemon, 1 tablespoon lime liqueur and 2 tablespoons chicken or white stock. Blend the resulting purée with 1¼ cups basic suprême sauce (see below).

2 Thin the sauce with ⅔ cup chicken or white stock and ⅓ cup dry sherry; season with salt and pepper to taste.

Serve with shrimp, chicken, veal, and pork chops.

Mornay Sauce

1 Place 2 egg yolks and ⅔ cup of light cream in a bowl. Stir well and dilute with ⅔ cup of cold suprême sauce, adding ⅓ cup of grated Parmesan or Cheddar cheese.

2 Pour the mixture into 1¾ cups of suprême sauce and thin to the required consistency with ⅔ cup of milk.

Serve with fish, vegetables, eggs, pastas, veal and chicken.

Suprême Sauce

1 Use the same ingredients as for German Sauce but omit the egg yolks; add 1¼ cups heavy cream with the stock.

2 Boil the sauce for 20 minutes, then season with salt and pepper to taste. The sauce should have an extra creamy consistency.

Serve as a base for Chaudfroid Sauce (see recipe page 132) with chicken dishes, and to blend with fillings for vol-au-vents or with vegetables.

Hot Mushroom Mousse with Cream Sauce

2 lbs. very fresh, white mushrooms
¾ cup butter
1 lemon, halved
4 shallots, or 1 medium onion, finely chopped
1 small clove garlic, peeled and crushed
¾ lb. cooked ham, ground
2 tablespoons finely chopped parsley
2 cups fine breadcrumbs
¼ cup light cream
salt and pepper
pinch nutmeg
2 tablespoons brandy
4 eggs
For the Sauce:
3 tablespoons butter
3 tablespoons flour
1 tablespoon tomato paste
⅔ cup light cream

1 Reserve 12-15 of the best mushrooms and set them aside for the garnish; finely chop the rest.

2 Melt ¼ cup butter in a sauté pan. Add the chopped mushrooms, the strained juice from the 2 lemon halves, and the chopped shallots or onion, and sauté over high heat until the mixture is completely dry — about 5 minutes.

3 Stir in the crushed garlic, ground ham, 1 tablespoon chopped parsley, breadcrumbs, cream, salt and pepper, nutmeg and brandy and cook over moderate heat for 5 minutes, stirring from time to time.

4 Separate 2 of the eggs and stir the yolks, together with the 2 whole eggs, lightly beaten, into the mushroom mixture during the last 2 minutes of cooking. Take the pan off the heat and check the seasoning; cool.

5 Preheat the oven to 350°F.

6 In a clean dry bowl whip the 2 egg whites until stiff. Using a metal spoon or spatula, fold the egg whites into the cooled mushroom mixture. Do not beat or the air trapped in the egg whites will be forced out.

7 Grease a 2-lb. capacity Charlotte mold or baking dish, turn the mousse mixture into it. Stand the mold or dish in a roasting pan, filled with enough hot water to come two-thirds of the way up the mold, and cook in the preheated oven for 45 minutes. After 30 minutes, increase the oven temperature to 400°F.

8 Meanwhile, prepare the sauce. Melt 4 tablespoons butter in a small saucepan. Add the flour and stir to make a roux, but do not let it brown. Stir in the tomato paste and then the cream. Bring to a boil, boil for 5 minutes, stirring continuously, until smooth and creamy. Check the seasoning.

9 Heat the remaining butter in a pan and toss the reserved mushrooms in it until lightly browned.

10 When cooked, turn out the mousse onto a hot serving dish. Pour on the hot sauce, garnish with the whole mushrooms and sprinkle with the remaining chopped parsley. Serve at once.

Serves 4

Tip: Alternatively, put the mushroom mixture into individual dishes (use ramekins or dariole molds) and cook in the oven as for a large mousse, for the same length of time; then turn out and serve as individual mousses.

To turn out a hot mixture: slide a knife around inside the mold to free the mixture cleanly, then invert, with a plate over the top, tap sharply once or twice and the mixture will slide out cleanly.

Hot mushroom mousse with cream sauce is a stunning yet economical dish to make

Look 'n Cook Chicken with Chaudfroid Sauce

1 Ingredients for chicken chaudfroid: chicken with giblets, bouquet garni, onion, celery and carrot. Place the ingredients in a pan with the water and cook gently until the chicken is tender **2** Melt the butter, stir in the flour and cook the roux until sandy in texture. Add the stock **3** Take the pan off the heat and stir in the cream. Add seasoning **4** Add half the gelatin to the sauce, stir until dissolved, then season and simmer for 15 minutes **5** Pour the sauce through a strainer to remove any lumps **6** Dissolve the rest of the gelatin in

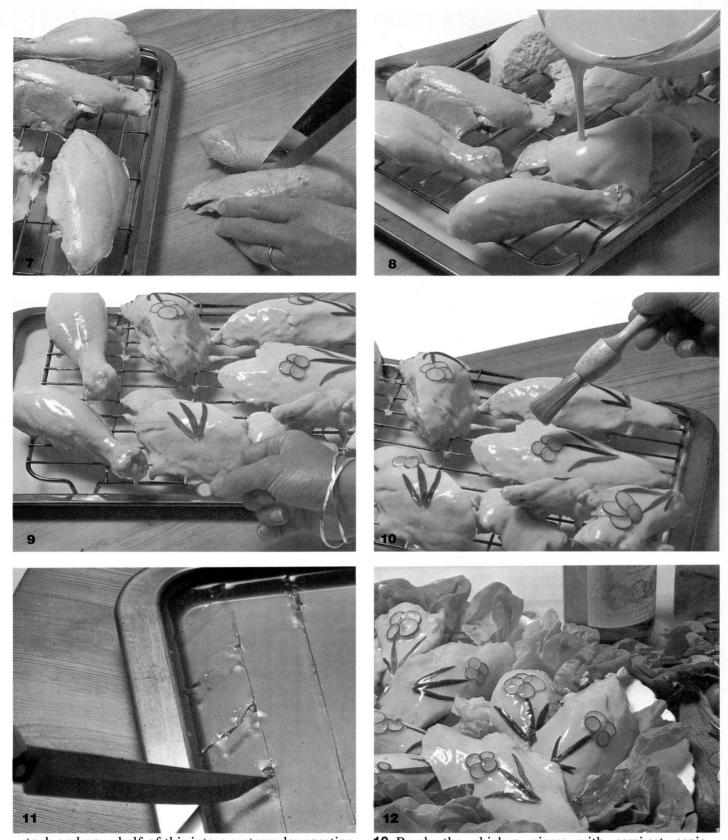

stock and pour half of this into a rectangular roasting pan and let set **7** Place the cooked chicken on a cooling rack and cut it into portions **8** Coat the chicken with the warm sauce **9** Chill the chicken and then decorate it with radish flowers and tarragon leaves

10 Brush the chicken pieces with semi-set aspic
11 Chop the set aspic or cut into geometrical shapes
12 The decorated chicken pieces served on a bed of lettuce leaves

Poached Eggs with Braised Endive in Suprême Sauce

½ cup butter
1 lb. Belgian endive, washed, trimmed and cut into 1-inch pieces
salt and pepper
1 teaspoon sugar
4 eggs
4¼ cups water
2 tablespoons white vinegar
4 slices bread, 1½ inches thick
⅔ cup suprême sauce (see page 128)

1 Melt 3 tablespoons butter in a sauté pan. Add the endive, cover and braise over low heat for 7-8 minutes or until tender. Then season with salt and pepper to taste, add the sugar and cook further, uncovered, until the endive breaks down to a purée.

2 While the endive is cooking, soft-poach the eggs in the water to which the vinegar has been added. Bring the water to a boil, then lower the heat until just below the simmering point.

3 Break 1 egg into a cup; lower the lip of the cup close to the surface of the water and slide the egg carefully into the water; then spoon the white up and over the yolk and cook for 3 minutes. Lift out the egg with a slotted spoon, trim the white neatly, then slide the egg into a bowl of warm water. Repeat the poaching process with the remaining eggs.

4 Hollow out the center of each piece of bread, but without cutting all the way through. Spread inside and out with the remaining butter and toast until golden.

5 Fill the toast 'nests' with hot endive purée and top with a drained egg. Arrange on a serving dish, cover with hot suprême sauce and serve.

Serves 4

Tip: Shelled hard-boiled eggs can be substituted for soft-poached eggs if preferred.

Chicken with Chaudfroid Sauce

2 small or 1 large roasting chicken, with giblets
8½ cups water
1 leek, sliced
1 carrot, sliced
2 branches celery, sliced
bouquet garni
salt and pepper
sprig tarragon

For the Chaudfroid Sauce:
¼ cup butter
½ cup flour
1¼ cups light cream
2 tablespoons lemon-flavored gelatin
pinch nutmeg
½ cup dark sherry

1 Wash the chicken and the giblets to remove all traces of blood. Place the chicken in a large saucepan (side by side if using 2). Cover with water.

2 Parboil the giblets (without the liver) in a pan of salted water for 5 minutes. Rinse in cold water, drain and add to the chicken.

Poached eggs in suprême sauce — a stylish way to dress up soft-poached eggs

3 Add the sliced leek, carrot and celery to the chicken, together with the bouquet garni. Season with salt and pepper and bring the liquid to a boil gently. Simmer for 45 minutes. Remove the pan from the heat and cool the chicken in the liquid until both are completely cold. Take out the chicken and chill in a refrigerator for at least 4 hours.

4 Boil the giblets, vegetables and liquid for 1 hour to concentrate the flavor, then strain and reserve the liquid.

5 To make the chaudfroid sauce: melt the butter in a saucepan, stir in the flour and cook the roux for 2 minutes until it has a sandy texture. Gradually stir in 1¼ cups of the reserved liquid, whisking gently to form a smooth velouté sauce. Pour in the cream and season to taste.

6 Dissolve half of the gelatin in the hot sauce, stirring all the time. Season with salt, white pepper and nutmeg. Simmer for 15 minutes, then strain through a conical fine strainer.

7 To make the aspic: pour $1\frac{3}{4}$ cups of the rest of the reserved liquid into a saucepan with $\frac{1}{2}$ cup dark sherry and a sprig of tarragon. Boil for 2 minutes, then remove the tarragon. Rinse the tarragon in cold water and drain. Place all the leaves in a dish. Meanwhile, dissolve the rest of the gelatin in the tarragon stock, simmer for 5 minutes and set aside until cold.

8 To decorate the chicken: place the chicken(s) on a cooling rack over a deep tray. Carve into 4 portions, and skin them. Discard unwanted bones.

9 Coat each piece of chicken with warm chaudfroid sauce (if it is too thick, thin it with a little stock). Chill the chicken in the refrigerator for 20 minutes to set the sauce, then decorate each piece with 3 tarragon leaves.

10 Glaze the chicken with a little semi-set aspic, set aside to firm, then carefully lift onto a serving dish, using 2 spatulas. Decorate with lettuce leaves, cucumber slices, tomatoes and slices of green pepper.

11 Pour the rest of the aspic into an oblong tray $1\frac{1}{2}$ inches deep and allow to set. When firm, cut the aspic with a knife into geometrical shapes or dice, or chop; turn out onto dampened wax paper and cut with a pastry cutter into small halfmoon shapes. Place the aspic

gelatin shapes around the dish.

Serves 4–8

Tip: If you use a boiling hen or capon for this dish, the breast can be sliced into thin escalopes after cooking and each slice coated with chaudfroid sauce. Instead of tarragon, you could substitute 3-4 drained, canned asparagus tips: place them on top of each chicken piece, securing them in position with a little semi-set aspic.

Chicken with chaudfroid sauce — an eye-catching dish to serve for a cold buffet

Brown Sauces

Basic Brown Sauce

¾ cup flour
½ cup beef drippings
2 medium carrots, coarsely sliced
2 medium onions, coarsely sliced
2 branches celery and trimmings, coarsely sliced
¼ lb. lean bacon, chopped
bouquet garni
1 clove garlic
¼ cup tomato paste
4¼ cups brown stock
salt and pepper
pinch of mace

1 Brown the flour on a baking sheet for 15 minutes at 400°F.; do not brown it too much. Remove. Heat half of the drippings in a heavy-based pan and stir in the baked flour. Cook the roux for 3 minutes to a sandy texture. Cool.

2 In another pan heat the remaining drippings and brown the vegetables and bacon for 8 minutes, keeping the lid on the pan throughout. Add the bouquet garni, garlic and the tomato paste. Drain off the surplus fat. Pour in the brown stock, bring to a boil for 1 hour. This reduces (evaporates) the stock and concentrates its flavor; skim from time to time.

3 Stir the cold roux into the boiling stock, then stir with a whisk to avoid lumps. Simmer for another hour, skimming from time to time, until the sauce is clear (a chef would simmer this sauce for as long as 4 hours, but this is not necessary for home cooking).

4 Strain the sauce and season with salt, pepper and mace. Thin with 1¼ cups of brown stock, or beer, wine, cider or fruit juice if preferred, and boil for another 30 minutes, adjusting the seasoning at the last moment.

Makes 2¼ cups

Conil Brown Sauce

¼ cup butter or fat
¼ cup onions, chopped or diced
½ cup carrots, chopped or diced
½ cup celery, chopped or diced
½ cup leeks, chopped or diced
½ cup flour
¼ cup tomato paste
3 beef bouillon cubes or 1½ tablespoons beef extract
4½ cups water
bouquet garni
1 sprig fresh mint
1 clove garlic
salt and pepper
pinch mace

1 Heat the butter in a heavy-based pan, add the vegetables, cover, and steam until soft. Then remove the lid and brown a little.

2 Stir in the flour to absorb the butter and cook the roux for 2 minutes. Stir in the tomato paste and cook a further minute.

3 Crumble the bouillon cubes in the water and add to the pan, together with the bouquet garni, mint and garlic.

4 Stir the sauce a little and boil for 30 minutes. Strain, then simmer for 15 minutes. Season with salt, pepper and mace. Diluted with a thin stock, this makes a quick, thick gravy.

Makes 2¼ cups

Demi-glace Madeira Sauce

1 Thin 2¼ cups basic brown sauce with ⅔ cup brown stock and ⅔ cup Madeira, stirring in 1 teaspoon beef extract.

2 Boil the sauce for 15 minutes to reduce by one-third, to give a thinner, glossier and more aromatic mixture than the basic brown sauce.

Serve with meat, poultry and game.

Makes about 4¼ cups

Demi-glace Sherry Sauce

1 Use the same ingredients as for demi-glace Madeira sauce but substitute medium dry sherry for Madeira and flavor with a sprig of mint and sage.

Serve with meat, poultry and game.

Makes about 4¼ cups

Bordelaise Sauce

¼ cup sweet onions or shallots, finely chopped
6 black peppercorns, crushed
1 sprig thyme
1 bay leaf
⅔ cup light red wine
1¼ cups demi-glace Madeira or sherry sauce

1 Place onion in a saucepan with peppercorns, thyme, bay leaf and wine. Boil for 5 minutes, then add demi-glace sauce.

2 Boil a further 30 minutes and pour through a fine conical strainer. Serve with Steak Bordelaise.

Makes 2¼ cups

Tip: This sauce can also include diced or sliced poached beef marrow, but this does tend to make the sauce richer and greasy.

Burgundy Sauce

¼ lb. mushroom caps
¼ cup butter
¼ lb. pearl onions, peeled
2¼ cups Bordelaise sauce, using a
  good red Burgundy wine
salt and pepper
1 tablespoon brandy

1 To prepare the garnish: wash mushrooms and remove stalks (these can be used to make a mushroom-flavored stock). Melt the butter, put in the onions and brown for 4 minutes. Drain off the fat.

2 Pour in the Bordelaise sauce and boil for 10 minutes until the onions are almost soft. Strain the sauce.

3 Reheat the sauce and add the mushroom caps. Boil for 3 minutes. Check the seasoning, adding salt and pepper to taste, then pour in the brandy. Serve with chicken (as in coq au vin), veal and beef dishes.

Makes 2¼ cups

Chasseur Sauce

2 tablespoons butter mixed with 2
  tablespoons oil
½ cup shallots or onions, peeled
  and chopped
⅔ cup white mushrooms, trimmed
  and sliced (stalks optional)
⅔ cup dry white wine
2¼ cups demi-glace or plain
  brown sauce
½ cup fresh tomatoes, skinned,
  seeded and coarsely chopped
salt and pepper
1 tablespoon chopped parsley and
  tarragon leaves

1 Heat the butter and oil in a sauté pan and cook the shallots for 2 minutes without coloring them. Add the mushrooms and cook a minute longer.

2 Strain off the butter/oil and pour in the wine. Reduce the sauce by boiling hard for 4 minutes, then stir in the demi-glace sauce and tomatoes and simmer for 15 minutes. Season with salt and pepper.

3 Add the chopped parsley and tarragon before serving.

Serve with veal escalopes or chops, lamb noisettes and sautéed chicken.

Makes about 2¼ cups

Basquaise Sauce

1 Cut in halves 1 sweet red and 1 green pepper, seed and mince finely.

2 Scald and drain the peppers, then add to 2¼ cups chasseur sauce and simmer for 10 minutes. Season with salt, pepper and garlic salt.

Serve with chicken, veal and pork chops.

Makes about 2¼ cups

Devilled Sauce (Sauce Diable)

½ cup shallots or sweet onions,
  peeled and finely chopped
⅔ cup dry white wine
2 tablespoons wine vinegar
6 white peppercorns, crushed
1 dried chili, seeded
2¼ cups demi-glace or plain brown
  sauce
salt and pepper

1 Boil the shallots in a saucepan with the wine, vinegar, peppercorns and chili until reduced (evaporated) by half.

2 Stir in the demi-glace or brown sauce and simmer for 15 minutes. Season with salt and pepper, then strain through a fine strainer.

Serve with broiled chicken legs, broiled ham steaks or fish.

Makes 2¼ cups

Poivrade Sauce

2 tablespoons oil
½ cup onions, peeled and diced
½ cup carrots, peeled and diced
½ cup celery, peeled and diced
⅔ cup dry white or red wine
¼ cup wine vinegar
3 peppercorns, crushed
bouquet garni
2¼ cups demi-glace or plain brown
  sauce
salt and pepper
ground mace or nutmeg

1 Heat the oil in a heavy-bottomed saucepan and sauté the vegetables until soft, keeping the lid on the pan throughout. Drain off the oil and add the wine, vinegar, peppercorns and bouquet garni.

2 Reduce the liquid by half by boiling hard for 8 minutes, then stir in the demi-glace sauce. Simmer for 30 minutes and season with salt, pepper, and ground mace or nutmeg to taste. Strain into a sauce boat.

Serve with game such as rabbit or venison.

Makes 2¼ cups

Reform Sauce

1 Cut into very thin, short strips ¼ cup of each of the following: hard-boiled egg white, dill pickles and beets, mushrooms, truffles (optional) and salted cooked tongue.

2 Add to 2¼ cups poivrade sauce.

Serve with lamb cutlets and chops.

Makes 2¼ cups

Sharp Sauces

Piquant Sauce

¼ cup onions or shallots, peeled
  and chopped
¼ cup malt, wine or cider vinegar
2¼ cups demi-glace or plain brown
  sauce
3 tablespoons dill pickles, chopped
1 tablespoon pickled capers
1 tablespoon chopped parsley and
  tarragon leaves, mixed
salt and pepper

1 Boil the onions in the vinegar for 4 minutes to reduce the liquid by half, then stir in the sauce and simmer for 15 minutes.

2 Add the dill pickles, capers, parsley and tarragon, and season with salt and pepper to taste.

Serve with prepared cooked meat dishes, boiled beef, ham and pork.

Makes about 2¼ cups

Robert Sauce

Use the same ingredients as for piquant sauce but omit the dill pickles and capers; at the last moment, take the pan off the heat and mix in 1 teaspoon prepared mustard to prevent curdling.

Serve with broiled pork chops, broiled duck, and any other fatty meat.

Makes about 2¼ cups

Tomato Sauces

Tomato Sauce

2 tablespoons oil
2 tablespoons butter
⅓ cup celery, peeled and diced
½ cup carrots, peeled and diced
¼ cup onions, peeled and diced
⅓ cup bacon, diced
¼ cup flour
6 tablespoons tomato paste
5 cups white stock or 3 chicken
  bouillon cubes dissolved in water
bouquet garni
1 sprig mint
salt and pepper
pinch paprika
½ tablespoon sugar

1 Heat the oil and butter in a large saucepan and sauté the vegetables and bacon for 15 minutes.

2 Add the flour, cook for a further 5 minutes, then stir in the tomato paste; cook for 5 more minutes.

3 Stir in the stock, add the bouquet garni and mint, and bring to a boil. Simmer for 1 hour.

4 Season with salt, pepper, paprika and sugar, then strain through a fine conical strainer.

Serve with pasta, eggs or hamburgers, and also vegetables, including beans.

Makes about 4 cups

Roman Sauce

2 tablespoons oil
⅔ cup white mushrooms, chopped
¼ cup shallots or onions, peeled and
  chopped
½ cup ham, chopped
½ cup fresh tomatoes, skinned,
  seeded and chopped
1 clove garlic, peeled and chopped
2 tablespoons tomato paste
2¼ cups tomato sauce
salt and pepper
1 tablespoon chopped parsley,
  mint, tarragon

1 Heat the oil in a pan and sauté the vegetables for 5 minutes. Then add the ham, tomatoes and garlic and cook for another 10 minutes.

2 Stir in the tomato paste and sauce and simmer for 10 minutes. Then season with salt and pepper and add the parsley, mint and tarragon.

Serve with scaloppini, steaks and cauliflower.

Makes about 2¼ cups

Portuguese Sauce

1 To 2½ cups basic tomato sauce add ½ cup of skinned, seeded and chopped tomatoes, and 2 chopped cloves of garlic.

2 Bring the sauce back to a boil for 10 minutes. Season to taste with salt and pepper.

Serve with meat, eggs and fish.

Makes 2½ cups

Neapolitan Sauce

1 To 1¼ cups basic tomato sauce, add ½ lb. of fresh, skinned, seeded and chopped tomatoes.

2 Season with salt and pepper and reboil for 5 minutes. Add mint or oregano to flavor.

Serve with meat, fish, eggs and pasta.

Makes 2½ cups

Barbecue Sauces

American Barbecue Sauce

2 tablespoons butter
1½ tablespoons oil
1 medium onion, chopped
⅓ cup vinegar
⅓ cup soy sauce
1 clove garlic, peeled and crushed
1 teaspoon allspice
1 teaspoon salt
pinch pepper
pinch cayenne pepper
1 tablespoon tomato paste
1½ tablespoons honey
1 tablespoon sugar
1½ cups pineapple juice

1 Heat the butter and oil together in a pan, add the onion and cook gently until the onion is soft and tender but not brown. Add the rest of the ingredients and bring to a boil. Boil for 10 minutes.

2 Remove the pan from the heat, cover with a lid and cool. When cold, strain the sauce and store it in a screw-top jar. Use to marinate steaks or any meat for broiling; soak them for 15 to 20 minutes in the sauce before cooking.

Makes about 2½ cups

To Prepare Chilies

Fresh Chilies: soak in cold salted water for 1 hour to help temper their hot flavor, then drain. Cut in half and discard stem, seeds and pith. Avoid handling chilies as much as possible as their pungent oils can burn and irritate your skin.

Canned Chilies: rinse under cold running water, then drain. Use as required.

Dried Chilies: wash in cold water, cut away stem, seeds and core if necessary. Put in a dish, add 2 teaspoons vinegar and pour on about 6 cups of water for every 1 cup dried chilies. Leave for 30-40 minutes, then drain.

Mexican Barbecue Sauce

3 sweet red peppers, skinned (see below) and chopped
3 small fresh green chilies, seeded and chopped
salt
6 cloves garlic, peeled
1¼ cups olive oil
6 onions, peeled and finely chopped
3 lbs. ripe tomatoes, skinned, seeded and diced
¼ cup sugar
3 tablespoons vinegar
bouquet garni
½ tablespoon saffron

1 Put the chopped pepper and chili in a mortar, together with a pinch of salt and the garlic.

2 Pound these ingredients, adding some of the oil drop by drop. When it has acquired a very smooth, paste-like consistency, set aside.

3 Heat 1 tablespoon olive oil in a skillet. Add the onions and sauté until they are golden brown.

4 When the onions are a deep golden brown, sprinkle them with the sugar. Leave to caramelize, watching that the sugar does not burn. Remove from heat, add the vinegar and diced tomatoes.

5 Add the bouquet garni to the mixture, cook over low heat for about 20 minutes, stirring frequently with a wooden spoon, to make a thick tomato mixture.

6 Remove the bouquet garni from the tomato mixture and rub through a strainer, or mix in a blender to a purée. Put the chili paste in the blender at the same time if liked.

7 Put the mixture into a small saucepan and add the saffron and the chili paste, if not already included. Cook for 2 minutes, beating with a whisk. Remove the pan from the heat and leave to cool.

8 Just before serving, incorporate the rest of the oil, little by little (as for mayonnaise), while beating the sauce with a whisk. Serve cold or chilled with grilled meat or fish.

Makes about 1¼ cups

Honolulu Sauce

1¼ cups pineapple juice
¼ lb. canned pineapple chunks, drained
1¼ cups thickened gravy
1 teaspoon prepared mustard, or to taste
2 tablespoons finely chopped red pepper

For the chili paste:
1 tablespoon fresh green chilies, seeded and chopped
1 tablespoon fresh gingerroot, peeled and grated
1 tablespoon of garlic, peeled and grated
⅓ cup finely chopped onion
⅓ cup wine vinegar
¼ cup sugar
1 teaspoon salt
⅓ cup lemon juice
pinch turmeric

1 Put all the chili paste ingredients, together with 2 tablespoons pineapple juice, in a blender and mix until smooth.

2 Blend in the remaining pineapple juice, add the salt and transfer the mixture to a saucepan. Bring to a boil and boil for 20 minutes. Stir in the mustard and pineapple, heat through and serve at once, with the chopped red pepper sprinkled on. Serve with broiled pork, ham, or roast duck or goose.

Makes about 1¼ cups

Steak Chasseur

⅓ cup butter
4 sirloin steaks, round-cut and
  each weighing about ½ lb.
sprigs watercress
1 tablespoon finely chopped
  parsley and tarragon leaves

For the Chasseur Sauce:
1¼ cups mushrooms, cleaned and
  chopped
¼ cup shallots or onions, peeled and
  finely chopped
⅔ cup dry white wine
1¼ cups demi-glace sauce
1 tablespoon tomato paste
salt and pepper

1 To make the chasseur sauce:
heat 2 tablespoons butter in a sauté
pan. Add the mushrooms and
shallots and soften but do not let
them brown. Stir in the wine and
cook, uncovered, until the liquid
has evaporated to half its quantity.

2 Stir in the demi-glace sauce and
tomato paste and simmer the sauce
for about 5 minutes to mellow the
flavors. Check the seasoning.

3 Heat 4 tablespoons of the butter
or oil in a skillet. When hot, sauté
the steaks for about 5-8 minutes on
each side, according to how rare
you like your steak. Season with
salt and pepper to taste, then take
out the steaks and arrange on a hot
serving platter. Pour the sauce on
the steaks, garnish with the watercress and sprinkle with the parsley
and tarragon.

Serves 4

Beef and Pork Meatballs in Tomato Sauce

1 medium onion, peeled and
  coarsely chopped
1 medium carrot, peeled and
  coarsely chopped
2 branches celery, peeled and
  coarsely chopped
2 cloves garlic
⅓ cup oil
1 lb. lean ground beef
½ lb. pork sausage meat
1 egg, beaten
½ cup fresh white breadcrumbs
salt and black pepper
pinch oregano, basil or mint
pinch each paprika, ground ginger
  and mace
1 tablespoon freshly chopped
  parsley
½ lb. spaghetti
1¾ cups tomato sauce

1 Pass all the vegetables twice
through a grinder or mix in a food
processor or blender. Heat the oil in
a saucepan and sauté the vegetables, with the lid on, for 5 minutes
to concentrate the flavor.

2 Remove the mixture from the
heat and place in a large bowl with
the beef and sausage meat. Combine well and bind the mixture with

*Beef and Pork Meatballs in
Tomato Sauce. Serve with
spaghetti or potatoes for a dish
with a different taste*

the egg and breadcrumbs. Season with salt, pepper, oregano, paprika, ginger, mace and chopped parsley.

3 Preheat the oven to 350°F.

4 Divide the mixture and roll into small balls, about 1 inch in size, on a work surface sprinkled with flour for easier handling.

5 Grease a roasting pan and place the meatballs on it at regular intervals. Bake for 30 minutes in the preheated oven.

6 Meanwhile, cook the spaghetti in a large pan of boiling water for 10-12 minutes or until just tender. Drain and turn into a hot serving dish; dot with butter.

7 Remove the meatballs when cooked and place on the spaghetti. The tomato sauce can either be poured on the meatballs or served separately, together with grated Parmesan, Gruyère or Cheddar cheese.

Serves 6

Chaudfroid Sauce

1 To every 2½ cups sauce — this can be béchamel, velouté, suprême, brown or tomato — add 1¼ tablespoons gelatin. Dissolve the gelatin in a little of the hot sauce, then add to the rest of the sauce and bring to a boil; boil for 2-3 minutes. Cool a little, then strain through a conical strainer before use.

2 While still warm, pour the chaudfroid sauce over the cold cooked pieces of fish or meat to coat. Allow to cool and firm, then glaze with a little semi-liquid gelatin and let set. Use for cold dishes and salads (see recipe for Chicken with Chaudfroid Sauce on page 132).

Makes 4¼ cups

Tips: Always make sure any food to be coated with chaudfroid sauce or mayonnaise is completely dry or the sauce will slide off.

Emulsified Sauces

Hollandaise and Béarnaise sauces and their derivations are made in smaller quantities than other sauces, because they must not be left standing for very long at room temperature. Like fresh cream they are susceptible to bacterial spoilage. Unfortunately, they cannot be refrigerated in the basic form because the butter hardens and solidifies the sauce.

Use only fresh eggs and good quality unsalted butter. Serve the sauces within 2 hours of making and always try to make them at the last possible moment. And of course, all equipment — whisks, bowls, etc. — should be spotlessly clean.

Basic Hollandaise Sauce

4 egg yolks
¼ cup cold water
1 tablespoon white vinegar
½ lb. butter, melted
juice 1 lemon
salt and white pepper
pinch cayenne

1 Whip the egg yolks, water and vinegar together in a stainless steel bowl (a metal bowl is the best conductor of heat).

2 Place the bowl over a deep pan of boiling water, making sure that the bottom of the bowl does not touch the water — egg yolks coagulate at 140°F., a temperature which is lower than that of boiling water. Beat lightly until the eggs are cooked to the consistency of a custard sauce. Mix well, stirring up from the bottom of the bowl and scraping down any sauce that adheres to the sides.

3 Remove the bowl from the heat. Stir for another 5 minutes while gradually pouring in the melted butter, and whisking all the time to obtain a thick sauce.

4 Add the juice of the lemon and season to taste. This sauce should be served immediately, and will not keep for longer than 2 or 3 hours.

Makes about 1¼ cups

Béarnaise Sauce

1 tablespoon chopped shallots
pinch chopped tarragon
6 finely crushed white peppercorns
3 tablespoons wine vinegar (preferably tarragon vinegar)
1¼ cups basic Hollandaise sauce
pinch chopped parsley

1 Place the shallots, half the tarragon, and the vinegar in a small pan. Bring to a boil and boil briskly until the vinegar has almost evaporated. Remove the pan from the heat.

2 Add the mixture to the Hollandaise sauce and then strain the sauce through cheesecloth into a bowl. Add the rest of the tarragon and the chopped parsley and mix.

Serve with broiled meat or fish steaks.

Makes 1¼ cups

Variations

Mock Hollandaise

1 To 1¼ cups basic Hollandaise sauce, add 1¼ cups velouté or white sauce. Check the seasoning.

Serve with eggs, vegetables and fish.

Mousseline Sauce

1 Whip 1¼ cups cream.

2 Add the cream to 1¼ cups Hollandaise sauce.

Serve with eggs, vegetables and fish.

Paloise Sauce

1 To 1¼ cups Hollandaise sauce, add 1 tablespoon finely chopped blanched mint.

Serve with eggs, vegetables and fish.

Conil Sauce

1 In a pan mix 2 tablespoons of mixed chopped parsley, tarragon, chervil and mint, 2 tablespoons dry vermouth, 1 teaspoon tomato paste and 1 peeled garlic clove. Bring to a boil and simmer for 1 minute.

2 Rub the mixture through a strainer or mix in a blender and add the purée to 1¼ cups basic Hollandaise sauce.

Serve with broiled or grilled steaks and beef kebabs.

Rosalie Sauce

1 To 1¼ cups Conil sauce, add ⅔ cup velouté or white sauce.

2 Fold in ⅔ cup whipped heavy cream.

Serve with broiled veal chops, salmon steaks and broiled chicken.

Sophia Loren

1 To 1¼ cups basic Hollandaise sauce, add 1 teaspoon anchovy paste, a pinch of garlic salt, 2 tablespoons cream and a pinch of curry powder.

Serve with fish.

Vino Sauce

1 To 1¼ cups basic Hollandaise sauce, add 1 tablespoon mixed chopped herbs and 1 tablespoon sweet or dry sherry.

Serve with eggs, broiled fish, meat and vegetables.

Maltese Sauce

1 To 1¼ cups basic Hollandaise sauce, add the strained juice of 1 orange.

Serve with cold roast duck, oily fish.

Choron Sauce

1 To 1¼ cups basic Hollandaise sauce, add 1 tablespoon catsup and 1 teaspoon tarragon vinegar.

Serve with broiled fish, meat and poultry.

Quantities
All the sauces on this page make 1¼ cups.

Asparagus with Mousseline Sauce

4 lbs. (approx. 50 spears) green asparagus
coarse salt

For the Mousseline Sauce:
¾ cup butter
3 eggs
1 tablespoon heavy cream
small sprig chervil
juice 1 lemon
salt and pepper

1 Prepare the asparagus.

2 Boil a large pan of salted water. Tie the asparagus in bundles and place them carefully in the boiling water. Cover and cook for 12-20 minutes. The cooking time depends on the freshness and thickness of the asparagus. Test to see if it is cooked by pricking the green part with the point of a knife.

3 Once the asparagus is cooked, lift it out, and rinse in cold water.

4 To prepare the Mousseline Sauce: put the butter into a small saucepan, let it melt gently, then turn off the heat. Let it rest for several minutes. Skim it with a small spoon to take off the particles which have risen to the top. Carefully pour the melted butter into a dish, leaving only the milk-like liquid in the bottom of the saucepan.

5 Break and separate the eggs. Put the yolks into a bowl placed over a pan of boiling water. Add 1½ tablespoons of water and beat until the mixture becomes thick and comes away from the bottom of the pan.

6 Add the melted butter to this egg yolk-water mixture (sabayon) beating continuously. Take the sauce off the heat.

7 Pour the cream into a bowl and beat it until it has doubled in volume. Add it to the warm sauce off the heat, mixing carefully with a wooden spoon.

8 Wash and dry the chervil and chop finely. Add the lemon juice and the chervil to the sauce with salt and pepper. Mix carefully and keep warm over the hot water.

9 Heat some water and put the asparagus in it for 2-3 minutes to reheat.

10 Put a folded napkin on a heated serving dish. Warm a sauce boat.

11 Strain the asparagus, remove the string and put the spears into the folded napkin (this will absorb any liquid). Pour the sauce into the sauce boat and serve.

Serves 4

Tips: Keep the cooking juice of the asparagus to make a soup.

The asparagus and mousseline sauce can be blended together to make a rich asparagus purée sauce.

1 Clarify the butter by melting it slowly. Let it stand then skim to remove any scum from the surface. Pour the butter into a dish very slowly so that the milk-like mixture will be left in the saucepan **2** Break the eggs, separating the yolks from the whites. Put the yolks into a saucepan. Place it in a double boiler (or over hot water) and add water **3** Keep whisking the mixture over the heat until it thickens and the bottom can be seen during the whisking **4** Add the clarified butter to this mixture in a slow steady stream from a ladle and keep whisking all the time **5** Prepare the whipped cream: put the cream into a small bowl, beating until it has doubled in volume and has a light consistency **6** Add the whipped cream to the hot sauce off the heat. Mix the cream and the sauce together very carefully

Look 'n Cook Hollandaise, Béarnaise and White Butter Sauces

1 To make Hollandaise sauce: melt the butter in a deep, heavy-based saucepan over a gentle heat, or use a double boiler. Skim off the froth which forms **2** Break the eggs and separate the whites from the yolks. Put the yolks in a metal bowl with the cold water and the vinegar **3** Place the bowl over a deep pan of boiling water, making sure that the bowl does not actually touch the water. Beat the mixture lightly until thick and creamy **4** Remove the bowl of sauce from the heat and con-

tinue stirring while gradually adding the melted butter in a thin stream. Add the lemon juice and seasoning **5** To make Béarnaise sauce, place the chopped shallots, crushed peppercorns, half the tarragon and the vinegar in a small pan and boil briskly until the vinegar has almost evaporated **6** Make Hollandaise sauce and add the melted butter to it (see steps 1-4). Then add the chopped shallots, tarragon and peppercorn mixture **7** Strain the sauce through fine cheese-

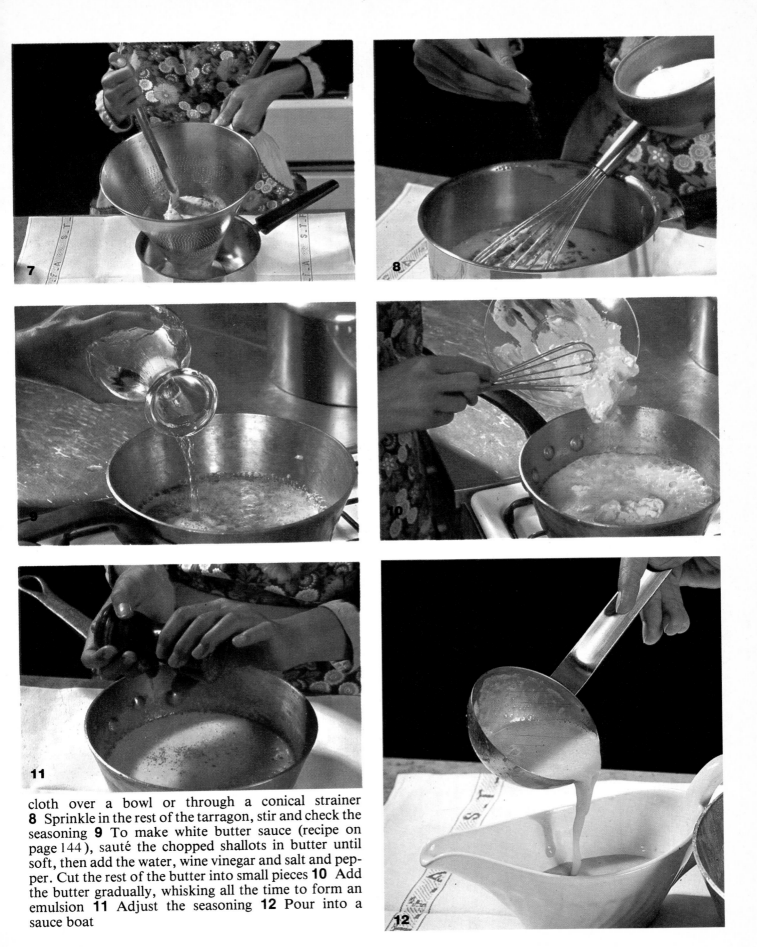

cloth over a bowl or through a conical strainer
8 Sprinkle in the rest of the tarragon, stir and check the seasoning **9** To make white butter sauce (recipe on page 144), sauté the chopped shallots in butter until soft, then add the water, wine vinegar and salt and pepper. Cut the rest of the butter into small pieces **10** Add the butter gradually, whisking all the time to form an emulsion **11** Adjust the seasoning **12** Pour into a sauce boat

Brown Butter Sauce

¼ cup butter
1 teaspoon cider vinegar
1 tablespoon chopped parsley

1 Heat the butter in a skillet until it begins to color.

2 Add the vinegar and the chopped parsley and mix. Pour the sauce immediately over the chosen dish.

Serve with plainly cooked fish

Tip: Stir in 1 tablespoon drained capers, if liked, just before serving.

White Butter Sauce

¼ cup clarified butter
¾ cup chopped shallots
¼ cup fish stock
¼ cup dry white wine
¼ cup white vinegar
pinch white pepper
pinch salt
¾ cup + 2 tablespoons sweet butter, softened

1 Put the clarified butter in a pan, add the chopped shallots and sauté gently until the shallots are soft.

2 Add the rest of the ingredients, except the butter, and cook for 5 minutes more until reduced to a syrupy consistency. Take off the heat and allow to cool.

3 Cut the softened butter into small pieces. When the shallot mixture is cool, add the butter, a piece at a time, whisking continuously to form an emulsion. Serve immediately.

Serve with plainly cooked fish

Makes about ¾ cup

Basic Sauce Mixtures

Before you can make some sauces, different kinds of mixtures must be assembled and prepared so you save time later on and the cooking can proceed smoothly.

Mushroom Duxelles

2 tablespoons oil
2 tablespoons clarified butter
½ cup finely chopped onion
3 tablespoons finely chopped shallots
1 lb. finely chopped mushrooms
salt and pepper to taste
2 tablespoons finely chopped parsley

1 Heat the oil and butter in a pan. Add the onions and shallots, cover, and cook them gently until soft but not colored.

2 Add the mushrooms and cook gently again, uncovered, until all the moisture has evaporated.

3 When dry, season the mixture with salt and pepper, stir in the parsley, then pour into a bowl and cover until required.

Add to sauces, white or brown; purée for use in soup, or sprinkle over fish dishes.

Green Herbs

1 Rinse and drain sprigs of fresh chervil, parsley or tarragon. Dry well in a cloth or on absorbent paper.

2 For chopped herbs: take off the leaves and chop them finely or coarsely (called *concassé* in French). Dry again on absorbent paper.

3 For whole leaves: take off the stems, put in a pan of boiling consommé or stock to scald, then drain and dry on absorbent paper. If the leaves are too large, tear them with your fingers; *chiffonnade* is the French term for this shredding or tearing process.

Use for decoration on cold dishes

Flavored Butters

Flavored Butters

As their name suggests, flavored, or compound, butters consist of softened butter blended with the chosen flavoring. Many butters are served as garnishes, toppings for broiled and fried meats and fish, while others are added to sauces to enhance their flavor and color.

You may find it more convenient to make up larger quantities of butters than those below, using ½ lb. butter for example, and all the other ingredients increased accordingly. Shape the finished butter into a sausage shape, wrap in foil and then store in the refrigerator or freezer until required.

Colbert Butter

¼ lb. butter, softened
1 tablespoon chopped tarragon
2 tablespoons chopped parsley
1 tablespoon lemon juice
3 tablespoons meat drippings

Mix all the ingredients into the butter and blend well.

Use with shellfish or broiled fish or meat, or add to fish sauces

Variation: When all the ingredients are blended, gradually beat in ¼ cup olive oil. Use with snails or scallops.

Maître d'Hôtel Butter

As for Colbert butter but omit the meat drippings and tarragon.

Kneaded Butter (Beurre Manié)

Cream 4 tablespoons butter with 4 tablespoons sifted flour.

Use for thickening sauces, stocks and stews

Shallot Butter

¼ cup chopped shallots
¼ cup red wine
3 tablespoons meat drippings
⅔ cup butter
3 tablespoons chopped parsley
1 tablespoon lemon juice
pinch salt
pinch pepper

1 Put the shallots in a pan with the red wine and boil together until the shallots are soft. Add the meat drippings and allow the mixture to cool.

2 Blend in the butter, parsley and lemon juice and season to taste.

Use with steaks or in sauces for broiled meat

Herb Butter

¼ lb. butter, softened
2 sprigs tarragon
2 sprigs parsley
1 tablespoon lemon juice or to taste
salt and pepper

1 Cream the butter in a bowl.

2 Chop the tarragon and parsley finely and mix into the butter. Add the lemon juice and the salt and pepper to taste.

Serve with broiled meat or fish

Meunière Butter

¼ lb. butter
1 tablespoon lemon juice

1 Put the butter in a pan and heat until the froth which forms dies down and the butter is lightly browned.

2 When the butter is clear, add the lemon juice.

Serve poured over fried food which has been sprinkled with chopped parsley.

Mayonnaise Butter

1 egg yolk
½ teaspoon dry mustard
salt and pepper
1 cup + 1 tablespoon oil
2 teaspoons vinegar or lemon juice
¼ cup butter, softened

1 Place the egg yolk in a bowl with the mustard and salt and pepper. Gradually mix in the oil, whisking the whole time, until the mixture thickens and all the oil is incorporated. Stir in the vinegar or lemon juice.

2 Cream the butter in a bowl. Mix into the mayonnaise and season again to taste.

Use to decorate canapés, hors d'oeuvre and open sandwiches

Tip: If using a blender to make the mayonnaise, use the whole egg.

Bercy or Bordelaise Butter

2 tablespoons chopped shallots
⅔ cup dry white wine
¼ lb. softened butter
pinch salt and white pepper
1 tablespoon lemon juice
1 tablespoon chopped parsley

1 Put the chopped shallots in a pan, add the white wine and bring to a boil. Boil for 5 minutes and then cool.

2 When the shallot mixture is cold, blend it with the butter, adding the rest of the ingredients as well. Cream well.

Use to garnish Steak Bordelaise or for blending into Bordelaise Sauce.

Garlic Butter

2-8 cloves garlic
¼ lb. butter, softened
salt and pepper to taste

1 Pound the cloves of garlic to a smooth paste either by using a garlic press or a pestle and mortar, or by firmly crushing the peeled cloves, sprinkled liberally with salt, with the flat blade of a knife until a pulp is obtained.

2 Cream the butter in a bowl, then mix it with the garlic and season to taste with salt and pepper.

Serve with broiled fish, steaks, hamburgers, lamb chops, boiled or baked potatoes, canapés and sandwiches

---

Clarified Butter

Melt a quantity of butter in a bowl placed over a pan of hot water. Cool, then put in the refrigerator to firm; turn out and scrape off the solids which have collected on the bottom of the cake of butter. The butter is then ready for use.

Tip: Thick solids coagulate to form caseins which caramelize during cooking and impart a bitter flavor to mixtures when heated at too high a temperature.

Cooking with Eggs

Eggs, which are one of the most nutritious foods available, are both versatile in and vital to cooking. They can be cooked in numerous ways for serving hot or cold as main course dishes, savories and appetizers; as preserves, desserts and in drinks, and used also as a garnish, a binding agent and for lightness

Fish and Pasta Florentine

This is a spectacular dinner party appetizer, especially if served in individual, shell-shaped, oven-proof dishes. Or serve as a "special" supper treat.

2 cups pasta shells or macaroni
3 hard-boiled eggs, chopped
1¾ cups white sauce
6 ozs. cooked smoked haddock, flaked
2 ozs. peeled, cooked, deveined shrimp
salt and pepper
10 oz. package frozen chopped spinach, thawed
½ cup grated cheese
few unpeeled shrimp, fresh or frozen and thawed (optional)

1 Cook the pasta shells in boiling salted water until just tender. Drain.

2 Mix the pasta with the hard-boiled eggs, white sauce, smoked haddock and peeled shrimp. Season to taste.

3 Spoon half the mixture into an ovenproof dish. Top with the spinach and then the remaining pasta and fish mixture. Sprinkle with the grated cheese.

4 Bake at 375°F. for 30 minutes. Serve hot, cut into wedges and garnished with the unpeeled shrimp.

Serves 4-6

Tip: If using packaged macaroni and cheese, make the pasta according to the directions and use only 1¼ cups white sauce.

Fish and Pasta Florentine — chopped hard-boiled eggs, smoked haddock, shrimp and pasta shells mixed in a rich white sauce and served on a bed of spinach

Boiled Eggs

Time Table for Boiling Eggs	Jumbo	Large	Medium
Eggs immersed in boiling water and gently simmered (soft-boiled)	3½ mins	3½ mins	3 mins
Eggs put into cold water, brought to a boil and gently simmered (uncovered) (soft-boiled)	3 mins after water has boiled	2¾ mins after water has boiled	2½ mins after water has boiled
Eggs placed in boiling water, covered and removed from the heat to prevent further boiling (soft-boiled)	8-9 mins	8-9 mins	7-8 mins (depending on temperature of eggs)
For eggs with hard-boiled whites and soft yolks	7 mins	7 mins in simmering water	6 mins
For true hard-boiled eggs	12 mins	11 mins in simmering water	10 mins

Eggs are never literally boiled: high temperatures toughen protein, and since the white of an egg is almost entirely protein, it will be spoiled if it is cooked at a very high temperature. An egg white coagulates at 140-143°F. and the yolk at 149°F.; therefore the temperature of boiling water (212°F.) is more than adequate to cook an egg. Also, if you use too high a temperature, the eggs will knock against each other in the bubbling water and the shells may crack. Cooking eggs without actually boiling them will prevent them from discoloring when they are exposed to the air.

Hard-boiled Eggs in Onion Sauce

4 small rolls
½ cup sliced onions
⅔ cup béchamel sauce (see page 124)
pinch salt and white pepper
4 hard-boiled eggs
2 tablespoons chopped parsley
¼ cup grated cheese

1 Split and hollow out the rolls.

2 Blanch the onions for 5 minutes, rinse in fresh water, then reboil in cold water till tender. Add to the béchamel sauce, reheat and season.

3 Dice the egg and blend with the sauce. Mix in the chopped parsley. Fill each roll half neatly. Sprinkle with grated cheese and melt cheese

under broiler.

Serves 4

Hard-boiled Eggs Bellevue

6 eggs
1 small head of lettuce
3 slices of cooked ham
sprigs of parsley, chervil and chives
few tarragon leaves
1 cup mayonnaise
20 hazelnuts, shelled
1 cup peeled, cooked, deveined shrimp
1 lemon
2 tomatoes
few olives
salt and pepper

1 Hard-boil the eggs for 10 minutes. Drain, cool and remove the shells.

2 Rinse and drain the lettuce leaves without breaking up the heart. Arrange 6 good leaves on a serving dish.

3 Cut the slices of ham in half and put half a slice on each lettuce leaf. Cover each with a cooked egg.

4 Rinse the parsley, chervil, chives

and tarragon under running water. Dry them and chop finely. Add them to the mayonnaise and mix well.

5 Coarsely crush the hazelnuts, and add them too, together with one-third of the peeled shrimp. Mix carefully.

6 Coat the eggs with this sauce, and top with the remainder of the shrimp.

7 Decorate the center of the dish with a few shrimp or cut the lemon and tomatoes into rounds and use them to decorate the edge of the dish. Place the little lettuce heart in the center and scatter with olives. Keep cool until ready to serve.

Serves 6

Tip: Eggs should never be placed in boiling water immediately after being removed from the refrigerator since the sudden change in temperature may cause the shells to crack. Allow eggs to stand at room temperature for an hour before cooking or immerse in tepid water for 2–3 minutes. If the shell has cracked, prick small holes in the wider end of the shell, and this should prevent the contents from oozing out while the egg is cooking.

Eggs Bellevue — a spectacular dish for a cold buffet. Hard-boiled eggs are coated with mustard mayonnaise and garnished with shrimp

Look 'n Cook Poached Eggs in Aspic

1 Add the vinegar (preferably distilled vinegar) to the boiling water **2** When the mixture is simmering, slip in the eggs one by one, taking care to put each in from the level of the water's surface **3** Check that they are cooked by pressing gently with a finger **4** Drain the eggs and im-merse in cold water **5** Still in the cold water, trim the eggs **6** Prepare aspic (1 tablespoon gelatin dissolved in $\frac{1}{4}$ cup cold water. Add 1 cup hot water or broth.) **7** Strain the gelatin **8** Put the molds on crushed ice or in ice water and pour a spoonful of gelatin into each **9** Prepare and

cut out the ingredients used for decoration: e.g., tomato, ham, hard-boiled egg white **10** Decorate the bottom of each mold and put in the eggs **11** Fill the molds with gelatin and let set in the refrigerator **12** Unmold onto lettuce leaves. Keep cold until served

Poached Eggs

Poached Eggs

1 Fill a sauté pan with hot water, adding 2 tablespoons wine vinegar and $\frac{1}{2}$ teaspoon salt per $4\frac{1}{2}$ cups water. Use a large, shallow pan or deep tray.

2 Bring to a boil and add the eggs (up to 8 at a time): break them into a saucer one at a time, then slip them into the sauté pan.

3 Simmer the eggs for 3-3$\frac{1}{2}$ minutes, turning them over when they begin to set, to wrap the white around the yolks.

4 Drain and refresh in cold water. Trim the excess white and keep eggs in cold water until required. To reheat, plunge in hot salted water and simmer for 1 minute.

Poached Eggs in Tomato Aspic

1 onion
$\frac{1}{4}$ cup butter
1$\frac{1}{2}$ lbs. very ripe tomatoes
salt and pepper
sprig thyme
3 tablespoons white vinegar to each
  4$\frac{1}{4}$ cups water
8 eggs
1 tablespoon gelatin
2 cups water
few sprigs fresh tarragon

1 Put 8 ramekins or individual molds into the refrigerator. Peel and chop the onion. Melt the butter in a small saucepan. When it is barely hot, put in the onion. Cover and cook slowly until the onion is soft.

2 Bring water to a boil. Plunge the tomatoes in for a few seconds, then drain, skin, remove the seeds and chop the flesh coarsely. Add this to the onion. Season with salt and pepper, and add a sprig of thyme. Cover the pan and cook gently for 20 minutes.

3 Prepare the poached eggs. Partly fill a large saucepan with water and add the vinegar, then bring to a boil. Break the eggs into separate cups; fill a bowl with cold water. When the pan of water reaches boiling point, slide the eggs in, putting the rim of each cup to the surface of the water. Simmer for 3 minutes.

4 After 3 minutes cooking, carefully remove the eggs with a slotted spoon. Check that they are cooked by pressing lightly with a finger. Plunge them into the cold water. Remove the white threads formed during cooking and trim them to an even, regular shape. Leave in the cold water.

5 Prepare the gelatin as instructed on the envelope, then cool.

6 When the tomatoes are cooked, rub them through a strainer or purée in a blender. Put the resultant purée back into the saucepan and reduce over brisk heat, stirring with a wooden spoon. When the tomato mixture becomes thick, take the pan off the heat. Add half the gelatin, stir vigorously and stand the saucepan in cold water.

7 Put crushed ice or ice water in a large container. Take the ramekins or molds out of the refrigerator and put them on ice or in the ice water. Put a spoonful of gelatin in each.

8 Wash and dry the tarragon and remove the leaves. Decorate the bottoms of the ramekins with the leaves.

9 Dry the eggs with a cloth or absorbent paper and put them on a cooling rack. When the tomato sauce has nearly set, pour it over the eggs in repeated layers to coat them well.

10 Put 1 tomato-covered egg into each of the ramekins or molds. Pour in the rest of the tomato aspic carefully, filling them completely. Put them in the refrigerator for several hours to set completely.

11 Unmold the eggs onto a serving dish and serve cold.
Serves 4

Tip: It is essential to dry the poached eggs completely or the tomato gelatin will slip off.

Egg Tips

1 If eggs are too cold, they will crack when boiled in the shell.

2 When cracking eggs, break them one by one into a cup before putting them into a bowl. This way, if one is bad, the others will not be spoiled by it.

3 Eggs may be kept at normal room temperature or, they can be stored in a refrigerator, where there is often a special rack provided to protect them from breakage, but make sure they are not near the freezer compartment. When possible, remove eggs from refrigerator about 1 hour before use, to allow them to return to room temperature. This makes them easier to whisk and helps to prevent cracking when they are boiled. Any dirty eggs should be wiped clean with a damp cloth before use.

4 Egg whites are used as clarifying agents, for instance, in making broth. The protein in the egg white coagulates and gathers the suspended particles, thus cleaning the liquid.

Eggs Hussar

6 tomatoes
salt and pepper
2 tablespoons oil
3 onions
2 tablespoons butter
½ lb. cooked ham
bunch parsley
4¼ cups water
2 tablespoons white vinegar
6 eggs

For the sauce:
¼ lb. lean bacon
1 large onion
1 carrot
¼ cup butter
sprig thyme
½ bay leaf
2 tablespoons flour
1¼ cups brown stock
1 tablespoon tomato paste
½ cup Madeira

1 Cut a slice from the end opposite the stalk of the tomatoes and scoop out the inside with a small spoon. Salt them to draw out excess moisture and turn upside down on a plate to drain until needed, then dry with absorbent paper. Preheat the oven to 375°F.

2 To make the sauce: dice the bacon. Peel and finely chop the onion. Peel and dice the carrot. In a sauté pan heat the butter for the sauce. Add the bacon, chopped onion, carrot, thyme and bay leaf. Cook gently until the onion is golden, stirring with a wooden spoon. Then sprinkle with flour and let the mixture brown. Gradually add the stock to the mixture, mix well and simmer gently for 20 minutes.

3 Put the tomatoes in an oven-proof dish, baste them with the oil, then place in the oven and cook for 20 minutes. Meanwhile, peel the remaining onions and slice them into rings. Heat the remaining butter in a pan and sauté the onion rings until golden.

4 Dice the ham. Wash, dry and chop the parsley.

5 Add the vinegar to a pan of water, bring to a boil and poach the eggs. Keep eggs hot in a bowl of warm water.

6 When the sauce is cooked, strain through a fine conical strainer, add the tomato paste, the Madeira and the diced ham. Adjust the seasoning and heat thoroughly.

7 Take the tomatoes out of the oven and arrange them on a hot serving dish. Put a poached egg in each tomato, topped with the onion rings. Pour the sauce and the diced ham into the center of the dish. Sprinkle with parsley and serve immediately.

Serves 6

Poached Eggs with Spinach

2 lbs. spinach
4¼ cups water
3 tablespoons white vinegar
4 eggs
3 tablespoons oil
2 slices bread
3 tablespoons butter

1 Rinse and trim the spinach and remove the tough stems. Drain.

2 Put the spinach into a saucepan with the water clinging to the leaves. Heat until cooked, about 10 minutes. Add salt to taste.

3 When the spinach is cooked, drain and cool, pressing out all excess water with the hands, then keep hot.

4 Heat the water in a large pan and add the vinegar. Break an egg into a cup and as soon as the water boils, slide in the eggs, putting the rim of the cup to the surface of the water. Simmer for 3 minutes.

5 Partly fill a bowl with warm water. When the eggs have been cooking for 4 minutes, lift them out with a slotted spoon. Check that they are cooked by pressing lightly with a finger, and plunge them into the warm water. Carefully cut off the white threads which will have formed during cooking.

6 Heat the oil in a skillet. Trim the crusts off the bread and cut the slices diagonally to make triangles. Put them in the hot oil and fry until golden.

7 Heat a serving dish. Add the butter to the spinach. Mix well together and place in the serving dish. Make 4 hollows in the spinach.

8 Dry the eggs with a cloth or absorbent paper. Put them in the hollows in the spinach. Insert the croûtons cornerwise in the spinach, so that they stand up. Serve hot.

Serves 4

Storage of eggs. They require a clean, cool storage place that is not too dry. A refrigerator with a temperature range of 35.5-39°F. is ideal, and not only for eggs but for cream, too.

Keep eggs away from any pungent smells, such as cheese, fish or any other strong-smelling food while in storage because they will absorb any odor through the porous shell.

Egg Cutlets

2 eggs, separated
⅔ cup béchamel sauce (see page 124)
pinch salt and pepper
pinch nutmeg
4 hard-boiled eggs
5 tablespoons diced mushrooms
¼ cup clarified butter
flour for dusting
¼ cup chopped nuts
2 cups dry breadcrumbs
1½ cups tomato sauce
sprig parsley

1 Blend the egg yolks with the cold béchamel sauce. Reheat gently without boiling. Season.

2 Dice the hard-boiled eggs. Lightly whip the egg whites.

3 Cook the mushrooms gently in clarified butter for 1 minute only. Combine mushrooms with the diced hard-boiled eggs.

4 Blend the mushroom mixture with the sauce, divide into 4 portions, and shape into ovals or cutlet form. Dust with flour, then dip in the beaten egg whites, then the nut and crumb mixtures to cover. Shake off any excess crumbs.

5 Deep-fry the cutlets for 4 minutes till golden. Drain on absorbent paper, then serve with a rich tomato sauce. Dish up and garnish with parsley.

Serves 4

Variations

Cromesquis Egg Fritters

1 Use the same ingredients as for Egg Cutlets (see recipe above), but add 2 tablespoons diced truffles, if liked. Shape the mixture into small, flat rounds.

2 Roll in sifted flour, then dip in batter. Deep-fry till golden, then drain on absorbent paper.

3 Garnish the fritters with a sprig of parsley and serve with tomato sauce.

Coddled Eggs

Coddled eggs are served in a special shallow dish which resembles a small soufflé dish. The ramekin is placed on a plate lined with a napkin. Eggs cooked in small ramekins are said to be "coddled."

1 Grease each ramekin with 1 tablespoon softened butter.

2 Crack an egg into a saucer and add to the ramekin.

3 Place the ramekin in a shallow tray or pan which is half-filled with hot water.

4 Cover with a lid and bring to a boil. Remove the lid and simmer for 2½–3 minutes until the egg white is set.

5 Cover with a little heavy cream and serve.

Tip: Do not season with salt.

Variations

Bergère

1 Grease a ramekin and add 2 tablespoons cooked ground lamb blended with some Chasseur sauce.

2 Crack an egg into a saucer and pour it on top of the mixture. Cook as outlined above.

3 Cover with Chasseur sauce.

Bordelaise

1 Place a slice of poached beef bone marrow inside a buttered ramekin.

2 Add an egg and cook as above.

3 Cover with Bordelaise sauce.

Capucine

1 Add a purée of cooked mushrooms and cream sauce to a buttered ramekin.

2 Add an egg and cook as above.

3 Cover with cream sauce.

Diane

1 Butter a ramekin and add 2 tablespoons ground cooked meat mixed with poivrade sauce.

2 Add an egg and cook as above.

3 Cover with poivrade sauce and top with a slice of mushroom.

Diplomate

1 Place a small piece of foie gras inside a buttered ramekin.

2 Add an egg and cook as above.

3 Pour on Madeira sauce.

Maryland

1 Place 3 tablespoons creamed sweet corn in a buttered ramekin.

2 Add an egg and cook as above.

3 Coat with a cream sauce and decorate with cooked sweet red peppers.

Soubise

1 Butter a ramekin and add 3 tablespoons cooked onion purée.

2 Add an egg and cook as above.

3 Coat with soubise sauce and decorate with a slice of mushroom or a strip of cooked red pepper.

Valentine

1 Place 3 tablespoons chopped tomato pulp inside a buttered ramekin.

2 Add an egg and cook as above.

3 Coat with espagnole sauce.

Egg Tip
A good egg pâté can be made by chopping hard-boiled eggs, mixing them with a little mayonnaise and cooked mushroom purée, and then blending whipped cream into the mixture. Serve chilled.

Quiche
(Basic Recipe)

2 eggs
1¼ cups milk
pinch salt
pinch nutmeg

1 Beat the eggs for 5 minutes, then blend into the milk. Preheat the oven to 400°F.

2 Season with salt and nutmeg, then strain and pour into the prepared crust until about two-thirds full. Bake in the preheated oven for 20 minutes, then reduce the oven temperature to 350°F. for the remaining 20-25 minutes baking time. Overall cooking time should be about 45 minutes. Serve hot or cold.

Makes enough to fill one 8-inch diameter pie crust

Variations

Bacon Quiche

Sprinkle ¼ lb. fried and crumbled bacon slices over crust. Pour in custard and bake as basic recipe.

Onion and Cheese Quiche

Sprinkle ½ cup grated cheese over crust, then top with a layer of sautéed sliced onions. Pour in custard and bake as basic recipe.

Tip: To thicken and enrich basic quiche add ⅔ cup thick béchamel sauce to basic custard.

―――――⌒⌒―――――

Quiche Lorraine

3 thin slices lean unsmoked bacon
¼ cup butter, melted
8-inch unbaked pie crust, 1½ inches deep
1 cup grated hard cheese
3 eggs, beaten
⅞ cup light cream
¼ cup milk
pinch salt and white pepper
pinch grated nutmeg

Quiche Lorraine — the classic French savory custard flan

pinch cayenne pepper (optional)

1 Scald the bacon and rinse, then cut into small pieces.

2 Set the oven at 375°F.

3 Brush melted butter over the bottom of the pie crust, then place on a greased baking sheet. Sprinkle grated cheese over the pastry, then layer with the bacon pieces.

4 In a bowl blend the beaten eggs, cream, milk and the seasonings. Pour half the custard only into the pie crust. Bake in the preheated oven for 20 minutes, then remove and add the rest of the custard and bake for another 20 minutes longer. Serve hot or cold.

Makes 6–8 portions

Tip: Quiche Lorraine lends itself to countless variations: the cheese or bacon can be omitted, or instead of bacon use corned beef or garlic sausage.

155

Look 'n Cook Flat Omelette

1 Peel the onions and chop finely. Cut the red and green peppers into halves, remove the seeds, wash and chop. Scald, peel, seed and finely chop the tomatoes **2** Add the chopped onions to hot, but not smoking, oil and cook until soft but not colored **3** Add the peppers and cook over moderate heat until soft **4** Add the chopped tomatoes with salt and pepper and cook uncovered, to evaporate some of the water from the vegetables. Remove from the heat **5** Break the eggs and beat with salt and pepper. Add a pinch of mixed

5

7

herbs and the mixed vegetables and beat again, with a fork **6** Place a skillet with 2 tablespoons of oil over medium-high heat. Pour in the prepared egg and vegetable mixture and stir in all directions to prevent sticking **7** When the bottom is cooked, turn like a pan-cake and cook the other side **8** When the second side is cooked, slide the omelette onto a heated serving dish. On no account leave it in the hot pan or it will overcook and dry

Omelettes

The term 'omelette' is derived from the Latin 'ova mellita', which, in the days of the Roman empire, consisted of a mixture of eggs and honey beaten together and baked.

Preparing the pan
Unless you have a non-stick omelette pan, it is best to prepare the pan you are going to use so that your omelettes are perfect every time. First of all, rub around the inside with coarse salt. Then cover the bottom of the pan with oil and heat it on the stove for about 5 minutes or until the oil is hot. Pour out the oil. The pan is now ready to use.

Mushroom Omelette

½ lemon
¾ lb. mushrooms
⅓ cup + 1 tablespoon butter
8 eggs
2 tablespoons cream
salt and pepper
small bunch parsley

1 Squeeze the half lemon.

2 Clean the mushrooms: cut off the base of the stalks and rinse the mushrooms rapidly (do not let them soak). Slice them into thin strips. Sprinkle the lemon juice over them.

3 Melt 2 tablespoons butter in a skillet and when it begins to turn golden put in the mushrooms. Cook until the juices have boiled away and the mushrooms are golden brown.

4 Cut about 2 tablespoons butter into small pieces.

5 Break the eggs into a bowl. Add the pieces of butter, the cream, salt and pepper. Beat with a fork. When the eggs are frothy, stop beating.

6 Warm a serving dish. Rinse and chop the parsley.

7 Melt the rest of the butter in the omelette pan and when it begins to turn golden pour in the egg mixture. Make the omelette.

8 When the omelette is done, i.e., set but still soft, put 3 spoonfuls of mushrooms over it. Fold it in half and slide it onto the serving dish.

9 Pile the rest of the mushrooms onto the dish around the omelette and sprinkle chopped parsley on top.

Serves 4

Mushroom Omelette makes an excellent family meal accompanied by home-fried potatoes and salad

Spanish Omelette with Spiced Sausage

3 onions
2 peppers
1 lb. tomatoes
2 cloves garlic
½ cup oil
bouquet garni
salt and pepper
7 ozs. chorizo (Spanish sausage)
⅔ cup white stock
8 eggs

1 Peel the onions. Mince one and shred the other two. Wash and dry the peppers, and cut them in halves. Remove the seeds and cut into thin strips. Skin and chop the tomatoes, discarding the seeds. Peel and crush the garlic.

2 To make the tomato purée: heat 2 tablespoons of the oil in a small sauté pan. Add the minced onion. Cook until golden brown, then add the tomatoes, the bouquet garni, and half of the crushed garlic. Season with salt and pepper. Cover and cook for 15 minutes over low heat.

3 In the meantime, cut the chorizo or other sliced sausage into thin slices.

4 Heat ¼ cup oil in a skillet. Add the chorizo, cook gently, then drain and keep warm.

5 Cook the shredded onions in the same oil until they are golden brown. Add the peppers and cook until soft. Season with salt and pepper.

6 When the peppers begin to brown, add the rest of the garlic. Cook for another 5 minutes then remove from the heat and keep hot with the chorizo.

7 Pour the tomato purée through a fine strainer. Return to low heat and thin with the stock. Adjust the seasoning and leave to cook over the low heat.

8 Break the eggs into a mixing bowl. Season with salt and pepper. Beat gently with a fork until frothy.

9 Heat the rest of the oil in an omelette pan. When it is hot, pour in the beaten eggs, and mix, scraping the bottom of the pan with a fork. Before the eggs start to solidify add the onions, the pepper and the chorizo, stirring all the time.

10 When the omelette is cooked, place it on a warm serving dish. Serve hot with the tomato sauce in a sauce boat.

Serves 4

Rolled Omelettes

2 tablespoons flour
3 beaten eggs
⅓ cup milk
2 tablespoons butter
pinch chopped parsley or mixed herbs
pinch salt and pepper

1 Sift the flour and add the beaten eggs and milk. Season with salt and pepper and strain.

2 Add a pinch of chopped parsley or mixed herbs for flavoring.

3 Melt the butter in an omelette pan and, when it is foaming, add the egg mixture. Stir it through and when it is cooked on one side, flip it like a pancake and cook until golden brown.

4 Remove the omelette from the skillet and spread with a filling. Roll up and serve.

Cheshire Style

1 Sprinkle ½ cup grated cheddar cheese onto the cooked omelette. Add a few drops of Worcestershire sauce.

2 Place under a hot broiler to melt the cheese.

3 Roll up and serve.

Rolled Herb Omelette

bunch of fresh mixed herbs (chives, chervil, tarragon etc.)
6 eggs
salt and pepper
1 tablespoon oil
2 tablespoons butter

1 Pick over the mixed herbs. Wash and dry them, then chop finely.

2 Break the eggs into a bowl. Add salt and pepper. Beat with a fork until the eggs are blended but not frothy.

3 Add the chopped herbs and mix in with the fork.

4 Melt the oil and butter together in an omelette pan until foaming and hot, then pour in the eggs. Stir in all directions with a wooden spoon or the back of a fork to prevent the cooked eggs from sticking to the pan.

5 When the omelette is cooked, but the eggs are still creamy, roll it up by tilting the pan and assisting the rolling with the wooden spoon or fork. Slide the rolled omelette to the edge of the pan.

6 Bring a heated serving dish to the edge of the pan. Lift the opposite side of the pan to turn out the omelette.

7 Serve immediately.

Serves 4

Tips: Always heat the serving dish, and if possible, the plates. Omelettes should be served either very hot or cold.

If intending to serve an omelette cold, cook it more thoroughly. It should be quite set and no longer creamy.

Cold omelettes make excellent picnic fare. They can also be served as a sandwich filling either whole in a French loaf or sliced and packed into rolls.

Look 'n Cook Mayonnaise

7

8

9

1 The ingredients needed to make the four mayonnaise variations — tartar sauce, garlic mayonnaise, rémoulade mayonnaise, catsup: olive oil, peanut oil, vinegar, mustard, white pepper, salt, egg, catsup, capers, lemon, garlic, chives, tarragon and parsley **2** Break the egg, separating the white from the yolk. Place the yolk in a deep mixing bowl **3** Add the mustard to the egg yolk **4** Make the mayonnaise by stirring in the peanut oil. Add only a little of the oil at a time, beating continuously with a wooden spoon. Alternatively, you can use a hand whisk or an electric mixer for the blending operation **5** When the mayonnaise is of a firm consistency, add freshly ground white pepper **6** Add salt **7, 8** and **9** Then add either vinegar, or lemon, or catsup according to the type of mayonnaise you wish to make **10** If making a tartar sauce, chop the chives, tarragon and parsley **11** Mix the chopped herbs into the stiff mayonnaise **12** Finally, add the capers to this mixture **13** For garlic mayonnaise, use olive oil instead of peanut **14** Mince the cloves of

▶

10

11

12

Look 'n Cook Mayonnaise (continued)

13

14

15

16

17

18

19

20

garlic finely **15** Mix the minced garlic into the stiff mayonnaise **16** To make the rémoulade: hard-boil the eggs, allow them to cool, then remove the shells. Cut the cold eggs into halves **17** Remove the egg yolks and place them in a bowl **18** Mash them with a fork **19** Add the mustard **20** Make the rémoulade with peanut oil. Decorate the finished rémoulade with a little chopped yolk and white of egg **21** To rescue a curdled mayonnaise, mix an egg yolk with some mustard in a bowl, then pour in, one after the other in very small quantities, the 'turned' mayonnaise and a little oil. Keep stirring until the mayonnaise has returned to the correct consistency **22** The finished mayonnaise variations (left to right): catsup mayonnaise, garlic mayonnaise, rémoulade and tartar sauce (front)

Mayonnaise

Mayonnaise (Basic Recipe)

1 egg
1 teaspoon mustard
1 cup peanut oil
salt
freshly ground white pepper
1 teaspoon vinegar

1 Break the egg, separating the white from the yolk.

2 Put the yolk into a small deep bowl with the mustard.

3 Pour in the oil little by little, stirring continously with a wooden spoon, whisk or electric blender.

4 When the mayonnaise is stiff, add salt and pepper. Add the vinegar. Cover and put in a cool place until you wish to serve it.

Makes 1 cup

Tips: If the egg yolks are very pale, a little natural egg coloring or a pinch of turmeric powder will enhance the final color of the mayonnaise. A few drops of Tabasco can be added to give the mayonnaise a little more bite.

An extra egg yolk can be added to make the sauce a little thicker.

Variations

Lemon Mayonnaise

1 Prepare the mayonnaise as shown in the basic recipe. Replace the vinegar with the juice of ½ lemon. You can also peel a fresh lemon, cut the flesh into small cubes and add this to the mayonnaise at the time of serving.

Lemon Cream Mayonnaise

1 Prepare 1 cup of the basic mayonnaise, reducing the mustard to ½ teaspoon. Add the juice of 1 lemon. Put the mayonnaise in a cool place.

2 Pour ½ cup heavy cream in a deep bowl, and put this into another deep bowl filled with crushed ice.

3 Beat the cream until it forms peaks.

4 Fold into the mayonnaise immediately so that you have a frothy mixture. Pour this sauce into a sauce boat.

Tip: The whipped cream can be replaced by a stiffly beaten egg white.

Variations

Antiboise Mayonnaise

1 Chop 2 drained canned anchovy fillets.

2 Mix the anchovy fillets with 1 teaspoon anchovy paste, a pinch of garlic salt and a pinch of chopped tarragon.

3 Add this mixture to 1 cup of the basic mayonnaise.

Andalusia Mayonnaise

1 Purée 3 tablespoons sweet red peppers with a pinch of garlic salt.

2 Add the purée to 1 cup of the basic mayonnaise and garnish with 3 tablespoons chopped peppers.

Madrilène Mayonnaise

1 Chop 3 tablespoons ham and add a pinch of garlic salt and 1 teaspoon tomato paste.

2 Blend this mixture into 1 cup of the basic mayonnaise.

Britannia Mayonnaise

1 Place 1 teaspoon freshly chopped mint in a pan and add 1 teaspoon sugar. Add 1 tablespoon wine vinegar and simmer the mint for 10 minutes.

2 Add the mint and vinegar to 1 cup of the basic mayonnaise and stir in a drop of green edible food coloring to make the mayonnaise a pale green color.

Santa Lucia Mayonnaise

1 Mix together 3 tablespoons grated horseradish, ¾ cup fresh white breadcrumbs, 3 tablespoons shredded coconut, 2½ tablespoons lime juice, 1 teaspoon sugar and a pinch of cayenne pepper.

2 Blend these ingredients into 1 cup of the basic mayonnaise.

3 Just before serving beat ⅓ cup heavy cream and fold it into the mayonnaise.

Herb Mayonnaise (Sauce Verte)

1 To 1 cup of the basic mayonnaise add 3 tablespoons spinach purée and 1 tablespoon of mixed chopped fresh herbs, such as parsley, watercress, tarragon and chives.

Tartar Sauce

1 Prepare 1 cup of the basic mayonnaise. Rinse, dry and chop a small bunch of chives, tarragon and parsley. Mix the chopped herbs and some capers with the mayonnaise.

Catsup Mayonnaise

1 To 1 cup of the basic mayonnaise, add 3 tablespoons catsup or 1 tablespoon of tomato paste and a generous quantity of pepper.

> **Rescuing a Curdled Mayonnaise**
> Break an egg, separating the white from the yolk. Put the yolk with a little prepared mustard into a deep bowl. Add oil and the curdled mayonnaise alternately, little by little, stirring continuously with a whisk.

Soufflés

Salmon Soufflé

$\frac{1}{4}$ cup clarified butter
$\frac{1}{3}$ cup grated Parmesan cheese
4 peeled, deveined, cooked shrimp
$\frac{1}{2}$ cup béchamel sauce
4 egg yolks
$\frac{1}{4}$ lb. canned salmon, skin and
   bones removed
pinch of salt and white pepper
3 egg whites
juice 1 lemon
grated Parmesan cheese

1 Preheat the oven to 400°F. Butter 4 individual soufflé dishes with clarified butter. Sprinkle the insides with grated Parmesan cheese. Place 1 peeled shrimp in each dish.

2 Warm up the béchamel with 2 egg yolks and the dry fish paste. Season to taste, then remove from the heat and add the remaining 2 egg yolks and the lemon juice.

3 In a large bowl, beat the egg whites to a soft meringue, making sure the whisk and bowl are clean and that no specks of yolk are left in the whites.

4 Fold the egg whites lightly into the fish mixture, then fill the prepared dishes to the top. Level off with a spatula. Run the tip of your thumb all around the inside edge to form a hollow ring.

5 Place the dishes in a roasting pan of water and bake in the middle of the preheated oven for 15-18 minutes.

6 Remove the soufflés from the oven, sprinkle the tops with Parmesan cheese and serve.

Serves 4

Cheese and Tomato Soufflé

2 large ripe tomatoes, skinned, seeded and diced
4 eggs, separated
1 cup grated cheese
1 tablespoon light cream
salt and pepper
pinch grated nutmeg

For the Béchamel Sauce:
$\frac{1}{4}$ cup butter
$\frac{1}{4}$ cup flour
$1\frac{1}{4}$ cups milk

1 Prepare the béchamel sauce (see page 124).

2 Preheat the oven to 425°F. Butter a 6-cup capacity soufflé dish.

3 Put the egg whites into a large bowl. Take the sauce off the heat and beat in the egg yolks, grated cheese, diced tomatoes, cream, salt and pepper to taste and nutmeg.

4 Beat the egg whites until they stand in stiff peaks, then, using a metal spoon, carefully cut and fold them into the sauce until well combined. Quickly pour into the prepared dish and run the tip of your thumb around the rim, $\frac{1}{4}$ inch deep in the mixture so that it rises evenly. Cook in the oven for 25 minutes or until risen and golden. Serve immediately.

Serves 6

Salmon Soufflé — a delicious starter to any meal. Bake the mixture in smaller ramekins to serve as individual soufflés

Look 'n Cook Cheese Soufflé

10

1 Butter the inside of a soufflé dish 2 Sprinkle evenly with Parmesan cheese (or any finely grated cheese) 3 Melt the butter in a saucepan without allowing it to brown 4 Add the flour and mix with a wooden spoon to form a roux. Remove from the heat and allow the mixture to cool a little, then add the milk all at once 5 Return the pan to the heat and let the sauce thicken, stirring all the time until smooth. This takes about 10-15 minutes. Grate a little nutmeg into the sauce and season with salt and pepper. Remove the saucepan from the heat 6 Add the egg yolks to the sauce and mix well 7 Add the grated cheese and allow it to melt into the sauce, stirring all the time with a wooden spoon 8 Beat the egg whites with a pinch of salt until they are stiff 9 Fold the egg whites gently into the cheese sauce with a metal spoon 10 Pour the mixture into the buttered soufflé dish and smooth over the top. Place in a 425°F. oven and cook for 25 minutes. Then raise the temperature to 475°F. and cook for a further 5 minutes 11 Remove from the oven and serve immediately. The soufflé should be well-risen and should be able to stand for at least 5 minutes after baking without collapsing.

11

Cheese Soufflé

¼ cup butter
6 tablespoons flour
1¼ cups milk
pinch grated nutmeg
salt and pepper
1 cup grated cheese
4 or 5 eggs, depending on size, separated

1 Make a thick béchamel sauce: Melt 3 tablespoons butter in a saucepan without allowing it to brown. Add the flour and stir briskly with a wooden spoon so that the butter and flour are mixed to form a roux. Remove pan from heat and let the mixture cool a little. Then add the milk all at once. Return the pan to the heat. Let the sauce thicken for 10-15 minutes, stirring continuously until smooth. Add the nutmeg. Salt lightly and pepper generously.

2 Add the grated cheese to the sauce and let it melt while stirring it with a whisk or wooden spoon. It is now a Mornay sauce.

3 Taking the saucepan off the heat, add the egg yolks to the sauce and mix well.

4 Preheat the oven to 425°F. Butter a soufflé dish 7 inches in diameter and 4 inches deep with the remaining butter.

5 Add a pinch of salt to the egg whites. Beat them in a large bowl until they are stiff.

6 Using a metal spoon or spatula, fold the whites into the Mornay sauce very carefully.

7 Pour the mixture into the buttered soufflé dish and smooth over the top, making sure it is level. Then run the tip of your thumb around the inside of the dish, about ¼ inch deep in the mixture. This helps the soufflé to rise evenly. Put into the oven. Cook for 25 minutes, then, without opening the oven door, turn the temperature up to 475°F. Remove the soufflé from the oven after it has been in for 30 minutes.

Serves 4

Soufflé Omelettes

When preparing a soufflé omelette, the egg whites are beaten separately to provide maximum expansion of the mixture and to make the finished dish as light as possible.

(Basic recipe)
4 eggs
1 tablespoon flour
pinch salt and pepper
2 tablespoons butter

1 Crack the eggs, separating the egg whites from the yolks.

2 Add the flour to the yolks and blend. Season with a pinch of pepper.

3 Beat the egg whites until they stand in stiff peaks. Add a pinch of salt.

4 Gradually fold the yolk mixture into the beaten egg whites.

5 Melt the butter in an omelette pan and pour in the egg mixture. Cook for a few minutes until the bottom of the omelette is set and golden brown.

6 Place the pan in a preheated oven to 375°F. and cook for 2-4 minutes.

7 Remove and fold the omelette over. Bake for another 3 minutes.

8 Turn out onto a buttered dish and serve.

Tip: Various sweet (and even savory) fillings can be added to this omelette before it is folded. The favorites are cheese, jam and fruit fillings.

Variations:

Devonshire

1 Prepare the basic omelette mixture but add 3 tablespoons grated Cheddar cheese and 2 tablespoons sherry to the yolks.

2 Cook as above and sprinkle with more grated cheese.

3 Place under a broiler until the cheese begins to bubble and turn brown.

Crêpes

Crêpes with Soufflé Stuffing

2¼ cups crêpe batter
2 cups béchamel sauce
4 eggs, separated
⅓ cup Gruyère cheese, diced

1 Preheat the oven to 400°F. Heat a greased crêpe pan and add enough batter to cover the bottom. Cook the crêpe on both sides and repeat until the batter is used up, storing the crêpes in a flat pile as they are cooked.

2 Make the soufflé stuffing: blend the béchamel sauce with the egg yolks and the diced cheese. Beat the egg whites in a clean bowl until stiff and then fold them gently into the cheese mixture.

3 Place a little of the filling on each crêpe and then fold it over to enclose the mixture completely. Place the filled crêpes on a buttered oven-proof platter and place them in the oven for 12 minutes to cook the filling.

Makes 16

1 Prepare the batter 2 Make the crêpes 3 Prepare the filling: mix the béchamel sauce, egg yolks and diced Gruyère cheese 4 Beat the egg whites until stiff and then fold them gently into the cheese mixture 5 Place a little of the filling on each crêpe, fold over to enclose the mixture completely 6 Arrange the filled crêpes on a buttered oven-proof platter and bake in the oven

Cheese Savories

Swiss Potato Pancake

2 lbs. baked potatoes
salt and pepper
¼ cup butter
¼ cup oil
1 cup grated Swiss cheese

1 When the baked potatoes are cool, cut each into two and scoop out the pulp and mash coarsely. Season with salt and pepper.

2 Melt the butter and the oil in a skillet 9 inches in diameter. Mix the mashed potato with ¾ cup of the grated cheese. Spread evenly across the pan. When the potato pancake is golden brown underneath, turn and cook the other side.

3 Sprinkle with the remaining grated cheese and place under a hot broiler until the cheese melts and bubbles. Cut the pancake into 4 and serve with broiled meat or salad.

Serves 4

Corn Gnocchi Mamaliga

4¼ cups water
pinch salt
2⅓ cups fine cornmeal
pinch ground nutmeg
¼ cup butter
3 tablespoons grated Parmesan
   cheese
pinch garlic salt

1 Pour the water into a large saucepan, add the salt and bring to a boil.

2 Stir in the cornmeal with a wooden spoon and boil. Add the garlic salt and nutmeg and cook for 15 minutes over low heat, stirring constantly, until the mixture thickens to a pouring consistency.

3 Butter a baking pan (using half the butter) and pour in the mixture. Leave until it is completely cold and set. Preheat the oven to 425°F.

4 Remove and cut into small squares and replace, overlapping, in the buttered pan.

5 Dot with the remaining butter and sprinkle with the grated cheese.

6 Place in the preheated oven for 10 minutes to brown. Serve as an entrée or with meat.

Gruyère Fritters

2 eggs
pepper to taste
1 cup fine dry breadcrumbs
deep fryer and oil
¾ lb. Gruyère cheese

1 Break the eggs into a bowl. Add pepper and beat with a fork.

2 Put the breadcrumbs into a deep plate.

3 Cut the rind off the Gruyère cheese. Cut the cheese into small sticks about ½ inch thick.

4 Beat the eggs again. Dip the small sticks of Gruyère cheese into the beaten egg, making sure they are well coated. Roll them in the breadcrumbs, shaking them to get rid of the excess. Heat the oil in the deep fat fryer and when hot, add the fritters.

5 Drain the fritters on absorbent paper as soon as they are golden. Cover the serving dish with a white paper napkin and arrange the fritters on top. Serve piping hot.

Serves 4

Avocado Grill

¼ lb. bacon
4 soft rolls
1 large avocado
2 teaspoons prepared mustard
1½ cups grated Cheddar cheese
1 tomato, sliced
8 olives (black or green)

1 Cut the bacon into strips and fry until crisp. Keep hot.

2 Split each roll lengthwise into two and toast and butter.

3 Remove the pit from the avocado, peel and slice the fruit thinly.

4 Place the avocado slices on the toasted rolls and spread lightly with mustard, saving some slices for the garnish.

5 Sprinkle with grated cheese, making sure that the avocado is well-covered.

6 Place under a hot broiler until the cheese melts and bubbles.

7 Decorate with the bacon strips and thin, twisted slices of avocado. Garnish with sliced tomatoes and olives.

Serves 8

Puffed Cheese Fritters

1 cup water
large pinch salt
pinch pepper
¼ cup + 1 tablespoon butter
1 cup flour
oil for deep frying
5 eggs (or 6 if small)
¾ cup grated Cheddar or Parmesan
   cheese

1 Make the choux pastry: measure out the water. Pour it into a saucepan and add the salt and the pepper.

2 Cut the butter into large pieces and add to the saucepan. Sift the flour onto a large sheet of paper.

3 Put the saucepan containing the water, salt, pepper and butter over high heat and boil. Watch it carefully as the liquid rises up like milk.

4 Heat the oil in the deep fat fryer.

5 Take the saucepan off the stove and add the flour all at once.

6 Put the saucepan back on the stove and stir briskly with a wooden spoon to dry out the paste. It should come away from the sides of

the saucepan. Take the pan off the heat.

7 Break 1 egg into a cup. Add it to the paste and beat it in very well. Do the same with the other eggs. The pastry should be soft but not liquid.

8 Add the grated cheese to the mixture.

9 When the oil is hot (but not smoking) add small spoonfuls of

Avocado Grill — soft rolls covered with slices of avocado and topped with mustard, cheese and crispy bacon strips

pastry, a few at a time.

10 When the fritters are nicely golden (this takes about 3 minutes), take them out of the oil and drain them on absorbent paper.

11 Serve the fritters piping hot.

Serves 6

Look 'n Cook Puffed Cheese Fritters

1 The ingredients: butter, flour, eggs, grated cheese, salt, water and oil. Weigh the butter and the flour **2** Measure the water and pour it into a saucepan **3** Cut up the butter into pieces. Put these into the saucepan **4** Bring the mixture to a boil (be careful, it rises up like milk). Heat the oil **5** Sift the flour **6** Take the saucepan off the heat and add the flour all at once **7** Stir briskly with a wooden spoon to blend it well and so that the mixture comes away from the side of the pan and curls round the spoon **8** Break an egg. Add it to the

mixture off the heat. Blend it in well. Add the other eggs, one by one, in the same way **9** Add the cheese and mix well. Add pepper and stir again **10** Using 2 small spoons, drop small quantities of the mixture at a time into the hot fat. The fritters should not touch each other **11** Let them fry. They turn themselves when one side is done **12** Lift the fritters out with a slotted spoon and drain on absorbent paper

Look 'n Cook Cheese Fondue

1 All the ingredients you will need to make the fondue
2 Grate the Swiss and Gruyère cheeses finely 3 Rub around the inside of the fondue dish (or a flameproof casserole) with a clove of garlic 4 Heat the white wine in a saucepan until it is warmed through and pour into the fondue dish over low heat 5 Add the grated cheese gradually, stirring constantly with a wooden spoon until the mixture thickens 6 Add the Kirsch and season with salt and freshly ground pepper. Add the cornstarch and bring to a boil, stirring all the time. Serve immediately with French bread

174

Cheese Fondue

Cheese Fondue

2¾ cups grated Swiss cheese
2¾ cups grated Gruyère cheese
1 clove garlic
1¼ cups dry white wine
1½ tablespoons Kirsch

pinch salt
freshly ground black pepper
1½ tablespoons cornstarch
1 crusty French loaf, cubed

1 Rub around the inside of a fondue dish, or flameproof casserole, with a clove of garlic.

2 Pour the white wine into a saucepan and warm through over low heat. Pour into the fondue dish.

3 Place the fondue dish over low heat or chafing flame and gradually add the grated cheese, stirring constantly with a wooden spoon.

4 When it thickens, add the Kirsch and freshly ground pepper. Season to taste.

5 Add the cornstarch and bring to a boil, stirring constantly.

6 Serve hot by dipping cubes of French bread, on long handled forks, into the fondue.

Serves 4

Tip: Fondues are great fun to serve instead of a dip when guests come for a meal or party. They are traditionally eaten in Switzerland on holidays. Use long-handled forks or skewers for spearing the cubes of bread.

Cheese Fondue — an increasingly popular dish for entertaining friends — which involves very little preparation time

Cheese and Pastry

Cheese Straws

$\frac{1}{2}$ lb. puff pastry, homemade or
  frozen and thawed
$\frac{1}{3}$ cup grated Parmesan cheese
$\frac{1}{2}$ cup grated Cheddar cheese
pinch cayenne
pinch paprika

1 Roll out the pastry to a rectangle about $\frac{1}{8}$ inch thick. Sprinkle on grated cheese to which the paprika and cayenne have been added. Fold in two and roll out again to the same thickness.

2 Set the oven at 400°F.

3 Roll out the pastry to the width of your baking sheet. Cut it into strips $\frac{1}{2}$ inch wide. Place on a board and twist with both hands, then place on a greased baking sheet.

4 Bake in the preheated oven for 8 minutes or until golden.

5 Cut the strips in regular lengths of 4 inches. Serve 12 per portion.

Makes about 32 straws

Tip: It is usual to bake some of the pastry in 2-inch rings into which bundles of cheese straws can be inserted (see photo). Serve them on a plate lined with a doily, if liked.

Savory Cheese and Spinach Puffs

1 lb. frozen puff pastry
5 ozs. spinach
1 cup sorrel
2 tablespoons butter
1$\frac{1}{4}$ cups well-drained cottage
  cheese
$\frac{1}{4}$ cup grated Gruyère cheese
pinch grated nutmeg
salt and pepper
1 whole egg plus 2 yolks

1 Thaw the frozen pastry for 1 hour at room temperature.

2 Pick over the spinach and the sorrel. Rinse and dry and chop coarsely.

3 Melt the butter without browning in a heavy sauté pan. Add the chopped spinach and sorrel. Cook for 7 minutes over low heat, stirring with a wooden spoon, then remove the pan from the heat.

4 Strain the cottage cheese into a bowl. Add the cooked spinach and sorrel, the grated Gruyère cheese, nutmeg, salt and pepper to taste. Mix well.

5 Add the whole egg and 1 yolk to this mixture. Mix with a wooden spoon until the mixture is smooth and firm. Preheat the oven to 450°F.

6 Divide the pastry dough in two. Roll out each piece to a rectangle about 4 × 7 inches.

7 Grease a baking sheet and place 1 rectangle on it. Spread with the filling to within $\frac{1}{2}$ inch of the pastry edge. Top with the remaining pastry rectangle and score the surface with a knife to make 10-12 portions. Pinch the edges to seal.

8 Beat the remaining egg yolk with 1 tablespoon water. Brush the top of the rectangle with this egg glaze.

9 Put the baking sheet into the oven and bake until the pastry is golden brown and well-risen (about 30 minutes). Take out and cut the pastry into portions with a sharp knife. Serve immediately.

Serves 6

Tip: If fresh sorrel is not available, substitute the same quantity of spinach.

Cheese Straws. Wrapped around sausages, cut into rounds or straw shapes — shown here are several ways of serving a basic cheese pastry

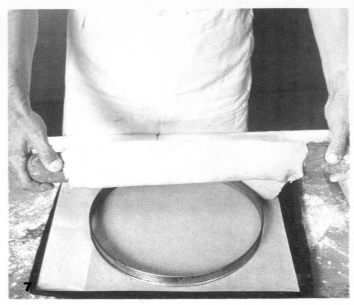

1 The ingredients: flour, butter (softened at room temperature), sugar, cottage or cream cheese, eggs, candied fruits, vanilla, brandy, salt **2** Make the pastry: break the eggs separating the whites from the yolks. Keep the whites that are not needed to one side **3** Whisk together the yolks, one white and the sugar **4** Add the softened butter. Stir with the whisk until the mixture is smooth **5** Add the flour and mix in. Roll the pastry into a ball and cool **6** Flour the pastry board. Roll out the pastry, adding flour as necessary **7** Cover the baking sheet with parchment paper. Put a springform-pan ring on top of it. Roll out the pastry and place this in the ring **8** Line the ring, making sure the pastry is pushed into the bottom and sides **9** Roll the excess pastry off the edges with the thumbs or a rolling pin. Prick the bottom of the pastry with a fork. Line with foil and bake "blind" (empty) **10** Prepare the filling: whisk together eggs and sugar, add the brandy and stir

Cheesecakes

Russian Cheesecake
Vatrouchka

For the Pastry:
3 egg yolks
1 egg white
1 cup superfine sugar
¼ lb. butter, softened
3¼ cups sifted flour

For the Filling:
dry cooking beans
½ lb. mixed candied fruits
(cherries, angelica and pineapple)
soaked in ¼ cup brandy
1 lb. cream cheese
1 cup superfine sugar
5 drops each vanilla, orange, and lemon extracts
2 eggs plus 2 yolks
1½ tablespoons brandy
1 teaspoon mixed allspice and coriander
4 egg whites
1 egg, beaten
¼ cup confectioner's sugar

◄ **11** Add the vanilla, stir again **12** Add the cottage or cream cheese and stir **13** Add the candied fruit. Mix it all together **14** Spread the filling on the bottom of the crust. Smooth the surface with a metal spoon **15** Roll out the leftover pastry into long even strips. Make a criss-cross pattern on top of the tart and brush the whole surface with beaten egg. Put the cheesecake in the oven **16** When cooked, dust with confectioner's sugar and serve

1 Butter a baking sheet and cover with a sheet of parchment paper. Butter a 10-inch springform-pan and place it on the baking sheet.

2 Place 3 egg yolks and 1 egg white (reserving the unwanted egg whites at this stage to use in the filling) in a pastry bowl. Whisk in the sugar for 4 minutes until white and fluffy.

3 Blend the soft butter into the egg mixture and whisk again for 3 minutes until the mixture is smooth.

4 Mix in the sifted flour and, with your hand, knead to a firm dough. Roll into a ball and place in the refrigerator for 1 hour.

5 Dust the pastry board and a rolling pin with flour and roll out the sweet pastry dough to a thickness of ¼ inch and 11 inches in diameter. Wrap it around the rolling pin for easy handling and unroll over the springform-pan ring. Press the pastry down well around the inside of the ring with your fingers and cut surplus pastry with a knife. Spread a piece of parchment paper inside. Fill with dry cooking beans and bake for 15 minutes at 400°F. Cool, and discard beans.

6 Roll all the pastry left over into a ball to be used later for the criss-cross pattern design.

7 Place 4 egg whites in a clean bowl and beat until the mixture forms stiff peaks when lifted with a whisk. Add only ¼ cup of superfine sugar, a little at a time, and whisk until the mixture is stiff. Blend in the cream cheese.

8 Place 2 whole eggs and 2 egg yolks in another bowl and flavor with the mixed spices, brandy and vanilla, lemon and orange extracts. Beat the mixture for 2 minutes.

9 Fold in the cream cheese mixture.

10 Add the candied fruits and chill.

11 Spread the cheese mixture

thickly into the baked pastry shell.

12 Roll the leftover pastry thinly on a floured board and cut into thin ½-inch strips (14 strips in all). Place the strips across the top in a criss-cross pattern. Brush the pastry strips with egg wash (1 beaten egg) and bake the cheesecake on the middle shelf for 35-40 minutes at 375°F. until golden brown.

13 Cool for 15 minutes, dust with confectioner's sugar and serve.

Serves 8–10

Variation

For a simpler cheesecake which is quicker to prepare, try this cold version:

1 Blend together ¼ lb. cream cheese with the juice and grated rind of 1 lemon.

2 Blend ¼ cup sugar and 1 tablespoon gelatin and dissolve in ⅔ cup of hot water.

3 Pour into the cream cheese mixture and blend well.

4 When cool, stir in ⅔ cup whipped heavy cream.

5 Mix ½ lb. of crushed graham crackers with ¼ lb. of melted butter and press down in a greased loose-bottomed springform-pan.

6 Fill with the cheese mixture and chill in the refrigerator.

Buying and Storing Cheese
Cheese must be enjoyed fresh. Buy only as much as you need. Fresh and soft cheeses should preferably be eaten on the day they are bought, or kept under refrigeration for a few days at most. Hard cheeses last longer, but they, too, should be kept under refrigeration at about 40-50°F., wrapped loosely in aluminum foil or plastic wrap. Take the cheese out of the refrigerator at least 1 hour before serving.

All about
Garden Vegetables

Vegetables have been an integral part of our diets since the beginning of time. In early days, people relied on root vegetables to eke out a starvation diet. Every laborer who had access to a plot of land grew what he could: carrots, onions, radishes, parsnips, and other root vegetables in addition to herbs grown for medicinal purposes.

Varieties of vegetables have been bred and brought to near perfection. French cooks have always had a reputation for cooking vegetables well, and often serve them as a separate course. The English, however, have a reputation for boiling vegetables until no hint of flavor is left.

We now have year-round access to fresh vegetables and good frozen or canned brands. We have become aware of their importance in creating a balanced, healthy diet. Through their alkalis, they help neutralize acids produced by proteins.

A diet rich in animal fats is currently thought to contribute to the high rate of heart disease endemic in the western world, and thus the substitution of vegetables and vegetable oils is recommended by many doctors. Vegetables, in addition to their dietary value, lend complementary flavors to other foods and, with their different colors and textures, can make a meal look as good as it tastes.

Vegetables are defined according to the way they grow:

Roots and tubers are cultivated in the ground. Potatoes, carrots, turnips, celeriac, beets, Jerusalem artichokes and rutabagas are all in this family. They all have a high carbohydrate value and contain vitamin C.

Fruits include tomatoes, eggplants and peppers, all high in vitamins A, B, C and E and abundant in minerals.

Leaves Lettuce, cabbage, spinach and chicory are just a few. They are rich in vitamin C, iron and calcium.

Legumes Peas, beans and lentils are full of protein and carbohydrates, plus vitamin B complex and iron. Soybeans are now widely accepted as a protein-substitute for meat.

Bulbs include onions and garlic.

Shoots Chives, leeks, celery, and asparagus are all shoots.

Flowers Cauliflower and broccoli are in this category.

Fungi Mushrooms and truffles are edible fungi.

As a general rule, buy vegetables of medium size, when they will have developed their flavor and still be tender.

To cook vegetables, clean them well, scrubbing if appropriate. If they can be eaten in their skins, do not peel them because much of their nutritional value is in the skin. If you must peel them, do so thinly.

Avoid overcooking vegetables — if possible, steam them. If they are to be boiled or simmered, use very little water, and after cooking, add the water to your stock pot. (Try cooking green vegetables in a stock made with half a chicken or vegetable bouillon cube, water and a little butter.)

To keep the color of green vegetables, before cooking them, blanch for 1 minute in a pan of boiling salted water, then plunge them immediately into cold water. *Never* use baking soda.

Root Vegetables

Carrot Casserole with Mushrooms in Sherry

1 lb. mushrooms
¼ cup butter
1 small onion, chopped
2 lbs. small carrots, sliced
1 tablespoon tomato paste
1½ cups water
1 chicken bouillon cube
⅔ cup sherry
salt and pepper
pinch each mace and oregano
1 tablespoon chives and parsley, chopped

1 Wash the mushrooms and trim the ends of the stalks.

2 Heat the butter and gently sauté the onion for 4 minutes without browning it.

3 Add to the onion, the carrots, tomato paste and water. Bring to a boil and boil for 30 minutes.

4 Crumble the bouillon cube into the mixture and add the sherry, seasoning, spices and mushrooms. Simmer for 10 minutes.

5 Place in a serving dish and sprinkle with the chopped chives and parsley.

Serves 4

Tips: The mushroom stalks can be trimmed from the raw mushrooms and used for making stuffing (chop them and blend with meat or breadcrumbs), or puréed for mushroom soup.

Carrot Casserole with Mushrooms in Sherry is a delicious accompaniment to roast pork or lamb

182

Look 'n Cook Chopping Vegetables

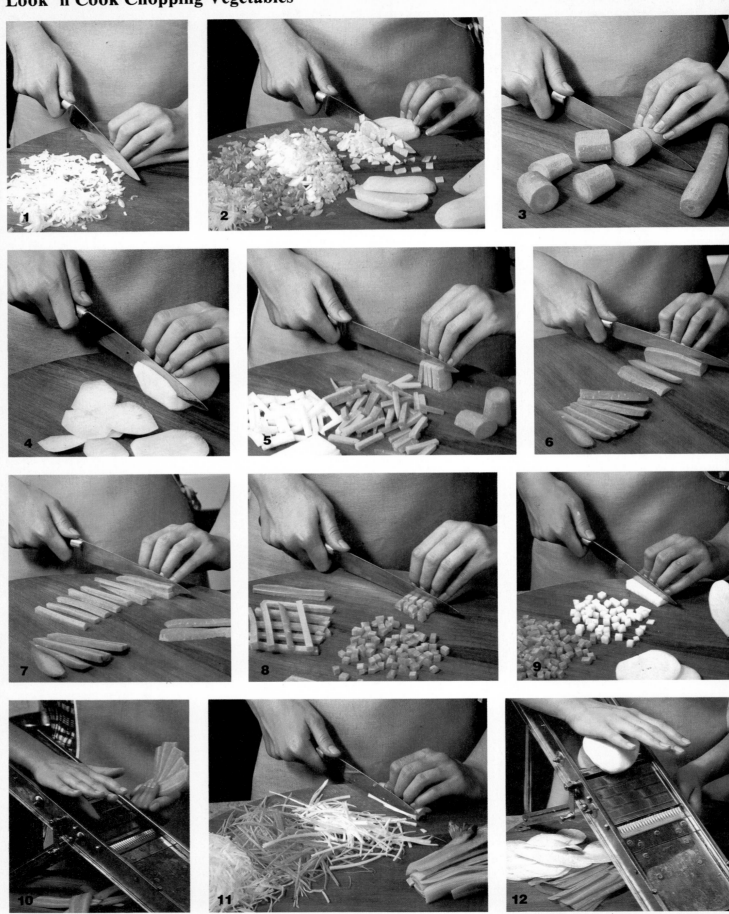

Paysanne

1 Slice the leeks into fine strips crosswise **2** Cut the carrots, turnips and potatoes into thin slices, then into small, irregular-shaped cubes. Use in soups which will not be strained — such as minestrone

Jardinière

3 Cut the peeled carrots into large pieces **4** Cut the turnips into thick, even slices **5** Cut the vegetables again into smallish sticks about ¾ inch long. Use with meat and fish dishes

Macédoine

6 Cut the carrots in slices lengthwise **7** Cut them again into thinner strips **8** Chop the carrots into even-size cubes **9** Cut the turnips in the same way. Use a macédoine of vegetables hot or cold in vegetable dishes and in salads with peas and green beans

Brunoise

10 Cut the carrots into very thin slices using a grater or a very sharp knife **11** Cut them into thin sticks and then into tiny cubes. Use in soups

Julienne

12 Slice carrots and turnips into thin slices **13** Use a sharp knife to cut them into very thin strips lengthwise **14** Cut the white part of the leek into thin strips

Mirepoix

15 Roughly chop some carrots, a branch of celery, a few parsley stems, a little thyme and a bay leaf. Use a mirepoix to flavor stocks and stews **16** The six classic ways of chopping vegetables displayed

Braised Sliced Carrots

1 lb. carrots, peeled and sliced
¼ cup butter
1 onion, chopped
2 cups water
salt and pepper
pinch sugar
pinch baking soda

1 Place the carrots in a pan with the butter and onion and sauté gently for 5 minutes with the lid on.

2 Pour in the water and add the seasoning, sugar and baking soda. Bring to a boil and simmer gently, uncovered, for about 35 minutes or until the carrots are tender and the liquid has almost evaporated.

Serves 4

Tip: A slice of bacon cooked with the carrots gives them a delicious meaty flavor.

In France, this dish is cooked in Vichy water because it contains the natural minerals which enrich and tenderize the carrots.

The baking soda can be omitted if the carrots are young and fresh.

Baked Turnip au Gratin

¼ cup butter
1 lb. peeled and sliced small white turnips
1 onion, chopped
½ lb. chopped mushrooms
1 clove garlic, chopped
⅔ cup plain yogurt
salt and pepper
½ cup fresh white breadcrumbs

1 Preheat the oven to 400°F.

2 Heat the butter in a skillet, add the turnips, onion, mushrooms and garlic and sauté gently for 4 minutes.

3 Stir in the yogurt and seasoning. Transfer the mixture to a small shallow ovenproof dish and sprinkle on the breadcrumbs. Bake in the preheated oven for 15 minutes.

Serves 4

Baked Parsnips with Radishes in Cream Sauce

6 large parsnips, peeled and cut in strips
¼ cup butter
¼ cup flour
2 cups milk
salt and pepper
¼ cup light cream
2 egg yolks
juice 1 lemon

For the Garnish:
6 radishes, diced
1 tablespoon chopped parsley and chervil
1 tablespoon chopped chives

1 Preheat the oven to 350°F. Boil the parsnips in salted water for 15 minutes. Drain.

2 Heat the butter in a pan and sauté the parsnips for 5 minutes then transfer them to a shallow ovenproof dish.

3 Add the flour to the butter left in the pan and cook for 1 minute. Blend in the milk to produce a smooth white sauce. Simmer the sauce for 10 minutes and season with salt and pepper.

4 Remove the pan from the heat and beat in the cream and egg yolks. Pour the sauce over the parsnips and bake in the preheated oven for 15 minutes.

5 Remove the dish from the oven and sprinkle the lemon juice over the parsnips. Garnish with the radishes and herbs and serve.

Serves 6

Tip: Enrich the flavor of this dish by including a little garlic, and for a touch of color, add 2 tomatoes, skinned, seeded and chopped.

Braised Parsnips with Chopped Eggs and Tomatoes

1 lb. peeled and sliced parsnips
¼ cup butter
1 medium onion, chopped
1 clove garlic, chopped
2 tomatoes, skinned, seeded and chopped
salt and pepper
2 hard-boiled eggs, chopped
1 tablespoon chopped parsley

1 Preheat the oven to 400°F. Boil the parsnips in salted water for 15 minutes only. Drain.

2 In a saucepan, heat the butter and sauté the onion and garlic for 4 minutes until tender but not colored. Add the tomatoes, parsnips and seasoning.

3 Transfer the mixture to a shallow ovenproof dish and bake in the preheated oven for 20 minutes. Serve sprinkled with the chopped egg and parsley.

Serves 4

Tip: For a more nutritious dish, add 1 cup diced mushrooms to the chopped eggs, and sprinkle with a little grated cheese.

Baked Parsnips with Radishes in Cream Sauce — an attractive and easy dish to prepare

Look 'n Cook Shaping Carrots and Turnips

1 Thinly peel, then wash and dry the carrots and turnips 2 Cut the carrots into even pieces about 1½–2 inches long 3 Split each piece into four (or according to the thickness of the carrot) 4 With a very sharp knife cut away the hard part in the middle of the carrot and pare off angles or sharp edges so that the pieces (shown in the bowl on the right) are smooth and neat 5 Trim the turnips so that every side is smooth 6 Cut the turnips into quarters, like the carrots, and pare away angles. If all the pieces of vegetables are an identical size and shape they look professional and attractive when served

Glazed Carrots with Grapes

1 lb. small carrots
1 cup water
¼ cup butter
1½ tablespoons sugar or honey
salt and pepper
**½ lb. purple or green grapes, or
 both, seeded**

1 Peel, wash and trim the carrots and cut them in quarters.

2 Put them in the water with the butter, sugar or honey, salt and pepper and bring to a boil. Boil until the liquid has almost evaporated and the carrots look glossy and tender.

3 Blanch the grapes, dipping them quickly in boiling water, and serve with the carrots.

Serves 4

Jerusalem Artichokes with Carrots and Rice

**1 lb. Jerusalem artichokes, peeled
 and sliced**
juice and rind 1 lemon
1½ cups sliced carrots
1¼ cups sliced onion
⅓ cup oil
⅓ cup rice
3⅔ cups water
1 teaspoon sugar
**1 tablespoon each chopped parsley
 and chopped mint**

1 Soak the sliced artichoke in the lemon juice.

2 Sauté the carrots and onion in the oil in a covered pan over low heat for 9 minutes until they are soft.

3 Add the rice and water and bring to a boil. Boil for 20 minutes.

4 Add the artichokes, lemon rind and sugar and cook for 5 more minutes.

5 Season and serve sprinkled with the chopped parsley and mint.

Serves 4

Sweet and Sour Beets with Orange Sauce

8 small beets
1 grapefruit
1 orange
1¼ cups water
1 chicken bouillon cube
salt and pepper
2 tablespoons sugar
2 tablespoons vinegar
pinch ground ginger
**1½ tablespoons cornstarch mixed
 with ⅓ cup water**

1 Preheat the oven to 400°F. Wash the beets. Bake them in their skins for 30 to 35 minutes.

2 Peel the grapefruit and orange, removing all the pith and white skin and reserving the peel. Separate into sections.

3 Cut a little of the orange rind into very narrow strips, put them in a pan, cover with water and boil for 8 minutes, then drain.

4 Peel the beets and put them in a saucepan with the water, the bouillon cube, seasoning, sugar, vinegar and ground ginger and boil for 5 minutes.

5 Add the cornstarch and water and boil for a further 3 minutes to thicken.

6 When the mixture is cold, serve it in a shallow dish garnished with orange and grapefruit sections.

Serves 4

Glazed Carrots with Purple Grapes is the ideal dish to serve with roast meat at a dinner party

The Squash Family

Stuffed Cucumber Alphonso

1 whole cucumber
salt and pepper
2 tablespoons butter
¾ cup grated Cheddar cheese

For the Rice Stuffing:
¼ cup oil
1 onion, chopped
4 mushrooms, chopped
½ cup pecans, chopped
⅔ cup long grain rice
1 clove garlic, peeled and crushed
1¼ cups water
1 chicken bouillon cube
pinch ground mace
2 tablespoons butter

1 Peel the cucumber and cut in two, lengthwise. Scoop out the seeds and cut each side into 2 pieces. Season.

2 Butter a shallow, ovenproof dish and place the cucumber pieces on the dish.

3 Preheat the oven to 400°F.

4 Prepare the rice stuffing. Heat the oil in a pan and sauté the onions, without coloring, for 4 minutes. Add the mushrooms and pecans, then stir in the rice. Simmer for 2 minutes.

5 Add the garlic and water, then crumble in the bouillon cube. Cover the pan and boil gently for 15 minutes. Season with salt and pepper and mace, then add the butter. The rice should have absorbed all the liquid. Remove the garlic.

6 Pile the rice stuffing into the cucumber pieces and sprinkle with the grated cheese. Bake in the oven for 20 minutes.

Serves 4

Eggplants au Gratin

2 lbs. of eggplant
¼ cup salt
4 lbs. of tomatoes
5 tablespoons oil
salt and pepper
2 cloves garlic
1 bunch parsley
oil for deep frying
½ cup grated Gruyère
   cheese

1 Peel the eggplants. Cut into slices about ½ inch thick. Sprinkle with salt and leave for 20 minutes, wash and dry.

2 Meanwhile, skin the tomatoes and cut into halves. Remove the seeds and chop the pulp.

3 Heat 4 tablespoons of the oil in a skillet. Add the tomatoes. Cook gently for 15 minutes, mashing from time to time with a fork. Season with salt and pepper to taste.

4 Peel and chop the garlic. Wash and chop the parsley. Add the garlic and parsley to the tomato sauce.

5 Heat the deep fat fryer to 360°F.

6 Lower the eggplant slices into the hot oil and fry until they are golden brown. Remove from the oil and drain.

7 Preheat the oven to 425°F.

8 Arrange the slices of eggplant and the tomato sauce in alternate layers in an ovenproof dish, finishing with a layer of tomato sauce. Sprinkle with the Gruyère cheese and trickle the remaining 1 tablespoon of oil onto the top. Brown in the oven for about 10 minutes.

Serves 6

Stuffed Zucchini with Sausage Meat

4 large firm zucchini
sprig parsley
¼ lb. butter
1 tablespoon milk
1½ cups fresh breadcrumbs
1 teaspoon chopped chives
pinch dried thyme
¼ lb. sausage meat

1 Wash and dry the zucchini. Cut them in half lengthwise and scoop out the insides. Chop the parsley.

2 Using 1½ tablespoons of the butter, grease an ovenproof dish. Arrange the halved zucchini in the dish.

3 Put the milk, ½ cup breadcrumbs and ¼ cup of the butter in a small pan. Add the parsley, chives and thyme and cook for a few minutes, stirring.

4 Preheat the oven to 425°F.

5 Remove the pan from the heat and thoroughly mix in the sausage meat. Fill the zucchini shells with stuffing.

6 Sprinkle the remaining fresh breadcrumbs over the zucchini halves. Cut the remaining butter into small pieces and dot over the top.

7 Put the dish toward the top of the oven and bake for 25 minutes or until the topping is golden and the zucchini are tender.

Serves 4

Stuffed Cucumber Alphonso — hollowed out cucumbers stuffed with rice and mushrooms, and topped with melted cheese

Beef Casserole with Eggplant and Chickpeas

1 cup canned chickpeas
2 lbs. braising or stewing beef,
  e.g. chuck steak
¼ cup oil
1 teaspoon paprika
4 cloves garlic, peeled and crushed
2 chopped onions
2 tablespoons tomato paste
6⅓ cups water
4 medium eggplants
salt and pepper
oil for deep frying

1 Cut the steak into 1½-inch chunks. Heat a little oil in a large pan, and brown the meat and the paprika for 5-10 minutes, stirring occasionally.

2 Strain off excess oil. Add the strained chickpeas, garlic, onions, tomato paste and water. Bring to a boil, cover and simmer gently for 2–2½ hours.

3 Meanwhile, slice the eggplants, place on a dish or wooden board and sprinkle liberally with salt. Leave for 30 minutes, then rinse and dry the slices.

4 Heat the oil in a deep fryer to 360°F. Deep fry the eggplant slices until golden brown. Drain on absorbent paper.

5 Add the eggplant slices to the beef casserole, and season to taste with salt and pepper. Simmer for another 30 minutes. Serve immediately in a heated serving dish.

Serves 6

Tip: Like many other dishes originating in North Africa and the Middle East, this casserole should contain plenty of richly flavored

liquid which may be eaten with a spoon, like a soup.

Ratatouille

2 large eggplants
4 medium zucchini
½ cup flour seasoned with salt
oil for deep frying
¼ cup cooking oil
1 onion, chopped
1 clove garlic, chopped
2 green peppers, split, seeded,
  cut in strips
4 tomatoes, skinned, seeded and
  chopped
2 tablespoons tomato paste
1 sprig mint leaves
pinch oregano or basil
salt and pepper

1 Peel the eggplants and cut diagonally in ½-inch slices. Slice the zucchini diagonally. Sprinkle the eggplant and zucchini with salt and let them stand for 30 minutes.

2 Rinse, drain and dry the slices. Dredge in the seasoned flour. Heat the deep fryer to 375°F and fry the eggplant and zucchini slices for 1 minute.

3 Drain and dry the fried slices and place in a casserole dish.

4 In a saucepan, heat the oil. Sauté the onion gently for 2 minutes. Add the garlic and green pepper, and sauté for 2 minutes, stirring frequently.

5 Preheat the oven to 350°F.

6 Add the chopped tomatoes, tomato paste, mint, oregano or basil, and a pinch of salt and pepper to taste. Cover and simmer gently for 10 minutes.

7 Pour this mixture over the eggplants and zucchini in the casserole dish. Mix them together lightly and

bake in the oven for 20-30 minutes. Serve hot or cold.

Serves 6

Eggplant and Mushroom Quiche

1 large eggplant
1 pie crust
2 eggs
1¼ cups milk
¾ cup grated cheese
salt and pepper
¼ lb. small mushrooms or 2
  tomatoes, sliced

1 Preheat the oven to 400°F.

2 Bake the eggplant in its skin for 20 minutes.

3 Meanwhile, roll out the pastry and use it to line a 7-inch pie pan. Cover pastry with foil or parchment paper, scatter in the dried beans or bread crusts to weigh the pastry down, and bake in the same oven for 15 minutes. Remove the paper and beans or crusts. Reduce the oven temperature to 350°F.

4 Scoop the pulp out of the baked eggplant skin, crush or blend to a purée, and spoon into the pastry shell.

5 Beat the eggs lightly and mix in the milk. Add the grated cheese, salt and pepper. Pour the mixture into the pastry shell. Arrange the mushrooms (or tomatoes) on top.

6 Bake for 30 minutes, until the top is golden brown. Serve hot or cold.

Serves 4

Eggplant and Mushroom Quiche is easy to prepare and makes a tasty supper snack or buffet dish

Peppers & Tomatoes

Vegetable Casserole with Caraway Biscuits

¼ cup oil
1 onion, chopped
1 green pepper, seeded and cut in strips
1 sweet red pepper, seeded and cut in strips
1 carrot, sliced
salt and pepper
⅔ cup dry white wine
⅔ cup water
1 tablespoon soy sauce

For the Caraway Biscuits:
2¼ cups flour
1 teaspoon baking powder
¼ cup butter
1½ teaspoons caraway seeds
⅔ cup milk

1 Heat the oil in a pan, add the onion and cook for 5 minutes until soft. Add the peppers and carrots, stir well and season.

2 Add the wine, water and soy sauce, mix and cook, covered, for 20 minutes or until the carrots are tender. Check the seasoning.

3 Place the mixture in a shallow dish and keep warm.

4 Make the caraway biscuits: preheat the oven to 400°F.

5 Sift the flour and baking powder into a bowl, add a pinch of salt and cut in the butter. Add the caraway seeds and enough milk to make a stiff dough. Roll out the dough to ¼ inch thickness and cut into rounds.

6 Place the rounds on a greased baking sheet and brush the tops with a little cold milk. Bake in the preheated oven for 15 minutes.

7 Arrange the cooked biscuits around the vegetable casserole and serve.

Serves 4

Vegetable Casserole with Caraway Biscuits — an economical casserole with a delicious biscuit topping

Vegetable Curry

5 new potatoes, peeled
2 cups water
¼ cup butter
¼ cup oil
2 onions, chopped
2 tablespoons curry powder
pinch paprika
1 sweet red pepper, seeded and
    diced
1 green pepper, seeded and
    diced
4 zucchini, sliced
4 tomatoes, quartered
1 clove garlic, crushed
1 tablespoon shredded coconut
2 tablespoons flour
1 chicken bouillon cube
1 tablespoon tomato paste
⅓ cup golden raisins
salt and pepper

1 Put the potatoes and water in a pan, add a little salt, and boil for 20 minutes. Strain the liquid into a bowl and reserve.

2 Heat the butter and oil together in a pan, add the onion and cook for 5 minutes until brown.

3 Add the curry powder and paprika and cook for 2 minutes. Add the peppers, zucchini, tomatoes, garlic, coconut, flour, bouillon cube, tomato paste and raisins and cook gently for 10 minutes. Add the potatoes and cook for a further 10 minutes to heat the potatoes through. Check the seasoning and serve the curry with boiled rice and salted peanuts.

Serves 6

Stuffed Peppers with Pine Nuts

5 tablespoons oil
2 onions, chopped

Vegetable Curry is a delicious mixture of tomatoes, peppers, potatoes and zucchini in a curry sauce

2 tomatoes, skinned, seeded and
    chopped
⅔ cup long grain rice
1 tablespoon chopped parsley
1 tablespoon raisins
1 tablespoon pine nuts
3 cups boiling water
salt and pepper
4 large green or red peppers
3 tablespoons breadcrumbs

1 Heat 3 tablespoons of the oil in a saucepan. Sauté the onions until softened. Add the tomato pulp and cook over low heat.

2 Add the rice, parsley, raisins and pine nuts to the tomato mixture and stir well. Cook, stirring, for 2 minutes. Pour in the boiling water and add salt and pepper to taste. Cover the saucepan and simmer for 15 minutes over low heat. All the water should be absorbed.

3 Preheat the oven to 425°F.

4 Wash and dry the peppers. Cut out a little lid at the stalk end. Remove the white pith and seeds. Salt and pepper the insides.

5 Fill the peppers with the rice mixture. Place them in a baking dish. Replace the lids. Sprinkle the peppers with breadcrumbs and then with the rest of the oil. Put the dish in the oven and cook for 15 minutes. Serve hot or cold.

Serves 4

Green Beans Old Style

¼ cup butter
¼ lb. unsmoked bacon slices, cut into strips
12 pearl onions, peeled
12 young carrots, peeled
2 lbs. green beans, washed
2½ cups water
bouquet garni
salt and pepper
pinch sugar
1 chicken bouillon cube
¼ cup light cream

1 Heat the butter in a pan and sauté the bacon for 2 minutes. Add the onions and lightly brown them. Add the carrots and simmer for 3 minutes.

2 Add the green beans and cover with the water. Bring to a boil and crumble in a bouillon cube. Add the bouquet garni, salt, pepper and sugar. Cook for 20 minutes until the vegetables are tender and the liquid has almost evaporated. Remove the bouquet garni.

3 Stir in the cream, check the seasoning and serve.

Serves 4

Tip: If you boil the green beans separately in salted water and add them to the other ingredients at the last minute, they will retain their green coloring. However, although this method improves the appearance of the dish there may be a loss of flavor.

Green Bean Fritters

2 lbs. green beans
½ cup flour seasoned with salt
2 eggs, beaten
oil for deep frying
pinch salt

1 Trim and wash the beans. Boil in salted water for 12 minutes and drain.

2 Dredge the beans in seasoned flour and then dip in beaten egg.

3 Heat the deep fryer to 375°F. Fry the beans until golden brown.

4 Drain on absorbent paper, sprinkle with salt and serve.

Serves 6

Green Beans with Ham, Mushrooms and Tomatoes

2 lbs. green beans
¼ cup butter
¼ lb. ham, cut into strips
1¼ cups mushrooms, sliced
4 tomatoes, skinned, seeded and chopped
salt and pepper
pinch garlic salt

1 Trim and wash the beans. Boil them in salted water for 20 minutes and drain.

2 Heat the butter in a skillet. Sauté the ham and mushrooms for 5 minutes. Add the beans and tomatoes, salt, pepper and garlic salt.

3 Simmer for 6 minutes, stirring occasionally and then serve.

Serves 6

Peas Westminster

2 mint leaves
2 tablespoons brown sugar
1 lb. peas
¼ cup butter
salt and pepper

1 Chop the mint leaves and mix them with the brown sugar.

2 Add the peas to boiling salted water and parboil for 5 minutes. Rinse in cold water. Drain.

3 Heat the butter in a pan, add the peas, chopped mint and seasoning and toss until heated through. Serve.

Serves 4

Petits Pois à la Sevigné

¼ cup butter
1¼ cups pearl onions
2½ cups mushrooms
1 lb. small peas
salt and pepper
pinch caraway seeds
1½ teaspoons sugar
½ cup dry white wine
¼ cup light cream

1 Heat the butter in a pan, add the onions and cook, covered, for 5 minutes without browning. Add the mushrooms and cook for 1 minute more.

2 Add the peas to boiling salted water and parboil for 5 minutes. Drain and add to the onions. Season and add the caraway seeds, sugar and wine. Boil gently for 8 minutes, then stir in the cream. Boil for 4 minutes. Serve, decorated with fried croûtons.

Serves 4

Peas Bonne Femme

½ cup pearl onions
1 lb. peas
¼ lb. lean slices bacon, cut into thin strips

1¼ cups water
1 chicken bouillon cube
bouquet garni
salt and pepper
2 tablespoons butter
¼ cup flour

1 Parboil the pearl onions for 5 minutes and drain.

2 Place the peas, onions and bacon in a pan, cover with water and sprinkle in the bouillon cube. Add the bouquet garni, season with salt and pepper and cook for 20 minutes with the lid on.

3 Cream together the butter and flour and add to the peas, a little at a time. Stir over low heat until the sauce thickens. Remove the bouquet garni and serve.

Serves 6

Petits Pois à la Française

1 lb. small peas
2 cups pearl onions, peeled
½ cup shredded lettuce leaves
salt and pepper
1½ teaspoons sugar
1¼ cups water or stock
2 tablespoons flour
2 tablespoons butter

Green Beans Old Style — beans, onions, baby carrots and bacon served in a creamy sauce

---

1 Place the peas in a pan, add the onions, lettuce, salt, pepper and sugar. Add the water or stock and cook gently for 10-15 minutes. Strain, reserving the liquid. Keep the peas warm.

2 Pour the liquid into a pan. Blend the flour and butter together and add this mixture to the liquid. Cook until thickened and add to the peas. Mix well and serve.

Serves 4

Cabbage & Spinach

Bubble and Squeak (Colcannon)

½ medium cabbage
3 tablespoons butter or bacon fat
1 small onion, finely chopped
leftover mashed potato equal to
    the amount of cabbage

1 Bring water to a boil in a saucepan.

2 Remove the core and any damaged leaves from the cabbage. Shred the cabbage.

3 Put the cabbage into the water and cook for 6-7 minutes. Drain well.

4 Heat the butter or bacon fat in a large skillet. Sauté the onion gently until softened. Add the cabbage and stir over low heat for 2 minutes.

5 Fold in the mashed potato until it is completely mixed with the cabbage. Press the mixture lightly into the skillet to form a large pancake.

6 Cook for 5 minutes or until the underside is lightly browned. Turn and brown on the other side for 5 minutes. Serve very hot.

Serves 4

Tip: The easiest way to turn Bubble and Squeak is to put a plate over it and invert the pan and the plate together so it falls out onto the plate with the browned side uppermost. Then slide it back into the pan.

This is an excellent way of using up leftover cooked cabbage and mashed potatoes.

Spring Green Cabbage and Celery Royal

2 lbs. green cabbage
¼ cup butter
4 branches celery, sliced
salt and pepper
pinch nutmeg
¾ cup salted peanuts

1 Discard the core of the cabbage and slice the leaves. Boil the cabbage in salted water for 10 minutes. Drain.

2 Heat the butter in a pan, add the cabbage and celery and cook for 5 minutes. Season with salt, pepper and nutmeg. Serve sprinkled with the salted peanuts.

Serves 4

Tip: To make this into a main dish, add ⅔ cup ham, cut in strips, to the cooked cabbage and cook for a few minutes until the ham is heated through.

Spinach with Walnuts and Anchovies

2 lbs. cooked leaf spinach
4 canned anchovy fillets, drained
¼ lb. butter
1 cup shelled walnuts
salt and pepper
pinch mace
⅓ cup grated Parmesan cheese

1 Squeeze any moisture from the spinach and chop. Chop the anchovy fillets.

2 Heat the butter in a pan, add the spinach and cook, covered, for 10 minutes. Add the walnuts. Season with salt, pepper and mace and simmer for a further 5 minutes.

3 Transfer the mixture to a shallow dish, sprinkle with the cheese and brown under the broiler for 3-4 minutes.

Serves 4

Tip: Adding nuts to vegetables increases the protein content of the dish. Any nuts can be used such as pecan nuts, peanuts, almonds and hazelnuts.

Sprouts and Rutabaga with Chestnuts

1 lb. rutabaga, peeled and cut in cubes
1 lb. Brussels sprouts, trimmed
3 cups chestnuts, canned or fresh and skinned
¼ lb. butter
1 onion, chopped
1 small sweet red pepper, seeded and chopped
2 branches celery, diced
salt and pepper
pinch grated nutmeg

1 Boil the rutabaga, sprouts, and chestnuts separately in salted water for 5 minutes, 8 minutes and 10 minutes respectively. Drain.

2 Heat the butter in a pan, add the onion and cook for 4 minutes without browning. Add the rutabaga, sprouts, chestnuts, pepper and celery, cover and simmer gently for 8 minutes. Season with salt, pepper and nutmeg and serve.

Serves 6

Tip: To give the sprouts a good color, rinse them in ice water after they have been boiled and drained.

Cabbage is not the boring vegetable which many people imagine it to be. It can, in fact, be used in a wide range of delicious, easily prepared dishes. Featured opposite are Spicy Red Cabbage with Sausages, Stuffed Cabbage Leaves and Cabbage Coleslaw with Scotch Eggs

Stuffed Cabbage Provençale

2-lb. cabbage
½ cup fresh breadcrumbs
1 cup milk
½ lb. salt pork, blanched and finely chopped
¼ lb. lean bacon, finely chopped
¼ lb. lean veal, finely chopped
2 medium onions, chopped
2 cloves garlic, peeled and crushed
2 sprigs parsley, chopped
2 tablespoons oil
1 egg yolk
2 tablespoons tomato paste
2 tablespoons butter

For the Tomato Sauce:
2 tablespoons oil
1½ lbs. tomatoes, skinned, seeded and chopped
1 onion, chopped
2 cloves garlic, peeled and crushed
1 carrot, sliced
pinch dried thyme
1 bay leaf
1 tablespoon chopped parsley
salt and pepper

1 Remove the outer cabbage leaves and cut into wide strips. Keep the heart intact.

2 Add the cabbage strips to a pan of boiling water and simmer for 10 minutes. Drain and dry.

3 Prepare the sauce. Heat the oil and add the tomatoes, onion, garlic, carrot, thyme, bay leaf and parsley. Season and cook gently, stirring occasionally, for 5 minutes. Increase the heat and cook until the liquid has evaporated.

4 Strain and set aside.

5 Soak the breadcrumbs in the milk. Finely chop the cabbage heart and mix with the salt pork, bacon, veal, onions, garlic and parsley and season to taste.

6 Heat the oil in a skillet. Fry the mixture for a few minutes, remove from the heat.

7 Add the egg yolk and the tomato paste and mix well.

8 Divide the stuffing between the cabbage strips and roll up to make small parcels. Tie with string.

9 Heat the butter in a pan and sauté the cabbage parcels until golden brown.

10 Coat with the tomato sauce, cover and simmer for 20 minutes.

Stuffed Cabbage Provençale — cabbage parcels with a meaty stuffing served in a piquant tomato sauce

11 Arrange on a serving dish.

Serves 4

Cabbage and Bacon Hotpot

2 lbs. unsmoked ham shank
1 lb. lean bacon slab
6⅓ cups water
2-lb. cabbage, washed and quartered
4 branches celery, halved
4 leeks, cleaned and halved
3 onions, peeled and studded with cloves
4 carrots, peeled and quartered
4 small turnips, quartered
bouquet garni
3 cloves garlic, peeled and crushed
salt and pepper
2 beef bouillon cubes
½ lb. beef sausages

1 Soak the ham and bacon in water overnight and drain.

2 Cover the meat with the water and bring to a boil, then simmer for 1½ hours, removing the surface scum.

3 Add the cabbage, celery, leeks, onions, carrots, turnips, bouquet garni and garlic. Season and crumble in the bouillon cubes. Bring to a boil, then simmer for 20 minutes until tender.

4 Meanwhile, broil the beef sausages for 20 minutes, slice thickly and keep warm.

5 Add the cabbage to the hotpot and cook for a further 15 minutes. Strain off the liquid and place the vegetables on a serving dish.

6 Remove the cooked meat and cut into thick slices. Arrange the meat and sausages on top of the vegetables and serve.

Serves 8

Cabbage and Bacon Hotpot is a hearty meal of vegetables, ham and sausages for the whole family

Cauliflower & Broccoli

Broccoli with Red Pepper

2 lbs. broccoli
2 branches celery
¼ cup butter
1 small sweet red pepper, seeded and chopped
2 tablespoons lemon juice
salt and black pepper

1 Wash and trim the broccoli, discarding any slightly wilted leaves. Drain. Bring a pan of salted water to a boil. Put in the broccoli and simmer for 10-15 minutes or until tender.

2 Meanwhile, rinse, drain and chop the celery. Melt the butter in a small pan. Cook for 1 minute.

3 Add the chopped pepper to the celery with the lemon juice, salt and pepper.

4 Drain the broccoli very well. Put into a heated serving dish. Pour the contents of the small pan over the broccoli and serve.

Serves 4

Broccoli Siciliana

1 lb. broccoli
1 onion, chopped
¼ cup oil
2 anchovy fillets, diced
⅔ cup white wine
salt and pepper
4 pitted black olives

1 Preheat the oven to 350°F. Wash the broccoli and trim surplus stalks.

2 Boil the broccoli in salted water

for 10 minutes, then drain. Place in a casserole.

3 Gently sauté the onion in the oil without browning and when it is tender, add the anchovies and cook for a further 2 minutes.

4 Pour the onion mixture over the broccoli. Cover with white wine and season to taste.

5 Bake, with the lid on, for 20 minutes.

6 Garnish with the olives.

Serves 4

Cauliflower Cheese with Potatoes

1 small cauliflower
4 large potatoes, peeled and sliced
6 tablespoons butter
6 tablespoons flour
1½ cups milk
pinch grated nutmeg
salt and pepper
1 cup grated cheese

1 Bring a pan of salted water to a boil.

2 Clean the cauliflower, break it into small florets and rinse them. Put the potatoes into the boiling water. Cook for 10 minutes, then add the cauliflower. Continue to cook until the cauliflower is just tender but still firm.

3 Meanwhile, make a white sauce with 3 tablespoons of the butter, the flour, milk, a pinch of nutmeg and salt and pepper to taste. Add half the cheese and stir well until it is melted. Keep hot.

4 Drain the potatoes and cauliflower. Keep hot.

5 Use half of the remaining butter to grease an ovenproof dish. Heat the broiler.

6 Spread the drained potatoes and cauliflower evenly in the buttered dish and cover with the cheese sauce.

7 Sprinkle the remaining grated cheese over the top. Cut the rest of the butter into small pieces and dot over the top. Put the dish under the broiler and brown.

Serves 4-5

Hungarian Style Cauliflower

1 medium cauliflower

For the Sauce:
¼ cup oil
1 medium onion, sliced
1 tablespoon paprika
1 lb. corned beef, cut into strips
2 tablespoons tomato paste
4 tomatoes, skinned, seeded and chopped
1 sweet red pepper, seeded and cut into strips
1½ tablespoons cornstarch
½ cup sour cream
salt and pepper
1 tablespoon chopped parsley

1 Remove the leaves, wash the cauliflower and boil for 20 minutes in just enough salted water to cover. Reserve ½ pint of the cauliflower water. Keep the cauliflower hot.

2 Meanwhile, heat the oil and sauté the onion gently without browning. Add the paprika, the beef, the tomato paste, the tomatoes and red pepper strips and cook for 4 minutes. Stir in the reserved cauliflower stock and boil for 8 minutes. Mix the cornstarch with the cream and stir into the sauce and boil for 3 minutes until it thickens. Season.

3 Sprinkle the cauliflower with chopped parsley and serve the sauce separately.

Serves 4

Hungarian Style Cauliflower — Cauliflower served with strips of red pepper and beef in a paprika-flavored sauce

Stem Vegetables

Hungarian Asparagus with Yogurt

2 lbs. (about 28 spears) asparagus
1 cup very dry bread
6 tablespoons butter
2 cups plain yogurt
½ cup light cream
1 teaspoon paprika
salt and pepper

1 Bring a pan of salted water to a boil.

2 Peel the asparagus and tie in bundles. Plunge them in the boiling water, tips up, and simmer for 20 minutes.

3 In the meantime, cut off and discard the crust of the dry bread and make into very fine crumbs in a blender or with a rolling pin.

4 Melt the butter in a skillet. When it begins to brown, add the breadcrumbs and cook till golden brown, stirring with a wooden spoon.

5 Preheat the oven to 425°F.

6 Sprinkle about half the breadcrumbs in the bottom of an ovenproof dish.

7 Drain the bundles of asparagus, untie the strings and arrange in the dish. Beat the yogurt, the cream and the paprika together and salt lightly but season liberally with pepper. Pour over the asparagus and cover with the rest of the breadcrumbs.

8 Brown in the oven for 10-12 minutes.

9 Remove from the oven and serve very hot in the same dish.

Serves 4

Asparagus with Cheese and Ham Sauce

3 lbs. very tender asparagus spears
6 eggs
½ cup Gruyère cheese, grated
1½ tablespoons butter

Hungarian Asparagus with Yogurt — the asparagus spears are baked in yogurt, topped with breadcrumbs and seasoned with paprika

For the Sauce:
3 slices cooked ham
¼ cup butter
½ cup flour
1 cup milk
¼ cup light cream
salt and pepper
pinch grated nutmeg

1 Bring salted water to a boil in a large pan.

2 Scrape the asparagus spears, or peel them if necessary. Trim them all to the same length and tie into several bundles to make it easier to remove them from the water. Put them into the boiling water, keep-

ing the tips above the water level, cook for 10-15 minutes or until tender.

3 Meanwhile, hard-boil the eggs. Drain the eggs and cool in cold water. Remove the shells and slice the eggs.

4 Roughly chop the ham for the sauce.

5 Make a white sauce with the butter, flour, milk and 1 cup of the cooking liquid from the asparagus.

6 Stir in the cream and season with

salt, pepper and a pinch of grated nutmeg.

7 Mix in the chopped ham.

8 Spread a few spoonfuls of the sauce on the bottom of a rectangular or oval ovenproof dish.

9 Preheat the oven to 425°F.

10 Drain the asparagus and untie the strings. Arrange a layer of asparagus in the ovenproof dish. Cover with slices of egg and then with a few spoonfuls of sauce. Repeat until all the ingredients are used up.

11 Sprinkle the top of the dish with the grated Gruyère cheese.

12 Melt the 1½ tablespoons butter and pour over the cheese. Cook in the oven until the cheese is beginning to brown (about 10 minutes).

13 Serve very hot in the same dish.

Serves 6

Asparagus au Gratin

2 lbs. asparagus (about 28 spears)
4 tomatoes
½ cup grated cheese
1 tablespoon chopped parsley
salt and pepper
¼ cup butter

1 Wash the asparagus. Trim any tough parts from the thick end of the stalks, and scrape the stems lightly with a potato peeler. Tie in bundles of about 8 stalks, and boil for 15 minutes in salted water.

2 Preheat the oven to 400°F.

3 Drain the asparagus and arrange the spears in rows in a lightly greased, ovenproof dish.

4 Slice the tomatoes, and lay the slices in overlapping rows between the asparagus heads. Sprinkle with the grated cheese and chopped parsley. Season with the salt and pepper, and bake in the oven for 10 minutes. Melt the butter and pour over the dish before serving.

Serves 4

Tip: The inedible, tough ends of asparagus stalks, together with the cooking water, can be used to make a delicious soup. Just blend with an equal quantity of white sauce and a little chopped ham. Blend the mixture to a purée and season to taste.

Asparagus au Gratin — the asparagus is baked in the oven with sliced tomatoes and grated cheese

Braised Onions with Golden Raisins

1 lb. small onions
1¼ cups water
1 cup white wine vinegar
3 tablespoons olive oil
4 tomatoes, skinned
salt and freshly ground pepper
⅓ cup golden raisins
bouquet garni

2 pinches sugar

1 Peel the onions, without cutting off the root ends. Put the onions into a pan with the water and vinegar. Stir in the olive oil. Bring to a boil and simmer gently.

2 Slice the tomatoes thinly. Add to

Braised Onions with Golden Raisins — the onions are braised in a tangy tomato and vinegar sauce

the onions with a pinch of salt and pepper.

3 Add the golden raisins, bouquet garni and sugar.

4 Return to a boil. Reduce the heat. Cover and cook slowly for about 30 minutes, stirring occasionally.

5 Remove from the heat and cool. Chill for at least 2 hours.

6 Before serving, remove the bouquet garni.

Serves 4

Braised Onions in Vermouth

60 very small onions
juice 4 lemons
¼ cup dry vermouth
2 tablespoons olive oil
2 tablespoons tomato paste
30 coriander seeds
½ teaspoon fennel seeds
½ teaspoon dried rosemary
pinch sugar
salt and pepper

1 Peel the onions, without cutting off the root ends.

2 Put the lemon juice into a saucepan with the vermouth, olive oil and tomato paste. Stir well.

3 Bring the vermouth mixture to a boil. Add the coriander seeds, fennel, rosemary, sugar and season with salt and pepper.

4 Reduce the heat and cook for a further 3 minutes. Add the onions, cover and simmer for about 25 minutes or until very tender.

5 Arrange the onions in a serving dish. Pour on a little of the liquid in which they were cooked.

6 Cool completely, then chill in the refrigerator. Serve very cold.

Serves 6

Stuffed Onions

6 large Spanish onions
½ lb. pork sausage meat
1 egg
¼ cup milk
1 tablespoon chopped parsley
salt and pepper
1 cup breadcrumbs
½ cup oil

1 Peel the onions. Cut off one third at their tip ends, leaving the two thirds of the stem end. Boil them in salted water for 15 minutes, then drain.

2 Preheat the oven to 350°F.

3 Squeeze out the center of each onion, leaving the outer layers to form a case. Chop the squeezed-out onion, put it in a bowl and blend well with the sausage meat, egg, milk and parsley.

4 Fill each onion shell with the sausage meat mixture. Place the onions in a shallow dish, sprinkle with breadcrumbs and pour a little oil over each.

5 Bake in the oven for 45 minutes. Serve with a tomato sauce.

Serves 6

Tip: Sweet and Sour Onions make an excellent accompaniment to boiled beef or ham. Cook peeled pearl onions in a mixture of water, vinegar and sugar in the proportions of 2:1:1.

Onions in Cream Sauce

coarse salt
18 medium onions
6 tablespoons butter
1 tablespoon sugar
½ cup dry white wine
⅞ cup heavy cream
salt and freshly ground pepper
pinch ground ginger

few sprigs chervil, chopped

1 Bring a large pan of water to a boil. Add a handful of coarse salt.

2 Peel the onions, without cutting off the root end. Drop them into the boiling water and simmer until they begin to soften. Drain.

3 Melt the butter in a heavy-bottomed saucepan. Add the onions. Sprinkle them with the sugar and let them caramelize, turning gently with a wooden spoon without breaking them.

4 When the onions are well and evenly browned, pour them into a heated serving dish and keep hot.

5 Pour the wine into the saucepan.

Stuffed Onions are filled with sausage meat and parsley, topped with breadcrumbs and baked until crispy

Stir quickly to mix with the caramelized juices. Stir in the cream and let the sauce thicken over low heat, stirring constantly.

6 Season to taste with salt and pepper and the ground ginger. Pour this sauce over the onions.

7 Sprinkle the onions with the chopped chervil and serve very hot.

Serves 6

207

Leeks in Tomato Sauce

2 lbs. small leeks, washed and
   trimmed
½ lb. sliced carrots
1¼ cups water
salt

For the Sauce:
¼ cup oil
1 cup chopped onions
¼ cup tomato paste
1½ tablespoons cornstarch
⅔ cup water
salt and pepper
pinch sugar
pinch grated nutmeg
pinch dried basil or oregano

1 Boil the leeks and carrots in the water, adding salt to taste, for 15 minutes. Drain, keep warm and reserve cooking liquid.

2 To make the sauce: heat the oil in a skillet and sauté the chopped onions until they are soft but not brown (about 10 minutes).

3 Add the tomato paste and the liquid in which the leeks were cooked. Bring to a boil and simmer for 10 minutes.

4 Blend the cornstarch with the water and stir into the sauce. Cook for a further 5 minutes, then add seasonings to taste. Pour over the leeks and carrots and serve.

Serves 4

Braised Fennel

1 bulb fennel, about 1 lb.,
   trimmed and quartered
1 carrot, chopped
1 onion, chopped
⅓ cup bacon fat or oil
1 chicken bouillon cube dissolved
   in 2 cups water
salt and pepper

For the Sauce:
2 tablespoons butter
¼ cup flour
2 tablespoons tomato paste

1 Preheat the oven to 350°F.

2 Parboil the fennel in salted water for 5 minutes. Rinse.

3 Lightly sauté the carrot and onion in the bacon fat or oil in a skillet. Add the drained fennel, pour on the chicken stock and transfer to an ovenproof dish. Braise, covered, for 1 hour in the oven.

4 To make the sauce, prepare a roux with the butter and flour and stir in the tomato paste. Pour on the braising liquid (strained). Bring to a boil and season to taste. Simmer for 15 minutes and pour over the fennel.

Serves 4

---

*Celery and Onion Casserole —
onions, bacon and celery in a
tomato sauce make a delicious
snack or accompaniment to meat*

Celery and Onion Casserole

¼ cup oil
½ lb. diced slab bacon
½ lb. pearl onions, peeled
1 bunch celery, about 2 lbs.,
   trimmed into 4-inch pieces
1 tablespoon tomato paste
2 chicken bouillon cubes dissolved
   in 1¾ cups water
bouquet garni
salt and pepper

1 Preheat the oven to 350°F.

2 Heat the oil in a skillet, add the bacon and sauté for 4 minutes. Remove and add the peeled onions, then the celery. Cook for 5 minutes.

3 Stir in the tomato paste and pour in the chicken stock; add bouquet garni. Season, replace the bacon, and transfer to an ovenproof dish. Cover and cook in the oven for 35 minutes.

Serves 4

Spanish Artichokes

6 large artichokes
¾ cup long grain rice
2 peppers
1 onion
3 tomatoes
¾ lb. smoked lean bacon
2 cloves garlic
bunch parsley
5 tablespoons olive oil
pinch saffron
salt and pepper
½ lemon

1 Trim the artichokes by cutting the stalk and leaves 1¼ inches from the base. (Use a serrated knife or scissors for the leaves.) Wash and drain them.

2 Boil salted water in a large saucepan. Put in the artichokes and boil for 15 minutes.

3 Meanwhile, wash the rice until the water is quite clear.

4 Put the rice in twice its volume of boiling salted water, and simmer for 12 minutes.

5 Drain the rice, rinse it under cold running water, then drain once more.

6 Wash and dry the peppers. Split them in two and remove the seeds and white fiber. Dice. Peel and chop the onion. Peel the tomatoes, cut them in quarters, remove the seeds, then dice them also. Dice the bacon finely. Peel and chop the garlic cloves. Wash, dry and chop the parsley.

7 Heat 2 tablespoons olive oil in a sauté pan. Put in the diced bacon, onion and peppers, and fry.

8 When they are golden-brown, add the diced tomatoes, garlic, parsley, saffron and rice. Season with salt and pepper. Stir for 3 or 4 minutes over moderate heat.

9 Drain the artichokes, and put them in cold water, then drain and dry. Pull the outside leaves apart and, with a small spoon, remove the hairy centers (chokes) and little leaves. Fill the artichokes with the rice mixture.

10 Heat the rest of the oil in a sauté pan. Put in the artichokes, cover and leave to finish cooking on low heat for 40 minutes.

11 Squeeze the half lemon. Heat a serving dish.

12 Halfway through the cooking, add the lemon juice and 3 tablespoons hot water to the artichokes.

13 Arrange the artichokes on a serving dish and serve very hot.

Serves 6

Artichoke Hearts with Herbs

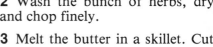

4 globe artichokes
½ lemon
large bunch chives, parsley and tarragon, mixed
3 tablespoons butter
salt and pepper

Trimmed and prepared artichoke in boiling water

For the blanching mixture:
2½ lemons
6⅓ cups water
1 tablespoon flour

1 Prepare the artichokes to give you 4 hearts (see page 55), then rub each heart all over with a ½ lemon. Prepare the blanching mixture with the lemons, water and flour and cook the hearts in the boiling liquid for 40 minutes or until tender. Drain them, rinse under cold water and cool.

2 Wash the bunch of herbs, dry and chop finely.

3 Melt the butter in a skillet. Cut the hearts into pieces and sauté them until they are golden-brown, then add the chopped herbs. Add a little pepper, mixing with the wooden spoon.

4 Warm a vegetable dish. Put in the artichoke hearts and serve hot.

Serves 4

Artichokes Stuffed with Vegetables

8 medium globe artichokes
1 lemon
4 onions
4 carrots
$\frac{1}{4}$ lb. lean bacon
scant 3 cups mushrooms
small bunch parsley
1 tablespoon olive oil
sprig sage
$\frac{1}{2}$ cup dry white wine
pinch dried thyme
salt and pepper

1 Break off the artichoke stems and rub each base with lemon. Also cut off the large leaves in a circle. Wash the artichokes under running water. Cook in boiling salted water for 25-30 minutes and then drain and keep hot.

2 Meanwhile, peel the onions and chop them roughly. Peel the carrots and cut them into matchsticks. Cut the bacon into small pieces. Prepare the mushrooms and cut into slices. Wash, dry and chop the parsley.

3 Fry the bacon and onions in the oil until the onions brown. Add the mushrooms, carrots, chopped pars-ley and sage. Let them brown also. Add the white wine and sprinkle in the thyme. Cover and simmer for about 20 minutes. Drain them and keep them hot.

4 Cut off the tops of the artichoke leaves and scoop out the choke. Stuff the artichokes with the bacon and vegetables.

Serves 8

Artichokes Stuffed with Vegetables — the shapely artichokes lend themselves to holding a variety of hot or cold fillings

All about Potatoes

Potatoes are part of the solanum family, which also includes tomatoes, eggplants—and deadly nightshade! Potatoes are an energy food—one of the cheapest we have. Although low in protein (3.8 percent), they are rich in carbohydrates, and contain vitamins B and C and iron (however, much of the vitamin C is lost in cooking). They provide an excellent food for a growing child. If a protein food

Potato and Leek Soup

such as eggs, cheese, fish or meat is included, potatoes are an invaluable aid toward a balanced diet.

Buy potatoes carefully—do not use them if their skins are green, if they are sprouting or suffering from frost damage. Store potatoes away from light—the cause of the inedible green patches—in an airy but not too cold place. At too low a temperature the potatoes can spoil and possibly freeze, which will give them a bitter taste.

It follows that the potatoes you put in your home freezer should either be cooked or partly cooked and wrapped (French fries are best frozen partly cooked). Commercial freezing is a different process.

Peeled potatoes should be kept in cold water or they will discolor. If peeled and left overnight in cold water, put them in the refrigerator, because they will ferment at room temperature.

Potatoes to be used for baking, for creamed or puréed dishes and for potato pancakes must be starchy when they are cooked. King Edwards, Majestics, the Dutch varieties, Idahos and Burbanks are all good examples of starchy potatoes which lend themselves to this form of cooking. Eat baked potatoes in their skins — this is where most of the vitamins, minerals and protein lie. Eat them with butter and Cheddar cheese, with blue cheese and sour cream, with freshly chopped chives or dill, and a generous sprinkling of salt and pepper. New potatoes boiled in their skins are delicious eaten hot with butter, salt, fresh mint or parsley — or as a potato salad, with mayonnaise or a vinaigrette dressing. Waxy, close-textured potatoes hold their shape after cooking; choose them to make chips, French fries, and the splendid sauté and gratin dishes you will find in this volume.

Throughout the centuries, botanists have been working toward perfecting the potato and eliminating the diseases to which it is prone. As a result, we now enjoy a wide range of varieties, with subtly different flavors and textures.

Boiled Potatoes

Potato and Leek Soup

2 small potatoes
$\frac{1}{2}$ lb. leeks
$\frac{1}{4}$ cup butter
1 tablespoon oil
$1\frac{1}{4}$ cups water
$\frac{2}{3}$ cup light cream
$\frac{2}{3}$ cup milk
salt and pepper
pinch nutmeg
1 tablespoon chopped parsley

1 Peel the potatoes. Slice and cut them into 1-inch strips.

2 Wash the leeks and trim off any wilted-looking leaves. Cut the leeks across in thin slices.

3 Heat the butter and oil in a saucepan and sauté the leeks for 2 minutes without browning them.

4 Add the potato strips, stir and cook for 2 minutes.

5 Add the water and boil for 12 minutes.

6 Stir in the cream and milk and reheat, then season to taste. Serve in a soup tureen, sprinkled with chopped parsley.

Serves 4

Tip: This soup can be blended, chilled and served cold with a sprinkling of chopped basil.

The Fisherman's Potato Hotpot

In many parts of the world the fisherman's diet has often been maintained with a fish and potato hotpot. Potatoes and onions are boiled for 10 minutes then white

fish steaks added and cooked like a hotpot, covered with a lid, for another 12 minutes. In just over 20 minutes a potato dish enriched with fish has been cooked.

On occasion, cider, wine or lemon juice is added with herbs to give the dish its characteristic distinction.

Potatoes Smitana

$1\frac{1}{2}$ lbs. new potatoes

For the Smitana Sauce:
2 tablespoons oil
2 tablespoons butter
1 medium onion, chopped
$1\frac{1}{4}$ cups light cream
salt and pepper
juice 1 lemon
1 tablespoon chopped parsley

1 Peel or scrape the potatoes.

2 Cook them in boiling salted water for 20 minutes.

3 Heat the oil and butter in a small saucepan. Gently sauté the onion for 2 minutes without coloring it.

4 Add the cream and season with salt and pepper. Boil for 5 minutes.

5 Remove from the heat and add the lemon juice.

6 Place the potatoes in a shallow dish, pour the sauce over them and sprinkle with chopped parsley.

Serves 4

Tip: When available, use sour cream for this sauce and omit the lemon juice.

Roast Potatoes au Gratin, Anna Potatoes and Potatoes Savoyarde — some delicious potato dishes

Potato and Onion Pancakes

4 medium-size potatoes
coarse salt
6 tablespoons butter
2 medium onions, chopped
salt and pepper
1 egg
pinch coriander and mace, mixed
½ cup flour
tomato slices and parsley

1 Scrub the potatoes. Put them into a saucepan, cover with cold water and add a handful of salt. Bring to a boil and simmer for 30 minutes.

2 Meanwhile, melt 2 tablespoons of the butter in a skillet. Add the onions and sauté gently until they are soft and brown. Season well with salt and pepper.

3 When the potatoes are cooked, drain and peel them. Work them through a food mill or strainer to make a purée.

4 Put the potato purée into a saucepan. Break the egg into the center, and stir over low heat until reheated and well mixed. Season generously with salt, pepper, and mixed spice.

5 Carefully stir the onions into the potato purée. Divide into 4 small heaps and flatten each into a small circle. Coat on both sides with the flour.

6 Melt the rest of the butter in a skillet. Put in the pancakes and fry until browned on both sides.

---

*Potato and Onion Pancakes —
the potatoes are first puréed, then
molded into flat cakes and
shallow-fried*

7 Drain them on absorbent paper. Arrange on a heated serving dish garnished with tomato slices and parsley.
Serves 4

Flavorings
To preserve all their flavor, boil and serve potatoes hot in their jackets. Potatoes which are to be sautéed or used in salads should be boiled in their skins, cooked, drained, peeled while they are warm and left covered in the refrigerator overnight so that they can be shaped without breaking.

The main flavoring for boiled potatoes is fresh butter, added at the last minute so that the heat of the potatoes melts it. Or add a few fresh mint leaves or freshly chopped parsley 5 minutes before they finish cooking.

Potato Casseroles

Lamb Navarin with New Potatoes

1¼ lbs. stewing lamb
salt and pepper
2 tablespoons butter
1 cup diced carrots
½ cup diced onion
¼ cup flour
1 tablespoon tomato paste
1 clove garlic
3⅔ cups beef stock
bouquet garni
1 lb. new potatoes
1 tablespoon chopped parsley

1 Preheat the oven to 350°F. Trim the meat into uniform pieces and season.

2 Heat the butter in an ovenproof casserole, add the meat and fry for 5 minutes. Add the chopped carrot and onion and cook for a further 3 minutes.

3 Drain off the surplus fat, add the flour and mix. Cook for 5 minutes until browned.

4 Add the tomato paste and garlic and then stir in the stock and seasoning. Add the bouquet garni, bring to a boil, skim, and cover with a lid. Cook in the preheated oven for 1½ hours.

5 Meanwhile, parboil the new potatoes in salted water for 10 minutes.

6 After 1½ hours, remove the casserole from the oven and add the potatoes. Return to the oven and cook for a further ½ hour or until the meat and potatoes are tender.

7 Arrange the meat and vegetables on a warm serving dish, correct the seasoning of the liquid and pour over. Sprinkle with the chopped parsley.

Serves 4

Lamb Navarin with New Potatoes is a tasty casserole of lamb, carrots and potatoes in a beefy sauce

Look 'n Cook Potato and Sauerkraut Hotpot

1 The ingredients: sauerkraut, frankfurters, meat, potatoes, bouquet garni, onions, garlic, wine, fat, peppercorns, juniper berries, carrots, bay leaves, cloves, seasoning **2** Wash the sauerkraut and then dry thoroughly, squeezing between the hands to remove excess moisture **3** Spread out the sauerkraut **4** Melt the chicken fat or butter in a pan and pour it over the sauerkraut. Mix well **5** Transfer half of the sauerkraut to

an ovenproof dish and add the carrots and the onions studded with cloves **6** Tie the garlic, peppercorns and juniper berries in a small piece of cheesecloth and add the bag to the sauerkraut with the bouquet garni, bay leaves and seasoning **7** Cover with the rest of the sauerkraut **8** Add the gin, if used, and the water and

Look 'n Cook Potato and Sauerkraut Hotpot (continued)

wine **9** Cover with foil and bake in the preheated oven for 20 minutes **10** Remove the foil and place the meat on top of the sauerkraut. Bring to a boil, cover and simmer for 1¼ hours **11** Lift out the meat; transfer to the oven to keep warm **12** Add the potatoes, cover again and simmer for 20 minutes or until the potatoes are cooked and the liquid has almost evaporated **13** Add the frankfurters to a pan of boiling water and simmer

14

15

16

for 8 minutes to warm through. Drain **14** When the potatoes are cooked, discard the carrots, bouquet garni, onions and cheesecloth bag. Pile the sauerkraut on a serving dish **15** Remove the meat from the oven and cut into neat slices **16** Arrange the meat slices around the sauerkraut with the frankfurters and potatoes

Potato and Sauerkraut Hotpot

2 lbs. canned sauerkraut
¼ lb. chicken fat or butter
6 black peppercorns
1 clove garlic, crushed
6 juniper berries or 2 tablespoons gin
4 carrots
2 onions, studded with 4 cloves
bouquet garni
2 bay leaves
salt and pepper
1¼ cups dry white wine
2½ cups water
1 lb. piece unsmoked ham or bacon
1½ lb. ham shank
6 medium-size potatoes, peeled
6 frankfurters

1 Preheat the oven to 400°F. Wash the sauerkraut and then drain, pressing well to remove moisture.

2 Place the dried sauerkraut in a dish. Warm the fat in a pan and mix it with the sauerkraut.

3 Tie the peppercorns, garlic and juniper berries in a small piece of cheesecloth. Transfer half of the sauerkraut to an ovenproof dish and add the cheesecloth bag, carrots, onions, bouquet garni, bay leaves and seasoning. Cover with the rest of the sauerkraut. Pour in the gin, if used, and the wine and water. Cover the dish with foil and bake for 20 minutes.

4 Remove the foil and add the meat. Bring to a boil, cover and simmer for 1¼ hours.

5 Lift out the meat and add the potatoes. Cover again and cook for 20 minutes or until they are cooked and the liquid has almost evaporated. Meanwhile, keep the meat warm in the oven.

6 Add the frankfurters to a pan of boiling water and simmer for 8 minutes until warmed through. Drain.

7 Discard the cheesecloth bag, carrots, bouquet garni and onions. Place the sauerkraut on a serving dish. Cut the meat into neat slices and arrange them around the pile of sauerkraut with the frankfurters and potatoes.

Serves 6

Tip: To save time, the meat can be cooked beforehand. Simply boil it in water for 1½ hours and then reheat by covering with cold water, bringing it to a boil and simmering for 20 minutes. If too salty, soak the meat in cold water overnight.

Farmhouse Potato and Chicken Casserole

6 tablespoons cornstarch
salt and pepper
4 chicken legs
¼ cup butter
2 tablespoons oil
6 medium-size potatoes, peeled and quartered
4 slices lean bacon, cut in strips
½ cup mushrooms, quartered
6 scallions
⅔ cup chicken stock
1 tablespoon chopped chives

1 Preheat the oven to 375°F. Season the cornstarch and use it to coat the chicken legs.

2 Heat the butter and oil in a pan, and fry the chicken legs until golden.

3 Remove the chicken from the pan and place in an ovenproof casserole with the potatoes.

4 Add the bacon, mushrooms and onions to the pan and sauté until golden. Add to the casserole. Pour the stock into the pan and bring to a boil, stirring. Pour the stock into the casserole. Cover the dish and bake in the preheated oven for 1 hour or until the chicken is tender.

5 Check the seasoning of the sauce and sprinkle the finished dish with the chopped chives.

Serves 4

Old Country Potato Hotpot

3 medium-size potatoes
1 onion
2 leeks, white part only
2 branches celery
1 chicken breast
1 slice unsmoked bacon
2 tablespoons butter
¼ cup oil
2 chicken bouillon cubes
4¼ cups water
salt and pepper
juice ½ lemon
⅔ cup light cream
1 tablespoon chopped parsley and chervil

1 Cut the potatoes, onion, leek and celery into thin strips, 2 by ¼ inches.

2 Skin the chicken breast and remove the bone. Cut the chicken and bacon into strips of the same size.

3 Heat the butter and oil in a pan, add the vegetable and meat strips and cook, covered, for 5 minutes.

4 Crumble the bouillon cubes into the water and add to the pan. Bring to a boil and simmer for 20 minutes.

5 Add seasoning and lemon juice. Stir in the cream and boil for 2 minutes more. Serve sprinkled with the chopped herbs.

Serves 4

Farmhouse Potato and Chicken Casserole — an economical family casserole of chicken, potatoes and mushrooms

Mashed Potatoes

For perfect mashed potatoes every time, drain the cooked potatoes thoroughly before mashing them. Return them to the pan and place over low heat, uncovered, for 3-4 minutes to evaporate the last drops of moisture.

Curried Shepherds Pie

3 medium-size potatoes
salt and pepper
2-4 tablespoons butter
a little milk
¾ tablespoon cornstarch
⅔ cup beef stock
3 tablespoons butter

½ cup onion, finely chopped
1 lb. ground cooked lamb
1 tablespoon curry powder

1 Cook the potatoes in boiling salted water until just tender. Mash with a fork or masher, adding butter and milk to give a smooth consistency. Season to taste.

2 Preheat the oven to 400°F. To the cornstarch add 5 tablespoons water and stir to make a smooth paste. Bring the stock to a boil, add the cornstarch and continue cooking until thickened.

3 Heat the remaining butter in a pan, add the chopped onion and sauté for 5 minutes without coloring. Add the ground meat and seasoning. Stir in the curry powder and add sufficient thickened stock to bind. Bring to a boil and simmer for 10-15 minutes.

Curried Shepherds Pie —curried lamb with a crisp potato topping is a variation on the traditional Shepherds Pie

4 Transfer the meat to a pie dish and arrange the potato on top. Make swirls on the top of the potato with a fork and place in the preheated oven for 10 minutes to brown.

Serves 4

Tip: Cooked beef can also be used in this dish. When using cooked meat, be sure to heat the meat thoroughly.

Coconut Potato Cake

3 medium-size potatoes, unpeeled
3 egg yolks
1 teaspoon lemon juice
1 tablespoon butter
¼ cup milk
salt
1 tablespoon grated cheese
5 tablespoons shredded coconut

For the Garnish:
slices bacon or sausage
strips red pepper
few stuffed olives

1 Preheat the oven to 350°F. Boil the potatoes in their skins until cooked. Drain.

2 Beat the egg yolks with the lemon juice. Grease an 8-inch pie plate with the butter. Peel the potatoes, mash and mix with the egg yolks, milk and salt. Beat for 1 minute.

3 Turn the potato into the pie plate, level the top and sprinkle with the cheese and coconut. Bake in the oven for 15-20 minutes until browned on top.

4 Turn the cake onto a warm dish and garnish with the meat slices, pepper strips and olives. Cut in slices to serve.

Serves 4

1 Peel and quarter some large potatoes. Place in cold salted water, bring to a boil and cook until just tender. Drain and place in a hot oven to dry **2** Work the potatoes through a food mill **3** and **4** For every 2 lbs. potatoes, mix in 4 tablespoons butter, 2 egg yolks, salt and pepper and grated nutmeg to taste. If liked, color some of the potato with tomato paste and a pinch of paprika **5** Spoon the potato into a piping bag fitted with a large star nozzle **6** and **7** Use the duchesse potato mixture to pipe attractive borders around a serving dish or around the edge of scallop shells **8** Or, pipe different shapes, such as swirls, cones and nests, onto a greased baking sheet. To make the nest, pipe a flat round for the base and then build up the sides, around and around **9** and **10** For better color, brush with beaten egg. Place the sheet in the oven to dry out the potato and brown the tops

Duchesse Potatoes

6 medium-size potatoes, peeled
2 egg yolks, beaten
¼ cup butter
salt and pepper
pinch grated nutmeg
1 egg, beaten

1 Preheat the oven to 400°F.

2 Boil the potatoes in salted water, when soft but not mushy, drain. Return to the pan, and shake gently over medium heat to dry thoroughly.

Duchesse Potatoes with Almonds — duchesse potato nests filled with chicken in a sherry sauce and topped with flaked almonds

3 Mash and blend in the egg yolks and butter. Season and add a pinch of nutmeg.

4 Pass the potatoes through a strainer or food mill.

5 Lightly oil a baking sheet. Fill a piping bag with the potato mixture and fit with a star-shaped nozzle. Pipe the mixture onto the sheet, forming small cones. Bake in the oven for 15 minutes.

6 Take out and brush the cones with the beaten egg. Return to the oven for 4-5 minutes to brown. Serve immediately.

Serves 6

Tip: Pipe duchesse potatoes in a variety of different shapes and sizes. Tiny rosettes, topped with grated cheese or chopped nuts, are delicious with cocktails.

Use your favorite pastry shell filling with duchesse potato nests. Any kind of creamy, savory mixture of meat, fish or vegetables is suitable.

Duchesse Potatoes with Almonds

2 cups duchesse potato mixture
1 beaten egg
2 tablespoons melted butter

For the Filling:
⅓ cup medium sherry
1⅓ cups diced, cooked turkey or chicken
1¼ cups white sauce
1 egg yolk

Duchesse Potatoes can be piped into decorative pyramids, glazed with beaten egg and browned in a hot oven

Duchesse Potato and Shrimp Scallops — the scallop shells are filled with shrimp and tomato sauce and surrounded with piped duchesse potato

¼ **cup heavy cream**
salt and pepper
pinch grated nutmeg
⅓ **cup sliced almonds, toasted**

1 Preheat the oven to 350°F.

2 Fill a piping bag with the duchesse potato mixture and fit it with a star-shaped nozzle. Pipe the mixture neatly onto a greased baking sheet to make six nest shapes.

3 Dry in the oven for 10 minutes, then brush the potato nests with the beaten egg. Return to the oven for 4-5 minutes. Take out and keep warm.

4 Next make the filling. Pour the sherry into a saucepan, add the turkey or chicken and bring to a boil. Stir in the white sauce and reduce heat to simmering. Take off the heat, blend in the egg yolk and cream and season with salt and pepper and grated nutmeg. Return to the heat, stirring all the time.

5 Fill each potato nest with the sauce and sprinkle on the sliced almonds. Brush the potato with the melted butter and return to the oven for 4-5 minutes. Serve immediately.

Serves 6

Duchesse Potato and Shrimp Scallops

4 scallop shells
1 cup duchesse potato mixture
1 beaten egg
2 tablespoons melted butter

For the Filling:
2 tablespoons oil
2 tablespoons butter
1 onion, finely chopped
1 tablespoon flour
4 tomatoes, peeled, seeded and chopped
1 tablespoon tomato paste
⅔ **cup water**
½ **chicken bouillon cube**
1 tablespoon anchovy paste
juice ½ lemon
salt and pepper
½ **lb. peeled, deveined shrimp**

1 Preheat the oven to 350°F.

2 Using a piping bag with a star-shaped nozzle, pipe the edges of the scallop shells with the duchesse potato mixture. Place them on a baking sheet and dry in the oven for 10 minutes. Remove and brush the potato with the beaten egg.

3 Now make the filling. Heat the oil and the butter in a skillet, and gently sauté the chopped onion until it is soft but not brown — about 5 minutes. Stir in the flour and cook for 2 minutes more.

4 Add the chopped tomatoes and the tomato paste. Pour in the water and add the crumbled ½ bouillon cube. Bring to a boil, then simmer for 5 minutes.

5 Flavor the sauce with the anchovy paste, lemon juice and salt and pepper to taste. Add the peeled shrimp, bring to a boil again, then cook gently for a further 5-6 minutes.

6 Increase the heat of the oven to 400°F.

7 Fill each scallop shell with the shrimp and tomato sauce inside the border of piped potato. Place them on the baking sheet and bake for 8 minutes, until the potato is golden brown. Take out, brush the potato with melted butter and serve immediately.

Serves 4

Baked Potatoes

Potatoes are delicious, peeled and baked in a sauce in the oven, or baked in their skins. You can eat the skin — it contains essential minerals and vitamin C. Baking potatoes in their skins retains all the goodness which can be lost by boiling or frying.

Always wash and scrub the potatoes well and make a cross-shaped incision or prick each potato with a fork before baking. If you prefer your potatoes soft-skinned, wrap each potato in aluminum foil. Baking the potato with a thin, metal skewer inserted through the center ensures that the heat is conducted right through the potato.

Potato Feast

Potatoes can make a main meal or an excellent party dish if baked in their skins and served with a variety of toppings, fillings and sauces. Here are some ideas for you to try out. They are sufficient to stuff or top 10 medium-size potatoes.

Sour Cream and Chive Topping

1 tablespoon chopped chives
⅔ cup sour cream or plain yogurt
salt and pepper

Potato Feast — serve baked potatoes as a party dish, with a variety of tasty fillings and toppings

1 Blend together the chives and sour cream. Season with salt and pepper.

2 Top each baked potato with a swirl of sour cream mixture or serve separately.

Bacon and Onion Topping

¼ lb. bacon slices
2 tablespoons bacon fat
½ cup chopped onions

1 Cut the bacon into thin strips.

2 Heat the bacon fat in a skillet and fry the bacon for 3 minutes. Remove and keep warm.

3 Add the onions to the skillet and sauté until soft and light brown. Drain off the fat and mix with the bacon.

4 Serve in a separate bowl or as a topping for baked potatoes. Alternatively, you can mix the bacon mixture with scooped out potato pulp and butter and replace inside the potato skin.

Tomato Fondue

2 tablespoons oil
1 small onion, chopped
1 clove garlic, peeled and chopped
4 tomatoes, skinned, seeded and chopped
⅔ cup mayonnaise
salt and pepper

1 Heat the oil in a skillet, add the chopped onions and sauté until soft. Add the garlic and tomatoes and simmer for 4 minutes. Cool and strain.

2 Blend this tomato mixture with the mayonnaise and season. Top each potato with the mixture or serve in a separate dish.

Baked Potatoes au Gratin

4 medium-size potatoes

For the Filling:
¼ cup butter
¼ cup chopped ham
1 tablespoon chopped chives
salt
freshly ground black pepper
1 cup grated Cheddar cheese
few sprigs parsley

1 Preheat the oven to 400°F.

2 Wash and scrub the potatoes. Prick the skins and place on a baking sheet. Bake in the oven for about 1 hour.

3 Cut the cooked potatoes lengthwise and scoop out the pulp. Place the potato pulp in a bowl and mix

Baked Potatoes au Gratin are filled with ham and chopped chives and topped with melted Cheddar cheese

with the butter, chopped ham and chives until it is soft and well blended. Season with salt and freshly ground pepper.

4 Place the potato mixture back inside the potato skins and sprinkle with the grated cheese.

5 Place under a hot broiler until the cheese is bubbling and golden brown. Top each potato with a sprig of parsley.

Serves 4

Tip: If you sprinkle a layer of coarse salt between the potatoes and the baking sheet it will prevent the potato skins from burning.

Potatoes Gratin Dauphinois

6 medium-size potatoes
1 clove garlic, peeled and crushed
¼ lb. butter, softened
2 eggs
2¼ cups milk
¾ cup light cream
salt and pepper
grated nutmeg
1 cup grated Gruyère cheese

1 Preheat the oven to 400°F.

2 Peel the potatoes, place in a pan of salted water and bring to a boil. Boil for 1 minute, then cool and slice thinly.

3 Rub the garlic around the inside of an ovenproof dish. Use ¼ cup butter to grease the dish.

4 Break the eggs into a bowl, add the milk, cream, salt and pepper and nutmeg and beat. Stir in ¾ cup of the grated cheese.

5 Cover the bottom of the greased dish with a layer of potato slices. Cover with a little of the cream and cheese mixture. Continue with alternate layers of potato and cheese until they are used up. Sprinkle the top with the remainder of the grated cheese and dot with butter.

6 Bake in the oven for 45 minutes. Cover with foil if it becomes too brown. Serve with roast meat or steak.

Serves 4

Tip: For delicious variations, try adding layers of sautéed, sliced mushrooms and chopped onions. Never use raw potatoes in this dish — very often they will cause the milk to curdle. Parboiling the potatoes first or thickening the milk with cornstarch will prevent this.

228

Baked Potatoes Stuffed with Shrimp

8 medium-size potatoes
¼ cup butter
⅔ cup plain yogurt
1 tablespoon catsup
½ lb. peeled shrimp
1 tablespoon chopped chives
salt and pepper
1 tablespoon paprika

1 Preheat the oven to 400°F.

2 Wash and scrub the potatoes and bake in the oven for about 1 hour.

3 Make a criss-cross on the top of each potato with a knife or prick skins with a fork. Remove most of the pulp and mix it in a bowl with the butter, yogurt, catsup, shrimp and chives. Season with salt and pepper.

Baked Potatoes Stuffed with Shrimp make an excellent party dish or supper snack

4 Place the mixture inside the potato skins and warm through in the oven. Sprinkle with paprika and serve.

Serves 4

Tip: A more sophisticated way to serve baked potatoes is to scoop out the potato pulp and mix with beaten egg, butter and light cream. Strain or blend the mixture to a purée. Fill the potato skin with shrimp, mushrooms or chicken in a sauce, and pipe the puréed potato mixture around the edge. Brush with beaten egg and broil until golden brown.

Roast Potatoes

Roast potatoes must be crisp and golden brown on the outside, starchy inside. Roast separately or with the meat and always baste during cooking. Large potatoes may be browned for a few minutes in beef drippings, then, after the drippings have been poured away, roasted in beef stock and meat glaze for 45 minutes until they are glazed, soft and brown. Other root vegetables such as parsnips, Jerusalem artichokes, carrots and sweet potatoes can also be roasted.

Traditional Sunday roast with roast potatoes

Roast Potatoes

8 small potatoes
1½ cups beef drippings
salt
¼ cup butter

1 Preheat the oven to 400°F.

2 Peel the potatoes and cut each in half lengthwise. Soak in a pan of cold, salted water.

3 Place the drippings in a shallow, ovenproof dish. Melt the drippings on top of the stove.

4 Dry the potatoes and place them in the dish. Season with salt and roast in the oven for 25 minutes, basting.

5 Drain off the drippings. Add the butter to the potatoes and roast for 5 minutes.

Serves 4

Honeyed Roast Potatoes

10 new potatoes
salt
⅓ cup oil
⅓ cup butter, melted
¼ cup honey

1 Preheat the oven to 400°F.

2 Place the potatoes in a pan of cold, salted water. Bring to a boil, then drain immediately.

3 Place the oil and 2 tablespoons of the butter in a shallow, ovenproof dish.

4 Season the potatoes with salt, and place them in the dish. Roast in the oven for 20 minutes.

5 Mix the remaining butter with the honey. Use it to baste the potatoes while they roast.

Serves 4

Sautéed Potatoes

Potatoes are excellent sautéed — that is, cooked in a skillet over high heat with the pan shaken so that the food literally jumps. (*Sauter* means "to jump" in French.) A mixture of oil and clarified butter makes an ideal cooking medium, and the potatoes may be raw or boiled and sliced. If you use raw potatoes, make sure that they are thoroughly dried on absorbent paper before they are cooked, and use a skillet with a lid. This speeds up the cooking and allows you to toss them in the fat more easily. When the po-tatoes are nearly cooked, try adding sliced onions, tomato pulp, chopped garlic or herbs.

Sautéed Potatoes with Chicken and Mushrooms in Sour Cream

2 tablespoons oil
3 medium-size potatoes, boiled and sliced
salt and pepper

For the Filling:
2 tablespoons butter
1 onion, chopped
1 cup mushrooms, sliced
1⅓ cups diced cooked chicken
½ cup sour cream
2 tablespoons medium sherry
pinch paprika

1 Heat the oil in a skillet. Sauté the potatoes until they are golden brown. Season, remove from the pan and keep hot.

2 In the same skillet, melt the butter and sauté the chopped onion gently for 4 minutes. Stir in the mushrooms and diced chicken and cook for 4 minutes.

3 Pour in the cream and the sherry, bring to a boil, and cook for a further 5 minutes.

4 Surround the mixture with the overlapping sautéed potatoes, sprinkle on the paprika and serve immediately, using the skillet as the serving dish.

Serves 4

Sautéed Potatoes with Chicken and Mushrooms in Sour Cream — the creamy sauce is surrounded by overlapping sautéed potatoes and served straight from the pan

Fried Potatoes

Crispy Pan-fried Potatoes with Bacon

¼ cup oil
¼ cup bacon fat or butter
4 slices bacon, cut into strips
1 onion, chopped
¾ cup mushrooms, sliced
3 medium-size cold boiled
  potatoes, sliced
salt and pepper

1 Heat the oil and fat in a skillet and fry the bacon until crisp (about 2 minutes). Remove from the pan and keep warm.

2 In the same pan, sauté the chopped onions and mushrooms for 2-3 minutes. Remove from the pan and keep warm.

3 Add the potatoes to the pan and sauté (with the lid on), turning them several times until they are golden brown.

4 Return the bacon, mushrooms and onions to the pan and season with the salt and pepper. Heat through. Serve immediately as a snack with sausages or hamburgers.

Serves 4

French Fried Potatoes

6 medium potatoes
deep fat bath
salt

1 Peel the potatoes, slice them lengthwise and then cut into strips. Put into a bowl of ice water for 10 minutes, then drain and dry well on absorbent paper.

2 Heat the fat to 375°F. Put a handful of potato slices into the frying basket (if used) and lower carefully into the fat. Fry for about 8 minutes (the potatoes should not brown at this stage). Drain on absorbent paper.

3 Continue to fry in this way until all the potatoes are partially cooked, then increase the heat to 400°F. Add all the potatoes and fry until they are crisp and golden brown (about 3 minutes).

4 Drain on absorbent paper, sprinkle with salt and serve at once.

Serves 4

Tip: Do not cover the potatoes with absorbent paper or the steam will not be able to escape and the potatoes will lose their crispness.

After the first stage in cooking, the fries may be left for a while and the second frying process carried out just before serving.

Crispy Pan-fried Potatoes with Bacon is a quick and easy to prepare meal for the whole family

Mushroom Stuffed Potato Pancakes

2⅔ cups potatoes, peeled and
  grated
2 eggs, beaten
salt and pepper
1 onion, chopped or grated
1 cup + 2 tablespoons sifted flour
1 teaspoon baking powder
⅓ cup milk
⅔ cup oil
1 tomato, quartered

For the Filling:
2 tablespoons oil
2 tablespoons butter
5 cups mushrooms, sliced
1 cup fresh breadcrumbs
1 tablespoon chopped parsley

salt and pepper
¼ cup heavy cream

1 Place the grated potatoes in a clean kitchen towel and gently squeeze out the moisture, then place in a bowl.

2 Blend in the beaten eggs, seasoning and chopped or grated onion. Add the flour and baking powder. Gradually add the milk, beating all the time, to form a thick batter.

3 Heat 2 tablespoons oil in a skillet. Drop in 2 or 3 spoonfuls of the mixture. When it is cooked underneath, turn the pancake over and cook the other side. Remove and keep warm. Repeat until all the

Mushroom Stuffed Potato Pancakes are pancakes with a difference — they are made with fried potato, not batter

mixture is used up (it should make 4 pancakes).

4 Meanwhile, make the filling. Heat the oil and butter in a skillet and sauté the mushrooms for 4 minutes until soft. Mix in the breadcrumbs, chopped parsley and seasoning. Then stir in the cream. Gently heat the filling through.

5 Place some mushroom filling in each pancake, fold over and serve. Garnish with tomato quarters.

Serves 4

1 Place the potatoes in salted water, bring to a boil and simmer until cooked **2** Sieve the potatoes, or mash until there are no lumps **3** Prepare the choux pastry: put the water, butter, salt and grated nutmeg in a pan and bring to a rolling boil **4** Sift the flour **5** When the water is boiling, remove the pan from the heat and add the flour, all at once, and beat **6** Return the pan to the heat and stir until the mixture no longer sticks to

233

the pan or wooden spoon **7** Away from the heat, beat in the eggs, one by one. The paste should be soft but not runny **8** Stir in the mashed potato **9** Add the Gruyère cheese (optional) **10** and **11** Heat the deep fryer and, using a spoon or a piping bag, add pieces of the potato/choux paste mixture and cook until golden brown **12** Put in a bowl and serve

Potatoes Dauphine

3 medium-size potatoes
1 egg yolk
2 tablespoons butter
salt and pepper
oil for deep frying

For the Choux Paste:
⅔ cup water
¼ cup butter
pinch salt
pinch grated nutmeg
1 cup + 2 tablespoons sifted
   all-purpose flour
2 eggs

1 Wash, peel and slice the potatoes. Boil in salted water for 15 minutes, then drain.

2 Mash the potatoes finely or pass through a strainer or food mill. Blend in a bowl with the egg yolk, butter and seasoning.

3 Make the choux paste. Place the water, butter, salt and nutmeg in a saucepan and bring to a rolling boil. Remove the pan from the heat and add the flour all at once. Beat until the mixture is thick and smooth and no longer sticks to the pan. Beat in the eggs, one by one, and continue beating until the mixture is smooth and soft, but not runny.

4 Mix the choux paste with the mashed potato mixture.

5 Heat the deep fryer to 350°F. Shape small, oval pieces of the dauphine mixture with a spoon and add, a few at a time, to the hot oil. Alternatively, use a piping bag to pipe the mixture into small cylindrical-shaped pieces.

6 Fry until golden brown. Drain on absorbent paper and serve immediately.

Serves 4

Tip: For a delicious alternative to Potatoes Dauphine, try Potatoes Lorette. Just add some grated Gruyère cheese to the choux paste/potato mixture before frying.

Fried Potato Allumettes

6 medium-size potatoes
oil for deep frying

For the Garnish:
4 tomatoes, peeled
10-15 anchovy fillets

Potatoes Dauphine are choux paste and mashed potato fingers, deep-fried until crisp and golden brown

1 tablespoon chopped parsley

1 Peel, wash and slice the potatoes. Cut into strips 2 inches long by ⅛ inch thick. Wash and dry on absorbent paper.

2 Heat the deep fryer to 375°F. Fry the potato strips until golden brown. Drain and arrange on a serving dish.

3 Meanwhile, cut the peeled tomatoes into halves and arrange around the potato allumettes. Garnish with the anchovy fillets and sprinkle with the chopped parsley.

Serves 4

Ham and Potato Pancakes

3 medium-size potatoes, cooked,
   mashed
½ cup mushrooms, finely chopped
⅓ cup ham, chopped
1 onion, finely chopped
¾ cup flour
2 tablespoons butter
1 egg, beaten
salt and pepper
½ cup oil

1 Mix together the mashed potato, mushrooms, ham and onion in a bowl. Add the flour, butter and beaten egg and stir until the mixture is smooth and well blended. Season with salt and pepper.

2 Place the mixture on a floured surface and roll it out like a large sausage until it is 3 inches in diameter. Cut into about 10 slices.

3 Heat the oil in a skillet, add the potato pancakes and fry on both sides until golden brown (about 3-4 minutes).

4 Serve the potato pancakes with coleslaw.

Serves 4

Look 'n Cook Potato Croquettes

1 Boil the potatoes in salted water 2 Dry the cooked potatoes on a baking sheet in the oven 3 Grate or grind the potatoes finely 4 Melt some butter in a saucepan and blend with the potato mixture 5 When the pulp is very hot, add the egg yolks in a continuous stream, stirring all the time 6 Oil a plate, cover with the potato mixture and leave to cool 7 and 8 Flour your hands and, when it is cool, roll out the mixture in-

to a long sausage shape **9** Cut the mixture at regular intervals **10** Dredge the croquettes in flour, then dip in seasoned, beaten egg **11** Roll the croquettes in breadcrumbs. Press with a knife so that the bread-crumbs stick to the croquettes **12** Place in a frying basket and cook in hot oil until well-browned. Serve immediately

Potato Croquettes

6 medium-size potatoes
salt and pepper
3 eggs
¼ cup butter
¼ cup flour
1 teaspoon oil
oil for deep frying
2 cups fresh breadcrumbs

1 Peel the potatoes and cut them into even-size pieces. Boil them in salted water for 20 minutes.

2 Drain the potatoes, place on a baking sheet in the oven to dry until the outsides become a little floury (about 10 minutes).

3 Separate 2 of the eggs.

4 Strain the potatoes into a pan and mix them with the butter over low heat. Increase the heat and continue to stir until hot.

5 Stirring all the while, slowly add the two egg yolks to the potato. Season with salt and pepper.

6 Spread the mixture on an oiled plate to cool.

7 Flour your hands and the working surface, take a handful of potato mixture, form it into a ball, then roll the ball under your hands into a long thin sausage shape, about 1 inch in diameter.

8 With a warm knife cut the potato roll into short lengths.

9 Heat the oil to 375°F. to deep fry the croquettes.

10 For the glaze, beat the whole egg with the egg whites, salt and pepper and a little oil. Spread the breadcrumbs on the work surface.

11 Dip the croquettes in the beaten egg then roll them gently in the breadcrumbs, pressing on the crumbs with a knife.

12 Dip the frying basket in the hot oil before adding the croquettes, then fry the croquettes briskly for about a minute until they are golden brown.

Makes about 16

Tips: The success of frying croquettes depends on the quality and condition of the fat used, whether animal or vegetable. Vegetable fats usually contain no moisture and can be heated to higher temperatures than animal fats. Also, they turn rancid less quickly — all fats exposed to the air tend to become rancid in time. Therefore, frying oil should always be stored in an airtight container. The temperature used when frying depends on the size of the portion to be fried — the smaller the portion, the hotter the fat. Remember that when cold potato is added to fat, the temperature of the fat is automatically lowered.

Fried potatoes, clockwise from top: potato croquettes, chips, fried potato and onion balls, potatoes Dauphine, croquettes, slices, allumettes and, in the center, French fries

All about Beef

Roast Rib of Beef

Beef has always enjoyed a sumptuous reputation — it became famous as the 'roast beef of Olde England' and was even knighted by King Henry VIII, after which the two hindquarters, including the legs, rump, sirloin and wing ribs, were always referred to as *Baronne de Boeuf*.

Beef is very nutritious and a good source of energy. It is rich in protein, vitamin B and iron. The price of beef varies with the cut. The most expensive are usually the most tender and can be quickroasted, fried or broiled. Tougher cheaper cuts require slower cooking methods to tenderize them but are just as nutritious.

Beef is extremely versatile and can be prepared and cooked in so many ways. You can roast, fry, broil, casserole, pot-roast, stew, boil, braise, stuff, smoke or salt it. It can be ground and made into hamburgers, or baked *en croûte* in pastry. Of course, the method of cooking you use will depend on the cut and quality of the beef and how much you can afford to spend.

Choosing Beef
When choosing beef, always take the color and texture into account. The lean flesh should be light rosy or cherry red in color, and the fat should be a creamy yellow. The lean meat should be marbled with fat — this is always a sign of good quality, tender meat. There should be a minimum of gristle. The texture will determine the tenderness of the meat — the most tender cuts such as sirloin spring back when touched.

Cuts of Beef
Different cuts will require different methods of cooking. Always be sure that you choose the right one. Cuts vary from one country to another, and even between areas and districts. Many cuts such as rib, chuck, leg, skirt, blade, shin, top round and brisket are very similar. The main differences lie in the cutting and terminology used, especially with steaks. The American equivalent of British fillet steak is tenderloin. As well as sirloin steak,

there are T-bone, Porterhouse, pin bone, and Club or Delmonico steaks. All these steaks are now popular.

Storing Beef
Store raw meat loosely wrapped in a cool place or refrigerator. Beef will keep in a refrigerator for 2-3 days. The most economical way to buy beef is in bulk if you have a freezer. The recommended storage time in a freezer is 8 months. Always thaw out frozen meat either in the refrigerator or at room temperature slowly. Never immerse in hot water to speed up the process. Once it is thawed, you should never refreeze the beef.

Seasoning Beef
Always season beef after cooking, especially roasting or broiling, with salt and freshly ground black pepper. Salt draws out the juices. For additional flavor you can season the beef with herbs or spices. Try rubbing the roast with garlic, onion, herbs or spices before cooking, or insert a clove of garlic or a small piece of onion into the meat itself.

Improving the Texture and Flavor of Beef
One way to improve the texture and flavor of cheaper cuts of meat is to marinate them for several hours. Try using wine, beer or cider or an acidic mixture of fruit juices and vinegar. You can tenderize a tough steak or roast with a ready-made tenderizer, which most supermarkets sell. These tenderizing powders are usually prepared from extract of figs, papain (an enzyme of papaya) and pineapple — the fresh juice of these fruits works equally well.

Larding Beef
You can lard tough, cheaper cuts of meat with a larding needle to tenderize them. Just push a larding needle through the meat with the grain, thread with fat and pull back through. This is explained in the step-by-step photo guide to larding on page 266. Introducing the fat into the flesh will moisten the meat during cooking.

Steaks

The most popular and well-known steak cuts are — in usual order of costliness — tenderloin, sirloin, rib, and rump. Being very expensive, tenderloin is graded into several different cuts.

An average beef tenderloin is 18-20 inches in length and tapers in width from 4 inches to 1 inch. A whole tenderloin weighs from 6-9 lbs. untrimmed, and when prepared for cooking, a tenderloin will weigh on average 3½-4 lbs.

The Châteaubriand is taken from the head of the tenderloin. A piece 4 inches is cut off, weighing from 12-16 ozs. It is wrapped with a cloth, and flattened until it is 2 inches thick, widening to double its original size at 8 inches in diameter. When cooked it is served in slices, and is always for two.

The Coeur de Filet or Medallion steak is cut 1 inch thick, and weighs ½ lb. It is cut from the heart of the tenderloin, and is also flattened to a diameter of 3 inches. The tenderloin steak is cut from the middle of the tenderloin, 2½ inches thick, about 4 inches in diameter, and weighs 7 ozs.

Sirloin steaks are tender and flavorsome. Entrecôte means 'between the ribs' but the term now includes any sirloin steak. Porterhouse is another cut of the sirloin. Rib steaks are large and tasty. The famous T-bone steak includes part of the tenderloin and sirloin. Rump steak is often hung to mature, producing a fine flavor.

The Tournedos is also cut from the middle of the tenderloin. It is tied in a blanched slice of bacon before cooking. It is cut 1½ inches thick, 3 inches in diameter, and weighs 5 ozs. Filet Mignon is cut from the thin end in a triangular shape, and weighs $\frac{1}{4}$ lb. This end of the tenderloin is also used for Strogonoff where the steak is cut into strips $1 \times \frac{1}{4}$ inch, or raw for Steak Tartare.

The cooking times will vary with the method used and the type and thickness of steak, but in general 2 minutes of cooking (1 minute each side) produces a rare steak, 4 minutes a medium steak, and 8-12 minutes a well-done one. Broiling is suitable for the best types of steak, while cheaper cuts may be fried very quickly.

Apollo Steaks

2 tablespoons oil
4 sirloin or rump steaks

For the Sauce:
1 lamb or beef kidney, skinned, cored and sliced
2 tablespoons butter
1 large onion, sliced
2 tomatoes, skinned, seeded and chopped
1 green pepper, seeded and chopped

Juicy Apollo Steaks are dressed with a richly flavored sauce of kidneys, green pepper, tomato and onion

$\frac{2}{3}$ cup red wine
$\frac{2}{3}$ cup beef stock
salt and pepper
pinch oregano

1 Sauté the sauce ingredients, except the wine, stock and seasonings, in a saucepan for 5 minutes until they are tender. Add the wine and stock, and season with salt, pepper and a pinch of oregano. Bring to a boil and simmer for 5 minutes to thicken.

2 Heat the oil in a skillet and fry the steaks for 2-8 minutes or according to taste. Pour the sauce over them and serve immediately. Serve with buttered new potatoes and a green or mixed salad.

Serves 4

Steak au Poivre Vert

4 sirloin steaks, ½ inch thick
¼ cup oil
pinch salt
¼ cup butter
3 tablespoons brandy
½ cup dry sherry or Madeira
1 medium onion, chopped
2 tablespoons green peppercorns,
  canned
2 tablespoons soy sauce
1 teaspoon vinegar
⅔ cup light cream
pinch paprika
1 tablespoon chopped fresh
  parsley

1 Trim the steaks of any excess fat and sinew. Brush with a little oil and season very lightly with salt.

2 Heat the rest of the oil and butter in a skillet and quickly fry the steaks on both sides to sear the flesh, for about 2 minutes. Pour in the brandy and ignite it. Almost immediately, pour in the sherry or Madeira to put out the brandy flames. Remove the steaks and keep them warm while cooking the sauce.

3 To the mixture in the pan add the onion, peppercorns, soy sauce, and vinegar. Boil for 4 minutes. Add the cream and paprika and boil briskly for another minute.

4 Return the steaks to the sauce to reheat for a minute on each side. Serve immediately, garnished with the chopped parsley.

Serves 4

Steak au Poivre Vert has the real taste of luxury, with brandy to flame, wine, and mildly spicy green peppercorns

Tips: Green peppercorns are the fresh berries of the spice more commonly used in its dried form as black or white ground pepper. They are available in canned form, and have a mild and aromatic flavor.

The given cooking times for sirloin steak are designed for a rare-cooked steak of ½ inch thick. Thicker steaks should be fried for twice the given length of time, or beaten with a rolling pin or meat mallet to the given thickness. For a medium-cooked steak, fry for 4 minutes. For a well-cooked steak, cover the skillet while frying for 4 or 5 minutes.

Entrecôte Bordelaise

4 sirloin steaks, about 1½ inches
  thick
2 tablespoons oil
salt and pepper
1 tablespoon chopped fresh
  parsley

For the Bordelaise Sauce:
4 shallots or 1 onion, chopped
¾ cup dry red wine
bouquet garni
3 tablespoons meat juice
¾ cup beef stock
1 tablespoon tomato paste
1 tablespoon beef fat
2 tablespoons flour

1 Brush the steaks with the oil and broil them for 8-12 minutes according to taste, turning once. Reserve the meat juices and keep the steaks warm.

2 To make the sauce, boil the shallot or onion in the wine, with the bouquet garni, for 5 minutes. Stir in the meat juice, beef stock and tomato paste.

3 Make a roux by rendering the beef fat and cooking the flour in it for 2 minutes. Remove from the heat and gradually stir in the wine and stock mixture to form a

smooth sauce. Simmer very gently for 20 minutes.

4 Season the steaks lightly with salt and generously with freshly ground black pepper. Pour the sauce over them and garnish with chopped parsley. Serve immediately.

Serves 4

Steak Manzanilla

2 rump steaks, about ½ lb. each
2 tablespoons oil
salt and pepper
2 slices Cheddar cheese, ⅛ inch
  thick
pinch paprika
4 anchovy fillets
2 stuffed green olives, sliced

1 Brush the steaks with oil and season with a little salt and plenty of freshly ground black pepper. Broil the steaks under high heat for 3-4 minutes on each side according to taste.

2 Place a slice of cheese on each steak, sprinkle with paprika and broil until the cheese is melted and just starting to brown.

3 Place the steaks on a warm serving dish. Decorate each steak with anchovy fillets, and slices of stuffed olive. Serve immediately.

Serves 2

Steak à l'Orange

4 sirloin steaks, ¾ inch thick
24 black peppercorns, crushed
rind 1 orange, cut in matchstick
  strips
1 tablespoon oil
⅔ cup dry sherry

4 fresh mint leaves
⅔ cup light cream

For the Marinade:
juice 2 oranges
2 cloves garlic, peeled and crushed
1 teaspoon fresh gingerroot, finely
  chopped
2 tablespoons soy sauce
¼ cup oil
2 tablespoons cider vinegar

1 Trim the steaks and rub the crushed black peppercorns into them.

2 Thoroughly blend the orange juice, garlic, ginger, soy sauce, oil, and vinegar to make a marinade. Soak the steaks in it for 20 minutes and then remove them, reserving the marinade.

Steak Manzanilla is an unusual dish featuring cheese and anchovies, which would also suit cheaper cuts of steak

3 Meanwhile, boil the orange rind for 8 minutes. Drain and rinse the strips in cold water and add them to the leftover marinade.

4 Fry the steaks in the oil until done to taste. Remove and keep warm. Pour the marinade into the pan and boil for 4 minutes to reduce. Add the sherry and mint leaves and boil for 3 minutes; then stir in the cream and boil 3 more minutes. Pour the sauce over the steaks and serve at once.

Serves 4

Sirloin with Peppercorns and Garlic

four ¾-lb. sirloin steaks, 1 inch thick
12 black peppercorns
4 cloves garlic, thinly sliced
⅓ cup oil
salt

1 Trim the fat from the steaks. Crush the peppercorns, using a rolling pin, and then sprinkle over both sides of the steaks, pressing well into the meat.

2 Make several slits in the surface of the steaks and insert the slices of garlic into the slits. Brush the steaks with oil and then cook them under a broiler, over a charcoal fire, or in a skillet. Cook for 2 minutes on both sides for rare meat, 4 minutes for medium or 8 minutes for well-done.

3 Season with salt and serve with watercress, French fries and a pat of garlic butter.

Serves 4

Rump Steak Royal

2-lb. rump steak in 1 piece
salt
1 teaspoon crushed peppercorns
3 tablespoons oil

Sirloin with Peppercorns and Garlic — try this deliciously different way of serving your steaks

2 cloves garlic, peeled and chopped
¼ cup peanut butter
⅔ cup dry vermouth

1 Season the steak with salt and peppercorns.

2 Heat the oil in a skillet and fry the steak. Cook for 6 minutes on either side for rare meat, 12 minutes for medium, 14 minutes for well-done.

3 Remove the steak from the pan and keep warm on a dish.

4 Mix the garlic and peanut butter and put in the skillet. Add the vermouth, stir and boil for 4 minutes. Pour over the steak.

5 Serve the steak whole and cut into 3 or 4 portions in front of the guests. Serve with a lettuce and orange salad.

Serves 3–4

Tournedos with Anchovy Butter

6 slices lean bacon (blanched)
6 tournedos steaks, $\frac{1}{4}$ lb. each,
 $1\frac{1}{2}$ inches thick
salt and freshly ground pepper
oil for frying steaks
6 green olives
6 anchovy fillets
2 tablespoons catsup

For the Anchovy Butter:
$\frac{1}{4}$ lb. butter
1 tablespoon chopped parsley
juice $\frac{1}{2}$ lemon
4 anchovy fillets, finely chopped
6 slices bread
2 tablespoons butter
2 tablespoons oil

1 Prepare the anchovy butter by creaming the butter with the parsley, lemon juice and anchovy fillets to form a paste. Roll the paste into a cylinder, wrap in parchment paper, and chill for 1 hour.

2 Make the croûtons by cutting six bread circles using a plain cutter of $2\frac{1}{2}$ inches. Put the butter and oil in a skillet and fry the bread on both sides until golden. Place the croûtons on a dish and keep warm.

3 Tie a slice of lean bacon around each steak and season. Heat some oil in the skillet and fry the steaks for 4-10 minutes, depending on whether you want the steaks rare, medium or well-done. If preferred, brush the steaks with oil, and broil. Remove the bacon. Place on the croûtons.

4 When ready to serve, cut slices off the roll of anchovy butter and place one on each steak. Place a green olive on each, surrounded by an anchovy fillet, and trickle a little catsup around as decoration. Serve at once with thin French fries as illustrated.

Serves 6

Tournedos with Anchovy Butter combines succulent steak with piquant anchovies, topped with green olives

South Seas Meatballs

1 lb. lean ground beef
1 beaten egg
pinch each salt and pepper
1 tablespoon oil
3 shallots, minced
2 tablespoons flour
1 lb. pineapple chunks
1 tablespoon soy sauce
1 teaspoon wine vinegar
½ green pepper, finely chopped
¼ cup almonds, blanched

1 In a large bowl blend the beef, beaten egg, salt and pepper. Make into 4 flattened balls, brush with oil and broil for 10 minutes, turning once. Keep warm.

2 Heat the oil in a skillet. Add the shallots and sauté gently for 3 minutes. Take out. Stir in the flour and cook the roux for 3 minutes more. Pour in the juice from the canned pineapple, and bring to a boil, stirring. Add the soy sauce and vinegar. Season to taste.

3 Add the shallots, pineapple chunks, green pepper and almonds. Place the meatballs in the pan and heat through, spooning on the sauce.

Serves 4

Brandy Steak with Mandarin Rice

¾ cup long grain rice
salt and pepper
2 tablespoons butter
11 ozs. canned mandarin oranges
4 tenderloin steaks, ¼ lb. each,
    1½ inches thick
4 slices lean bacon (blanched)
2 tablespoons butter
2 tablespoons oil
4 tablespoons brandy
½ cup light cream

Brandy Steak with Mandarin Rice; tender tournedos are flamed in brandy and flavored with mandarin oranges

1 Wash the rice and cook in salted boiling water for 20 minutes. Drain, and stir in the butter. Season and keep warm.

2 Meanwhile, heat the mandarin oranges in their syrup and drain. Keep the juice. Add the oranges to the rice. Keep warm.

3 Season the steaks, and tie a slice of bacon around each. Heat the butter and oil in a skillet, and shallow fry the steaks for 2-3 minutes on each side, if you like them rare. Cook longer if you prefer. If you want the steaks well done, put a lid on the pan.

4 Pour the brandy into the skillet and flame the steaks. Remove the steaks, discard the bacon, and put them on a dish and keep warm.

5 Pour the cream into the skillet, and mix with the meat juices, and boil for 2 minutes to make a smooth sauce. Remove from the heat, add 1 tablespoon of the mandarin juice and pour over the steaks. Serve at once with the mandarin rice, and a green salad.

Serves 4

South Seas Meatballs have a sweet-sour fruity flavor, and make a tasty supper for the family

Marengo Meatballs

1 large slice white bread
2 tablespoons milk
1½ lbs. lean ground beef
1 egg yolk
1 onion, finely chopped
pinch salt and pepper
1 tablespoon flour
¼ cup butter
⅓ cup dry white wine
4 large tomatoes, skinned,
  seeded and chopped
pinch sugar
1½ cups long grain rice
2 tablespoons light cream
1 tablespoon chopped parsley

1 Soak the bread in the milk for 5 minutes. Squeeze out, remove excess liquid and crumble into breadcrumbs.

2 In a mixing bowl, combine the beef, egg yolk, onion, salt and pepper and breadcrumbs. Divide into 6 and roll into flattened balls. Dust with the flour.

3 Heat the butter in a skillet and fry the meatballs for 10 minutes, turning them once. Pour on the wine, then add the tomatoes and a pinch of sugar. Bring to a boil, then reduce the heat and simmer for 25 minutes.

4 Meanwhile, place the rice in a pan of slightly salted water. Bring to a boil and cook for 15 minutes or until the rice is just tender. Drain. Heat the cream in a small pan and pour over the rice. Sprinkle with the parsley and arrange in the center of a serving dish surrounded by the meatballs and sauce.

Serves 6

Marengo Meatballs use ground beef with creamy rice for a nourishing and economical meal

Mushroom Burgers

2 tablespoons butter
2 tablespoons oil
2 onions, finely chopped
2 cups finely chopped mushrooms
pinch mixed herbs
1 clove garlic, peeled and crushed
1½ lbs. lean ground beef
pinch salt and pepper
2 tablespoons flour

1 Heat the butter and 1 tablespoon oil in a skillet. Gently fry the onions and the mushrooms for 5 minutes. Add the mixed herbs and the crushed garlic clove and cook for a further minute. Allow to cool.

2 In a bowl, combine the beef with the onion and mushroom mixture. Season. Divide into 8 balls, then flatten slightly. Dust with the flour.

3 Heat the rest of the oil in the pan and fry the mushroom burgers slowly for 4-6 minutes on each side.

Serves 4

Tip: To make a quick, tasty sauce, take the burgers out of the pan when they are cooked and keep hot. Pour away the oil and add ½ cup sherry, wine or fruit juice to the pan. Boil rapidly until the sauce is reduced by half and pour it over the burgers.

Mushroom Burgers are tasty and easy to make. Serve them with a big mixed salad and French fries

Meatballs with Zucchini

⅓ cup chickpeas, canned
  and drained
1 lb. lean ground beef
1 clove garlic, peeled and crushed
1 cup fresh breadcrumbs
⅓ cup hazelnuts, finely chopped
1 egg, beaten
1 small green seeded chili pepper,
  finely chopped
1 tablespoon chopped parsley
pinch cumin
salt and pepper
2 tablespoons flour
¼ cup oil

For the Sauce:
2 tablespoons oil
1 onion, chopped
1 clove garlic, peeled and crushed
4 zucchini, sliced
4 tomatoes, skinned, seeded
  and chopped

*Meatballs with Zucchini includes
other unusual vegetables —
chickpeas, hot chili pepper
and hazelnuts*

1¼ cups peas, fresh or frozen
1¼ cups water
1 chicken bouillon cube
1 tablespoon mixed mint and
parsley, chopped

1 Preheat the oven to 400°F.

2 Mash the chickpeas with a fork.
Place them in a mixing bowl, and
add the beef, garlic, breadcrumbs,
hazelnuts, beaten egg and chili pepper. Blend together well and add
the parsley, cumin, salt and pepper.
Shape into 8 slightly flattened balls
and dust with the flour.

3 Heat the oil in a skillet and fry
the meatballs for 6-8 minutes.
Drain and keep hot.

4 To make the sauce, pour off the
oil in which the meatballs were
cooked and wipe the pan clean.
Heat 2 tablespoons oil and gently
sauté the onion for 4 minutes, until
soft but not brown. Add the garlic,
zucchini, tomatoes and peas. Pour
on the water and crumble in the
bouillon cube. Bring to a boil, add
the parsley and mint and season to
taste. Transfer to a casserole, add
the meatballs, and place in the oven
for 20 minutes.

Serves 4

Tips: Try using equal quantities of
ground pork and beef for a good
texture as well as a delicious flavor.

For economy, replace ½ cup ground
meat with 2½ ozs. texturized vegetable protein.

Meatballs can be braised in the
oven or deep fried and any kind of
cereal binder can be used, such as
matzo meal, oats, cooked rice.

Look 'n Cook Boeuf en Brioche

1 Make two circles of sifted flour. Mix the yeast with water, pour into the smaller circle and mix with the flour **2** Put the yeast mixture into a small bowl in a warm place to rise. Break the eggs into the larger circle **3** Gradually mix the flour to a soft dough using the fingertips **4** Beat with an up and down, yo-yo like motion for 5-6 minutes until the dough no longer sticks to your fingers **5** Mix in the soft butter in small pieces. Cover with a cloth and leave to proof for 45 minutes **6** Heat the oil in a skillet and add the seasoned tender-

loin **7** Brown all over for 5 minutes to seal the juices, with a lid on. Roast in the oven for 15 minutes at 425°F. and then cool **8** Roll out the dough ¼ inch thick **9** Place the cold tenderloin in the center and brush with beaten egg. (Add flavored pastes at this stage if you wish). **10** Brush the dough with beaten egg and fold over the fillet **11** Fold over the other half making a large overlap, and turn over so that the seam is underneath **12** Trim off each end, sealing the tenderloin inside **13** Form into a loaf shape **14** Roll out the trim-

257

Look 'n Cook Boeuf en Brioche (continued)

mings and cut into strips. Brush the loaf with beaten egg **15** Arrange the strips decoratively **16** Brush them with beaten egg and place on a baking sheet and proof for 25 minutes. Prick in two or three places **17** Bake for 15 minutes at 425°F. and for 20 minutes at 375°F. Watch the pastry so that it does not burn. Remove from the oven and cool for 10 minutes **18** Carve in 1-inch slices and serve hot

Beef Italienne

1½-lb. tenderloin
4 strips bacon
⅓ cup oil
1 carrot, 1 onion and 2 celery
  branches, sliced

For the Gravy:
⅔ cup white wine
1 cup water
1 beef bouillon cube
bouquet garni
1 teaspoon cornstarch

1 Prepare the tenderloin by removing the tough skin carefully with a knife to avoid damaging the meat. Lay the bacon along the tenderloin and secure with string, tied at intervals of 1 inch.

2 Preheat the oven to 400°F.

3 Heat the oil in a skillet and brown the meat all over for 8 minutes to seal.

4 Transfer the meat to a roasting pan and add the carrot, onion and celery.

5 Roast for 40 minutes. Remove from the oven, discard the bacon, string, and vegetables. Place on a serving dish and keep hot.

6 To the juices in the roasting pan, add the wine, ⅔ cup water, bouillon cube, and bouquet garni and simmer for 15 minutes. Thicken with cornstarch mixed with the remaining water. Boil for 3 minutes, season and strain.

Serves 6

Beef Italienne could be the star attraction at a special dinner — superb tenderloin, flamboyantly garnished

Tip: As the photograph shows, the Beef Italienne may be garnished in several ways.

With small strips of fresh noodle dough deep fried until crisp and golden and arranged in heaps around the dish.

With globe artichokes, boiled in water and lemon juice, after the outside leaves and hairy choke have been removed. The artichokes may be filled with a duxelles of ham, mushrooms, onion and breadcrumbs, sautéed for 5 minutes.

The dish may be decorated with a few mushrooms, which have been scribed with the point of a knife blade, and then blanched in water with lemon juice or wine.

The garnishes should be prepared before the meat is cooked.

Look 'n Cook Preparing and Garnishing Rib of Beef

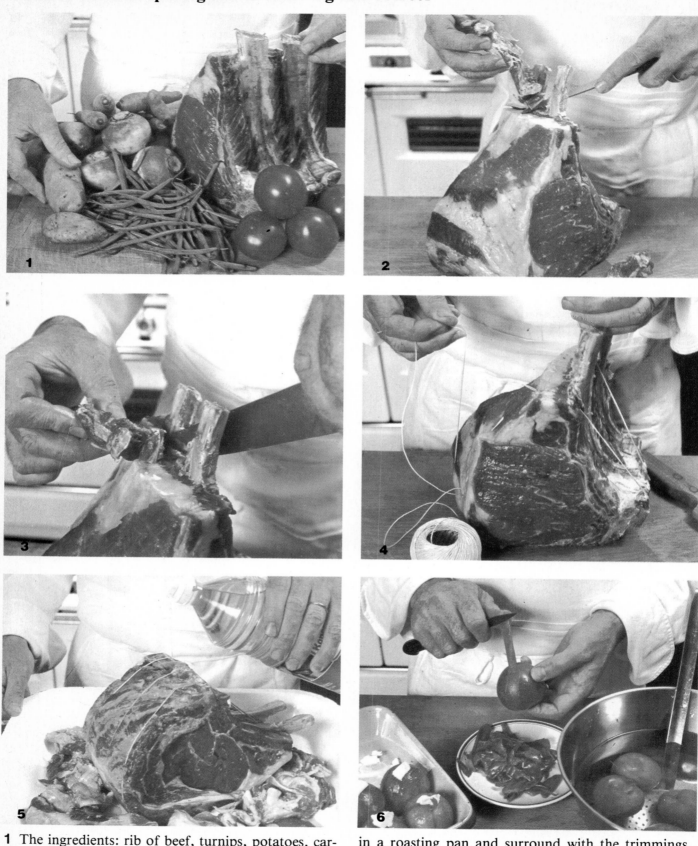

1 The ingredients: rib of beef, turnips, potatoes, carrots, green beans and tomatoes 2 and 3 Trim the rib for roasting. Expose the ends of the bones and remove the fat and trimmings. Reserve for use later 4 Tie the rib with trussing string to keep its shape 5 Place the rib in a roasting pan and surround with the trimmings, which will provide the gravy. Season lightly and pour on a little oil 6 Scald and skin the tomatoes. Place them in a greased ovenproof dish and dot with butter 7 Peel the carrots, turnips and potatoes and trim them

to a uniform size **8** Put each vegetable into a separate pan. Pour on enough water to cover and add a little butter and a pinch each salt and sugar. Cover, and put on to boil **9, 10** and **11** When the vegetables are tender, reduce the water in which they were cooked and glaze them with the sugar and butter. Brown the potatoes in a sauté pan with a little more butter **12** The finished dish: roast rib of beef, surrounded by vegetables, ready to carve and serve

Look 'n Cook Carving Rib of Beef

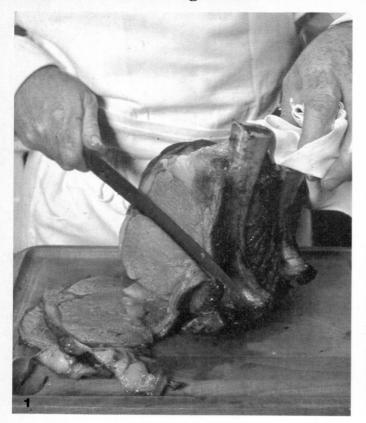

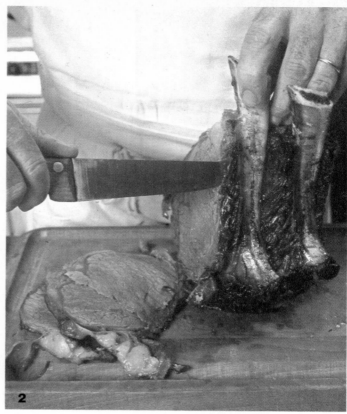

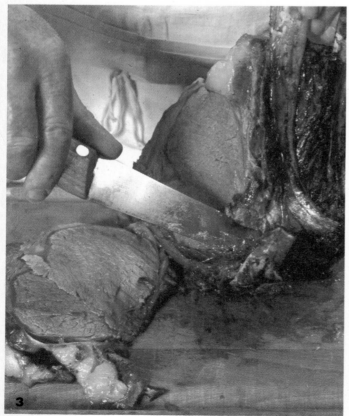

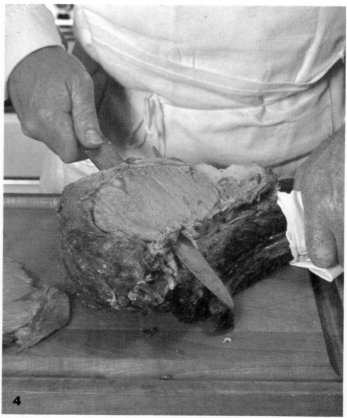

Beef ribs can be carved in two ways, vertically or horizontally **1** To carve vertically, hold the ribs upright on their base and cut regular slices until the knife meets the first bone **2** Start to remove the first bone by sliding the blade of the knife down between the bone and the meat **3** Complete the removal **4** To carve horizontally, place the ribs flat and slice from the thickest part of the roast **5** Continue until the knife reaches the nar-

row part and then the first bone. Cut out the bone by running the blade of the knife around it **6** Bend the bone back to separate it from the meat **7** Put the slices on the serving dish. Surround them with the vegetables such as those illustrated here **8** The completed dish with the sauce boat of gravy, peas, carrots, potatoes and tomatoes

Braised Beef

Braised meat is first seared in hot fat to seal in the juices, and then barely covered with a water-based liquid and cooked gently until tender. For additional flavor, the meat can be soaked in a marinade before it is cooked; the marinade liquid should always include vinegar, wine or fruit juice for the best flavor.

Beef Olives with Ham

4 thin slices of braising steak, $\frac{1}{4}$ lb. each, from leg or shoulder
4 thin slices cooked ham
1 small onion, chopped
1 clove garlic, chopped
few sage leaves, chopped
2 tablespoons chopped parsley
salt and pepper
$\frac{1}{4}$ lb. butter

Beef Olives with Ham uses a less expensive beef dressed up with a garnish of mushrooms and onions

$\frac{1}{2}$ cup oil
1 onion, coarsely chopped
1 carrot, coarsely chopped
1 tablespoon flour
$\frac{2}{3}$ cup red wine
$1\frac{1}{4}$ cups brown stock
1 tablespoon capers
$\frac{2}{3}$ cup long grain rice
2 cups pearl onions
$\frac{1}{2}$ lb. mushrooms

1 Preheat the oven to 350°F.

2 Beat the steaks until very thin. Place a slice of ham on each steak. Mix together the chopped onion, garlic, sage and half the parsley and divide the mixture between the steaks. Sprinkle with salt and pepper.

3 Roll up the steaks tightly and secure with string or toothpicks.

4 Heat $2\frac{1}{2}$ tablespoons of the butter and half the oil together in a pan, add the meat and fry briskly for 5 minutes.

5 Transfer the meat to a casserole dish. Add the chopped vegetables to the pan, and sauté gently, covered, for about 8 minutes or until soft. Sprinkle in the flour and cook for 1-2 minutes or until brown. Stir in the wine and stock and bring to a boil. Pour the contents of the pan over the meat, add the capers and season to taste. Cover the dish and cook in the oven for $1\frac{1}{4}$ hours.

6 Meanwhile, prepare the garnish. Boil the rice in salted water for 18 minutes, drain and blend in 4 tablespoons of the butter and salt and pepper. Heat the rest of the oil and butter in a pan and sauté the onions for 3 minutes until brown. Add the mushrooms and cook for 1 minute more. Cover the vegetables with water and boil for 6 minutes. Drain.

7 When the meat is cooked, arrange the rice on a warm serving dish, place the meat on top and garnish with the mushrooms and onions, and the rest of the parsley.

Serves 4

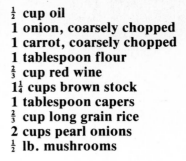

Braised Beef Home-Style

**2 lbs. braising beef from leg, in
  1 piece**
1 onion, finely sliced
**1 clove garlic, peeled and
  quartered**
bouquet garni
$\frac{1}{4}$ cup brandy
1$\frac{1}{4}$ cups dry white wine
$\frac{1}{4}$ lb. butter
2 onions, chopped
$\frac{7}{8}$ cup stock
pinch mixed spice
salt and pepper
1 lb. carrots, sliced
1 lb. green beans

*Braised Beef Home-Style provides
a hearty mixture of lean beef and
vegetables to satisfy a hungry
family*

1 Place the meat in a bowl, and
add the sliced onion, garlic, bouquet garni, brandy and two-thirds
of the wine. Leave to marinate for 3
hours.
2 Drain the meat, reserving the
marinade, and dry. Melt half the
butter in a flameproof casserole,
add the meat and fry briskly until
browned all over. Add the chopped
onion and fry until golden-brown.
Strain the reserved marinade and
add it to the pan with the stock,
mixed spice and salt and pepper to

taste. Cover and cook gently for 2
hours.
3 Melt the remaining butter in a
separate pan, add the carrots and
fry gently until browned. Add just
enough water to cover, then cook
gently until the carrots are tender.
Cook the beans in salted water until
tender, then drain.
4 When the meat is cooked, add
the vegetables to the casserole,
cover and cook for a further 15
minutes.
5 Drain the meat and carve into
neat slices. Arrange on a warm
serving dish and surround with the
vegetables and gravy. Serve hot
with roast potatoes.
Serves 6

265

Look 'n Cook Boeuf à la Mode

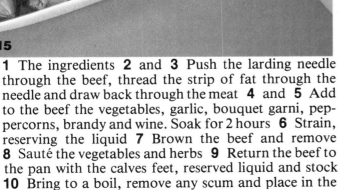

1 The ingredients **2** and **3** Push the larding needle through the beef, thread the strip of fat through the needle and draw back through the meat **4** and **5** Add to the beef the vegetables, garlic, bouquet garni, peppercorns, brandy and wine. Soak for 2 hours **6** Strain, reserving the liquid **7** Brown the beef and remove **8** Sauté the vegetables and herbs **9** Return the beef to the pan with the calves feet, reserved liquid and stock **10** Bring to a boil, remove any scum and place in the oven. Glaze the onions and carrots **11** After 1½ hours, transfer the beef to another casserole. Dice the meat from the calves feet and add **12** Add the glazed carrots and onions **13** Strain over ¾ of the gravy and complete the cooking **14** Reduce (evaporate) the rest of the gravy and use to glaze the cooked beef **15** and **16** Serve the beef with the vegetables and the juices left in the casserole

Boeuf à la Mode

1 lb. salt pork
salt and pepper
2 tablespoons chopped parsley
4½ lbs. braising beef
2½ cups red wine
bouquet garni
1½ lbs. carrots
1 shallot, sliced
2 large onions, sliced
2 cloves garlic, crushed
6 peppercorns
¼ cup brandy
½ cup oil
2 calves feet, cut in half (optional)
4¼ cups beef stock
¼ lb. butter
1 teaspoon sugar
12 pearl onions
3 tablespoons cornstarch mixed
  with ⅔ cup water (optional)

1 Cut the pork fat into strips, ½ inch thick. Season and sprinkle on the parsley. Lard the beef at regular intervals with the strips (see pages 266-267).

2 Place the meat in an earthenware dish with the wine and bouquet garni. Cut half the carrots in slices across and add them to the dish with the shallot, onions, garlic, peppercorns and brandy. Leave in the refrigerator for 2 hours, turning from time to time.

3 Preheat the oven to 350°F. Strain the meat and vegetables, reserving the liquid. Heat the oil in an oven-proof casserole, add the beef and cook quickly for 10 minutes until browned. Lift out the meat and sauté the strained vegetables and bouquet garni for 5 minutes.

4 Return the beef to the pan, add the calves' feet and pour in the reserved liquid and the beef stock. Season and bring to a boil. Remove any scum, cover the dish and cook in the oven for 2-2½ hours.

5 Heat half the butter in a pan, add the rest of the carrots, the sugar and enough water to cover. Cook until

the liquid has evaporated. In a separate pan, heat the rest of the butter, add the onions and enough water to cover and cook for 8 minutes.

6 After the meat has been cooking for 1½ hours, remove from the oven and transfer the beef to another casserole. Dice the meat of the calves' feet and discard the bones. Add the diced meat to the beef with the glazed carrots and onions. Strain the gravy and add about three-quarters to the beef. Cover again and return to the oven for the rest of the cooking time.

7 Boil the rest of the gravy for 5 minutes to reduce it. Season.

As a variation of Boeuf à la Mode, chuck may be braised in stout instead of wine. This gives it a darker color and a rich malty flavor. It may be served cold in its gravy

8 Place the cooked meat on a serving dish and coat with the reduced gravy. Return to the oven for a few minutes to glaze.

9 Surround the meat with the vegetables, coat with the gravy and serve hot. The gravy can be thickened with flour if liked.

Serves 8

All about Beef Stews and Casseroles

Daube of Beef in Red Wine

Beef Stews

Stews and casseroles provide the best methods of cooking tougher cuts of beef. They all involve slow cooking at a low heat with a measured volume of liquid: (that is, one cup meat to one cup liquid) although you can use a pressure cooker. You can use a covered pan on the stove and simmer at 180°F. but for best results, cook in a casserole in an oven preheated to 350°F.

The cooking liquor should be slightly acid, to help tenderize the meat. Include a little wine, cider, beer, tomato paste or fruit juice. The meat can be marinated first, and the marinade included in the cooking liquor. For a better flavor, fry the meat quickly in fat to brown it and seal in the juices. Root vegetables and onions which are added for flavor should be lightly fried, too, before you add stock and any aromatic herbs you may wish to include. Flour for thickening can be added when the meat is browned, or as a roux stirred into the cooking liquor when the stew is nearly done. A stew cooked with beans makes a meal in itself.

Cuts suitable for stewing come from muscular areas, such as leg and shoulder. Rump steak, top round, flank, skirt, and chuck steak are all good and economical. Variety meats lend themselves to slow cooking. Oxtail provides a rich stew and ox kidney and liver, which tend to be strongly flavored, are often cooked with stewing beef or bacon.

Stews have the great merit of being suitable for cooking in advance, for reheating or freezing. Many casseroles improve with reheating because their sauce continues its work of tenderizing even as it cools.

Beef Burgundy

½ cup oil
2 lbs. top round, cut into 1-inch cubes
1 carrot, thinly sliced
1 large onion, thinly sliced
¼ cup flour
2 cups dry red wine
salt and pepper
2 cloves garlic, peeled and crushed
bouquet garni
1 cup pearl onions, peeled
1 tablespoon sugar
¼ cup butter
¼ lb. lean bacon, cut in strips
1 cup mushrooms, chopped

1 Heat three-quarters of the oil in a heavy stewpan, put the pieces of beef into it and brown over high heat. Remove the meat, then pour out any remaining oil and add the slices of carrot and onion. Let them brown lightly, then add the flour and cook it, stirring constantly with a wooden spoon.

2 Mix in all the wine. Bring it to a boil and allow at least a third of it to evaporate on high heat. Return the meat to the pan and add enough cold water to cover it. Add salt, pepper, the garlic and the bouquet garni. Cover and cook gently for 2½ hours.

3 Put the pearl onions in a pan with the sugar, the butter and enough water to cover. Cover and cook until the water has evaporated. When a golden caramel mixture remains, roll the small onions in it and place to one side.

4 Heat the rest of the oil in a pan and lightly fry the bacon. Drain and reserve. Fry the mushrooms in the same oil and reserve.

5 When the stew is cooked, strain the sauce, then return it to the pan. Add the pearl onions, bacon and mushrooms and cook for a further 10 minutes.

Serves 6

Czardaz Beef with Caraway Rice

2 tablespoons oil
2 lbs. stewing beef, cut into 1-inch cubes
3 branches celery, chopped
1 large onion, sliced
⅔ cup water
½ beef bouillon cube
1 lb. canned pineapple chunks, with juice
1 tablespoon chopped parsley
pinch sugar
1 tablespoon tomato paste
few drops Worcestershire sauce
salt and pepper
1½ cups long grain rice
2 tablespoons butter
2 teaspoons caraway seeds

1 Preheat the oven to 350°F.

2 Heat the oil in a skillet. Brown the meat in it, remove and place in a casserole. Add the celery and the onion to the oil and sauté for 3 minutes, then add to the casserole.

3 Pour the water into a pan, bring to a boil and crumble in the bouillon cube. Drain the pineapple and add the juice to the stock with the parsley, sugar, tomato paste, Worcestershire sauce and salt and pepper to taste. Pour over the meat in the casserole, cover, and cook for 1½ hours, adding more stock if necessary.

4 15 minutes before the end of cooking, add the pineapple.

5 To cook the rice, first place it in a strainer and wash it thoroughly under cold running water. Remove any discolored grains. Place it in a large pan of boiling, slightly salted water. Boil for 12 minutes or until the rice is tender. Turn off heat and steam covered for 10 minutes. Gently stir in the butter and the caraway seeds.

Serves 6

Czardaz Beef with Caraway Rice is a fruity casserole with a Russian flavor which will delight your family and friends

Austrian Beef Casserole with Horseradish Sauce

2 lbs. stewing beef
¼ cup oil
6 small onions
6⅓ cups water
3 beef bouillon cubes
bouquet garni
6 leeks

For the Horseradish Sauce:
⅔ cup water
2 tablespoons white vinegar
⅔ cup horseradish, scraped
⅔ cup cooking apple, peeled and cored
½ cup fresh white breadcrumbs
¼ cup light cream

1 Cut the meat into 1½-inch cubes.

2 Heat the oil in a heavy pan and brown the meat, covered with a lid, for 8 minutes. Stir often.

3 Slice the onions and add to the meat, and brown for 3 minutes.

4 Cover with the water mixed with the beef cubes and bouquet garni.

5 Wash the leeks, split into four, tie in a bundle and put with the meat.

6 Bring to a boil, and remove the scum as it rises, with a spoon. Simmer for 2-2½ hours until the meat is tender.

7 Meanwhile, put the water and vinegar in a bowl and grate the horseradish and apple into it. Soak for 1 hour. Drain the liquid off, and mix the breadcrumbs and cream into the mixture. Place in a bowl.

8 When the meat is cooked, the broth may be strained off and served separately as soup. Remove the leeks, discard the string, and place on top of the meat.

Serves 6

Beef Niçoise is a casserole from the Mediterranean, cooked in wine and garnished with tomatoes and black olives

Tip: In Central Europe the broth would be served with liver dumplings.

Beef Niçoise

2 lbs. stewing beef
¼ lb. lean bacon
¼ cup oil
4 onions, sliced
2 cloves garlic, peeled and crushed
bouquet garni
¼ cup flour
1¼ cups wine
1¼ cups water
1 beef bouillon cube
2 tablespoons tomato paste
6 tomatoes, skinned, seeded and chopped
salt and pepper
1 tablespoon chopped parsley
6 black olives

1 Cut the meat into 1-inch cubes and the bacon into strips.

2 Heat the oil in a thick pan. Brown the beef and bacon for 8 minutes, covered with a lid. Stir often.

3 Add the onion, garlic and bouquet garni, cook for 4 minutes. Sprinkle on the flour, cook for 1 minute.

4 Add the wine, water, bouillon cube, tomato paste and chopped tomatoes. Season. Bring to a boil and simmer for 1½-2 hours until the meat is tender. Or cook in the oven with a lid on at 350°F. for the same time.

5 When ready to serve, add the chopped parsley and olives.

Serves 6

Austrian Beef Casserole with Horseradish Sauce is a tasty way of serving beef, with leeks and a creamy sauce

Look 'n Cook Daube of Beef with Red Wine

1 The ingredients 2 Cut the lean salt pork and white salt pork fat into strips. Put the pork fat in a dish, sprinkle with brandy and chopped parsley and chill 3 Cut the meat into cubes, and thread each piece with a strip of fat 4 Place the ingredients in a bowl, and add the mushrooms 5 Pour on the red wine, oil and brandy. Season and marinate for 2 hours. Remove the meat and salt pork and dry. Put some oil in the casserole and

brown the meat **6** Add the vegetables and brown. Add the marinade and water **7** Bring to a boil and cook in the oven for 2½ hours at 350°F. **8** When the meat is tender, remove the fat with a ladle, and remove the bouquet gar-

ni and pork rind **9** Place the meat on a serving dish and pour the sauce over. Sprinkle with the parsley and serve with new potatoes.

Daube of Beef with Red Wine

½ lb. lean salt pork
½ lb. salt pork fat (optional)
¼ cup brandy or port
1 tablespoon chopped parsley
4 lbs. top round of beef
3 large carrots, chopped
3 large onions, chopped
3 large tomatoes, chopped
3 cloves garlic, crushed
8 mushrooms
½ bottle red wine
½ cup oil
salt
12 peppercorns, crushed
pinch mixed spice
1¼ cups water
bouquet garni
2 tablespoons flour (optional)

1 Cut the lean salt pork into strips, and scald by plunging in boiling water for 1 minute. Cool.

2 Cut the pork fat (if used) into strips 2 x ¼ inches, sprinkle with a few drops of brandy and a pinch of parsley. Chill for ½ hour.

3 Cut the meat into 1½-inch cubes. If using the pork fat, take a larding needle, and thread each piece with a strip of fat.

4 Place the salt pork and the meat in a bowl with the carrots, onions and tomatoes, garlic, and mushrooms.

5 Pour on the wine, brandy and half of the oil. Add salt, the peppercorns and the mixed spice and marinate for 2 hours. Remove the meat and dry on absorbent paper.

6 Preheat the oven to 350°F.

7 Put the remainder of the oil in a thick pan, add the meat and salt pork and brown for 5 minutes. Add the vegetables and brown for 3 minutes. Add the marinade, water, and bouquet garni and bring to a boil. Put in the oven with a lid on and cook for 2½ hours, or until the meat is tender.

8 When cooked, remove the fat from the surface carefully with a ladle. Remove the bouquet garni.

9 If you wish, thicken the daube with the flour mixed with ½ cup water and cook for 2 minutes, stirring gently.

10 Place the meat on a serving dish, pour on the sauce and sprinkle with the remainder of the chopped parsley. Serve with new potatoes.

Serves 8

Steak Romanov

1 lb. Filet Mignon
¼ cup oil
1 medium onion, or 3 shallots, chopped
1 tablespoon paprika
2 tablespoons tomato paste
⅔ cup water
⅔ cup whipping cream
1 tablespoon vodka
salt and pepper

1 Remove the skin and fat from the meat and cut into cubes ¾ inch thick.

2 Heat the oil in a skillet. Brown the meat for 4 minutes, stirring constantly. Remove from the pan.

3 In the same pan, fry the onions gently for 2 minutes without coloring.

4 Sprinkle on the paprika and add the tomato paste and cook for 2 minutes, stirring.

5 Add the water and boil for 5 minutes. Beat the cream until stiff, add to the pan and boil for 2 minutes.

6 Reheat the meat in the sauce for 3 minutes. Remove from the heat.

7 Just before serving, add the vodka and check the seasoning. Serve with boiled rice.

Serves 4

Variation

This recipe for Steak Romanov is given as an illustration of a style of cooking steak in a skillet in front of guests. Because it is cooked in only a few minutes, tenderloin must be used so that the meat is both cooked and tender.

The Russians tend to use sour cream, rather than the fresh cream we have used, and they call it Sauce Smitane. If you wish to try this, you can buy sour cream, or make your own by adding a few drops of lemon juice to the fresh cream.

To make Sauce Smitane, gently sauté some chopped onions in butter. Add wine and reduce. Pour in the sour cream and boil for a few moments. Strain through a sieve and add lemon juice. Try this sauce with beef, or with chicken, veal or lamb.

Another Russan variation on Steak Romanov would be to use caraway seeds instead of paprika, and to add a little kummel, which is a liqueur flavored with caraway seeds.

The classic dish of Beef Strogonoff is another variation of a dish to be cooked in public. For this the tenderloin is cut into thin strips and cooked with mushrooms and sour cream. The dish was created by the head chef of the Count Strogonoff in the 1880s in Russia. The dish was almost unknown in Europe, until the great mass of Russian emigrants came to France after the Russian Revolution. The dish then became very popular in the big hotels of the French Riviera in the 1920s and gradually spread through Europe as the head waiters of famous restaurants enjoyed the drama of preparing this dish, flaming in brandy, before honored customers. Brandy is the traditional spirit used, although other spirits may be added.

1 Cut the tenderloin into cubes **2** Heat the oil in a skillet and brown the meat, stirring constantly **3** Remove the meat from the pan **4** Fry the chopped onions gently, sprinkle on the paprika and add the tomato paste and stir. Cook for 2 minutes. Add the water **5** Add the cream, stir and boil **6** Reheat the meat in the sauce. Remove from the heat, add the vodka and season

Country Beef and Olive Casserole

1½ lbs. stewing beef
2 tablespoons oil
3 carrots, sliced
2 small onions, quartered
1 branch celery, sliced
1 clove garlic, peeled and crushed
¼ cup flour
1¼ cups water
⅔ cup sherry
1 lb. canned tomatoes
1 beef bouillon cube
1 bay leaf
few sprigs parsley
salt and pepper
6 stuffed green olives, sliced

1 Cut the beef into 1½-inch cubes.

2 Preheat the oven to 350°F.

3 Heat the oil in a saucepan and fry the meat until browned. Remove from the pan.

4 Add the carrots, onions, celery and garlic to the pan. Sauté over low heat for 5 minutes.

5 Stir in the flour and cook gently for a few minutes, then add the water, sherry and canned tomatoes. Crumble in the bouillon cube and stir well. Add the bay leaf and parsley and season with salt and pepper.

6 Bring to a boil, stirring all the time until it thickens. Transfer to an ovenproof dish, cover with a lid and cook in the oven for 2½ hours. Remove the bay leaf and parsley. Stir in the olives and serve with green beans and boiled potatoes.

Serves 4

Country Beef and Olive Casserole has a distinctive Spanish flavor with its tomatoes and stuffed olives

Sweet and Sour Beef

4 beef sausages
2 tablespoons oil
1 onion, chopped
½ lb. diced, boiled beef

For the Sauce:
1¼ cups water
½ cucumber, cut into chunks
2 branches celery, sliced
1 carrot, cut into thin strips
¼ cup soy sauce
1 beef bouillon cube
1 clove garlic, peeled and chopped
1 tablespoon fresh gingerroot, peeled and chopped
1½ tablespoons honey
2 tablespoons vinegar
1½ tablespoons cornstarch
salt and pepper

1 Broil or fry the sausages. Cool and cut in thick slices.

2 Heat the oil and fry the onion until soft, then add the beef and sausages. Fry for 5 minutes.

3 Bring the water to a boil, and cook the cucumber, celery and carrot for 5 minutes so that they are still crisp.

4 Add the soy sauce and crumble in the bouillon cube. Add the garlic, ginger, honey and vinegar and stir well. Mix the cornstarch with a little water and stir into the sauce. Boil for 3 minutes until it thickens, stirring all the time. Stir in the sausage, beef and onion mixture and simmer for 10 minutes.

5 Arrange on a serving dish, surrounded by boiled rice.

Serves 4

Tip: For a sweeter and more colorful sauce, try adding strips of sweet red pepper, pineapple chunks and tangerine sections to the sauce before serving.

Sweet and Sour Beef, Curried Meat Balls and Beef Farmhouse Pie are three supper dishes for cold evenings

Look 'n Cook Beef Goulash

1 The ingredients **2** Peel the onions and slice them finely **3** Cut the meat into 1-inch cubes **4** Sauté the onion in the oil for 4 minutes until pale brown **5** Add the cubed meat, reduce the heat and cook gently for 8 minutes, stirring from time to time **6** While the meat is cooking, remove the seeds from the pepper and cut the flesh into shreds. Skin, seed and chop the tomatoes **7** Add the paprika, cumin, garlic, seasoning and mar-

joram to the pan and cook for 1 minute **8** Add the
tomatoes and pepper and cook for another 10 minutes
9 Stir in the wine and water and crumble in the beef
bouillon cubes. Cook gently for 1½ hours **10** Boil the
potatoes **11** Thicken the goulash and add the lemon
juice to the cream **12** Serve the goulash with the sour
cream and the potatoes

Beef Goulash

⅓ cup oil
3 medium onions, thinly sliced
1½ lbs. stewing beef (chuck steak) cut in 1-inch cubes
1 tablespoon paprika
pinch cumin
2 cloves garlic, crushed
salt and pepper
pinch marjoram
3 tomatoes, skinned, seeded and chopped
1 green pepper, shredded
⅔ cup red wine
4¼ cups water
2 beef bouillon cubes
4 medium-size potatoes, peeled
3 tablespoons flour
juice half lemon
⅔ cup light cream

1 Heat the oil in a pan and sauté the onion for 4 minutes until pale brown. Add the meat, reduce the heat and cook gently for 8 minutes, stirring from time to time.

2 Add the paprika, cumin, garlic, seasoning and marjoram and cook for 1 minute more. Add the tomatoes and pepper and simmer for another 10 minutes. Stir in the wine and water and crumble in the bouillon cubes. Cook gently for 1½ hours.

3 Toward the end of the cooking time, boil the potatoes in salted water for 18 minutes.

4 When ready to serve, dissolve the flour in ⅔ cup water, stir into the meat and cook for 2-3 minutes until thickened.

5 Add the lemon juice to the cream. Serve the goulash with the sour cream and the boiled potatoes.

Serves 6

Tip: Shell pasta or rice can be served with this dish in place of the boiled potatoes, if preferred.

Beef Casseroles

Hungarian Meatballs Casserole

1 lb. ground beef
½ cup breadcrumbs
1 egg
salt and pepper
1 tablespoon chopped parsley
½ cup flour
¼ cup oil
3 large onions, sliced
2 tablespoons paprika
¼ cup tomato paste
2 tablespoons flour
1 bouillon cube
1¼ cups boiling water
pinch caraway seeds (optional)
3 medium-size potatoes, sliced

1 Mix the ground meat, breadcrumbs, egg, salt and pepper, and parsley in a bowl. Make 12 meatballs and dust with the flour.

2 Preheat the oven to 375°F.

3 Heat most of the oil in a skillet, brown the meatballs and place in a casserole.

4 To make the sauce, slice the onions, and brown in the rest of the oil. Add the paprika and tomato paste and cook for 2 minutes. Sprinkle on the flour. Stir; cook for 1 minute.

5 Add the bouillon cube mixed with the boiling water. Season and add the caraway seeds.

6 Pour the sauce over the meatballs. Arrange slices of potato around the dish and bake for 45 minutes.

Serves 4

Hellenic Casserole

1 lb. eggplant, peeled, sliced
¼ cup oil
2 large onions, thinly sliced
1 clove garlic, crushed
1 lb. ground beef
2 tablespoons tomato paste
salt and pepper
1¼ cups boiling water
1 beef bouillon cube
3 medium-size tomatoes, sliced
3 medium-size potatoes, sliced
2 eggs
⅔ cup light cream
½ cup grated cheese
3 tablespoons grated Parmesan cheese

1 Sprinkle the eggplant with salt and leave for ½ hour. Wash off the bitter juices and dry.

2 Heat the oil in a skillet and cook the eggplant slices for ½ minute on each side. Remove from the pan.

3 Preheat the oven to 350°F.

4 Fry the onions and garlic until golden-brown. Add the ground meat and brown, stirring. Add the tomato paste and cook for 2 minutes. Season. Add the boiling water mixed with the bouillon cube. Simmer for 10 minutes.

5 Arrange the eggplant, meat and onions, sliced tomatoes and sliced potatoes, in layers in a casserole and bake for 35 minutes.

6 Beat the eggs with the cream and stir in the cheese. Pour on the casserole and return to the oven for 20 minutes until the topping is golden-brown.

Serves 4

The center of our table shows, from top to bottom: Hungarian Meatballs Casserole, Steak and Kidney Pudding, Hellenic Casserole

Quick Chicken and Beef Casserole

1¼ cups white sauce
¼ cup dry sherry
salt and pepper
⅔ cup cooked beef, cut into strips
1 small dill pickle, sliced
⅔ cup cooked chicken, diced
⅔ cup sliced mushrooms
⅔ cup ham, cut into strips
½ cup almond halves

1 Heat the white sauce and stir in the sherry and season with salt and pepper.

2 Preheat the oven to 350°F.

3 Place the beef and dill pickle in the bottom of an ovenproof dish. Pour in half of the white sauce. Put a layer of chicken, mushrooms and ½ cup of the ham on top. Pour on the remaining white sauce and sprinkle with the almonds and ham strips.

4 Place in the oven and warm through for 15 minutes.

Serves 4

Tip: This casserole is especially quick to make and all sorts of left-over meat could be used such as pork or turkey or even veal. For extra body, mix in some canned butter beans.

Mexican Hotpot

2 tablespoons oil
1 large onion, chopped
1 green pepper, seeded and chopped
1 sweet red pepper, seeded and chopped
1 lb. ground beef
pinch paprika
pinch chili powder
¼ cup flour
2 tablespoons tomato paste
1¾ cups water
1 beef bouillon cube
bouquet garni
salt and pepper
1 cup canned kidney beans, drained

1 Heat the oil in a saucepan and fry the onion until soft. Add the green and red peppers and cook for 1 minute. Add the ground beef and brown for 5 minutes, stirring occasionally.

2 Stir in the paprika, chili powder and flour and cook for 2 minutes. Add the tomato paste and water, and crumble in the bouillon cube. Bring to a boil, stirring all the time, then add the bouquet garni, lower the heat and cook gently on top of the stove for 30 minutes.

3 Season with salt and pepper to taste and add the drained kidney beans. Continue cooking for another 5 minutes until the kidney beans are heated through, then serve with plain boiled rice.

Serves 4

Tip: If you like really hot spicy food, try increasing the amount of chili powder and adding some corn for a more authentic South American flavor.

Beef Cobbler

¼ cup oil
1½ lbs. stewing beef, cubed
1 onion, chopped
1 carrot, chopped
¼ cup flour
2 tablespoons tomato paste
1¼ cups water
1¼ cups beer
1 beef bouillon cube
1 clove garlic, peeled and crushed
pinch rosemary
salt and pepper
1 tablespoon milk
1 tablespoon chopped parsley

For the Cobbler Topping:
1½ cups self-rising flour
pinch salt
2 branches celery, finely minced
2 tablespoons chopped parsley
3 tablespoons butter
½ cup milk

1 Heat the oil in a pan and brown the stewing beef for 5 minutes. Add the onion and carrot and cook for 2-3 more minutes until soft. Stir in the flour and cook for a further minute.

2 Preheat the oven to 350°F.

3 Add the tomato paste, water and beer and crumble in the bouillon cube. Add the garlic and rosemary and bring to a boil.

4 Transfer to an overproof casserole dish and place in the oven for 1¼ hours.

5 Meanwhile, make the cobbler topping. Mix together the flour, salt, celery and parsley in a bowl. Rub in the butter until the mixture resembles fine breadcrumbs. Add the milk, a little at a time, and mix well to make a soft dough.

6 Knead the dough lightly on a floured surface and roll out ¾ inch thick. Using a 3-inch cutter, cut out as many circles as you can. Then, using a ½-inch cutter, cut a hole in the center of each dough circle.

7 Increase the oven temperature to 425°F. Remove the casserole and season to taste. Arrange the dough rings, overlapping each other, around the top and brush with milk.

8 Bake for a further 20 minutes until the topping is golden-brown. Garnish with chopped parsley.

Serves 4

Mexican Hotpot, Beef Cobbler and Quick Chicken and Beef Casserole are all deliciously different ideas for casseroling beef

Beef Hotpots

Hotpot Parisienne

3 cups cooked lima beans
1½ lbs. stewing beef, cut into
  1-inch cubes
¼ cup oil
2 onions, chopped
1 clove garlic, crushed
2 tablespoons flour
1 tablespoon tomato paste
1¼ cups water
⅔ cup white wine
bouquet garni

sprig rosemary
salt and pepper
2 zucchini, sliced
4 tomatoes, quartered

1 If using dried beans, soak them overnight in water, then bring to a boil and simmer until tender. Rinse and drain.

2 Preheat oven to 350°F. Brown the meat in the oil for 5 minutes in a saucepan. Add the onion and garlic and cook for 2 minutes. Sprinkle in the flour and cook for 2 minutes to brown it. Stir in the tomato paste and then pour in the water and wine. Season with the bouquet garni, rosemary, salt and pepper. Bring it to a boil and simmer for 10 minutes.

Hotpot Parisienne makes a colorful and economical dish for a dinner party — serve with boiled or savory rice

3 Transfer the mixture to an earthenware pot. Add the beans, cover, and bake in the oven for 1½-2 hours.

4 Remove the hotpot from the oven, add the zucchini and tomatoes, and return to the oven for 15 minutes. Check seasoning, and serve hot.

Serves 6

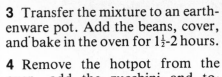

Beef in Cider Hotpot

3 tablespoons butter
1½ lbs. top round, cut into thin
  slices
1 large onion, sliced
2 large carrots, peeled and sliced
2 turnips, peeled and diced
6 tablespoons flour
1¾ cups cider, or 1¼ cups apple juice
  with ⅔ cup water and 1 tablespoon
  vinegar
salt and pepper
1 beef bouillon cube, crumbled
3 medium-size potatoes, peeled
  and thinly sliced
¾ cup grated cheese

1 Preheat oven to 350°F. Melt the butter and fry the beef slices for 5 minutes. Remove. Add the onion, carrots and turnips to the pan and sauté gently for 10 minutes. Stir in the flour for 1 minute. Remove from heat and pour in the cider or apple juice. Bring to a boil, then add seasoning and the bouillon cube. Cook for 5 minutes.

2 Pour into an earthenware pot and arrange the potato slices on top. Cover and cook in the oven for 1½-2 hours. Increase the oven temperature to 400°F. Sprinkle the grated cheese on top and bake for 15-20 minutes uncovered until the cheese is golden-brown. Serve.

Serves 4

Beef in Cider Hotpot is a delicious variation on the traditional hotpot — the beef is cooked in cider and topped with cheese

Beef Fondues

Sukiyaki

1 cup rice
salt
3 cups finely shredded green
  cabbage
1 large leek, cleaned and sliced
  diagonally
8 ozs. canned water chestnuts
2 large carrots, thinly sliced
5 radishes, sliced
4 unbroken egg yolks

1 lb. tenderloin, cut in ⅛-inch slices
  about 2 inches long

For the Stock:
2½ cups water
2 beef bouillon cubes
¼ cup soy sauce
⅔ cup dry sherry

1 Boil the rice in salted water until just tender. Rinse and drain. Prepare the vegetables and arrange in a wide dish.

2 At the table, serve each diner with a bowl of rice and a side dish containing an unbroken egg yolk. Bring the water to a boil in the fondue pot. Crumble in the bouillon cubes and stir to dissolve. Pour in the soy sauce and sherry,

---

Sukiyaki is a traditional Japanese dish — the guests cook their own meat and help themselves to dips and vegetables

bring back to a boil and keep just under boiling point.

3 Place pieces of each vegetable in the stock, and a piece of meat for each diner in the middle. Diners may remove the meat when it is cooked to their individual taste — a couple of minutes should be enough. Serve the vegetables, also cooked to taste, on the rice, and dip the pieces of meat in the egg yolk before eating. Replenish the stock with vegetables and meat as required.

Serves 4

Beef Fondue with Dips

1¼ cups mayonnaise
1 teaspoon curry powder or 1
  tablespoon curry sauce
1 clove garlic, crushed
1 tablespoon chopped fresh
  parsley and chives
3 cups water
2 beef bouillon cubes
⅔ cup dry sherry
bouquet garni
2 fresh mint leaves
salt and pepper
1 lb. tenderloin, diced

1 Divide the mayonnaise between 2 dishes. Into one, mix the curry powder or sauce to make a curry dip. Into the other stir the garlic, parsley and chives to make a garlic herb dip.

2 At the table, boil the water, add the bouillon cubes, sherry, bouquet garni, mint leaves, and season to taste. Keep just below boiling point. Diners take a piece of meat on a fondue fork and leave it in the stock 2-5 minutes until cooked to taste. Dip the meat into one of the dips before eating.

Serves 4

Tip: Other fondue sauces include horseradish, tomato, mustard or tartar.

Beef Fondue with Dips is fun to eat — diners boil meat at the table and flavor it with dips and sauces

Economy Beef

Texturized soy protein (or textured vegetable protein) has proved of great help to cooks to stretch meat further and thus economize, especially with beef. It reduces the need for starchy additives like potato and has the same nutritional value as meat. Its neutral taste absorbs the flavor of whatever it is cooked with. To increase its flavor, fry at the same time as the beef.

Curried Beef and Golden Rice

1 cup long grain rice
pinch turmeric
½ lb. ground beef
1 carrot, diced
1 tablespoon curry powder
1 teaspoon shredded coconut
2 tablespoons raisins
1 apple, peeled, cored and diced

1 Boil the rice in plenty of salted water to which a good pinch of turmeric has been added. Simmer until tender, rinse and drain. Keep warm.

2 Make the basic ground beef, according to the recipe, but add the diced carrot to the onion before frying, and stir in the curry powder when browning the meat. Stir in the coconut, raisins and apple after adding the soy protein.

3 Arrange the rice around the edge of a large dish, and pour the curry into the middle. Serve hot.

Serves 4

Basic Ground Beef

1 large onion, chopped
2 tablespoons oil
1 lb. ground beef
¼ cup flour
2 tablespoons tomato paste
1¼ cups water
1 beef bouillon cube
salt, pepper, pinch mace
½ cup reconstituted texturized soy protein

1 Fry the onion gently in the oil until soft. Stir in the beef and flour and cook until browned. Add the tomato paste and continue to cook for 2 minutes.

2 Pour in the water, in which the bouillon cube has been dissolved, and season with salt, pepper and a pinch of mace. Add the soy protein. Simmer for ½ hour, stirring from time to time.

Serves 4

Beef and Vegetable Vol-au-vent

one 6-inch pastry shell
½ lb. ground beef
½ cup frozen peas
2 zucchini, peeled and sliced

1 Preheat the oven to 425°F. Bake the pastry shell for 20-25 minutes or until golden-brown. Keep warm.

2 Meanwhile, prepare the basic ground beef, according to the recipe. While it is cooking, add the peas to boiling, salted water. Bring back to a boil, add the zucchini and cook them together for 4 minutes.

3 When the beef is cooked, stir in the peas and zucchini and pour the mixture into the pastry case. Serve immediately.

Serves 4

Stuffed Crêpes

½ lb. ground beef
½ green pepper, diced
1 cup corn kernels
1 teaspoon chili powder
1¼ cups crêpe batter
1 cup grated cheese

1 Make the basic ground beef as in the recipe, but add the diced green pepper to the onion before frying, and add the corn and chili powder with the soy protein.

2 Meanwhile, make 4 crêpes from the batter. Preheat the oven to 400°F. When the beef is cooked, spoon ¼ of the mixture into the middle of each crêpe and roll them up. Arrange the rolls in a greased shallow dish and sprinkle the grated cheese over them. Bake for 20 minutes until the cheese is melted and golden. Serve immediately.

Serves 4

Beef Brunchies

½ lb. ground beef
3 tablespoons sweet pickle or mango chutney
2 hard-boiled eggs, chopped
4 slices toasted bread
½ cup grated cheese

1 Make the basic ground beef as in the recipe. When cooked, stir in the sweet pickle or chutney and the chopped eggs.

2 Make the toast and spoon ¼ of the beef mixture onto each slice. Sprinkle the grated cheese over them and serve.

Serves 4

Reading clockwise: Stuffed Crêpes, Beef and Vegetable Vol-au-vent, Beef Brunchies and Curried Beef and Golden Rice

Beef España

1 lb. stewing beef

For the Sauce:
2 tablespoons oil
1 medium onion, chopped
2 tablespoons flour
2 tablespoons tomato paste
1 clove garlic, peeled and crushed
1¼ cups water
1 beef bouillon cube
¼ cup medium sherry
salt and pepper
12 green olives, stuffed
sprig rosemary

1 Preheat the oven to 400°F.

2 Slice the boiled beef thickly and place in an ovenproof dish.

3 To make the sauce, heat the oil in a skillet and fry the onion lightly for 5 minutes, until tender and slightly brown. Stir in the flour and cook for 1 minute more. Stir in the tomato paste and garlic and pour on the water. Crumble in the bouillon cube and bring to a boil. Add the sherry and simmer for 15 minutes. Pass the sauce through a strainer.

4 Season to taste. Scatter the olives over the beef, pour on the sauce and place the dish in the oven for 20 minutes. Garnish with a sprig of rosemary and serve hot.

Serves 4

Tip: You can replace the olives with dill pickles or capers.

Beef España is a quick and easy way of using up boiled beef in a sherry-flavored sauce with olives

Spanish Pie

1½ lbs. stewing beef, cut in ¾-inch cubes
¼ cup flour
1 teaspoon salt
pinch pepper
3 tablespoons lard or shortening
2 large onions, finely sliced
2 branches celery, sliced
⅔ cup water
½ beef bouillon cube
¾ cup tomatoes, skinned, seeded and chopped
1 tablespoon tomato paste
20 green olives, stuffed
¾ lb. puff pastry dough
1 egg, beaten

1 Preheat the oven to 325°F.

2 Coat the beef cubes with the flour, seasoned with salt and pepper. Heat the lard in a skillet and quickly brown the meat in it. Remove and place in a casserole. Sauté the onion and celery in the fat for 3 minutes, then add to the meat. Boil the water in a pan and crumble in the ½ bouillon cube. Pour into the casserole and stir in the tomatoes and tomato paste. Cover and cook for 2 hours or until the meat is tender. Take out of the oven, add the olives and check the seasoning. Turn into a 2½-pint pie dish. Leave to cool.

3 Turn the oven up to 425°F.

4 Roll out the puff pastry dough to a thickness of ⅛ inch on a floured board. Place over the pie dish, trim, and seal the edges. Brush with the beaten egg. Make 2 small slits in the center of the pie and bake for 45 minutes.

Serves 6

All about Veal
Veal in Vermouth and Tuna Sauce

Veal is the meat of the young milk-fed calf of up to 3 months in age, although animals of up to 1 year may be sold as veal.

Veal is at its best from May to September. When choosing veal, the flesh should be pale pink, moist, firm and smell pleasant. The fat should be white and slightly pinkish. The connective tissue should be gelatinous (which will disappear during cooking) but not hard or bubbly. If very white meat is desired for a fricassée, or blanquette, the veal may be soaked in salted water to remove the blood, and even bleached with a little lemon juice in the water.

The cuts of veal are similar to those of beef, with chuck, ribs, loin and legs providing the most commonly used cuts. The chuck can be used for roasts, bone-in chops, veal cubes, veal patties, and lower quality cutlets. The ribs can be used for rib chops and high quality roasts such as split veal rack and crown roast. The loin, which includes the loin eye muscle and the tenderloin, provides steaks, loin chops, medallions of veal, and rolled roasts. The legs supply the highest quality veal cutlets, which are pounded and prepared for dishes such as veal scallopine and veal parmigiana, and can also be boned, rolled, and tied for roasting. Shank is used for stews and the famous Osso Buco. Foreshank and breast provide meat for stews and rolled roasts.

The liver and kidneys are renowned for their high quality. Calf's head and feet may be boiled and served with a sharp vinaigrette sauce.

Veal is an expensive meat and is probably best known for the world-famous Wiener Schnitzel. To make a Wiener Schnitzel cutlet, only 3 ozs. of meat are used. It is flattened out and cooked very briefly in a mixture of oil and butter.

The meat has very little fat and tends to be rather bland and lacking in flavor. For this reason, interesting sauces are often made to go with veal, and pot roasting on a bed of vegetables, or braising, is a better, more tasty way to cook veal than a simple roast.

Veal Roasts

Veal in Vermouth and Tuna Sauce

2 lbs. boned rolled leg of veal
2 tablespoons butter
2 tablespoons oil
1¼ cups water

For the Marinade:
2¼ cups dry vermouth
2 tablespoons vinegar
1 large onion, sliced
1 large carrot, sliced
2 cloves garlic, peeled and chopped
salt and pepper
pinch basil

For the Sauce:
5 ozs. tuna
4 anchovy fillets
3 egg yolks
yolks of 2 hard-boiled eggs
juice 1 lemon
1 tablespoon olive oil
½ tablespoon wine vinegar
salt and pepper
1 dill pickle, sliced
2 tablespoons capers

1 Mix the marinade ingredients and leave the veal to marinate for 2 hours. Remove the meat and dry with absorbent paper.

2 Put the butter and oil in a saucepan and brown the meat. Add the marinade and water, bring to a boil and simmer for 1 hour. Allow to cool in the marinade. If convenient, this part may be done the day before.

3 Remove the meat, and wipe it.

4 Strain the marinade and reduce by fast boiling until 1¼ cups remain. Cool.

5 Make the sauce by mixing the tuna fish, anchovy fillets, egg yolks, hard-boiled egg yolks, lemon juice, olive oil and vinegar. Add the marinade and blend to a smooth, thick sauce, in a blender if possible. Season with salt and pepper, and add the pickle and capers.

6 Cut the veal in thin slices, arrange on a dish, and pour on the sauce. Serve with a rice salad.

Serves 6-8

Veal Vesuvio

1 tablespoon butter
2 tablespoons flour
⅔ cup stock
1¼ cups milk
pinch salt, nutmeg, pepper
juice 1 lemon
¼ cup corn kernels
2 lbs. boned rolled breast of veal
6 ozs. sliced ham
few sprigs watercress
salt and pepper
¼ cup oil
1¼ cups water

1 To make the sauce, make a roux and add the stock. Boil for 10 minutes, add the milk, seasoning and lemon juice. Simmer for 5 minutes. Add the corn.

2 Preheat the oven to 400°F.

3 Unroll the meat, spread with the ham slices, reserving one for decoration, and watercress leaves. Spread with half of the sauce and season. Roll the meat and tie with string. Season and brush with oil.

4 Roast the meat for 1 hour. Add 1¼ cups water to the pan, and cook for ½ hour, basting with the liquid. When cooked, place the meat on a dish.

5 Reheat the remaining sauce and pour over the meat. Decorate with the slice of ham and sprigs of watercress.

Serves 6-8

Veal Vesuvio takes some culinary skill, but the end result makes it all very worthwhile

Veal with Lemon Sauce

2 lbs. veal loin, rump or rolled
  boned shoulder
¼ up oil
2 onions, 2 carrots, 2 branches
  celery, diced
2 lemons
1¼ cups stock
pinch thyme
1 bay leaf
salt and pepper
¼ cup sherry
1 teaspoon cornstarch
¼ cup water
pinch caraway seeds

1 Preheat the oven to 375°F.

2 Brown the veal in the oil in a flameproof casserole, then remove the veal.

3 Put the diced onions, carrots and celery in the casserole, and place the meat on top.

4 Add the finely chopped rind of one lemon.

5 Pour the stock, the juice of the 2 lemons, thyme and bay leaf onto the meat and season. Cover and cook in the oven for 1½ hours.

6 Remove the meat and keep warm.

7 Strain off the liquid and reduce it by fast boiling to 1¼ cups. Add the sherry and boil for 5 minutes. Mix the cornstarch and water and use to thicken the sauce.

8 To serve, carve the meat in slices, arrange on a dish with saffron flavored rice and sprinkle the veal

---

Veal with Lemon Sauce is served with savory saffron rice and makes an extra special roast meal

with caraway seeds. Serve the sauce separately.

Serves 8

Creole Veal with Avocados

¼ cup oil
3 lbs. loin of veal, boned
2 onions, sliced
2 carrots, sliced
¼ cup butter
½ cup flour
1 cup milk
2 tablespoons cream
1 avocado
1 cup + 2 tablespoons rum
juice 2 lemons
cayenne pepper, salt and pepper
1 lb. puff pastry
1 beaten egg

1 Preheat the oven to 375°F.

2 Heat the oil in a casserole and brown the meat for 10 minutes and remove.

3 Gently sauté the onions and carrots and place the meat on top. Cover and cook for 1½ hours. Cool.

4 Make 1 pint of thick white sauce using the butter, flour, milk and cream but reserving 2 tablespoons of cream. Cool and add 1 mashed avocado and flavor with rum, half the lemon juice, cayenne pepper, salt and pepper.

5 When the meat and sauce are cold, roll out the pastry ¼ inch thick.

6 Preheat the oven to 400°F.

7 Slice the meat in ½-inch slices and sandwich some sauce between. Press together in the shape of the roast and place on the pastry. Brush the pastry with beaten egg, and wrap around the meat. Turn over, and trim the ends. Brush with beaten egg. Decorate with leaves cut from pastry trimmings, and brush with egg. Let rest for 20 minutes, and bake for 25 minutes.

8 Meanwhile, thin the remainder

Veal en Croûte, in its succulent pastry, is an impressive dish to serve at dinner parties

of the sauce with the remainder of the lemon juice and cream.

9 Just before serving, garnish the roast with slices of avocado. Serve cold with the sauce.

Serves 8

Veal en Croûte

1½ lbs. loin of veal
¼ cup oil
salt and pepper

To make the Flavored Paste:
6 ozs. calves liver
1 large onion
6 ozs. mushrooms
1 egg
1 cup breadcrumbs
1 clove garlic, chopped
1 tablespoon parsley
salt and pepper
1 lb. puff pastry
1 beaten egg

1 Preheat the oven to 400°F.

2 Brush the loin of veal with oil. Season with salt and pepper and place in a roasting pan. Roast for 1 hour. Cool.

3 To make the flavored paste, remove the skin from the raw calves liver and grind. Chop the onion and mushrooms finely, and mix with the egg, breadcrumbs, garlic, parsley and seasoning. Mix with the liver to a smooth paste.

4 When the meat is cold, roll the pastry to an oblong ¼ inch thick. Place the veal in the middle and brush with beaten egg. Spread the paste thickly over it. Brush the pastry with beaten egg. Wrap around the meat with a wide overlap. Turn over so that the seam is underneath, and trim off the ends, making a loaf shape.

5 Place on a greased tray, and brush the outside with beaten egg. Roll out the trimmings to make leaves and place on top for decoration, brushing again with beaten egg. Let rest for 20 minutes.

6 Bake for 25 minutes. Serve hot or cold.

Serves 6

Braised Veal in Mushroom Sauce

2½ lbs. boned and rolled veal roast
  (leg or shoulder)
6 tablespoons butter
2 shallots, chopped
2 onions, chopped
1 sprig thyme
1 bay leaf
salt and pepper
1⅔ cups cider
½ lb. mushrooms, chopped
1 egg yolk
½ cup light cream
2 tablespoons chopped parsley

1 Fry the veal gently in ¼ cup of the butter until browned on all sides. Lift out. Sauté the shallots and onions in the same fat until softened.

2 Return the veal to the pan and add the thyme, bay leaf, salt and pepper to taste and the cider. Bring to a boil, cover and cook over low heat for 1½ hours.

3 Fry the mushrooms in the rest of the butter for 3-4 minutes.

4 When the veal has cooked for 1½ hours, add the mushrooms to the pan and continue cooking for a further 10 minutes.

5 Drain the veal and place on a serving dish. Keep warm. Discard the thyme and bay leaf.

6 Beat the egg yolk with the cream. Beat into the cooking liquid and cook gently until thickened. Cover the meat with this sauce, sprinkle with the parsley and serve hot.

Serves 6

Roast Veal Steaks Parisienne

2 lbs. loin of veal, cut in 6 steaks
salt and pepper
¼ lb. butter

1¼ cups dry white wine
5 potatoes, cut into balls
6 small onions
½ cup light cream
2 slices cooked ham, diced
3 cups fresh mushrooms, cooked, diced
6 cooked artichoke hearts
sprig parsley, chopped

1 Preheat the oven to 400°F. Season the veal steaks and spread them with half of the butter. Cook in the oven for ½ hour, turning once to brown both sides. During the cooking, use the wine to baste the meat.

2 Meanwhile, fry the potato balls and onions, covered, in the rest of the butter for 10 minutes. Drain and keep hot.

3 When the meat is cooked, drain the gravy into a pan and bring to a boil. Add the cream and boil for 5 minutes. Season.

4 Place the steaks on an ovenproof dish and pour a little of the sauce on. Mix the ham and mushrooms and pile on top of the artichoke hearts. Arrange these around the meat and place in the oven for 12 minutes to heat through.

5 Decorate the dish with the potato and onions and sprinkle with the parsley. Serve the rest of the sauce separately.

Serves 6

Shoulder of Veal in Vermouth

3 lbs. boned shoulder of veal
¼ cup brandy
salt and pepper
¼ cup milk
2 cups fresh breadcrumbs
5 ozs. cream cheese
1 cup finely chopped mushrooms
½ lb. chopped cooked ham
1 tablespoon chopped parsley
1 large clove garlic, chopped
2 onions, chopped

1 egg
1½ tablespoons butter
2 tablespoons oil
1¼ cups dry white vermouth
⅔ cup light cream

1 Place the veal in a dish, spoon on the brandy and season with salt and pepper. Let marinate, turning once.

2 Pour the milk over the breadcrumbs. Let it soak in, then squeeze the bread dry.

3 Put the cream cheese, mushrooms, ham, breadcrumbs, parsley, garlic and onions in a bowl. Add the egg and season with salt and pepper. Mix thoroughly.

4 Spread this stuffing thinly over the inside of the veal. Roll up and tie securely with kitchen string.

5 Heat the butter and oil in a large pan. Add the meat and brown on all sides. Add the vermouth, cover and leave to cook over low heat for about 1½ hours.

6 Place the meat on a heated serving dish and keep hot.

7 Add the cream to the pan. Mix quickly with a wooden spoon over a brisk heat. Correct the seasoning, pour the sauce into a sauce boat and serve with the veal.

Serves 7-8

For Extra Flavor
The delicate flavor of veal can be enhanced by cooking it with aromatic vegetables such as carrots, celery and onions, and with fragrant herbs including basil, rosemary and marjoram. To add flavor to the gravy served with veal roasts, you may use veal stock, but may also try incorporating dry white wine, sherry or even vermouth for a really impressive sauce.

Roast Veal Steaks Parisienne are garnished with artichoke hearts topped with ham and mushrooms

Cutlets and Steaks

Veal cutlets, which come from the leg of the calf, are considered particularly choice cuts since they contain no fat or gristle. They are cut about $\frac{1}{4}$ inch thick and are then usually beaten with a mallet or rolling pin until very thin.

Scaloppines and cutlets are similar cuts of veal but differ in the way in which they are cut from the main joint: scaloppines are cut against the grain of the meat whereas cutlets are cut with it.

We have included in this section one recipe which uses veal loin steaks. The loin is a prime cut and so the steaks can be very expensive; pork loin steaks would make a suitable alternative, but the cooking time should be lengthened to ensure that the meat is cooked through.

Veal Steaks with Jerusalem Artichokes

$\frac{1}{4}$ cup oil
$\frac{1}{4}$ cup butter
Six $\frac{1}{2}$-lb. veal loin steaks, $\frac{1}{2}$ inch thick

For the Sauce:
1 onion, chopped
bouquet garni
$\frac{2}{3}$ cup dry vermouth
1 bouillon cube
$\frac{2}{3}$ cup water
juice $\frac{1}{2}$ lemon
$1\frac{1}{2}$ tablespoons cornstarch

For the Garnish:
$\frac{1}{4}$ cup butter
2 lbs. Jerusalem artichokes, cut in halves
1 onion, chopped

1 Heat the oil and butter in a pan, add the veal steaks and cook for 12-14 minutes over low heat and covered with a lid. Turn the steaks over once or twice during the cooking time. Remove the steaks and keep them warm.

2 Make the sauce. Using the fat left from cooking the meat, sauté the onion for 5 minutes and then remove surplus fat. Add the bouquet garni and vermouth and boil for 8 minutes.

3 Dissolve the bouillon cube in the water, add the stock to the pan and boil for 4 minutes more. Season to taste and add the lemon juice.

4 Mix the cornstarch with 6 tablespoons water and add to the sauce. Boil for 1 minute until thickened. Strain the sauce and pour a little of the sauce over the veal.

5 For the garnish, heat the butter in a pan and sauté the Jerusalem artichokes for 6 minutes, covered with a lid. Add the chopped onion and cook for 2 minutes more. Drain off the fat, add $\frac{1}{2}$ cup of the sauce and simmer for 5 minutes. Season.

6 Serve the veal steaks with the garnish and pour the rest of the sauce into a sauce boat.

Serves 6

Wiener Schnitzel

4 veal cutlets
6 tablespoons flour, lightly salted
1 egg, beaten
$\frac{3}{4}$ cup fine dried breadcrumbs
$\frac{1}{4}$ cup butter
4 slices lemon

1 Place the veal cutlets between 2 sheets of dampened parchment paper and beat with a mallet or rolling pin until very thin, $\frac{1}{8}$ inch thick.

2 Coat the veal with the seasoned flour, then dip in the beaten egg and the breadcrumbs until thoroughly coated.

3 Melt the butter in a large skillet. Add the veal and fry over moderate heat until golden-brown on both sides, turning once during cooking.

4 Transfer the veal to a warm serving dish and serve immediately, garnished with the lemon slices. Serve with new potatoes tossed in parsley and a green salad.

Serves 4

Veal Cutlets in Marsala

4 veal cutlets
$\frac{1}{4}$ cup butter
$\frac{1}{2}$ cup Marsala
$\frac{3}{4}$ cup gravy or thickened stock
pinch cayenne pepper

1 Place the veal cutlets between 2 sheets of dampened parchment and beat with a mallet or rolling pin until they are $\frac{1}{8}$ inch thick.

2 Heat the butter in a skillet and fry the cutlets until well browned. Transfer them to a warm serving dish and keep hot.

3 Add the Marsala to the fat in the pan and boil for 5 minutes, stirring well. Add the gravy or stock and cayenne, mix well and pour the sauce over the veal.

Serves 4

Veal Cutlets Milanese

8 asparagus spears
4 veal cutlets

¼ **cup butter**
1 teaspoon cornstarch
¼ **cup port**
3 tablespoons light cream
sprig tarragon, finely chopped
pinch paprika
salt and pepper

1 Cook the asparagus in boiling salted water for 15-20 minutes.

2 Meanwhile, place the veal cutlets between 2 sheets of dampened parchment paper and beat with a mallet or rolling pin until very thin. Heat the butter in a skillet and fry the cutlets over low heat for 5-8

Veal Steaks with Jerusalem Artichokes is a dish that shows how well veal combines with less familiar vegetables

---

minutes on each side or until cooked through.

3 Mix the cornstarch and the port. Drain the cutlets and arrange them on a heated serving dish. Keep hot.

4 Pour the cream into the skillet and stir well to mix with the pan juices. Add the tarragon. Boil for 2

minutes, then add the cornstarch mixed with the port. Simmer, stirring, until thickened. Add the paprika and the salt and pepper to taste.

5 Drain the asparagus and arrange around the cutlets. Pour the sauce over the top and serve very hot.

Serves 4

Tip: The asparagus must be very carefully drained to ensure that no extra water is added to the sauce—otherwise it will become diluted.

Veal Rib Chops

Veal rib chops can be either broiled or fried. It is important to differentiate between rib chops and loin chops— many people confuse the two. Rib chops are taken from the best rib part of the animal and usually weigh about 10 ozs. and are $\frac{1}{2}$ inch thick. Frying is the best method of cooking them. Season the rib chops with salt and pepper, dredge with flour and brown the rib chops on both sides. Then fry gently, covered with a lid, for 15 minutes. Use clarified butter or oil and butter mixed for the best results and flavor. When the rib chops are cooked, drain off the butter, remove the rib chops and pour a little white wine, sherry or Madeira into the pan. Add some rich brown sauce with sliced cooked mushrooms and boil for 5 minutes. Serve with the rib chops.

Veal Cutlets Provençale

4 tomatoes
salt and pepper
3 tablespoons olive oil
four $\frac{1}{2}$ lb. veal cutlets
$\frac{1}{2}$ cup flour
$\frac{1}{4}$ lb. butter
$\frac{1}{3}$ cup green olives, pitted and blanched
1 clove garlic, peeled and crushed
1 bunch parsley, chopped

1 Preheat the oven to 375°F.

2 Wash the tomatoes and place them in an ovenproof dish. Sprinkle with salt and pepper and pour in the oil. Place in the oven for about 10 minutes.

3 Tenderize the cutlets by beating with a mallet or rolling pin. Season with salt and pepper and dredge with flour.

4 Melt half of the butter in a skillet and fry the cutlets for about 5 minutes on each side until browned and cooked.

5 Arrange the cutlets in a dish, place the olives and baked tomatoes around the edges. Keep warm.

6 Melt the rest of the butter in a pan and sauté the garlic and parsley for a minute, stirring all the time. Pour this butter mixture over the cutlets and serve at once.

Serves 4

Veal Rib Chops with Mushrooms

$\frac{1}{4}$ lb. butter
$3\frac{3}{4}$ cups sliced mushrooms
salt and pepper
four $\frac{1}{2}$ lb. veal rib chops
2 tablespoons brandy
$\frac{1}{2}$ cup light cream
1 tablespoon chopped parsley

1 Melt the butter in a skillet. Add the sliced mushrooms and salt and pepper and fry until tender. Remove from the pan and keep warm.

2 Season the rib chops with salt and pepper and place in the pan. Fry gently until browned on both sides and cooked through.

3 Warm the brandy and pour it over the chops. Ignite and, when the flames die down, transfer the chops to a heated serving dish and keep warm.

4 Add the cream to the pan and boil for 2 minutes to thicken, stirring all the time. Taste the sauce and correct the seasoning.

5 Arrange the mushrooms around the veal chops. Pour the sauce over the chops and sprinkle with the chopped parsley. Serve very hot with sautéed potatoes.

Serves 4

Tip: Veal rib chops are delicious when dredged with flour and fried and served on a bed of green beans, as shown in the picture. Pour the butter and meat juices over the veal and sprinkle with chopped parsley. This makes a very quick and easy meal to prepare.

Veal Chops Portuguese

six $\frac{1}{2}$ lb. veal rib chops
salt and pepper
$\frac{1}{2}$ cup flour
$\frac{1}{4}$ cup oil
1 onion, sliced
1 red pepper, seeded and sliced
2 tomatoes, skinned, seeded and chopped
2 cloves garlic, peeled and chopped
pinch rosemary
$\frac{1}{2}$ cup corn kernels
$\frac{2}{3}$ cup dry sherry
$\frac{2}{3}$ cup water
1 chicken bouillon cube
salt and pepper
pinch paprika

1 Sprinkle the rib chops with salt and pepper and dredge with flour. Heat the oil in a skillet and fry the chops for 5 minutes on each side until browned. Transfer the chops to a shallow ovenproof dish and keep warm.

2 Preheat the oven to 375°F.

3 Sauté the onion in the same pan for 5 minutes until soft. Add the sliced pepper and fry for a further 2 minutes. Add the tomatoes, garlic, rosemary and corn and stir well. Pour in the sherry and water and sprinkle in the bouillon cube. Season with salt and pepper and paprika, and boil for 5 minutes.

4 Pour the sauce over the veal and braise gently in the oven for 35 minutes, covered with a lid. Serve with plain boiled rice.

Serves 6

Veal Chops Bonne Femme

four ½-lb. veal rib chops
salt and pepper
½ cup flour
¼ lb. clarified butter or butter and
   oil mixed
2 small boiled, cold potatoes,
   thinly sliced
1 cup pearl onions
½ cup sherry
⅔ cup rich brown sauce
1 tablespoon chopped parsley

Veal rib chops look as good as they taste if served with a colorful vegetable, such as these tender green beans

1 Sprinkle the rib chops with the salt and pepper and dredge with flour.

2 Preheat the oven to 400°F.

3 Heat the butter in a skillet and gently fry the rib chops on both sides for a few minutes.

4 Place the rib chops on an oven-proof dish in the oven to continue cooking.

5 Fry the potatoes in the same pan until golden-brown, remove and keep warm. Then sauté the onions for 2 minutes. Transfer the onions to a saucepan of water and boil until soft.

6 Drain off the butter and pour the sherry into the pan. Add the brown sauce and bring to a boil, stirring all the time.

7 Arrange the rib chops on a serving dish, surrounded by the fried potatoes and onions. Cover with the sauce and sprinkle with chopped parsley.

Serves 4

Stuffed Veal

These dishes use cutlets in a different way by stuffing them with interesting fillings, rolling them up into little parcels, and then gently braising them. The long slow cooking means that it is not necessary to use expensive cuts and the cutlets can be cut from any part, such as the chuck.

Veal Paupiettes

5 ozs. lean pork or veal trimmings
1 egg
1¼ cups slightly whipped all-
   purpose cream
4 veal cutlets, 6 ozs. each
salt, pepper, and nutmeg
2 tablespoons butter
¾ cup white wine

1 Chop and grind the pork or veal trimmings. Put in a bowl, add the egg and mix well. Stir in ¼ cup of the cream and chill to make a firm paste.

2 On a wet board, beat the cutlets to make them very thin. Season with salt, pepper and nutmeg.

3 Spread the stuffing on the cutlets, roll up and tie with string.

4 Heat the butter and brown the paupiettes all over.

5 Add the rest of the cream and the white wine and stir carefully. Bring to a boil and simmer the paupiettes for 1 hour.

6 Remove the paupiettes. Discard the string and keep hot.

7 Reduce the sauce to 1¼ cups by fast boiling, and pour over the paupiettes.

Serves 4

Hungarian Veal Paupiettes

½ cup sausage meat
½ cup ground ham
1 egg
salt and pepper
6 cutlets, ¼ lb. each
½ cup flour
¼ cup oil
1 lb. carrots
¼ lb. lean bacon
¼ cup butter
¾ cup white wine
½ lb. pearl onions
1¼ cups stock
1 tablespoon chopped parsley

1 Blend the sausage meat, ham, egg and seasoning to a smooth paste. Chill.

2 On a wet board, flatten the cutlets by beating to make them thin. Spread the filling on each cutlet. Roll up and tie with string, and dip in flour.

3 Heat half of the oil in a pan and brown the paupiettes for 4 minutes, covered with a lid. Remove and put in a casserole.

4 Slice the carrots. Cut the bacon into strips.

5 Heat the butter and rest of the oil and fry the bacon for 1 minute, then add the carrots. Sauté for 3 minutes, then add the bacon and carrots to the veal.

6 Add the white wine and bring to a boil. Cover the dish and simmer for 1 hour.

7 Meanwhile, boil the pearl onions in stock for 2 minutes.

8 Remove the paupiettes, discard the string.

9 Reduce the sauce by fast boiling to 1¼ cups.

10 Serve the paupiettes surrounded by the bacon, carrots and onions. Pour on the sauce. Sprinkle with parsley.

Serves 6

Veal with Olives

2 large onions, chopped
¼ cup butter
¼ lb. calves liver
¼ lb. lean bacon
1 cup olives, pitted
¼ lb. veal trimmings
1 cup breadcrumbs
1 egg
salt and pepper
6 veal cutlets, 6 ozs. each
1 carrot, chopped
1 tablespoon flour
½ cup white wine
1 cup stock
2 tablespoons tomato paste
bouquet garni

1 Sauté one chopped onion in 2 tablespoons of the butter and brown lightly. Put in a bowl. Briefly fry the calves liver to brown and remove.

2 Mince the bacon, one third of the olives, veal trimmings and liver, and add to the onions. Add the breadcrumbs and egg.

3 On a wet board, beat the cutlets to make them thin. Spread with the stuffing. Roll up and tie with string.

4 Brown the paupiettes all over in the remainder of the butter. Remove and put in a casserole.

5 Add the other chopped onion and carrot and brown. Stir in the flour and brown. Add the white wine, stock and tomato paste. Add the bouquet garni, salt and pepper.

6 Pour over the paupiettes and cook for 1 hour. Add the remainder of the olives 10 minutes before the end.

7 Remove the paupiettes. Discard the string, and arrange on a dish. Reduce the sauce to 1¼ cups and pour over.

Serves 6

Hungarian Veal Paupiettes, stuffed with sausage meat, wins compliments from guests at the dinner table

Look 'n Cook Veal Paupiettes

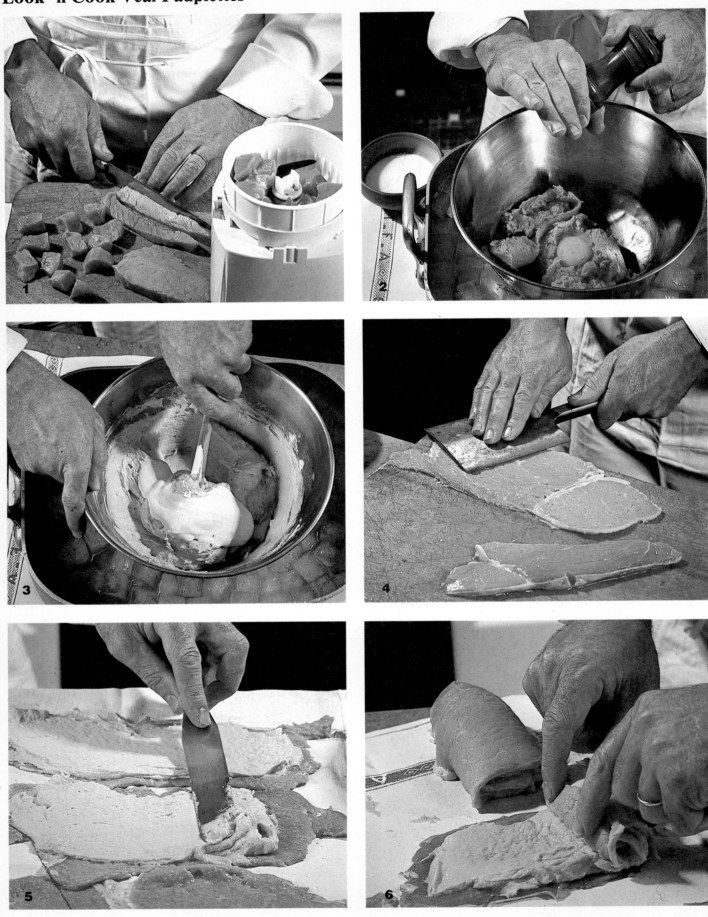

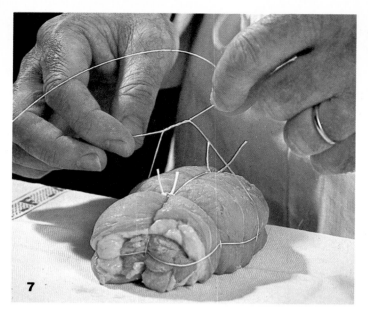

1 Chop the lean pork or veal trimmings to be used for the stuffing and put through a grinder **2** Place in a bowl and keep cool over ice cubes or chill in a refrigerator when made. Add 1 egg and season with salt and freshly ground pepper **3** Add the cream gradually and stir to make a smooth firm paste and chill until used **4** On a wet board, beat the cutlets until they are very thin **5** Place on a cloth to dry and then spread the chilled stuffing carefully on each cutlet **6** Roll up tightly **7** Tie up securely with string into neat parcels **8** Heat a mixture of butter and oil and brown the paupiettes all over, covered with a lid **9** Add the cream and white wine. Stir carefully, season and add a bouquet garni, bring to a boil and simmer for 1 hour **10** When the paupiettes are tender, remove from the pan. Carefully remove all the string and arrange on a dish. Reduce the sauce by fast boiling to 1¼ cups and check the seasoning and pour over the paupiettes and serve hot

Veal Stews

Blanquette de Veau

2 lbs. stewing veal from neck or
   shoulder
salt and pepper
2 large carrots
1 large leek
1 branch celery
2 cloves garlic
bouquet garni
1 onion studded with 2 cloves
$\frac{1}{4}$ lb. butter
$\frac{1}{2}$ cup flour
1 lb. small onions
1 lb. mushrooms
juice $\frac{1}{2}$ lemon
2 egg yolks
$\frac{2}{3}$ cup heavy cream
pinch nutmeg

1 Cut the veal into 1½-inch cubes.
Place in a saucepan, cover with cold
water and bring to a boil. Drain and
rinse in cold water, removing any
scum. Return the meat to the pan,
cover with water, season with salt
and pepper. Bring to a boil, then
simmer.

2 Slice the carrots in 4 lengthwise,
trim and clean the leek, chop the
celery and garlic. Add these vegetables, with the bouquet garni and
the onion studded with 2 cloves, to
the meat. Cover and simmer gently
for 1¼ hours.

3 Make a roux with half of the butter, and the flour. Cook for 2
minutes and leave to cool.

4 Sauté the small onions in half of
the remaining butter. Blanch the
mushrooms in the other half of the
butter, the lemon juice and 2 tablespoons water, until tender. The
liquor may be added to the stew.

5 Take the meat from the pan and
keep warm. Remove the vegetables

and strain the sauce. Pour some of
the liquid onto the roux and blend
to produce a thin, smooth sauce.
Bring to a boil, adjust seasoning.

6 In another bowl beat together
the egg yolks and cream with a
pinch of nutmeg. Stir in ½ cup of the
sauce. Pour this mixture into the
stew sauce, stirring briskly with a
sauce whisk to a thick, smooth
sauce.

7 Return meat, mushrooms and
small onions to a pan and pour the
sauce over them through a sieve.
Reheat without bringing to a boil.
Arrange the meat and vegetables in
a heated serving dish, pour the
sauce over them, and serve hot.

Serves 8

Veal Fricassée

2 onions, chopped
1½ lbs. stewing veal cut in 1¼-inch
   cubes
$\frac{2}{3}$ cup white wine
1 bay leaf
pinch thyme
salt and pepper
$\frac{1}{4}$ cup flour
2 tablespoons butter
2 tablespoons milk
$\frac{1}{4}$ lb. mushrooms

1 Preheat oven to 325°F. Place the
veal, onions, wine, herbs, and
seasoning to taste in a casserole,
cover and cook in the oven for
about 1¼ hours or until the meat is
tender. Remove the meat, strain
liquid.

2 Make a roux of the flour and
butter and cook for 2 minutes.
Remove from the heat, add the
milk to make a smooth paste, and
stir in the cooking liquid to make
up 1¼ cups of smooth sauce.

3 Pour the sauce over the veal in
the casserole, add the mushrooms,
and return to the oven for 20
minutes. Serve hot.

Serves 4

Mediterranean Veal Stew

1½ lbs. shoulder veal cut in 1¼-inch
   cubes
3 onions, chopped
3 tablespoons oil
$\frac{1}{4}$ cup flour
juice 1 lemon
1¼ cups white meat stock
2 cloves garlic, peeled and
   chopped
1 lb. tomatoes, skinned, seeded
   and chopped
2 green peppers, seeded and
   sliced
2 cups peas
salt and pepper
$\frac{2}{3}$ cup pitted green olives
$\frac{1}{2}$ cup light cream

1 Fry the meat and onions in the
oil until lightly browned. Add the
flour and stir while cooking for 2
minutes.

2 Stir in the lemon juice, stock,
garlic, tomatoes, green peppers,
peas and seasoning to taste. Bring
to a boil, cover and simmer gently
for 25 minutes.

3 Dip the olives into boiling water
for 1 minute, drain and chop them
roughly. Add them to the pan and
continue to cook for 15 minutes.

4 Remove the meat and vegetables
and transfer them to a heated serving dish. Add the cream to the pan
and boil, stirring constantly, for 5
minutes to thicken. Pour the sauce
over the meat and serve at once.

Serves 4

Serbian Veal with Yogurt

2 green peppers, seeded and
   diced
2 tablespoons oil
1½ lbs. shoulder veal

1 Cut a lemon in two and squeeze the juice out **2** Put the butter into a heavy-based saucepan. Break it into pieces with a wooden spoon. Pour in the lemon juice. Melt the butter, stirring. Do not allow the mixture to

brown **3** Add the turned mushroom heads and the water. Simmer gently without a lid **4** When the mushrooms are tender, remove them from the pan

2 large onions, quartered
¼ cup shortening
salt and pepper
1 cup white meat stock
1 tablespoon paprika
4 large tomatoes, peeled, seeded and chopped
1¼ cups yogurt

1 Sauté the diced green peppers in the oil for 10-15 minutes over low heat.

2 Cut the meat into ¼-inch slices. In a saucepan, sauté the veal and onions in the shortening until lightly browned. Season with salt and pepper, pour in the stock, add the paprika and bring to a boil. Cover and simmer for 20 minutes.

3 Add the tomatoes to the green peppers and cook for 10 minutes over low heat, stirring constantly.

4 Remove the veal and onion from the saucepan, leaving the liquid, and place in a warm serving dish. Strain the green pepper and tomato, arrange around the meat, and pour any remaining vegetable liquid into the meat liquor.

5 Stir the yogurt into the liquor over heat, and beat for 2 minutes with a whisk. Pour over the veal.

Serves 4

Look 'n Cook Blanquette de Veau

1 Place veal in a saucepan, cover with cold water and bring to a boil **2** Drain and rinse in cold water. Return veal to pan, cover with water and season. Bring to a boil **3** Slice carrots, trim and clean leek, prepare onion, bouquet garni, celery, garlic. Add vegetables to meat

and simmer 1¼ hours **4** Make a roux from the butter and flour. Cook 2 minutes and let cool **5** Sauté the small onions in butter **6** Poach the mushrooms in butter, water and lemon juice until soft. Add the liquor to the stew **7** Remove meat from pan and reserve. Dis-

card vegetables. Strain cooking liquor through a sieve **8** Pour part of the liquor on the roux. Bring to a boil, stirring, and add more liquor if needed to make a smooth thin sauce **9** Mix cream and egg yolks with some of the sauce. Add to the sauce, beating to thicken

10 Combine meat, mushrooms and onions and pour the sauce over them through a sieve. Reheat without boiling **11** and **12** Place meat mixture in a dish, pour on the sauce and serve hot

Veal Marengo

2 lbs. stewing veal (from the
  shoulder)
¼ cup oil
¼ cup butter
2 large onions, finely chopped
½ cup flour
1¼ cups white wine
4 tomatoes, skinned, seeded and
  chopped
2 cloves garlic, crushed
bouquet garni
salt and pepper
1 lb. scallions
1 tablespoon butter
1 tablespoon sugar
3 cups mushrooms
4 slices white bread
1 tablespoon chopped parsley

1 Cut the veal into 1-inch cubes.
Brown it quickly in half the oil and
butter, mixed. Add the chopped
onions and cook them gently with
the meat until soft. Dust with flour
and cook until it just browns.

2 Add the white wine and stir to
absorb any juices which are stuck
onto the pan. Mix in the tomatoes,
garlic and bouquet garni, cover
with water, and season with salt
and pepper. Bring to a boil, cover
the pan and simmer over low heat
for 1-1¼ hours.

3 Peel the scallion bulbs, cutting
away the green leaves, and sauté
bulbs to light golden in the butter
and sugar.

4 Quarter the mushrooms and fry
them gently in the other half of the
oil and butter mixture.

5 Cut the bread into heart-shaped
croûtons, and fry them until crisp
and golden-brown in the rest of the
oil and butter.

6 Add the scallions and mushrooms to the meat and simmer for 5
minutes more. Chop the parsley
and dip the pointed end of each
croûton in the meat sauce and then

in the parsley. Serve in a deep,
heated dish, garnished with the
croûtons.

Serves 8

Veal Shoulder Riviera with Noodles

1½ lbs. veal shoulder in 2-
  inch thick pieces
6 ozs. veal kidney, sliced
¼ cup oil
1 large onion, chopped
3 carrots, scraped and sliced
2 branches celery, sliced
⅔ cup white wine
⅔ cup white meat stock
1 clove garlic, crushed
2 cups noodles
¼ cup butter
⅓ cup grated Parmesan
salt and pepper
¼ cup light cream
large pinch paprika
parsley to garnish

1 Brown the veal shoulder and
kidney in the oil for 8 minutes,
turning the shoulder pieces once.
Add the vegetables, cover and
simmer gently for 10 minutes.

2 Pour in the wine and stock, add
the garlic and season to taste. Simmer for 1½ hours.

3 Boil the noodles in salted water
for 8-10 minutes until tender. Drain
them and stir in the butter,
Parmesan cheese, and a pinch of
salt and pepper.

4 Stir the cream and paprika into
the meat mixture. Bring back to a
boil and remove from heat.

5 Arrange the noodles around a
heated serving dish and fill the center with the meat and sauce. Garnish with sprigs of parsley, and
serve at once.

Serves 4

Crêpes Corsican Style

2 eggs
1 cup flour
1¼ cups milk
¼ cup butter
1 large onion, chopped
½ cup diced mushrooms
¾ cup ground cooked veal
pinch curry powder
1 clove garlic, chopped
1 tablespoon tomato paste
1 tablespoon flour
salt and pepper
pinch oregano

For the Sauce:
1 egg yolk
1 teaspoon prepared mustard
1¼ cups white sauce
½ cup grated cheese
pinch paprika

1 Combine the eggs, flour and
milk into a smooth batter and make
6 crêpes, about 6 inches wide.

2 Melt the butter and sauté the
chopped onion for 5 minutes until
soft. Add the mushrooms and sauté
for 1 minute. Blend in the ground
veal, curry powder, garlic, tomato
paste, flour, salt and pepper to
taste, and oregano. Cook gently for
8 minutes, and leave to cool.

3 Divide the mixture between the
crêpes. Roll up each crêpe and
place in a a shallow ovenproof dish.

4 Blend the egg yolk and mustard
and mix in the white sauce. Stir in ¾
of the grated cheese, and season
with salt, pepper and a pinch of
paprika. Pour the sauce over the
crêpes, sprinkle on the rest of the
cheese, and place dish under the
broiler until browned. Serve hot.

Serves 3

---

*Veal Shoulder Riviera with
Noodles (left), and Crêpes
Corsican Style (right) are two
tasty ideas for lunch*

Look 'n Cook Veal Marengo

1 The main ingredients: veal, bread, tomatoes, onions, mushrooms, herbs and garlic **2** Cut the veal into cubes and brown quickly in oil and butter **3** Cook the chopped onions gently with the meat **4** Dust with flour and cook gently to brown **5** Add the white wine and stir to absorb any juices stuck to the pan. Add tomatoes, garlic, bouquet garni and hot water to cover, and season. Bring to a boil, cover and simmer for 1-1¼ hours **6** Peel the scallion bulbs and brown in butter and sugar **7** Clean the mushrooms, quarter and sauté them in butter **8** Cut the bread into heart-shaped croûtons. Fry to golden-brown **9** Add the mushrooms and scallions to the meat and simmer for 5 minutes. Chop the parsley **10** Serve in a deep, heated serving dish. Dip the point of each croûton in the sauce and then in the chopped parsley. Arrange the croûtons around the dish. Serve very hot

Osso Buco with Artichoke Hearts

2 tablespoons flour
salt and pepper
8 slices veal shank 1 inch thick
2 tablespoons butter
1 large onion, sliced
2 cloves garlic, peeled and crushed
2 carrots, sliced
2 branches celery, finely chopped
¾ cup dry white wine
4 large tomatoes, skinned,
  seeded and chopped
1 tablespoon tomato paste
1 bay leaf
pinch dried rosemary
8 canned artichoke hearts
juice and grated peel 1 lemon
1 tablespoon chopped parsley

1 Season the flour with salt and pepper. Dredge the veal in it. Heat the butter in a skillet and brown the veal. Take out and place in a heavy-based pan.

2 Lightly sauté the onion, garlic, carrots and celery in oil, then add to the meat.

3 Pour the wine over the meat and vegetables. Bring to a boil, then lower heat to simmering. Stir in the tomatoes, tomato paste, bay leaf and rosemary. Season to taste. Cover and let simmer for 1 hour or until the meat is tender.

4 Add the drained artichoke hearts and the juice and grated rind of the lemon. Cook for 10 minutes more. Immediately before serving, sprinkle on the chopped parsley. Serve with plain boiled potatoes, rice or noodles and a crisp green salad.

Serves 4

Tips: This dish can also be made using veal shank cut 2 inches thick. Allow one per portion and cook for 1½ hours.

The marrow inside the shinbone is delicious: eat it with the stew.

Shoulder of Veal Paysanne

20 pearl onions
20 small carrots
salt and pepper
3 lbs. shoulder of veal cut in 2-inch
  pieces
¼ cup flour
2 tablespoons butter
1½ cups water
1 chicken bouillon cube
bouquet garni
20 small new potatoes
1 lb. green peas, fresh or frozen

1 Carefully peel the onions, leaving them whole. Peel and trim the carrots.

2 Season the veal and dredge in the flour. Heat the butter in a skillet and brown the meat in it. Transfer to a heavy-based stewing pan. Sauté the onions and carrots in the butter for 1 minute, then add to the meat.

3 Pour on the water, crumble in the bouillon cube and bring to a boil. Reduce heat at once, add the bouquet garni and check seasoning. Cover and simmer gently for 30 minutes.

4 Peel the new potatoes and add them to the pan with the peas. Add more stock, if necessary, so the vegetables are just covered. Replace the lid on the pan and simmer again for 45 minutes to 1 hour, until the meat is tender.

Serves 6

Veal Hotpot

1½ lbs. leg of veal
¼ lb. bacon
2 medium potatoes
1 medium carrot
1 large onion
1 green or red pepper
1 clove garlic
4 tomatoes
salt and pepper
2 tablespoons flour
2 tablespoons oil
1 tablespoon tomato paste
bouquet garni
pinch paprika
2½ cups water
1 chicken bouillon cube

1 Preheat the oven to 350°F.

2 Cut the veal and the bacon into 2-inch cubes. Peel and quarter the potatoes and carrot. Slice the onion and seed the pepper, cutting it into 2-inch strips. Peel and crush the garlic. Skin, seed and quarter the tomatoes.

3 Season the veal and dredge in the flour. Heat the oil in a skillet and fry the meat until browned. Remove and place in a casserole. Lightly fry the bacon, onion and pepper. Add the garlic, potatoes and carrot and fry for 2 minutes more. Transfer to the casserole.

4 Stir in the tomatoes, tomato paste, the bouquet garni and the paprika. Bring the water to a boil in a pan, crumble in the bouillon cube, and pour over the meat. Cover tightly and place in the oven for about 1 hour or until the veal is tender.

Serves 4-5

Using Pork Shoulder
Dishes which use shoulder or leg of veal can be made more interesting by using half the quantity of veal and making up the difference with pork shoulder. This shoulder has a higher proportion of meat to bone for the same weight and so will work out more economically. Pork and veal combine well together, the pork adding a considerable amount of flavor while the veal supplies the gelatinous ingredient necessary for a good gravy.

Osso Buco is a traditional veal stew from Italy, usually garnished with parsley, lemon and garlic

Cold Veal

Cold Veal Galantine

one ½-lb. eggplant
1 lb. ground stewing veal
½ lb. ground pork
¼ cup ground bacon
1 onion, chopped
1 cup fresh breadcrumbs
1 tablespoon chopped parsley
salt and pepper
pinch curry powder
pinch garlic salt
1 egg, beaten
6 slices cucumber
3 radishes, sliced

1 Preheat the oven to 400°F.

2 Bake the eggplant in its skin for 15 minutes. Cut in two and scoop out the pulp. Mix in a bowl with the meat, onion, breadcrumbs and parsley, salt and pepper, curry powder and garlic salt. Blend in the beaten egg.

3 Place the meat mixture in a greased, oblong bread pan. Stand the pan in a roasting pan half-filled with water and bake for 1½ hours. Cool and turn out onto a dish. Garnish with the cucumber and radishes.

Serves 6

Veal Roulade

six ¼-lb. veal cutlets
salt and pepper
¼ cup flour
¼ cup oil

For the Stuffing:
5 ozs. diced liver
1 onion, chopped
¼ cup flour
1 egg, beaten
12 asparagus tips, fresh or frozen

For the Chaudfroid Sauce:
1¼ cups white sauce
⅔ cup chicken stock
2 teaspoons unflavored gelatin

1 Beat each cutlet thinly with a mallet or rolling pin on a wet board. Season and dredge with flour.

2 Heat the oil in a skillet and fry the cutlets for 5 minutes on each side. Then cool.

3 Fry the diced liver in the same pan for 4 minutes, add the onion and cook for a further 4 minutes. Stir in the flour and cook for 1 minute.

4 Grind the stuffing mixture finely — twice if necessary — and blend with the beaten egg.

5 Spread this liver stuffing over each cutlet, roll up tightly and wrap in foil. Chill overnight, remove foil and place on a rack.

6 Heat the white sauce. Heat the stock and add the gelatin. Simmer for 2 minutes. Blend half of the gelatin stock with the white sauce and put the remainder aside for glazing and allow to cool.

7 Coat each stuffed veal roll evenly with the chaudfroid sauce. Let cool and set. Then brush with the gelatin. Decorate each roll with two asparagus tips and serve.

Serves 6

Cold Veal Galantine makes a tasty summer lunch; it is also ideal for picnics and buffet parties

Poultry

All kinds of chicken and fowl, turkeys, ducks, geese, and Cornish hens are classed as poultry. They are available fresh or frozen (and sometimes smoked), either whole or as separate pieces, so ensuring a good all-year-round supply. Most poultry is sold oven-ready — cleaned, plucked and trussed — but should you have to prepare a freshly-killed bird yourself, there are full step-by-step photo guides on the following pages

Poultry Tips

Hanging and Storing. Freshly-killed poultry is usually plucked before hanging but should not be cleaned; hang a fowl, by its feet and protected from flies, for 2-3 days in a cool place.

Plucking and Singeing. Feathers are most easily removed while a fowl is still warm. Spread out a large cloth or paper and pluck into this: hold the fowl firmly, then take a few feathers at a time — too many can cause the skin to tear — and tug them sharply toward the head, in the opposite direction to which they lie. Large wing feathers may need plucking singly with pliers. Singe off single hairs or down by holding the fowl over an open flame, while turning it quickly.

For details of trussing and preparing giblets, see following pages.

Frozen Poultry. Frozen birds are usually sold trussed and ready for stuffing; the giblets are wrapped inside the body cavity, so remove them before cooking. All frozen poultry must be thawed completely before cooking; otherwise the inside will be partially cooked when the outside is done, thus running the risk of leaving possible food-poisoning bacteria active. This is especially important when cooking large turkeys.

As a general rule, thaw frozen birds 5 hours per lb. in the refrigerator or in a cool place, or follow the instructions on the wrapper.

Some frozen turkeys are self-basting, meaning they are impregnated with fat to keep them moist during cooking.

Carving Poultry. As soon as the fowl is cooked, let it stand for about 15 minutes to allow the juices to settle; this makes carving easier. Always remove trussing string first.

Sit the fowl on a non-slip surface, with the neck end and breast diagonally toward you. With the flat of the knife firmly against the breast, level the leg outward to reveal the thigh joint; cut through with the knife. Separate the drumstick from the thigh by cutting through its joint. Steady the wing with the fork, then cut through the joint, taking a little breast meat at the same time. Ease the wing away from the body and sever it completely. Repeat both processes for the other leg and wing.

Carve thin slices of breast meat, parallel with the breastbone, including stuffing if used.

ROASTING TABLE FOR POULTRY

Type of bird (unstuffed)	Weight and Servings	Average Time and Oven Temperature
CHICKENS		
Pullet 6-8 weeks old	1-2 lbs. *Serves 1-2*	40-50 mins. at 375°F.
Broiler or Spring 10-12 weeks old	2½ - 3½ lbs. *Serves 3-4*	50-60 mins. at 375°F.
Roaster	3-6 lbs. *Serves 4-6*	20 mins. per lb. plus extra 20 mins. at 400°F.
Capon Young neutered cockerel especially fattened	8-10 lbs. *Serves 6-10*	25 mins. per lb. plus extra 25 mins. at 325°F.
TURKEYS	up to 10 lbs. *Serves 8-12*	slow roast 20 mins. per lb. plus extra 20 mins. at 325°F.
	10-14 lbs. *Serves 12-16*	slow roast 18 mins. per lb. plus extra 18 mins. at 325°F.
	over 14 lbs. *Serves 16-25*	slow roast 15 mins. per lb. plus extra 20 mins. at 325°F.
		Fast roast all turkey weights at 450°F., allowing 2¾ hours, 3 hours, and 3¾ hours overall respectively.
DUCKS including Duckling 2-3 months old	3-6 lbs. *Serves 2-4*	25 mins. per lb. at 400°F.
GEESE	6-12 lbs. *Serves 4-10*	Slow roast 30 mins. per lb. at 350°F.
		Fast roast 15 mins. per lb. at 400°F.
CORNISH HENS	2-3 lbs. *Serves 2-3*	45-60 mins. at 400°F.

NB: For stuffed birds, weigh before stuffing and increase overall roasting time by 15-45 minutes, according to weight of bird.

Chicken Roast & Braised

Roast Chicken with Almonds

$\frac{1}{3}$ cup currants
2$\frac{1}{2}$-3 lb. chicken, oven-ready
salt and pepper
sprig thyme
$\frac{1}{4}$ lb. butter
3 tablespoons water
1$\frac{1}{3}$ cups long grain rice
about 2$\frac{1}{4}$ cups chicken stock — about
    equivalent to 1$\frac{1}{2}$ times volume
    of rice
$\frac{1}{3}$ cup blanched almond halves
1 tablespoon pine nuts

1 Wash the currants and let them soak in a bowl of tepid water. Preheat the oven to 400°F.

2 Cut open the gizzard and remove the pouch. Remove the spleen from the liver, being careful not to let it split open, and discard. Cut away any greenish parts which may be sticking to the liver and which would give a bitter taste. Wash and dry the chicken and giblets.

3 Season the inside of the chicken with salt and pepper. Put in the sprig of thyme, 2 tablespoons of butter and the liver. Rub the chicken with 2 more tablespoons butter. Season the outside. Place the chicken in a roasting pan. Pour the water into the pan, put it in the oven and let it cook for 1 hour. Baste from time to time and turn it around so it cooks evenly.

4 Thirty minutes before the chicken is ready, measure the rice. Boil the stock, adding the prepared giblets. Melt the remaining butter in a stewpan. Add the dry rice and cook over moderate heat. Stir with a wooden spoon until the grains become transparent. Pour in the boiling stock, cover the pan and simmer until all the liquid is absorbed.

5 Place the almonds in a nonstick skillet and heat, stirring frequently until they are golden-brown.

6 Warm a serving dish and sauce boat. Drain the currants.

7 When the rice is cooked, place it on the serving dish. Add the currants and pine nuts and mix them carefully into the rice. Spread the browned almonds on top.

8 Drain the chicken and place it on top of the rice.

9 Pour 2-3 tablespoons of hot water into the roasting pan. Stir vigorously with a spoon to dissolve all the meat juices. Pour the liquid into the sauce boat and serve hot.

Serves 4

Roast Chicken with Almonds — served on a bed of almonds, pine nuts and raisins

Chicken in Wine with Mushrooms

3½ lb.-chicken, oven-ready
⅓ cup butter
1 clove garlic
2 onions
sprig thyme
1 bay leaf
1 cup dry white wine
salt and pepper
½ lb. mushrooms, wiped and
    trimmed
juice 1 lemon
1¼ cups light cream

1 Brown the chicken in 4 tablespoons butter. Peel and chop the garlic and the onions. Put the chicken, together with the garlic and onions, in a large pan with the sprig of thyme, bay leaf and the white wine. Season with salt and pepper, cover and cook gently for about 1 hour.

2 About 20 minutes before the end of the cooking time, heat the remaining butter in a pan, add the strained lemon juice and heat, stirring continuously without letting the mixture color. Add the mushrooms, then enough cold water just to cover them. Reduce (evaporate) the liquid to about half its quantity, with the lid off the pan. As soon as the mushrooms are tender, take them off the heat.

3 Remove the chicken from the pan and place on a hot serving dish. Discard the bay leaf and thyme.

4 Reduce the cooking juices a little, then stir in the cream. Pour the sauce over the chicken. Arrange the drained mushrooms all around.

Serves 6

Scandinavian Roast Chicken

Traditionally, the chicken was wrapped up with pine needles and left for 24 hours for the flavor to infuse.

24 juniper berries
3-lb. chicken, oven-ready
½ teaspoon salt
pepper
4 shallots
3 tablespoons butter

1 Pound the juniper berries in a mortar or chop in a blender and put aside half until the following day.

2 Insert a little of the remaining crushed juniper berries in the chicken and rub the outside with the rest. Season with salt and pepper.

3 Preheat the oven to 400°F.

4 Peel the shallots and chop them coarsely.

5 Heat the butter in a skillet. As soon as it stops frothing, add the shallots and brown them.

6 Add the reserved crushed juniper berries. Cook the mixture gently for 1 minute over low heat, stirring all the time.

7 Pour half the juniper- and shallot-flavored butter into a roasting pan. Place the chicken on top, and baste with the rest of the butter. Put the chicken into the oven and cook for 45-60 minutes, turning and basting the chicken from time to time.

8 Serve straight from the oven.

Serves 4

Tip: Scandinavians serve this dish with potatoes baked in ashes and then basted with cream.

Chicken with Mustard

3-lb. chicken, oven-ready
⅞ cup oil
salt and pepper
1 egg
1½ tablespoons Dijon-style mustard
1 cup dry white breadcrumbs
2 tablespoons white vinegar
1 teaspoon capers, drained and
    chopped
small bunch parsley, finely
    chopped

1 Preheat the oven to 325°F.

2 Put the chicken in a roasting pan. Baste it with 2 tablespoons of oil. Season it with salt and pepper. Cook for 30 minutes in the oven.

3 Boil some water in a small saucepan. Hard-boil the egg for 10 minutes. Put it into cold water. Shell it. Halve it. Remove the yolk and place the yolk in a bowl. (Use the white for other purposes.)

4 When the chicken has been cooking for 30 minutes, take it out of the oven. Spread 1 tablespoon of the mustard over the chicken. Sprinkle the breadcrumbs over it. Put it back into the roasting pan and cook for a further 15 minutes.

5 Add the rest of the mustard to the egg yolk. Blend in the vinegar. Add the rest of the oil a little at a time, stirring continuously with a wooden spoon. Add the chopped capers and parsley to the sauce. Add salt and pepper to taste and mix again.

6 Warm a serving dish and a sauce boat. Place the chicken on it. Pour the sauce into a sauce boat and serve hot.

Serves 4

Scandinavian Roast Chicken with juniper berries–a deliciously different way with chicken

Look 'n Cook Trussing a Chicken

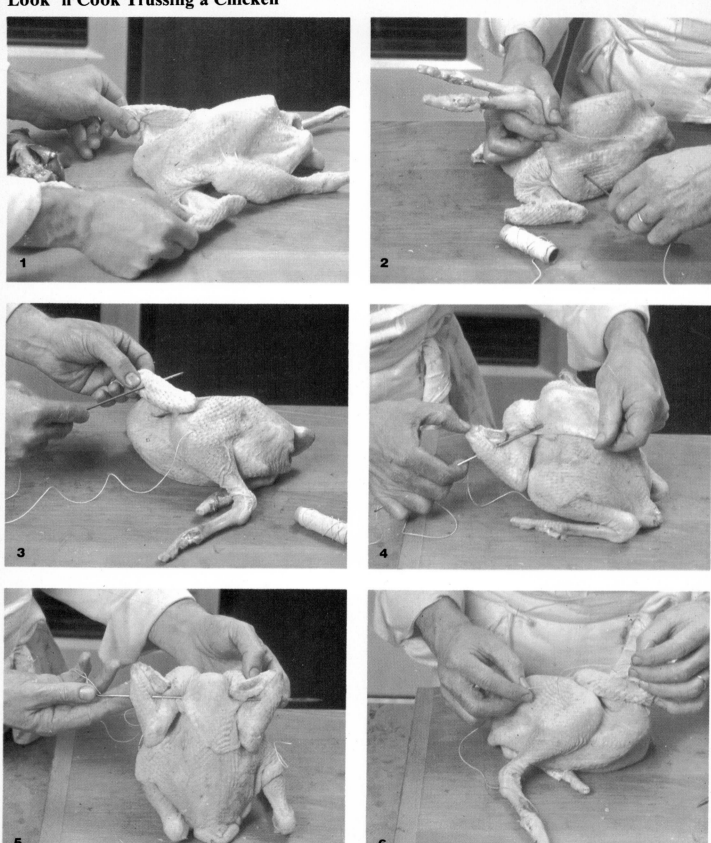

1 Place the chicken on its back. Spread the four limbs quite flat **2** Pull up the legs to lie along the body of the chicken. With a trussing needle threaded with kitchen string, pierce through the thigh of one leg and the body of the chicken, level with its backbone, then out through the other thigh. Pull out the needle and pull

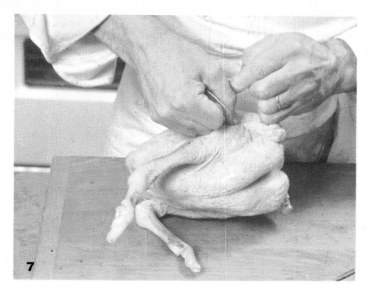

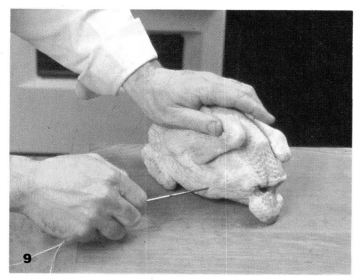

through the string **3** Place the chicken breast-down. Pierce through one wing with the needle **4** Pull the flap of skin from the neck over the back of the chicken and pass the needle through it and the body and out through the other side **5** Pass the needle through the second wing and pull the string through **6** With one hand, hold the end of the string which is coming out of the leg and with the other hand hold the thread coming out of the wing **7** Pull these two ends tightly **8** Tie them together with a double knot without relaxing the tension. This will secure the wings firmly in position **9** Hold the legs against the sides of the chicken. Pass the needle through the back from one side to the other, keeping as close as possible to the backbone; pull the string through without letting the needle become unthreaded **10** Still holding the legs in position, pass the needle again through the chicken from one side to the other, but this time over the drumstick and under the breastbone so that the legs are secured. Pull tightly and tie again with a double knot **11** How the trussed chicken should look —

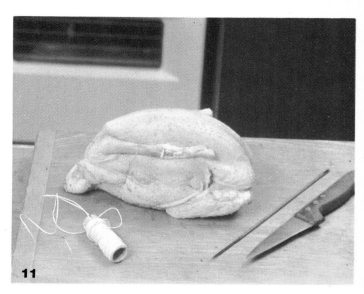

neat and tidy — together with the essential trussing needle, thread and knife

Spit-roast Chicken with Tarragon Stuffing

2½-lb. chicken, oven-ready and
 including its liver
bunch tarragon
3 tablespoons butter
salt and pepper

1 Wash and dry the tarragon. Strip off the leaves and chop them. Put them into a bowl with half of the butter and the chicken liver. Work the mixture with a fork until it has a paste-like consistency. Add salt and pepper. Put the mixture into the chicken.

2 Truss the chicken (instructions on pages 324-325).

3 Soften the rest of the butter in a bowl with a wooden spoon. Season the outside of the chicken with salt and pepper and coat it with the softened butter.

4 Heat the rotisserie unit (spit roaster) or broiler.

5 Pierce the chicken with the skewer or kebab stick. Place it in position on the rotisserie (spit roaster) or under the broiler and cook for about 50 minutes, basting occasionally, above a dish or drip tray. If using a broiler, turn and baste from time to time so it cooks evenly.

6 Warm a serving dish and a sauce boat. When the chicken is cooked remove the skewer or kebab stick. Cut and pull out the trussing thread. Place the chicken on the dish.

7 Pour 2 tablespoons of hot water into the drip tray. Stir vigorously with a wooden spoon to dissolve all the meat juices and pour the liquid into the sauce boat. Serve this dish with watercress and creamed potatoes.

Serves 4

Spanish Chicken with Red Peppers

1 onion
3 red peppers
1¼ cups long grain rice
⅔ cup butter
2 tablespoons olive oil
scant 1 cup diced chorizo (Spanish
 hot red pepper sausage)
small bouquet garni
3-lb. chicken, oven-ready
1 cup cooked young peas
salt and pepper
⅓ cup dry white wine
1¼ cups chicken stock
1-2 tablespoons light cream,
 optional

1 Preheat the oven to 375°F.

2 Peel the onion and chop it finely. Cut the red peppers in half and remove the seeds and white membranes; dice the flesh. Use a cup or bowl to measure the volume of the rice and then put 1½ times its volume in water in a pan and add salt. Set aside.

3 Melt 3 tablespoons butter in a skillet over medium heat. Add 1 tablespoon olive oil and when the butter is hot, add the onion and the diced peppers. Sauté them together for 2 minutes, then stir in the chorizo and brown for 1 minute.

4 When this mixture is ready, add the dry rice. Mix together so that the rice absorbs the flavor from the fried ingredients. Transfer to a casserole, then pour the prepared salted water over the rice mixture. Add the bouquet garni and bring to a boil.

5 Cover with the lid, put in the oven and leave for 18 minutes.

6 When the rice is cooked add 3 tablespoons butter and mix well with a fork until it is all melted. Stir in the cooked tiny young peas, mixing gently.

7 Remove one-quarter of the prepared rice and spread it out on a plate to cool. This will be the stuffing for the chicken. Put the rest of the rice, covered with foil, to one side and reheat in the oven about 30 minutes before the final cooking.

8 Stuff the chicken with the cooled rice. Then truss the bird (see pages 324-325).

9 Heat 1 tablespoon olive oil and the remaining butter in a stewpan.

10 Rub salt into the chicken and place the bird in the stewpan over low heat until it is browned all over (this takes about 15-20 minutes).

11 When the chicken is golden-brown, pour in the white wine, then the stock. Season with pepper, cover and finish cooking over gentle heat for 50 minutes. Reheat the rice.

12 Warm a large, preferably round, serving dish and sauce boat.

13 When the chicken is done, lift it out of the cooking juices. Snip and remove the trussing string and set the chicken aside but keep it warm.

14 Boil the cooking juices rapidly until the quantity is reduced by half. Check the seasoning, then strain the sauce through a conical sieve or fine strainer into the sauce boat. Stir in the cream, if liked. Keep warm.

15 Arrange the hot rice mixture in a ring around the edge of the serving dish. Place the stuffed chicken in the center and give it an attractive, bright glaze by spooning a little of the sauce over it. Serve hot.

Serves 4

Tip: If you cannot buy chorizo sausage use a boiling sausage instead such as knockwurst, together with a good pinch of cayenne pepper and ½ teaspoon paprika.

Spicy Roast Chicken with Peanuts

1 teaspoon paprika
pinch cayenne pepper
pinch ground ginger
salt and pepper
3 tablespoons oil
3 generous cups shelled peanuts
3½-lb. chicken, oven-ready
¼ lb. butter
few slices dry white bread
2 tablespoons light rum

1 In small bowl put the paprika, cayenne pepper, ginger and salt. Add the oil and beat together well.

2 Put ½ cup peanuts through a small mill or work in a blender.

Add the resulting powder to the oil and spice mixture. Preheat the oven to 400°F.

3 Wash, drain and wipe the chicken and season the inside with salt and pepper and truss (pages 324-325). Coat the bird all over with the spicy oil and nut mixture, place it in a roasting pan and put in the oven to cook.

4 Put another ½ cup peanuts through the small mill or work in a blender and mix this powder into half of the butter. Add a little salt.

5 Toast the slices of dry bread and spread them with the prepared peanut butter mixture.

6 Put the remaining butter in a small skillet and when it is just

Spicy Chicken with Peanuts — chicken coated with a delicious mixture of pepper, ginger and ground peanuts

golden add the rest of the peanuts. Fry them.

7 Put the toast on a baking sheet in the top of the oven and cook briefly, or until the peanut butter topping is browned and bubbling.

8 When the chicken is done, pour over the rum and ignite.

9 Arrange the chicken on a hot serving dish and sprinkle on the fried peanuts. Arrange the baked peanut bread slices around the chicken and serve.

Serves 6

Chicken Stuffed with Ham

4-lb. chicken
2 ozs. salt pork
2 tablespoons olive oil

For the stuffing:
¼ lb. bacon
1 onion
2 shallots
small bunch parsley
¼ lb. lean veal
2 cloves garlic
pinch each nutmeg and ginger
¼ teaspoon thyme
pinch crushed bay leaf
1 cup dry white breadcrumbs
3 tablespoons milk
1 egg
salt and pepper
2-4 slices cooked ham

For the garnish:
2 lbs. green peppers
2 lbs. tomatoes
2 onions
2 cloves garlic
few sprigs parsley

1 Wash, drain and wipe the chicken. Prepare the giblets and reserve the gizzard, first removing pouch and liver. Wash and dry the chicken.

2 Make the stuffing. Dice the bacon. Heat some water in a saucepan and as soon as it is boiling, put in the bacon pieces and blanch them for about 5 minutes. Drain them, cool them in cold water, and dry them.

3 Peel the onion and cut in quarters. Peel the shallots. Wash and dry the parsley.

4 Work in a blender or through a grinder the following stuffing ingredients: the bacon, lean veal, chicken gizzard and liver, the onion, shallots and parsley.

5 Peel and finely mince the cloves of garlic. Add them to the rest of the stuffing ingredients, together with the mixed spice, thyme and bay leaf.

6 Rub the dry breadcrumbs through a sieve. Moisten them with the milk and then squeeze out any excess liquid.

7 Add the whole egg to the breadcrumbs and mix well. Fold into the stuffing ingredients. Season with salt and pepper to taste and mix well to obtain an even consistency.

8 Wrap the stuffing in the slices of ham, and slide them into the chicken. Sew up the opening with a trussing needle and string so that the stuffing does not escape.

9 Cut the salt pork into small pieces. Heat the oil in a large flameproof casserole. Add the diced salt pork and melt over low heat. Put the chicken into the casserole and brown it over moderate heat, so that it is sealed on all sides. Cover the pan and let the chicken cook for about 45 minutes.

10 Meanwhile, prepare the garnish. Wash and dry the peppers. Cut them in half, remove the membranes and take out the seeds. Cut them into strips. Skin the tomatoes by placing in a bowl of boiling water, let stand for 1-2 minutes, then drain and skin; take out the seeds and dice the pulp. Peel the onions and cut them in quarters. Peel and crush the garlic. Wash, dry and chop the parsley.

11 When the chicken has cooked for about 45 minutes, add the onions, green peppers and garlic. Season with salt and pepper to taste and sauté for 15 minutes.

12 Then mix in the tomatoes and chopped parsley. Cover and finish the cooking (about 15 minutes).

Chicken Stuffed with Ham — a tasty stuffing made with bacon, veal, spices and herbs

13 Heat a serving dish. Remove string.

14 Arrange the chicken on the hot dish, surround it with the garnish and serve hot.

Serves 6

Chicken Stuffed with Raisins

1 cup raisins
½ cup dry sherry
1 large onion
2¼ cups long grain rice
3 tablespoons oil
¾ cup slivered almonds
pinch ginger
pinch powdered saffron
¼ teaspoon chili powder
pinch each nutmeg and clove
salt and pepper
4-lb. chicken, oven-ready
⅓ cup butter

1 Wash the raisins and soak them for 30 minutes in the dry sherry.

2 Peel and chop the onion. Measure the amount of rice and boil twice its volume of water.

3 Heat the oil in a stewpan. Add the almonds and chopped onion and sauté them until golden.

4 Add the rice to the onion and almond mixture and fry, stirring constantly with a wooden spoon, until the grains of rice are opaque. Pour in the boiling water, cover the pan and cook over very low heat for about 18 minutes.

5 Mix the spices in a bowl — ginger, saffron, chili and mixed spices. Add a little salt and pepper. When the rice is cooked, mix in the spices and raisins. Preheat the oven to 400°F.

6 Fill the inside of the chicken with part of the prepared rice and keep the rest hot in a warm oven.

7 Sew up the opening in the chicken so that the stuffing does not leak out.

8 Melt the butter in a roasting pan, add the chicken and roast for about 1½ hours, or until cooked. Baste the chicken occasionally during roasting.

9 Remove trussing string. Put the cooked chicken on a flat serving dish surrounded by the rice which has been kept hot. Serve hot.

Serves 6

Chicken with Cider

4-lb. chicken
5 cooking apples
1 cup walnuts
2 tablespoons parsley, chopped
2 slices bacon
1 small onion
1½ cups fresh white breadcrumbs
1 egg
½ teaspoon cinnamon or ginger
1 tablespoon dark brown sugar
¼ lb. butter
2-3 shallots
sprig fresh thyme
2 cloves
salt and pepper
2 cups cider
⅔ cup light cream

1 Preheat the oven to 375°F.

2 Peel, core and quarter the apples. Place them in a bowl of lightly salted water to prevent browning.

3 Roughly chop the shelled walnuts.

4 Remove the rind from the bacon and chop it finely. Peel and dice the onion. Melt 1 oz. of the butter in a frying pan, and fry the bacon and onion gently until they are softened.

5 Rinse two-thirds of the apples to remove the salty water. Grate the apples into a bowl, add the bacon, onions, walnuts, parsley, breadcrumbs, beaten egg, half of the cinnamon, seasoning and half of the sugar. Mix well. Stuff the chicken with this mixture, and sew it up with a trussing needle, to prevent the stuffing coming out during cooking.

6 Put the chicken in the roasting pan and spread it with half of the butter. Put into the oven and roast for about one and three-quarter hours, or until the chicken is cooked. 15 minutes before the end of cooking, rinse the remaining apple quarters and place them in the roasting pan around the chicken. Pour on the cider, and baste both the chicken and apples with the cider.

7 Meanwhile, peel and mince the shallots finely. Heat the rest of the butter in a large pan. Add the chopped shallots and sauté for 5-6 minutes on low heat, then add the cloves, pepper and remaining sugar. Stir in the cream, and heat gently for 5 minutes.

8 When the chicken is cooked, remove it from the roasting pan with the apples. Remove trussing string. Skim off any excess fat from the pan juices, then gradually pour the juices into the sauce.

9 Serve the chicken on a warm plate surrounded by the apple quarters, with the sauce poured over it.

10 When the chicken is cooked, add the cream and shake the pan to mix the sauce well. Taste and adjust the seasoning with salt and pepper and a pinch of cinnamon or ginger.

11 Transfer the chicken to a hot serving dish, or carve and arrange the pieces on a hot serving dish, surrounded by the apple quarters and the sauce. Serve immediately.

Serves 6

Look 'n Cook Glazed Onions

1 Peel the pearl onions carefully, leaving all the layers joined at the root end. Cut off the stem down to the onion. Wash the onions in clear water **2** Put the onions into a small thick-bottomed saucepan, and add just enough cold water to cover the onions **3** Add a large lump of butter and bring to a boil **4** Add the finely powdered sugar **5** Heat until all the liquid has been absorbed. The simmering heat should be just enough to make all the water evaporate and not enough to make the onions fall to pieces **6** When all the liquid has been absorbed and the caramel becomes golden brown, shake the saucepan around in a circle so that the onions roll around and are coated in the glaze

Roast Chicken with Caramelized Onions

3-lb. chicken, oven-ready
sprig thyme
sprig rosemary
salt and pepper
1 tablespoon oil
⅔ cup butter
¼ lb. bacon
4 medium-size potatoes, peeled
  and diced
20 pearl onions
2 teaspoons sugar
½ lb. button mushrooms
bunch parsley

1 Preheat the oven to 425°F. Prepare the giblets Rinse the herbs and place them inside the chicken, season with salt and pepper and truss the chicken (see pages 324-325).

2 Place the chicken on its side in a roasting pan. Coat it well with the oil. Spread 2 tablespoons butter on top. Season with salt and pepper. Put the roasting pan into the oven. After 15 minutes turn the chicken onto its other side, basting with the cooking juices (if necessary add a spoonful of boiling water). Fifteen minutes later, turn the chicken onto its back again and leave it until it is completely cooked, basting often (about 25 minutes).

3 Meanwhile, cut the bacon into thin strips. Heat 2 tablespoons of butter in a skillet and fry the pieces of bacon in it. Put them to one side of the pan and keep the fat.

4 Fry the diced potato in the fat left in the skillet.

5 Peel the onions, being careful to keep them whole. Place them in a pan large enough for them to cover the bottom but not sit on top of each other. Add 4 tablespoons butter, a pinch of salt, the sugar and enough water to cover half the depth of the onions. Cover the pan and bring to a boil. The onions are cooked when the water has completely evaporated and the sugar has caramelized. Only cook them long enough to soften but still stay whole. Roll them in the caramelized juices to glaze them.

6 Cut off the ends of the mushroom stalks. Wash the mushrooms quickly and wipe dry. In a second skillet fry them in the rest of the butter over high heat. When all the natural moisture from the mushrooms has evaporated, transfer them to the pan of fried bacon and potatoes. Wash the parsley, dry and chop it.

7 When the chicken is cooked take it out of the roasting pan and keep it warm in the oven on a serving dish. Heat the roasting pan and skim off the fat from the cooking juices; deglaze the juices by stirring in a little boiling water. Leave this gravy to simmer for 2 minutes.

8 Reheat the skillet of bacon, potatoes and mushrooms as well as the pan of caramelized onions. Pour the gravy into the sauce boat. Spoon the vegetable garnish around the chicken. Remove trussing string. Sprinkle on the parsley and serve immediately.

Serves 6

Roast Chicken with Caramelized Onions, also garnished with bacon rolls, sautéed potatoes and mushrooms

Roast Chicken with Blue Cheese Stuffing

1½ ozs. Roquefort or other blue cheese
4 ozs. Swiss cheese
⅓ cup butter
3-lb. chicken, oven-ready
sprig thyme
salt and pepper
1 tablespoon light cream

1 Preheat the oven to 400°F. Blend the cheeses with 2 tablespoons butter. Stuff the inside of the chicken with this mixture. Add a sprig of thyme.

2 Truss the chicken (see page 324). Grease a roasting pan with half the rest of the butter. Season the outside of the chicken with salt and pepper.

3 Place the chicken in the greased roasting pan. Put a few knobs of butter on the chicken. Place the pan in the oven and cook the chicken for 50 minutes.

4 Skim off the fat from the juices in the roasting pan and then stir in the cream. Place the chicken on a warm serving dish. Remove the trussing string. Pour the sauce in a sauce boat and serve with the chicken.

Serves 4

Chicken Cooked in Salt

3-lb. chicken, oven-ready
1 teaspoon brandy
pepper
10 lbs. kosher salt

1 Preheat the oven to 475°F.

2 Pepper the interior of the chicken. Pour the brandy into it.

3 Spread 4 lbs. of kosher salt on the bottom of an ovenproof dish, and place the chicken on it. Cover with the rest of the salt. Do *not* put a lid on the pot. Put it in the oven and cook for 1½ hours without opening the door.

4 Warm a serving dish.

5 When it is cooked, take the chicken out of the pot. Break the crust of salt with a hammer and cut up the chicken. Arrange the pieces on the hot dish and serve immediately.

Serves 4

Tip: The oven should be extremely hot when the chicken is put in so that the salt will firm up properly.

If the stewing pot is covered while cooking, the humidity from the chicken will not escape and the salt will melt and will penetrate the flesh.

Break up the lumps of salt and use again for the same dish.

Roast Chicken with Pineapple

3-lb. chicken, oven-ready
salt and pepper
1 lemon, cut in half
2 oranges
½ cup light rum
¼ cup butter, melted
2 teaspoons sugar
1 small pineapple

1 Season the inside of the chicken with salt and pepper. Rub 1 lemon half over the skin so that it absorbs the juice; reserve the lemon. Squeeze the juice from the remaining half lemon and set aside.

2 Peel 1 orange. Remove the membranes between the sections so that the flesh alone remains. Chop this coarsely. Sprinkle 2 tablespoons rum and 1 tablespoon lemon juice over the orange pieces. Fill the chicken with the prepared orange pieces and leave the chicken in the refrigerator until the next day.

3 An hour and a quarter before the time to serve the chicken, put it in the roasting pan in an oven preheated to 425°F. (The oven should be hotter than is usually needed to roast a chicken, because of its cold stuffing). After 20 minutes, sprinkle salt and pepper over the outside of the chicken and pour the melted butter over it. Return the chicken to the oven.

4 Squeeze the reserved lemon half. Put the juice into a small saucepan with the sugar. Heat, stirring, until it is a fairly dark-colored caramel.

5 Remove ends of the pineapple, then cut away the prickly skin. Slice it, and cut away or stamp out the fibrous core with a pastry cutter. Collect any juice that runs out and add it to the lemon caramel.

6 Pour this lemon sauce and the remaining rum alternately over the chicken. Ten minutes before serving, put the pineapple slices in the roasting pan to heat through.

7 Remove the chicken from the oven and cut up into pieces. Arrange them on a hot serving dish, surrounded by pineapple slices. Add the cooking juices from the pan and the juice squeezed from the other orange to the sauce. Correct the seasoning and pour into a sauce boat. Serve with rice.

Tip: An alternative presentation is to put the rice on a serving dish and place the whole chicken in the center, with the pineapple slices surrounding it. For added color heat a few candied cherries with the pineapple slices, then place them in the center of some of the pineapple rings and around the chicken.

Serves 6

Chicken Portions

Chicken with Caramelized Apples

4 chicken pieces
3 onions
3 tablespoons oil
salt and pepper
1 teaspoon paprika
½ teaspoon ground ginger
1 teaspoon ground coriander
pinch ground saffron
2¼ cups water
3 firm dessert apples
¼ cup butter

1 Lightly fry the peeled and sliced onions in oil. Add the chicken pieces and brown.

2 Season the chicken with the salt, pepper, paprika, ginger, coriander and saffron. Pour in the water and simmer for 30 min.

3 Meanwhile, wash and dry the apples. Cut them in half without peeling, and core them. Heat the butter in a skillet. Add the apple halves and brown them over high heat.

4 Preheat the oven to 350°F.

5 After the chicken has simmered for 30 minutes, place the pieces in an ovenproof dish. Add the caramelized apple halves. Pour over the cooking juices from the pan. Cover the dish with foil and pierce a few holes in it. Place the dish in the oven and let the chicken cook for 30 minutes more. Serve at once.

Serves 4

Chicken with Green Peppers and Paprika Rice

½ lb. bacon
¼ cup butter
2½ lb. oven-ready chicken, cut into serving pieces
¼ teaspoon salt
freshly ground black pepper
1 large onion, peeled and chopped
1 teaspoon flour
1 cup wine, red or white
1 bay leaf
2¼ cups chicken stock
3 green peppers, halved, cored and seeded
1 teaspoon paprika
1 cup long grain rice

1 Preheat the oven to 350°F. Gently fry the bacon in a deep skillet or stewpan. When the fat has run from the bacon, remove it and pour all but 1 tablespoon of the fat from the pan. Put half the butter in the pan, add the chicken pieces and brown them evenly on all sides. Remove the pieces and season them with salt and pepper.

2 Fry half the onion in the same fat for 3 minutes or until soft. Stir in the flour and cook the roux slowly for a few minutes; then stir in the wine and the bay leaf. Cook over a high heat to reduce the wine to about ½ cup. Add ½ cup of the stock and bring to a boil.

3 Put the chicken pieces, bacon and any juices left in the pan in a casserole, cover with a lid and cook in the oven for 50 minutes or until the chicken is tender.

4 Heat the remaining butter in a pan and add the green peppers cut into 1-inch squares and the remaining onion. Fry over moderate heat for 5 minutes, then stir in the paprika and the rice. Stir over moderate heat for 3 minutes, then add the remaining chicken stock, boiling; cover and simmer for 20 minutes. Discard the bay leaf.

5 Serve the chicken from the casserole, with the rice served separately.

Serves 4

Chicken Waterzoi

2 large carrots
8 leeks
4 branches celery
¼ cup butter
salt and pepper
bunch parsley
4-lb. chicken, oven-ready
6⅓ cups chicken stock
3 egg yolks
¾ cup heavy cream
juice 1 lemon

1 Peel the carrots; trim and clean the leeks and celery. Wash them, dry and chop finely. Heat the butter in a stewpan, add the prepared vegetables and let soften over low heat for about 15 minutes. Season lightly. Wash the parsley, dry, chop and add three-quarters of it to the pan of vegetables.

2 Cut the chicken in pieces (see pages 334-335). Put half the vegetables into a casserole. Cover with the chicken pieces and then with the remaining vegetables. Place over low heat for 10 minutes, then gradually pour in the chicken stock. Cover and cook slowly for at least 50 minutes or until the chicken pieces are very tender.

3 Place the pieces of chicken on a heated serving dish. Beat the egg yolks with the cream and the juice of the lemon. Pour this mixture into the casserole while stirring with a wooden spoon. Heat for a few minutes, stirring continuously, but do not allow to boil. Pour the thickened vegetable soup into a hot tureen and sprinkle with the remaining chopped parsley.

4 Serve some of the soup in wide soup bowls, topping each one with a piece of chicken.

Serves 6

Look 'n Cook Cutting up an Uncooked Chicken

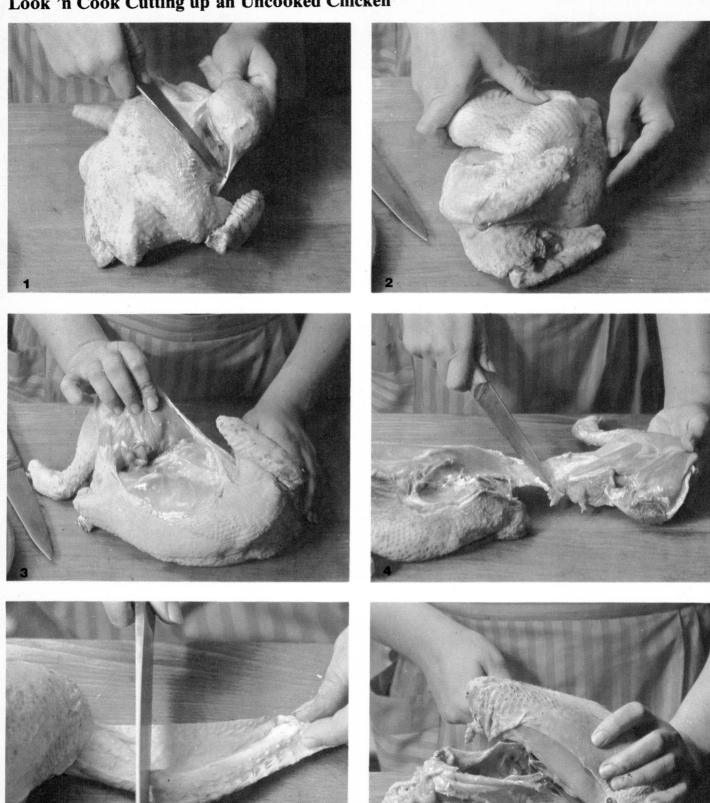

1 Place the chicken on its back, with the parson's nose towards you. Lift one leg and pull it away from the body of the chicken. Cut the skin between the body and the leg **2** Pull the joint out of place by swinging the leg from right to left **3** Pull up the leg so that the thigh joint and bone can be seen **4** Cut through the ball and socket joint and detach each leg **5** Cut off the wings at the center of the joints **6** Cut through the carcass parallel to the breast **7** Detach it by carving carefully along next to the backbone **8** Cut the two sides of the

334

breast (the fillets or suprêmes) in two along the breast-bone, which in a young chicken, will be quite pliable and split easily **9** Carefully pull away the rib cage **10** Cut off the ends of each drumstick **11** Using a sharp knife, cut out the large bones from the legs. Insert the knife into the leg and, keeping the blade as close to the bone as possible, cut all around the bone which can then be pulled away **12** The 6 chicken pieces are now ready to use

Chicken in the Pot

4-lb. stewing chicken, oven-ready
  and with a few extra giblets
  (necks, wings, bones and
  gizzards)
bouquet garni
sea salt
1 lb. carrots
1 lb. turnips
3 leeks
1 branch celery
3 medium-size potatoes
6 slices whole wheat bread
1¾ cups grated Gruyère cheese

1 Cut up the chicken into 10 pieces (see page 334). Put them into a large stewpan. Add the giblets. Cover with cold water and bring to a boil. Drain the chicken meat and rinse under cold water. Put back into the pan with about 9 cups cold water. Add the bouquet garni and a handful of sea salt and boil again, skimming now and then.

2 Peel the carrots and the turnips. Wash them. Cut up both vegetables into equal size.

3 Carefully trim and wash the leeks and the celery. Cut them into 2 or 3 pieces. Tie them together in bundles with string.

4 After the chicken has been cooking for 45 minutes, add the carrots, turnips and bundles of leeks and celery. Let cook for about 1 hour (the time will depend on the age and size of fowl). Check if the chicken is done by piercing the thigh with the point of a knife or trussing needle; the flesh should no longer feel firm.

5 Peel the potatoes. Wash them and cut them up into pieces the same size as the carrots and turnips. Put them into a saucepan. Cover with cold water. Add a little sea salt and cook for about 20-25 minutes or until tender.

6 Preheat the oven to 375°F. Cut the slices of bread in half. Put them on a rack in the oven to allow them to dry.

7 Put the grated cheese into a small bowl. Put the bread on a plate. Warm a deep serving dish.

8 Just before serving, drain the chicken pieces. Put them into the warm dish. Arrange the carrots and turnips all around them. Remove the string from the leeks and celery. Drain the potatoes. Put the rest of the vegetables on the plate. Sprinkle with a little stock from the pot and serve piping hot with the baked bread and Gruyère cheese.

Serves 6

An impressive party dish, Devilled Chicken with Coconut combines a mixture of spices with fresh coconut

Devilled Chicken with Coconut

4-lb. chicken, oven-ready
8 peppercorns
2 cloves
½ teaspoon ground ginger
½ teaspoon ground cinnamon
salt and pepper
3 onions
1 fresh coconut (full of milk)
1¼ cups water
½ cup oil
2 tablespoons butter
pinch cayenne pepper

1 Cut the chicken into pieces. (See p. 334).

336

2 Crush the peppercorns with the cloves, ginger and cinnamon. Add salt and mix well.

3 Spinkle this spicy mixture over the chicken pieces, turning them so that they are well impregnated.

4 Peel and finely chop the onions.

5 Pierce one of the coconut 'eyes' and drain off the milk; reserve. Cut open the coconut, scoop out the flesh and grate finely.

6 Boil the water in a small saucepan, add half of the grated coconut and then simmer for 5 or 6 minutes.

7 Take the saucepan off the heat and leave the coconut in the water.

8 Heat the oil in a pan, add the chopped onions and chicken pieces, and brown over low heat; then continue to cook for 35 minutes, stirring frequently. At the end of this time the chicken pieces should be evenly browned.

9 Strain through cheesecloth the water in which the coconut has been sitting, squeezing well. Mix this coconut milk with the milk taken from the coconut.

10 Heat a serving dish.

11 Drain the chicken pieces and arrange them on the dish. Keep hot.

12 Pour the coconut milk into the pan and boil gently until reduced (evaporated) by half.

13 Meanwhile, heat the butter in a small pan. When it starts to go a deep yellow, add the rest of the grated coconut and brown over low heat, while stirring with a wooden spoon.

14 Salt and pepper the coconut milk sauce, season with a pinch of cayenne pepper and pour over the chicken.

15 Sprinkle the chicken pieces with the browned coconut and serve hot.

Serves 6

Pan-fried Chicken with Pasta

4-5 lb. chicken, oven-ready
salt and pepper
2 tablespoons flour
¼ cup butter
2 tablespoons oil
4 cups fresh pasta (ribbon noodles, spaghetti, macaroni)
½ lb. mushrooms
3 shallots
½ cup brandy
½ cup dry white wine
½ lb. canned tomatoes
sprig tarragon, chopped
½ cup chicken stock
¼ lb. bacon
¼ lb. diced ham

1 Cut up the chicken into pieces (see page 334). Season the pieces with salt and pepper. Roll them in the flour. Put them in a pan with half the butter and all the oil and cook them for 20 minutes until brown and tender. Take out and keep hot.

2 Put the fresh pasta into a large saucepan of salted, boiling water. Let the pasta cook for about 10 minutes or until just tender (time will depend on the shape and thickness of the pasta).

3 Trim and wash the mushrooms. Sauté them in the same pan used to brown the chicken pieces.

4 Peel and chop the shallots. Add them to the mushrooms and let them soften for 1 minute. Pour in the brandy. Heat it and then ignite it. Add the white wine. Stir. Add the tomatoes, tarragon and stock. Let it reduce (evaporate) by one-third over high heat.

5 Brown the bacon in the rest of the butter. Add the ham and heat.

6 Drain the pasta and put into a deep serving dish or vegetable dish. Mix in the bacon and the ham. Arrange the chicken on a separate serving dish and cover it with the sauce. Serve at once.

Serves 4

Portuguese Chicken Stew with Fried Eggs

3½-lb. oven-ready chicken, cut up into pieces
¼ lb. butter
½ cup dry white wine
2 small onions, peeled and finely chopped
1 teaspoon salt
freshly ground black pepper
1 chicken liver
4 eggs

1 Put the chicken pieces into a pan, half the butter, the wine, chopped onions, salt and pepper. Cover and simmer over low heat for about 45 minutes or until the chicken is tender. Remove the chicken from the pan and keep it warm.

2 Rub the chicken liver through a sieve into the cooking liquid. Heat and stir without boiling. Return the chicken pieces to the pan to reheat. Then arrange on a heated serving dish.

3 Fry the eggs in the remaining butter and serve them with the chicken pieces. Serve the sauce in a sauce boat. Serve boiled rice separately.

Tip: Instead of the chicken liver, the chicken can be flavored with 2 tablespoons tomato paste and thickened with a little cornstarch or with a combination of 2 egg yolks mixed with 2 tablespoons heavy cream. Do not let the sauce boil if egg yolks are used or else they will curdle and the sauce will separate.

Serves 4

Chicken Breasts with Spinach

2 lbs. spinach
salt and pepper
1 shallot
1 tablespoon oil
⅔ cup butter
4 chicken breasts (or duck or
  turkey breasts — see Tip)
7 tablespoons flour
3 cups milk
2 egg yolks
1 cup grated Gruyère cheese

1 Cut out the tough stalks and discard any wilted spinach leaves. Wash the spinach thoroughly in several changes of water.

2 Put the undrained spinach into a pan, add salt, cover with a lid and cook slowly for about 10 minutes or until cooked (there's sufficient water on the leaves to cook them). Then rinse under cold water, drain well and squeeze out all the moisture with the hands. Peel and chop the shallot.

3 Heat the oil and 2 tablespoons butter in a stewpan. When the butter is melted, place the chicken breasts in the pan and fry them over medium heat until they are just golden but not brown. Season with salt and pepper. Continue to cook slowly until they are cooked; turn them after 10 minutes and then add the chopped shallot.

4 Slowly melt 5 tablespoons butter in a saucepan. Add the flour and stir and cook for 2 minutes but do not let the roux brown. Then remove the pan from the heat, pour in the milk and blend until smooth, add the salt and pepper, return the pan to the heat, bring to a boil and cook for 5 minutes.

5 Chop the spinach roughly. Preheat the oven to 425°F.

6 Heat the rest of the butter in a saucepan. When it is just melted, add the spinach. Stir well and season with salt and pepper to taste. Heat the spinach through, then put into an oven-to-table dish. Place the chicken breasts on top and, leaving the door open, warm the dish in the oven.

7 Pour the sauce into the pan in which the chicken breasts were cooked. Boil for 2 minutes, stirring vigorously to dissolve any juices that are stuck to the bottom of the pan. Beat in the egg yolks and the Gruyère cheese. Coat the chicken with this sauce.

8 Bake in the top of the hot oven for about 10-15 minutes or until browned. Serve straight from the oven.

Tips: If using frozen, chopped spinach put it into a strainer to thaw, if time permits. Then squeeze the moisture out and heat gently as given in the method above. Or put the frozen spinach into a pan over low heat until thawed.

Cooked chicken breasts, or thick slices from the cooked breasts of duck or turkey can be used. In that case, in step 3, fry lightly until the meat is heated through.

Serves 4

Chicken with Paprika Sauce

½ cup flour
½ cup milk
2-lb. oven-ready chicken, cut
  in half
salt and pepper
6 tablespoons butter
oil for frying

For the sauce:
2 onions
¼ cup butter
2 tablespoons flour
salt
1 teaspoon paprika
1¼ cups heavy cream or cream and
  milk mixed

1 Put the flour in a deep plate or dish. Pour the milk into a bowl and dip the 2 halves of chicken in it. Drain them well, then season with salt and pepper and roll them in the flour.

2 Heat the butter with some oil in a skillet. Use enough oil to make a depth of about ¼ inch. Brown the chicken halves on both sides. Reduce the heat and continue to fry the chicken for about 45 minutes or until tender, depending upon size.

3 Meanwhile, prepare the sauce. Peel the onions and cut them into thin slices. Heat the butter in a pan and soften the onions over a gentle heat without browning. Add the flour, salt and paprika to taste and stir with a wooden spoon over a low heat. Mix in the cream or cream and milk mixture and continue to mix until the sauce is smooth and thick. Keep hot in a double boiler.

4 When the chicken halves are cooked, drain them on absorbent paper and put on a heated dish. Pour the sauce into a sauce boat. Serve them both hot.

Serves 4

Chicken Breasts with Mushrooms

4 chicken breasts, with wing bones
  attached
salt and pepper
pinch ground thyme
2 slices ham
scant 1 cup flour
¼ cup butter
¼ cup Madeira

For the sauce:
¼ lb. lean bacon
1 onion
1 carrot
1 small branch celery
½ lb. mushrooms
¼ cup butter
1 tablespoon flour
1¼ cups stock

3 Heat the butter in a stewpan, add the breasts and fry them over moderate heat for 25 minutes, turning them several times.

4 Meanwhile, make the sauce. Wash, dry and finely dice the bacon. Peel and chop the onion. Peel, wash, dry and finely dice the carrot. Wash, dry and thinly slice the celery. Trim the mushroom stalks. Wash and slice the mushrooms.

5 Heat the butter for the sauce in a pan. Add the mushrooms, cook for 10 minutes, then drain and keep hot.

6 In the same butter, sauté the bacon, onion, carrot and celery, stirring them with a wooden spoon.

7 When these sauce ingredients are golden-brown, add the flour and cook until nut-colored. Then stir in the chicken stock and half the Madeira. Add the bouquet garni, tomato paste and meat juice, with salt and pepper to taste, and continue to cook slowly for 20 minutes.

8 Heat a serving dish.

9 Arrange the chicken breasts on the hot serving dish, first taking out the toothpicks. Pile the mushrooms in the center of the dish and keep hot.

10 Pour the remaining Madeira into the pan used for cooking the chicken breasts and boil for 2 minutes, scraping up the juices on the bottom of the pan.

11 Strain the sauce through a conical strainer, pressing it down well, into a pan. Return it to the stove, add the cooking juices scraped from the pan and boil the sauce for 2 minutes.

12 Wash, dry and finely chop the parsley.

13 Pour the sauce on the chicken breasts, sprinkle with chopped parsley and serve immediately.

Serves 4

½ **cup Madeira**
bouquet garni
1 tablespoon tomato paste
2 tablespoons meat glaze
bunch parsley

1 Cut off and discard the tips of the wings. Remove the skin from the wings, cut the flesh on the inside and take out the bone. Continue the slit the length of the breast, and open out the breasts. Season inside and out with salt and pepper and sprinkle lightly with thyme.

Chicken Breasts with Mushrooms — chicken breasts stuffed with ham and cooked in a mushroom and Madeira sauce

2 Cut the slices of ham in half and slide them into the chicken breasts. Fold together and secure with wooden toothpicks. Dip the stuffed breasts into the flour and shake off any excess.

339

Chicken with Apples

3 onions
5 tablespoons oil
3-4 lb. oven-ready chicken, cut
  into pieces
salt and pepper
1 teaspoon paprika
1 teaspoon ground ginger
pinch ground saffron
bunch coriander leaves or 1
  teaspoon ground coriander
2¼ cups water
2 lbs. apples
¼ cup butter

1 Peel the onions and cut them into rounds.

2 Put the oil in a large pan and brown the chicken pieces and then the sliced onions.

3 Season with salt, pepper, paprika, ginger and saffron. Add the washed coriander leaves or ground coriander seeds, then the water and cook with the lid off for 30 minutes.

4 Meanwhile, halve the apples, leaving the skins on but removing the core and seeds.

5 Put the butter in a skillet and brown the apple pieces over high heat. Take them off the heat when they are lightly caramelized.

6 Preheat the oven to 350°F.

7 Arrange the apples and chicken pieces in an oven-proof dish, and pour the cooking liquid from the chicken over them. Cover with foil, pierced with several holes.

8 Put the dish into the oven and cook for 30 minutes. Serve the chicken in its cooking dish.

Serves 4-5

Southern Fried Chicken

¾ cup flour
¼ teaspoon salt
1 cup milk
1 egg
2 tablespoons vegetable oil
3-lb. frying chicken, cut into
  serving pieces
oil for frying

Southern Fried Chicken — pieces of chicken dipped in batter and fried until tender

1 Mix the flour, salt, milk, egg and oil in a bowl and beat with a wire whisk to obtain a smooth batter. Dip the chicken pieces in the batter and, immediately after coating, fry in hot oil 375°F. for about 30 minutes, or until the chicken is almost tender.

2 Remove the chicken from the fat and drain on paper towels. Turn up heat to 400°F. and fry the chicken for a further 5 minutes until the batter is crisp and golden.

Tip: Serve the chicken in a wicker basket with French fried potatoes and corn bread, or with a salad. For variety, trickle a little liquid honey over the chicken just before serving.

Serves 6

Chicken in Piquant Sauce

2½-lb. chicken, oven-ready
½ cup vinegar
1 lemon
1 bay leaf
sprig thyme
1 clove garlic
salt and pepper to taste
¼ cup flour
2 tablespoons oil
2 tablespoons butter
1 onion
2 shallots
2 tablespoons brandy
⅞ cup red wine
4 tomatoes
2 tablespoons chopped parsley

For the kneaded butter:
1 tablespoon butter
2 tablespoons flour

1 Cut up the chicken into pieces (see page 334). Put pieces into a plastic bag.

2 Put the vinegar into a bowl. Squeeze the juice from the lemon and add to the vinegar, together with the bay leaf and sprig of thyme. Peel and crush the garlic. Add with the salt and pepper. Mix all together and put into the bag of chicken pieces.

3 Seal the bag and then turn it over and over until all the pieces are well coated. Leave the chicken in a cool place for 3 hours, turning the bag from time to time.

4 Then drain and pat dry the chicken pieces with absorbent paper. Roll them in the flour. Heat the oil and butter together in a pan, put in the chicken pieces and brown them for about 20 minutes. Remove them and keep warm.

5 Peel the onion and shallots. Chop finely and put into the pan in which the chicken was cooked. Allow to soften for 1-2 minutes, then pour in the brandy, heat a little and ignite.

6 Pour in the red wine. Skin, chop and add the tomatoes. Add the chopped parsley. Boil quickly for 10 minutes to reduce and concentrate the sauce.

7 Mix the butter and flour together with a fork or by hand to make the kneaded butter. Remove the sauce from the heat and cool for 1-2 minutes. Using a whisk, beat in the kneaded butter bit by bit to thicken the sauce. When all has been incorporated let the sauce boil and thicken for 5 minutes.

8 Coat the chicken pieces with the sauce and serve hot.

Serves 4

Coq au Vin

Coq au vin is a traditional French dish: chicken pieces are cooked in a rich red wine sauce with onions, carrots and mushrooms. The chicken is first sealed all over in a frying pan and a little brandy can be poured in at this stage and then ignited.

This dish is relatively inexpensive to make, but if a fairly good quality wine is used, the taste will be so much better. And if left overnight and then reheated the next day, the flavors of coq au vin are greatly enhanced.

¼ **lb. lean salt pork or bacon slices**
2 small carrots
18 pearl onions
2 tomatoes
6 chicken pieces
salt and pepper
2 tablespoons brandy
1½ **tablespoons flour**
3 cups red wine
**1 tablespoon freshly chopped
   parsley**
½ **teaspoon dried thyme**
1 bay leaf
½ **lb. mushrooms**

1 Cut the pork or bacon into thin strips. Peel and slice the carrots. Peel the onions. Skin and chop the tomatoes, discarding the seeds.

2 Put the pork or bacon in a flame-proof casserole and fry to brown the meat. Add the carrots and onions and sauté gently for 5 minutes, turning frequently. Remove from the pan with a slotted spoon and set aside.

3 Add the chicken to the pan and fry until golden on both sides. Sprinkle with salt and pepper to taste. Warm the brandy, pour over the chicken, then ignite.

4 Add the tomatoes and cook for a few minutes, then return the pork and vegetables to the pan. Sprinkle with the flour, then fry for a few minutes, stirring constantly.

5 Add the remaining ingredients except the mushrooms and bring to a boil, stirring constantly. Cover and simmer for 30 minutes.

6 Wipe the mushrooms, trim the stalks and slice or quarter them if large. Add to the casserole and continue cooking 15 minutes more or until the chicken is tender.

7 Remove the bay leaf, taste and adjust the seasoning, then serve straight from the casserole.

Serves 6

Look 'n Cook Chicken and Ham Quenelles

Look 'n Cook Chicken and Ham Quenelles (continued)

1 Ingredients for quenelles **2** Grind meats **3** Make the panada **4** Blend egg whites, lemon juice and cream; mix in the meat; refrigerate. Combine the cold panada with the chicken and ham mixture and refrigerate **5** Using 2 tablespoons scoop out the mixture a little at a time and mold into 2 oz. ovals; dip the spoons into warm water each time to prevent the mixture from sticking. Butter a flameproof dish and place the quenelles in it **6** Decorate each quenelle with a small piece of truffle, if liked **7** Make the roux for the Divine Sauce **8** Strain the chicken stock **9** Add tomato paste to the roux, then gradually stir in the stock and cold milk until you have a smooth sauce; simmer for 5 minutes. Cook the mushrooms for the garnish in the sherry and lemon juice, then strain the liquor into the white sauce; season with salt and pepper, and mace or nutmeg. Boil for 5 minutes, then stir in the light cream and boil again for 3 minutes **10** Pour the remaining chicken stock over the quenelles, bring to a boil, then finish the cooking in the oven for 3 minutes **11** Drain and transfer the quenelles to a serving dish **12** Strain the sauce, check the seasoning and pour over the quenelles **13** Finish cooking the quenelles in a hot oven for about 10 minutes, then serve at once

Gratin of Chicken and Ham Quenelles with Divine Sauce

Quenelle is derived from an old French word meaning rabbit because originally quenelles were made with rabbit meat, but any kind of fish or meat may be used. The mixture is then shaped into ovals before poaching. In the recipe below, the choux paste used to bind the chicken and ham forcemeat is called a panada.

3-lb. roasting chicken, oven-ready
$\frac{1}{4}$ lb. ham
2 egg whites
juice and grated rind $\frac{1}{2}$ lemon
$\frac{2}{3}$ cup heavy cream
about 4 cups chicken stock, made with the carcass (for the sauce and for poaching quenelles)

For the Choux Paste:
$\frac{1}{4}$ cup butter
6 tablespoons flour
$\frac{2}{3}$ cup cold milk
2 egg yolks

For the Divine Sauce:
2 tablespoons butter
$\frac{1}{4}$ cup flour
1 tablespoon tomato paste
$\frac{2}{3}$ cup chicken stock (reserved from overall quantity)
$\frac{2}{3}$ cup cold milk
$\frac{2}{3}$ cup dry sherry
juice $\frac{1}{2}$ lemon
salt and pepper
pinch mace or nutmeg
$\frac{2}{3}$ cup light cream

For the Garnish:
5 ozs. white mushrooms (optional)
finely chopped parsley and tarragon, mixed (optional)

1 First make the quenelles forcemeat. Remove the chicken skin, then remove the flesh from the bones, scraping them clean. Set aside the flesh, and use the skin and cartilaginous parts for making the stock.

2 Cut the ham in small cubes; grind the chicken and ham together in a food processor or with a hand grinder.

3 In a mixing bowl blend together the egg whites, lemon juice and rind, then gently blend in $\frac{2}{3}$ cup heavy cream. Blend in the chicken and ham, then refrigerate the mixture while preparing the choux paste for binding it.

4 Prepare the choux paste: melt the butter in a pan and stir in the flour. Allow to cook without coloring for 2 minutes until the roux looks like wet sand, then gradually pour in the cold milk, stirring gently to form a smooth paste. The paste will form itself into a dough and come cleanly away from the sides of the pan. When it no longer sticks to the pan, remove from the heat and cool; then blend in the 2 egg yolks. Allow the mixture to cool completely in the refrigerator, then combine with the raw chicken and ham mixture, beating it to a smooth paste. Refrigerate again for 15 minutes.

5 Using a tablespoon, scoop out the mixture a little at a time, and mold into ovals, using another tablespoon in reverse to give the quenelles an egg shape. Dip the spoons each time in warm water to prevent the mixture from sticking. Butter a deep flameproof dish and place the quenelles in it, one at a time.

6 Then store in the refrigerator for 20 minutes to harden the quenelles while you prepare the sauce.

7 To make the Divine Sauce: melt the butter in a pan and add the flour. Cook the roux gently to a sandy texture, without coloring, for 1 minute. Add the tomato paste, gradually stir in the $\frac{2}{3}$ cup stock, followed by the cold milk until you have a smooth sauce; simmer for 5 minutes.

8 Wash and slice the button mushrooms for the garnish, or leave them whole, minus the stalks, if very tiny. Boil them in the sherry and lemon juice for 4 minutes. Strain the liquor into the white sauce, season with salt and pepper and a pinch of mace or nutmeg. Boil for 5 minutes, add the light cream, give it a stir and boil again for 3 minutes longer.

9 Preheat the oven to 350°F. Pour the rest of the chicken stock over the quenelles; bring to a boil gently, then finish the cooking in the preheated oven for 3 minutes, covering the dish with buttered parchment paper; grease an ovenproof serving dish.

10 Drain the quenelles carefully with a slotted spoon and place them on the greased dish; turn the oven to 400°F. Pour the cream sauce through a conical strainer and check the seasoning. Surround the serving dish with the mushrooms, if used.

11 Pour the sauce over the quenelles; finish cooking in the hot oven for about 10 minutes. Serve at once, with the mushroom garnish and sprinkled with the chopped parsley and tarragon mixture, if liked.

Serves 8

Grilled Chicken

Grilled or Broiled Chicken with Onion

3-lb. chicken, oven-ready
2 tablespoons oil
salt and pepper
2½ tablespoons butter
2 onions
8 small tomatoes
1 tablespoon prepared mustard
1 tablespoon heavy cream
2½ cups dry white breadcrumbs
bunch watercress

1 Cut up the chicken (see pages 334-335).

2 Heat the grill or broiler. Preheat the oven to 400°F.

3 Baste the chicken with half of the oil. Season with salt and pepper. Place it on the grill or under the broiler, skin side up, and grill or broil it on both sides, turning it a quarter of a turn every 2 minutes. Total time is about 8 minutes each side.

4 Place the chicken in an oven-proof dish and cook in the oven for 30 minutes.

5 Peel and grate the onions. Melt the butter in a skillet. Add the grated onion and cook over low heat until soft, with the consistency of a purée.

6 Wash and dry the tomatoes; slice them in half, and cover them in the rest of the oil. Put them in a roasting pan, add salt and pepper, and put them in the oven to cook.

7 Put the onion purée into a bowl. Add the mustard and cream. Mix them well. Put the breadcrumbs on a large plate.

8 When the chicken has been cooking for 30 minutes, drain it. Cover it with the onion and mustard mixture. Then coat both sides with the breadcrumbs, pressing them on well. Put it back in the roasting pan and baste it with the cooking juices. Let it cook for another 10 minutes.

9 Wash and drain the watercress. Warm a serving dish.

10 When the chicken is cooked, put it on the serving dish. Place the baked tomatoes and cress around it. Pour the juices from the dish over the chicken and serve hot.

Serves 4

Grilled or Broiled Chicken with Mustard

3-lb. frying chicken, cut into
   serving pieces
5 tablespoons butter
2 tablespoons mild mustard
1 teaspoon Worcestershire sauce
1 teaspoon chopped rosemary
2 tablespoons finely chopped
   parsley
½ teaspoon salt
freshly ground black pepper

1 Preheat the oven to 400°F. Put the chicken pieces into a buttered flameproof dish and dot with 2 tablespoons butter. Bake in the oven for 20 minutes.

2 Mix the remaining butter with the rest of the ingredients. Brush half the mixture over the chicken pieces and grill or broil for 12 minutes. Turn the chicken over, brush with the remaining butter mixture, and grill or broil for a further 12-15 minutes or until the chicken is tender.

3 Serve with a green salad.

Serves 4

Provençal Split Chicken

3-lb. chicken, oven-ready
3 shallots
2 cloves garlic
3 lemons
1 tablespoon crushed thyme and
   rosemary
⅓ cup oil
salt and pepper
small bunch watercress

1 Cut up the chicken (see pages 334-335).

2 Peel the shallots and the garlic. Chop them finely. Squeeze 2 of the lemons and pour the juice into a bowl; add the shallots and garlic, the thyme and rosemary and the oil. Add salt and pepper. Stir the marinade with a fork.

3 Place the prepared chicken flat in a deep dish. Pour on the marinade and let marinate for 3 hours in a cool place.

4 Heat the broiler. Drain the chicken and reserve the marinade. Place the chicken in the broiler pan, skin side down. Put it under the broiler and broil it under high heat. Turn the bird after about 15 minutes. Baste it with the marinade and let it cook for a further 15 minutes.

5 Warm a serving dish. Place the well-browned chicken on it, spoon on the cooking juices and serve hot, garnished with lemon quarters and small bunches of watercress.

Serves 4

Spatchcock
The French phrase for this method of preparing a chicken is *en crapaudine*: the split bird has its legs and wings tucked in to resemble a flattened toad — *crapaud* being the French word for a toad.

Chicken Stews

Rumanian Chicken Stew

3 lbs. chicken pieces
1 teaspoon salt
black pepper
¼ teaspoon dried marjoram
½ teaspoon paprika
¼ cup butter
2 tablespoons oil
2 onions
2 carrots
1 leek
1 lb. canned butter beans
½ cup stock
1 teaspoon lemon juice

1 Dry the chicken pieces and rub them with the salt, pepper, marjoram and paprika mixed together.

2 Heat half the butter and the oil in a skillet. Fry the chicken pieces for about 10 minutes, turning them as necessary to brown all over. Peel the onions and cut into rings. Peel the carrots and slice them. Trim off the green part and wash the leek well to remove soil, then cut it into rings. Drain the beans.

3 Heat the remaining butter in a clean pan. Add the onion slices and sauté until they are golden-brown. Add the carrots, leek and beans and cook over low heat for 15 minutes. Add the chicken pieces and the stock. Cover the pan with its lid. Simmer for 1 hour or until tender.

4 Taste for seasoning and adjust if necessary. Add the lemon juice and serve at once.

Serves 4-6

Chicken Fricassée with Walnuts

3 shallots
¾ cup walnuts
3-lb. chicken, oven-ready
6 tablespoons butter
2 tablespoons flour
1 tablespoon paprika
½ cup dry white wine
2¼ cups chicken stock
salt and pepper
1 tablespoon tomato paste

1 Peel the shallots and chop them finely. Chop the walnuts.

2 Cut the chicken into serving pieces (see pages 334-335).

3 Heat the butter in a sauté pan and when hot, brown the pieces of chicken, 2 or 3 at a time. Then add the shallots and leave them to brown. Sprinkle with the flour and the paprika. Stir and cook for 2 minutes.

4 Add the white wine and stock together with the salt and pepper. Add the tomato paste and the walnuts. Blend well together, bring to a boil, then cover the pan, reduce the heat, and simmer for 40 minutes.

5 Heat a serving dish.

6 Taste and adjust the seasoning. Pour the fricassée into the serving dish and serve hot.

Serves 4

Rumanian Chicken Stew — a homey chicken and vegetable stew

Fricassée of Chicken with Paprika

2½-lb. chicken, oven-ready
salt and pepper
3 medium onions
3 tablespoons lard
1 teaspoon paprika
1 teaspoon caraway seeds
1 cup chicken stock
1¼ cups fresh tomato sauce
8 medium potatoes
½ cup plain yogurt
1 tablespoon heavy cream
1 tablespoon flour

1 Cut the chicken into 8 pieces and season.

2 Peel the onions and cut into thin slices.

3 Melt the lard in a sauté pan. Add the sliced onions and the chicken pieces. Cook until golden-brown, stirring often, and until the chicken is done (about 15 minutes).

4 When the chicken and onions are brown, sprinkle them with the paprika. Add the caraway seeds and stir for 1 minute with a wooden spoon to incorporate them.

5 Add the stock and the tomato sauce. Season with salt and pepper and cook over a low heat for 1 hour.

6 Peel and wash the potatoes. Steam or boil them.

7 Heat a deep serving dish.

8 Drain the pieces of chicken, arrange them on the serving dish and surround with the cooked potatoes.

9 Mix together the yogurt, the cream and the flour and pour into the sauce. Blend over low heat, without boiling, stirring with a wooden spoon until the sauce thickens (3-4 minutes).

10 Pour the sauce over the chicken pieces and serve hot.

Serves 4

Poached Chicken

Chicken Mousse

2 chicken pieces
1¼ cups chicken stock
⅔ cup milk
1 bay leaf
few peppercorns
2-3 slices onion
2 hard-boiled eggs

For the béchamel sauce:
½ tablespoon butter
1 tablespoon flour
salt and pepper
1 tablespoon unflavored gelatin
bunch watercress
1 medium onion
⅔ cup heavy cream
few sprigs parsley

1 Put the chicken joints in a pan and add enough chicken stock to cover. Bring to a boil, then reduce the heat and poach, with the lid on, until the chicken is tender — about 30 minutes for legs, 25 minutes for breast meat. Drain, reserving ⅔ cup of the stock. Put the milk in a pan, together with the bay leaf, peppercorns and slices of onion and heat just to boiling point; take off the heat and set aside to infuse for about 10 minutes. Strain, reserving the milk.

2 Slice the hard-boiled eggs and place them in the bottom of a lightly oiled 8-inch ring mold.

3 Make the béchamel sauce: melt the butter in a pan, stir in the flour to make a roux and cook for 1 minute, stirring all the time. Take the pan off the heat and blend in half the reserved milk. Stir in the rest of the milk until smooth. Return the pan to the heat and cook slowly until the sauce thickens, stirring continuously. Add salt and pepper to taste and leave to cool.

4 In a pan, dissolve the gelatin in a little of the reserved chicken stock and leave for about 5 minutes or until spongy. Then heat gently until the gelatin is completely dissolved, stirring all the time. Take the pan off the heat and cool slightly.

5 Wash and chop half the watercress; peel and slice the onion; stiffly whip the cream.

6 Remove the meat from the chicken pieces; put in a blender and blend with the rest of the chicken stock to a smooth purée. Add this mixture to the cooled béchamel sauce.

7 When the gelatin is at the point of setting but still liquid, stir it into the sauce (it is important to blend in the gelatin so it sets evenly without lumps). Cut and fold in the cream and chopped watercress as lightly as possible. Check the seasoning, then pour the mousse into the mold and place it in the refrigerator to set.

8 When firm, place your chosen serving dish on top of the mold, invert, tap sharply on the bottom and the mousse should slide out without damage. Garnish the center with the remaining watercress, the onion slices and parsley. Serve chilled.

Serves 4

Fresh Tomato Sauce

Peel and chop 1 carrot and 1 onion; sauté in 2 tablespoons butter for 5 minutes. Stir in 2 tablespoons flour, then add 1 lb. skinned and chopped tomatoes, 1¼ cups stock, 1 bay leaf, ½ teaspoon sugar, salt and pepper to taste. Bring to a boil, cover and simmer 45 minutes; sieve, reheat and check seasoning. Use as required.

Makes about 2 cups

Chicken Mousse and Chicken with Orange Sauce — two mouthwatering dishes using poached chicken pieces

Chicken with Orange Sauce

4 chicken pieces (see p. 334)
1 bay leaf
few peppercorns
4¼ cups chicken stock or water
few sprigs watercress

For the orange sauce:
3 tablespoons butter
¼ cup flour
scant 2¼ cups cooking liquid
juice and grated rind 2 oranges
1 tablespoon medium sherry
salt and pepper

1 Put the chicken pieces, bay leaf and peppercorns in a pan and add enough chicken stock or water to cover. Bring to a boil, reduce the heat and poach, with the lid on, for 30-45 minutes or until the chicken is tender. Strain, reserving 2½ cups of the cooking liquid. Keep the chicken hot.

2 To make the sauce: melt the butter in a small pan, stir in the flour to make a roux and cook gently for 1 minute, stirring all the time. Take the pan off the heat and blend in half the reserved cooking liquid. Stir in the rest of the liquid until smooth and return the pan to the heat. Cook the sauce until it thickens, stirring continuously. Add the juice and grated rind of the oranges, the sherry and salt and pepper to taste.

3 Place the chicken pieces on a warm serving dish, pour on the sauce and garnish with watercress sprigs and segments of the oranges.

Serves 4

Cold Chicken Tonnato is a delicious standby for hot weather eating. This version is derived from the classic Italian recipe, Veal in Tuna Fish Sauce (Vitello Tonnato)

Chicken Tonnato

1 onion
1 branch celery
4 whole chicken breasts, skinned and boned
2¼ cups chicken stock
salt and pepper
pinch thyme
few sprigs parsley
½ bay leaf
⅔ cup white wine (optional)

For the sauce:
7½ ozs. tuna
6 canned flat anchovy fillets
2 tomatoes
1¾ cups mayonnaise
2 tablespoons lemon juice
3 tablespoons capers

For the garnish:
few anchovy fillets
few capers
crisp lettuce leaves

1 Peel and halve the onion. Wash well and halve the celery.

2 Place the chicken breasts, chicken stock, onion, celery, seasoning, herbs, wine and enough water to cover in a large pan and bring to a boil. Simmer very gently for 20-30 minutes, depending on the size of the chicken breasts, until tender and cooked.

3 Remove the chicken breasts from the pan with a slotted spoon and let cool.

4 To make the sauce: drain the tuna fish and anchovy fillets. Wash and thinly slice the tomatoes. In a blender, blend the mayonnaise, tuna fish, anchovy fillets, lemon juice and capers until smooth and well combined.

5 Place the cooled chicken breasts on a serving dish and spoon the sauce over them to cover. Garnish with more anchovy fillets and capers and arrange tomato slices around them. Serve on a bed of crisp lettuce leaves and any remaining sauce.

Serves 4

Chicken Cutlets with Mushrooms and Almonds

¼ lb. butter
1 cup plus 2 tablespoons flour
1¼ cups chicken stock (in which the chicken was poached)
¾ lb. mushrooms
white meat only from 2½-lb. chicken, poached in stock
¼ lb. ham
3 eggs
1 cup heavy cream
2 tablespoons finely ground almonds
2 tablespoons brandy
salt and pepper
1 teaspoon paprika
pinch each nutmeg and clove
1 cup dry white breadcrumbs
¾ cup slivered almonds
3 tablespoons white port

1 Melt one-third of the butter in a small pan, add ½ cup plus 1 tablespoon flour, and stir over low heat to make a white roux.

2 Mix the roux with the stock and cook for 10 minutes on very low heat, stirring frequently with a wooden spoon.

3 During this time, trim the bottom of the mushroom stalks, wash the mushrooms briefly, dry and coarsely chop one-third of them. Slice the rest finely.

4 Heat 1 tablespoon butter, add the chopped mushrooms, and fry until all the liquid from them has evaporated.

5 Dice the white chicken meat and chop the cooked ham.

6 Break 1 egg into a bowl and beat in half the cream and the ground almonds.

7 Take the pan of sauce off the heat and stir in the egg and cream liquid, the chopped mushrooms, chopped ham, diced chicken and the brandy. Season with salt, pepper, paprika and mixed spice.

8 Return the pan to low heat for 3 minutes, mixing well with a wooden spoon.

9 Lightly butter a large dish, pour in this mixture to a depth of about 1¼ inch and let cool and set completely.

10 Heat 2 tablespoons butter in a small pan and sauté the sliced mushrooms.

11 Preheat the oven to 400°F.

12 Cut the cold meat mixture into four and shape each piece into an oval cake about ¾ inch thick. Curve one of the sides and make it thinner at one end to make into the shape of a cutlet.

13 Break the remaining eggs into a bowl and beat well together.

14 Dip the "cutlets" into the rest of the flour, then in the beaten egg, and coat them with the breadcrumbs.

15 Heat the rest of the butter in a skillet, add the egg and breadcrumbed cutlets and brown on each side over not too high a heat.

16 Put the slivered almonds to brown in the hot oven, then turn off the heat but leave the door closed.

17 Heat a serving dish.

18 Drain the cutlets on absorbent paper and arrange them on the hot serving dish.

19 Put the cutlets into the still hot oven, but with the door open.

20 Stir the port into the leftover drippings from cooking the cutlets, scraping the bottom of the pan with a wooden spoon, and cook for 2 minutes over high heat. Add the rest of the cream, season with salt and pepper, and stir over medium heat until the mixture thickens but doesn't boil.

21 Take the serving dish from the oven, surround the cutlets with the sliced mushrooms and coat with the sauce. Sprinkle with slivered almonds and serve very hot.

Serves 4

Chicken Sautés

Sautéed Chicken in Cream Sauce

2½ lbs. chicken pieces
salt and pepper
2 tablespoons oil
2 tablespoons butter
½ lb. mushrooms
3 shallots
½ cup dry white wine
⅞ cup sour cream

1 Season the chicken pieces.

2 Heat the oil and butter in a sauté pan over high heat. Sauté the pieces of chicken in the butter for about 15-20 minutes, without letting them brown. Turn the pieces and let them cook over low heat for 15 minutes, without a lid.

3 Meanwhile, trim, wash, dry and slice the mushrooms. Peel the shallots and grate them.

4 Heat a serving dish. Remove the chicken pieces from the pan. Arrange them on the serving dish and keep them warm.

5 Put the mushrooms into the pan. Sauté them for 5 minutes but don't let them brown. Then add the shallots and let them soften for 2 minutes over low heat. Add the white wine. Stir in all the cooking juices at the bottom of the pan and let the liquid reduce by about half over high heat.

6 Add the cream. Stir vigorously and let the mixture reduce by about half its quantity over high heat. Taste the sauce and adjust the seasoning. Coat the chicken with the sauce and serve hot.

Serves 4

1 The ingredients required for this dish **2** Season each piece of chicken with salt and pepper **3** Heat a mixture of oil and butter in a pan. Brown the chicken pieces lightly on the outer, skin-covered sides **4** Turn the chicken pieces over and let them to cook over low heat, without a lid **5** Wash and slice the mushrooms. Grate the shallots **6** Take the chicken pieces out of the pan and arrange them on a warm serving dish. Add the mushrooms to the fat in which the chicken pieces have been cooking and sauté them, without letting them brown **7** Add the grated shallots and let them soften, without browning them **8** Add the white wine and heat until the juice reduces **9** Add the cream and stir. Let the mixture reduce again to half its volume **10** Adjust the seasoning, if necessary, by adding salt and pepper, and stir again **11** Coat the chicken pieces with the sauce

Sautéed Chicken in Rich Cream Sauce

3-lb. chicken, oven-ready
salt and pepper
2 tablespoons oil
¼ cup butter
¾ lb. mushrooms
3 shallots
½ cup dry white wine
1 egg yolk
juice ½ lemon
pinch ground nutmeg
3 tablespoons flour
1¼ cups heavy cream
¾ cup grated cheese

1 Cut up the chicken (see pages 334-335). Season with salt and pepper.

2 Pour the oil in a skillet. Add half the butter and heat. When hot put in the chicken pieces and sauté for about 10 minutes on each side.

3 Meanwhile, trim the mushroom stalks. Wash the mushrooms quickly, dry and slice them. Peel and chop the shallots.

4 Remove the chicken pieces from the skillet after 10 minutes or so and keep them warm. Add the mushrooms to the same skillet and fry them for 5 minutes. Then add the shallots and soften over low heat for 2 minutes.

5 Pour in the white wine and stir, scraping the bottom of the pan to dissolve the cooking juices; then reduce the liquid to about half its quantity over high heat.

6 Preheat the oven to 425°F.

7 Put the egg yolk into a cup. Mix it with the lemon juice and nutmeg. Using a fork work the rest of the butter thoroughly with the flour on a plate.

8 Add the kneaded butter to the sauce bit by bit, whisking vigorously. Boil it for 1 minute, then add the egg and lemon mixture, still whisking the mixture, and without letting it boil. Stir in the cream.

9 Arrange the chicken pieces in a heated ovenproof serving dish. Coat them with the cream sauce. Sprinkle with the grated cheese and put the dish in the oven to brown. When golden and bubbling on top, serve the chicken at once.

Serves 4

Sautéed Chicken with Grape Juice

2½-lb. chicken, oven-ready
salt and pepper
2 tablespoons chicken fat
2 shallots
few tarragon leaves
12 mushrooms
¼ lb. bacon
few sprigs parsley
2 cloves garlic
¼ cup grape juice
2 tablespoons heavy cream

1 Cut up the chicken (see pages 334-335) and season with salt and pepper.

2 Heat the chicken fat in a stewpan and when it is hot put in the chicken pieces, skin side down, and cook over slow heat for about 15 minutes; then turn and cook for 15 minutes more.

3 Peel and mince the shallots. Wash the tarragon leaves, dry and chop them finely. Trim, wash, dry and chop the mushrooms. Cut the bacon into thin strips.

4 Wash and dry the parsley. Peel the garlic. Chop the parsley and garlic together. When the chicken is cooked arrange it on a dish and sprinkle with the parsley and garlic. Keep warm.

5 Put the shallots, tarragon, mushrooms and bacon into the pan in which the chicken was cooked. Cook slowly for about 10 minutes, then add the grape juice and cook for a further 10 minutes. Then add the cream, bring to a boil and reduce to about half its volume.

6 Pour the sauce over the chicken and serve hot.

Serves 4

Sautéed Chicken in Rich Cream Sauce

Sautéed Chicken in Avocado Sauce

3-lb. chicken, oven-ready
salt and pepper
½ teaspoon ground ginger
2 tablespoons oil
⅓ cup butter
4 avocados (1 very ripe)
3 shallots
½ lb. mushrooms
pinch cayenne pepper
½ cup dry white wine
scant cup heavy cream

1 Cut up the chicken (see pages 334-335). Season the pieces with salt, pepper and ginger.

2 Heat the oil and half the butter in a pan. Sear the chicken pieces, skin side down, in hot fat for about 10 minutes without letting them brown. Turn over the pieces and let them cook over low heat for another 10 minutes, without a lid.

3 Halve the avocados and remove the seeds. Put the very ripe one to one side. Scoop out small balls, using a potato or melon baller, from the other three. Rub any pulp remaining from these, together with the very ripe avocado pulp, through a fine mesh strainer. Peel and finely chop the shallots. Wash, dry and slice the mushrooms.

4 Melt the rest of the butter in a skillet. Add the avocado balls and season them with salt, pepper and cayenne pepper. Let the balls brown over low heat, shaking the skillet gently so as not to crush them.

5 Remove the chicken pieces from the pan when cooked, arrange them on a heated ovenproof serving dish and keep hot in a warm oven, with the heat turned off.

6 Put the chopped shallots and the sliced mushrooms in the pan and let them soften. Add the white wine and let it reduce (evaporate) over high heat. Stir in the cream and the avocado purée.

7 Arrange the avocado balls around the chicken. Cover with the sauce and serve hot.

Serves 4

Spiced Chicken with Tomato Sauce

4 boneless chicken portions
salt and pepper
2 pinches ground ginger
⅓ cup rum
1 large onion
½ cup oil
1 teaspoon curry powder
pinch cayenne pepper
scant 1 cup chicken stock
½ cup raisins
1⅓ cups long grain rice
5 thin bacon slices
5 bananas
2 hard-boiled eggs

For the spicy tomato sauce:
2 shallots
2 tablespoons oil
¼ cup tomato paste
scant 1 cup chicken stock
ground ginger to taste
1 tablespoon honey
2 tablespoons white vinegar
1 bouquet garni

1 Place the chicken flat on a cloth, skin side down, then sprinkle with salt, pepper, a pinch of ginger and 1 tablespoon rum.

2 Roll up as tightly as possible and tie securely with kitchen string. Rub the remaining ginger into the exposed skin.

3 Peel the onion and chop finely.

4 Heat half the oil in a pan. Add the chicken and fry until browned on all sides. Add the onion and fry until golden, stirring constantly.

5 Stir in the curry powder, cayenne and stock. Cover and cook gently for 30 minutes.

6 Meanwhile, put the raisins in a bowl, stir in the remaining rum, then let soak.

7 Prepare the tomato sauce: peel and chop the shallots. Heat the oil in a pan, add the shallots and sauté gently till golden-brown. Stir in the tomato paste and stock, then season to taste with salt, pepper and ginger. Mix the honey with the vinegar, then stir into the pan and add the bouquet garni. Cook gently for 10 minutes.

8 While the sauce is cooking, rinse the rice, and cook it in boiling salted water. When cooked, drain and keep warm.

9 When the chicken is cooked, remove from the pan with a slotted spoon, discard the string and keep the chicken hot. Boil the cooking liquid until reduced by half, then add to the tomato sauce. Taste and adjust seasoning, then remove the bouquet garni.

10 Drain the raisins and reserve the rum, stir the raisins into the sauce. Return the chicken to the pan, pour on the reserved rum, heat through, then ignite.

11 Heat the remaining oil in a separate skillet, add the bacon and fry until crisp and brown. Remove from the pan with a slotted spoon and keep hot.

12 Peel the bananas, add to the pan and sauté until lightly colored on all sides.

13 Put the rice on a warm serving platter, then arrange the bacon and bananas on top.

14 Chop the eggs finely. Arrange the chicken pieces over the bacon and bananas, then sprinkle with the egg.

15 Serve immediately with the tomato sauce separate.

Serves 4

Look 'n Cook Sautéed Chicken with Mushrooms

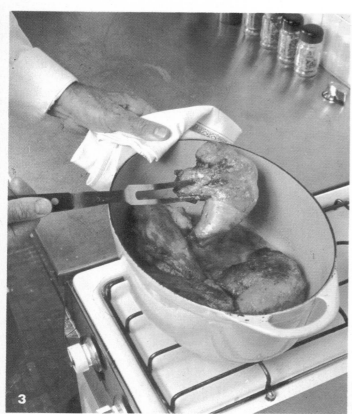

1 Season the chicken pieces with salt and pepper. Roll them in flour **2** Heat a mixture of oil and butter in a deep pan. Put in the chicken, skin side down, and brown for about 10 minutes **3** Turn the pieces and brown on the other side for another 10 minutes or so **4** Meanwhile, trim and wash the mushrooms, dry and slice them. Peel and finely mince the shallots. Remove the chicken from the pan and sauté the mushrooms in

the same fat **5** Add the shallots and let them soften for 1 minute over low heat **6** Add the brandy and ignite, then stir in the white wine **7** Add the chopped tomatoes and tarragon, and the veal or chicken stock.

Reduce (evaporate) over high heat, uncovered **8** Adjust the seasoning. Place the chicken on a hot serving dish and cover with the sauce

Sautéed Chicken with Mushrooms

2½ lbs. chicken pieces
salt and pepper
1 cup flour
2 tablespoons oil
2 tablespoons butter
½ lb. mushrooms
3 shallots
½ cup brandy
½ cup dry white wine
8 ozs. canned tomatoes, drained
sprig tarragon
1 cup chicken stock

1 Season the pieces of chicken and roll them in the flour.

2 Put the oil and butter into a sauté pan; over high heat brown the chicken for about 10 minutes, then turn and brown on the other side for another 10 minutes.

3 While the chicken is cooking, trim the mushroom stalks. Wash, dry and slice the mushrooms. Peel and finely mince the shallots.

4 Take the pieces of chicken out of the pan as they are cooked; the quicker cooking wings first, then the legs, etc. The wings shouldn't take longer than 15 minutes, the legs about 20 minutes. Keep them warm. Add the mushrooms to the pan and sauté quickly. Add the shallots, reduce the heat and soften them for 1 minute.

5 Pour in the brandy and ignite it. Add the wine and stir to dissolve the meat juices.

6 Chop the drained tomatoes roughly and add them to the pan. Chop the tarragon. Add the tarragon and the stock. Let the mixture reduce over high heat, uncovered, for 10 minutes.

7 Warm a serving dish. Arrange the pieces of chicken on it. Taste and adjust the seasoning of the sauce. Cover the chicken with the sauce and serve hot.

Serves 4

Turkey Roasts and Stews

All kinds of turkey products — both cooked and uncooked, are available to cooks today, thus offering plenty of scope for inventive dishes as well as for all-time favorites.

Uncooked Turkey

Whole turkeys (fresh or frozen) can reach giant proportions but for most of us a mini bird of between 6-8 lbs. oven-ready, is a popular choice. Just right for family gatherings or picnics, when value for money is often an important consideration.

Apart from whole turkey, it can also be bought as:

Portions: breasts, drumsticks, thighs (some already boned and stuffed), wings (either whole or the tips only).

Turkey roasts: these are boned and rolled white and dark meat roasts, wrapped in pork fat and deep frozen — thaw and cook as for ordinary roasts.

Assorted packs of ground and chunked meat, giblets and livers are also available. These are ideal for making stews, casseroles, soups and stocks, or for pâtés and risotto.

Cooked Turkey Products

For lazy cooks, there is a choice of various cooked boneless turkey rolls: some are already sliced, others may be cured or smoked. All will give plenty of lean meat with no waste. Some convenience foods may also be cooked.

Convenience foods

There are a host of these turkey products — uncooked, ready-cooked, and others requiring nothing more than heating through, or deep frying. Choose from turkey meat loaves and pâtés, burgers, crispy fries, fingers, croquettes and sausages.

Stuffing a Turkey

When stuffing a turkey for roasting, allow about 1 lb. stuffing for the neck end of a bird weighing up to 14 lbs. — double the quantity for larger turkeys — and allow about 1-2 lbs. for the body cavity, according to the size of the bird. Vary the flavors if using two stuffings: chestnut or veal forcemeat, say, for the neck end and sausage meat for the body cavity.

Roasting a Turkey

There are many theories on the best way to roast a turkey, but whichever way you choose, make sure the breast is amply covered with softened fat (butter, margarine or drippings) to keep it moist and tender during cooking. For extra flavor lay slices of bacon on top as well.

Cover the bird with several thicknesses of foil to prevent the flesh drying out and toughening, but remove the coverings for the last 30-40 minutes so the bird can crisp and brown, and be basted with its cooking juices.

Wrap foil around the leg ends so they don't burn during roasting, then dress them with paper turkey frills for serving at the table.

Roast Turkey with Link Sausage

1 lb. fresh chestnuts
4 large potatoes
7-8 lb. turkey
salt and pepper
¼ cup oil
¼ lb. butter
3 large onions

1 lb. carrots
½ cup dry white wine
2 teaspoons sugar
¾ lb. pearl onions
¾ lb. bacon
1 lb. link sausage
½ cup chicken stock

1 Preheat the oven to 400°F.

2 Peel the chestnuts and cook until tender (see box).

3 Peel the potatoes.

4 Stuff the turkey with the potatoes, truss securely with kitchen string (see pages 324-325), then sprinkle salt and pepper all over the bird. Put the turkey in a roasting pan, pour on half the oil, then dot with half the butter. Roast in the preheated oven until golden brown.

5 Meanwhile, peel the large onions and 2 carrots and slice finely. Place them around the turkey, continue roasting until the vegetables are browned, then add the wine. Continue roasting for about 1½ hours or until the turkey is tender, basting frequently. Cover with foil if the skin becomes too brown during cooking.

6 Meanwhile, peel and dice the remaining carrots. Put in a pan with enough water just to cover, then add salt, half the sugar and 2 tablespoons butter. Cover with foil and cook over high heat until the carrots are tender and have absorbed all the liquid. Do not allow the carrots to brown.

7 Peel the small onions, then caramelize them with water and the remaining sugar and butter as for the carrots.

8 Cut the bacon into neat strips and blanch in boiling water for 3 minutes. Drain, rinse under cold running water, then drain again.

9 Slice the link sausages into 1¼-inch lengths.

10 Heat the remaining oil in a skillet, add the bacon and fry until brown. Add the link sausage and

fry until brown, then drain off any excess fat. Add the caramelized carrots and onions and stir well to mix. Drain the chestnuts and add to the pan to heat through. Transfer the mixture to an ovenproof dish and keep hot in the oven.

11 To test to see if the turkey is cooked, prick the thickest part of the thigh: the juices should run clear. Remove the trussing string from the turkey, and take out the potatoes. Put the turkey on a warm serving platter and keep hot.

12 Transfer the roasting pan to the top of the stove and skim off the fat from the cooking juices. Add the stock, then boil until the liquid is reduced by a quarter. Taste and adjust the seasoning, then pour through a fine strainer into a sauce boat.

13 Arrange the link sausage and vegetable garnish around the turkey and serve hot with the sauce separate.

Serves 8

Cooking Fresh Chestnuts
Slit the brown outer skin and put the chestnuts into cold water. Bring to a boil and cook for 5 minutes, then drain and remove the outer and inner skins. Return the chestnuts to the pan, cover with stock and simmer for about 30 minutes or until tender.

Roast Turkey with Link Sausage — garnished with chestnuts, sausages, carrots, onions and bacon strips

Turkey Roast with Fruit Sauce

2 tablespoons butter
5½-lb. white meat turkey roast
1 red pepper
1 small green pepper
1 onion
8 ozs. canned mandarin oranges (juice reserved)
8 ozs. canned sweet corn (juice reserved)

For the sauce:
2 teaspoons cornstarch
reserved juice from mandarin oranges
reserved juice from canned sweet corn
1 tablespoon vinegar
1 teaspoon sugar
1 teaspoon Worcestershire sauce
1-2 tablespoons sherry

1 Preheat the oven to 375°F. Spread the butter over the turkey roast then wrap it in foil to make a parcel. Place in a roasting pan and roast for 1½ hours.

2 Wash, seed and core the peppers; peel and chop the onion. Drain the mandarins and corn, reserving the juices. Mix the mandarins, corn, peppers and onion together.

3 To make the sauce: mix the cornstarch with a little water to make a smooth paste. Blend the juice from the mandarins and corn with the vinegar, sugar, Worcestershire sauce, sherry and cornstarch and heat until thickened, stirring well. Add the fruit and vegetables.

4 Remove the turkey roast from the oven and unwrap the foil. Pour a little of the sauce all over and around the turkey and cover again with the foil.

5 Replace the turkey in the oven and cook for a further 1-1½ hours or until the turkey is tender and cooked through.

6 Unwrap the turkey and place it on a serving dish surrounded by its fruity sauce and serve the rest of the sauce separately.

Serves 6-8

Turkey en Croûte with Ratatouille

2 tablespoons butter
5½-lb. white meat turkey roast
2 pie crusts, homemade or frozen and thawed

For the stuffing:
1 medium onion
1½ cups mushrooms
1 egg
3 cups fresh white breadcrumbs
pinch thyme
pinch sage
2 tablespoons finely chopped parsley
salt and pepper

For the ratatouille:
½ lb. zucchini
2 eggplants
1 sweet red pepper
1 green pepper
2 medium onions
4 tomatoes
oil for frying

For the garnish:
parsley sprigs

1 Preheat the oven to 325°F.

2 Spread the butter over the turkey roast, then wrap in foil to make a parcel and place in a roasting pan. Put in the oven and roast for about 2 hours.

3 To make the stuffing: peel and finely chop the onion. Wipe and finely chop the mushrooms. Beat the egg. Mix the stuffing ingredients together with enough of the beaten egg to bind.

4 Wash all the vegetables for the ratatouille. Trim and slice the zuc-chini; slice and chop the eggplant; seed and core the peppers and cut the flesh into strips; peel and chop the onions; quarter the tomatoes.

5 Remove the turkey from the oven and open up the foil. Leave until cool enough to handle, then remove the string and the outer layer of skin. Spread some of the stuffing in a thick layer over the turkey roast but leave the ends free.

6 Roll out the pastry thickly ($\frac{1}{4}$-$\frac{3}{8}$ inch) into one large oblong to fit the roast and its stuffing. Place the turkey roast, upside down, on the pastry, so you can spread stuffing on the other side as well.

7 Spread on the remaining stuffing, dampen the ends of the pastry and fold it over to make a "pastry parcel," seal the edges and ends together well, then turn it over again so the lengthwise seam is underneath. Turn the oven to 375°F.

8 Brush the parcel and the remaining beaten egg, and decorate the top with leaves from any remaining pastry. Brush with egg and then bake the parcel on a greased baking sheet for about 35 minutes or until the pastry is golden-brown and the turkey is cooked. Serve either hot or cold, garnished with sprigs of parsley.

9 For the ratatouille: heat the oil and sauté the zucchini, eggplant, peppers and onion until softened and slightly browned. Add the tomatoes and cook for a further 5 minutes. Season to taste and serve.

Serves 6-8

Turkey Roast with Fruit Sauce — the mandarin oranges provide a delicious contrast of flavors

Turkey Escalopes

An escalope is a thin slice of prime-cut meat (usually veal) which is beaten flat and often fried in shallow fat. Boned chicken and turkey breasts make ideal escalopes, which may also be stuffed and rolled and then fried or braised.

To Prepare Escalopes
Place the meat between 2 pieces of wax paper — the moisture helps to prevent sticking — and, using a rolling pin or mallet, beat flat until the meat is doubled in size and almost wafer-thin.

Hawaiian Turkey Escalopes

1⅛ cups long grain rice
4 turkey escalopes
salt and pepper
½ teaspoon ground ginger
⅓ cup butter
¼ cup brandy
½ cup grated fresh or shredded coconut
1 teaspoon curry powder
¼ cup stock
1 tablespoon lemon juice
3 tablespoons pineapple juice
¼ cup sour cream
pinch cayenne pepper
4 slices pineapple, fresh or canned

1 Wash the rice well in several changes of cold water. Cook in boiling, salted water for about 12 minutes or until tender.

2 Meanwhile, rub the salt, pepper and ginger well into both sides of the escalopes.

3 Melt ¼ cup butter in a pan, add the escalopes and sauté over high heat until golden-brown on both sides. Lower the heat, then cook for 15 minutes or until the meat is tender.

4 Pour the brandy over the turkey, heat through, then ignite.

5 Meanwhile, melt the remaining butter in a skillet, add the coconut and sauté until golden-brown. Set aside. Drain the escalopes, then arrange on a serving dish, surrounded by the rice.

6 Stir the curry powder into a little turkey cooking liquid, then return to the pan with the stock, the pineapple juice and lemon juice. Cook over high heat, stirring with a wooden spoon to loosen the pan juices and sediment. Add the sour cream and cayenne pepper and beat well. Taste, and adjust the seasoning, then add the pineapple and heat for 1-2 minutes.

7 Arrange the pineapple slices over the escalopes, then pour on the sauce. Sprinkle with the coconut and serve immediately.

Serves 4

Turkey with Olives

1¾-lb. turkey breast
1½ cups pitted green olives
1 egg
½ teaspoon ground ginger
salt and pepper
flour, for dredging
2 tablespoons butter
2 tablespoons oil
¾ cup sweet white wine
1 cup fresh orange juice
½ cup chicken stock
½ cup pitted black olives

1 Cut 6 large thin slices from the turkey breast, then beat them between 2 sheets of wax paper until very thin.

2 Mince the remaining turkey meat finely. Mince the green olives finely and beat the egg. Put the turkey and half the olives in a bowl, then add the beaten egg, ginger and salt and pepper to taste. Stir well to mix.

3 Divide the mixture equally between the turkey slices, then roll up and secure with toothpicks. Dredge the rolls with flour.

4 Heat the butter and oil in a skillet, add the turkey rolls and sauté gently until browned on all sides. Remove from the pan with a slotted spoon and place in a casserole dish.

5 Add the wine, orange juice and stock to the skillet. Bring to a boil, scraping up the sediment from the bottom of the pan with a wooden spoon. Boil for 5 minutes.

6 Meanwhile, preheat the oven to 350°F.

7 Mince the black olives finely, then sprinkle over the turkey with the remaining green olives. Pour on the sauce, then cover and cook in the preheated oven for about 45 minutes until the turkey is tender when pierced with a skewer.

8 Place the turkey rolls on a warm serving platter, remove the toothpicks and cut the meat into neat slices.

9 Taste and adjust the seasoning of the sauce, then spoon a little sauce over the meat. Serve hot with the remaining sauce separately.

Serves 6

Turkey Escalopes with Spring Vegetables

4 turkey escalopes (see p. 362)
1 teaspoon dried savory
1 teaspoon dried thyme
salt and pepper
2 leaves fresh sage
½ bay leaf
1 cup milk
1 lb. young fresh peas
1 head lettuce
8 small carrots
8 pearl onions
¼ lb. lean bacon
¼ lb. butter
1 sprig fresh savory (optional)
1 teaspoon sugar
1 egg plus 1 egg yolk
1 tablespoon paprika
1 cup flour
1 cup dried breadcrumbs
2 tablespoons sour cream

1 Sprinkle both sides of the escalopes with the dried savory, thyme and salt and pepper to taste. Rub the seasonings into the meat with the fingertips.

2 Put the escalopes in a large shallow dish. Place the sage leaves and bay leaf on top, add a little milk, then marinate for 2 hours.

3 Meanwhile, shell the peas. Wash the lettuce without detaching the leaves, drain thoroughly, then cut into quarters. Peel the carrots, then cut into julienne strips (matchsticks). Peel the small onions. Dice the bacon.

4 Melt half the butter in a skillet, add the onions and bacon and sauté gently until lightly colored. Add the peas, carrots, fresh savory, sugar, salt and pepper, then cover and cook gently for 1 hour. Add the lettuce for the final 15 minutes of cooking.

5 Twenty minutes before the end of cooking, drain the escalopes and dry thoroughly on absorbent paper.

6 Beat the egg lightly with the paprika and salt and pepper. Coat the escalopes first in the flour, then in the beaten egg, then in the breadcrumbs.

7 Melt the remaining butter in a skillet. Add the escalopes and fry gently until tender and golden-brown on both sides.

8 Drain the vegetables, reserving the cooking liquid, then arrange on a warm serving dish.

9 Beat the egg yolk and sour cream together, then stir into the reserved cooking liquid. Cook over low heat until well blended, stirring constantly. Do not allow to boil.

10 Taste and adjust the seasoning of the sauce, then pour over the vegetables. Arrange the escalopes on top and serve immediately.

Serves 4

Stuffed Turkey Rolls

¾ lb. onions
¼ lb. butter
salt and pepper
pinch grated nutmeg
1 egg
⅞ cup heavy cream
4 large turkey escalopes
  (see p. 362)
4 thin slices bacon
4 thin slices cheese
2 tablespoons oil
½ cup dry white wine
¾ lb. mushrooms
2 shallots

1 Peel the onions and chop finely. Melt 3 tablespoons butter in a skillet, add the onions and sprinkle with salt and pepper to taste. Cover and cook over gentle heat until soft, then add the nutmeg and cool.

2 Transfer the onions to a bowl, then stand in a larger bowl filled with crushed ice. Add the beaten egg and stir well to mix. Let chill for a few minutes, then beat in half the cream a little at a time. Chill.

3 Flatten the escalopes with a rolling pin. Sprinkle with salt and pepper.

4 Spread half the onions on the escalopes, then put a slice of bacon on each and cover with a slice of cheese. Spread the remaining onions on top, then roll up the escalopes, tucking in the ends to secure the stuffing. Tie with kitchen string.

5 Heat the oil and 1½ tablespoons of the butter in a heavy-bottomed saucepan. Add the turkey rolls and sauté gently until golden-brown on all sides.

6 Pour in the wine, cover and cook gently for 45 minutes until tender, basting occasionally.

7 Meanwhile, wipe the mushrooms, trim the stalks, then slice finely. Peel and mince the shallots. Melt the remaining butter in the skillet, add the mushrooms and shallots and cook over high heat until the moisture has evaporated. Add salt and pepper to taste.

8 Remove the turkey from the saucepan with a slotted spoon. Remove the string, then place the turkey on a warm serving dish and keep hot. Pour the remaining cream into the saucepan, then stir with a wooden spoon to loosen the pan juices and sediment. Add the mushrooms and shallots, then boil for 1-2 minutes stirring constantly.

9 Taste and adjust the seasoning of the sauce, then pour on the turkey and serve immediately.

Serves 4

Look 'n Cook Stuffed Turkey Rolls

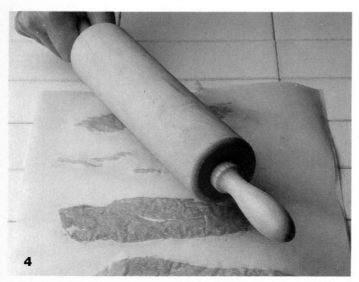

1 Ingredients for turkey rolls **2** Soften chopped onions in butter, then add nutmeg **3** Beat half the cream into onion and egg mixture **4** and **5** Beat out escalopes and season. Top them with bacon, cheese and remaining onion **6** Roll up escalopes and secure **7** Fry turkey rolls till golden **8** Pour in wine, cover

and cook gently till tender **9** Sauté shallots and mush-rooms; season **10** and **11** Stir cream, then mush-room mixture into pan juices; heat, then pour on turkey rolls

Creamed Turkey

3 tablespoons butter
1 small onion
2 cups button mushrooms
¼ cup flour
1½ cups turkey or chicken stock
1¾ cups heavy cream
½ teaspoon salt
freshly ground pepper
½ teaspoon chopped rosemary
juice 1 lemon
3-4 cups leftover cooked turkey

1 Peel and finely chop the onion. Wipe and thinly slice the mushrooms. Cut the turkey meat into small pieces.

2 Heat the butter in a large pan and sauté the onion carefully until it is soft. Add the mushrooms and sauté for a further 2 minutes.

3 Stir in the flour and cook for a few minutes. Add the stock and then the cream gradually, stirring until the sauce thickens.

4 Stir in the salt, pepper, rosemary, lemon juice and turkey, and simmer over low heat for 5 minutes. Serve with fluffy rice or on toast triangles if liked.

Serves 6

Turkey Divan

1 lb. fresh broccoli or 2 packages frozen
4 cups cooked turkey

For the cheese sauce:
3 tablespoons butter
6 tablespoons flour
1⅓ cups milk
½ cup grated cheese
salt and pepper

1 If using fresh broccoli, trim the thick stem ends and cut the large sprigs in half. Cook in boiling salted water for 8-10 minutes or until just tender. If using frozen broccoli, cook according to the package instructions. Drain the broccoli. Cut the cooked turkey meat into strips.

2 To make the cheese sauce: melt the butter in a pan, stir in the flour and cook for 1 minute, stirring continuously. Take the pan off the heat and blend in half the milk. Stir in the rest of the milk, return the pan to the heat and bring to a boil, stirring. Cook for 2 minutes until the sauce is thick.

3 Remove the pan from the heat and stir in half the cheese and season to taste.

4 Preheat the oven to 400°F.

5 Arrange the broccoli and turkey in layers in a greased ovenproof dish, spoon the cheese sauce on the top and sprinkle with the remaining cheese. Bake in the oven for 15 minutes or until hot and browned.

Serves 4

Tip: Do not overcook the broccoli or the tops will become too soft and break off.

Creamed Turkey — diced turkey meat in a rich cream sauce, flavored with rosemary

Roast Duck

Long Island ducks are most popular in the United States. They are descendants of ducks which were brought from China to New York City in 1873.

Ducks can weigh as much as 7 lbs., but for the cook, the smaller ducklings, up to 4 lbs. are preferable because they are more tender and less fatty. Ducks on the market are usually only 10-12 weeks old.

If a duck is excessively fatty, pinch the skin together between your forefingers, so it's clear of the meat, and pierce all over with a sharp knife. This will make the fat run out freely, without the meat juices escaping.

Estimating Quantities
As the ratio of bone to flesh is so much greater in a duck than in other poultry such as chicken, allowance must be made for this when estimating the weight of duck to buy. The following chart is a guide to the average number of portions that can be carved from different weights:

Weight of Bird	Portions without bone — each about $\frac{1}{4}$ lb.
$4\frac{1}{2}$ lbs.	6
$5\frac{1}{2}$ lbs.	$7\frac{1}{4}$
$6\frac{1}{2}$ lbs.	$9\frac{3}{4}$

Duck with Peaches

2-lb. can peach halves
$\frac{1}{2}$ lemon
$4\frac{1}{2}$-lb. duck, oven-ready
salt and pepper
2 cloves
pinch cinnamon
$\frac{1}{4}$ cup white vinegar
3 tablespoons butter
pinch cayenne pepper

1 Drain the peach halves, reserving the syrup. Squeeze the half lemon, reserving the juice.

2 Season inside the duck with salt and pepper and fill it with 6 half peaches, the cloves, cinnamon and salt and pepper. Then add 2 tablespoons vinegar.

3 Heat the butter in a large pan and when it begins to brown, add the duck.

4 Brown the duck over low heat, turning it frequently until it is golden-brown on all sides. Cover and leave to cook for about 50 minutes.

5 Add the rest of the vinegar, the other peach halves, sliced, the lemon juice and $\frac{2}{3}$ cup of the reserved peach syrup, and finish the cooking (another 20-25 minutes).

6 Before serving, heat a serving dish and sauceboat. Put the duck in the center of the dish. Surround it with the peaches.

7 Adjust the seasoning of the sauce, and add a pinch of cayenne pepper. Pour the sauce into the sauceboat. Serve the duck and sauce together.

Serves 6

Duck with Peaches — duck dressed up with a succulent but simple sauce made with canned peaches

Duck in Liqueur with Mixed Vegetables

4-lb. duck, oven-ready
½ teaspoon salt
freshly ground pepper
½ lb. bacon
1 small turnip
4 carrots
18 pearl onions
3 tablespoons butter
1 clove garlic
1 bay leaf
½ teaspoon thyme
½ teaspoon marjoram
3 sprigs parsley
½ cup dry white wine
3 tablespoons anise liqueur
1 lb. canned peas, drained

1 Preheat the oven to 375°F. Wash the duck and dry it thoroughly. Prick with a fork all over the skin and into the fat underneath it. Season inside and out with salt and pepper and truss it (see pages 324-325).

2 Cut the bacon into small pieces. Peel the turnip and carrots. Cut the turnip into wedges and the carrots into ¼-inch pieces. Peel the onions and garlic; crush the latter.

3 Fry the bacon in a large flameproof casserole. When the fat has run from the bacon, remove bacon. Add the butter. When the fat is hot, brown the duck in it and leave it breast side up.

4 Add the turnip wedges, onions, carrots, bay leaf, garlic, thyme, marjoram and parsley. Cover with the lid and cook in the preheated oven for 1 hour.

5 Pour the fat from the pot and add the wine and liqueur. Cover again and cook for 20 minutes more. Add the peas and cook 10 minutes longer.

6 Serve the duck whole or cut into serving pieces. Strain the vegetables and arrange them around the duck. Skim the surplus fat off the sauce, then strain it and serve separately in a sauce boat.

Serves 6

Honey-glazed Duckling with Grapefruit and Orange

5-lb. fresh duckling, oven-ready, with giblets
salt
1 medium carrot
1 medium onion
2 branches celery
1 tablespoon oil

For the Fruit Sauce:
2 teaspoons sugar
⅔ cup fresh orange and grapefruit juice, mixed
2 tablespoons white vinegar
1 tablespoon tomato paste
⅔ cup Madeira or sherry
⅔ cup water
1 chicken bouillon cube
1 clove garlic
sprig fresh mint
bouquet garni

For the Glaze:
⅓ cup honey
2 tablespoons vinegar
¼ cup cornstarch
⅔ cup cold water
salt and pepper
pinch nutmeg
1 orange
1 grapefruit

1 Preheat oven to 400°F. Wash the duck, drain and wipe dry. Season inside and out with salt only. Set aside for 15 minutes. Scald the neck, wings and gizzard, and place in a roasting pan.

2 Peel and quarter the carrot and onion, cut the celery in slivers, and place on top of the giblets.

3 Brush the duck with oil and place it on top of the vegetables. Roast the duck for 35 minutes. Pour off most of the fat in the pan and reduce the heat to 350°F. Cook for another hour, basting from time to time and removing excess fat to prevent burning. When done, drain the duck of its juices, cavity downward, lift out and keep warm. Remove all fat from the pan.

4 To make the sauce, place the roasting pan on top of the stove and boil down the remaining drippings for 5 minutes until almost reduced to a glaze. At the same time cook the sugar in a corner of the pan until it turns to caramel; then immediately add the orange and grapefruit juices, and the vinegar, and boil for 2 minutes. Stir in the tomato paste, wine, water and crumbled bouillon cube.

5 Peel and crush the garlic, add with the sprig of mint and bouquet garni. Boil for 15 minutes.

6 To glaze the duck, boil the honey and vinegar in a small pan and pour on the duck. Return the duck on a tray to the oven at 350°F for 5 minutes to make the glaze. Take out the duck as soon as it is glossy.

7 Blend the cornstarch with the remaining cold water and pour into the sauce to thicken it when boiling. Leave to clear for 5 minutes, then strain and season with salt, pepper, and a pinch of nutmeg.

8 Peel the rind of the orange and grapefruit, without the white pith. Cut peel into short, very thin strips. Boil them in water for 10 minutes, rinse, drain and add to the sauce. Skin the sections, remove any seeds, and reserve for the garnish.

9 Place the duck on a shallow serving dish. Pour some of the sauce over the duck, with the rest in a sauce boat. Serve the bird, garnished with sections of orange and grapefruit.

Serves 4

Honey-glazed Duckling, with a decorative garnish of tangy orange slices and grapefruit sections

Duck with Grapes and Mint

salt and pepper
4½-lb. duck, oven-ready
¼ cup butter
2 carrots
2 onions
¼ lb. lean bacon
1 lemon
1 tablespoon sugar
½ cup stock or dry white wine
½ cup white grape juice
2 tablespoons vinegar
8 mint leaves
2 lbs. large green grapes

1 Salt and pepper the inside of the duck and truss it (see pages 324-325).

2 Preheat the oven to 475°F. Prick all over the skin of the duck with a fork (see page 367). Put the duck onto the grid of the roasting pan and when the oven is very hot, put it in. Leave for 15 minutes to melt the excess fat. Remove the duck from the oven and wipe it with absorbent paper. Turn off the oven and shut the oven door.

3 Melt the butter in a large pan. Add the duck and brown on all sides, turning it frequently without piercing the skin (about 15 minutes).

4 While the duck is sizzling, peel the carrots and onions, and chop them finely. Chop the bacon. Squeeze the juice from the lemon.

5 When the duck is golden-brown, take the pan off the heat and put the duck into a warm oven so that it will not get cold.

6 Put into the large pan the chopped carrots, onions and bacon and brown them.

7 When these ingredients start to brown, sprinkle with sugar and leave to caramelize slightly.

8 Add the stock or white wine, grape juice, 2 tablespoons lemon juice, the vinegar, pepper and the mint leaves.

9 Put the duck back into this sauce, cover the pan and finish the cooking over low heat (about 30 minutes). Heat the serving dish and sauce boat.

10 Meanwhile, wash and dry the grapes, skin and remove the seeds.

11 Strain the sauce, then put back in the pan.

12 Pour the grapes into the sauce and reheat for 1 minute.

13 Carve the duck quickly, and arrange the pieces on the hot serving dish. Take out the grapes with a slotted spoon and garnish the duck with them. Pour the rest of the sauce into the sauce boat.

14 Serve the duck and sauce with shell pasta or new potatoes.

Serves 5-6

Potato Straw Nests and Honeycomb Nests

2 lbs. potatoes
oil for deep frying

1 Peel the potatoes, then without rinsing slice them with a mandoline (vegetable slicer). Use the comb-shaped blade for the potato straws, and the fluted blade for the honeycomb shapes. With the latter, press the potato flat onto the blade, turning the hand gently to the right, then gently to the left, thus using the whole potato. Do the same with the other potatoes.

2 Heat the oil to 360°F.

3 Fill a large nest shape with the potato straws, distributing them equally throughout. Keep it in shape by pressing a smaller one into it. If making honeycomb shapes, overlap the pieces in the larger shaped basket — by doing this, the pieces will lightly weld themselves on top of each other. Then squeeze into it the smaller basket shape.

4 Plunge the filled basket into the fat when quite hot and keep squeezing the two baskets together throughout the cooking, i.e. for 5 to 6 minutes. Cook until the nest comes away by itself when the smaller basket is removed. Let the nest drain on absorbent paper.

5 Put into a nest cherries, plums, orange quarters, peaches etc; dauphine potatoes; or small pieces of any fried food.

Serves 4

Roast Duckling with Apricot Stuffing

4-lb. duckling
apricot stuffing (see recipe on page 384)
3 tablespoons butter
3 tablespoons honey
2 tablespoons vinegar
1 bunch watercress

1 Preheat the oven to 350°F.

2 Wash and dry the duck well on absorbent paper.

3 Spoon the apricot stuffing into the cavity of the duckling, then truss securely with kitchen string (see pages324-325). Place on a rack in a roasting pan, then prick all over the skin with a skewer, taking care not to puncture the flesh itself.

4 Melt the butter until just liquid but not oily.

5 Mix together the vinegar, butter and honey, then brush over the skin. Roast in the preheated oven for 1½ hours or until the duckling is tender. Brush the juices over the bird again 15 minutes before the end of the cooking time.

6 Remove the trussing string from the duckling, let stand for 15-20 minutes, so the juices can settle, before carving. Then place on a warm serving platter. Serve at once garnished with watercress.

Serves 4

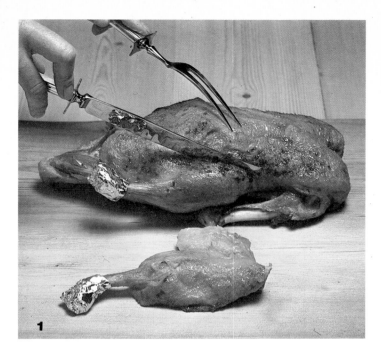

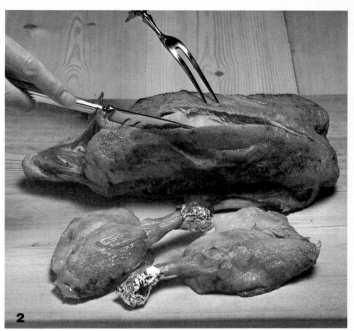

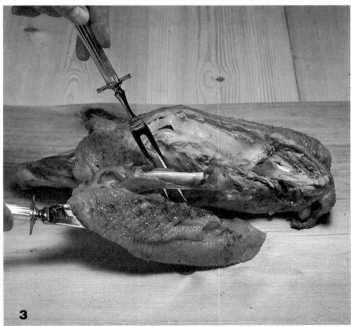

1 The English-style method of carving a duck. First, detach the leg by cutting downward, parallel to the body wall behind the knee joint. Twist the leg away from the body slightly to expose the ball and socket joint and cut through this to sever the leg completely **2** After removing the 2 legs, carve the breasts. Cut along the center of the breastbone and then down toward the back, easing the flesh away from the rib-cage with the knife. **3** The breast meat is removed in 1 piece with the wing attached **4** The 4 portions of duck arranged on the serving dish **5** The French-style of carving: the leg is detached in the same way. The wing is removed next and then the breast meat is cut into slices, usually about 3 slices from each breast

371

Braised Duck

Braised Duck with Apricots

5-lb. duck, oven-ready
salt and pepper
pinch ground allspice
¼ cup butter
1 tablespoon oil
1¼ cups chicken or white stock
⅔ cup dry white wine
1 lb. fresh apricots, or canned
   halves, drained
juice and grated rind 1 lemon
1 teaspoon vinegar
1 tablespoon apricot brandy
   (optional)
2 tablespoons brandy (optional)

1 Preheat the oven to 375°F.

2 Rub the prepared duck with salt, pepper and allspice.

3 Heat the butter and oil in a large skillet, then put in the duck and brown on all sides. Lift it out of the skillet and place in a large flame-proof casserole.

4 Pour the stock and wine into the skillet and heat until the liquid reaches boiling point. Remove from the heat and pour this mixture over the duck. Cover the casserole and place in the preheated oven for 1½-2 hours.

5 Meanwhile, wash and halve the apricots, discarding the pits. After the duck has been cooking for 1 hour, add half the fresh or canned apricots to the roasting pan. Baste them with the stock mixture, and cook.

6 When the duck is cooked, lift it onto a serving dish and keep warm. Strain the cooking liquid and skim off all but 1 tablespoon of the fat.

Rub the cooked apricots through a strainer and reserve the purée.

7 Pour the cooking juices into a small pan, and boil until the liquid has reduced by one-third. Stir in the apricot purée, the lemon rind and juice, and the white vinegar.

8 Arrange the remaining apricot halves around the duck. Bring the brandies to a boil and immediately pour them on the duck. If liked, the brandy may be ignited for effect. Serve at once, with the sauce in a sauce boat.

Serves 4

Roast Duckling with Turnips

3-lb. duckling, oven-ready
salt and pepper
½ cup butter
2 carrots
2 onions
2 tomatoes
few sprigs parsley
2 cloves garlic
some chicken giblets
sprig thyme
½ bay leaf
½ cup dry white wine
¾ cup water
2 lbs. small turnips
4 teaspoons sugar
7 ozs. shallots or pearl onions
1 tablespoon cornstarch
2 tablespoons Madeira or dry
   sherry

1 Preheat the oven to 425°F. Season the duck inside and outside with salt and pepper. Truss it (see pages 374-375) then spread it with 2 tablespoons butter. Place it on one side in a roasting pan.

2 Peel and wash the carrots and the large onions and cut them into large pieces. Wash the tomatoes and cut them in quarters. Wash the parsley. Peel and crush the garlic.

3 When the duck starts to brown, place the giblets around it, together with the carrots and onions. Let

them brown slightly. When it has been cooking for 25 minutes, turn the duck onto its other side. With a small ladle, remove the fat which has run from the duck. Add the tomatoes, parsley, garlic, thyme and bay leaf. Pour in 7 tablespoons white wine and the water. Cook for another 25 minutes, basting the bird now and then with the pan juices.

4 Peel and wash the turnips, cutting them into wedges. Place them in a heavy skillet with 3 tablespoons butter, a pinch of salt, half the sugar and just enough water to cover the turnips. Cover with foil. Bring to a boil and cook over moderate heat. The turnips should be cooked when all the water has evaporated and they are coated with a sticky brown glaze.

5 Take the duck from the oven and turn it on its back; cook for another 20 minutes, basting several times. If it begins to brown too much, cover it with foil.

6 Peel the shallots or pearl onions and glaze them in the remaining butter and sugar in the same way as for the turnips.

7 When the duck is cooked, put it on a serving dish or in a casserole and keep warm. Pass the cooking juice through a fine mesh strainer into a saucepan. Skim off the fat. Mix the cornstarch with the rest of the white wine. Pour this mixture into the saucepan and mix with a whisk. Cook for 5 minutes, then add the Madeira or dry sherry to the sauce.

8 Mix together the glazed turnips and the shallots or pearl onions. Pour the sauce over them. Simmer gently for 4-5 minutes. Arrange them around the duck and serve very hot.

Serves 4

Roast Duck with Turnips — a home-style meal well suited to serving in an earthenware casserole

Roast Goose

A mature goose weighs between 12-14 lbs. so choose smaller, younger fowl to be sure of tenderness. You can recognize tenderness by the pliability of the breastbone.

Before roasting a goose, pinch together the skin on the breast, then prick all over with a fork; this will allow the natural fat to run out during cooking.

Roast Goose with Prune and Apple Stuffing

8-9 lb. goose, oven-ready
salt and pepper
pinch garlic salt
pinch ground ginger
goose giblets
1 large carrot
1 large onion
little melted goose fat
2 tablespoons tomato paste
  diluted with 2 tablespoons
  vinegar
¼ teaspoon gravy coloring
pinch mace
¼ cup melted goose fat (optional)
¼ cup flour (optional)

For the Stuffing:
2 small tart apples
1½ cups canned prunes with the
  juice
1 egg
4 cups fresh brown breadcrumbs
¼ cup melted butter
pinch cinnamon and coriander
2 tablespoons brown sugar
juice and grated rind 1 lemon

1 Wash, clean and wipe the goose. Thoroughly season it inside and out with salt, pepper, garlic salt and ginger. Prick the skin without touching the meat to allow the seasoning to penetrate. Let stand for 20 minutes.

2 Make the stuffing: peel, core and quarter the apples. Drain the canned prunes, reserving the juice. Remove the pits from the prunes. Beat the egg. In a bowl, blend the brown breadcrumbs, melted butter, beaten egg, spice, sugar and juice and grated rind of the lemon. Gently but thoroughly combine the prunes and apples with this mixture.

3 Spoon some of the stuffing inside the cavity of the goose and the rest inside the neck cavity (turn the goose on its back to do this). Fold the neck flap over the backbone and secure it with a skewer or kitchen string. Preheat the oven to 375°F.

4 Wash the giblets, put them in a pan and cover with cold water. Bring to a boil and then drain and rinse in cold water. Peel and quarter the carrot and onion. Put them with the giblets in a roasting pan and place the goose on top. Brush a little melted goose fat all over the goose. Roast in the preheated oven for 1 hour, basting from time to time with a little water and the fat of the goose. After 1 hour, turn the bird on its side and cook for a further 15 minutes. Then turn it on the other side and cook for 15 minutes more. Reduce the oven temperature to 325°F. for the rest of the cooking time. The goose should be ready after a total cooking time of 2½ hours. To test if the bird is cooked, pierce the thickest part of the leg with a skewer: the juices should run clear.

5 When cooked, lift the goose from the pan and drain all juice into the pan. Keep the goose warm while making the gravy.

6 Remove all the fat from the roasting pan, leaving only the meat juices. Pour the juices into a saucepan. Dilute ⅔ cup of the reserved prune juice with ⅔ cup water and add this mixture to the meat juices. Stir in the tomato paste and vinegar, the gravy coloring, salt, pepper and the mace. Bring to a boil and boil for 15 minutes. Strain into a bowl.

7 The gravy can be served thin and clear as it is. If preferred, it can be thickened as follows. Mix the melted goose fat and the flour together in a pan and cook until a light brown. Take the pan off the heat and gradually add the juices. Return the pan to the heat, bring to a boil and cook for 3 minutes until thickened. Strain the gravy.

8 Carve the goose (see page 371) by removing the legs first; then slice the breast and leg meat as for duck, cutting 4 thin slices from each breast. Garnish each portion with some of the stuffing and serve the gravy separately.

Serves 4

Roast Goose with Apple and Walnut Stuffing

1 lb. fresh chestnuts
5-lb. goose

For the Stuffing:
1 lb. pork sausage
2 onions
2 branches celery
½ cup walnuts
2 cooking apples
1 egg
¼ cup butter
1 teaspoon dried sage
salt and pepper

1 Peel the chestnuts and cook until tender (see page 359).

2 To make the stuffing, fry the sausage meat gently for about 10 minutes until lightly colored, stirring occasionally. Remove from the heat and drain off the excess fat.

3 Peel the onions and mince. Chop the celery and walnuts. Peel and core the apples, then slice finely. Beat the egg.

4 Melt half the butter in a pan, add the onions, celery and walnuts and sauté gently until softened and lightly colored. Add the apples and cook for a few minutes more.

5 Remove the pan from the heat, then stir in the sausage meat, beaten egg, sage and salt and pepper to taste.

6 Preheat the oven to 400°F.

7 Spoon the stuffing into the cavity of the goose, then truss securely with kitchen string (see pages 324-325). Place the goose on a rack in a roasting pan, prick all over with a skewer, then brush with the remaining fat.

8 Roast in the preheated oven for 1¾ hours or until the juices run clear when the thickest part of the thigh is pierced with a skewer.

9 Five minutes before the end of the cooking time, drain the chestnuts and heat in a pan of hot water.

10 When the goose is cooked, remove the string and place the goose on a warm serving platter. Drain the chestnuts and arrange around the goose.

11 Serve hot with giblet gravy, chestnuts and Brussels sprouts.

Serves 6

Roast Goose — straightforward to cook and a splended dish to serve. A tart sauce like gooseberry helps to take the edge off the natural fattiness of the bird

Cornish Hens

Cornish Hens Véronique

2 Cornish hens, oven-ready
salt and pepper
4 slices bacon
¼ cup butter
2 tablespoons butter
¼ cup flour
1¼ cups dry white wine
1¼ cups stock made with giblets
  and chicken bouillon cube
pinch nutmeg
½ cup heavy cream
juice ½ lemon
¼ lb. green seedless grapes

1 Preheat the oven to 400°F.

2 Wipe the hens inside and out, and season them inside and out with salt and pepper. Wrap the bacon slices around the fowl breasts and secure with string. Spread the ¼ cup butter on top of the hens, then place them in a roasting pan, resting on their sides. Cook on 1 side for 10 minutes, then turn over onto the other side for another 10 minutes, then on their backs for the rest of the cooking time. Baste them with melted butter from time to time. Cook them in the oven for about 45 minutes. Remove the bacon slices about 20 minutes before the end of cooking.

3 Meanwhile, melt 2 tablespoons butter in a pan, stir in the flour and

mix thoroughly for about 2 minutes until it has a light brown, sandy texture. Gradually pour in the white wine and stock, stirring constantly. Taste and season with salt and nutmeg, and simmer for a further 10 minutes. Strain and boil again for 5 minutes. Stir in the cream and boil to reduce the sauce another 5 minutes. Then add the lemon juice.

4 When the hens are cooked, quarter them, and place the pieces in a casserole or shallow ovenproof dish; pour on the sauce.

5 To prepare the garnish: skin the grapes and remove the seeds. Scatter the grapes over the hens and serve at once with boiled rice.

Serves 4

Pot Roast Cornish Hen

2½-lbs. Cornish hen, oven-ready
salt and pepper
pinch mace
¼ cup butter
2 tablespoons lard
1 medium carrot
1 small onion
2 branches celery
2 tablespoons oil
1 bouquet garni

For the Gravy:
1 small slice bacon
giblets including neck and gizzard
¼ cup dry sherry
1¼ cups water

For the Garnish:
bunch watercress

1 Wash and dry the hens, then season inside and out with salt, pepper and mace. Rub the breast and

legs with a mixture of butter and lard.

2 Peel the carrot and onion, then cut in small cubes. Wash and dice the celery. Heat the oil in a pan, add the vegetables and brown them for 1-2 minutes. Place the vegetables in a casserole large enough to hold the hens.

3 Preheat the oven to 400°F.

4 Dice the bacon. Wash the giblets, put in a pan of cold water and bring to a boil. Rinse in cold water and drain. Add them to the vegetables with the diced bacon and bouquet garni. Spoon them over the bottom of the casserole.

5 Place the guinea hen(s) on the bed of vegetables, cover with a lid and roast in the preheated oven for 30 minutes. During the cooking time turn around to allow legs and breast(s) to roast evenly and stay moist. Remove the lid after 30 minutes to allow the heat to brown quickly. At this stage add the sherry and cook for another 15 minutes.

6 Remove the hen(s), and let it stand for 15 minutes, then carve in portions (see page 371) and place on a platter. Pour the contents of the casserole into a saucepan with the water and boil it for 15 minutes. Strain the gravy and skim off most of the fat; check the seasoning. If the gravy is too pale, add ½ teaspoon gravy coloring. Pour the sauce into a sauce boat.

7 Garnish the Cornish hen with watercress and serve with bread, sauce, and a green salad if liked.

Serves 4

Cornish hens are tender, and have a slightly gamey flavor. They are now available all year round, and may be roasted, braised, sautéed, pan fried or broiled. In fact, they are as versatile a bird as a chicken or turkey.

Cornish Hens Véronique cooked in a classic white sauce and garnished with seedless green grapes

Poultry Stuffings

Cranberry Stuffing

1 medium onion
2 tablespoons butter
½ lb. cranberries, fresh or frozen and thawed
⅓ cup honey or sugar
½ lb. pork or beef sausage meat
1 cup fresh white breadcrumbs
1 beaten egg
salt and pepper
pinch cinnamon
pinch pepper
juice and grated rind 1 orange
1 tablespoon freshly chopped parsley

1 Peel the onion and chop finely. Melt the butter in a sauté pan and sauté the onion for 5 minutes until soft but not colored. Add the cranberries and sauté for 2 minutes until lightly cooked. Remove the pan from the heat, add the honey or sugar, and cool.

2 In a bowl combine the sausage meat, crumbs and beaten egg. Season with salt, pepper, the juice and rind of 1 orange, and parsley.

3 Stir in the cranberry mixture as lightly as possible so as not to crush the cranberries too much.

Use for turkey, capon and Cornish hens.

Apricot Stuffing

⅓ cup dried apricots
½ cup cider
1 medium onion
¼ cup butter
1 cup fresh white breadcrumbs
1 tablespoon fresh chopped mint and parsley
¼ lb. pork or beef sausage meat, or mixture of both
1 egg
salt and black pepper
pinch mace
pinch allspice

1 Soak the dried apricots in the cider for 2 hours, then drain, reserving the liquid, and chop the apricots. Peel the onion and chop.

2 Heat the butter in a pan and brown the onion slightly for 2 minutes; add the crumbs and apricots, cook for 5 minutes, then remove the pan and cool.

3 Combine all the stuffing ingredients in a bowl, together with the reserved liquid, and blend thoroughly to form a smooth but firm paste.

Use for ducks, geese and Cornish hens

Lemon, Rice and Raisin Stuffing

1 medium onion
5 tablespoons oil
⅓ cup long grain rice
¾ cup white mushrooms
1 cup hot water
1 chicken bouillon cube
salt and pepper
¼ cup seedless white raisins
grated rind and juice 1 lemon

1 Peel and chop the onion. Heat the oil in a heavy-based pan and sauté the onion for 3 minutes without coloring. Add the rice, stirring it into the oil, and cook until translucent — about 5 minutes.

2 Wash, drain and slice the mushrooms, and add to the rice mixture; cook for 1 minute only. Pour in the hot water and crumble in the bouillon cube. Season to taste with salt and pepper and boil covered for 20 minutes.

3 Scald and drain the raisins and stir into the rice mixture, together with the lemon juice and grated rind. Steam off heat covered for 5 minutes and serve.

Use for ducks, geese and Cornish hens

Potato and Onion Stuffing

¼ cup butter
½ cup onion, chopped
1 medium cooked potato, diced
½ lb. sausage meat
salt and pepper
1 egg, beaten
pinch sage and parsley

1 Heat the butter in a pan, add the onions and sauté them until tender but not brown. Add the diced cooked potato, toss together and then cool.

2 Blend the sausage meat with salt and pepper, the beaten egg and the sage and parsley. Incorporate the cooled potato mixture and season to taste.

Use with all types of poultry

All about Fish

Fish can add variety to your daily menu. There is a wide range of fish (and shellfish) to choose from, with many different tastes and textures, from the kings of fish, salmon and trout, through flat fish, halibut and sole, and oily fish, mackerel and herring, to the tiny sardines. Whether planning an everyday meal or a dinner party, there is always a fish to suit the occasion.

Your choice of fish will probably depend on the occasion and how much money you wish to spend but all fish, no matter what the cost, contain many vital nutrients. Fish is made up of protein, fat and water and also contains vitamins and minerals. For example, 8 ozs. herring contains: $23\frac{1}{2}$ g protein; $14\frac{1}{2}$ mg calcium; 200 i.u. vitamin A; 1300 i.u. vitamin D; 2 mg iron; 0.05 mg vitamin B.

Protein Cod is very rich in protein, particularly the liver and the roe. The protein content in salmon and trout is higher still, but a little lower in white fish. A rich egg sauce will increase the protein content in a white fish dish.

Fat The fat content in fish varies greatly according to species, and accounts for the wide variation in calories provided by fish. Fish of the cod family contain less than one percent fat while halibut has 2 to 5 percent fat. Fatty fish such as salmon, mackerel or herring are always relatively fatty but the fat content varies with the season and spawning cycle—herring can contain as little as 5 percent or as much as 22 percent fat. Fat in fish is not localized, as it is in meat, but is distributed throughout. In certain areas however, particularly just below the skin, the fat content is higher than elsewhere. The fat of fish is also easily digested.

Vitamins The flesh of fatty fish contains a little vitamin A and is rich in vitamin D. The lean fish have almost no vitamin A or D in the flesh. Fish oils, found in the liver, provide a reliable source of vitamins A and D — these vitamins are more concentrated in the livers of fatty species. Livers of halibut and tuna are especially rich in both vitamins A and D. Fish, like meat, is a good source of niacin and provides riboflavin as well. The proportions of the different vitamins vary with the species and a certain amount is lost in cooking.

Minerals All fish are good sources of phosphorus, iodine, copper and fluorine. Most of the calcium in fish is found in the bones and, for this reason, it is wise to include the softened bones when eating canned fish. The iron content of fish is rather low and the diet should provide other sources of this mineral. Shellfish, such as oysters and clams, which are eaten whole, provide more iron than other fish.

Fish is cooked and eaten all over the world, whether grilled over a primitive wood fire, or served in a delicious wine sauce with truffles by a great French chef. The supply of various kinds of fish and their abundance during different seasons of the year is reflected in the market price. Although prices of some fish are high during off-season periods or because of scarcity, on average, fish are an economical food source. Fish can be especially delicious if served with a rich wine sauce to add extra flavor.

Fish is not only nourishing and tasty but also more digestible than meat. To obtain the same benefit as from meat, fish should be eaten in larger quantities — 2 lbs. cod equals 1 lb. meat.

Whatever the method of preparation, fish nearly always tastes best when it is fresh from the sea. There are exceptions: sole is less tough if allowed to stand on ice for a day or two, and salmon will improve in flavor if kept on ice for several days.

Choosing and Buying Fish
The quality of fish is largely determined by its freshness. Always make sure that the fish you buy are fresh. Check that the skin is shiny and bright and the scales do not cling tightly. The gills should be a clear bright red, free from shine. They should not be pink, grey or brownish-green. The eyes should be bright, clear and full — not faded, cloudy or sunken. The flesh should be firm and elastic to the touch and should not separate easily from the bone. Above all, the fish should not smell strongly or unpleasantly — it should have only a mild, characteristic odor.

Methods of Cooking Fish
These depend on the nature of the fish and on the recipe. Sometimes a combination of several methods is required to complete one fish dish. The chief methods used are:

Boiling: applicable to large or small pieces, or whole fish, which are completely immersed in the cooking liquid.

Boil Point 'Au Bleu': the fish must be alive. It is cooked in clear stock with vinegar.

Poaching: the fish is placed in only a little liquid and the liquor is used as a base for the sauce.

Stewing: a form of poaching. Fish cooked in this way are served as soup in clear broth, or styled 'en matelote,' in which case the broth is thickened with a roux or cream.

Shallow frying: the fish is cooked with a little fat in a skillet. When cooked in clarified butter and finished with 'beurre noisette,' the method is called 'à la Meunière.'

Deep frying: the fish is completely immersed in fat or oil, usually coated in batter, crumbs or seasoned flour and milk.

Baking: the fish is baked in leaves or foil.

Roasting: cooked in the oven and basted with fat.

Braising: baked in the oven with a little liquor on a bed of root vegetables.

Grilling: cooked on a charcoal grill or broiler.

Au Gratin: the fish is cooked until the moisture has evaporated and the top is browned to form a crust.

In salted water: this procedure varies according to the size and cut of the fish. With whole fish, immerse in cold, salted water or court bouillon, bring to a boil and simmer until the fish is cooked. With cut fish, immerse the fish in boiling, salted water and simmer for a few minutes.

Saltwater Fish

Atlantic	Pacific
Alewives	Anchovies
Bass	Cod
Catfish	Flounder
Cod	Halibut
Cusk	Herring
Eels	Ling Cod
Flounder	Rockfish
Haddock	Salmon:
Hake	(Chum)
Halibut	(Coho)
Herring	(Pink)
Mackerel	(Spring)
Pollock	(Sockeye)
Ocean Perch	Skate
Salmon	Sole
Shad	Trout
Skate	Tuna:
Smelts	(Albacore)
Sole	
Swordfish	
Tuna	

Fillet of Flounder Tivoli

four ¼-lb. fillets of flounder, sliced into small pieces
½ cup flour
pinch salt and pepper
¼ cup oil
½ cup sliced, white leeks
⅓ cup chopped, skinned tomatoes
2 chopped mint leaves
1 pinch ground thyme
⅔ cup cider

3 tablespoons tomato paste
1 chicken bouillon cube
pinch dill

1 Wash and drain the fish fillets and sprinkle with seasoned flour.

2 Heat the oil in a skillet and fry the fish fillets for 3 minutes. Remove and keep warm.

3 Add the leeks and sauté for 3 minutes. Add the chopped tomatoes, mint, thyme, cider, tomato paste and bouillon cube and stir

Fillet of Flounder Tivoli prepared in a tangy apple cider sauce, with tomatoes and leeks to complement the delicate flavor of the flounder

well. Boil for 5 minutes to reduce the liquid. Season well.

4 Reheat the fish fillets and place on a warm serving dish. Pour on the sauce and serve with a sprinkling of dill.

Serves 4

385

Fish Stocks & Sauces

Fish Stocks and Sauces

When making fish stock, do not use the bones of oily fish, which are not suitable for white sauces. A fish stock must be neutral with a sweetish taste. Sautéeing bones and onions in clarified butter produces a good flavor but tends to color the sauce.

Fish sauces must always be more acidic than those served with meat and poultry. This can be done by adding the juice of 1 lemon per $4\frac{1}{2}$ cups of sauce and also some dry white wine — sweet wine tends to make the sauce grey in color. White wine vinegar is always preferable to cider vinegar when used with fish stock.

Basic Fish Stock

1 lb. fish heads, bones and
 trimmings
2 tablespoons butter
2 tablespoons oil
1 carrot, sliced
1 onion, sliced
$3\frac{2}{3}$ cups water
$1\frac{1}{4}$ cups dry white wine
bouquet garni
pinch salt and pepper
1 chicken bouillon cube

1 Wash the fish heads and trimmings well.

2 Heat the butter and oil in a large pan and add the sliced carrot and onion. Cover and cook gently for 5 minutes.

3 Add the fish trimmings to the

vegetables in the pan. Cook for 5 minutes.

4 Pour in the water and wine and add the bouquet garni. Season. Cook for 15 minutes.

5 Crumble in the bouillon cube and simmer for 5 minutes.

6 Strain through clean cheesecloth or a fine strainer, cover and cool. Refrigerate until required.

Makes $3\frac{2}{3}$ cups

Tip: Fish stock should always be used the same day or frozen.

Basic White Wine Sauce

2 tablespoons butter
$\frac{1}{4}$ cup flour
$2\frac{1}{2}$ cups fish stock
$\frac{1}{2}$ cup chopped shallots
$\frac{2}{3}$ cup dry white wine
4 egg yolks
$\frac{2}{3}$ cup light cream
pinch salt and pepper
pinch cayenne pepper
juice $\frac{1}{2}$ lemon

1 Melt the butter in a saucepan and stir in the flour. Cook the roux for 3 minutes.

2 Add the fish stock gradually, stirring all the time, until the velouté sauce is smooth. Simmer for 20 minutes.

3 Boil the shallots in the wine until soft and add to the velouté sauce. Simmer for 15 minutes.

4 Blend the egg yolks with the cream and some of the sauce until well mixed. Pour into the velouté sauce and reheat, but do not allow the sauce to boil.

5 Season with salt and pepper and stir in the cayenne pepper and lemon juice.

Makes about $3\frac{2}{3}$ cups

Fillet of Cod Véronique

four 6-oz. fillets of cod
pinch salt and pepper
$\frac{1}{4}$ cup butter
$\frac{2}{3}$ cup dry white wine
$1\frac{1}{4}$ cups velouté sauce
$\frac{1}{4}$ cup light cream
pinch cayenne
juice $\frac{1}{2}$ lemon
$\frac{1}{3}$ lb. skinned and split
 seedless green grapes

1 Preheat the oven to 400°F.

2 Wash and dry the cod fillets. Season with salt and the pepper.

3 Butter a shallow baking dish and arrange the fish fillets in it, side by side.

4 Pour in the dry white wine and velouté sauce, and cover with damp parchment paper.

5 Bake in the oven for 15 minutes. Remove the paper and pour off the liquor into a saucepan. Keep the fish warm.

6 Boil the liquor to reduce by half and stir in the cream, whisking all the time. Season with salt, pepper and cayenne and stir in the lemon juice.

7 Arrange the fish in a clean shallow dish. Pour on the sauce, and decorate with a border of grapes.

Serves 4

Tips: A fish sauce should always be made with ingredients which will enhance the flavor of the fish used. Aromatic herb sauces are best with oily fish such as sardines, trout or mackerel. The best stock you can make for a fish sauce is usually made from the liquid in which the fish is poached. A fish liquor of wine and onions infused with a bouquet garni can constitute the base for a delicious sauce. Thicken with a mixture of egg yolks and cream, or simply blend with a basic white sauce.

1 As a preliminary to making Poached Fish (see p. 394) make the fish stock. Ingredients: fish trimmings, butter, carrot, onion, white wine, bouquet garni, salt and pepper **2** Wash the fish and cut off heads, bones and trimmings **3** Heat some butter and oil in a large pan.

Add the carrots and onions and cook for 5 minutes. Add the fish trimmings and cook another 5 minutes **4** Add the water and wine and bouquet garni. Cook for 15 minutes, then crumble in the bouillon cube. Simmer 5 minutes

Braised Fish

Haddock with Anchovies

3 lbs. haddock
salt and pepper
6 canned anchovy fillets, drained
½ cup fine breadcrumbs
6 tablespoons soft butter
1 tablespoon chopped parsley
grated rind 1 lemon

1 Preheat the oven to 400°F.

2 Clean and wash the fish. Season with salt. Make several small incisions across the backbone of the fish with a sharp knife. Cut the anchovy fillets into thin strips and place in the slits.

3 Place the fish in a greased baking dish and sprinkle with the breadcrumbs. Melt 2 tablespoons butter and baste the fish.

4 Bake the fish for 20 minutes, basting it occasionally.

5 Cream the chopped parsley with the remaining butter and the grated lemon rind. Season with salt and pepper. Place in the refrigerator until firm but still pliable. Turn onto a sheet of aluminum foil and roll into a cylindrical shape. Refrigerate again. When really cold, cut into thin, round slices.

6 Serve the fish with the rounds of parsley butter and coleslaw tossed in a vinaigrette dressing.

Serves 4

---

*Haddock with Anchovies —
served with a salad of finely
grated carrot, white cabbage and
beets tossed in French dressing*

Fillet of Sole Bonne Femme

6 tablespoons butter
¼ cup chopped shallots
1 tablespoon chopped parsley
1¼ cups sliced, white mushrooms
¼ lb. fillets of sole
salt and pepper
⅔ cup dry white wine
⅓ cup fish stock
⅔ cup velouté sauce
juice ½ lemon
pinch cayenne pepper

1 Preheat oven to 400°F.

2 Butter a shallow baking dish with 1 tablespoon butter. Sprinkle with the chopped shallots, parsley and sliced mushrooms.

3 Season the fillets of sole with salt and pepper and arrange them in the baking dish.

4 Add the wine, fish stock and

velouté sauce and heat the dish on top of the stove until the liquor is boiling.

5 Cover the dish and place in the oven for 8 minutes.

6 Keeping the fillets warm, pour the liquor into a pan and boil to reduce by one-third.

7 Cut the butter into small pieces and whisk it in, one piece at a time, until it is all blended and the liquor is creamy.

8 Check the seasoning and add the lemon juice.

9 Place the fish on an ovenproof serving platter and cover with the sauce. Sprinkle with cayenne pepper and place under the broiler for a few seconds to brown it. Decorate with sautéed mushrooms.

Serves 4

Tip: To make Sole Bercy, a delicious alternative to Sole Bonne Femme, just follow the recipe as indicated but omit the mushrooms.

Fillet of Lemon Sole Stockholm

¼ **cup butter**
2 tablespoons chopped onions
four 6-oz. fillets of lemon sole
salt and pepper
pinch paprika
⅔ **cup dry white wine**
1¼ **cups velouté sauce**
⅓ **cup light cream**
pinch dill
8 peeled, cooked shrimp

1 Preheat the oven to 400°F.

2 Grease a shallow baking dish with butter and sprinkle with chopped onions.

3 Arrange the fish fillets in the dish and season with salt, pepper and paprika.

Fillet of Lemon Sole Stockholm, cooked in white wine and cream, and served with whole shrimp and buttered rice

4 Add the wine, cover with a sheet of parchment paper and bake for 15 minutes.

5 Pour off the fish liquor into a pan and stir in the velouté sauce and cream. Cook over low heat, stirring constantly, for 10 minutes.

6 Check the seasoning and pour on the fish. Sprinkle with dill and garnish with the peeled shrimp. Serve with buttered, boiled rice.

Serves 4

Tip: Baking with dry heat is impossible for fish, thus no fish can be 'baked' without a certain amount of moisture. Always remember to add sufficient moisture to make up the loss from evaporation during the cooking process. To ensure that the moisture is retained either baste occasionally or cover the fish with foil or parchment paper.

Cod Manuella

eight ¼-lb. cod fillets
¼ cup flour
salt and pepper
¼ cup oil
1 onion, chopped
1 zucchini, peeled and sliced
3 tomatoes, peeled and chopped
1 red pepper, seeded and
  chopped
1 tablespoon tomato paste
1 tablespoon wine vinegar
⅔ cup dry sherry
⅔ cup water
1 chicken bouillon cube
pinch garlic salt
1 tablespoon chopped parsley

1 Clean and wash the cod fillets and cut into small pieces. Season the flour and sprinkle it over the cod.

2 Heat the oil and sauté the onion, sliced zucchini, chopped tomatoes and red pepper until soft (about 8 minutes).

3 Stir in the tomato paste, vinegar, sherry and water. Crumble in the bouillon cube and boil for 12 minutes, stirring from time to time.

4 Place the fish fillets on top. Season with salt and pepper and cover with a lid. Simmer gently on top of the stove for 12 minutes.

5 Pour into a serving dish and sprinkle with chopped parsley.

Serves 4

Cod Manuella — a Spanish dish in which cod is poached with zucchini, tomatoes and red peppers in a delicious sherry sauce

Fish Stuffings

Both stuffings are enough for 4 whole small fish or 4–6 fillets.

Mousseline Stuffing

1 cup raw finely ground cod
1 egg white
⅓ cup heavy cream
salt and pepper

1 Mix the fish paste with the egg white in a bowl. Place inside a larger bowl containing crushed ice and chill for at least 1 hour.

2 Add the heavy cream gradually, stirring all the time, then season with salt and pepper.

Herb and Breadcrumb Stuffing

1 cup coarsely ground haddock
1 tablespoon chopped parsley
1 small onion, grated
1 cup fresh white breadcrumbs
1 whole egg
salt and pepper
pinch of garlic salt

1 Mix the ground fish, chopped parsley, grated onion and breadcrumbs together.

2 Blend with the beaten egg and season with salt and pepper and the garlic salt. Use as a stuffing for any fish — whole round or flat fish and fillets.

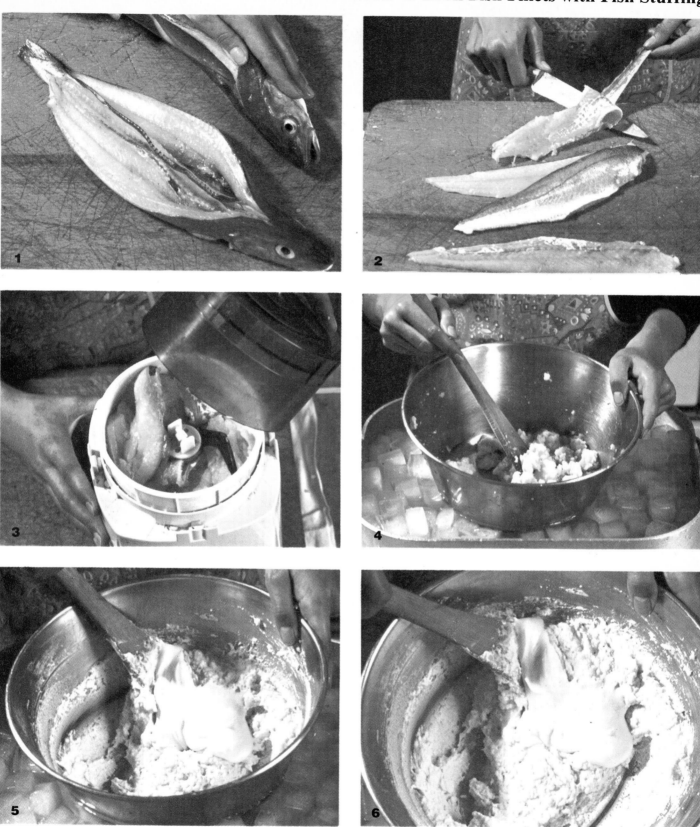

1 Wash the cod, cutting along the backbone to fillet it **2** Remove the skin from the fillets **3** Chop up the flesh in a food mill or blender to obtain a very fine paste. Season with salt and pepper **4** Place the fish paste in a bowl and blend with the egg white. Put this bowl in another larger bowl full of crushed ice. Chill the mixture for at least an hour **5** and **6** Add the heavy cream, spoonful by spoonful, to the mousseline stuffing. Mix thoroughly with a wooden spoon **7** Flatten the fillets with a wooden mallet or rolling pin or a wide-

Look 'n Cook Stuffed Fillet of Sole (Paupiettes)

bladed knife. Season them, turn over and repeat the flattening process **8** Spread the stuffing over the fillets **9** Roll the fillets up from the tail end. Do not squeeze them—the stuffing will ooze out **10** Tie the stuffed fillets with string. Make 2 turns and one knot **11** Butter an ovenproof dish and sprinkle with chopped shallots.

Place the stuffed fillets, upright and tightly packed, on top **12** Pour in the white wine and fish stock. Cover with a lid or aluminum foil and cook for 20 minutes in the oven. Remove the string. Make a sauce with the fish liquor and eggs. Pour over the stuffed fillets and serve.

Stuffed Fillet of Sole with White Wine Sauce (Paupiettes de Sole)

For the Stuffing:
1 slice bread
½ lb. haddock fillets
6 tablespoons butter
pinch grated nutmeg
1 egg, beaten
salt and pepper

For the Sauce:
eight 3-oz. fillets of sole
2 tablespoons chopped shallots
1 cup dry white wine
1 cup fish stock
1 tablespoon butter
2 tablespoons flour
2 egg yolks
juice 1 lemon
salt and pepper

1 Soak the bread in a little water and mash it with a fork. Put the haddock fillets through a food mill or in a blender. (If using a blender, add 1-2 tablespoons water or milk.)

2 Heat 2 tablespoons butter in a small saucepan and add the soaked, crumbled bread. Stir with a wooden spoon until blended but do not brown.

3 Melt the remainder of the butter in a small saucepan over low heat.

4 In a bowl mix the ground haddock and breadcrumb mixture. Add the melted butter, grated nutmeg, beaten egg, and season with salt and pepper. Blend well together.

5 Preheat the oven to 400°F.

6 Flatten the fillets of sole on both sides with a wooden mallet or a rolling pin. (First place the fish between two pieces of parchment paper or foil, so that it does not stick to the board or the mallet.) Then season them with salt and pepper.

7 Spread the stuffing over the fillets and roll them up from the tail end. Be careful not to squeeze them, or the stuffing will ooze out. Tie them with string.

8 Butter a small, round ovenproof dish (about 6 inches in diameter) and sprinkle with the chopped shallots. Arrange the stuffed fillets on top, standing upright and packed in tightly, very close to each other.

9 Pour on the wine and fish stock. Cover with a lid or aluminum foil and cook in the oven for about 20 minutes.

10 Blend the butter and flour together to make a firm paste.

11 Remove the string from the stuffed fillets. Arrange them on a serving dish and keep warm.

12 Pour off the fish liquor into a saucepan and boil to reduce by one third. Add the butter paste (*beurre manié*), a little at a time, stirring constantly to make a thick, smooth sauce.

13 Beat the egg yolks with the lemon juice and add to the sauce.

Adjust the seasoning. Heat gently over low heat, stirring constantly until the sauce coats the back of the spoon. Do not allow it to boil.

14 Pour the sauce over the stuffed fillets. Serve with crescents of puff pastry (*fleurons*) and baked potatoes or plain rice.

Serves 4

Tip: Lemon sole or flounder could both be substituted for sole in this dish. Also, a mousseline stuffing could be used, as shown in the step-by-step picture sequence, instead of the coarser breadcrumb-based stuffing.

Fillets of Sole, paupiette style, may be stuffed with a mixture of either breadcrumbs and fish or ground haddock and cream

393

Fish and Wine

Poached Flounder

3 lbs. flounder
¼ cup butter
¼ cup chopped shallots
1 tablespoon freshly chopped
 mixed tarragon, parsley, chives,
 mint

For the Fish Stock:
2 tablespoons butter
2 tablespoons oil
1 carrot, sliced
1 onion, sliced
1¼ cups water
1¼ cups dry white wine
bouquet garni
1 chicken bouillon cube

For the Sauce:
2 tablespoons cornstarch
⅔ cup heavy cream
2 egg yolks
2 tablespoons butter
salt and pepper
juice ½ lemon
pinch cayenne pepper

1 Preheat the oven to 400°F. Fillet and skin the fish. Wash the fillets and cut them into suitably sized portions. Heavily butter the bottom of a shallow ovenproof dish and sprinkle in the chopped shallot and the herbs. Place the fish pieces on top.

2 Make the fish stock: heat the butter and oil together in a pan, add the carrot and onion, cover and cook gently for 5 minutes. Wash the fish bones, skin and head, add them to the vegetables and cook for 5 minutes more. Stir in the water and wine and add the bouquet garni. Cook the stock for a further 15 minutes, then crumble in the bouillon cube. Simmer for 5 minutes and then strain the stock over the fish pieces. Cover with buttered parchment paper and bake in the preheated oven for 15 minutes.

3 Remove the dish from the oven, discard the parchment paper and lift out the pieces of fish with a slotted spoon. Arrange the fish on a serving dish and keep it warm.

4 Strain the fish stock into a pan and place over high heat. Boil for 8 minutes until reduced by half.

5 Make the stock: mix the cornstarch with the cream and add to the reduced stock, whisk continuously. Heat gently until the sauce thickens slightly, stirring all the time. Take the pan off the heat and whisk in the egg yolks and the butter, cut into small pieces. Whisk until the ingredients are well incorporated. Season the sauce with salt and pepper and add the lemon juice and cayenne pepper.

6 Pour the sauce over the fish pieces and place under a hot broiler for a few minutes to brown the top. Serve with boiled new potatoes, cauliflower or asparagus tips.

Serves 6

Tips: If any of the sauce is left over, try blending it with an equal quantity of white sauce and using this to cover mild-flavored vegetables such as cauliflower, leeks, celery, turnips. You can also use it with hard-boiled eggs and with rice.

Many types of fish can be used for this dish, including sole, salmon, cod and tuna. But make sure that you always use dry white wine and fresh herbs.

This dish can also be served cold: allow to cool and blend the sauce with a quarter as much mayonnaise or salad dressing. Place the fish on a bed of sliced cold cooked potato and pour on the sauce. Decorate with fresh lettuce leaves, tomatoes and cucumber.

Norwegian Baked Cod with Peppers

1 lb. cod fillet
salt and pepper
grated rind and juice ½ lemon
⅔ cup dry white wine
½ green pepper
½ sweet red pepper
¼ cup tomato paste
2 tablespoons flour
½ cup light cream
1 onion, chopped
2 cloves garlic, chopped
pinch paprika
pinch chopped thyme
½ cup Cheddar or Parmesan cheese
2 tablespoons fresh breadcrumbs

1 Preheat the oven to 400°F. Cut the fish into ½-inch slices and place them in an ovenproof dish. Season the fish with salt and pepper and add the lemon juice and white wine. Remove the membranes and seeds from the peppers and cut the fish into strips. Place the strips on top of the fish.

2 Mix together the tomato paste, grated lemon rind, flour, cream, chopped onion, chopped garlic, paprika and chopped thyme. Pour the mixture over the fish.

3 Sprinkle the fish with the cheese and breadcrumbs and bake in the preheated oven for 20-25 minutes.

Serves 4

Molded Cod and Shrimp in Aspic

¼ cup short grain rice
1¼ cups fish stock
1 egg yolk
⅔ cup flaked, cooked cod
¼ lb. cooked, peeled, deveined
  shrimp
pinch nutmeg
salt and pepper
1 cup chicken stock, or water with
  1 chicken bouillon cube added
¼ cup gelatin

For the Garnish:
cucumber and lemon slices

1 Put the short grain rice and fish stock in a pan, bring to a boil and simmer for 10 minutes.

2 Add the egg yolk, flaked cod, shrimp, nutmeg and salt and pepper and blend well.

3 Put the chicken stock, or water and bouillon cube, in a pan and bring to a boil. Take off the heat, add the gelatin and stir until dissolved. Cool.

4 Pour half the dissolved gelatin in an 8-inch ring mold, place the mold in a bowl of ice and tilt it so that the gelatin coats the sides and base of the mold as it cools.

5 Add the rest of the dissolved gelatin to the fish mixture and blend well. Pour into the mold and leave in the refrigerator for 1 hour to set.

6 Invert the mold onto a serving dish and decorate with cucumber and lemon slices.

Serves 6

Tip: Tarragon leaves may also be used to decorate the ring, in which case add 1 teaspoon tarragon vinegar to the fish mixture before chilling.

Molded Cod and Shrimp in Aspic — a perfect picnic treat which can be prepared in advance

Broiling is one of the best methods of cooking fish. It is especially suited to oily fish: herring, mackerel, sardines, trout, salmon, shad and others. When broiling a whole, round fish, first clean it, if necessary (the fish dealer will usually do this for you), then scale, wash and dry. If you like, the head and tail can be removed, although it is usual to leave them on both broiled and fried fish. The practice of cutting the tail into a deep V-shape is known as 'Vandyking.' Score the fish on both sides by making 2-3 diagonal cuts with a knife: this helps it to cook evenly, without burning the outside and leaving the inside half-raw. Brush it with oil or clarified butter, sprinkle with salt, a little prepared mustard or lemon juice — or top with a delicious savory butter. Line the broiler with foil so that the fishy smell doesn't linger in your kitchen after cooking. Broil at a high temperature, turning the fish once, carefully, and brushing the second side with oil. Allow 8 minutes to cook a fish 1 inch thick. For a special decorative touch, heat a skewer in an open flame till red-hot; then mark the fish with a criss-cross pattern just before serving. Serve broiled fish with a piquant sauce — the sharpness takes the edge off the richness of the fish — or one with a garlic or herb base, or topped with pats of savory butter, and accompany with plain boiled potatoes or rice.

White fish is also excellent broiled, especially if it has been lightly marinated first to bring out its flavor. Steep it in a mixture of oil, lemon juice or wine vinegar, seasoned with salt and pepper. Add crushed garlic, a little sugar, soy sauce, sliced onion, a pinch of cayenne and fresh herbs such as tarragon, fennel or thyme: the combinations are endless.

Broiled fish is rich in protein and vitamins, and is a vital part of a calorie-controlled, low fat diet. Serving fish as kebabs or with an oriental sauce is an original variation on plain broiled fish, and both make excellent party dishes.

Baltic Cod Kebabs

14 ozs. cod fingers or fillets
4 pearl onions
4 firm tomatoes, skinned and halved
4 mushrooms, washed
1 teaspoon chopped dill
1 sprig parsley
1 lemon, cut in wedges
For the Marinade:
$\frac{1}{3}$ cup olive oil
juice 1 lemon
2 teaspoons Worcestershire sauce
salt and pepper

1 Cut the fish into 1-inch cubes and place in a bowl.

2 Mix the marinade ingredients together and pour over the cubes of cod. Soak in the marinade for 30 minutes.

3 Parboil the pearl onions for 5 minutes.

4 Skewer the cod cubes, tomatoes, mushrooms and onions on four long, metal skewers. Brush with the remaining marinade and season.

5 Place under a broiler or over a grill or barbecue for 8-10 minutes. Brush with oil or melted butter from time to time.

6 Sprinkle the cooked kebabs with chopped dill and garnish with parsley and lemon wedges. Serve with tartar sauce and plain boiled rice.

Serves 4

Baltic Cod Kebabs — marinated pieces of cod threaded on skewers with mushrooms, onions and tomatoes and broiled or barbecued

Skillet-fried Fish

Fish, skillet-fried, should be tasty, crisp and fresh. All kinds of fish lend themselves to this method of cooking, from herring or trout to fillets of flounder or sole; and cod or haddock steaks. First clean and dry the fish, scaling and gutting if necessary. Then coat it in seasoned flour, or matzo or corn meal. (This seals in its flavor, and prevents it from sticking to the pan.) Make sure the fish is evenly coated — shake off excess flour. Heat a heavy frying pan or skillet and pour in enough oil to reach a depth of about $\frac{1}{4}$ inch. When the oil is very hot, place the fish in it and fry it quickly, turning it once, for 2 minutes. Lower the heat, and let it cook thoroughly. Drain and dry on absorbent paper. Serve immediately, with a tangy tartar sauce, French fries or creamed potatoes, seasonal vegetables, and a generous wedge of lemon.

You may fry in cooking fats (shortening) or use a mixture of oil and clarified butter. Fish dipped in beaten egg, then rolled in fine breadcrumbs or oatmeal (after being ground) is especially delicious fried. Fried fish is a perennial family favorite — but when it is cooked à la Meunière, it becomes a classic of French cuisine. Coat the fish evenly with seasoned flour, then cook it gently in clarified butter which is hot, but not brown. (Add a little oil.) When it is ready, keep the fish hot, squeeze the juice of $\frac{1}{2}$ lemon over it, and sprinkle with chopped parsley. Melt a little butter until it is frothy and lightly colored and pour it on the fish. Fish Meunière can be adapted to a range of recipes, and each different garnish — like tomatoes, capers, or shrimp and mushrooms — has its own title in classic French cookery.

Trout with Almonds. Coat the fish with seasoned flour and skillet-fry. Then sprinkle with lightly-toasted, sliced almonds and serve garnished with lemon slices

Sautéed Salmon with Creamed Mushrooms

2 tablespoons butter
¾ cup flour
⅓ cup water
⅔ cup light cream
salt and pepper
1-2 tablespoons dry sherry
½ lb. mushrooms, cut in
  quarters, and sautéed in butter
6 salmon steaks, ½ lb. each
½ cup oil
1 lemon
lettuce leaves

1 Melt the butter in a pan, add 4 tablespoons flour and cook the roux for 1 minute. Take the pan off the heat and blend in the reserved liquid from the mushrooms, the water and the cream. Cook the sauce for 5 minutes without boiling, add salt and pepper and the sherry and simmer for a further 10 minutes. Add the mushrooms and heat for 3 minutes more.

2 Season the rest of the flour and dust the salmon steaks with the flour.

3 Heat the oil in a pan, add the steaks and sauté for 4-5 minutes on each side until golden-brown. Place the steaks on a serving dish and spoon a little of the sauce on each one. Garnish with the lemon, cut into an attractive shape, and the lettuce leaves.

Serves 6

Sautéed Salmon with Creamed Mushrooms. The mushroom, sherry and cream sauce complements the flavor of the salmon

Flounder Fillets with Shrimp

2 tablespoons flour
½ cup breadcrumbs
salt
2 eggs, well beaten
4 fillets of flounder
2 tablespoons oil
⅔ cup butter
½ lb. cooked, peeled, deveined shrimp
1 lemon

1 Put the flour on one plate and the breadcrumbs on another. Add salt to the eggs.

2 Salt the fillets of flounder, and dip them, on both sides, into the flour. Shake them gently to get rid of the excess flour, then dip them into the beaten egg, and lastly into the breadcrumbs. Press the breadcrumbs firmly onto the fish.

3 Put the fillets on a plate and place in the refrigerator for 10 minutes.

4 Heat the oil and 3 tablespoons butter in a skillet and sauté the fillets of fish for 2 or 3 minutes on each side, turning them carefully with a spatula.

5 Remove from the skillet and arrange them on a heated serving dish. Keep hot.

6 Melt 3 tablespoons butter over low heat in a small saucepan. Pour in the shrimp and shake the pan until all are coated with butter (2 or 3 minutes).

7 Arrange a row of shrimp down the middle of each fillet and keep hot.

8 Heat the rest of the butter in the same saucepan until it is a nutty brown, and pour this over the fish fillets.

9 Cut the lemon into quarters. Garnish the dish with the lemon quarters and serve very hot.

Serves 4

Flounder Fillets with Shrimp — deep-fried flounder decorated with shrimp tossed in melted butter

Look 'n Cook Trout Meunière

1 Heat a mixture of butter and oil in a large, oval skillet and, when foaming, add the floured trout. Arrange side by side and cook gently on one side **2** Turn the trout over and cook the other side **3** Arrange the cooked trout on a warm serving dish and sprinkle with chopped parsley **4** Heat the remainder of the butter in a pan until frothing and pour over the trout **5** Garnish the dish with peeled lemon slices and more chopped parsley. Serve with sautéed mushrooms

Trout Meunière

four ½-lb. trout
salt and pepper
½ cup flour
⅔ cup butter
¼ cup oil
2 lemons
1 tablespoon chopped parsley

1 Wash and dry the trout and season with salt and pepper.

2 Roll the trout in flour and shake off the excess.

3 Heat 4 tablespoons butter and the oil in a large, oval skillet. When foaming, add the trout and cook gently on both sides.

4 Meanwhile, cut vertical grooves in the skin of a lemon and slice thinly. Peel another lemon and cut into slices.

5 Arrange the cooked trout on a buttered serving dish and sprinkle with the chopped parsley. Keep hot.

6 Heat the remainder of the butter in a pan until it is frothing and pour over the trout. Garnish with the lemon slices.

Serves 4

Tip: Sole or flounder can be used as a substitute for trout. Use the fish whole and do not remove the white skin or cut off the fillets. Cook in the same manner as for trout.

Variations

Belle Meunière: Garnish the trout with peeled, seeded tomatoes and sautéed mushrooms.

Bretonne: Garnish the trout with peeled shrimp and sliced sautéed mushrooms.

Doria: Decorate the trout with chopped, sautéed cucumber.

Marseillaise: Garnish with sautéed eggplants, tomatoes and garlic butter.

Flounder in Black Butter

2 lbs. flounder
¼ lb. butter
2 tablespoons vinegar
2 tablespoons capers
1 tablespoon chopped parsley

For the Stock:
2¼ cups water
⅓ cup vinegar
1 onion, chopped
1 carrot, chopped
bouquet garni
salt and pepper

1 Cut the flounder into equal-size pieces.

2 Put all the ingredients for the stock in a large pan and boil for 10 minutes (until the onion and carrot are soft).

3 Add the fish and poach for 5-6 minutes. Remove the flounder, drain well and place in a serving dish. Keep hot.

4 Heat the butter in a skillet until it is brown and foaming — almost black. Add the vinegar immediately and pour on the fish.

5 Sprinkle with capers and chopped parsley and serve.

Serves 4

Skillet-fried Mullet

four ½-lb. red mullet
2 tablespoons seasoned flour
¼ cup oil
¼ lb. butter
4 bananas
2 ears of fresh corn
2 tablespoons chopped parsley

1 Clean and wash the mullet and turn in seasoned flour.

2 Heat the oil and 4 tablespoons butter in a skillet and cook the mullet gently on both sides until cooked. Arrange in a serving dish and keep hot.

3 Split the bananas in two and heat the remainder of the butter in a pan. Fry the bananas until soft.

4 Place the corn in a saucepan and cover with water. Boil for 5-8 minutes, slice into 8 pieces and season.

5 Sprinkle the mullet with chopped parsley and serve with the corn slices and fried bananas.

Serves 4

Sole Murat

This famous recipe was created by M. Dinan who was chef to Marshall Murat and later to Napoleon when he was imprisoned on St. Helena.

¾ lb. fillets of sole
¼ cup flour
3 medium-size potatoes, boiled
½ lb. artichoke hearts
¼ cup butter
¼ cup oil
salt and pepper
juice 1 lemon
1 tablespoon chopped parsley

1 Cut the fillets into strips ¼ inch wide by 2 inches long and dredge with flour.

2 Cut the potatoes and artichokes into strips — the same size as the sole strips.

3 Heat the butter and oil in a skillet and sauté the strips of sole, potatoes and artichokes for 8-10 minutes. Cover the pan with a lid and toss from time to time. Season with salt and pepper.

4 Arrange the sautéed strips in a serving dish and sprinkle with lemon juice and chopped parsley.

Serves 4

Deep-fried Fish

Deep-fried fish, coated with crisp batter or egg and breadcrumbs and served piping hot, is an irresistible family dish. Deep-frying is a good way of cooking white and oily fish, either whole, if small, or as fillets, strips, fish-balls and made-up mixtures like croquettes, patties and fish cakes.

You need a deep-fat fryer with a basket inside to hold the fish. You may use any vegetable oil or solid cooking shortening, but do not mix the two. Never fill the pan more than half-full of oil or fat, as it can very easily splatter. Make sure the cooking fat is completely clean.

To prepare fish for frying

1 Egg and crumb method: wash and dry the fish completely — hot fat and water do not mix and splattering will occur. Dust the fish evenly with flour (shake off the excess) and dip it first in beaten egg, then in fine breadcrumbs (they can be white or brown).

2 Batter method: coat the floured fish in a savory batter (see page 410) seasoned to your taste.

Heat the oil or fat to 375°F. — check with a frying thermometer or by putting in a cube of bread which should turn brown within 1 minute and the oil or fat bubble around it as soon as it is submerged. Dip the basket into the hot fat or oil (this prevents food sticking to it), then lower the fish into the fryer. Fillets take 3-4 minutes to cook; thicker fish 5-6 minutes. When the fish is crisp and golden, take it out carefully, drain and dry thoroughly on absorbent paper. Serve immediately.

Never overfill the frying basket, as too much food causes a reduction in temperature, resulting in soggy or undercooked food. And *never* leave the fryer over heat unattended. Make sure the handle is turned inward and away from you, so there is no danger of knocking it over.

Deep-frying is a particularly tasty way of cooking white fish such as haddock or cod.

Fried White Fish

oil for deep frying
four ½-lb. fillets of white fish
1 cup beer
3 tablespoons flour
bunch parsley
2 lemons
salt

1 Heat the oil to 375°F.

2 Clean the fish fillets. Wash and dry them. Put them into a dish and cover with beer.

3 Pour the flour onto a plate, dip the drained fish into it and shake to remove excess flour.

4 Dip the basket into the hot oil and then lower the fish into the basket. Leave until the fish are cooked through and browned (about 4-5 minutes).

5 Wash and dry the parsley and untie the bunch.

6 Wash and dry the lemons. Cut into halves, serrating the edges. Heat a serving dish.

7 When the fish are cooked, drain them and place on a serving dish. Salt them, then arrange the half lemons around the dish.

8 Lower the parsley into the oil. Leave for about 2 seconds, then drain it. Decorate the plate with the fried parsley.

9 Serve very hot.

Serves 4

Tip: The oil should be very hot, but not boiling. Serve with fluffy mashed potatoes.

Fried Sardines (or Smelts)

16 large fresh sardines (or smelts)
handful sea salt
1 tablespoon dry breadcrumbs
1 tablespoon light cream
1 egg, separated
1 clove garlic, chopped
2 shallots, chopped
1 tablespoon chopped chives
1 tablespoon chopped chervil
salt and pepper
1¼ cups flour

oil for deep frying
1¼ cups milk
bunch parsley

1 Wash and dry the sardines. Place them in an earthenware dish. Sprinkle with the sea salt. Leave them for 4 hours in a cool place.

2 Mix the breadcrumbs and cream in a bowl. Add the egg yolk and mix again.

3 Add the garlic, shallots, chives and chervil to the cream and breadcrumbs. Add salt and pepper. Mix thoroughly with a wooden spoon.

4 Pour the flour onto a plate. Heat the oil to 375°F.

5 Clean the sardines if necessary. Gut them, cut out the backbone and fill with the cream stuffing. Reshape and secure the sardines with a wooden toothpick.

6 Put the stuffed sardines back into the earthenware dish, cover with the milk. Then dry them and dip into the flour one by one. Put them into the frying basket. Gently shake the basket to remove excess flour.

7 Lower the basket into the hot oil and fry until brown.

8 Heat a serving dish. Wash the parsley, dry well.

9 When the fish have browned, drain them and arrange on the serving dish.

10 Lower the parsley into the oil. Fry for 2 minutes, then drain it and arrange with the fish.

11 Serve very hot.

Serves 4

Deep-Fried Sole or Flounder with Zucchini Fritters

1¼ cups flour

2 eggs
1⅔ cups milk
1 tablespoon chopped parsley
1 garlic clove, peeled and crushed
salt and pepper
oil for deep frying
2 large zucchini, thinly sliced
four ½-lb. sole or flounder fillets
2 lemons

1 Preheat the oven to 275°F.

2 Prepare the batter for the zucchini. Sift ¾ cup of the flour into a bowl. Add the eggs and mix well together. Gradually stir in ⅞ cup of the milk. Add the chopped parsley, garlic and salt and pepper to taste. Mix well.

3 Half fill a deep fat fryer with oil and heat to 375°F.

4 Dip zucchini slices in flour, then coat with batter and lower into the oil. Cook for 3-4 minutes.

5 When the fritters are well browned, take them out of the oil, drain them on absorbent paper, put them into a heated vegetable dish, and keep them warm in the oven.

6 Rinse and dry the fish fillets. Pour the rest of the milk into a bowl. Spread the rest of the flour on a plate.

7 Dip the fillets into the milk, then coat them in the flour. Shake to remove excess flour. Dip the basket in the hot oil and then lower the fish into the basket and cook until brown on both sides.

8 Cut the lemons into halves (with a zig-zag edge, if liked).

9 Drain the fillets and arrange them on a white napkin on a heated serving dish. Place a lemon half on each fillet. Serve very hot with the zucchini fritters.

Serves 4

Tip: The fritter batter should be a lot thicker than pancake batter, so add a little extra flour if necessary.

Fish Tempura

Tempura is the Japanese name for a dish of lightly-fried pieces of meat, fish, poultry or vegetables, served straight from the pan with a soy sauce dip or raw vegetable salad.

2 lbs. fish fillets (e.g. haddock, mullet, cod, halibut)
juice 1 lemon
½ cup seasoned flour
oil for deep frying

For the Batter:
⅔ cup water
1 egg, beaten
1 tablespoon oil
¾ cup flour
pinch salt and pepper

1 Mix all the ingredients for the batter in a bowl.

2 Cut the fish fillets into small squares, cubes or strips. Sprinkle with the lemon juice and coat in the seasoned flour.

3 Heat the oil to 375°F. Dip the fish pieces in the batter and then fry in the hot oil for 3-4 minutes. Drain and dry on absorbent paper. Serve with mayonnaise dips, vegetable salads, and a tartar, horseradish or chili sauce.

Serves 4

Tartar Sauce
Blend ⅔ cup mayonnaise with 1 tablespoon chopped parsley, dill pickles and capers.

Horseradish Sauce
Blend ⅔ cup mayonnaise with 1 tablespoon grated horseradish.

Chili Sauce
Blend ⅔ cup mayonnaise with ½ teaspoon Tabasco sauce and 1 tablespoon chopped chives.

Red Pepper Dip

2 tablespoons soy sauce
1 teaspoon vinegar
juice 1 orange
1 small onion, finely chopped
salt and pepper
1 teaspoon sugar
⅔ cup mayonnaise
scant ½ cup finely chopped sweet red pepper
3 tangerine sections

1 Mix together the soy sauce, vinegar, orange juice, onion, salt and pepper and sugar in a blender or a bowl.

2 Lightly blend in the mayonnaise, then add the red pepper and tangerine sections.

Makes ⅔ cup

Pineapple Dip

⅔ cup mayonnaise or salad dressing
2 tablespoons chopped pineapple
2 tablespoons soy sauce
1 clove garlic, chopped
⅓ cup pineapple juice

1 Work all the ingredients, except the mayonnaise or salad dressing, in a blender or in a bowl.

2 Blend in the mayonnaise or salad dressing.

Makes ⅔ cup

Fish-balls Chinese-style

1 onion, peeled
1 lb. white fish (e.g. haddock, cod, sole) skinned and bones removed

2 cups crushed saltines or breadcrumbs
1 teaspoon sugar
salt and pepper
1 egg, beaten
½ cup seasoned flour
oil for deep frying

For the Batter:
1 egg
1 cup + 2 tablespoons flour
⅔ cup flat beer or water

1 Combine the ingredients for the batter in a bowl to form a smooth but fairly liquid batter. Leave for 20 minutes before using.

2 Grate the onion into a bowl. Grind the fish and add to the onion. Blend in the crushed crackers or breadcrumbs, sugar, salt and pepper to taste and the beaten egg. Grind again to obtain a smooth paste.

3 Divide the mixture into small dumplings and coat with seasoned flour, then dip in the batter.

4 Heat the oil to 375°F. Then fry the dumplings a few at a time for 3 minutes or until crisp and golden. Drain on absorbent paper. Serve at once with a sweet 'n sour sauce.

Serves 4

Vegetable accompaniments
You can serve almost any raw vegetables with Fish Tempura, such as carrots, turnips and cucumber, all cut in floral shapes. All vegetables must be raw or, at the most, scalded, so that they keep their color and taste. To scald, plunge into boiling salted water for 30 seconds.

Fish Tempura — small pieces of fish cooked quickly in hot oil and served with various vegetables and sauces

Beer Batter

2¼ cups flour
pinch salt
⅔ cup flat beer
1 egg yolk
⅔ cup milk
2 egg whites
2 tablespoons oil

1 Sift the flour and salt into a bowl.

2 Mix the beer, egg yolk and milk together and then blend this mixture into the flour to obtain a smooth batter. Cover the bowl with a cloth and let the batter stand at room temperature for 1 hour.

3 When the batter is ready, beat the egg whites until they stand in soft peaks. Add the egg whites and the oil to the batter and use immediately.

Makes about 1¼ cups

Fish Fritters. The recipe for Beer Batter given above can be used to coat all kinds of fish, meat and vegetables for deep-frying.

Vegetable Fritters

Many different vegetables can be deep-fried and served as fritters. Coat the vegetable pieces in seasoned flour, dip them in batter and fry for a few minutes in fat heated to 375°F. Try using slices of eggplant cut diagonally or lengthwise strips of zucchini. Sprouts, cauliflower, broccoli and root vegetables, such as parsnips, carrots, turnips and rutabagas, make excellent fritters but parboil them first in salted water until tender.

French Fried Onions

1 lb. large onions, sliced across in rings
⅔ cup milk
½ cup flour
salt
oil for deep frying

1 Separate the onion slices into rings. Place the rings in a bowl, cover with cold water and soak for 10 minutes. Drain well.

2 Dip the onion rings in the milk and then drain in a colander. Sift the flour and a pinch of salt onto a plate. Coat the onion rings in the seasoned flour.

3 Heat the oil to 375°F. Add the onion rings and fry for 3 minutes or until golden. Drain them on absorbent paper and use as a garnish for deep-fried fish.

Makes about 1 lb.

French Fried Parsley

bunch parsley
oil for deep frying

1 Wash the parsley well, drain and dry on a cloth. The parsley must be as free from moisture as possible.

2 Heat the oil to 400°F. and add the parsley sprigs. Allow them to fry for only 15 to 20 seconds. Drain and dry on absorbent paper. Use for garnishing fried fish.

Rolled Scrod

4 scrod (young cod)
2 eggs
2 tablespoons oil
salt and pepper
1 cup flour
3 slices fresh bread
oil for deep frying
few sprigs parsley

1 Trim, clean and wash the scrod. Carefully split them along the backbone with a filleting knife. Slip the filleting knife through to separate the two fillets. Cut out the backbone close to the head with kitchen scissors. Dry the fillets.

2 Prepare the coating. Put the eggs, oil and some salt and pepper in a deep plate. Beat with a whisk. Spread the flour on a plate. Make crumbs from the bread, and pour onto another plate.

3 Dip the scrod successively in the flour, the beaten egg and the breadcrumbs. Press on the crumbs gently with the blade of a knife, then roll up the fillets to the outside of either side of the head. Keep them in place with a skewer or wooden toothpick.

4 Heat the oil in the deep fat fryer to 375°F.

5 Carefully lower the rolled-up scrod into the hot oil and fry until golden-brown. Drain them on absorbent paper and keep hot.

6 Toss the parsley into the oil and fry for 2 seconds. Drain and decorate the serving dish with it. Serve with a tomato sauce.

Serves 4

Fried Smelts

1 lb. smelts
1 cup + 2 tablespoons flour
1 cup milk or beer
oil for deep frying
1 bunch parsley
2 lemons
salt

1 Clean, wash and dry the fish.

2 Pour the flour into a bowl.

3 Put the fish in a deep dish and soak in the milk or beer.

4 Heat the oil in a deep fat fryer to 375°F.

5 Drain the fish in a colander. Shake them, then toss them in the flour. It is best to do this gradually so the flour does not get too wet and clot on the fish. Toss the fish so that they are evenly covered. Then empty them back into the dried colander to remove any excess flour. Wash and dry the parsley. Cut the lemons into quarters.

6 Put the fish into the frying basket and lower into the hot oil. When the fish are golden and have risen to the surface, drain and dry them on absorbent paper. Add salt.

7 Fry the parsley for 2 or 3 seconds. Drain it.

8 Heat a serving dish. Put the fish on it. Decorate with the fried parsley and lemon quarters. Serve immediately.

Serves 4

Tip: It is not practical to clean very small fish, but they should be thoroughly washed.

1 Put the smelts in a container and cover with milk. For a variety of flavor, some of the fish can be soaked in beer in a separate container **2** Pour the flour into another container. Drain the fish and then, with the hands, toss them in the flour **3** Put the fish in a perforated basket (the one from the fryer, for example). Shake the fish to remove any excess flour **4** The fish are now ready for frying **5** Heat the oil. Lower the

basket into the hot, but not smoking oil **6** When the fish are cooked, raise the basket and rest the loops on the handles of the fryer, so that the oil can drain **7** Dry the fish on absorbent paper, put them onto a plate and lightly salt them **8** Fry the parsley in the same oil **9** Arrange the fish on a hot serving dish. Decorate with the parsley and lemons cut into quarters

Look 'n Cook Fried Fish Fingers

1 Take fillets of cod or haddock. Cut them into long pieces (fingers). Marinate them in the oil, lemon and parsley mixture 2 Prepare the batter 3 Beat the egg whites until stiff and fold into the batter 4 Heat up the frying oil. Drain the pieces of fish. Dip them in the batter 5 Lower them into the hot oil and let them brown 6 Drain and serve with fried parsley

Fish Croquettes

1 tablespoon oil
1 onion, chopped
1 shallot, chopped
1 cup mushrooms, chopped
2 sprigs parsley, chopped
1 cup milk
¼ cup flour
salt and pepper
freshly grated nutmeg
1 cup ground fish fillets (any white fish)
oil for deep frying

1 Heat the oil in a pan, add the chopped vegetables and parsley and cook gently without browning. Warm the milk.

2 Stir in half the flour and cook for a few seconds, stirring constantly with a wooden spoon.

3 Stir in the milk gradually. Season with salt and pepper to taste and add a little grated nutmeg.

4 Stir in the ground fish and cook gently for 10 minutes, stirring constantly. Remove from the heat and leave to cool.

5 Heat the oil to 375°F.

6 Shape the fish mixture into croquettes, then roll them in the remaining flour.

7 Deep-fry the croquettes in the hot oil until golden, then drain on absorbent paper and serve hot with a tomato sauce.

Serves 4

Deep-fried Kedgeree in Pastry Casing

¼ lb. flaked cooked haddock
⅓ cup cooked rice
½ cup cooked peas
⅔ cup diced cooked carrots
⅓ cup canned baked beans in tomato sauce
⅓ cup chopped raw onion
1 hard-boiled egg, coarsely chopped
salt and pepper
pinch curry powder
½ lb. puff pastry, homemade or frozen and thawed
oil for deep frying

1 Place the haddock, rice, peas, carrots, baked beans, onion, egg, salt, pepper and curry powder in a bowl and mix thoroughly.

2 Roll out the puff pastry thinly (⅛ inch thick). Cut the pastry into 4 rounds, each about 6 inches in diameter.

3 Place 3 large spoonfuls of the kedgeree mixture on each pastry round. Brush the edges of the pastry with water and fold over to make a half-moon shape and enclose the stuffing. Press the edges together to seal.

4 Heat the oil to 375°F. Add the pastry cases and fry for 4 minutes or until golden.

5 Drain and serve with tomato curry sauce or lemon wedges.

Serves 4

Indian Fish Cutlets

3 cups cooked rice
½ lb. any cooked fish
2 tablespoons curry powder
3 eggs
salt and pepper
1 cup fresh breadcrumbs
5 tablespoons shredded coconut
1 cup + 2 tablespoons seasoned flour
oil for deep frying

1 Grind the rice and fish together twice. Add the curry powder, 1 egg and seasoning and mix well. Form the mixture into 4 cutlet shapes.

2 Beat the remaining eggs. Mix the breadcrumbs and shredded coconut. Coat the cutlets in the seasoned flour, then dip in the beaten egg and then roll in the breadcrumbs.

3 Heat the oil to 375°F, add the cutlets and fry for 5 minutes. Serve with a wedge of lemon.

Serves 4

Fried Cod Fingers

1 lemon
2 lbs. cod fillets, skinned
¼ cup oil
¼ cup chopped parsley and chervil
freshly ground pepper and salt
oil for frying

For the Batter:
1 cup + 2 tablespoons flour
2 eggs, separated
½ cup beer

1 Squeeze the lemon. Cut the cod fillets into strips (fingers). Place in an earthenware dish. Pour the lemon juice and the oil over them. Sprinkle with the chopped parsley and chervil, some pepper and a little salt. Mix very carefully and leave to soak.

2 Pour the flour into a bowl. Put the egg yolks into the middle with a pinch of salt. Using a whisk, mix in the flour a little at a time. When the batter becomes too thick, dilute it with the beer to obtain a type of thick pancake batter. Let stand.

3 Meanwhile, beat the egg whites until firm. Add to the batter and fold in with a metal spoon or spatula, giving a very light batter. Heat the oil in a deep fat fryer to 375°F.

4 Drain the cod strips well, dip into the batter and lower into the hot oil.

5 Drain the strips on absorbent paper when they are golden. Serve immediately, very hot, with mayonnaise, a tartar sauce or fried parsley.

Serves 6

Baked Fish

Baking Fish

Baking is one of the most versatile methods of cooking. Fish may be baked simply, with a little butter, lemon juice and parsley; in a variety of different liquids such as stock, wine, apple cider, or cream; or stuffed, in a rich sauce. Baking retains the flavor of the fish supremely well, and cooking smells are kept to a minimum.

Arrange the fish attractively in a casserole — which can also be used as a serving dish. Always preheat the oven. Set it at 350°F. for dishes to be cooked in a covered casserole; 400°F. if you want a golden brown or gratinéed surface.

The possibilities for experimenting with different ingredients, herbs and seasonings are almost limitless. Sousing is a form of baking: cook at 350°F. and allow the fish to cool in spiced vinegar.

Cooked 'en papillote,' the fish is placed on a sheet of aluminum foil or parchment paper, covered with a garnish, rich or simple. The sheet is folded to make an airtight parcel and the fish cooks in its own juices in the oven. Serve the fish in its wrapping on each plate. This method of cooking is excellent as part of a calorie-controlled diet.

A popular American method of cooking fish is 'planking.' The fish is partially grilled or broiled, then transferred to an oiled oak plank, and baked. The plank imparts a delicious, barbecue-like flavor and aroma — and makes an impressive dish to present to guests, especially if the platter is decorated with a piped border of duchesse potatoes before it is placed in the oven.

Serve boiled or creamed potatoes with baked fish — or make a rice pilaf. A crisp green salad is an excellent accompaniment.

Baked Fish Fillets in Sour Cream

four 5-oz. fish fillets
salt and pepper
¼ cup oil
¼ cup chopped chives
⅔ cup sour cream
1 bay leaf
pinch caraway seeds (optional)
pinch paprika
sprig parsley
4 lemon wedges

1 Set the oven at 400°F.

2 Place the fish fillets on a buttered, shallow dish. Season with salt and pepper and brush with oil. Bake for 5 minutes in the preheated oven.

3 Add the chopped chives, sour cream, bay leaf and caraway seeds, cover with a lid, return to the oven and bake for 15 minutes at the same temperature.

4 Serve the fish in the same dish, with boiled new potatoes and turnips. Sprinkle with paprika just before serving and decorate with parsley and lemon wedges.

Serves 4

Baked Mackerel Stuffed with Apple

four ½-lb. mackerel
¼ lb. butter
1 cup celery, finely chopped
1 apple, peeled and finely chopped
small onion, chopped

1 cup fresh breadcrumbs
1 tablespoon chopped parsley
salt and pepper
pinch ground ginger
juice and grated rind 1 lemon

1 Preheat the oven to 350°F.

2 Using a sharp knife, remove the backbones from the fish without damaging the flesh. Open out the fish to form a pocket for the stuffing, and clean it thoroughly.

3 Make the stuffing. Melt ¼ cup butter in a saucepan and sauté the celery, apple and onion for 4 minutes. Stir in the breadcrumbs and chopped parsley. Season with salt and pepper and add the ginger, grated lemon rind and juice.

4 Spread the filling evenly on each mackerel, and fold over. Melt the remaining butter in a pan and use to brush the mackerel. Wrap them in foil and bake in the oven for 20 minutes.

Serves 4

Baking en Papillote

A papillote is a heart-shaped piece of parchment paper or aluminum foil, well-oiled or buttered, and folded around the ingredients to be cooked. This method of cooking is advantageous because it ensures that the fish simmers in its own juices and thus does not lose its own distinctive flavor.

Many fish can be cooked in this way — trout, red mullet, sole or pompano to name but a few. Really, the term only implies half-cooking because the fish used is often pre-cooked before it is placed in the paper bag or foil.

Always serve papillotes in their puffed-up paper shells and let your guests cut them open themselves at the table with a knife. If you use aluminum foil, remove the fish from the foil to serve.

Mexican Baked Cod

four ½-lb. cod steaks
salt and pepper
⅔ cup medium dry sherry
¼ cup grapefruit juice
pinch paprika
bouquet garni
¼ cup oil and butter
1 onion, chopped
4 tomatoes, skinned, seeded and
　chopped
1 red pepper, seeded and
　chopped
¾ cup corn kernels
1 cup fresh breadcrumbs
1 tablespoon chopped parsley

1 Preheat the oven to 400 F.

2 Wash and dry the cod steaks. Season with salt and pepper and place in a shallow ovenproof dish. Pour on the sherry and grapefruit juice. Add a pinch of paprika and the bouquet garni.

3 Bake in the oven for 15 minutes.

4 Meanwhile, heat the butter and oil in a saucepan and sauté the chopped onions until soft. Add the tomatoes, red pepper and corn. Season with salt and pepper and simmer for 8 minutes.

5 When the fish are cooked, remove from the oven. Place the cod steaks on a serving dish and keep warm. Drain off the fish liquor and add to the sauce.

6 Boil the sauce for 4 minutes, season to taste and remove from the heat. Stir in the breadcrumbs and chopped parsley, and pour over the cod steaks.

7 Serve with boiled potatoes or rice.

Serves 4

Mexican Baked Cod — the cod steaks are cooked in sherry and grapefruit juice and served in a tomato sauce

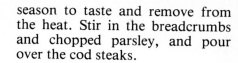

Herring with Apples in Cider

2 lbs. fresh herring, filleted
½ cup flour
1 tablespoon prepared mustard
salt and pepper
1 onion, sliced
2 apples, peeled and sliced in
　rings
3 cups potatoes, thinly sliced
1¼ cups apple cider
1¼ cups water
1 tablespoon cider vinegar
1 bay leaf
¼ lb. butter
1 tablespoon chopped parsley

1 Preheat the oven to 400°F.

2 Wash and drain the herring fillets and coat with flour. Spread the mustard on the fleshy side. Season with salt and pepper.

3 Place the fish fillets, side by side, in an oblong, shallow dish and cover with alternate layers of sliced onion, apples and potatoes. Season with salt and pepper.

4 Pour in the apple cider, water and cider vinegar. Add the bay leaf and dot the top with small pieces of butter.

5 Bake in the oven for 45-50 minutes. Sprinkle with parsley before serving.

Serves 4

Polynesian Baked Mackerel

four ½-lb. mackerel
salt and pepper
¼ cup butter
2 cups mushrooms, sliced
1 sprig thyme
1 bay leaf
1 lemon

For the Marinade:
⅔ cup pineapple juice
⅔ cup dry white wine
1 tablespoon soy sauce
1 clove garlic, crushed
1 medium onion, chopped
salt and pepper
1 teaspoon sugar

1 Preheat the oven to 400°F.

2 Clean and wash the fish. Make 4 slits in each mackerel. Season with salt and pepper and place in a shallow dish.

3 Place all the ingredients for the marinade in a blender and blend. Transfer the marinade to a pan and boil for 5 minutes.

4 Slice the mushrooms and heat the butter in a small pan. Add the mushrooms and sauté for 1 minute and place around the fish, with thyme and bay leaf.

5 Pour on the marinade and bake in the oven for 25 minutes. Baste with the liquid from time to time.

6 Serve with wedges of lemon.

Serves 4

Polynesian Baked Mackerel — the mackerel are marinated in pineapple juice and white wine and baked with mushrooms

Portuguese Stuffed Flounder Rolls

eight ¼-lb. fillets of flounder or
  lemon sole, skinned
¼ cup butter
½ lb. cooked, peeled, deveined
  jumbo shrimp
1 lemon

For the Stuffing:
1 hard-boiled egg
1 sprig watercress
¼ cup butter
¼ cup oil
1 onion, chopped
2 cups fresh breadcrumbs
1 egg, beaten
juice and grated rind 1 lemon
salt and pepper

For the Sauce:
1¼ cups velouté sauce
1 tablespoon tomato paste
2 tablespoons dry sherry
juice ½ lemon
salt and pepper

1 Preheat the oven to 350°F.

2 Tap each fillet gently with a rolling pin to break down the fibers.

3 Chop the hard-boiled egg and watercress and mix well with the other stuffing ingredients to form a paste.

4 Spread the stuffing evenly over each fish fillet. Roll up the fillets and place upright in a shallow oven-proof dish. Season, dot with butter and bake for 15 minutes.

5 Meanwhile, make the sauce. Boil the velouté and stir in the tomato paste, sherry and lemon juice. Season to taste.

6 Pour the sauce over the cooked, rolled fillets and decorate with the shrimp and lemon wedges.

Serves 4

Portuguese Stuffed Flounder Rolls are stuffed with bread-crumbs, watercress and lemon and then covered in a sherry sauce

Baked & Braised Fish

Halibut in Wine

four ½-lb. halibut steaks, about 1 inch thick
½ lemon
salt and pepper
1 tablespoon oil
⅔ cup dry vermouth

1½ cups heavy cream
¼ cup butter
½ lb. button mushrooms, sliced
1 onion, chopped
¼ lb. cooked, peeled, deveined shrimp
2 tablespoons tomato paste
pinch cayenne pepper
1 tablespoon brandy

1 Preheat the oven to 400°F. Rub the steaks with the lemon. Salt and pepper lightly.

2 Place the fish steaks in an oiled ovenproof dish and pour over the vermouth and 1¼ cups heavy cream.

3 Cover the dish with aluminum foil and place in the preheated oven for 20 minutes.

4 Heat 2 tablespoons butter in a pan, add the mushrooms and sauté for 2 minutes. Add salt and pepper and the rest of the cream. Keep warm.

5 In a separate pan, melt the rest of the butter, add the onion and mushrooms and sauté, covered, for 6 minutes. Add the remaining ingredients and cook for 2 minutes. Add the cream. Taste and correct the seasoning.

6 Transfer the halibut to a warm serving dish and cover with the sauce. Serve with boiled potatoes and a green salad.

Serves 6

Halibut in Wine — halibut baked with shrimp in a rich, creamy sauce flavored with vermouth and brandy

Baked Bass with Mushroom and Olive Stuffing

one 4-lb. bass, cleaned, scaled
1¼ cups dry white wine
1¼ cups water
1 onion, sliced
1 carrot, sliced
bouquet garni
1 clove garlic, crushed
1 bulb fennel, sliced
salt and pepper

For the Stuffing:
¼ cup oil
1 onion, chopped
½ lb. chopped mushrooms
4 cups fresh breadcrumbs
1 tablespoon chopped parsley
4 pitted olives, chopped

For the Garnish:
6 mushrooms

6 black olives, pitted
6 green olives, pitted
4 tomatoes
1 lemon

1 Preheat the oven to 400°F. Place the bass in a shallow ovenproof dish and add the wine, water, onion, carrot, bouquet garni, garlic, fennel and seasoning. Cover with parchment paper and bake in the preheated oven for 30 minutes.

2 Remove the dish from the oven, discard the bouquet garni and lift out the vegetables. Chop them coarsely and put on one side to use in the stuffing. Place the fish on an oval serving dish and reserve the stock. Reduce the oven temperature to 350°F.

3 Make the stuffing: heat the oil in a pan and add the chopped onion and mushrooms. Cook for 5 minutes and then add the chopped, cooked vegetables, the bread-crumbs, salt and pepper, parsley and chopped olives. Mix well.

4 Cut the tops of the mushrooms in swirls using a zesting knife and then boil the mushrooms for 4 minutes in a little of the reserved fish stock.

5 Surround the bass with the stuffing. Decorate with the black and green olives and the cooked mushrooms.

6 Place the 4 tomatoes for the garnish in boiling water for 1 minute, remove and peel off the skins. Cut the lemon in a decorative shape and

Baked Bass with Mushroom and Olive Stuffing is served surrounded by stuffing, and garnished with peeled tomatoes, olives and lemon waterlilies

place the tomatoes and lemon on the dish. Return the dish to the oven for 12 minutes to heat. Serve with boiled potatoes.

Serves 6

Bass or Snapper
à la Dugleré

one 2-lb. bass or snapper, cleaned and scaled
¼ cup butter
4 tomatoes, skinned, seeded and chopped
2 onions, chopped
2 shallots, chopped
1 clove garlic, chopped
bouquet garni

salt and pepper
1¼ cups dry white wine
2 tablespoons flour
pinch cayenne pepper
1 tablespoon chopped parsley

1 Wash and dry the fish. Either leave it whole or cut it into 6 steaks. Do not separate these but leave them together.

2 Preheat the oven to 375°F. Liberally butter an oval ovenproof dish with 1 tablespoon of the butter. Arrange half the chopped tomatoes, onions and shallots and the bouquet garni on the bottom of the dish. Place the fish on top. Cover it with the rest of the tomatoes, onions and shallots. Season with salt and pepper. Sprinkle the wine over the top. Cut 2 tablespoons of the butter into small pieces and scatter them over the fish. Cook in the preheated oven for 30 minutes.

3 When the fish is cooked, transfer it carefully from the cooking dish to

The ingredients for Bass or Snapper Dugleré. The bass is cooked in white wine, with tomatoes and shallots

a heated oval serving dish. Keep warm.

4 Pour the cooking juices and vegetables into a saucepan and bring to a boil. Boil until reduced by one-quarter. Discard the bouquet garni. Knead the rest of the butter with the flour to make a paste. Whisk this into the cooking juices and simmer until thickened.

5 Correct the seasoning and add the cayenne pepper.

6 Coat the fish with the sauce and serve immediately, sprinkled with the chopped parsley.

Serves 4

1 Clean, scale and wash the salmon. Place it in a fish kettle or large pan and cover with cold water. Add sea salt and thin slices of lemon with the pith and peel removed. Simmer gently without letting the water boil for 5 minutes per lb. Let it cool in its own liquor until quite cold **2** Drain the cooked salmon **3** Carefully remove the skin with a thin-pointed knife **4** Make some aspic and, when it is almost set, coat the fish with the aspic **5** Decorate the salmon with strips and small pieces of tomato and tarragon and coat with more aspic

to fix the decorations in place. Remove the decorated salmon from the grid and place on a large serving dish **6** Surround the fish with stuffed tomatoes, stuffed eggs and parsley **7** To serve the fish, cut off fillets, parallel to the backbone, with a knife and fork **8** When all the flesh has been taken off the first side, remove the fish bones by lifting up the backbone from the tail toward the head. Cut off the remaining fillets

Serving poached fish

Serve poached freshwater fish in their own court bouillon in a shallow dish. The court bouillon should always be clear — never cloudy. Serve with sliced carrots, sliced cooked onions and boiled potatoes and garnish with bay leaves and parsley. Alternatively, pour warm melted butter over the fish or, if you prefer a sauce, try a Hollandaise and decorate with lemon waterlilies.

Trout Soup Solianka

four ½-lb. trout
4¼ cups water
1 bouquet garni
1 chicken bouillon cube
¼ cup butter
1 carrot, thinly sliced
1 branch celery, thinly sliced
1 clove garlic, crushed
¼ cup flour
1 tablespoon tomato paste
salt and pepper
juice 1 lemon
1 tablespoon chopped parsley and dill
1 tablespoon capers
6 stuffed olives, sliced

1 Clean and fillet the fish, and cut each fillet into 3 pieces. Keep the heads, bones and trimmings to make the fish stock.

2 Place the fish bones with a bouquet garni in a saucepan of water, crumble in the bouillon cube and boil for 20 minutes.

3 Heat the butter in a saucepan and sauté the sliced carrot, celery and garlic for 15 minutes. Add the flour and cook for 3 minutes. Strain off the fish stock and add to the sautéed vegetables. Stir in the tomato paste and boil for 15 minutes until the vegetables are almost soft. Add the fish and simmer for 15 minutes. Season to taste.

4 Stir in the lemon juice, chopped parsley and dill and garnish with the capers and olives. Serve with rye bread and butter.

Serves 4–6

Poached Trout

four whole trout
2 carrots, sliced
2 onions, chopped
1 branch celery, thinly sliced
bouquet garni
1 sprig mint
6 peppercorns
4¼ cups water
2 tablespoons vinegar
salt and pepper
2 lemons

1 Clean and wash the fish.

2 Make the court bouillon: place the carrots, onions, celery, bouquet garni, mint and peppercorns in a large saucepan. Add the water and vinegar and boil for 15 minutes.

Trout Soup Solianka is garnished with capers and stuffed olives. Serve each dish with a swirl of sour cream

3 Place the trout in the court bouillon and simmer for 10 minutes.

4 Cut the lemons into wedges. Arrange the poached trout on a serving dish, pour on a little court bouillon and decorate with the lemon wedges. Serve with boiled new potatoes and melted butter or Hollandaise sauce.

Serves 4

Tip: This basic recipe for court bouillon stock can be used for all poached fish.

Salmon Mousse

1 lb. salmon, poached
2 tablespoons butter
¼ cup flour
1¼ cups milk
salt and pepper
pinch paprika
1 tablespoon tomato paste
1 teaspoon anchovy paste
juice ½ lemon
¼ cup dry sherry
pinch cayenne pepper
1¼ cups whipped heavy cream

For the Aspic:
1¼ cups water
½ cup gelatin
1 chicken bouillon cube
juice ½ lemon

For decoration:
¼ cucumber, sliced
12 cooked peeled, deveined
  shrimp
6 stuffed olives

1 Remove the bones and skin from the salmon. Chop the flesh.

2 Heat the butter in a saucepan, add the flour and cook for 2 minutes. Stir in the milk.

3 Place the chopped salmon in the sauce and cook for 10 minutes. Season with salt and pepper and a pinch of paprika. Stir in the tomato paste, anchovy paste, lemon juice, sherry and cayenne pepper. Simmer for 8 minutes. Blend or pass through a food mill. Allow the salmon purée to cool a little and stir in the whipped cream.

4 Make the aspic. Boil the water and stir in and dissolve the gelatin, bouillon cube and lemon juice. Simmer for 5 minutes and allow to cool a little.

5 Stir half of the aspic into the salmon purée.

6 Cover the base of a 5-cup mold with aspic, ⅛ inch thick, and allow to set. Then line the sides of the mold with aspic and set.

7 Dip the decorative garnishes — the cucumber, shrimp and olives — in a little tepid aspic and arrange inside the mold on the bottom and sides in an attractive pattern. Allow to set and then dab with the remaining aspic. Allow to set.

8 Pour in the salmon purée and chill in the refrigerator for 2 hours.

9 Stand the mold on a plate and hold under running, slightly tepid tap water. Gently loosen the mold and ease off. Be careful not to use excessive force or the mousse will fall apart.

10 Garnish with sliced cucumber, shrimp and olives.

Serves 6

Savory Pike with Walnuts

2 lbs. whole pike, or salmon
salt and pepper
½ cup flour
¼ cup oil
1 cup celery, sliced
1 cup carrots, sliced
1 cup onions, sliced
1¼ cups mushrooms, sliced
¾ cup walnuts, chopped
⅔ cup dry white vermouth
⅔ cup water
1 chicken bouillon cube
1 cup grated cheese

1 Preheat the oven to 400°F.

2 Clean the fish and cut either into small pieces across the bone or into steaks. Season with salt and pepper and dredge with flour.

3 Heat the oil in a skillet and brown the fish for 5 minutes on each side. Place the fish pieces in a shallow, ovenproof dish.

4 In the same skillet sauté the celery, carrots, onions and mushrooms for 4 minutes. Pour the sautéed vegetables over the fish pieces and sprinkle with the walnuts. Add the vermouth and water and crumble in the bouillon cube.

5 Bake in the oven for 20 minutes. Remove and sprinkle with the grated cheese. Place under a hot broiler until brown and bubbling and serve immediately.

Serves 4

Carp in Mandarin Sauce

2 lbs. carp or catfish
1 green pepper, seeded and cut
  into strips
1 sweet red pepper, seeded and
  cut into strips
2½ cups court bouillon
1 small can mandarin oranges
dash Tabasco sauce
1 tablespoon tomato paste
¼ cup sugar
salt and pepper
1½ tablespoons cornstarch
⅓ cup light cream
1 teaspoon horseradish
4 sprigs watercress

1 Preheat the oven to 400°F.

2 Clean, wash and fillet the carp.

3 Place the fish fillets in a shallow, ovenproof dish. Cover with the pepper strips and pour in the court bouillon.

4 Open the can of mandarin oranges, strain off the juice into a bowl, retaining the sections for decoration, and blend in the Tabasco, tomato paste and sugar. Season with salt and pepper. Pour over the fish and bake in the oven for 25 minutes.

5 Drain off the fish liquor, transfer the cooked fish to a clean serving dish and keep hot. Boil the liquor to reduce it by half.

6 Mix together the cornstarch and light cream and stir into the reduced fish liquor. Add the horseradish and heat through.

7 Decorate the fish with the sections of mandarin oranges and sprigs of watercress. Serve the sauce separately.

Salmon Mousse is ideal for lunch on hot, summer days or as a mouth-watering dish for any dinner party

Serves 4

Salmon Steaks with Spinach

6 tablespoons butter
2 carrots, thinly sliced
2 onions, thinly sliced
2 branches celery, thinly sliced
4 salmon steaks

For the Court Bouillon:
1 onion, cut into quarters
1 branch celery, thinly sliced
few sprigs parsley
1 carrot, thinly sliced
½ bay leaf
1 lb. fish trimmings
½ cup dry white wine
2¼ cups water
salt and pepper

For the Spinach Purée:
2 tablespoons butter
2 lbs. spinach leaves, washed and
  coarsely chopped
salt and pepper
pinch grated nutmeg
2 tablespoons flour
2 tablespoons light cream

1 To make the court bouillon, place the onion, celery, parsley, carrot, bay leaf, fish trimmings, white wine and water in a large saucepan. Season with salt and pepper and boil for 20 minutes.

2 Heat the butter in a saucepan and sauté the sliced vegetables over low heat for 8 minutes, until soft.

3 Strain off the court bouillon. Place the salmon steaks on top of the sautéed vegetables and cover with the court bouillon. Simmer for 15 minutes.

4 Make the spinach purée: heat the butter in a sauté pan and sauté the spinach for 10 minutes, covered, over low heat. Season with salt, pepper and nutmeg.

5 Sprinkle with the flour and stir in the cream. Simmer for several minutes.

6 Remove the skin and bones from the salmon steaks and arrange on a large serving dish. Arrange the spinach purée on one side of the dish, and the sautéed vegetables on the other. Garnish the salmon steaks with thin strips of carrot and lemon slices. Serve with a Hollandaise or shrimp sauce.

Serves 4

Tips: Fish trimmings may be bought from a fish store. Alternatively, buy 1 lb. of a cheap white fish.

Sorrel makes an excellent substitute for spinach.

Crayfish Bordelaise

36 crayfish (shrimp may be
  substituted)
2 carrots, diced
2 onions, chopped
4 shallots, chopped
juice ½ lemon
¼ lb. butter
sprig of thyme
½ bay leaf
bouquet garni
1½ cups mushrooms, chopped
salt and pepper
pinch cayenne pepper
pinch paprika
3 tablespoons brandy
⅔ cup dry white wine
1¼ cups water
1 chicken bouillon cube
3 tablespoons cornstarch
1 cup light cream
1½ tablespoons tomato paste
1 tablespoon parsley, chopped

1 Clean and gut the crayfish. Gently twist and pull out the fin from under the tail.

2 Sprinkle the chopped carrots, onions and shallots with lemon juice.

3 Heat ¼ cup butter in a sauté pan. Add the chopped vegetables, thyme and bay leaf and cook over low heat (with the lid on).

4 Meanwhile, heat the remaining butter and sauté the chopped mushrooms.

5 Add the crayfish to the sautéed vegetables and season with salt and pepper, cayenne pepper and paprika. Sauté briskly over high heat, stirring frequently, until the crayfish have turned red all over.

6 Add the brandy, sautéed mushrooms, wine and water. Crumble in the bouillon cube and cook for 15 minutes over moderate heat. Then drain the crayfish, arrange in a deep serving dish and keep hot.

7 Boil the sauce to reduce it by half. Blend the cornstarch with a little cream and stir into the reduced sauce. Add the remainder of the cream and the tomato paste. Boil for a few minutes over high heat. Correct the seasoning.

8 Pour the sauce over the crayfish, sprinkle with chopped parsley and serve.

Serves 6

Tips: All crustaceans such as lobster and large shrimp can be cooked in a similar manner. It is the shell — not the flesh — which gives the sauce its distinctive flavor. The sauce can be made into a bisque, a kind of shellfish soup, by mixing it with béchamel or velouté sauce and adding lobster meat or shrimp and so on. Crayfish Bordelaise may be served as an appetizer or as a main dish. The usual accompaniment is boiled rice.

Salmon Steaks with Spinach are garnished with spinach purée and sautéed vegetables and served with a Hollandaise sauce

Fish Dumplings

Forcemeats are usually made from ground white fish, such as cod, and combined with breadcrumbs or a thick white sauce, egg yolks and seasonings. Shellfish can also be used but if you want to economize, mix it with a cheaper fish. Use the forcemeat for stuffing whole fish or paupiettes or shape into dumplings, cover with fish stock and poach for 10 minutes. Serve the dumplings hot as a garnish for fish dishes or cold as an hors d'oeuvre.

Basic Fish Forcemeat

1 lb. ground white fish
⅔ cup thick white sauce
¼ cup butter, softened
salt and pepper
pinch grated nutmeg
2 eggs, beaten
juice ½ lemon

1 Pound the ground fish to a paste with a rolling pin or blend.

2 Add the thick white sauce and butter and blend well. Season with salt and pepper and nutmeg.

3 Beat in the eggs and then add the lemon juice.

4 Use as a stuffing for fish or shape into dumplings and poach.

Serves 4

Tip: Serve the dumplings with a sauce. Wine or shellfish flavored sauces such as shrimp or lobster sauces are delicious.

Dumplings are an ideal way of using up leftover fish, or making a little fish go a long way. Any fish can be used.

Quenelles

1 lb. raw white fish
¼ cup butter
1 cup + 2 tablespoons flour
½ cup water
salt and pepper
pinch grated nutmeg
2 egg whites
1¼ cups heavy cream
1¼ cups fish stock
1 tablespoon chopped parsley

1 Skin and bone the fish and grind the fish flesh twice.

2 Melt the butter in a pan, add the flour and cook the mixture for 3 minutes, stirring continuously. Add the water and mix well to form a stiff paste. Cool.

3 Add the ground fish to the paste and either pound with a rolling pin or blend.

4 Season with salt and pepper and grated nutmeg and mix in the egg whites. Chill the mixture thoroughly by placing in the refrigerator or freezer.

5 When the mixture is icy cold, blend in the cream and shape the mixture into quenelles. Take a spoonful at a time and, using two spoons, shape the mixture until it is oval.

6 Place the quenelles in a large, buttered pan or baking dish. Cover with the fish stock — the quenelles should be totally immersed.

7 Bring the stock to a boil, and then simmer on top of the stove for 10 minutes until the quenelles are cooked.

8 Place the quenelles in a shallow serving dish and cover with Nantua sauce. Sprinkle with chopped parsley and serve with boiled rice or duchesse potatoes.

Serves 6

Mushroom Fish Stuffing

½ lb. ground white fish, e.g., cod, haddock
4 soft herring roe
1½ cups fresh breadcrumbs
⅓ cup milk
¼ cup butter
¼ cup shallots, chopped
⅓ cup dry white wine
1¼ cups mushrooms, chopped
1 tablespoon chopped parsley
salt and pepper
2 eggs, beaten
juice ½ lemon

1 Blend the ground fish with the soft herring roe, breadcrumbs and milk. Grind again or place in a blender and blend.

2 Melt the butter in a pan and sweat the shallots for 2 minutes with the lid on. Add the wine and chopped mushrooms, and boil for 3 minutes.

3 Pour onto the fish mixture and stir in the chopped parsley and salt and pepper. Blend well and gradually add the eggs and lemon juice until all the moisture has been absorbed by the breadcrumbs and fish. If the mixture is too moist, add more crumbs — it should be of a firm, but moist consistency.

4 Use as a stuffing for fish or poach as dumplings.

Serves 4

Tip: Use this mushroom fish stuffing in savory, stuffed crêpes. Make the crêpes and roll up the stuffing inside. Cover with a cheesy Mornay sauce, sprinkle with grated cheese and place under a hot broiler until the crêpes are bubbling and golden-brown.

Quenelles are delicious fish dumplings, usually served in a Nantua sauce with plain, boiled rice

Salmon Loaf

6⅓ cups water
pinch salt
½ cup long grain rice
½ lb. salmon, drained
1 sweet red pepper, seeded and
   chopped
10 pitted green olives
4 hard-boiled eggs, chopped
¼ cup mayonnaise
1 teaspoon tomato paste
juice ½ lemon
¼ cup butter, softened
1 small head lettuce, washed and
   diced
small pinch parsley

1 Boil the water in a saucepan and add the salt and rice. Cook for about 20-25 minutes, drain and cool.

2 Flake the salmon with a fork. Add the chopped red pepper and olives, rice and hard-boiled eggs.

3 Blend the mayonnaise with the tomato paste and lemon juice, and stir in the salmon mixture.

4 Butter inside an oblong mold (or cake pan) with the butter. Pour in the salmon mixture, pressing it down well. Chill in the refrigerator for 2 hours.

5 Cover a serving platter with the lettuce leaves and turn out the salmon loaf onto them. Decorate with parsley and serve immediately.

Serves 4

Salmon Pastry Envelopes

½ lb. mushrooms, chopped
juice ½ lemon
1 lb. canned salmon
¼ cup butter

6 shallots or onions, peeled and
   chopped
¼ cup flour
½ cup light cream
2 eggs, beaten
4 sprigs parsley, chopped
1 lb. puff pastry, frozen and
   thawed

1 Preheat the oven to 350°F.

2 Place the chopped mushrooms in a small bowl and marinate in the lemon juice.

3 Drain the salmon and put aside the fish juice in a small bowl. Remove the bones and pound the flesh finely with a rolling pin or pestle.

4 Heat the butter in a skillet. Add the shallots or onions and the mushrooms which have been soaked in lemon juice. Sauté for 3 minutes, then add the salmon, stirring briskly over high heat.

5 Stir in the flour and cook for 3 minutes, then add the salmon juice and cream, stirring all the time. Stir in 1 beaten egg and the chopped parsley when the sauce has thickened, and remove from the heat.

6 Roll out the puff pastry ⅛ inch thick and cut into rectangles 3 inches across by 4 inches long.

7 Place some of the salmon filling on the middle of each rectangle and moisten the pastry edges. Fold over and pinch together to seal the parcels. Brush with beaten egg.

8 Place the parcels on a greased baking sheet and bake for 15-20 minutes. Serve hot or cold.

Serves 6

Coulibiac

Coulibiac is a traditional, hot, Russian fish pie usually made with salmon. It is served with sour cream.

¼ cup butter
1 medium onion, chopped
1 cup long grain rice
4¼ cups water
1 chicken bouillon cube
2 lbs. puff pastry, frozen and
   thawed
½ lb. salmon, flaked
juice 1 lemon
1¼ cups mushrooms, sliced
salt and pepper
2 hard-boiled eggs, sliced
1 egg, beaten

1 Preheat the oven to 400°F.

2 Heat the butter in a saucepan and sauté the onion until soft. Add the rice and simmer for 3 minutes until transparent. Add the water and crumble in the bouillon cube. Bring to a boil, then simmer for 20 minutes, until the rice is cooked.

3 Roll out the pastry into an oblong shape on a floured board until it is ⅛ thick. Place a layer of the cooked rice in the center, then a layer of salmon. Pour on the lemon juice and top with the sliced mushrooms. Season with salt and pepper. Cover with more rice and arrange the slices of hard-boiled eggs along the top.

4 Wrap the pastry over so that it resembles a bread loaf and place on a greased baking sheet. Brush the top with beaten egg and make a decorative pattern with a fork.

5 Bake in the oven for 30 minutes. Serve with a dish of sour cream or shrimp sauce.

Serves 6

Tips: Coulibiac can be served with a sour cream sauce — *smitana*. To make this, just boil up a few shallots in a cup of white wine, stir in some sour cream and season with salt and pepper.

Another way to make Coulibiac is to use biscuit dough instead of puff pastry.

All about Lamb
Roast Shoulder of Lamb

Lamb used to be referred to as "spring lamb" when it was only home-produced. However, the advent of refrigeration meant that it could be shipped around the world and eaten at all times of the year. Lamb is only called "lamb" from five months to a year and a half. After that it is referred to as mutton.

Choosing Lamb

You should always look carefully at the color and texture of the meat when buying lamb. Good quality lamb is light pink and lean with firm fat — the younger the animal, the paler the meat. In an older animal it may be light red. The color of the fat varies too. Freshly butchered young lamb, available in the spring and early summer, has a creamy fat, while the fat of older lamb is firm and white.

Cuts of Lamb

The cuts of lamb, unlike beef, are international and thus the same throughout the world. Lamb is easy to cook as it has a distinctive flavor and natural fat. Thus most cuts are tender and not tough. In England, the United States and Australia, most people prefer lamb well cooked. However, in France and other parts of Europe it is usually eaten slightly underdone and still pink in the center. Lamb is very versatile and most cuts can be cooked by both dry and moist cooking methods.

Loin: This is a prime cut which is usually roasted, either on the bone or boned, stuffed and rolled. The loin is also cut up and served as chops. Other cooking methods for loin are pot-roasting and braising. When cooking loin, you should allow 12 ozs. per person on the bone, and 4-6 ozs. off the bone.

Leg: This is another cut which is usually roasted, braised or pot-roasted. It is often boned and stuffed but the meat can also be cut off the bone and used in stews and casseroles, pies and kebabs. If you intend to roast a leg, always allow 12 ozs. meat on the bone per person.

Shoulder: This is a large cut which is often more flavorsome than the leg. It is inclined to be more fatty. Shoulder can be stuffed with various exciting stuffings and roasted. Allow 12 ozs. of meat on the bone per person.

Breast of Lamb: This is a cheap and rather fatty cut which is often boned, stuffed and rolled. It is then roasted or braised, stewed or boiled. You should allow 8-12 ozs. of meat per person, on the bone.

Back of Neck: This is inexpensive and probably the most versatile cut of all. It is the cut next to the loin and can be roasted, stewed or braised. Allow 12 ozs. per person.

Chops: These are cut from the loin; the ones nearest to the leg are known as chops. They are usually broiled or fried but they are also often used in casseroles. Allow 1-2 chops per person.

Cutlets: These come from the rack and can be broiled or fried. They have little lean meat and a longish bone. Allow 1-2 per person.

Neck Middle and Neck End: These are all cheap cuts which are suitable for stews and casseroles. They have little meat and a high proportion of fat and bone. Allow 8-12 ozs. meat on the bone per person.

Sauces and Stuffings

Roast lamb is traditionally served with mint jelly or red currant jelly, Cumberland or onion sauce. Lamb is delicious when stuffed. Be adventurous and try some new fruity stuffings made with apricots, prunes, apples and dried fruit. Rice can be used for stuffing lamb — try mixing it with herbs and nuts for a change from the usual thyme and parsley or sage and onion.

Crown Roast of Lamb

This is a very special and well-known lamb dish which always looks impressive at dinner parties. Most butchers will prepare a crown roast for you if you give them a couple of days' warning. It consists of two pieces of the rack which are usually taken from opposite sides of the animal. It is served stuffed in the center and the bones are decorated with cutlet caps.

Roasting Lamb

Always roast with the thickest layer of fat on top so that the roast will be automatically basted during cooking. You can try dusting the basted skin of the lamb with seasoned flour. This will absorb excess fat and make the top crisp and golden.

Herbs and Lamb

Herbs go very well with lamb and you should try roasting or casseroling it with different herbs and combinations. Thyme, oregano, marjoram, basil, savory, rosemary, parsley and mint all enhance its flavor. Garlic is also a good flavoring — try rubbing your roast with it, or inserting a clove into the meat itself. Do not overdo the flavoring as lamb has a rather delicate flavor and you may disguise it altogether. Herbs should only be used to complement it.

Storing Lamb

The cheapest way to buy lamb, of course, is to buy in bulk and store it in your freezer. However, if you cannot afford to do this, uncooked meat should keep in the refrigerator for 3-4 days. Do not store the lamb in its wrapping paper. Instead, put it on a plate and cover with some thin plastic wrap — leave the ends open for ventilation. Always wrap cooked lamb before placing in the refrigerator, otherwise it will dry out.

Two examples of the varied dishes which can be prepared from lamb: a stuffed roast leg, and cutlets from the rack served with caper sauce

Leg of Lamb

Traditionally served, a roast leg of lamb with roast potatoes, peas, mint sauce, red currant jelly, or cranberry sauce, is very popular.

We also realize that you may want to know of other unusual ways of cooking a leg of lamb and so we offer you many different and interesting recipes. We show you how to add a delicate flavor by inserting slivers of garlic into cuts in the flesh. In another recipe we explain how to lard a leg of lamb with bacon strips to give a gamey venison flavor. Lamb can be marinated and spread with a sauce made with sour cream before cooking as a change. Or it can be served, Spanish-style, with tomatoes and olives and flavored with rosemary. You will know when a leg of lamb is cooked because the juice will run clear if the meat is pierced with a sharp knife. If you use a meat thermometer, the internal temperature of the meat (not near a bone) should read 180°F.

To calculate cooking times, allow 20 minutes per lb., and 20 minutes more for a cut on the bone. Allow 25 minutes if the roast is boned, and 30 minutes if the roast is boned and stuffed and make sure you add the weight of the stuffing to the weight of the roast. When you buy a leg of lamb, allow 12 ozs. for each person for meat on the bone, and 4-6 ozs. if the roast has been boned.

Pot Roast Lamb

salt and pepper
4-lb. leg of lamb, boned, rolled
 and tied
2 cloves garlic
¼ cup butter
2 tablespoons oil

3 carrots, sliced
3 onions, sliced
3 leeks, sliced
2 cups beef stock
1 lb. cooked lima beans
1½ cups water
½ tablespoon cornstarch

1 Season the leg of lamb and insert slices of garlic into cuts in the flesh.

2 Heat 2 tablespoons butter and the oil in a casserole, and brown the lamb all over for 8 minutes. Remove. Brown the carrots, onions and leeks in the same fat for 5 minutes. Pour off the fat. Return the lamb to the casserole. Add the stock and bring to a boil, and simmer for 2 hours.

3 Heat the beans in the rest of the butter and season with salt and pepper. Keep warm.

4 When the meat is cooked, remove from the casserole and keep warm. Pour off the fat, add 1¼ cups of the water and boil for 5 minutes. Thicken with the cornstarch mixed with the rest of the water. Boil for 5 minutes, strain and season.

5 To serve, slice the meat and arrange on a dish, surrounded by the beans. Serve the gravy separately.

Serves 8

Roast Lamb with Lemon Sauce

3-lb. leg of lamb
2 cloves garlic, sliced
salt and pepper
¼ cup oil
¼ cup butter
2 carrots, sliced
2 branches celery, sliced
1 onion, chopped
2 lemons

1 cup + 2 tablespoons water
½ cup sugar
1 tablespoon vinegar
½ tablespoon cornstarch

1 When buying the leg of lamb, ask the butcher to cut out the bone and to trim the knuckle.

2 Preheat the oven to 400°F.

3 Make cuts in the flesh and insert the slices of garlic. Season the leg, smother with the oil and butter and place in a roasting pan on a bed of carrots, celery, onion, 1 sliced lemon and the bone.

4 Roast for 1¼ hours (allowing 20 minutes per lb. and 20 minutes more) basting from time to time. When cooked, let set for 10 minutes, then place on a clean platter and keep warm.

5 Make the gravy. During the roasting time, cut the other lemon into segments, and simmer for 8 minutes in 1 cup of the water with the sugar and vinegar.

6 When the roast has been removed, put the roasting pan on top of the stove over gentle heat for 2 minutes to allow the sediment to settle. Carefully pour off the fat, leaving the sediment and juices. Cook for 3 minutes until brown, then add 1¼ cups of lemon liquid (add water if necessary to make up the amount). Stir and scrape the pan to loosen the browned sediment, and cook for 8 minutes. Thicken with the cornstarch mixed with 3 tablespoons of the water. Cook for 5 minutes to clear. Strain.

7 To serve, decorate the leg of lamb with a cap around the bone, and pour a little sauce over it. Arrange the lemon segments on top. Serve the rest of the sauce separately. Serve with boiled rice, sprinkled with chopped parsley.

Serves 6

An unusual and different way of serving roast leg of lamb is on a bed of beans

Braised Lamb in Wine

4 cloves garlic
4-lb. leg of lamb
½ cup oil
2 onions, chopped
2 carrots, diced
½ cup white wine
4¼ cups stock
bouquet garni
salt and pepper

1 Preheat the oven to 400°F.

2 Cut each clove of garlic into four and insert each into a gash cut in the leg of lamb.

3 Heat the oil in a skillet and brown the lamb on all sides for 8 minutes. Remove and place in a casserole.

4 Brown the onions and carrots and add to the lamb.

5 Pour the white wine and stock into the casserole. Add the bouquet garni, salt and plenty of pepper and bring to a boil. Cover and put in the oven for 2 hours.

6 When the meat is cooked, remove from the casserole and keep warm. Strain the liquid from the casserole into a saucepan. Remove the fat and boil until only 1¼ cups remain.

7 The lamb may be served sliced, with a little sauce poured over it, or carved at the table.

Serves 6–8

Festive Leg of Lamb

½ lb. canned pineapple slices with juice
4-lb. leg of lamb
salt and pepper
candied cherries for decoration

1 Preheat the oven to 400°F.

2 Remove the juice from the can of pineapple slices.

3 Put the lamb in a roasting pan and pour over the pineapple juice. Season with salt and pepper.

4 Roast in the preheated oven allowing 20 minutes per 1 lb. and 20 minutes more, basting occasionally with the juice.

5 When cooked, place on a dish and garnish with halved pineapple slices with a cherry between each. Serve with roast potatoes.

Serves 6–8

Stuffed Leg of Lamb

2 tablespoons currants
6 tablespoons butter
1 onion, chopped
4 apples, peeled, cored and diced
¾ cup long grain rice
salt and pepper
4-lb. leg of lamb, boned
½ cup oil
½ cup stock
juice 1 lemon

1 Preheat the oven to 400°F.

2 Soak the currants in water.

3 Heat the butter in a skillet. Sauté the onion gently, add the apples and cook until all the liquid evaporates.

4 Boil the rice for 10 minutes.

5 Mix the onion and apples with the drained currants and the rice. Season with salt and pepper. Stuff the leg with the mixture and sew up the opening. Season and brush with oil.

6 Roast for 2¼ hours in all, 35 minutes at 400°F. and for 1 hour 40 minutes with the temperature reduced to 350°F.

7 When the leg is cooked, remove from the pan and put on a serving dish. Make a gravy with the juices in the pan and the stock and flavor with lemon juice.

Serves 6–8

Normandy Lamb

1 clove garlic
4-lb. leg of lamb
salt and pepper
1 teaspoon thyme
6 tablespoons butter
1 cup cider
1 teaspoon flour
¼ cup apple brandy or brandy
⅔ cup light cream

1 Preheat the oven to 400°F.

2 Insert the clove of garlic, peeled, into the knuckle end of the leg of lamb with the point of a knife. Salt and pepper the meat generously and sprinkle with thyme. Rub in well so that the flavors sink into the meat.

3 Heat the butter, reserving 1 teaspoon, in a casserole. Add the lamb and brown all over for 8 minutes. Cover and cook, allowing 20 minutes per lb. and 20 minutes more, basting with half of the cider from time to time.

4 Blend the 1 teaspoon flour with 1 teaspoon butter for a "beurre manié" to thicken the gravy later on.

5 When the lamb is cooked, pour on the apple brandy or brandy and ignite. Then place the meat on a serving dish and keep warm.

6 Pour the remainder of the cider into the pan. Boil for 2 minutes, scraping the casserole to loosen the browned sediment.

7 Add the cream and stir for 1 minute, then add the "beurre manié" and cook gently until it thickens.

8 Serve the sauce separately with the lamb.

Serves 6–8

Stuffed Leg of Lamb. The stuffing is a tasty mixture of raisins, apple and onion.

Glazed Lamb with Sherry Sauce

3½-lb. boned leg of lamb
¼ lb. lean bacon, chopped or
  ground
1 cup breadcrumbs
1 egg, beaten
salt and pepper
pinch dried thyme and rosemary
1¼ cups dry sherry
1¼ cups water
3 carrots, cleaned and chopped
2 branches celery, chopped
few sprigs each fresh parsley and
  tarragon
1 clove garlic, crushed
2 tablespoons oil
¼ cup butter
⅔ cup sour cream
1 tablespoon prepared mustard
1 egg yolk
1 teaspoon chopped fresh parsley

1 Ask the butcher to bone the leg of lamb for you. Mix the bacon, breadcrumbs, egg, seasoning and herbs to a paste and use it to stuff the leg. Tie the meat into shape with kitchen string and marinate it for 5 hours or overnight in the sherry, water, vegetables, fresh herbs and garlic, turning it from time to time to soak all sides.

2 Preheat the oven to 400°F. Drain the leg from the marinade and dry it. Brush it with the oil and butter, season with a pinch of salt and pepper, and roast for 35 minutes.

3 Meanwhile, drain the vegetables from the marinade, reserving both. Place the vegetables under the leg and continue to roast for 15 minutes.

4 Reduce the oven temperature to 350°F. Pour the marinade around the leg, cover and cook for 1 hour.

5 Mix the sour cream, mustard, egg yolk and parsley. Remove the meat from the oven and pour the vegetables and cooking liquid into a pan. Turn the oven up to 425°F. Spread the sour cream mixture over the leg and return to the oven for 10 minutes until it is golden brown.

6 Meanwhile, boil the marinade to reduce it to a thicker consistency. Strain the vegetables out and pour the sauce into a sauce boat. Remove the string. Serve the meat on a heated dish with the sauce.

Serves 8

Leg of Lamb Minorca

3½-lb. leg of lamb
2 cloves garlic
salt and pepper
2 sprigs fresh rosemary
2 onions, chopped
3 carrots, quartered
2 tablespoons oil
6 tablespoons butter
1¼ cups rosé wine
2 tablespoons tomato paste
1 cup sliced mushrooms
12 stuffed green olives
1½ tablespoons cornstarch
3 tablespoons water
12 cherry tomatoes

1 Remove the bone or ask the butcher to do it for you, and keep it. Cut the garlic into slivers and insert them into slits on the surface of the meat. Season with salt and pepper, and rosemary sprigs.

2 Preheat the oven to 375°F. Place the onions and carrots in a roasting pan with the bone. Brush the roast with oil and 4 tablespoons of the butter and set it on the vegetables. Roast for 45 minutes.

3 Add the wine and tomato paste, cover and continue to cook for 45 minutes.

4 Remove the meat from the roasting pan and keep it warm. Take the bone and carrots from the liquid. Boil the liquid to reduce (evaporate) it.

5 Sauté the mushrooms in the rest of the butter for 5 minutes. Add to the sauce with the green olives. Thicken the sauce with cornstarch dissolved in the water.

6 Broil the tomatoes for 5 minutes. Arrange them around the roast on a serving dish. Put 2 tomatoes on a kebab skewer with a few stuffed olives and stick it into the meat to decorate. Pour the sauce over the roast and serve.

Serves 6–8

Lamb Espagnola

4-lb. leg or shoulder of lamb
2 cloves garlic, crushed
1 teaspoon mixed thyme and dill
few sprigs fresh rosemary
¼ cup sherry
¼ cup water
12 very small onions, peeled
6 stuffed green olives, sliced

1 Place the lamb in a roasting pan. Spread the crushed garlic and dried herbs evenly over the surface and arrange rosemary sprigs on top and underneath. Pour the sherry over the meat and let stand for 3 hours.

2 Preheat the oven to 375°F. Add the water to the roasting pan and arrange the peeled, whole onions around the roast. Roast in the oven for 20 minutes per lb. and 20 minutes more, basting from time to time.

3 Set the lamb on a heated serving dish and arrange the onions around it. Stir the sliced olives into the cooking juices and pour the liquid over the roast.

Serves 6–8

*Leg of Lamb Minorca. The roast
is covered with a sauce of
mushrooms and olives*

Shoulder of Lamb

Shoulder of lamb is a popular cut which has a higher proportion of fat than the leg but greater flavor. The cut is sold both on the bone and with the bones removed, ready for stuffing.

Shoulder of lamb can be used in four main ways: cut into chops which can be broiled or braised; stuffed to be roasted or braised; cut into cubes for stews, curries or blanquettes; and ground to make meatballs, burgers or sausages which can be broiled, fried or baked.

For the traditional roast, allow 12 ozs. of meat on the bone per person and a cooking time of 20 minutes per lb. plus an extra 20 minutes. Spread the meat with a little butter and oil and season with salt and pepper. Roast at 400°F. for the first 30 minutes, then reduce the temperature to 350°F. for the rest of the cooking time.

Lamburgers Capucine

3 cups ground shoulder of lamb
1 onion, chopped
1 egg
salt and pepper
1 cup breadcrumbs
¼ cup flour
4 slices bacon
¼ cup butter
¼ cup oil
1 cup sliced mushrooms
1 green pepper, sliced

1 Combine the meat, onion, egg, seasoning, breadcrumbs, and flour and shape into 4 burgers. Wrap each with a slice of bacon and secure with kitchen string.

2 Heat the butter and oil in a pan, add the lamburgers, cover with a lid and cook for 8-10 minutes, turning from time to time until golden-brown and cooked through.

3 Lift from the pan, remove the string and place on a warm serving plate. Sauté the mushrooms and pepper in the same pan for 4 minutes and use to garnish the lamburgers.

Serves 4

Variation

Preheat the oven to 400°F. Combine the lamb, onion, eggs, seasoning, breadcrumbs and flour in the same way as for the lamburgers. Cut four thick slices from a large zucchini and remove the seeds. Parboil the rings in salted water, drain and place in a casserole dish. Fill the rings with the lamb mixture, cover and bake in the preheated oven for 20 minutes.

Andorran Shoulder of Lamb

4-lb. shoulder of lamb, bones and fat removed
2 tablespoons butter
2 tablespoons oil
1 cup stock
1 cup dry white wine
½ cup anisette

For the Stuffing:
½ lb. sausage meat
1 egg, beaten
1 tablespoon brandy (optional)
1 cup chopped mushrooms
2 sprigs thyme, finely chopped
sprig rosemary, finely chopped
1 tablespoon chopped parsley
1 shallot, chopped
1 clove garlic, peeled and chopped
salt and pepper
2 tablespoons butter
1 tablespoon oil

For the Tomato Sauce:
3 tablespoons oil
1 onion, chopped
4 large tomatoes, skinned and chopped
1 clove garlic, peeled
1 chili, seeded and chopped
1 tablespoon sugar
1 sprig thyme

1 To make the stuffing, mix all the ingredients, except the butter and oil, together in a bowl.

2 Heat the butter and oil in a pan, add the stuffing and cook for 7-8 minutes until golden brown.

3 Spread the lamb flat on the work surface. Spread the stuffing over the meat, to within 1¼ inches of the edge. Roll up the meat and secure with kitchen string.

4 Heat the butter and oil in a heavy-based pan and fry the meat until golden brown all over. Pour in the stock and white wine, cover and leave to cook over low heat for 2¼ hours.

5 Meanwhile, prepare the tomato sauce. Heat the oil in a pan, add the onion, tomatoes, garlic, chili, sugar and thyme and season with salt and pepper. Cook over high heat until golden brown, then reduce the heat, cover and cook over low heat for 40 minutes.

6 Pour the sauce through a fine conical strainer, cover and return to low heat. If the sauce becomes too thick, add a few spoonfuls of the cooking liquor from the meat.

7 When the meat is cooked, transfer it to a heated serving dish and pour the sauce into a sauce boat.

8 Just before serving, warm the anisette, sprinkle it over the meat and ignite it. Serve with rice, noodles or green beans.

Serves 6–8

In front, Roast Shoulder of Lamb and, behind, Andorran Shoulder of Lamb and Lamburgers Capucine

Spring Lamb in Mushroom Sauce

**4-lb. shoulder of spring lamb,
 boned**
salt and pepper
pinch thyme
1 lb. mushrooms
⅔ cup butter
2 large onions, chopped
2 tablespoons flour
2 tablespoons heavy cream
1 cup fresh breadcrumbs
2 tablespoons oil
2 cups pearl onions
bouquet garni
⅔ cup stock

1 Cover the working surface with a cloth and spread the meat out on it, skin downward. Open up the meat and season the inside with the salt and pepper and thyme. Roll the

Spring Lamb in Mushroom Sauce is stuffed, rolled and roasted, then carved and served with mushrooms and onions

shoulder and put aside while preparing the stuffing.

2 Rinse, dry and chop half of the mushrooms. Melt 2 tablespoons butter in a saucepan and sauté the onions and mushrooms over a low heat until soft.

3 Remove the onions and mushrooms from the pan and blend in a blender to form a purée.

4 Return the purée to the pan and add the flour. Cook for 1 minute over low heat, stirring all the time. Gradually stir in the cream, then the breadcrumbs. Correct the seasoning.

5 Preheat the oven to 400°F.

6 Unroll the shoulder of lamb, spread with the onion and mush-

room mixture, then roll it up again and tie it with string.

7 Place the lamb on a roasting pan and smother it with oil and 6 tablespoons of the butter. Season well and place in the oven. After 35 minutes, reduce the temperature to 350°F. Continue to roast gently for another 1½ hours.

8 Heat the remaining butter in a pan and sauté the rest of the mushrooms and the pearl onions until golden brown. Add the bouquet garni, season and pour in the stock. Cover and cook over low heat for 15 minutes.

9 When the lamb is cooked, carve it and serve on a heated serving dish, surrounded by the mushroom and onion garnish.

10 If you like, you can make a gravy with the meat juices and the stock and pour it over the meat.

Serves 6

Shoulder of Lamb with Apricot Stuffing

4-lb. shoulder of lamb, boned
salt and pepper
2 tablespoons oil
¼ cup butter
⅔ cup chicken stock
¼ cup syrup from canned apricots
1 tablespoon wine vinegar
1½ tablespoons cornstarch
12 canned apricot halves

For the Apricot Stuffing:
¾ cup dried apricots
½ cup pork sausage meat
½ cup beef sausage meat
1 cup fresh white breadcrumbs
1 egg, beaten

1 Soak the dried apricots for several hours or overnight in water. When they are soft, drain and chop finely.

2 Preheat the oven to 400°F. Blend the ingredients for the stuffing to make a thick smooth paste.

3 Spread open the boned shoulder of lamb, season, and cover the inside evenly with stuffing. Roll it up and tie it into shape with fine string. Place in a roasting pan and brush with oil and butter.

4 Roast the meat for 20 minutes, then lower oven heat to 350°F. Continue to cook for 1½ hours, basting frequently.

5 Remove the meat from the roasting pan and drain off the excess fat. Add the stock, syrup and vinegar, season, and boil for several minutes to reduce. Thicken with the cornstarch dissolved in a little water.

6 Place the stuffed lamb on a serving dish or carving board and surround it with the canned apricot halves. Serve each portion with an apricot half and sauce.

Serves 8

Shoulder of Lamb is especially satisfying when stuffed with Chestnuts (on the left) or Apricots (on the right)

Shoulder of Lamb with Chestnut Stuffing

salt and pepper
4-lb. boned shoulder of lamb
2 tablespoons oil
¼ cup butter
⅔ cup stock

For the Chestnut Stuffing:
1 cup sausage meat
1 cup peeled chestnuts, chopped
1 egg, beaten
¼ cup flour
1 tablespoon sherry

1 Preheat oven to 400°F. Blend stuffing ingredients.

2 Season the lamb and spread the stuffing evenly over the inside. Roll and tie. Brush with oil and butter and roast, basting frequently, for 1¾ hours. After 20 minutes reduce the oven heat to 350°F.

3 Remove the meat from the pan and drain off excess fat. Add the chicken stock, season, and boil for 5 minutes to reduce. Serve the gravy with the meat.

Serves 8

Breast of Lamb

Breast of lamb is usually considered one of the cheapest cuts of lamb. There is no need for it to taste improvised, however; carefully cooked, it is worthy of a place on any table.

Breast of lamb should be boned — the butcher will usually do this — and it is generally stuffed, rolled and roasted. Because lamb breast contains little lean meat it is best stuffed with a sausage meat mixture, but a wide variety of flavors can be incorporated. Rich and fruity stuffings may be used. The stuffing should be spread on the inner side of the breast, or placed in a 'pocket' between the meat and inner skin layers. Season the meat well before stuffing.

Norfolk Parcel

2-lb. boned breast of lamb, cut in 4
  equal pieces
2 tablespoons oil
2 tablespoons butter

For the Stuffing:
2 large onions, chopped
2 tablespoons fat
⅔ cup chicken stock
1 cup sausage meat
2 cups fresh breadcrumbs
salt and pepper
1 tablespoon fresh sage, finely
  chopped
1 tablespoon chutney

1 Trim any excess fat from the meat, and beat it lightly with a rolling pin or meat mallet. Preheat the oven to 400°F.

2 To make the stuffing, sauté the onion gently in the fat until soft but not browned. Add the stock and boil for 5 minutes, until the liquid is well reduced (evaporated). Remove

Norfolk Parcel makes a meaty meal. Tie it as shown at right, and roast it to juicy crispness as seen above

from the heat and stir in the sausage meat, breadcrumbs, a pinch of salt and pepper, the sage and the chutney. Blend well to make a thick paste.

3 Divide the stuffing into 4 and spread it over the pieces of meat. Place the pieces of meat on top of each other to make a sandwich, and tie them together neatly with fine string. Season with salt and pepper and brush the oil and butter over the top and sides.

4 Roast the meat parcel in the oven for 20 minutes. Then turn the oven temperature down to 350°F. for

1½–2 hours, basting the meat frequently. Place the meat on a heated serving dish. Strain fat from the cooking juices and pour the rest over the meat. Serve.

Serves 6

Saddle of Lamb

The saddle is cut from the rack to the end of the loins and includes the chops and the kidneys. This large roast usually weighs about 7 lbs. A short saddle weighs about 2-5 lbs. and is without the chops.

To roast, the saddle should be skinned and the kidneys removed. Any excess fat and sinews should be cut away. The flaps should be cut off, leaving about 6 inches on each side, so that they meet in the middle. The bone should be removed. The saddle may also be cooked by pot roasting or braising.

There are two ways of carving a saddle on the bone. It may be carved lengthwise, either side of the backbone, or a deep cut is made on both sides of the backbone and the whole section of meat freed from the bone. The meat is then cut in thick slices.

Waipura

2½-lb. saddle of lamb, boned and skinned
½ tablespoon chopped parsley
1 clove garlic, crushed
salt and pepper
one ¾ pork fillet
¼ cup butter

1 Ask the butcher to bone and skin the saddle of lamb.

2 Preheat the oven to 400°F.

3 Sprinkle the meat with the parsley, garlic, salt and pepper, and use the pork fillet to fill the cavity left by the removal of the backbone. Roll up and tie with string.

4 Place in a roasting pan, and smother with the butter. Roast for ½ hour, then reduce the heat to 350°F. for 1¼ hours (allowing 30 minutes to 1 lb. plus 20 minutes more.)

5 When cooked, let stand for 15 minutes. Make a gravy from the juices in the pan. Serve with roast potatoes and a green salad.

Serves 6

Soubise Saddle of Lamb

2½-lb. saddle of lamb
salt and pepper
¼ cup butter
1 cup onion purée
2 cups thick white sauce
2 egg yolks
⅓ cup white wine
1½ tablespoons grated Parmesan cheese

1 Preheat the oven to 400°F.

2 Place the saddle in a roasting pan. Season and spread with butter. Roast for ½ hour, then reduce the heat to 350°F. for 40 minutes (allowing 20 minutes for every 1 lb. and 20 minutes more).

3 Mix the purée of onions with the white sauce and egg yolks, and season.

4 Remove the loins by making a deep cut along the backbone and slipping the knife underneath. Carve them into thick slices.

5 Increase the oven temperature to 425°F.

6 Spread the slices of meat with half of the sauce and sandwich together to the original shape and place on the bones.

7 Dilute the remainder of the sauce with the white wine and pour over the saddle. Sprinkle with Parmesan cheese. Brown in the oven for 8 minutes until golden brown.

Serves 4

Britannia Saddle of Lamb

2½-lb. saddle of lamb
½ cup brandy
1 teaspoon mixed allspice and coriander
6 tablespoons butter
1 cup ground lean pork
¼ lb. ground liver
2½ cups white breadcrumbs
2 eggs, beaten
¼ cup chopped parsley
2 tablespoons chopped fresh mint
1 teaspoon rosemary
salt and pepper
¾ lb. pieces salt pork
¼ lb. tongue or ham, cut in strips

1 When buying the saddle of lamb, ask the butcher to bone it completely, leaving enough flap to wrap under the saddle and enclose the stuffing.

2 Remove the underfillets and marinate them with a little of the brandy and mixed spice for ½ hour. Sauté them in 2 tablespoons of the butter for 5 minutes.

3 Make the stuffing by mixing the ground lean pork and liver with the breadcrumbs, eggs and chopped parsley, mint, rosemary and brandy. Season with salt and pepper.

4 Preheat the oven to 400°F.

5 Spread the pieces of salt pork on a board and place a layer of stuffing on top, then arrange a few strips of tongue and the underfillets and continue until all is used. Wrap in the salt pork to make a sausage shape, the same length as the saddle and about 3 inches in diameter.

6 Turn the saddle upside down on the board, and place the filling inside. Cover with the two flaps of

the saddle. Season and tie firmly with string at 1-inch intervals.

7 Place the saddle in a roasting pan and smother with the rest of the butter and roast for 30 minutes, then reduce the heat to 350°F for 1¼ hours (allowing 30 minutes to 1 lb. and 30 minutes more).

8 Remove the saddle, discard the string, and keep meat warm. Make gravy from the juices in the pan. Serve with mint jelly and red currant sauce.

Serves 4

Springtime Saddle of Lamb

2½-lb. saddle of lamb
salt and pepper

Springtime Saddle of Lamb is a delicious combination of the best meat and the best vegetables of the season

6 tablespoons butter
½ lb. green beans
12 asparagus spears
½ lb. small carrots
1 teaspoon sugar
3 small onions, peeled
2 cups peas
4 new potatoes
sprig mint
1 tablespoon chopped parsley
1 bunch celery
6 tomatoes

1 Preheat the oven to 400°F.

2 Place the saddle in a roasting pan. Season with salt and pepper and smother it with 4 tablespoons of the butter. Roast for ½ hour, then reduce the heat to 350°F. for 40 minutes, basting from time to time.

3 Meanwhile, trim the beans. Scrape the asparagus and tie in bundles.

4 Put the carrots in a saucepan with the sugar and onions, and cover with water. Boil for 15 minutes. Add the peas and cook for 8 minutes until the water has almost evaporated. Then add the remaining butter.

5 Boil the new potatoes with the mint, until cooked, and drain. Mix with the carrots and peas, season with salt and pepper and sprinkle with parsley. Keep warm.

6 Boil the asparagus in salted water for 15 minutes, drain, remove the string, and keep warm.

7 Boil the celery in salted water for 15 minutes, drain and keep warm.

8 Drop the tomatoes in boiling water for 2 minutes, then peel and keep warm in the oven.

9 When ready to serve, arrange the saddle on a large platter and surround with the asparagus, celery, tomatoes, new potatoes, carrots, onions, peas and beans. Sprinkle with chopped parsley.

Serves 4

Rack of Lamb

The neck of lamb is seldom sold as a complete cut and is more usually divided into three: the end and middle, which are best used for stewing, and the rack which can be cooked in a number of ways but is particularly good roasted.

Two racks are used to make the traditional crown roast and guard of honor. The roasts are cut (your butcher will do this) and the ends of the rib bones are stripped of skin and fat; the bone tips then form the points of the crown or the interlacing blades of the Guard of Honor.

Crown Roast of Lamb

2 racks of lamb, cut
2 teaspoons butter
1 cooking apple, peeled, cored and chopped
½ lb. pork sausage meat
2 tablespoons fresh breadcrumbs
1 tablespoon chopped parsley
1 tablespoon finely chopped mint candied cherries

1 Preheat the oven to 350°F. Trim the skin and fat from the ends of the rib bones so that 1 inch of the bone protrudes. Place the two racks back to back with the bones curving upward and outward. Secure with kitchen string.

A decorative, delicious Crown Roast of Lamb makes an eye-catching centerpiece for that very special occasion

2 Heat the butter in a pan and sauté the apple. Add the sausage meat, cook for 2-3 minutes, then stir in the rest of the ingredients.

3 Place the stuffing in the cavity of the crown. Cover the tips of the bones with foil and roast in the preheated oven for 30 minutes per lb. plus 30 minutes.

4 Decorate the bone ends with cutlet caps and cherries and serve with roasted potatoes.

Serves 6–8

Guard of Honor

2 racks of lamb, cut
salt and pepper
few parsley sprigs

1 Preheat the oven to 350°F.

2 Trim the skin and fat from the ends of the rib bones so that about 3 inches of bone protrudes. Stand the joints together in a roasting pan with the bone ends criss-crossing. Secure with kitchen string.

3 Sprinkle with salt and pepper, cover the ends of the bones with foil, and bake in the preheated oven for about 1½ hours.

4 Decorate with the parsley sprigs and serve with creamed potatoes and peas.

Serves 6–8

Braised Stuffed Lamb

2½-lb. rack of lamb, boned
¼ cup oil
2 tablespoons butter
1 lb. small onions
¾ lb. carrots, quartered
1 beef bouillon cube
1¼ cups water
1½ tablespoons cornstarch

Guard of Honor looks as grand and festive as its name suggests, and would honor a special dinner party

For the Stuffing:
2 tablespoons butter
6 tablespoons chopped onion
¾ lb. sausage meat
1 teaspoon chopped parsley
pinch mixed rosemary and dill
pinch thyme
salt and pepper
1 egg

1 Preheat the oven to 400°F.

2 Prepare the stuffing: heat the butter in a pan, add the chopped onion and cook for 5 minutes. Mix in the sausage meat, herbs and seasoning and blend well. Cover with a lid and cook for 5 minutes more. Remove from the heat and blend in the egg to make a smooth paste.

3 Spread the stuffing over the meat, roll up and secure with kitchen string. Brush with a little oil and brown in the preheated oven for 20 minutes.

4 After this time, reduce the heat to 350°F. and continue cooking for one hour more, brushing with more oil if necessary.

5 Meanwhile, heat the butter in a pan and sauté the small onions until brown (about 4 minutes). Cover the onions with water and boil for 8 minutes until tender. Drain and keep hot.

6 Boil the carrots in salted water for about 20 minutes until tender. Drain and keep hot.

7 Twenty minutes before the meat has finished cooking, dissolve the beef bouillon cube in the water and pour it over the meat. Return the meat to the oven for the rest of the cooking time.

8 When the meat is cooked, lift it from the roasting pan, transfer to a serving dish and keep hot while preparing the gravy.

9 Place the roasting pan with the cooking juices on a burner and boil for 5 minutes. Season, strain and thicken with the cornstarch dissolved in 6 tablespoons of water.

10 Surround the meat with the carrots and onions, pour on a little of the gravy and serve the rest in a sauceboat.

Serves 6

450

Carving Lamb

Carving may look easy but it is more difficult than it appears. It is very important that you have a really sharp carving knife, with a 10-inch blade. Always sharpen the knife before carving with a traditional steel or an electric knife sharpener. You may have an electric carving knife — these are really good and enable you to carve meat very thinly and thus it will go further.

Always use a carving fork with a thumb guard and, if possible, place the roast on a spiked carving platter so that it does not slip. Allow the meat to stand for about 15 minutes before carving it. Carve thin, consistent slices. When possible, cut the lamb against the grain. This will give you more tender slices.

When a roast is carved well, it looks more attractive and the meat goes further. There are no hard and fast rules. It depends on the position of the bones and the way in which the meat and fat are distributed. You will probably find that it is much easier to carve if you are standing up. Always use a long, even sawing action and keep the blade at the same angle. Do not press down on the meat too much or you will squeeze out the juices. Serve the carved meat on very warm plates.

Leg of Lamb: Carve the leg with the round side uppermost, inserting the fork near the knuckle. Make the first cut down to the bone diagonally. Cut out a thick wedge-shaped slice, then carve slices from either side of the cut. Turn the leg over and carve in long slices parallel to the leg bone.

Shoulder of Lamb: Carve the shoulder downward towards the knuckle end. Turn over and carve downward in long slices.

Loin of Lamb: Ask your butcher to cut through the sections of the backbone, then it can be divided into chops.

Rack or Neck of Lamb: Your butcher will cut this joint for you (saw along the backbone to release the meat from the bone). Remove the bone from the cooked meat and carve between the ribs.

Look 'n Cook Carving Shoulder of Lamb

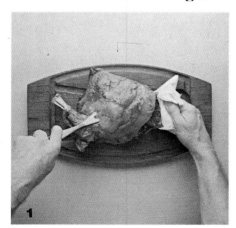
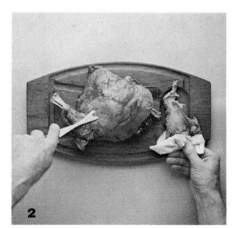
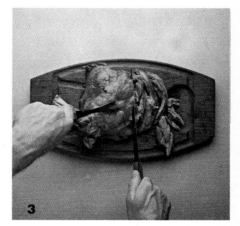

1 Using your left hand, insert the carving fork into the shoulder. With your right hand, grip the exposed blade bone **2** Twist the blade bone until free and then pull out **3** Carve downard diagonally from one end to the other **4** Turn and slice parallel until you reach the bone at the end **5** The finished carved roast

Look 'n Cook Carving Leg of Lamb

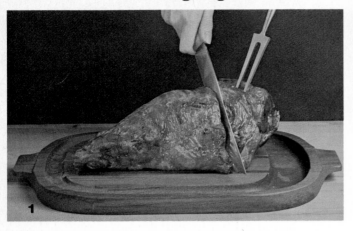

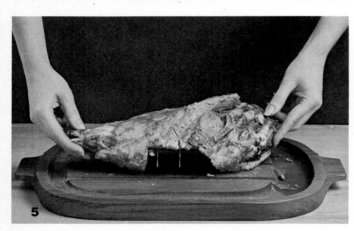

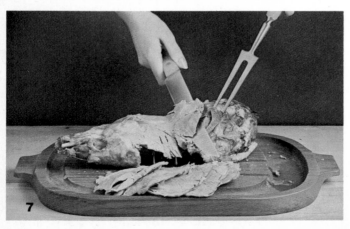

1 Spear the leg of lamb with a carving fork in your left hand. Taking the carving knife in your right hand, cut downward through the middle of the leg **2** Carve in slices, drawing the knife diagonally down through the leg. Then cut across the bottom of the wedges horizontally **3** Using both the fork and knife, lift out the carved middle slices and arrange on a serving dish or individual plates **4** Carve diagonally down through the bottom of the lamb under the bone **5** Lift the leg of lamb off the spikes and turn it over. Replace it on the spikes **6** Carve diagonally down through the leg, holding it with the fork **7** Slice through towards the bone until all the lamb has been carved. Arrange the meat on hot individual plates or a large heated serving dish

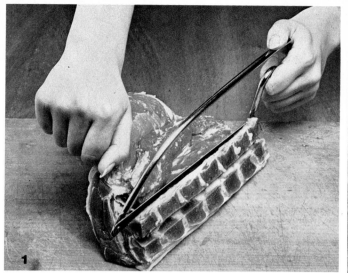

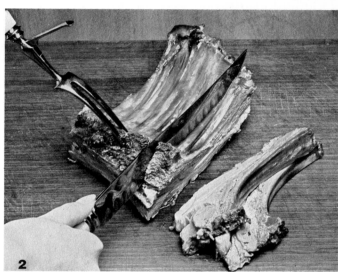

1 Before cooking the loin, cut through the bone. This will make carving easier. Remove the central bone **2** When the loin is cooked, carve into neat slices **3** The carved roast

1 Before cooking the rack, cut the roast by sawing along the backbone **2** When the meat is cooked, carve downward between the rib bones to form cutlets **3** The carved rack of lamb

453

Loin of Lamb

The loin of a lamb is half of the saddle, cut lengthwise through the spine. It is a meaty and well-flavored cut and is hence quite expensive. It may be roasted on the bone or with the bone removed — the butcher will do this for you. When boned, with the long flap of the breast, it is sometimes stuffed and rolled, tied in shape with string and roasted. It is also used without the breast flap.

Beswick Lamb

3-lb. loin of lamb, boned
2 tablespoons butter
2 tablespoons oil
1 lb. garden peas
1 sprig mint
6 scallions
¼ cup sherry
juice 1 orange

For the Stuffing:
2 slices bacon, chopped
2 lamb kidneys, skinned, cored
  and chopped
¼ cup butter
1 onion, finely chopped
1 cup chopped mushrooms
salt and pepper
1 teaspoon tomato paste
1 cup fresh breadcrumbs

1 To make the stuffing, fry the chopped bacon and kidney in the butter for 3 minutes. Then stir in the onion and cook another 3 minutes. Add the mushrooms and sauté 2 minutes. Season, stir in the tomato paste and the breadcrumbs, and stir to bind all ingredients together to a loose mixture, adding a little melted butter if necessary. Allow the stuffing to cool.

2 Preheat the oven to 400°F. Spread the stuffing on the inside of

Beswick Loin of Lamb is served with peas and red currant jelly for a dinner party or an extra-special occasion.

the loin of lamb, roll up the meat and tie it with fine string. Place it in a roasting pan, brush with butter and oil and season. Roast it for 1–1½ hours.

3 Boil the peas in salted water with a sprig of mint and the scallions until tender. Drain and pile the peas on a heated serving dish.

4 When the meat is cooked, carve it into slices and arrange them on the bed of garden peas.

5 Strain off excess fat from the cooking juices. Pour the sherry and orange juice into the roasting pan and boil for 3 minutes. Season to taste. Pour the sauce into a sauce boat and serve with the meat, peas, and some red currant or cranberry jelly.

Serves 8

1 The ingredients **2** Cut the shoulder of lamb into cubes and prepare the beef, kidneys and bacon **3** Prepare the marinade and soak the meat for 3 hours. Drain and dry on absorbent paper **4** Cut the tomatoes in quarters, trim the scallions and cut the pepper into squares **5** Stick the ingredients on the skewers alternating the meat with the garnish **6** Brush with oil and grill over charcoal

Kebabs and Grills

Shish kebab are the Turkish words for cooked meat (kebab) on the skewer (shish). In Turkey and all over the Middle East people eat shish kebab at home, in cafés, and even from street vendors. There, lamb is the most popular meat and a shish kebab of lamb liver and kidneys is considered the greatest delicacy. Sometimes the fat from bacon is needed to moisten the chunks of lean meat as they are grilled or broiled and the kebabs need to be brushed with oil.

The meat is usually mixed with vegetables, such as onions, mushrooms, green peppers and tomatoes. If using small whole tomatoes it is wise to put them on either end of the skewer so that they receive less heat and remain firm. Fruit makes an interesting addition, and chunks of pineapple, firm apricots and pieces of peach or apple work well.

Kebabs are always marinated in a mixture of wine, oil and vinegar with additions of garlic and herbs. Using a marinade helps to tenderize the meat as well as to impart extra flavor. It is important that the cubes of meat should be the same size so that they will be cooked at the same time.

Lemon Kebabs

2 slices lean bacon
1¼-lb. leg of lamb, cut in 1-inch cubes
4 onions, quartered
2 tomatoes, quartered
1 green pepper
8 bay leaves
8 mushrooms
¼ cup oil

Lemon Kebabs are colorful and ideal to prepare for a party or when your friends drop in unexpectedly

1 teaspoon cornstarch
3 tablespoons water
1 cup long grain rice, boiled
2 tablespoons butter

1 Blanch the bacon in boiling water for ½ minute. Drain and dry on absorbent paper. Cut into strips 1 inch wide.

2 Soak the lamb cubes (which may be cut in half if preferred) and the bacon strips in the marinade for 3 hours. Drain and dry on absorbent paper.

3 Stick on skewers the lamb and bacon alternately with the onions, tomatoes, green pepper, bay leaves, and mushrooms.

4 Brush the kebabs with oil.

5 Cook under a broiler or over charcoal for 8 minutes.

6 Meanwhile, boil the marinade for 5 minutes until 1¼ cups are left. Thicken with the cornstarch mixed with water and cook for 2 minutes until clear. Season.

7 Serve the kebabs on a bed of plain boiled rice mixed with the butter and seasoned, with the sauce separately.

8 To serve each guest, place some rice on a plate and then arrange the meat and garnish on the rice, removing the skewer carefully.

Serves 4

Mixed Grill Kebabs

4 slices lean bacon
4 lamb kidneys, quartered
1 lb. lamb shoulder, cut into 16 cubes
$\frac{1}{4}$ lb. rump steak, cut into 4 cubes
12 scallions
1 green pepper, seeded
4 tomatoes, quartered
1 tablespoon oil
1 teaspoon cornstarch
3 tablespoons water
pinch cayenne or chili pepper

For the Marinade:
1$\frac{1}{4}$ cups vermouth
2 tablespoons oil
1 tablespoon vinegar
6 crushed black peppercorns
1 bay leaf
pinch tarragon
pinch thyme

1 Blanch the bacon in boiling water for $\frac{1}{2}$ minute. Drain and dry.

2 Mix the marinade.

3 Skin the kidneys and remove the core. Put the meat in the marinade for 3 hours.

4 Trim the scallions and cut the green pepper into squares.

5 Stick the meat on the skewers, wrapping some of the pieces of kidney in bacon, with the onions, peppers and tomatoes.

6 Brush with oil and cook under the broiler for 8 minutes.

7 Boil the marinade for 5 minutes. Thicken with the cornstarch and water and boil for 2 minutes. Season.

8 Serve with rice and the sauce.

Serves 4

Spanish Kebabs with Olives

2 slices lean bacon

2 loin chops, cut in cubes
2 tomatoes
2 mushrooms
6 olives
1 tablespoon oil
1 teaspoon cornstarch
3 tablespoons water

For the Marinade:
$\frac{3}{4}$ cup tomato juice
$\frac{1}{3}$ cup dry sherry
juice of 1 lemon
1 tablespoon oil
1 tablespoon vinegar
1 chili
1 red pepper
1 onion
2 cloves garlic
pinch oregano

Spanish Kebabs with Olives are an attractive and quick meal for busy working mothers to prepare and cook

1 Blanch the bacon in boiling water for $\frac{1}{2}$ minute. Drain and dry.

2 Blend all the ingredients for the marinade.

3 Marinate the bacon and lamb for 1 hour. Drain and dry.

4 Stick the meat and bacon, rolled, on two of the skewers, and put the tomatoes, mushrooms and olives on the other skewers. Brush with the oil.

5 Cook the meat under the broiler for 8 minutes, and the garnish for 5.

6 Meanwhile, boil the marinade until 1$\frac{1}{4}$ cups remain. Thicken with the cornstarch and water.

7 Serve the kebabs on rice with sauce.

Serves 2

Chops and Cutlets

Chops and Cutlets

Chops are cut across the saddle and split in the middle of the backbone. Each chop includes the meat of the loin and a small piece of the tenderloin as well. Lamb loin chops correspond to T-bone steaks in beef. A chop cut across the saddle can be either cut single, 1 inch thick, or double, 1½ inches thick.

When boned, a chop or cutlet becomes a noisette — a little 'nut' of tender meat, or in butcher's terms, the 'eye' of the meat. When boned and rolled (like a Tournedos in beef) it is called a rosette.

The end loin chops are the cheapest because they include part of the pelvic bone. There are only 2 or 3 on each animal. They are usually cut diagonally and weigh 10 ozs. each.

Cutlets are cut from the 13 ribs of the lamb. There are 7 at the rack and it is usual for a butcher to remove one bone without meat, leaving 6 cutlets of equal thickness. A butcher should remove the backbone.

In double cutlets, the rib is cut between two bones and the butcher will then usually remove one rib bone. If wished, the cutlet may then be flattened slightly to make a wider piece of meat.

Lamb Cutlets Reform

4 double cutlets
3 cups breadcrumbs
2 tablespoons chopped ham
2 teaspoons chopped parsley
salt and pepper
pinch of cloves
1¾ cups flour seasoned with salt
and pepper
2 eggs, beaten
¼ lb. butter

For the Reform Sauce:
3 tablespoons carrot, minced
3 tablespoons onion, minced
3 tablespoons celery, minced
½ bay leaf
sprig thyme
1 tablespoon butter
1 tablespoon lemon juice
6 peppercorns, crushed
1¼ cups brown sauce
1 tablespoon port
1 tablespoon red currant jelly

For the Garnish:
½ small cooked beet
hard-boiled white of ½ egg
1 small dill pickle
1 mushroom
2 tablespoons ham
2 tablespoons tongue

1 When you buy the double cutlets ask the butcher to remove one of the bones from each.

2 To make the Reform Sauce: sauté the carrot, onion, celery, bay leaf and thyme in the butter in a pan for 3 minutes. Drain off the fat. Add the lemon juice and crushed peppercorns, and cook until the liquid has evaporated by two thirds.

3 Add the brown sauce, and simmer for ½ hour. Remove any scum from the surface.

4 Add the port and red currant jelly. Bring to a boil and strain through a fine sieve. Keep warm.

5 Prepare the garnish by cutting the ingredients into matchstick size.

6 Put the breadcrumbs, ham, parsley, seasoning and pinch of clove in a bowl and mix well.

7 Flatten each cutlet slightly, and dip each in the seasoned flour, and in the beaten egg.

8 Press the breadcrumb mixture well into both sides of the cutlets. If you like, add a professional touch by making criss-cross lines on each side with the blade of a knife.

9 Heat the butter in a pan and sauté the cutlets for 4-5 minutes on each side.

10 Just before serving, add the garnish to the sauce and reheat. Serve separately, with the cutlets placed on a dish.

Serves 4

Worcestershire Cutlets

4 double cutlets
20 asparagus spears
2 tablespoons oil
2 strips sweet red pepper

For the Sauce:
⅔ cup tomato sauce
⅔ cup brown sauce
2 teaspoons Worcestershire sauce
2 tablespoons pineapple juice
salt and pepper

1 When you buy the cutlets, ask the butcher to remove one bone. Scrape the tip of the remaining bone clean.

2 Scrape the asparagus and boil for 15 minutes. Drain and keep warm.

3 To make the sauce, heat the tomato and brown sauces. Add the Worcestershire sauce and pineapple juice. Check the seasoning. Keep warm.

4 Season the cutlets, brush with oil and broil or sauté for 4-5 minutes on each side.

5 Place the cutlets on a serving dish, with a paper cap on each bone tip, and garnish with the asparagus decorated with the strips of pepper. Serve the sauce separately.

Serves 4

Worcestershire Cutlets with asparagus may look plain but taste delicious in their spicy, tangy gravy

Chops Royale

4 double chops
2 tablespoons oil
salt and pepper
pinch mace
4 large onions
1 cup flour
½ cup milk
oil for deep frying
4 mushrooms
4 tomatoes
bunch watercress

1 Brush the chops with oil, season with salt and pepper and a pinch of mace, and grill or broil for 12-15 minutes, turning once.

2 Meanwhile, cut the onions into rings, dip in flour, then milk, then flour again, and deep fry for ½ minute. Drain on absorbent paper.

3 Brush the mushrooms with oil and grill for 2 minutes. Make two cross cuts on the top of each tomato, brush with oil and grill for 2-3 minutes until the skin blisters.

4 When ready to serve, garnish the chops with the mushrooms, tomatoes, onion and watercress.

Serves 4

Chops with Barbecue Sauce

1 onion, chopped
1 branch celery, chopped
1 clove garlic, crushed
2 tablespoons butter
1 teaspoon dry mustard
1 teaspoon brown sugar
½ teaspoon Tabasco
1¼ cups tomato juice
1 teaspoon Worcestershire sauce
juice ½ lemon
1 teaspoon vinegar
1 bay leaf
4 double chops, grilled

1 Sauté the onion, celery and garlic in the butter for 5 minutes. Add the

Chops Royale are a great idea for barbecue parties along with kebabs and different sauces and spicy dips

remaining ingredients and simmer for 15 minutes. Remove the bay leaf.

2 Serve the chops on a dish and the sauce separately.

Serves 4

Noisettes Provençale

1 rack of neck, including the two cutlets of the middle neck, to give 6 noisettes

½ cup oil

For the Provençale Sauce:
3 small onions, sliced
1 clove garlic
1 teaspoon flour
1 tablespoon tomato paste
⅔ cup stock
3 tomatoes, skinned, seeded and chopped
bouquet garni
salt and pepper

1 Bone the noisettes of lamb by holding the rack upright and with a sharp knife gently and carefully detaching and scraping the meat from the top to the middle of the back bone until the meat is detached. Roll the belly flap around the meat and secure with wooden toothpicks or string.

2 In a skillet sauté the sliced onions and clove of garlic for 5 minutes in 2 tablespoons of the oil. Sprinkle on the flour and cook for 1 minute. Stir in the tomato paste and stock and simmer for 10 minutes. Add the tomatoes, bouquet garni and seasoning and simmer for 15 minutes until the sauce is thick. Remove the bouquet garni and check the seasoning.

3 Season the noisettes with salt and pepper and fry for 12-15 minutes in the rest of the oil. When cooked, remove the toothpicks or string.

4 To serve, place the sauce on a dish and put the noisettes on top. Serve with plain boiled potatoes.

Serves 3

Noisettes with Cream Cheese

1 rack from neck end
salt and pepper
⅓ cup oil
3 ozs. cream cheese
4 slices lean bacon
1 large onion, chopped
½ lb. fresh or canned tomatoes
1 tablespoon chopped basil

1 Bone the rack of neck to give 4 noisettes. Fold the belly flap around and tie up with string. Season with salt and pepper. Put half the oil in a skillet and brown the noisettes on both sides. Cool.

How to bone a noisette.
1. Holding the rack of neck upright, carefully detach and scrape the meat from the tip to the middle of the backbone until the meat is detached 2. Roll the belly flap around the meat and secure with toothpicks (or pieces of string may be used) at intervals of 1 inch, and cut the noisettes 1 or 1½ inches thick 3. Noisettes of Lamb served with a rich delicious Provençale Sauce

2 Preheat the oven to 375°F.

3 Spread each noisette with some of the cream cheese, and wrap each in a slice of bacon, held in place with a wooden toothpick.

4 Place in a roasting pan, with the oil from the skillet and roast for 45 minutes in the oven.

5 Put the rest of the oil in a skillet and sauté the onion for 5 minutes. If the tomatoes are fresh, skin them. Add the tomatoes to the pan. Season with salt and pepper. Add the basil and simmer for 15 minutes. Strain the sauce, check the seasoning and keep warm.

6 When ready to serve, place the noisettes on a dish, having removed the string and toothpick. Serve the sauce separately. Serve with boiled potatoes, or with noodles tossed in butter.

Serves 2

Look 'n Cook Lamb Curry with Coconut

1 The ingredients of the curry: lamb, apple, orange, pineapple, banana, onion, garlic, rice, shredded coconut **2** Peel, core and dice the apple. Cut orange peel into matchstick strips **3** Peel and finely chop the onion and the garlic. Chop the parsley **4** With a mortar and pestle crush the mustard seed and black pepper and mix the garlic with them **5** Pour hot water onto the shredded coconut and let stand **6** Heat the oil in a heavy pan and brown the lamb **7** Turn the pieces while cooking until browned on all sides **8** Add the onions and diced apple to the pan and mix with the meat

Look 'n Cook Lamb Curry with Coconut (continued)

15

16

17

9 and **10** Add the spices; stir well **11** Mix in the parsley and orange rind **12** Boil the coconut in the water for 2 minutes. Strain through a cloth, squeezing to obtain all the juice **13** Pour the coconut liquid into the curry **14** Add salt and check seasoning. Simmer gently **15** Boil the rice in salted water until it is tender **16** Slice the bananas and chop some pineapple **17** Serve the curry in a large dish with the rice, fruit and chutney placed in individual side dishes

Lamb Curry with Coconut

1 large apple
rind 1 orange
1 large onion
4 cloves garlic
2 tablespoons chopped fresh
  parsley
1 teaspoon each: mustard seed,
  black pepper
1 cup hot water
1¼ cups shredded coconut
¼ cup oil
1½ lbs. lean lamb (shoulder or leg)
  cut in 1¼-inch cubes
1 teaspoon each: ground fenu-
  greek, turmeric, coriander,
  cumin
½ teaspoon each: cayenne pepper,
  ginger
salt
1 cup rice
2 bananas
3 slices pineapple

1 Peel, core and dice the apple. Slice the orange rind into match-stick strips. Peel and chop the onion and garlic; chop the parsley.

2 Crush the mustard seed and pepper and add the garlic to them. Pour hot water onto the shredded coconut and let it stand.

3 Heat the oil in a heavy pan and gently fry the pieces of lamb, stirring to turn them and brown them on all sides. Meanwhile, boil the water and coconut for 2 minutes, then strain through a clean cloth, squeezing the coconut to extract all the juices.

4 Stir in the apple, onion, and all the spices, stirring to spread them over the meat. Add the parsley and orange rind.

5 Pour the coconut liquid into the curry, add a pinch of salt and adjust seasoning to taste. Bring to a boil and cover. Simmer over low heat for 40-50 minutes until lamb is cooked, stirring from time to time and adding a little water if it becomes dry.

6 Boil the rice in salted water until it is just tender. Rinse and drain.

7 Peel and slice the bananas; cut the pineapple into small chunks. Put rice, bananas and pineapple into side dishes. Transfer the curry to a large serving dish. Serve at once with fruit chutney and other curry accompaniments.

Serves 6

Lamb Chops Orléans

8 lamb chops
salt and pepper
5 tablespoons butter
4 thin slices dry bread
2 tablespoons oil
4 shallots, chopped

For the Sauce:
3 tablespoons butter
1 small carrot, finely diced
1 onion, chopped
¼ cup flour
1⅓ cups stock
4 chicken livers
2 tablespoons heavy cream
2 tablespoons apple brandy or
  brandy

1 To make the sauce, melt the butter in a sauté pan and sauté the carrot and onion until they are browned. Sprinkle with the flour and cook, stirring, until brown. Stir in the stock and cook for 10 minutes.

2 Meanwhile, blend the chicken livers and mix them with the cream and brandy. Beat well.

3 Strain the stock mixture and put aside.

4 Rub the lamb chops on both sides with salt and pepper. Melt 3 tablespoons of the butter in a skillet, add the chops and cook until browned on both sides and tender.

5 Meanwhile, cut the crusts off the bread and cut each slice into 2 triangles. Heat the rest of the butter with the oil in another pan and fry the bread triangles until golden brown. Drain.

6 Drain the chops and arrange them on a heated serving dish. Keep hot.

7 Add the shallots to the butter left from cooking the chops and cook for 1 minute. Add the strained stock mixture, stirring well. Reduce the heat so that the sauce does not boil and stir in the chicken liver mixture. Beat until heated through, then pour over the chops.

8 Arrange the bread triangles around the edge of the dish and serve very hot.

Serves 4

Lamb Scaloppines

2 lbs. thin slices lamb, from the leg
½ cup flour seasoned with salt and
  pepper
2 tablespoons oil
2 onions, finely chopped
3 large tomatoes, skinned,
  seeded and chopped
1 tablespoon tomato paste
1¼ cups white wine
2 cups finely sliced mushrooms
1 green pepper, seeded and
  sliced

1 Tenderize the slices of lamb with a meat mallet or rolling pin. Dust them with the seasoned flour.

2 Heat the oil in a skillet, add the lamb slices and brown quickly on both sides.

3 Add the remaining ingredients and cook over gentle heat for 15 minutes. Serve with boiled rice.

Serves 6

Ground Lamb

Oriental Lamb Puffs

2⅔ cups leftover roast meat
1 onion, chopped
1 clove garlic, crushed
3 tablespoons pineapple, cubed
2 cups breadcrumbs
1 egg
1 tablespoon chopped ginger
1 tablespoon soy sauce
salt and pepper
½ cup flour seasoned with salt and
   pepper
oil for deep frying

For the Batter:
1 cup flour
1 egg

1½ cups milk mixed with water

1 Make the batter and beat until smooth.

2 Grind together the meat, onion, garlic and pineapple and combine with the breadcrumbs, egg, ginger, soy sauce and seasoning.

3 Divide into 20 balls, coat in seasoned flour and the batter and fry at 375°F for 2 minutes until golden brown.

Serves 4

Ground Lamb Cutlets with Asparagus

½ lb. ground lamb from the shoulder

Oriental Lamb Puffs are crispy deep-fried lamb fritters served with tomato sauce on a bed of boiled rice

½ lb. sausage meat
1 cup breadcrumbs
1 egg
1 small onion, chopped
2 tablespoons raisins
1 tablespoon fresh parsley
1 tablespoon corn kernels
1 sweet red pepper, ¼ cut in strips,
   ¾ chopped
½ cup flour seasoned with salt and
   pepper
⅓ cup oil
12 asparagus spears

For the Sauce:
1 onion, chopped
1 slice lean bacon, diced
1 clove garlic
1 tablespoon flour
2 tablespoons tomato paste
⅔ cup white wine
1¼ cups stock
1 bay leaf

1 Combine the lamb and sausage meat and breadcrumbs with the egg, onion, raisins, parsley, corn kernels and ¼ of the chopped red pepper. Divide into 6 portions and shape each into a "cutlet" shape. Dip in seasoned flour and brown in ¼ cup of the oil for 6 minutes. Then place in a casserole.

2 To make the sauce, heat 2 tablespoons of the oil and sauté the onion, bacon, garlic and half of the diced red pepper for 5 minutes. Sprinkle on the flour, add the tomato paste, white wine and stock. Season and add the bay leaf. Simmer for 5 minutes.

3 Preheat the oven to 375°F.

4 Pour the sauce over the cutlets and braise in the oven for 30 minutes.

5 Meanwhile, scrape the asparagus, tie, and boil for 15 minutes.

6 When ready to serve, arrange the cutlets in a dish, pour on the sauce and garnish with the asparagus and strips of red pepper.

Serves 4

Scotch Eggs

1 lb. ground lamb
1 large onion, grated
1 cup fresh breadcrumbs
few drops Worcestershire sauce
salt and pepper
2 eggs, beaten
4 hard-boiled eggs, shelled
⅓ cup dried breadcrumbs
oil for deep frying

1 Mix together in a bowl the lamb, grated onion, breadcrumbs and Worcestershire sauce. Season with the salt and pepper and bind the mixture with one of the beaten eggs.

2 Divide the mixture into four portions and mold each around a hard-boiled egg. Dip in the rest of the beaten egg, then coat with breadcrumbs.

3 Heat the oil in a deep fat fryer and, when hot, fry the kiwi eggs for 5-7 minutes until crisp and golden brown. Cool and cut into halves or quarters. Serve with a green or mixed salad.

Serves 4

Sicilian-style Lamb Loaf

¼ cup shortening
3 bay leaves
6 slices very lean ham
1 lb. ground lamb
⅓ lb. ground lamb liver
¼ cup texturized vegetable protein
⅓ cup warm water
1 egg, beaten
2 tablespoons dry sherry
1 small onion, chopped
1 clove garlic, crushed
½ cup corn kernels
½ cup cooked peas
¼ sweet red pepper, chopped
⅓ cup diced small dill pickle
salt and pepper
1 tablespoon wine vinegar

Look 'n Cook Scotch Eggs

1

2

3

1 Mix together the ground lamb, chopped onions, and breadcrumbs in a bowl. Season with salt and pepper and Worcestershire sauce and bind with the beaten egg 2 Divide the mixture into four and mold it around each hard-boiled egg 3 Dip each Scotch Egg in beaten egg and coat with breadcrumbs. Deep fry in hot oil for 5-7 minutes.

juice and grated rind 1 lemon
1 orange, thinly sliced
12 juniper berries

1 Grease an oblong 1-quart oven-proof dish with the shortening.

2 Preheat the oven to 350°F.

3 Place 3 bay leaves in the bottom of the dish, then line with the slices of ham.

4 In a large bowl, mix together the lamb and liver. Soak the texturized vegetable protein in the warm water and add to the bowl. Bind with the beaten egg.

5 Mix in the sherry, onion, garlic, corn, cooked peas, red pepper and pickle. Season with the salt and pepper and stir in the wine vinegar and lemon juice and rind.

6 Place the filling in the lined dish and stand the dish in a shallow tray, half-filled with water.

7 Bake in the oven for 1¼ hours. Remove and cool. Then chill in the refrigerator and, when cold, decorate with the slices of orange and juniper berries. Serve it sliced like a meatloaf for lunch or a picnic.

Serves 8

Lamb Turnovers

½ lb. puff pastry, fresh or frozen
  and thawed
⅔ cup ground cooked lamb
1½ tablespoons apple chutney
2 tablespoons diced apple
1 tablespoon grated onion
1 egg, beaten
salt and pepper
pinch cumin

1 Roll out the pastry on a floured

surface, $\frac{1}{8}$ inch thick and, using a saucepan lid, cut out 4 circles.

2 Preheat the oven to 400°F.

3 In a large bowl, mix together the ground lamb, chutney, diced apple and grated onion. Bind with most of the beaten egg (put a little of it aside to glaze the pastry). Season with salt and pepper and a pinch of cumin.

4 Divide the mixture into four portions and place one in the center of each pastry circle. Wet the edges of the pastry with water and fold over, pressing the edges firmly together. Then crimp the edges.

5 Place the turnovers on a greased baking sheet and bake on the middle shelf of the oven for 20 minutes until well-risen and golden brown.

Serves 4

Lamb Braid

1 lb. ground lamb
2 onions, chopped
$\frac{1}{2}$ cup fresh breadcrumbs
1 tablespoon tomato paste
1 tablespoon Worcestershire sauce
2 eggs, beaten
salt and pepper
$\frac{1}{2}$ lb. puff pastry, fresh or frozen
  and thawed

1 Mix together the ground lamb, onions, breadcrumbs, tomato paste, Worcestershire sauce and one of the beaten eggs. Season with salt and pepper.

2 On a floured surface, roll out the pastry into an oblong $\frac{1}{8}$ inch thick.

3 Place the lamb mixture in the center and, with a knife, cut diagonal strips from the center to

1 Mix the ground lamb, onions, breadcrumbs, tomato paste, Worcestershire sauce and beaten egg together. Season with salt and pepper **2** Roll out the pastry and place the lamb mixture in the center **3** With a sharp knife, cut strips diagonally from the center to the edge of the pastry along each side and dampen the edges with water **4** Fold the end strips over and fold the others alternately across the filling **5** Place on a baking sheet, brush with eggwash and bake 30 minutes

the edges along each side. Dampen the edges with a little water.

4 Fold the pastry at each end and then fold the strips over alternately so that they meet in the center.

5 Preheat the oven to 425°F.

6 Place the Lamb Braid on a greased baking sheet and brush with the remaining beaten egg. Bake in the oven for 15 minutes, then reduce the temperature to 350°F. Cook for a further 30 minutes. Serve hot with fresh vegetables.

Serves 4

Tip: To make this dish more economical and to give it a smoother texture, try mixing pork sausage meat with the ground lamb. For a different flavor, why not add a little chopped liver? The addition of herbs such as rosemary, or even spices, make the Lamb Braid taste delicious.

Lamb en Croûte

Both lamb roasts and cutlets can be served en croûte in crisp golden puff pastry. If you use a boneless leg of lamb or loin roast, then make sure that the meat is well cooked before encasing it in the pastry. Cutlets need only be quickly browned on each side.

Lamb Capricio Pie

pastry for two 9-inch pie crusts
½ lb. ground cooked lamb
⅓ lb. pork sausage meat
¼ lb. ground cooked lamb liver
1 small onion, chopped
8 stuffed olives, sliced
2 eggs, beaten
⅔ cup dry sherry
1½ cups fresh breadcrumbs
salt and pepper
pinch curry powder

1 Preheat the oven to 400°F.

2 Roll out the pie crust dough ⅛ inch thick and 16 inches long by 8 inches wide.

3 Cut the pastry into 2 squares and use one to line a greased square cake pan. Prick the pastry all over with a fork and bake for 15 minutes. Remove from the oven and cool.

4 Meanwhile, mix all the other ingredients together in a large bowl. Reserve a little beaten egg for glazing the pie.

5 Fill the baked crust with the filling and cover with the uncooked square of dough. Crimp the edges of the pie together and glaze with beaten egg.

6 Bake in the oven for 20 minutes. Serve cold with salad.

Serves 6-8

Lamb Cutlets en Croûte stretch a little meat around a large family —serve them with fresh garden vegetables

Lamb Cutlets en Croûte

4 lamb cutlets
2 tablespoons butter
1 tablespoon oil
1 small onion, chopped
¼ cup chopped mushrooms
¼ cup fresh breadcrumbs
1 teaspoon mixed dill and thyme
salt and pepper
1 egg, beaten
½ lb. puff pastry, fresh or frozen
  and thawed
few sprigs parsley

1 Trim the cutlets to expose 2 inches of bone at the narrow end. Melt the butter and oil in a skillet and brown the cutlets on both sides. Drain on absorbent paper and cool.

2 Cook the onions and mushrooms in the remaining butter and oil until soft. Place in a bowl with the breadcrumbs and herbs and mix together well. Season with the salt and pepper and bind with some of the beaten egg.

3 Preheat the oven to 425°F.

4 Roll out the pastry on a floured surface into a large oblong, ⅛ inch thick. Cut into 4 strips.

5 Season the cutlets with salt and pepper and spread each with the stuffing mixture on one side only. Wrap a strip of pastry around each cutlet, working from one end to the other and seal the ends well.

6 Brush with the remaining beaten egg and place on a baking sheet. Bake in the oven for 15 minutes, then reduce the heat to 350°F. Continue cooking for another 15 minutes until golden brown, then remove and arrange on a serving dish. Garnish with sprigs of parsley and serve with buttered peas and carrots and roasted potatoes.

Serves 4

All about Lamb Stews and Casseroles

Spring Hotpot

Lamb Stews

Stews have the great merit of being suitable for cooking in advance, for reheating or freezing.

A stew is a combination of meat and vegetables cooked on top of the stove. There are three kinds of stew, one brown and two white. For the brown stew the meat is always seared first to seal the juices. It is then thickened by flour sprinkled on the meat or by a roux or cornstarch.

The stew may be given a good brown color by the addition of $\frac{1}{4}$ teaspoon of commercial "browning," or you can use the same amounts of molasses and vinegar to darken the stew without sweetening it.

In a white stew, the meat is first boiled in water. A roux is added to the stew and diluted with the stock, and mixed with some milk. The stew may be further enriched with cream or a thickener of egg yolks and cream.

The other type of white stew is a fricasée in which the meat is lightly pan fried to sear, but not to color. The meat is then dredged with flour and liquid added.

A sauté is another variety of stew in which the meat is cooked as dry as possible. The meat is browned and cooked, with a lid on, in its own juices until almost tender.

Stews are cooked on top of the stove and it is necessary to use a heavy dutch oven or pot.

If you do not have a suitable pot, it may be best to start the stew in a saucepan on top of the stove, and then to put the meat and vegetables in an ovenproof dish and finish the cooking in the oven.

Navy Bean Lamb Stew

1¼ lbs. stewing lamb
2 tablespoons shortening
2 slices lean bacon
8 pearl onions
1 clove garlic, crushed
¼ cup flour
3⅔ cups stock
salt and pepper
bouquet garni
½ lb. navy beans, soaked overnight
1 carrot, chopped
1 large onion, chopped
1 tablespoon tomato paste
1 tablespoon vinegar
1 tablespoon chopped parsley

1 Cut the meat into cubes.

2 Heat the shortening in a pan and add the bacon, diced (keep the bacon rind to cook with the beans) and the pearl onions. Brown slightly and remove from the pan.

3 In the same pan, brown the meat. Drain off half the fat, add the garlic and flour and stir for 1 minute.

4 Add the stock and bring to a boil. Season, skim off any scum. Add the bouquet garni, cover with a lid and simmer for 1½ hours.

5 Preheat the oven to 350°F.

6 Drain the soaked beans, reserving the liquid. Put the beans in clean water and bring to a boil. Throw the water away. Put the beans in an ovenproof dish with the chopped carrot, onion, bacon rinds, tomato paste and vinegar. Add some of the original liquid to cover and bake in the oven for 1 hour. When the beans are tender, remove the bacon rinds, and season with salt and pepper.

7 To serve, either combine the beans with the meat in one dish, or serve separately, sprinkled with chopped parsley.

Serves 4

Lamb and Pasta Stew

salt and pepper
2 zucchini, cut in chunks
¼ cup oil
4 thick chops
1 onion, chopped
¼ cup flour
2 tablespoons tomato paste
1¼ cups stock
juice 2 oranges
1 tablespoon thin strips of orange peel
2½ cups pasta wheels
1 tablespoon chopped fresh mint
few mint leaves

1 Sprinkle salt on the zucchini and leave for ½ hour. Rinse off the bitter juices and dry.

2 Preheat the oven to 350°F.

3 Heat the oil and brown the chops. Remove from the pan and place in an ovenproof dish.

4 In the same pan, sauté the onion for 3 minutes; stir in the flour and cook for 1 minute. Add the tomato paste and cook for 1 minute. Stir in the stock and orange juice and boil for 15 minutes. Season with salt and pepper and strain over the chops.

5 Meanwhile, blanch the strips of orange peel in boiling water for 6 minutes. Drain and add to the meat.

6 Put the meat in the oven to cook for 1 hour.

7 During this time, boil the pasta for 8 minutes. Drain and add to the stew with the zucchini 15 minutes before the end of the cooking time.

8 When ready to serve, check the seasoning, sprinkle with chopped mint and garnish with a few whole leaves for decoration.

Serves 4

Lamb and Pasta Stew is a good way of serving lamb with mint and oranges which makes an ideal lunch or supper dish

Lamb Stew with Celery and Pepper

2 lbs. lean stewing lamb cut into
  1-inch cubes
¼ cup oil
2 onions, chopped
1 sweet red pepper, diced
1 branch celery, diced
1 tablespoon tomato paste
⅓ cup medium sherry
salt and pepper
pinch ground mace
2½ cups beef stock
1½ tablespoons cornstarch
⅓ cup cold water
½ teaspoon gravy browning
  (optional)
1 cup long grain rice

1 Brown the meat in the oil in a heavy-bottomed casserole. Add the onions, pepper and celery and sauté gently for 4 minutes.

2 Add the tomato paste, sherry and seasoning. Stir. Add the meat stock.

3 Cover and stew gently for 1½ hours on low heat or until the meat is tender.

4 To thicken, prepare a roux by combining the cornstarch and water to a smooth paste. Add the browning, if used, and pour the roux into the stew. Stir and simmer for 10 minutes.

5 Cook the rice in boiling, salted water. Serve the casserole steaming hot on a bed of rice.

Serves 6

Lamb Stew with Celery and Pepper tastes as good as it looks with meaty chunks and vegetables on a bed of rice

Lamb Stew Jardinière

⅓ cup oil
2-lb. leg of lamb cut into 1-inch
  cubes
1 onion, chopped
2 tablespoons tomato paste
1 beef bouillon cube
1¼ cups cider
3⅔ cups water
salt and pepper
½ lb. pearl onions
½ lb. peas
1 teaspoon sugar
1 tablespoon butter
½ lb. baby carrots, quartered
½ lb. turnips, cut into strips
¼ cup flour

1 Heat ¼ cup of the oil in a pan and brown the lamb for 8 minutes. Place the meat in a casserole.

2 In the same oil, sauté the chopped onion until tender. Stir in the tomato paste and cook for 1 minute. Add the bouillon cube, cider and water and season. Boil for 10 minutes.

3 Pour the sauce over the meat. Cover and simmer for 1½ hours.

4 Boil the pearl onions and peas until tender in water seasoned with salt, pepper and half the sugar. Drain, toss in butter and keep warm.

5 Boil the carrots and turnips separately in water seasoned as for the peas and onions. Drain.

6 Mix the remaining oil and flour over low heat for 3-4 minutes. Add a little of the stew gravy, stir and simmer for 10 minutes.

7 Pour into the stew and stir over low heat for 5 minutes.

8 Pour the stew into the center of a shallow dish and surround with the vegetables.

Serves 6

Latin American Bean Stew

½ lb. navy beans, soaked overnight
8½ cups water
¼ cup oil
2-lb. lean shoulder of lamb, cut in cubes
1 large onion, chopped
1 branch celery, sliced
2 eggplants, peeled and cubed
1 bay leaf
3 cloves garlic, chopped
2 red chilies, sliced
¼ cup tomato paste
⅔ cup white wine
salt and pepper
1½ tablespoons cornstarch (optional)

1 Place the beans in a pan, add 3¾ cups of the water and bring to a boil. Remove any scum as it rises, reduce the heat and simmer for 1 hour until almost tender.

2 Meanwhile, heat the oil in an ovenproof casserole and cook the lamb for 5 minutes to brown it. Add the onion and celery and cook for a further 2 minutes. Add the eggplant, bay leaf, garlic and chilies and cook for 1 minute. Stir in the tomato paste, the rest of the water and the wine and simmer for 1½ hours.

3 Drain the beans and add them to the stew after the 1½ hours. Season and simmer for 20 minutes.

4 If liked, thicken the stew with the cornstarch mixed with ⅓ cup water.

5 Serve the stew in the casserole dish.

Serves 6

Oriental Stew (left) and Latin American Bean Stew (right) are just two of the delicious stews made with lamb

Variation

Oriental Stew

1 Omit the beans from the recipe for Latin American Bean Stew and cook the lamb in the same way but simmer for 1¾ hours.

2 Meanwhile, mix ⅔ cup pineapple juice, 1 teaspoon sugar, 1 tablespoon vinegar and 2 tablespoons soy sauce together in a pan. Add ½ lb. (4 cups) mushrooms and 1 sweet red pepper, diced. Bring to a boil and boil for 5 minutes.

3 Add the mushroom and pepper mixture to the lamb stew ½ hour before it has finished cooking.

4 Heat 2 tablespoons oil and a pan and stir fry 1 cup bean shoots for 1-2 minutes.

5 Stir the bean sprouts into the stew, check the seasoning and garnish with 6 olives. Serve with toasted peanuts.

Lamb and Shrimp Spanish-style

¼ cup oil
2-lb. boned lamb cutlets, cut in
  small, thin slices
1 large onion, sliced
12 stuffed olives, sliced
2 cloves garlic, chopped
1¼ cups water
⅔ cup medium dry sherry
1 bay leaf
pinch saffron
½ cup long grain rice
2 tomatoes, skinned, seeded and
  chopped
1 small sweet red pepper, seeded
and chopped
1⅓ cups peeled shrimp
1½ cups sliced mushrooms
salt and pepper
1 tablespoon chopped parsley

1 In a large sauté pan, heat the oil and cook the lamb for 8 minutes, covered with a lid.

2 Add the onion, cook for 1 minute, then add the olives, garlic, water, sherry, bay leaf and saffron, and bring gently to a boil. Reduce the heat and simmer for ½ hour.

3 Add the rice, tomatoes and pepper and simmer for 20 minutes.

4 Add the shrimp and mushrooms, season and cook for 4 minutes more. Sprinkle with the chopped parsley and serve.

Serves 6

Lamb Bourguignonne

2 lbs. lean shoulder of lamb, cut
  in 1-inch cubes
¼ cup oil
3 slices bacon, diced
2 onions, chopped

Lamb Bourguignonne is a dish for special occasions which is marinated in red wine, then served on a bed of rice

2 tablespoons tomato paste
1 teaspoon molasses
⅔ cup long grain rice
¼ cup butter
6 mushrooms, sliced
salt and pepper
pinch mixed mace and coriander

For the Marinade:
1¼ cups red wine
⅔ cup water
1 bay leaf
2 cloves garlic, crushed
bouquet garni
2 tablespoons vinegar

1 Mix the ingredients for the marinade. Place the lamb in a bowl, pour on the marinade and soak for 3 hours.

2 Lift the meat from the marinade and dry it. Heat the oil in a pan and cook the lamb and bacon for about 6 minutes until browned. Add the onions and cook for a further 3 minutes.

3 Add the marinade, tomato paste and molasses and bring to a boil. Reduce the heat and simmer for 1½ hours.

4 Meanwhile, cook the rice in boiling salted water, drain and mix with half of the butter.

5 Sauté the mushrooms in the rest of the butter for 2 minutes.

6 When the stew has finished cooking, discard the bay leaf and bouquet garni. Add the mushrooms, check the seasoning and add a pinch of mixed spice. Arrange the boiled rice on a serving platter and pour the lamb bourguignonne over it.

Serves 6

Lamb Portuguese

2¼ lbs. lamb from leg, loin or
  shoulder, cut in 1-inch cubes
¼ cup flour
salt and pepper
¼ cup oil
1 cup chopped onion
¼ cup tomato paste
3⅔ cups water
1 cup red wine
3 tablespoons vinegar
bouquet garni
pinch fresh rosemary
pinch summer savory
1 clove garlic, chopped
½ lb. navy beans, soaked overnight

1 Roll the lamb in the flour seasoned with salt and pepper. Shake to remove any excess.

2 Heat the oil in a heavy-bottomed casserole dish and lightly brown the meat. Add the onion and stir over moderate heat for 5 minutes.

3 Add the tomato paste, water, wine and vinegar. Stir. Add the bouquet garni and season with salt, pepper, rosemary, summer savory and garlic. Cover and stew over low heat for 1 hour.

4 While the stew is cooking, boil the soaked beans in salted water for 10 minutes. Remove the scum from the surface, reduce the heat and simmer for a further 40 minutes.

5 Drain the beans and add to the casserole. Check the seasoning. Cook for a further ½ hour or until the meat and beans are tender.

Serves 6

Tips: Dishes described as "Portuguese" are strongly flavored with tomato. You may either increase or decrease the amount of tomato paste used according to taste. Ideally, fresh tomatoes should be used. In this recipe, you may substitute 1 lb. of skinned, seeded and chopped tomatoes for the tomato paste.

Lamb Blanquette

2 lbs. lamb from the shoulder cut
  into 1-inch cubes
2 medium onions
2 cloves
½ bunch celery, diced
1 bay leaf
pinch fresh thyme
salt and pepper
⅔ cup dry white wine
2 tablespoons butter
¼ cup flour
juice ½ lemon
2 cloves garlic, crushed
pinch cayenne pepper
2 egg yolks
⅓ cup light cream
1 teaspoon chopped parsley

1 Place the lamb in a large saucepan. Stud each onion with a clove and add to the meat with the celery, bay leaf, thyme, salt and pepper. Pour in the wine, and enough water to cover the ingredients. Cover and cook on low heat for 1½ hours.

2 Strain, reserving 2½ cups of the stock. Remove the onions and place the celery and meat in a casserole dish.

3 Melt the butter and stir in the flour. Simmer on low heat and continue to stir until a smooth paste is formed. Bring the reserved stock to a boil and gradually add to the roux sauce, stirring all the time. Check the seasoning. Stir in the lemon juice, crushed garlic and cayenne pepper.

4 Beat the egg yolks and cream together in a bowl. Add ⅔ cup of the sauce to the mixture and blend well.

5 Gradually pour the mixture into the sauce, stirring all the time. Simmer for 5 more minutes.

6 Add the sauce to the meat and reheat. Sprinkle with chopped parsley and serve.

Serves 4

Lamb Bordelaise

1½ cups mushroom caps
3 potatoes
½ cup oil
1½ lbs. lean lamb from the
  shoulder, cut into 1½-inch cubes
salt and pepper
1 onion, chopped
bouquet garni
4 cloves garlic, chopped
1¼ cups beef stock
⅔ cup dry white wine
oil for deep frying
1 tablespoon chopped parsley

1 Thoroughly wash the mushroom caps. Drain, dry and cut into quarters.

2 Peel, wash and cut the potatoes into balls one inch in diameter, with a potato or melon baller.

3 Heat the oil in a pan and add the meat. Cover and sauté for 12 minutes or until browned. Season. Add the onion and bouquet garni. Stir and cook for 5 more minutes.

4 Add the mushrooms and garlic and cook for a further 2 minutes. Remove any excess fat from the pan.

5 Add the stock and wine. Stir and cook on low heat for 40 minutes or until tender.

6 About 10 minutes before the lamb is ready to serve, heat the deep fat fryer to 375°F. and deep-fry the potato balls for 4 minutes or until cooked and golden brown. Drain and keep warm.

7 Pour the lamb into a shallow serving dish. Serve garnished with the chopped parsley and surrounded by the potato balls.

Serves 4

Spicy Lamb Curry

¼ cup oil
2 lbs. lamb cutlets
1 large onion, chopped
1 apple, peeled, cored and sliced
2 cups water
⅔ cup shredded coconut
2 teaspoons curry powder
pinch cumin
pinch paprika
¼ cup flour
¼ cup tomato paste
⅔ cup pineapple juice
1 bay leaf
3 tablespoons mango chutney
salt and pepper
½ cup blanched almonds

For the Garnish:
2 bananas, sliced
1¼ cups shredded coconut
½ cup pineapple chunks
⅓ cup mango chutney
⅓ cup peach chutney

1 Heat the oil in a heavy saucepan and fry the lamb cutlets for 8 minutes until browned. Remove.

2 Sauté the onion and apple until soft.

3 Meanwhile, bring the water to a boil and soak the coconut in it for 3-4 minutes.

4 Add the curry powder, cumin, paprika, flour and tomato paste to the pan. Cook for 3 minutes.

5 Add the coconut water, pineapple juice and bay leaf and bring to a boil, stirring all the time. Add the mango chutney and seasoning and simmer for 1½ hours.

6 Sprinkle with the almonds and serve with boiled rice, bananas, coconut, pineapple, mango and peach chutney arranged around the curry in small bowls.

Serves 4–6

Spicy Lamb Curry is served in the traditional manner and surrounded by side dishes: chutneys, coconut and boiled rice

Lamb Curry

2 lbs. shoulder of lamb
2 tablespoons oil
2 large onions, sliced
2 tablespoons curry powder
1 tablespoon turmeric
1 teaspoon ground ginger
⅔ cup beef stock
salt and pepper
1 tablespoon tomato paste
3 tablespoons mango chutney
2 tablespoons raisins
⅔ cup sour cream
⅓ cup split almonds
½ lemon, sliced

1 Cut the lamb off the bone and remove the fat. Cut it into 1-inch cubes.

2 Heat the oil in a heavy saucepan and sauté the onions until soft. Add the lamb and brown it all over.

3 Stir in the curry powder, turmeric and ginger. Cook for 3 minutes.

4 Stir in the stock and season with the salt and pepper. Add the tomato paste and bring to a boil, stirring all the time.

5 Add the mango chutney and raisins and simmer, covered with a lid, for 45 minutes until the meat is tender.

6 Stir in the sour cream and most of the almonds. Simmer gently for 10 more minutes.

7 Arrange the curry on a serving dish, surrounded by a ring of boiled rice. Sprinkle with the remaining almonds and decorate with slices of lemon. Serve with side dishes such as coconut, mango chutney, sliced tomatoes, bananas, chopped apple, cucumber and orange sections.

Serves 4–6

Lamb Casseroles

A casserole differs from a stew by being cooked in the oven rather than on top of the stove, and by containing considerably less liquid. A casserole can be made using better cuts of meat, such as chops, and so takes less time to cook than a stew.

A hotpot is a form of casserole which is cooked in clear broth and relies upon the inclusion of potatoes, beans or lentils for its thickening.

Types of meat suitable for hotpots include cutlets or diced shoulder of lamb, and all cuts of mutton.

Lancashire Hotpot

1½ lbs. lamb chops
1 tablespoon flour seasoned with salt and pepper
2 tablespoons oil
4 medium onions, sliced
2 lamb kidneys, skinned, cored and sliced
2 cups sliced mushrooms
1 parsnip, sliced
4 potatoes, sliced
2¼ cups stock

1 Preheat the oven to 350°F.

2 Trim any excess fat from the lamb chops and coat them in the seasoned flour.

3 Heat the oil in a pan, add the lamb and cook for a few minutes until browned on both sides.

4 Arrange the lamb, onions, kidneys, mushrooms, parsnip and potatoes in layers in a large casserole, finishing with a layer of potatoes. Pour in the stock and cover.

5 Bake in the preheated oven for 2 hours. After this time, remove the lid and cook for a further ½ hour to brown the potatoes.

Serves 4

Casserole of Lamb Polish-style

1½ lbs. stewing lamb, cut into cubes
⅓ cup oil
2 onions, chopped
1 teaspoon paprika

Lancashire Hotpot is a famous old English dish which was traditionally made with oysters

pinch caraway seeds
¼ cup flour
2 tablespoons tomato paste
2½ cups water
1 bay leaf
salt and freshly ground black pepper
4 potatoes
4 fresh tomatoes, skinned, halved and seeded
⅔ cup sour cream or yogurt

1 Preheat the oven to 375°F.

2 Remove any fat from the meat. Heat the oil in a heavy casserole and add the meat. Cover and cook for 8 minutes, stirring from time to time, until the meat is evenly browned. Add the chopped onions and cook for 2 minutes more.

3 Sprinkle in the paprika, caraway seeds and flour and add the tomato paste. Stir and cook for 1 minute. Pour in the water and add the bay

479

leaf. Bring to a boil, season and place in the preheated oven for ¾–1 hour.

4 Meanwhile, boil the potatoes in salted water for about 20 minutes or until tender.

5 Five minutes before the casserole has finished cooking, remove from the oven and add the drained potatoes. Decorate with the halved tomatoes and return to the oven for the rest of the cooking time.

6 Serve the casserole with the sour cream or yogurt poured over the top or served separately.

Serves 6

Casserole of Lamb Polish-style is nourishing and cheap. The sour cream topping turns it into something very special

Yugoslavian Casserole

2 onions, thinly sliced
2 peppers, seeded and sliced
⅔ cup oil
4 tomatoes, skinned, seeded and chopped
salt and pepper
½ cup long grain rice
1¾ lbs. lamb shoulder, cubed
1¼ cups hot water
1 teaspoon paprika

1 Gently sauté the onions and peppers in 3 tablespoons of the oil for 10 minutes. Add the tomatoes, cook for 2 minutes and season. Place half the mixture in an ovenproof casserole.

2 Preheat the oven to 350°F. Heat 3 tablespoons oil in the pan and fry the rice for 2 minutes. Add the rice to the casserole and cover with the rest of the tomatoes.

3 Brown the meat in the rest of the oil, season and add to the casserole. Add the water, cover and bring to a boil. Cook in the oven for 1½ hours.

4 Sprinkle with the paprika and serve.

Serves 5

Lamb and Cabbage Casserole

3 lbs. boneless shoulder of lamb
2 tablespoons oil
2 lbs. cabbage
2 teaspoons salt
1¾ cups hot beef stock
1 bay leaf
a little fresh chopped parsley

1 Cut the lamb into cubes. Heat the oil in an ovenproof casserole, add the lamb and fry briskly until browned on all sides. Remove from the pan and pour off the oil.

2 Wash and trim the cabbage, separating the leaves. Put the lamb and cabbage in alternate layers in the casserole, sprinkling each layer with salt.

3 Pour in the stock, add the bay leaf and bring to a boil. Reduce the heat, cover and cook gently for 1½ hours or until the lamb is tender, adding a little more water if the meat becomes dry during cooking.

4 Remove the bay leaf, taste and adjust the seasoning. Sprinkle with the parsley and serve hot.

Serves 6

1 The ingredients: lamb loin chops, potatoes, to-matoes, zucchini, onions, garlic, parsley, white wine, milk and cheese **2** Dredge the chops with flour and shallow fry until browned on both sides. Place them in a shallow ovenproof dish **3** Blanch the zucchini and cover the chops **4** Sauté the onions until soft, then add the chopped tomatoes, garlic, water, wine, bouillon cube and seasoning. Simmer for 5 minutes **5** Pour the

481

5

7

6

8

tomato and wine mixture over the zucchini in the dish **6** Cover with a layer of thinly sliced blanched potatoes, overlapping each other **7** Make a basic roux and then

a white sauce by adding milk. Stir in a little cheese and then pour the sauce over the potatoes **8** Sprinkle with the remaining cheese, then bake for about 45 minutes

Loin Chops Catalonia

6 lamb loin chops
¼ cup flour seasoned with salt and pepper
¼ cup oil
3 onions, sliced
4 tomatoes, skinned, seeded and chopped
1 clove garlic, crushed
⅔ cup white wine
⅔ cup water
1 chicken bouillon cube
salt and pepper
bouquet garni
4 zucchini, sliced
3 potatoes
⅔ cup white sauce
¾ cup grated Cheddar cheese

1 Dredge the lamb chops in the seasoned flour. Heat the oil in a skillet and fry the lamb chops until well-browned on both sides. Remove them from the pan and arrange in the bottom of a shallow ovenproof dish.

2 Preheat the oven to 350°F.

3 In the same oil, sauté the onions until soft, then add the chopped tomatoes and garlic. Pour in the wine and water and crumble in the bouillon cube. Season with salt and pepper and add the bouquet garni. Simmer for about 5 minutes.

4 Meanwhile, blanch the zucchini in boiling water for 3-4 minutes and arrange over the lamb chops in the dish.

5 Pour the tomato and wine mixture over the top.

6 Blanch the potatoes in boiling water for 4 minutes. Cut in thin slices and arrange them, overlapping, across the top of the dish.

7 Heat the white sauce and stir in ½ cup of the grated cheese. Blend and pour the sauce over the potatoes. Sprinkle with the remaining grated cheese.

8 Bake in the oven for 45 minutes.

Serves 6

Lamb and Rice Casserole is an exciting new idea for serving lamb with cooked rice and fresh vegetables

Lamb and Rice Casserole

2 tablespoons oil
¼ cup butter
2 onions, chopped
2 large carrots, chopped
1 branch celery, chopped
2 leeks, cleaned and sliced
6 lamb chops
¼ cup flour seasoned with salt and pepper
sprig thyme
1 bay leaf
salt and pepper
pinch nutmeg
2¼ cups water
1 chicken bouillon cube
1½ cups rice
1 cup peas

1 Heat the oil and butter in an ovenproof casserole dish. Gently sauté the onions, carrots, celery and leeks until tender, stirring from time to time.

2 Preheat the oven to 375°F.

3 Dredge the lamb chops in the seasoned flour. Remove the fried vegetables from the casserole and keep warm. Pan-fry the lamb chops until well-browned on both sides. Return the vegetables to the casserole, add the thyme, bay leaf, salt and pepper and nutmeg.

4 Pour in the water and crumble in the bouillon cube. Bring to a boil, check the seasoning, then bake in the oven for 30 minutes.

5 Remove and stir in the rice. Bring to a boil on top of the stove, add the peas and cover with a lid. Replace in the oven and bake for a further 20 minutes until the rice is tender. If necessary, you can add extra stock during cooking if the rice absorbs too much liquid.

Serves 6

Algerian Lamb Casserole

¼ cup oil
2 lbs. lamb cutlets
1 lb. onions, sliced
3 medium-size potatoes, peeled
  and thinly sliced
2 cups water
⅔ cup white wine
bouquet garni
pinch cumin
salt and pepper
1 bay leaf

1 Preheat the oven to 350°F.

2 Heat the oil in an ovenproof dish and brown the lamb cutlets on both sides. Add the onions and sauté until soft.

3 Cover with the sliced potatoes, water and white wine. Add the bouquet garni, cumin and salt and pepper. Stir in the bay leaf and cover with a lid.

Algerian Lamb Casserole brings a taste of North Africa to your dinner table, flavored with wine and cumin

4 Bake in the oven for 1¼–1½ hours until the lamb is tender and the potatoes are cooked through. Check the seasoning and serve with cooked fennel, celery, carrots or squash.

Serves 4–6

Tips: The Algerians usually serve this dish with couscous, a type of semolina which is cooked in twice its volume of stock with boiled vegetables such as celery, fennel, carrots, chick peas and squashes. You can make a spicy sauce from the stock with Tabasco sauce. Just crush a clove of garlic and mix with ½ teaspoon cumin, 2 tablespoons tomato paste, ½ teaspoon oil and a good pinch of chili powder. Mix in a little salt and dilute into the stock with a pinch of basil.

North African Cooking
Lamb and mutton are widely eaten in North Africa and are usually roasted over glowing charcoal fires. Meat is seasoned and flavored with delicate herbs and spices and served with a cool yogurt dressing. Oregano and cumin are ideal for enhancing the flavor of lamb. Stews, hot-pots and casseroles are popular since they can be cooked in a single pot over an open fire, thus conserving fuel. Eggplants are the most widely eaten vegetables and are stuffed, puréed, stewed and fried. You can prepare a delicious lamb casserole with eggplants, cumin, cinnamon and wine. Add a generous sprinkling of herbs and whatever vegetables you fancy. Chickpeas can be used too.

Casserole of Lamb Basquaise

2 lbs. shoulder of lamb
¼ cup oil
3 large onions, quartered
1 green pepper, seeded and cut
  in strips
⅔ cup diced lean bacon
4 large mushrooms, sliced
2 cloves garlic, crushed
⅔ cup dry white wine
1¼ cups water
1 chicken bouillon cube
bouquet garni
sprig tarragon
4 large tomatoes, skinned,
  seeded and chopped
salt and pepper
3 tablespoons cornstarch

1 Cut the lamb into ½ inch cubes.

2 Preheat the oven to 375°F.

3 Heat the oil in a saucepan and sauté the onions and pepper until soft. Add the lamb and bacon, cover with a lid and cook for 3 minutes. Then add the sliced mushrooms and garlic.

4 Pour the wine and water into the pan and crumble in the bouillon cube. Add the bouquet garni, tarragon and chopped tomatoes and season with salt and pepper.

5 Transfer to an ovenproof casserole dish, cover with a lid and cook in the oven for 1¼ hours. The meat should be tender and the liquid reduced.

6 Mix the cornstarch with a little of the liquid from the casserole and stir into the dish. Bring to a boil on top of the stove, stirring all the time, until the sauce thickens. Serve the casserole with boiled rice or roasted potatoes.

Serves 6

Tip: For a different flavor, try substituting red wine, dry sherry or vermouth for white wine in this casserole. The addition of basil or oregano will give it a taste of the Mediterranean.

Dijon Lamb Hotpot

2 tablespoons oil
6 lamb cutlets
2 branches celery, sliced
4 carrots, sliced
1 rutabaga, cut in chunks
2 onions, chopped
1¼ cups water
⅔ cup dry white vermouth
pinch marjoram
pinch thyme
salt and pepper
pinch cumin
1 tablespoon vinegar
1 tablespoon honey
1 chicken bouillon cube
1 teaspoon prepared Dijon
  mustard

1 Heat the oil in a skillet and fry

Dijon Hotpot comes all the way from France with tasty lamb cutlets in an unusual wine and mustard flavored sauce

the cutlets for about 5 minutes until browned.

2 Preheat the oven to 375°F.

3 Place the browned cutlets in an ovenproof dish and cover with the vegetables. Pour in the water and vermouth. Sprinkle in the herbs and season with salt and pepper. Stir in the cumin, vinegar and honey. Crumble in the bouillon cube.

4 Cover with a lid and bake in the oven for 1½ hours until the meat and vegetables are tender.

5 Stir the mustard into the stock until well blended with the liquid. Serve hot with boiled rice or potatoes.

Serves 6

Tip: If you prefer a casserole-type dish in a thick sauce to a hotpot such as this one which is served in a thin gravy, you can always thicken the liquid with cornstarch.

Turkish-style Moussaka

6 small eggplants
salt and pepper
½ cup oil
3 tomatoes, skinned, seeded, and chopped
2 onions, chopped
1¼ cups sliced mushrooms
1½ lbs. ground lamb
3 cloves garlic, crushed
2 tablespoons chopped parsley
2 eggs, beaten
½ cup flour

1 Preheat the oven to 425°F.

2 Slice 4 of the eggplants in half. Make an incision around the sides with a knife. Then make a criss-cross pattern.

3 Season them with salt and pepper and fry in 2 tablespoons of the oil for a few minutes. Scoop out the pulp.

4 Heat 1 tablespoon of oil in a pan and sauté the tomatoes.

5 Using the same amount of oil, sauté the onions until tender in another pan. Meanwhile, sauté the mushrooms in 1 tablespoon oil.

6 In a large bowl, mix together the lamb and garlic with the sautéed onions and mushrooms, and one third of the cooked tomatoes. Mix in the crushed garlic and parsley and bind with the beaten eggs, and 4 tablespoons flour.

7 Peel the remaining eggplants and slice thinly. Season and toss in the remaining flour. Fry them in the rest of the oil for 1 minute.

8 Butter a deep ovenproof dish and line the sides with the eggplant skins. Fill the dish with alternate layers of the lamb mixture and fried sliced eggplant. Cover the top with more skins.

9 Bake in a shallow pan of water for 45 minutes. Surround with the remaining tomato pulp.

Serves 6

Greek-style Moussaka

2 eggplants, peeled and sliced
2 zucchini, sliced
1 teaspoon salt
2 tablespoons flour
oil for deep frying
3 medium-size potatoes, sliced
6 tomatoes, skinned and sliced
½ cup grated cheese

For the Filling:
¼ cup oil
1 onion, chopped
1 lb. ground lamb
1 clove garlic, crushed
¼ cup flour
2 tablespoons tomato paste
pinch each oregano and mace
salt and pepper
⅔ cup stock

For the Cheese Sauce:
1¼ cups white sauce
½ cup grated cheese
1 egg yolk
juice and rind 1 lemon

1 Sprinkle the eggplants and zucchini with salt. Leave 10 minutes, then wash and dry.

2 Parboil the zucchini for 3-4 minutes. Coat the eggplants with flour and deep fry for 30 seconds.

3 Make the filling. Heat the oil and sauté the onion until soft. Add the lamb, garlic, flour, tomato paste, herbs and seasoning. Pour in the stock, boil, then simmer for 10 minutes.

4 Blanch the potatoes.

5 Preheat the oven to 375°F.

6 Place alternate layers of the meat mixture, zucchini, eggplant, tomatoes and potatoes in a deep casserole.

7 Make the white sauce, stir in the cheese, egg yolk and lemon juice and rind. Simmer gently, then pour over the moussaka. Sprinkle with grated cheese and bake for 30 minutes.

Serves 6

Lamb Cobbler

¼ cup oil
1 onion, chopped
1½ lbs. ground lamb
¼ lb. chopped lamb liver
¼ cup flour
¼ cup tomato paste
1¼ cups stock
salt and pepper
pinch rosemary
1 teaspoon prepared mustard
2 tablespoons chopped dill pickle

For the Topping:
3 cups self-rising flour
pinch salt
¼ lb. butter
⅓ cup water
1 tablespoon milk

1 Heat the oil in a pan and sauté the onion until soft. Add the lamb and liver and cook for 5 minutes.

2 Stir in the flour and tomato paste and cook for 2-3 minutes. Then pour in the stock and add the salt and pepper and rosemary.

3 Preheat the oven to 375°F.

4 Mix the mustard and pickle into the lamb mixture and pour into a shallow ovenproof dish. Cool.

5 Meanwhile, make the topping. Sift the flour and salt together and cut in the butter. Add enough water to form a stiff dough.

6 Knead the dough a little on a floured board and roll out ¼ inch thick. With a round pastry cutter cut the dough into rounds to form small biscuits. Arrange these biscuits, overlapping each other, around the top of the casserole dish. Brush with milk.

7 Bake in the oven for 30 minutes.

Serves 6

All about Pork
Sautéed Pork Cutlets

Pork has a distinctive flavor which is quite different from other meats. As well as tasty roasts and chops, there are bacon, ham and many types of sausage.

Choosing Pork

The lean meat should always be pale pink in color, without gristle and firm to the touch. It should be marbled a little with milky-white fat, and the outer fat should be firm and white. If you are buying a ham with skin or rind, make sure that there are no hairs and that it is not too thick. If you like crackling on your roast, ask the butcher to score the rind for you.

Storing Pork

Pork is available all year round, fresh or frozen. Of course, if you have a freezer you would be well advised to buy in bulk. Roasts and chops will store in a freezer for about 4 months. Pork can be stored in a refrigerator for 2-3 days, or in a cool place for about 24 hours.

Cuts of Pork

Pork is available in a variety of cuts and should always be cooked thoroughly. It can be roasted, grilled, broiled, fried, casseroled, cured, boiled and made into sausages. Here are the best-known cuts:

Loin: This is usually considered to be the choicest cut. It is also the most expensive. It can be roasted whole on the bone or boned, rolled and stuffed. It is also cut up into loin and rib chops. When roasting loin, allow ½ lb. on the bone per person, and 4-6 ozs. boned per person.

Ham: This is another expensive cut which is lean and tender. It is usually roasted either on the bone or boned and stuffed. It comes from the top end of the hind leg and can also be cut into steaks.

Leg: This is a very large roast which is often cut in two and then roasted. It can be roasted on the bone or stuffed and rolled. Generally, it has more flavor when roasted on the bone.

Spare Ribs: These are usually associated with Chinese and Oriental cooking. However, they are growing more popular in the West. They are usually roasted, marinated, or grilled or broiled. They should not be confused with rib chops, which come from the loin.

Chops: Rib and loin chops both come from the loin and are about 1 inch thick. They are usually grilled, broiled, fried or baked.

Cutlets: These lean pieces of meat are taken from the spare rib and have very little bone. Like chops, they can be fried, grilled, broiled or casseroled.

Blade: This is a cheaper cut which can be roasted or braised on or off the bone.

Belly: This is a very fatty cut which can be roasted entirely or cut into slices. Because it is so fat, it is cheap and sold either fresh or salted.

Shoulder Hock: This cut comes from the foreleg and is sold both fresh and salted. It is suitable for roasting, braising and stewing. If you are a crackling lover, this is the cut for you as it has a very large area of rind.

Suckling Pig: This is a young pig which is slaughtered between three weeks and two months. It can be spit-roasted.

Sauces and Flavorings

Pork is traditionally served with applesauce. Spices such as cloves and paprika go well with pork in either a marinade or a tart apple sauce. Herbs such as thyme, sage, rosemary and garlic all enhance the flavor of pork. Pork is a favorite meat in oriental dishes and is often served with ginger, soy sauce or pineapple. You can make a delicious marinade for a roast or chops with these ingredients. Or why not try cooking your roast the Italian way? Just make some small cuts in the lean meat and insert some slivers of garlic. Sprinkle with oregano and roast as normal. The end result tastes and looks delicious. Or you can try making a sticky glaze for a pork roast with honey, orange or pineapple juice and spices such a powdered cloves, ginger or cinnamon.

Chops and Cutlets

Both loin and rib pork chops come from the loin. Pork chops can be broiled, fried or casseroled in many different ways. In this section, we give you recipes for all three. Pork chops are most economical when served in a sauce or casserole to make them go further.

Fruity Pork Chops

four 6-oz. pork chops
salt and pepper
¼ cup oil
pinch oregano
½ sweet red pepper, cut in strips
½ cup long grain rice
½ lb. seedless green grapes, halved

1 Sprinkle the pork chops with salt and freshly ground black pepper.

2 Heat the oil in a skillet and gently fry the chops until brown on both sides. Sprinkle in the oregano.

3 Add the strips of red pepper and sauté until soft.

4 Meanwhile, cook the rice in boiling salted water until tender, but still firm.

5 Add the halved grapes to the pork and peppers and heat through.

6 Arrange the rice on a heated serving dish and arrange the chops in the center. Spoon the peppers and grapes over the top and serve.

Serves 4

Fruity Pork Chops are served on a bed of plain rice with sautéed strips of red pepper and juicy green grapes

Barbecued Pork Cutlets

¼ cup oil
6 pork cutlets
¼ cup butter
1 small onion, chopped
½ cup water
2 tablespoons brown sugar
½ teaspoon prepared mustard
salt and pepper
1 tablespoon vinegar
1 tablespoon tomato paste
2 tomatoes, skinned, seeded
 and chopped
1 teaspoon Worcestershire sauce
⅓ cup catsup
pinch paprika

1 Heat the oil and fry the pork cutlets until well browned on both sides.

2 Meanwhile, make the barbecue sauce. Melt the butter in a saucepan and sauté the onion until soft. Add the water and stir in the brown sugar, mustard, seasoning and vinegar. Bring to a boil, then simmer for 5 minutes.

3 Add all the remaining ingredients, stir well and simmer for 15 minutes.

4 Serve the pork cutlets with the barbecue sauce on a bed of plain boiled rice.

Serves 6

Tips: You can make the sauce more appealing by adding sliced mushrooms or peppers. If you like red-hot food, why not add a few drops of hot sauce? Or you can make a more fruity version with cooked plums, pineapple or fresh chopped peaches and apricots.

You can remove the meat from the chops, of course, and use it skewered as kebabs. Or why not try marinating the chops in soy sauce, pineapple juice, oil and garlic for a more oriental flavor?

Pork in Cider brings the flavor of the countryside to your dinner table with its fresh vegetables and fruity taste

Pork in Cider

½ cup oil
2 carrots, diced
2 onions, diced
1 clove garlic, crushed
2 shallots, chopped
1 branch celery, thinly sliced
½ cup flour
3 tomatoes, skinned, seeded,
 and chopped
1¼ cups cider
bouquet garni
1 cup canned creamed corn
salt and pepper
six ½-lb. pork cutlets
1 tablespoon chopped parsley

1 Heat half of the oil in a saucepan and gently sauté the carrots, onions, garlic, shallots and celery until tender.

2 Sprinkle in half of the flour, stir and cook for 1 minute. Add the tomatoes and cider and bring to a boil. Add the bouquet garni and

corn and season with salt and pepper. Simmer for 15-20 minutes.

3 Coat the cutlets in the remaining seasoned flour and heat the rest of the oil in a pan. Pan fry the cutlets for about 10 minutes until browned on both sides.

4 Preheat the oven to 350°F.

5 Remove the cutlets from the pan and arrange in an ovenproof dish. Cover with the sauce and check the seasoning. Bake in the covered ovenproof dish for 20 minutes.

6 Sprinkle with parsley and serve with boiled new potatoes.

Serves 6

Tip: If you have no cider, you can always use apple juice or white wine or a mixture of both. Fresh sliced apples will bring out the fruity flavor. Fresh corn on the cob or canned corn will give the casserole a more crunchy texture.

Pork with Rice and Peppers is an easy and tasty dish to prepare which is ideal for quick, filling family meals

Pork with Rice and Peppers

6 pork cutlets
½ cup seasoned flour
¼ cup oil
1 onion, chopped
1 green pepper, seeded and cut in strips
1 sweet red pepper, seeded and cut in strips
1 clove garlic, crushed
½ cup water
salt and pepper
¾ cup long grain rice
¼ cup butter

1 Coat the pork cutlets in the seasoned flour. Heat the oil in a skillet and cook the cutlets for about 10 minutes until browned on both sides.

2 Remove the cutlets and keep warm. Sauté the onion, green and red peppers and garlic until soft. Then return the cutlets to the pan and add the water and seasoning. Bring to a boil, then simmer, covered with a lid, for 20 minutes.

3 Meanwhile, cook the rice in boiling salted water until tender. Drain and place in a buttered mold. Press it down firmly and unmold onto a serving dish.

4 Surround the molded rice with the cutlets, peppers and onions and serve immediately.

Serves 6

Tips: You can use either pork chops or cutlets for this dish. It tastes especially delicious if served in a tomato sauce. Just add some skinned, seeded and chopped tomatoes, tomato paste, sliced mushrooms and a pinch of basil. For a special occasion, substitute white wine or dry sherry for the water.

491

Pork Chops with Cider Cream Sauce

4 pork chops
2 tablespoons flour
salt and pepper
¼ cup butter
1 large onion, chopped
1½ cups sliced mushrooms
1¼ cups cider
¼ cup heavy cream
1 tablespoon chopped parsley

1 Coat the pork chops in half the flour seasoned with salt and pepper. Melt the butter in a large skillet and fry the pork chops slowly until cooked through. Remove the chops from the pan and keep them warm.

2 Add the onion to the meat cooking juices and sauté gently for 3 minutes.

3 Stir in the mushrooms and cook for another 3 minutes.

4 Stir in the rest of the flour and cook for 1 minute. Take the pan off the heat and stir in the cider to make a smooth sauce. Return the pan to the heat and stir for 1 minute.

5 Over low heat, stir in the cream and season with salt and pepper. Heat to just below the boiling point. Pour the sauce over the pork chops, garnish with the chopped parsley, and serve at once.

Serves 4

Pork Chops with Cider Cream Sauce — an impressive combination — enriched with thick cream and sliced mushrooms

Pork Chops à l'Orange

4 thick pork chops
1 onion, finely chopped
¼ cup butter
¼ cup oil
1 cup fresh breadcrumbs
salt and pepper
pinch dried sage
grated rind and juice 1 orange
2 tablespoons flour
1¼ cups chicken stock

1 Cut a pocket in each pork chop by making a slit in the same direction as the bone, cutting from the fat side through to the bone.

2 Sauté the chopped onion in half of the butter and oil for 5 minutes until softened but not browned.

3 Stir in the breadcrumbs, salt and pepper to taste, sage, and the grated orange rind, so that the mixture absorbs the cooking fats and forms a thick paste. If necessary, remove from the heat and use the milk to bind the mixture.

4 Preheat the oven to 325°F. Stuff ¼ of the breadcrumb mixture into each chop, securing if necessary with a wooden toothpick. Arrange the chops in an ovenproof dish and keep warm.

5 Heat the rest of the butter and oil in the pan, scraping up any residue. Cook the flour for 1–2 minutes. Remove from the heat and stir in the stock and orange juice and bring to a boil, stirring all the time.

6 Pour the thickened sauce over the chops, cover, and cook in the oven for 15 minutes. Serve with buttered green beans.

Serves 4

Pork Roasts

The following recipes show just how many ways there are of serving pork roast aside from the traditional applesauce.

Pork with Pineapple

6 tablespoons butter
⅓ cup oil
2-lb. loin pork roast
salt and pepper

⅔ cup water
1 small pineapple, cut into chunks, or ½ lb. canned pineapple pieces, drained

For the Gravy:
1 tablespoon flour
⅓ cup water
2 tablespoons Worcestershire sauce
⅓ cup pineapple juice
1 tablespoon cornstarch

1 Preheat the oven to 375°F. Melt the butter in a saucepan and combine it with the oil.

2 Remove the backbone and all the rind from the pork itself. Season the meat with salt and pepper and

Pork with Pineapple — crisp, roast pork with fresh or canned pineapple chunks in a delicious, golden gravy

brush all over with half the butter and oil mixture. Place the pork on a rack in a roasting pan and roast in the oven for 1½ hours or until the meat is well cooked. Baste from time to time with the water, to ensure the meat does not dry out.

3 Meanwhile, heat the remaining butter and oil in a pan and sauté the pineapple pieces for 3 minutes on both sides or until golden. Remove from the pan and keep warm.

4 When the meat is cooked, prepare the gravy. Remove most of the fat from the meat juice. Add the flour and stir over a low heat for 3-4 minutes until browned. Add the water, Worcestershire sauce, and the pineapple juice. Bring to a boil and simmer for 5 minutes, stirring all the time. Thicken with the cornstarch mixed with a little water. Check the seasoning.

5 Place the meat on a heated serving platter, surround it with the pineapple pieces and, just before serving, pour on the gravy.

Serves 8

Braised Leg of Pork

3-lb. shoulder of pork
1¼ cups dry white wine
⅓ cup brandy
2 shallots, sliced
1 clove garlic, crushed
2 carrots, sliced
1 bay leaf
sprig thyme
sprig parsley
salt and pepper
2 tablespoons fat
½ cup brown breadcrumbs
¼ cup water
1 teaspoon cornstarch

1 Preheat the oven to 450°F. Trim the pork all around. Remove all the rind and some of the fat.

2 Place it in a large bowl and cover

it with the wine, brandy, shallots, garlic, carrots, bay leaf, thyme and parsley. Cover and marinate for 6 hours, turning it from time to time.

3 Wipe it, season it to taste with salt and pepper and place it in a roasting pan. Add the fat and sear the meat in the oven for 30 minutes. Strain off any excess fat.

4 Reduce the heat to 350°F. Add the vegetables and herbs and baste the meat with the marinating liquor from time to time, until it is cooked. The cooking time will depend on the weight of the leg. Allow at least 30 minutes per lb. When cooked, sprinkle the meat with the brown breadcrumbs.

5 Strain the juices into a saucepan. Season, add the water and boil it for 5 minutes. If necessary, thicken with the cornstarch mixed with a little water. Serve the sauce in a gravy boat with the meat.

Serves 8–10

Pork with Rosemary — an unusual way of serving a roast by pot-roasting in white wine with mushrooms and celery

Pork with Rosemary

2 lbs. lean boned shoulder or loin of pork
salt and pepper
⅔ cup butter
1 carrot, sliced
1 large onion, chopped
1 branch celery, diced
¾ lb. mushrooms
1¼ cups water
⅔ cup dry white wine
2 sprigs rosemary
1 clove garlic, crushed

1 Preheat the oven to 375°F. Season the meat.

2 Melt half of the butter in a flameproof casserole. Add the meat and brown it on all sides. Remove the casserole from the heat.

3 In a separate pan melt the remaining butter. Add the carrot and sauté for 5 minutes. Add the onion and celery and sauté for a further 5 minutes. Finally add the mushrooms, cover and cook on low heat for 2 minutes.

4 Pour the contents of the pan into the casserole. Add the water, wine, one rosemary sprig and the garlic. Check the seasoning. Cover and cook in the oven for 1½ hours or until the meat is well cooked.

5 Serve garnished with the second sprig of rosemary.

Serves 6

Stuffed Pork with Eggplant

2½ lbs. boneless loin of pork, rind
  and some fat removed
salt and pepper
1 lb. onions, chopped
1 clove garlic, crushed
2 tablespoons oil
8 tomatoes, skinned, seeded and
  chopped
1 teaspoon chili powder
⅓ cup raisins
1 cup cooked rice
1 egg, beaten
⅔ cup dry white wine
⅔ cup stock
2 eggplants, peeled and sliced
¼ cup flour
oil for deep frying

1 Preheat the oven to 375°F. Cut the pork almost in half lengthwise and season.

2 Sauté the onions and garlic in the oil until soft. Add the tomatoes and chili powder and simmer for 5 minutes. Add the raisins.

3 Blend half the tomato mixture with the rice and egg and place the stuffing on the pork. Fold over the meat and tie at intervals. Place in a roasting pan and cook in the oven for 1 hour.

4 Pour out the fat which has collected in the roasting pan. Mix the remaining tomato mixture with the wine and stock and add to the pan. Return to the oven for 30 minutes or until the meat is cooked. Baste occasionally, adding more wine to the sauce if it becomes too thick.

5 Meanwhile, soak the eggplants in salted water for 15 minutes, then drain and dry. Coat with the flour and deep fry until golden. Keep warm.

6 Remove the string from the roast and place the meat in a serving dish. Pour the sauce around it and add the eggplant slices.

Serves 6–8

Stuffed Pork with Eggplant. A tomato and chili mixture is used in both the sauce and the filling

Pork with Prune and Almond Stuffing

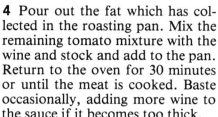 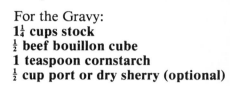

2 lbs. boned loin of pork, rind
  and some fat removed
salt and pepper
½ cup long grain rice

For the Stuffing:
¾ cup pitted prunes, cooked
½ cup slivered almonds
2 cups fresh breadcrumbs

For the Gravy:
1¼ cups stock
½ beef bouillon cube
1 teaspoon cornstarch
½ cup port or dry sherry (optional)

1 Preheat the oven to 375°F.

2 Spread the meat flat and season the inside. Combine the ingredients for the stuffing and place along the center of the meat. Roll up and secure with string. Season the outside of the meat and roast in the preheated oven for 1¼ hours, basting from time to time with a little water.

3 Meanwhile, cook the rice in boiling salted water until tender. Drain and keep warm.

4 Place the stock in a pan, crumble in the bouillon cube and bring to a boil. Add the cornstarch, mixed with a little water, and cook for a few minutes more. Season the gravy and add the port or sherry, if used.

5 Place the rice on a serving dish and place the roast pork on the top. Serve with the gravy and applesauce.

Serves 6

Tip: You can substitute other nuts such as chopped walnuts for the almonds in the stuffing.

Pork with Prune and Almond Stuffing, on a bed of rice, is served with a deliciously rich wine-flavored gravy

495

1 Remove the backbones from the two pork loins **2** Cut 1½ inches of the fat from the ends of the bones **3** Trim away the sinew from between the bones **4** Bend the two cuts around to form the crown shape and secure with string **5** Place the crown in a roasting pan and brush all over with the melted butter **6** Wrap aluminum foil around the ends of the bones to prevent them from burning during the cooking **7** Heat the rest of the butter in a skillet, add the onion and celery and sauté until they are soft **8** Add the sausage meat and

cook until the fat runs out of the meat **9** Drain the excess fat from the pan **10** Add the breadcrumbs, rosemary, parsley, seasoning and stock and mix well **11** Place the stuffing mixture in the center of the crown and cover with a circle of aluminum foil to prevent drying out. Roast in the oven, allowing 30 minutes per lb. **12** Remove from the oven, discard the pieces of foil and place a cutlet cap on the end of each bone **13** Garnish roast with peas and roast potatoes and serve.

498

Crown Roast of Pork

2 loins of pork, each containing 8
  chops, (see page 497)
¼ cup melted butter
1 onion, finely chopped
2 branches celery, finely chopped
1 cup pork sausage meat
2 cups fresh breadcrumbs
1 teaspoon rosemary
2 tablespoons finely chopped
  parsley
½ teaspoon thyme
salt and pepper
¼ cup chicken stock

1 Remove the backbone from the loins. Cut 1½ inches of the fat away from the ends of the bones. Trim away the sinew from between the bones.

2 Bend the 2 loins around to form the crown and secure with string. Place the crown in a roasting pan and brush all over the outside with the melted butter. Wrap pieces of aluminum foil around the ends of the bones to prevent them from burning.

3 Preheat the oven to 350°F. Prepare the stuffing: heat the remaining butter in a skillet, add the onion and celery and sauté until they are soft.

4 Add the sausage meat and cook until all the fat has run out of the meat. Drain the excess fat from the pan.

5 Stir in the breadcrumbs, rosemary, parsley, thyme, seasoning and stock and mix.

6 Place the stuffing in the center of the crown and cover the stuffing with a circle of foil.

7 Roast the crown in the oven, allowing 30 minutes per lb.

8 Before serving, remove the pieces of foil and place a cutlet cap on the end of each bone. Serve the crown roast garnished with peas and roast potatoes.

Serves 8

Loin of Pork
Spanish-style

1 lb. navy beans, soaked overnight
2 cloves garlic, crushed
1 bay leaf
¼ cup olive oil
2 onions, sliced
2 lbs. boned loin of pork, cubed
½ lb. chorizo (spicy Spanish
  sausage) cut in ¾-inch slices
½ lb. smoked lean bacon, cut in
  small strips
3 tomatoes, skinned, seeded and
  chopped
1 tablespoon paprika
pinch saffron
4¼ cups boiling water
salt and pepper
2 cups green beans, trimmed and
  cut in 1¼-inch lengths
small green cabbage, quartered
6 eggs

1 Drain the navy beans, rinse and place in a pan. Cover with fresh cold water and add 1 clove of garlic and the bay leaf. Bring to a boil, reduce the heat and simmer for 1 hour.

2 Heat the oil in a pan and add the onion, pork, chorizo, bacon, the remaining garlic and the tomatoes. Add the paprika and saffron and cook gently for 7 or 8 minutes, stirring constantly.

3 Pour in the boiling water, season with salt and pepper and cook over low heat for 45 minutes.

4 When the navy beans have cooked for 1 hour, drain and add them to the pork and simmer for 30 minutes more, or until tender.

5 Add the green beans and cabbage and cook for 20 minutes.

6 Meanwhile, cook the eggs in boiling water for 10 minutes, cover with cold water and then remove the shells.

7 Transfer the pork mixture to a heated serving dish and garnish with the hard-boiled eggs. Serve very hot.

Serves 6

Pork Orloff

¼ cup butter
few bacon pieces
3 lbs. loin of pork
1 onion
1 carrot, sliced
1 bay leaf
bouquet garni
salt and pepper
3 tablespoons grated Parmesan
  cheese
2 tablespoons butter, cut in pieces

For the Purée:
¼ cup butter
1 tablespoon oil
4 onions, chopped
1 lb. mushroom caps, diced
⅔ cup thick white sauce
⅔ cup heavy cream
pinch grated nutmeg
3 tablespoons grated Parmesan
  cheese

1 Heat the butter in a pan, add the bacon and pork and cook until browned. Add the onion, sliced carrot, bay leaf, bouquet garni and seasoning and then cover with water. Cover the pan and cook slowly for 1¾ hours.

2 Meanwhile, make the purée. Heat the butter and oil in a pan and sauté the chopped onion for 10 minutes, without browning. Add the diced mushrooms and cook for 1 minute.

3 Strain off the fat and add the white sauce and cream. Mix well and season with salt, pepper and nutmeg. Stir in the cheese and cook for 3 minutes. Cool.

4 Preheat the oven to 450°F. Lift the pork from the pan and carve it into thick slices. Spread each slice with purée and replace the slices to resemble the original roast.

5 Cover with the remaining purée and sprinkle with the grated Parmesan cheese and the pieces of butter. Return to the oven for 5-10 minutes to brown.

Serves 6–8

Look 'n Cook Boned Blade of Pork with Apricot and Walnut Stuffing

1 Score the rind of the boned pork with a sharp knife and set the roast aside **2** Peel and finely chop the onion **3** Sauté the onion in the butter over low heat until soft and lightly golden in color **4** Finely chop the apricots and walnuts and mix with the onion, breadcrumbs, parsley and salt and pepper to taste **5** Bind with the egg and mix well **6** Place the stuffing on the inner side of the meat and press it down well **7** Roll the meat up and tie it tightly with string **8** Brush the skin all over with the oil **9** Rub the skin well with salt to ensure a crisp crackling **10** Serve the stuffed pork with boiled, sliced leeks

501

Pickled Pork with Saffron Rice

3 lbs. pork loin, boned
1 tablespoon saltpeter
1 lb. coarse salt
1 teaspoon ground ginger
salt and pepper
4 cloves
2 cups long grain rice
¼ teaspoon ground saffron
¼ cup butter

1 Buy the pork loin the day before the dish is to be served. Rub saltpeter over it. Put a layer of coarse salt in an earthenware bowl. Lay in the meat and cover with the rest of the salt. Leave it for 24 hours in a cool place.

2 Remove the pork from the salt, wash it thoroughly in cold water and dry it.

3 Preheat the oven to 375°F. Spread out a cloth and put the meat onto it, fat side down. Sprinkle with the ginger and pepper to taste. Roll it up, seasoned side inside, tying it tightly with string.

4 Using the point of a sharp knife, cut the fat in criss-cross lines forming a diamond pattern. Stud the meat with the 4 cloves and season with pepper.

5 Pour ½ cup of warm water into a roasting pan with a rack. Place the meat on the rack and roast in the oven for about 1¼ hours or until cooked through.

6 Put the rice into a pan with 5 cups cold water, the saffron and salt to taste. Cover and cook for 20 minutes, steaming covered off the heat until the rice is tender and the water absorbed. Add the butter, season with pepper and fluff up with a fork.

7 Arrange the sliced pork on the rice to serve.

Serves 8

Boned Blade of Pork with Apricot and Walnut Stuffing

4 lbs. blade or shoulder of pork, boned
1 onion, finely chopped
1 tablespoon butter
⅓ cup dried apricots, soaked in water overnight and finely chopped
12 walnut halves, finely chopped
1 cup fresh white breadcrumbs
1 tablespoon chopped parsley
salt and pepper
1 egg
1 tablespoon oil
1 teaspoon salt

1 Preheat the oven to 450°F. Score the rind of the pork with a sharp knife.

2 Sauté the onion gently in the butter until lightly golden.

3 Mix together the apricots, walnuts, onion, breadcrumbs, parsley and salt and pepper to taste. Mix in the egg.

4 Place the stuffing on the inner side of the meat. Roll up the meat and tie tightly with string. Place in a buttered roasting pan, brush with the oil and rub the salt into the skin.

5 Roast for 30 minutes or until the surface has crackled. Turn the oven to 375°F and roast for another hour.

Serves 6

Flemish Pork with Red Cabbage

2¼ lbs. pork loin
salt and pepper
pinch each cinnamon and coriander
¼ cup oil
1 small red cabbage, shredded
1 onion, chopped
1 clove garlic, finely chopped
½ cup vinegar
2 apples, peeled, cored and thinly sliced
1 tablespoon sugar
1 teaspoon chopped parsley
½ beef bouillon cube dissolved in 1¼ cups water
1 tablespoon tomato paste
2 teaspoons cornstarch, mixed with water

1 Preheat the oven to 375°F. Remove the rind from the pork and season with salt, pepper and mixed spice. Brush with oil and place on a rack in a roasting pan. Roast in the preheated oven for 1¼ hours, basting frequently with 1 cup water.

2 Place the cabbage in an earthenware bowl with the onion, garlic, vinegar and 2½ cups water. Let stand for 15 minutes.

3 Add the apples to the cabbage with the sugar and seasoning. Transfer to a stainless steel pan, bring to a boil and simmer for 20 minutes.

4 Transfer the pork to a serving dish. Surround with the cabbage in its liquid and sprinkle with parsley.

5 Pour off the fat from the roasting pan, retaining the meat juices. Add the stock and tomato paste, bring to a boil and simmer for 5 minutes. Add the cornstarch to the pan and simmer for 1 minute, stirring. Season and strain into a sauce boat to serve.

Serves 6

Tips: To save time, instead of pickling a loin of pork, you can buy a ham. If you are not a lover of red cabbage, don't ignore this recipe. You can substitute green cabbage and omit the vinegar. However, if you do use red cabbage and want to make this dish extra special, use red wine instead of water.

Pork Piedmontese

¼ cup oil
1½ lbs. lean pork, cut into cubes
2 tablespoons flour
1 tablespoon tomato paste
1¼ cups water
⅔ cup dry white wine
⅓ cup light cream
juice 1 lemon
pinch oregano
salt and pepper
3 medium zucchini

For the Stuffing:
¼ lb. calves liver
salt and pepper
2 tablespoons flour
2 tablespoons oil
1 onion, chopped
2 thin slices bacon
¾ cup mushrooms, finely sliced
1 tablespoon Parmesan cheese
¼ cup dry white wine
⅓ cup heavy cream

Pork Portuguese, served with rice pilaf, is a tasty way of serving pork in white wine with tomatoes, celery and peppers

1 Preheat the oven to 350°F. Heat the oil in a pan. Add the meat and brown for 12 minutes. Sprinkle in the flour and stir. Cook for one minute, then add the tomato paste, water and wine. Bring to a boil and simmer for 15 minutes. Stir in the cream, lemon juice and oregano. Season and transfer to a casserole. Bake in the preheated oven for one hour or until the meat is tender.

2 Meanwhile, cut the zucchini in half lengthwise. Cook them for 5 minutes in boiling salted water. Drain and keep warm.

3 If necessary remove the membrane from the liver. Cut it into small cubes and roll in seasoned flour.

4 In a separate pan, heat the oil. Add the onion and sauté until it is soft. Add the bacon, liver, mushrooms and Parmesan cheese and cook for 5 minutes on moderate heat. Pour in the wine and cream. Stir and simmer for a further 5 minutes. Check the seasoning.

5 With a spoon scoop out the seeds from the zucchini halves. Place the zucchini on a warm serving dish and spoon the stuffing mixture into the cavities. Surround with the hot pork casserole and serve.

Serves 6

Tips: You can use this tasty stuffing for other vegetables besides zucchini. Try using it in eggplants or even red and green peppers. To give it an even richer, more distinctive flavor, substitute a fortified wine such as sherry or port for the white wine.

503

Pork Paupiettes Braised in Beer

1 lb. lean loin of pork
salt and pepper
2 tablespoons fat
3 carrots
1 lb. small onions
$\frac{1}{4}$ cup flour
1 tablespoon tomato paste
1$\frac{2}{3}$ cups brown stock
1$\frac{1}{4}$ cups beer
bouquet garni

For the Stuffing:
2 tablespoons chopped onion
1 tablespoon oil
1 cup white breadcrumbs
1 teaspoon chopped parsley
pinch thyme
$\frac{1}{2}$ egg to bind
2 chopped apricots
4 chopped walnut halves
2 teaspoons butter

1 Cut the meat across the grain into 4 thin slices and pound them. Trim to approximately 5 inches × 4 inches and chop the trimmings into small pieces. Season the meat slices.

2 Prepare the stuffing. Sauté the onion in the oil until it is soft. Combine the onion with all the other ingredients and mix in the chopped pork trimmings. Spread a quarter of the stuffing down the center of each meat slice. Roll them up and tie with string.

3 Heat the fat in a pan. Add the paupiettes and lightly brown them all over. Then add the carrots and onions and continue cooking until the meat is golden all over. Remove from the heat.

4 Drain off the fat and pour 2 tablespoons into a clean pan. Add the flour and stir over low heat until you have a brown roux. Mix in the tomato paste and allow to cool. Boil the stock and add it to the pan with the beer. Bring the sauce to a boil, remove any scum, season and pour over the meat.

5 Add the bouquet garni, cover and allow to simmer on low heat for 1-1$\frac{1}{2}$ hours.

6 Remove the string and place the paupiettes on a warm serving dish. Surround with the vegetables and pour on the sauce.

Serves 4

Pork Alentago

1$\frac{1}{2}$ lbs. lean pork tenderloin, boned
$\frac{3}{4}$ cup dry white wine
2 cloves garlic, crushed
2 bay leaves
1 teaspoon paprika
salt and pepper
2 slices bacon, diced
4 slices white bread
1 clove garlic, halved
2 tablespoons oil
10 ozs. cleaned mussels or clams

1 Cut the pork into 1-inch cubes.

2 Combine the wine, garlic, bay leaves and paprika in a bowl. Season with the salt and pepper and add the pork. Cover tightly with plastic wrap or foil and refrigerate for 24 hours.

3 Fry the bacon in a heavy skillet until the fat runs out.

4 Drain the pork cubes, dry them thoroughly and brown in the bacon fat. Cover and cook over very low heat for 30 minutes.

5 Strain the marinade and add the liquid to the pan. Simmer uncovered for 20 minutes.

6 Meanwhile, remove the crusts from the bread and rub with the garlic clove. Heat the oil in a pan and sauté the bread until it is brown. Place the bread slices in a shallow casserole and keep warm.

7 Add the mussels or clams to the pork and marinade and cook thoroughly. Pour the pork and shellfish over the bread and serve.

Serves 4

Pork Canton

1$\frac{1}{2}$ lbs. lean ground pork
$\frac{1}{2}$ cup chopped onions
salt and pepper
$\frac{1}{4}$ teaspoon fresh gingerroot, minced
1 egg, beaten
2 tablespoons oil

For the Sauce:
$\frac{1}{2}$ cup chopped onion
2 branches celery, diced
2 tablespoons cornstarch
$\frac{1}{4}$ teaspoon fresh gingerroot, chopped
2 tablespoons sugar
1 tablespoon soy sauce
1 cup chicken stock
$\frac{1}{2}$ cup peach juice
$\frac{1}{4}$ cup vinegar
$\frac{1}{2}$ lb. canned peaches, drained and diced

1 Combine the pork, onion, salt, pepper and ginger in a bowl. Bind with the beaten egg.

2 Roll the ground mixture into balls approximately 1$\frac{1}{2}$ inches in diameter.

3 Heat the oil in a skillet and cook the meatballs for about 10 minutes or until done. Remove the meat from the pan and drain well.

4 Prepare the sauce. Drain all but 1 tablespoon of fat from the pan. Sauté the onion and celery in the fat until the onion is transparent.

5 Combine the remaining ingredients, except the peaches, and pour into the pan. Stir and cook until the sauce is thick and clear.

6 Finally, add the meatballs and diced peaches. Cover and simmer gently for 10 minutes to allow the sauce flavor to impregnate the meat. Serve with hot rice or noodles.

Serves 6

Pork Paupiettes Braised in Beer are stuffed with fruit, nuts and herbs and cooked in a tasty, beer-flavored stock

Oriental Pork

Sweet 'n Sour Pork

1 lb. pork tenderloin, cubed
2 tablespoons sherry
1 tablespoon soy sauce
¼ teaspoon sugar
¼-inch piece fresh gingerroot,
 grated
salt and pepper
4 branches celery, sliced
1 sweet red pepper, seeded and
 diced
8 scallions, cut into 2-inch pieces
¼ cucumber, cut into wedges
3 tablespoons oil
½ lb. pineapple chunks with juice
6 tablespoons cornstarch
¼ cup vinegar

½ cup sweet white wine
1 tablespoon brown sugar
oil for deep frying

1 Mix the pork with the sherry, soy sauce, sugar and ginger. Add pepper to taste and mix well. Marinate for 30 minutes.

2 Sauté the vegetables in the oil until soft but not brown. Drain the pineapple reserving the juice and add the chunks to the pan. Stir-fry for 2 minutes.

3 Mix 2 tablespoons of the cornstarch with the vinegar, and stir into the pan with pineapple juice, wine and sugar. Season and simmer for 2 minutes, stirring.

4 Heat the oil for deep frying. Remove the pork from the marinade and add the marinade to the sauce.

5 Coat the pork in the remaining cornstarch and fry it in the hot oil.

Pork and Bamboo Shoots. Sliced pork tenderloin stir-fried with onion and garlic in a pineapple and ginger sauce

Drain well.

6 Serve the pork on a bed of fried noodles with the sauce.

Serves 4

Pork and Bamboo Shoots

3 tablespoons oil
1 onion, chopped
1 clove garlic, crushed
1 lb. pork tenderloin, thinly sliced
½ lb. bamboo shoots, thinly sliced
1 teaspoon cornstarch
½ teaspoon ground ginger
1 teaspoon soy sauce
½ teaspoon anchovy paste
⅔ cup pineapple juice
pepper

1 Heat the oil in a skillet and sauté the onion and garlic until soft but not brown. Add the pork and stir-fry until browned.

2 Add the bamboo shoots to the pan, cover and cook gently for 10 minutes.

3 Mix the constarch, ginger, soy sauce and anchovy paste with enough pineapple juice to make a smooth paste. Add to the pan with the remaining juice and simmer gently, uncovered, for 15 minutes.

4 Season with pepper and serve with rice.

Serves 4

Sweet 'n Sour Pork — traditional Chinese Food, which is becoming increasingly popular in countries all over the world. Serve it on a bed of fried noodles, with fried rice, boiled noodles and chopped mangoes

Spareribs Tahiti

2 lbs. pork spareribs
½ cup vinegar
1¼ cups water
¾ cup catsup
¾ cup brown sugar
1½ teaspoons soy sauce
2 large pinches salt
3 tablespoons cornstarch
¼ cup water

1 Preheat the oven to 325°F. Divide the meat into individual ribs. Pour the vinegar and water over them in a roasting pan and bake for 1 hour. Skim off any fat from the liquid, strain the liquid and reserve.

2 Stir the catsup, brown sugar, soy sauce and salt into the cooking liquid. Mix the cornstarch with the 4 tablespoons of water and add to the liquid. Stir over heat to thicken.

3 Pour the sauce over the spareribs and return them to the oven to bake for 30 minutes or until browned. Serve immediately with rice.

Serves 4

Stir-fried Pork with Nuts

½ lb. pork tenderloin
4 small carrots, cut in matchstick strips
3 tablespoons oil
pinch salt
1 onion, thinly sliced
1 clove garlic, crushed
2 thin slices fresh gingerroot, peeled and finely chopped
½ red pepper, seeded and sliced
¼ cup blanched almonds or cashews
½ cup chicken stock
2 tablespoons soy sauce
1 tablespoon sherry
1½ tablespoons cornstarch

1 Cut the pork into thin slices across the grain of the meat. Blanch the carrots in boiling water for 4 minutes, refresh in cold water and drain.

2 Heat half the oil in a pan or wok. Add the pork and salt and stir-fry for 3 minutes. Remove the meat from the pan with a slotted spoon and keep warm.

3 Heat the rest of the oil in the pan. Add the onion, garlic and ginger, and stir-fry for 1 minute. Then add the pepper, carrot and nuts and stir-fry for another minute. Add the stock, soy sauce and sherry, and bring to a boil, stirring.

4 Lower the heat and return the pork to the pan. Cover and cook gently for about 5 minutes or until the pork is tender.

5 Mix the cornstarch to a paste with a little water, and add until the sauce thickens. Serve at once.

Serves 3

Pacific Pork

1½ lbs. pork tenderloin
¼ cup flour
2 tablespoons shortening or lard
1 cup pineapple juice
½ cup crushed canned pineapple
½ teaspoon each salt, pepper, ground ginger, allspice
1½ tablespoons cornstarch
2 tablespoons water

1 Preheat the oven to 350°F. Cut the tenderloin into 6 pieces, and coat them with flour.

2 Melt the fat in a skillet and brown the pork lightly. Transfer the pork to an ovenproof dish. Combine the pineapple juice and fruit, salt, pepper, ginger and allspice. Pour the mixture over the meat and bake uncovered for 45 minutes or until the meat is tender.

3 Remove the meat to a serving dish and keep warm. Pour the rest of the cooking liquid into the pan and thicken with the mixture of cornstarch and water. Pour the sauce over the meat and serve.

Serves 6

Pork Vindaye

1 lb. spare ribs or blade of pork
2 onions
2 cloves garlic
1 sweet red pepper
2 tablespoons oil
2 teaspoons vinegar
1 tablespoon curry powder
2 teaspoons ground ginger
salt
1 cup water

1 Cut the meat into large chunks or, if using spare rib chops, remove excess fat and cut them in half.

2 Finely chop the onions and garlic. Seed the red pepper and chop. Mix these together with the oil and vinegar and pound to a paste with a pestle and mortar.

3 Stir in the curry powder, ginger and a good pinch of salt. Coat the pieces of meat with this mixture and place them in a large saucepan. Pour in the water, cover, and simmer for 2 hours. Serve with golden rice — boiled with a pinch of turmeric to color it.

Serves 4

Pork Vindaye — large chunks of pork cooked gently in a spicy curry-flavored coating until succulently tender

508

Saté

This is a traditional Indonesian dish of small pork kebabs served with a spicy peanut sauce, always featured among the many accompaniments on an Indonesian table.

1 lb. pork loin
¼ cup soy sauce
¼ cup sherry
1 clove garlic, crushed
1 thin slice fresh gingerroot, finely chopped
1 teaspoon curry powder
2 tablespoons oil
⅔ cup fresh peanuts, finely chopped
1 teaspoon honey
few drops chili sauce
1 teaspoon catsup
1 teaspoon lemon juice
¼ cup peanut butter
1 teaspoon cornstarch

1 Cut the pork into 1¼-inch cubes.

Mix together the soy sauce, sherry, garlic, ginger, curry powder and oil, and marinate the pork pieces in this for 3 hours, basting from time to time.

2 Strain the meat from the marinade and thread the pieces onto kebab skewers. Broil the kebabs, turning frequently, until browned on all sides.

3 Meanwhile, pour the marinade into a saucepan and add the rest of the ingredients except the cornstarch. Heat gently, stirring to blend them into a smooth sauce. Thicken if required with the cornstarch mixed with a little water.

4 Take the cooked pork from the kebab skewers. Arrange the meat around a heated serving dish, and pour the peanut sauce into the middle. Use toothpicks to dip the meat

---

A traditional Indonesian Rice Table with the famous Saté (foreground), Indonesian Rice (center), jumbo shrimp, curried chicken and bean sprouts

pieces into the sauce. Serve with Indonesian Rice.

Serves 4

Indonesian Rice

½ cup long grain rice
pinch turmeric
2 tablespoons oil
⅓ cup fresh peanuts, skinned
1 teaspoon cumin seeds
1½ tablespoons shredded coconut
salt and pepper

1 Boil the rice in salted water with a pinch of turmeric. Rinse and drain.

2 Heat the oil in a skillet. Add the rice and stir-fry for 3 minutes. Add the other ingredients, stir well and fry for another 3 minutes.

Serves 4

2 eggs
salt and pepper
pinch cayenne pepper
$\frac{1}{2}$ cup grated Cheddar cheese

1 After making the pie crust, allow it to stand for 20 minutes.

2 Prick the sausages and broil them for 4 minutes to brown the outsides.

3 Preheat the oven to 425°F. Grease an 8-inch flan pan. Roll out the dough to $\frac{1}{8}$ inch thickness and use it to line the flan pan. Prick the dough with a fork and bake empty in the preheated oven for 12 minutes. Cool. Reduce the oven temperature to 350°F.

4 Combine the white sauce and the eggs, season to taste and add half of the cheese. Pour the mixture into the flan and arrange the sausages on top. Sprinkle with the rest of the cheese and bake for 30 minutes.

Serves 4

Sausage Cheese Flan combines hearty sausages with a light and tasty cheese mixture, to make a perfect supper

Sausage Pie

two 8-inch pie crusts
2 tablespoons shortening
$\frac{1}{2}$ lb. beef and pork link sausages
3 eggs
$\frac{1}{4}$ lb. pork sausage meat
1 tablespoon chopped parsley
1 onion, chopped
3 tablespoons fresh white breadcrumbs
2 tablespoons brandy or sherry
salt and pepper
pinch paprika
pinch mace or nutmeg
pinch garlic salt

1 Preheat the oven to 375°F. Roll out the dough to $\frac{1}{8}$-inch thickness and divide in two. Grease an 8-inch

pie plate with the shortening and line the bottom with one piece of the dough. Trim, and prick the base with a fork.

2 Broil the sausages for 3 minutes to brown the outsides. Cut into thick chunks and cool.

3 Beat 2 of the eggs and combine with the sausage meat, parsley, onion, breadcrumbs, brandy or sherry, salt, pepper, paprika, mace or nutmeg, and garlic salt. Blend in the chunks of sausage and place the mixture in the pie plate.

4 Cover with the remaining piece of dough. Beat the remaining egg and use to glaze the surface of the pie. Decorate with pastry trimmings and brush again with the beaten egg. Flute the edges of the pie with a fork to seal.

5 Bake in the preheated oven for 40 minutes and serve hot or cold.

Serves 6

517

Sausage and Mushroom Pie

1 lb. pork sausages
¼ cup butter
2 onions, sliced
⅓ cup flour
1¼ cups milk
1¼ cups stock
salt and pepper
1 cup sliced mushrooms
¾ lb. puff pastry
1 egg, beaten

1 Preheat the oven to 400°F.

2 Prick the sausages and broil them until golden.

3 Melt the butter in a pan and sauté the onions and mushrooms for 5 minutes. Stir in the flour and cook for 1 minute more.

4 Gradually blend in the milk and stock and bring to a boil. Stir until thickened and then add the seasoning.

5 Place the sausages in a pie plate and pour on the mushroom sauce. Roll out the puff pastry, cover the dish with it and trim off any excess pastry. Brush the top with the beaten egg and bake the pie for 40 minutes. Serve piping hot.

Serves 6

Tip: This pie can be stored in the freezer. Freeze it uncooked, and when ready to use, cook in an oven preheated to 425°F. for 45-50 minutes.

Vary the vegetables used in the sauce — try sweet corn, carrots or peas.

Sausage Rolls

1 lb. pork sausage meat
1 lb. puff pastry
1 egg, beaten

Sausage and Mushroom Pie holds a rich, chunky filling in a creamy sauce, topped with a light pastry shell

1 Preheat the oven to 425°F.

2 Roll the sausage meat into a long strip 24 inches long.

3 Roll out the pastry to ⅛-inch thickness and cut it into 2 strips 12 inches × 4 inches. Cut the sausage meat in half and place one half on each strip of pastry. Brush the edge of the pastry with beaten egg and fold over. Crimp the edge with a fork. Cut into pieces about 2½ inches long and brush with beaten egg.

4 Place the rolls on a greased baking sheet and bake for 15 minutes. Serve hot.

Makes 16 sausage rolls

Savory Bouchées

1 small onion, chopped
2 tablespoons oil
1 clove garlic, chopped
½ lb. pork sausage meat
¼ cup dry sherry
salt and pepper
1 tablespoon chopped parsley
1 lb. puff pastry
2 tablespoons shortening
1 egg, beaten
6 stuffed olives

1 Preheat the oven to 425°F.

2 Sauté the onion in the oil for 3 minutes. Add the garlic and meat and cook for 15 minutes, covered with a lid. Add the sherry, seasoning and parsley and keep the mix-

Sausage Rolls, left, and Savory Bouchées, right, are ideal party dishes, tasty and neat for eating with your fingers

ture hot while making the bouchée cases.

3 Roll out the pastry to ⅛-inch thickness. Cut 12 rounds using a 2½-inch cutter. Grease a baking sheet with the shortening and place 6 rounds on the sheet. Press a 1½-inch cutter into the center of the remaining rounds to give 6 rings. Dampen the edge of the rounds with water and place the rings on top. Press together to seal. Brush the tops with the beaten egg and bake in the oven for 15 minutes until golden and puffy.

4 Fill the bouchées with the sausage mixture, top each one with a

stuffed olive and serve hot.

Makes 6

Easter Pie

4 cups flour
9 eggs
½ lb. butter, softened
1½ lbs. pork sausage meat
1 tablespoon chopped parsley
½ teaspoon salt
pinch freshly ground black pepper
1 teaspoon mixed mace and coriander
pinch cayenne pepper
1 egg yolk, beaten
2 tablespoons shortening

1 Form the flour into a ring on the work surface. Break in 2 eggs and

add the softened butter. Mix together with the fingers, adding 1-2 tablespoons water, and knead the dough for 2-3 minutes until smooth. Roll the dough into a ball and place it in a cool place or in the refrigerator for 30 minutes.

2 Cook 5 of the eggs in boiling water for 10 minutes, drain and cover them with cold water to cool.

3 In a bowl, combine the sausage meat with 2 of the eggs and the parsley, salt, pepper, mixed spice and cayenne. Mix well.

4 Shell the hard-boiled eggs to prevent them from discoloring; cover them with cold water until needed.

5 Halve the dough and roll out each piece to a rectangle about ½ inch thick.

6 Place half of the meat mixture along the center of one piece of dough and arrange the hard-boiled eggs along the top of the meat. Cover the eggs with the rest of the meat mixture, making sure the eggs are well covered at the sides.

7 Brush the border of dough around the meat with the egg yolk and place the second piece of dough over the top. Trim off the excess dough and crimp the edges of the parcel with the fingers to seal. Pinch together at intervals to produce a fluted edge. Preheat the oven to 350°F.

8 Brush the whole parcel with more egg yolk. Roll out the dough trimmings to ⅛ inch thickness and cut out decorative leaf shapes. Arrange some into roses and place the roses and the leaves on the top of the Easter Pie. Brush the decorations with more beaten egg yolk.

9 Grease a baking sheet with the shortening and place the pie on the sheet. Bake in the preheated oven for 1 hour. Allow to cool and decorate with sprigs of parsley. Serve cold.

Serves 8

Look 'n Cook Easter Pie

1 The ingredients **2** Form the flour into a continuous ring on the work surface. Break in 2 of the eggs **3** Add the softened butter and a little water and mix with the fingers. Knead the dough for 2-3 minutes until smooth.

Roll the dough into a ball and place it in the refrigerator for 30 minutes. Meanwhile, cook 5 of the eggs in boiling water for 10 minutes. Drain and cover with cold water to cool **4** Combine the sausage meat, 2 of the eggs,

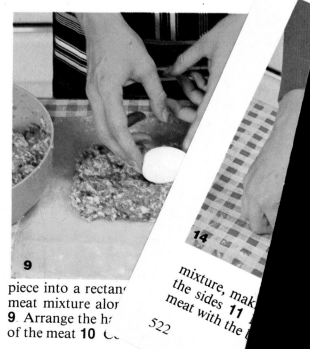

parsley, salt, pepper, mixed spice and cayenne **5** Mix the ingredients well **6** Shell the eggs and, to prevent them from discoloring, cover them with cold water until needed **7** Cut the dough in half and roll out each

piece into a rectan[...] meat mixture alor[...] **9**. Arrange the h[...] of the meat **10** C[...]

mixture, mak[...] the sides **11** [...] meat with the [...]

522

Look 'n Cook Easter Pie (continued)

ing sure that the eggs are well covered at
Brush the border of dough around the
beaten egg yolk **12** Cover the meat with the second piece of dough **13** Trim the edges of the dough with a knife **14** and **15** Crimp the edges with the fingers to seal and then pinch the dough together at

intervals to produce a fluted edge **16** Brush all over the outside of the pie with the egg yolk **17** Roll out the dough trimmings to $\frac{1}{8}$ inch thickness and cut out decorative leaf shapes. Form some of the leaves into roses and arrange the roses and leaves on the top of the pie. Brush with egg yolk **18** Bake the pie for 1 hour and then cool. Transfer to a serving dish and decorate the dish with sprigs of parsley. Serve cold

All about
Ham and Bacon

Ham steaks with pineapple

Who could resist a delicious pearly pink, succulent ham as in our cover picture? In this volume we deal with ham, ham shank and bacon and give you exciting recipes for all three. But first we must distinguish between them.

Both the shank and ham come from the hind leg of the pig, whereas bacon comes from the body. Ham is removed from the hind leg before salting and is then cured. Some hams such as Parma ham (prosciutto) are smoked and then eaten raw. Bacon is the salted flesh which may be smoked or unsmoked. Smoked bacon keeps longer than the unsmoked types.

Choosing Ham and Bacon

When buying cooked sliced ham, it should have pink-colored flesh and very white fat. Make sure that it is moist and not dried out. Bacon should smell pleasant and have firm white fat and pink lean flesh. If unsmoked, the rind should be pale and creamy; if smoked, a golden-brown.

Storing Bacon and Ham

Store bacon and ham in a refrigerator. Always wrap it in foil or plastic wrap to keep it fresh. Wax paper is not very satisfactory as it will allow the bacon to dry out. You can store bacon and ham for up to a week in the refrigerator. You can, of course, freeze it.

Types of Ham

There are many different types and varieties of ham which you can buy, both imported and home-produced. You can buy country hams such as the Virginia and Kentucky varieties. These may be cured in many ways. Of course, there are also the smoked hams which are thinly sliced and eaten raw such as the famous Italian Parma ham (prosciutto) and the French Bayonne ham, which is salted and smoked with herbs.

Glazes for Fresh Hams: Your ham will taste even more delicious if you make a glaze for it. Boil the ham for half the cooking time, then bake in the oven and, half an hour before removing the ham, score the fat in a diamond pattern. Stud each diamond with a clove and baste with a glaze. You can make a glaze with a little honey mixed with orange juice and grated rind or pineapple juice and brown sugar. You can even add some wine or cider and spices such as ginger, allspice or ground cloves. Maple syrup or honey mixed with spices makes a sweeter alternative.

Cuts of Bacon

These tend to vary and may be either smoked or unsmoked. Although most people tend to associate bacon slices with breakfast-time and the delicious aroma of sizzling bacon wafting around the house, bacon can be served in a variety of ways and in different dishes. It can be fried, broiled, roasted or boiled depending on the cut. The breakfast slices are back, streaky or middle cut, all of which may be smoked or fresh. Back is the leanest, streaky is streaked through with fat, while middle cuts consist of long slices of streaky and back combined. Collar and hock are the most common cuts of bacon. They tend to be fairly inexpensive and are suitable for boiling. Collar can also be roasted or braised. Usually they are boned and prepared by the butcher or supermarket and therefore there is little effort involved in cooking them. They can be eaten either hot or cold and there is very little waste on them.

Hams are both economical and versatile. Don't fall into the trap of thinking that you can only serve them cold with salad. They can be served hot or cold with a variety of flavorings, glazes and sauces — fruity ones are especially good. Syrup or honey mixed with fruit juices and spices makes a delicious glaze, and should give the meat itself a subtle flavor.

Hams

Ham with Cranberries

4-lb. fresh cured or cooked ham
cloves for decoration

For the Glaze:
$\frac{1}{4}$ lb. butter
$\frac{1}{3}$ cup corn syrup
1 teaspoon cinnamon
pinch chili powder
1 teaspoon prepared mustard

For the Cranberry Sauce:
3 cups cranberries
2 tablespoons brown sugar
$\frac{3}{4}$ cup water
pinch ground ginger
1 teaspoon cornstarch

1 Soak the ham in cold water overnight. Drain, place in a large saucepan and cover with water. Bring to a boil, then simmer for about $1\frac{1}{4}$ hours. (This step may be eliminated if ham is cooked.)

2 Remove the ham from the pan and carefully peel off the skin and trim any excess fat. With a knife, make a criss-cross pattern across the fat. Place a clove in the center of each diamond.

3 Preheat the oven to 350°F.

4 Make the glaze. Place all the ingredients except the mustard in a pan and bring to a boil. Boil the glaze for 2-3 minutes, then remove from the heat and add the mustard.

5 Brush the glaze over the ham so that it is coated evenly. Place the ham in a shallow roasting pan and bake in the oven for about 45 minutes until crisp and golden-brown.

6 Meanwhile, make the cranberry sauce. Place the cranberries, sugar, ⅔ cup of the water and ginger in a pan and bring to a boil. Boil for 5 minutes. Mix the cornstarch with the remaining water and stir into the sauce. Boil for another 3-4 minutes until the mixture is clear.

7 Serve the glazed ham hot or cold with the cranberry sauce and cole-slaw.

Serves 8

Glazed Ham with Cranberries has a crisp, golden exterior, studded with cloves, and is served with fresh cranberry sauce

Maple Baked Ham

3-lb. cooked or cured ham
1 onion
6 peppercorns
1 bay leaf
cloves for decoration
⅓ cup maple syrup
½ teaspoon ginger
pinch nutmeg
pinch allspice

1 Place the ham in a large pan, cover with cold water and bring to a boil. Remove the scum from the top and add the onion, peppercorns and bay leaf. Simmer, covered with a lid, for 1½ hours. Cool in the liquid, then drain. (This step may be eliminated if ham is cooked.)

2 Remove the skin and score the fat in a criss-cross pattern. Stud each diamond shape with a clove.

3 Preheat the oven to 375°F.

4 Mix together the maple syrup and spices. Place the ham in a roasting pan and brush with the glaze.

5 Bake for about 1 hour until the ham is crisp and well glazed.

Serves 8-10

Cinnamon Ham with Apricots

4-lb. cooked ham
½ lb. canned apricot halves, drained

For the Glaze:
1 teaspoon prepared mustard
¼ cup softened butter
3 tablespoons honey
pinch ground cinnamon
pinch ground ginger
2 tablespoons brandy

1 Preheat the oven to 375°F. Combine the mustard with the softened butter, honey, cinnamon, ginger and brandy. Place the ham in a roasting pan, spread the glazing mixture over the surface of the meat and place in the oven for 5-8 minutes to caramelize the glaze.

2 Remove the ham from the oven and decorate with the drained apricot halves. Serve cold with a salad of lettuce, celery and apple mixed with a yogurt dressing.

Serves 8

Tip: A cooked ham can be glazed in a number of ways and is therefore a very versatile dish to prepare. The basic glaze can be varied to include the ingredients you have or the flavors you prefer. In this recipe, for instance, try using a different spirit and change the fruit used for decoration — try peaches, oranges or papayas.

Ham with Orange

15-lb. fresh or cooked ham
24 cloves
½ cup brown sugar
pinch ground cinnamon
2 teaspoons dry mustard
2¼ cups white wine
bouquet garni

2 onions, sliced
2 carrots, sliced
¼ cup tomato paste
1 tablespoon cider vinegar
3 tablespoons cornstarch
⅔ cup water
4 oranges, sliced
8 candied cherries

1 Cover the ham with cold water and leave to soak for 6 hours.

2 Drain and rinse the ham and place it in a large pan. Cover with cold water and bring to a boil, removing any scum as it rises. Simmer for 3½ hours or until tender. (If ham is cooked, steps 1 and 2 may be eliminated.)

3 Peel off the skin and place the ham in a deep roasting pan. Make sure ham is cool.

4 Preheat the oven to 350°F. Make regular criss-cross lines, 1 inch apart, on the surface of the ham and press a clove into each intersection.

5 Mix the sugar, cinnamon and mustard and sprinkle this mixture over the ham. Place in the oven for 1 hour.

6 After the ham has baked for 20 minutes, pour on the wine and add the bouquet garni, onions, carrots, tomato paste and vinegar and return the pan to the oven for the remaining 40 minutes. Baste the meat frequently to prevent it from drying out.

7 Lift the ham from the pan and keep it warm while preparing the sauce. Pour the contents of the roasting pan into a saucepan and boil for 10 minutes. Thicken with the cornstarch mixed with the water.

8 Place the ham on a serving plate and decorate it with the orange slices and cherries. Decorate the end of the bone with a paper cap. Strain the sauce and serve it with the ham.

Serves 25-30

Tip: Score the oranges from one end to the other before slicing: this will give the slices a decorative serrated edge.

Ham Mousse

2 tablespoons unflavored gelatin
2 tablespoons medium sherry
⅓ cup stock
1 cup ground cooked ham
⅔ cup white sauce
salt and pepper
pinch grated nutmeg
pinch paprika
⅔ cup heavy cream
1 tablespoon oil

1 Place the gelatin in a bowl, pour in the sherry and soak for a few minutes to soften the gelatin.

2 Bring the stock to a boil and pour it over the gelatin. Stir until dissolved.

3 Stir the ham and the white sauce into the gelatin and stock mixture and then season with salt and pepper. Add a pinch of grated nutmeg and paprika.

4 Transfer the mixture to a pan and bring to a boil. Simmer for 5 minutes, then cool.

5 Once the ham mixture is cold, whip the cream until it is stiff and fold it in.

6 Oil a 3¾-cup mold and place the ham mixture in it. Place in the refrigerator for at least 2 hours to chill it thoroughly.

7 Turn the mousse onto a flat plate and serve with a salad of lettuce and avocado, garnished with orange and grapefruit sections.

Serves 4

Ham with Orange. What an impressive centerpiece for a buffet or reception — and one you can easily make yourself

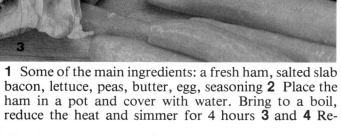

1 Some of the main ingredients: a fresh ham, salted slab bacon, lettuce, peas, butter, egg, seasoning **2** Place the ham in a pot and cover with water. Bring to a boil, reduce the heat and simmer for 4 hours **3** and **4** Re-

move the brown ends of the lettuce stalks. Peel the carrots and onions. Cut the bacon into strips and cut the carrots into matchsticks. Blanch the bacon strips **5** and **6** Immerse each head of lettuce in boiling water for 2

Look 'n Cook Ham Ile de France (continued)

minutes. Drain. Holding them by the stalks, plunge each one into cold water 3 or 4 times to remove any sand. Drain again, press the leaves together and tie with string

7 Fry the bacon in a flameproof dish. Arrange the lettuce on top. Cover and cook for 45 minutes **8** Cook the carrots and onions separately in butter and water

10

11

12

9 Cook the peas in boiling water, flavored with butter, savory, salt and sugar **10** When the ham is cooked, drain it, place it on a board and with a large knife, peel off the skin **11** and **12** Remove the excess fat from the meat. Place the leg in a large roasting pan and pour on the Madeira. Make sure the whole leg has a coating of the wine before baking. Place in the oven to glaze **13** While the ham is cooking, baste it frequently with

13

14

15

16

the Madeira. When ready it should have a golden glaze
14 Halve the lettuces lengthwise. Remove the stalks carefully with a knife and fold each portion in half
15 Heat the ham juices with half the cream. Whisk the

remaining cream with the egg yolk and add this to the sauce **16** Arrange the vegetables around the ham and serve the peas and sauce separately

Ham Ile de France

one 13-lb. fresh or cooked ham
6 heads lettuce
1½ lbs. carrots, peeled
½ lb. bacon slab
¼ lb. butter
1 lb. small onions
salt and pepper
1 tablespoon sugar
2 lbs. peas
pinch savory
1¼ cups Madeira
1 cup + 2 tablespoons light
  cream
1 egg yolk

1 Cover the ham with water and simmer for 4 hours. (This step may be eliminated if a cooked ham is used.)

2 Trim the stalks of the lettuces. Cut the carrots into matchsticks.

Cut the bacon into strips and blanch in boiling water for 30 seconds. Rinse and drain.

3 Plunge each head of lettuce into boiling water for 2 minutes and drain. Holding the stalk, dunk each into cold water 3-4 times to remove sand. Press the leaves together firmly and tie with string.

4 Melt 2 tablespoons butter in a pan. Fry the bacon for 5 minutes, place the lettuces on top, just cover with water and simmer, covered, for 45 minutes.

5 Place the carrots and onions in separate pans and just cover them with water. Add seasoning, 1 teaspoon sugar and 2 tablespoons butter to each pan. Cover and simmer,

Cold Glazed Ham is surrounded by orange cups stuffed with rice, olives and fresh fruit in a tangy vinaigrette dressing

until the water has evaporated. Keep warm. Cook the peas in water seasoned as for the carrots and onions, but add the savory.

6 Preheat the oven to 375°F. When the ham is cooked, skin it and remove the excess fat. Sprinkle it with Madeira and glaze in the oven for 30 minutes, basting frequently.

7 Drain and cut the lettuces in half lengthwise. Remove the stalks and fold each portion in half. Place the meat on a serving dish with the lettuce, carrots and onions. Drain the peas and bacon and combine in a bowl.

8 Pour the ham juices into a pan, add half the cream and boil for 2 minutes. Blend the remaining cream with the egg yolk and gradually stir it into the pan. Season, strain and serve with the meat and vegetables.
Serves 12-14

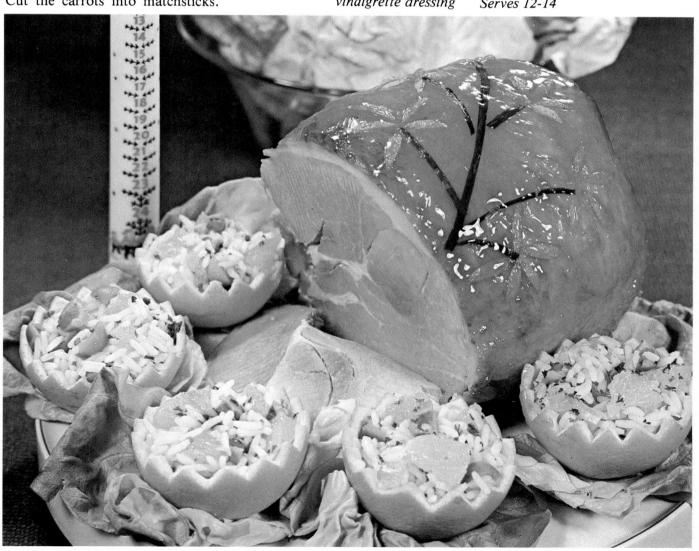

Fiesta Ham

4-lb. fresh or cooked ham
1¾ cups apple juice
1 onion, finely sliced
freshly ground black pepper
2 tablespoons honey
3 dessert apples
2 tablespoons brown sugar
2 tablespoons butter
2 tablespoons oil
12 stuffed green olives

1 Cover the ham with cold water and leave to soak for 12 hours. Drain.

2 Place the ham in a pan and pour on the apple juice. Add the onion and pepper, cover and simmer, allowing 20 minutes per lb. plus 20 minutes.(Steps 1 and 2 may be eliminated if cooked ham is used.)

3 Preheat the oven to 425°F. Remove the ham from the pan and allow to cool slightly. Remove the skin and score the fat diagonally in a diamond pattern. Place the ham in a shallow ovenproof dish and brush the surface with the honey. Place in the preheated oven for about 15 minutes until golden brown.

4 Core the apples and, leaving them unpeeled, cut them across in rings. Toss the apple rings in the sugar.

5 Heat the butter and oil in a pan and fry the apple rings, turning once, until golden.

6 Place the ham on a serving dish and surround it with the apple rings. Place each olive on a toothpick and push the sticks into the meat in the center of the scored diamond shapes. Serve.

Serves 10

Tips: Apples combine well with other fruit such as blackberries, currants and black cherries, so try reducing the amount of apple juice and making up the difference with another fruit juice; add a pinch of cinnamon, too. And for more festive occasions, try adding 2 tablespoons apple brandy to the juice.

Mustard Ham

one 12-lb. cooked ham
1¼ cups stock
⅔ cup pineapple juice
¼ cup dry mustard
1 tablespoon cornstarch
2 egg yolks
2 tablespoons Dijon mustard
1½ cups fine dry breadcrumbs

1 Remove the rind and the most of the fat from the ham and place the meat in a roasting pan. Set the oven temperature to 425°F.

2 In a bowl, mix the dry mustard, cornstarch, egg yolks and Dijon mustard and beat until smooth. Spread the mixture over the top and sides of the ham.

3 Sprinkle on the breadcrumbs and place the ham in the oven for about 30 minutes or until the top is browned and crisp.

Serves 24

Tips: This recipe is sufficient for a large number of people, but if your numbers are smaller, cut the finished ham into 3 and freeze the smaller pieces. If well sealed, the hams should keep for up to 6 months.

Ham Port Maillot

one 5-lb. fresh or cooked ham
salt and pepper
1 lb. carrots, cut in sticks 1½ × ¼ inch
1 lb. turnips, cut in sticks 1½ × ¼ inch
1 lb. green beans
1 lb. frozen peas
1 tablespoon sugar
1¼ cups medium sherry
¼ lb. butter

1 Cover the ham with cold water and soak for 6 hours, changing the water frequently.

2 Place the ham in a large pan and cover generously with cold water. Simmer, allowing 40 minutes per 2 lbs. (These first two steps may be eliminated if cooked ham is used.)

3 Bring a large pan of salted water to a boil, add the carrots and cook for 8 minutes. Add the turnips and cook for a further 5 minutes. Add the beans and peas. When all the vegetables are cooked, drain them, run cold water over them and drain again.

4 Preheat the oven to 375°F.

5 Peel off the rind and place the ham in a deep ovenproof dish. Sprinkle it with the sugar and place in the oven for 10 minutes to caramelize the sugar. Pour on the sherry and return to the oven for a further 10-15 minutes, basting occasionally and taking care not to let it burn.

6 Meanwhile, melt the butter in a pan and add the drained vegetables, salt and pepper. Heat through, stirring from time to time.

7 Place the ham on a large serving dish, with the vegetables. Pour the sauce from the dish into a sauce boat and serve hot.

Serves 10–12

Cold Glazed Ham

1¼ cups water
2 tablespoons unflavored gelatin
2 tablespoons sugar
1 tablespoon port
salt and pepper
4-lb. cooked ham
1 green leek leaf
4 oranges
4½ cups cooked rice
1 small onion, chopped
8 stuffed green olives chopped
1 teaspoon chopped parsley
2 tablespoons vinaigrette dressing
6 lettuce leaves

1 Make the aspic: boil the water and remove the pan from the heat. Dissolve the gelatin and sugar in the water. Add the port, season and cool. Brush the ham with half the aspic and allow it to set.

2 Scald the leek leaf and cut it into strips. Remove the skin from one orange and cut out 25 small petal shapes. Dip these in the remaining aspic and decorate the ham with a floral pattern. Allow to set before recoating the meat.

3 Making zig-zag incisions, cut 3 oranges into halves. Remove the fruit and white flesh from the skins. Dice the fruit and combine it with the rice, onion, olives, seasoning and parsley. Toss this mixture in the vinaigrette and spoon it into the orange halves.

4 Place the ham on a bed of lettuce leaves. Surround with the orange salads and serve.

Serves 6

Glazed Ham with Pineapple

3-lb. cooked or fresh ham, halved
bouquet garni
½ cup brown sugar

Glazed Ham with Pineapple cleverly imitates the real fruit and makes a tasty, attractive dish for buffet parties

1 tablespoon prepared mustard
¼ lb. butter
1 teaspoon combined allspice and coriander
salt and pepper
cloves for decoration
2 canned pineapple rings
½ lb. canned pineapple chunks, drained

For the Sauce:
¼ cup sugar
¼ cup vinegar
⅓ cup medium sherry
1¼ cups beef stock
⅔ cup pineapple juice
1 tablespoon rum
6 coriander seeds, crushed
2 teaspoons cornstarch
⅓ cup water

1 Drain and wrap each ham in a piece of cheesecloth. Secure with string. Place them in a large pot and cover with water. Add the bouquet garni, bring to a boil and simmer for 1 hour. Remove from the heat and allow the meat to cool in the liquid. (This step may be eliminated if cooked ham is used.)

2 Blend the sugar, mustard, butter, mixed spice and seasoning in a bowl.

3 Drain and dry the hams. Spread them with the glaze and, with a knife, make a lattice pattern all over. Stud each intersection of lines with a clove. Preheat oven to 375°F.

4 Place them in a roasting tray and braise in the preheated oven for 20 minutes or until the glaze is golden.

5 While the ham is baking, prepare the sauce. Boil the sugar and vinegar, stirring all the time until the sugar has caramelized. Still stirring, add the sherry, stock, pineapple juice, rum, coriander seeds and seasoning. Boil for 10 minutes and thicken with the cornstarch mixed with the water.

6 Remove the ham from the oven. Heat the tip of a skewer over a flame and singe the lines of the pattern to a dark brown. (This is optional and purely for decoration.)

7 Place a pineapple ring on top of each ham, surround with pineapple pieces and serve with the hot sauce.

Serves 6

Ham with Chablis

1½ teaspoons butter
four ¼-inch thick slices cooked
  ham
¾ cup Chablis or other dry white
  wine
3¾ cups trimmed and finely sliced
  mushrooms
1 clove garlic, chopped
2 shallots, chopped
salt and pepper
1 cup sour cream

1 Preheat the oven to 400°F.

2 Butter an ovenproof dish and
place the slices of ham in it. Pour in
¼ cup of the Chablis, cover the dish
and place in the oven for 10 minutes.

3 Place the mushrooms, garlic and
shallots in a sauté pan, pour on the
rest of the wine and season. Bring
quickly to a boil, then simmer for
10 minutes.

4 Add the sour cream and boil for
5 minutes.

5 Remove the ham from the oven
and add the cooking juices to the
mushrooms. Boil the sauce again
for 5 minutes.

6 Place the slices of ham in a deep
serving dish, pour on the sauce and
serve hot.

Serves 4

Cranberry Glazed Ham

2 tablespoons melted butter
2 teaspoons prepared mustard
black pepper
4 ham steaks
1 cup cranberries
1 cup sugar
grated rind and juice 1 orange

1 Mix the butter, mustard and
pepper. Brush the steaks with the
mixture and broil on one side for 5
minutes. Turn over, brush again
and broil until tender.

2 Mix the cranberries, sugar and
orange rind and juice in a pan. Let

*Ham Florentine. The slices of
ham surround a spinach and
cream filling and are served with a
rich, Madeira-flavored sauce*

stand for 5 minutes.

3 Simmer the cranberries gently
for 5 minutes or until they pop.

4 Garnish the ham with the cranberries and serve with noodles.

Serves 4

Ham Florentine

2 tablespoons oil
¼ cup butter
1 carrot, diced
1 onion, chopped
2 slices of lean bacon, cut in pieces
2 tablespoons flour
1¼ cups chicken stock
½ cup Madeira
salt and pepper
pinch thyme
1 bay leaf
4 lbs. spinach, cooked and
  chopped
½ cup heavy cream
6 thick slices cooked ham

1 Heat the oil with half the butter
and sauté the carrot, onion and
bacon until slightly browned.
Sprinkle in the flour and cook for 2
minutes more, stirring. Mix in the
stock and Madeira, season and add
the thyme and bay leaf. Cover and
cook for 25 minutes.

2 Preheat the oven to 400°F. Mix
the spinach with the cream and seasoning. Divide the spinach between
the slices of ham and roll them up.
Place in an ovenproof dish greased
with the rest of the butter.

3 Strain the sauce and pour half
over the rolls. Place in the oven for
10 minutes, then serve with the rest
of the sauce.

Serves 6

*Ham with Chablis is expensive to
make but never fails to impress
your guests at that special
occasion or dinner*

536

Ham and Leek Mornay

4 young leeks
4 large slices ham
2 tablespoons butter
1¼ cups white sauce
1 cup grated Cheddar cheese
salt and pepper

1 Preheat the oven to 375°F. Trim and remove the outer leaves of the leeks. Cut off the green part and cook the white part for 15 minutes in boiling salted water.

2 Roll a slice of ham around each leek. Grease a shallow ovenproof casserole dish with half the butter, and place the leeks inside. Add ¾ cup of the cheese to the white sauce and season it.

3 Pour the cheese sauce over the leeks. Sprinkle with the remaining cheese and dot with the rest of the butter.

4 Bake in the preheated oven for 15 minutes and serve.

Serves 4

Ham and Apple Casserole

¼ cup butter
2 onions, sliced
2 apples, peeled, cored and sliced
4 ham steaks
¼ cup flour
1¼ cups cider
⅔ cup chicken stock
salt and pepper
pinch ground cloves
½ teaspoon dry mustard
2 cups canned corn, drained
½ cup raisins
1½ cups mushrooms, washed and sliced

1 Preheat the oven to 375°F. Melt the butter in a pan. Sauté the onions and apples until soft. Add the ham slices and brown on both sides. Transfer the ham to a flame-proof casserole.

2 Add the flour to the pan and stir over low heat for 2 minutes. Add the cider and stock and bring to a boil, stirring all the time.

3 Simmer and add the seasoning, mustard, corn, raisins and mushrooms. Cook for 1 more minute and pour the contents of the pan into the casserole dish. Cover and cook in the oven for 45 minutes or until well cooked.

Serves 4

Ham Jambalaya

¼ cup oil
1 lb. cooked ham, diced
1 onion, finely chopped
2 cloves garlic, crushed
1 tomato, peeled, seeded, and chopped
2 cups long grain rice
3 cups water
1 chicken bouillon cube
pinch turmeric
salt and pepper
14 ozs. canned pineapple chunks with their juice
1 cup peeled shrimp
1 egg
⅔ cup fine dry breadcrumbs
2 tablespoons butter

1 Heat the oil in a saucepan, add the ham and fry gently for 5 minutes. Add the onion, garlic and tomato and sauté for 5 more minutes. Add the rice, water, stock cube, turmeric, salt and pepper.

2 Drain the pineapple pieces, and retain ⅔ cup of the juice. Add this to the pan.

3 Bring to a boil, cover and cook gently for 15 minutes.

4 Stir in the shrimp and heat through. Check the seasoning. Place the rice on a serving dish.

5 Dry the pineapple pieces. Beat the egg. Dip the pineapple in the egg and roll each piece in the breadcrumbs.

6 Melt the butter in a skillet, add the pineapple pieces and fry until golden on both sides.

7 Spoon the pineapple onto the rice and serve.

Serves 6

Ham with Wine and Tomato

¼ cup butter
6 large slices cooked ham
6 shallots, chopped
⅓ cup dry white wine
4 tomatoes, skinned, seeded and chopped
2 teaspoons tomato paste
salt and pepper
⅔ cup heavy cream
1 sprig parsley

1 Preheat the oven to 375°F. Butter a small baking dish. Roll the ham slices into cylinders and place them side by side in the dish. Dot the ham with 1 tablespoon of butter and place it in the oven for 15 minutes or until heated through.

2 Meanwhile, gently melt the remaining butter in a skillet and sauté the shallots for 3 minutes.

3 Add the wine and boil for 2 minutes before adding the tomatoes and tomato paste. Season. Allow the sauce to boil for 5 more minutes while gradually stirring in the cream. Check the seasoning.

4 Pour the sauce over the ham, and garnish with the parsley.

Serves 6

Ham with Wine and Tomato is served with a quickly prepared onion and tomato sauce which is enriched with wine and cream

Ham and Olives en Croûte

2-lb. fresh ham, soaked overnight
1 lb. frozen puff pastry, thawed
2 tablespoons brown sugar
2 teaspoons French-style mustard
8 stuffed green olives, chopped
a little beaten egg

1 Place the soaked ham in a saucepan. Cover with cold water, bring to a boil and simmer for 1 hour.

2 Remove the ham from the pan and cool slightly. Remove the skin and excess fat and allow to cool completely.

3 Preheat the oven to 425°F. Roll the pastry out to a circle large enough to wrap the ham.

4 Mix the sugar, mustard and olives and spread on top of the ham. Place it sugar side down on the pastry. Fold the pastry up over the ham, sealing the seams together with beaten egg.

5 Place the ham, seams downward, on a flat baking sheet. Make a small hole in the top and decorate with leaves made from pastry trimmings. Brush with egg.

6 Bake for 25-30 minutes, until the pastry is golden.

Serves 6

Ham and Olives en Croûte proves how versatile ham can be, and looks and tastes good as well as being economical

Ham and Chestnuts en Croûte

3-lb. fresh ham, soaked overnight, or cooked ham
1 tablespoon butter
1 onion, chopped
1 cup canned unsweetened chestnut purée
$\frac{1}{4}$ cup crunchy peanut butter
$\frac{1}{4}$ teaspoon chopped fresh thyme
pinch ground cloves and allspice together
salt and pepper
2 teaspoons honey
2 eggs, beaten
1$\frac{1}{2}$ lb. frozen puff pastry, thawed

1 Place the soaked ham in a saucepan. Cover with cold water, bring to a boil and simmer for 1$\frac{1}{2}$ hours. (This step may be eliminated if a cooked ham is used).

2 Remove the ham from the pan. Cool. Remove the skin and excess fat and cool completely.

3 Preheat the oven to 425°F. Melt the butter in a small pan and saute the onion until soft. Drain and mix with the chestnut purée, peanut butter, thyme, spice, seasoning, honey and half of the beaten egg to bind.

4 Roll the pastry out to a circle large enough to wrap the ham.

5 Spread the mixture over the top and sides of the ham and place it, chestnut side down, on the pastry. Fold the pastry up over the ham, sealing the seams together with a little beaten egg.

6 Turn onto a flat baking sheet. Make a small hole in the top and decorate with leaves made from pastry trimmings. Brush all over with beaten egg.

7 Bake for 30-35 minutes, or until the pastry is golden brown.

Serves 8–10

Ham and Chestnuts en Croûte is a welcome change from the usual Sunday ham — serve it hot with a delicious brown gravy

Smoked Ham

Salted and smoked hams, including Virginia, Kentucky and Dijon, are boiled to serve either hot or cold as a much-prized dish. The curing of hams is a very specialized industry. The meat is covered with a mixture of salt, saltpeter and sugar and left for three days. It is then put into brine, washed and dried and finally smoked in a special chamber. It is usually necessary to soak smoked ham before cooking in order to remove the very salty flavor.

The best known and most popular variety of smoked ham is prosciutto from Parma in Italy. These pigs are fed on whey from the local cheese which contributes to its delicate flavor. Parma ham (prosciutto) can be bought in the delicatessen section, thinly sliced and ready to eat without further preparation or cooking. It must be kept well-covered in the refrigerator to prevent it from drying out.

Parma Ham Antipasto
Wafer-thin slices of translucent smoked ham wrapped loosely around fresh fruits must be the most refreshing and simple appetizer.

The ingredients should be touched as little as possible and served right away for them to be seen and eaten at their best. Each of the following fruit preparations is enough for 4 servings.

1 Peel 1 large or 2 small papayas, seed and cut into wedges. Wrap 1 or 2 slices of ham around each and garnish with thin slices of lemon and parsley sprigs.

2 Cut 8 fresh figs in half. Form 4 ham slices into cornet shapes and fill and garnish with the halved figs.

3 Remove the peel and seeds from half a small ripe honeydew melon. Slice it into 4 wedges and garnish each wedge with 1 or 2 slices ham and thinly sliced orange.

4 Halve two tiny cantaloupes, deseed and garnish each with 1 slice ham and a few seedless green grapes.

5 Peel 1 avocado, cut it into quarters lengthwise and brush it with lemon juice to keep it white. Arrange each quarter on a plate with 1 or 2 slices ham and garnish with black olives.

6 Peel 2 dessert pears, cut them in half lengthwise and remove the core using a teaspoon. Brush each half with lemon juice, fill with halved and deseeded black grapes and arrange each on a plate with a cornet of ham.

7 Peel and halve 2 peaches or nectarines, roll 1 or 2 slices ham around each half and garnish with tiny sprigs of watercress.

8 Halve 4 dessert plums and remove the pits. Arrange on the plate with slices of ham and garnish with orange sections.

Parma Ham Antipasto is a tasty, traditional northern Italian appetizer which can be served with figs, melon slices or papayas

All about Pasta

Pasta Paella

Pasta is the generic term for products made from a dough of durum flour, or semolina, mixed with eggs, oil and water. It is economical to use as there is no waste. It can be made at home and we give you the recipe below. It is sometimes blended with spinach to produce a green pasta or tomato paste for red pasta.

Pasta can be bought everywhere and there are many different sizes for different uses. The very small varieties of pasta can be used as a garnish in soups; there are other varieties, such as noodles, to be cooked plain as an accompaniment to a meat dish, or the pasta can be used for a main composite dish. Other varieties of pasta can be used to wrap around meat such as ravioli or cannelloni.

Pasta has been made for thousands of years — the Chinese were making it 6,000 years ago and travelers and explorers gradually introduced it into the West. Some stories say that Marco Polo brought it back with him from his travels, but historical research has shown that pasta was being eaten in Rome in 1284 some years before Marco Polo returned.

The Italians have made pasta their national dish and, apart from the well-known spaghetti, macaroni and ravioli, they have thought of many delightful names for the different shapes they now produce. They make pasta in the shape of butterflies (farfallette), shells (conchiglie), spirals (fusilli), wagon wheels (ruote) and even the alphabet letters our children love to find in soup.

Pasta is simple to cook in boiling salted water, and if you add a little oil to the water the pasta will not stick. The cooking time varies from 5 minutes for vermicelli to 18 minutes for thick macaroni. When cooked, it should be drained, returned to the pan with a pat of butter and some pepper. Pasta can be kept indefinitely in a cool cupboard, and is therefore an excellent food to have tucked away for unexpected guests.

The Italians cook pasta until it is *al dente* which means "to the tooth." They like to be able to bite into it, and prefer to eat it rather dry, tossed in a little oil, and sprinkled with grated Parmesan cheese.

Pasta Soups

Basic Pasta Dough

See pages 552-553 for step-by-step illustrations of this recipe

4 cups all-purpose bread flour
2 eggs, beaten
½ cup tepid water
½ tablespoon salt
2 teaspoons oil

1 Sift the flour into a circle. In the center, put the eggs, water, salt and oil.

2 If you wish, blend in a vegetable to color the pasta at this stage.

3 With your fingertips, wórk into a soft dough and shape into a ball.

4 On a floured surface, knead the dough until smooth and elastic. Wrap in a damp cloth and leave for 30 minutes.

5 Roll out to ⅛ inch thick and cut into the desired shapes.

6 Sprinkle a sheet of paper with flour or semolina and arrange the pasta on it and put in a warm place to dry.

7 When ready to cook, bring a large pot of water to a boil, add 2 tablespoons salt and 1 teaspoon of oil to prevent the pasta from sticking. Boil until the pasta is of the desired softness.

8 Drain, and return to the pan and mix with oil if you wish. Place in a serving dish and serve immediately.

Makes 1 lb. of pasta
Serves 6–8

Three Bean Spaghetti Soup

½ cup dried red kidney beans, soaked overnight
½ cup dried white beans, soaked overnight
2 onions, sliced
2 tablespoons oil
2 tablespoons tomato paste
3⅔ cups stock
salt and pepper
1 cup shelled broad beans
1 cup sliced mushrooms
½ cup spaghetti rings or macaroni

1 Simmer the dried beans, without salt, in water until soft — in separate pans, to avoid the red beans coloring the white. When soft, season with salt and drain.

2 In an ovenproof casserole, gently sauté the onions in the oil for 3 minutes. Add the tomato paste and cook for 1 minute. Stir in the stock, season, and bring to a boil, then simmer for 5 minutes.

3 Add the broad beans, mushrooms and pasta rings. Simmer for 10 minutes. Add the precooked dried beans and heat through. Check the seasoning, then serve.

Serves 6

Three Bean Spaghetti Soup is nourishing and warming on cold winter days and makes a tasty meal in itself

The addition of pasta to soup makes it both more visually attractive and more nutritious and filling. We give you recipes for thin soups such as Watercress and Vermicelli, and Chicken Noodle Soup — these will make good first courses for a dinner. There are also recipes for more substantial soups such as Three Bean Spaghetti Soup and Minestrone. These will make a quick and simple family meal if eaten with bread, cheese and fruit.

Minestrone Soup

¼ cup pork fat
⅓ cup diced bacon
2 tablespoons chopped onion
1 leek, white part, shredded
7¼ cups water
1 carrot, finely diced
1 turnip, finely diced
1 potato, finely diced
1 branch celery, finely diced
¾ cup shredded cabbage
2 tomatoes, skinned, seeded and chopped
¼ cup diced green beans
½ cup fresh peas
¼ cup rice or vermicelli
1 clove garlic, peeled
2 tablespoons ham fat
pinch basil or marjoram
1 teaspoon chopped parsley

1 Melt the pork fat in a large pan, add the diced bacon, chopped onion and shredded leek and cook gently for 5 minutes.

2 Add the water and bring to a boil. Add the carrot, turnip, potato, celery, cabbage and tomatoes. Cook for a further 25 minutes.

3 Add the green beans, the peas, and the rice or vermicelli and simmer gently for a further 45 minutes, skimming carefully from time to time.

4 Mash the garlic with the ham fat, the basil or marjoram, and the chopped parsley. Add this mixture to the soup, boil for 5 minutes and serve.

Serves 6

Tip: For extra flavor, a pinch of saffron powder can be added to the bacon and chopped onion.

Chicken Consommé Vermicelli

¾ lb. chopped or ground beef
pinch salt
1 egg white
7¼ cups cold chicken stock
¾ cup chopped mixed vegetables (onion, carrot, celery, leek)
bouquet garni
3-4 peppercorns
2 raw chicken legs
⅓ cup vermicelli

1 Thoroughly mix together the beef, salt, egg white and 1¼ cups of the cold chicken stock in a heavy-bottomed pan.

2 Add the chopped vegetables, the rest of the stock, the bouquet garni, peppercorns and chicken legs.

3 Bring slowly to a boil over gentle heat, stirring occasionally. Allow to boil rapidly for 5-10 seconds, then reduce the heat to a gentle simmer. Leave to simmer very gently for 1½–2 hours without stirring.

4 Meanwhile, cook the vermicelli in boiling salted water for 5 minutes, and drain.

5 When the soup is cooked, lift out the chicken legs, strain the soup through double cheesecloth and remove all the fat from the surface with absorbent kitchen paper. Adjust the seasoning. Remove the skin and bones from the chicken legs and dice the meat. Add the chicken meat to the soup and bring it back to a boil. Add the vermicelli, allow it to warm through, and serve.

Serves 6

Tip: To enrich the vermicelli, you can cook it in a little of the strained

soup rather than the salted water.

For economy, the chicken legs can be replaced by 2 chicken bouillon cubes.

Watercress and Vermicelli Soup

½ lb. watercress
7¼ cups water
1½ cups sliced potatoes
1 small onion, sliced
salt and pepper
2 egg yolks
⅓ cup vermicelli

1 Clean the watercress and reserve a few of the top leaves. Place the rest of the watercress in a pan, add the water, potatoes and onion and bring to a boil. Reduce the heat and simmer for about 15 minutes or until the potatoes are tender. Season to taste.

2 Whisk the egg yolks in a bowl and then gradually add the hot soup, whisking all the time. Return the soup to the pan and reheat, without boiling, until the soup is the consistency of custard.

3 Meanwhile, cook the vermicelli in boiling salted water for about 5 minutes and drain. Boil the reserved watercress leaves in salted water for 3 minutes and drain.

4 Add the vermicelli to the reheated soup, garnish with the boiled watercress leaves and serve.

Serves 6

Tip: The egg yolks add nutritional value to the soup, but they can be omitted if preferred.

Watercress and Vermicelli Soup is a sophisticated soup to serve at parties and special lunches and occasions

Pasta

Fettuccine Napolitana

¼ cup olive oil
2 onions, sliced
3 large tomatoes, skinned,
  seeded and chopped
1 clove garlic, peeled and crushed
pinch basil
pinch sugar
salt and pepper
pinch oregano
1 lb. fettuccine

1 Heat the oil in a skillet. Sauté the onions until they are soft but not colored. Add the tomatoes, crushed garlic, basil and sugar. Season to taste with salt and pepper. Simmer for 15 minutes, then add the oregano.

2 Bring a large pot of salted water to a boil. Add a few drops of oil and place the fettuccine in the pot. Boil for about 6 minutes. Drain and serve immediately with the sauce and a bowl of Parmesan cheese.

Serves 4

Bolognese Sauce

¼ cup olive oil
1 onion, chopped
1 branch celery, chopped
1 clove garlic, chopped
½ lb. ground beef
¼ cup ground chicken or calves
  liver
¼ cup flour
2 tablespoons tomato paste
1 beef bouillon cube
1¼ cups water
¼ cup dark sherry or Marsala
pinch each oregano, paprika and
  mace
salt and pepper

1 Heat the oil in a pan and sauté the onion, celery and garlic for 5 minutes until lightly browned.

2 Add the ground beef and liver and cook for a further 5 minutes.

3 Sprinkle in the flour and cook for 1 minute. Stir in the tomato paste and cook for 1 minute more. Dissolve the beef bouillon cube in the water and add the liquid to the pan with the sherry or Marsala. Add the oregano, paprika, mace and seasoning and simmer for a further 15 minutes.

Makes 2 cups

Spaghetti Amalfi

3 eggplants, diced
salt
¼ cup olive oil
1 onion, chopped
1 clove garlic, peeled and chopped
1 green pepper, seeded and
  diced
2 mushrooms, sliced
¼ cup flour
2 tablespoons tomato paste
⅔ cup water
1 chicken bouillon cube
pinch each basil, paprika, curry
  powder
pepper
½ lb. spaghetti
2 tablespoons butter
½ cup grated cheese

1 Sprinkle the diced eggplant with salt and let stand for 30 minutes. Rinse and dry.

2 Heat the oil in a pan and sauté the onion and garlic for 5 minutes without browning. Add the eggplant and mushrooms and simmer for 3 minutes more. Sprinkle in the flour and add the tomato paste and water. Crumble in the chicken bouillon cube and add the basil, paprika, curry powder and salt and pepper. Simmer for 12 minutes until thick.

3 Meanwhile, cook the spaghetti in salted water, drain and add the but-ter and grated cheese. Mix well.

4 Place the spaghetti on a serving dish, cover with the eggplant sauce and serve.

Serves 4

Spaghetti Flan

one 9-inch pie crust
¼ lb. spaghetti, broken into short
  lengths
¼ cup tomato sauce
4 slices bacon
1 onion, chopped
2 tablespoons butter
3 eggs, beaten
salt and pepper

1 Preheat the oven to 400°F. Line a flan dish with the crust, prick the base with a fork and bake in the oven for 10 minutes. When cooked, remove and reduce the oven temperature to 375°F.

2 Cook the spaghetti in boiling salted water until tender, then drain and mix with the tomato sauce.

3 Chop 3 of the bacon slices. Fry the chopped bacon and the onion gently in the butter for 5 minutes.

4 Remove from the heat and mix in the spaghetti in tomato sauce, the beaten eggs, and the seasoning. Pour the mixture into the flan crust. Cut the remaining slice of bacon into strips and arrange them in a lattice pattern over the top of the flan. Bake in the oven for 30 minutes.

Serves 4–6

Spaghetti Amalfi is served with a delicious tomato and eggplant sauce, and sprinkled with Parmesan

548

Spaghetti San Remo

¼ lb. spaghetti
3 tablespoons olive oil
2 onions, thinly sliced
2 cloves garlic, chopped
¼ lb. bacon slices, cut into ½-inch
  strips
½ lb. mushrooms
5 anchovy fillets
salt and pepper
6 stuffed green olives
1 tablespoon chopped parsley
⅓ cup grated Parmesan cheese

1 Boil the spaghetti in salted water for 15 minutes until cooked *al dente*.

2 Meanwhile, heat the oil in a skillet and sauté the onions 3 minutes. Add the garlic and sauté 1 minute. Stir in the bacon, mushrooms, and anchovy fillets, and cook for another 5 minutes. Season with salt and pepper.

3 Drain the spaghetti and rinse quickly with hot water. Place it in a heated serving dish. Pile the bacon mixture on top and garnish with the stuffed olives. Sprinkle with parsley and Parmesan cheese, and serve immediately.

Serves 2

Spaghetti with Clams

48 littleneck clams
bouquet garni
1 lb. spaghetti
⅓ cup olive oil
1 onion, finely chopped
2 cloves garlic, crushed
4 large tomatoes, peeled,
  seeded and chopped

4 leaves fresh basil, finely chopped
2 tablespoons butter
⅔ cup grated Parmesan cheese
salt and pepper

1 Wash the clams thoroughly in cold water and rinse 3 times to remove the sand. Put them in a large saucepan, cover with water and add the bouquet garni. Boil them for 5 minutes until all the shells are open. Remove them from the shells and rinse in cold water.

2 Boil the spaghetti in salted water for 10-15 minutes until cooked *al dente*. Drain and rinse.

3 To make the sauce, heat the oil and sauté the onions 4 minutes until soft. Add the garlic and sauté 1 minute. Stir in the tomatoes and basil and season. Simmer for 8 minutes.

4 Reheat the spaghetti in the butter and stir in ½ of the Parmesan. Mix the clams with the sauce and continue to simmer until they are hot. Pour the spaghetti into a warm serving dish, and stir in the clams and sauce gently. Sprinkle on the rest of the Parmesan or serve it separately. Serve at once.

Serves 8

Pesto Sauce
Finely chop ½ cup fresh basil leaves, 2 cloves garlic and ¼ cup pine nuts. Mix them together and add ⅓ cup grated Parmesan cheese. Gradually beat in ½ cup olive oil, and season. Serve with plain cooked spaghetti.

Spaghetti with Clams comes from Calabria in southern Italy — try substituting mussels for clams

Look 'n Cook Colored Noodles *See recipe for Basic Pasta Dough on page 544.*

1 Weigh the flour **2** Sift to remove any lumps **3** Add two eggs, water, oil and salt **4** Add strained cooked spinach at this stage to blend with the noodle dough to make green pasta **5** Or, combine tomato paste to make red pasta. Use the fingertips to make the dough **6** Knead each piece of dough on a floured surface until smooth and elastic and roll into a ball. Wrap in a damp cloth and leave for 30 minutes **7** Roll out the spinach

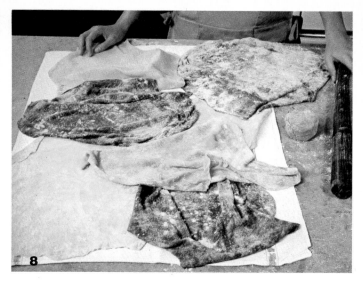

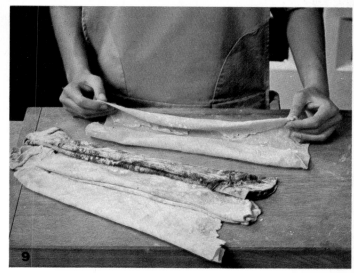

dough very thinly to $\frac{1}{8}$ inch thick **8** Roll out each ball of dough **9** Roll up each piece **10** Cut with a sharp knife into strips for noodles **11** Sprinkle a sheet of paper with flour or semolina and place the pasta on it and dry in a warm place **12** When ready to cook, boil a large amount of water in a pan, add salt and oil, and the pasta. Cook until "al dente" or as desired **13** Strain and place in a bowl **14** Mix gently with butter and pepper and serve with grated cheese or a sauce

Lasagne

Lasagne consists of flat sheets (about 5 inches square) or wide strips of pasta. It may be white, brown (wholemeal) or green (spinach flavored). It is usually cooked in layers with meat and sauce, and topped with grated cheese.

Lasagne Verde

6 ozs. green lasagne
salt

1 tablespoon butter
2½ cups thick Bolognese Sauce (see p. 548)
2½ cups white sauce
½ cup grated Parmesan or Romano cheese

1 Boil the green lasagne in salted water for 5 minutes or until tender. Rinse in cold running water, drain and dry.

2 Preheat oven to 375°F. In a buttered ovenproof dish arrange a layer of lasagne, topped by a layer of Bolognese Sauce and then one of white sauce. Repeat. Sprinkle the grated cheese over the top and bake for 30 minutes. Serve hot.

Serves 6

Spiced Lamb Lasagne is an ideal lunch or suppertime snack, served piping hot with a fresh mixed or green salad

Bacon and Mushroom Lasagne

½ lb. lean bacon, thinly sliced
1 onion, chopped
2 tablespoons olive oil
¼ cup flour
1 tablespoon tomato paste
salt and pepper
2½ cups beef stock
1 cup chopped mushrooms
6 ozs. lasagne
1¼ cups white sauce
1 cup grated cheese

1 Reserve 3 slices of bacon and chop the rest. Fry the chopped bacon with the onion in the oil until soft. Stir in the flour and cook for 1 minute. Stir in the tomato paste, season, and add the stock. Stir in the mushrooms, bring to a boil, cover and simmer for 10 minutes.

2 Boil the lasagne in salted water for 5 minutes or until tender and rinse thoroughly in running cold water. Drain and dry.

3 Preheat oven to 375°F. Arrange the bacon mixture and the lasagne in layers in an ovenproof dish, starting with bacon and finishing with lasagne. Cut the three remaining slices of bacon in half and arrange them over the dish. Pour on the white sauce, and sprinkle with the grated cheese. Bake in the oven for 30 minutes. Serve piping hot with broiled tomatoes.

Serves 6

Spiced Lamb Lasagne

1 onion, finely chopped
2 tablespoons oil
1 lb. ground lamb, raw or cooked
1 tablespoon chili powder
1 green pepper, seeded and chopped
1 tablespoon tomato paste
salt and pepper
1¾ cups beef stock
⅓ cup raisins
6 ozs. lasagne
1 cup plain yogurt
1 egg
1 tablespoon chopped walnuts
1 small sweet red pepper, seeded and cut in rings

1 Sauté the onion in the oil for 3 minutes until softened. Add the lamb and stir to brown it. Add ⅔ of the chili powder and cook for 1 minute. Add the green pepper, tomato paste, seasoning, stock and raisins. Bring to a boil, cover, and simmer for 15 minutes if using cooked lamb, or 40 minutes if using raw lamb.

2 Boil the lasagne in salted water for about 5 minutes or until just tender. Wash the lasagne briskly under cold running water to remove

Bacon and Mushroom Lasagne is an exciting variation on the traditional dish: layers of bacon and mushrooms

the starch and separate the strips. Drain and dry on a clean cloth or paper towel.

3 Preheat the oven to 375°F. Spoon a layer of meat sauce into the bottom of an ovenproof dish. Cover with a layer of lasagne. Repeat until the sauce and lasagne are all used, finishing with a layer of sauce on top.

4 Beat together the yogurt, egg, and chopped walnuts, adding the rest of the chili powder. Pour the yogurt mixture over the top of the dish. Arrange the rings of red pepper over the yogurt. Return to the oven and cook for another 20 minutes. Serve immediately with a crisp green salad.

Serves 6

Tip: Extra flavor may be given to lasagne dishes by brushing the pasta layers with butter while making up the dish.

Ravioli

Ravioli are small pasta pillows, stuffed with savory fillings: beef, chicken, veal, spinach, eggs and cheese can all be used in different combinations. They are usually served as an appetizer in a rich tomato sauce. Once the basic method of making ravioli has been learned — and it is quite easy — you will find that you can experiment with your own favorite combinations of fillings and flavors. A good tip to remember is that ravioli cooked and left overnight in the refrigerator with its accompanying sauce will be extra tender the next day.

The traditional way of serving ravioli is to drain it well, then toss it in butter, either plain or garlic-flavored, and then top it with grated cheese.

Ravioli

For the filling you can use one kind of meat alone or a combination, such as pork and veal.

1 lb. pasta dough
1 tablespoon olive oil
½ cup finely chopped onion
½ lb. ground pork, veal, beef or chicken
¼ cup cooked spinach
salt and pepper
pinch ground nutmeg
1 egg, beaten

1 Divide the dough into two equal portions. Roll each into a rectangle, ⅛ inch thick. Let rest in a cool place.

2 Heat the oil in a skillet. Gently sauté the onion until it is soft but not colored. Remove and lightly sauté the meat. Drain and place in a bowl with the onion and the spinach, from which all water has

Ravioli Sophia are stuffed with cheese and spinach purée, and served with a typical Italian tomato and mushroom sauce

been squeezed. Season with salt, pepper and nutmeg. Mince finely and mix with the beaten egg.

3 Either spoon the filling, or pipe it, in little walnut-size mounds at ½-inch intervals along one half of the dough. Brush with water between the fillings and cover with the second layer of dough. Mark the dough over the fillings with a pastry cutter turned upside down. Then, using a ruler and a serrated pastry wheel or ravioli cutter, cut the ravioli into squares. Line a baking sheet with wax paper and sprinkle with uncooked semolina. Place the squares on it and dry for 1 hour.

4 Bring a large pot of water to a boil. Add the ravioli and boil for 8 minutes. Refresh in cold water and drain.

5 Preheat the oven to 375°F. Place the ravioli in a buttered casserole and cover with tomato sauce. (Use the sauce described on page 548 for Fettuccine Napolitana.) Sprinkle with grated Parmesan cheese and bake for 20 minutes.

Makes 16

Ravioli Marinara with Eggplant

2 eggplants, sliced
salt
oil for deep frying
1 lb. pasta dough

For the Filling:
$\frac{1}{4}$ cup butter
$\frac{1}{2}$ cup flour
$\frac{1}{2}$ cup water
$\frac{3}{4}$ cup ground raw cod or other white fish
$\frac{1}{4}$ lb. peeled, deveined shrimp, finely chopped
pinch each salt and pepper
pinch sugar
juice $\frac{1}{2}$ lemon
pinch parsley and basil
1 egg, beaten

For the Sauce
$1\frac{1}{4}$ cups tomato sauce
$\frac{1}{4}$ cup light cream
$\frac{1}{2}$ cup grated Cheddar cheese

1 Sprinkle the eggplant with salt and put on one side for 20 minutes.

2 Roll out the dough as described in the basic recipe for ravioli.

3 To make the filling, heat the butter in a pan, add the flour and cook to a pale roux. Gradually pour on the water to form a stiff paste. Take off the heat and stir in the fish and the shrimp. Season, add the sugar, lemon juice and herbs. Add the beaten eggs.

4 Prepare, fill and cook the ravioli as described in the basic recipe.

5 Wipe the eggplants dry and dust lightly with flour. Heat the oil and deep fry for 30 seconds. Preheat the oven to 375°F. Prepare the tomato sauce as described in the recipe on page 548. Stir in the cream. Butter a shallow casserole and arrange the eggplant in two rows with the ravioli in its sauce in the middle. Sprinkle with the grated cheese and bake for 12 minutes.

Serves 6

Ravioli Sophia

1 lb. pasta dough

For the Filling:
$\frac{1}{3}$ cup finely chopped cooked spinach
$\frac{2}{3}$ cup cottage cheese
$\frac{1}{3}$ cup grated Parmesan cheese
2 egg yolks, beaten
$\frac{1}{4}$ cup flour
pinch salt and pepper
grated rind $\frac{1}{2}$ lemon

For the Sauce:
$1\frac{1}{4}$ cups tomato sauce
1 cup chopped mushrooms

1 Roll out the pasta dough as described in the previous recipe.

Ravioli Marinara with Eggplant makes a tasty meal which can be served as an appetizer

2 Squeeze all excess water from the spinach. In a bowl, combine it with the two cheeses, egg yolks, flour, salt, pepper and grated lemon rind.

3 Make and cook the ravioli as described in the previous recipe.

4 To make the sauce, follow the recipe described on page 548 for Fettuccine Napolitana, but add chopped mushrooms with the onions. Bake as in previous recipe.

Serves 6

Cannelloni

The very name 'cannelloni' is colorful and conjures up an image of Italy. Cannelloni are hollow pasta tubes, usually 4 inches long and 2 inches in diameter. They can be stuffed with a variety of meat, cheese or vegetable mixtures and are then coated with a sauce and baked. They are often topped with grated cheese. Always blanch the cannelloni in boiling salted water, to which has been added 1 tablespoon oil, for 5 minutes. The oil will prevent the cannelloni tubes from sticking together. Cannelloni can be served as an appetizer or as a main course with a green salad.

Cannelloni with Olives

6 cannelloni tubes
1 tablespoon olive oil
1 onion, chopped
½ lb. ground beef
1 tablespoon tomato paste
1 teaspoon basil
1 teaspoon sugar
8 stuffed olives
salt and pepper
1 tomato, thinly sliced

For the Sauce:
1¼ cups white sauce
½ teaspoon prepared mustard
salt and pepper
1 cup grated Parmesan cheese

1 Blanch the cannelloni in salted

Cannelloni with Olives makes a nourishing meal for lunch or supper, stuffed with ground beef in a cheesy sauce

boiling water for 5 minutes. Drain and place under running cold water until cool.

2 Heat the oven to 375°F.

3 Heat the oil in a skillet and sauté the onion until soft. Add the ground beef and cook until brown. Stir in the tomato paste, basil and sugar.

4 Chop 6 olives and add them to the beef mixture and season with salt and pepper.

5 Using a piping bag or spoon, fill the cannelloni tubes with the mixture. Place in a shallow ovenproof dish.

6 Heat the white sauce and flavor with the mustard and salt and pepper. Stir in most of the cheese, reserving a little for the top.

7 Pour the sauce over the cannelloni and sprinkle with the remaining cheese. Bake in the oven for 20 minutes.

8 Decorate the top with the remaining sliced olives and tomato and serve hot.

Serves 3–6

Tip: This dish can be served as an appetizer, in which case allow one cannelloni tube per person. If serving as a main course, allow two per person.

Cannelloni Fries

8 cannelloni tubes
1 tablespoon olive oil
1 sweet red pepper, seeded and chopped
1 cup chopped mushrooms
1¼ cups white sauce
¼ lb. chopped ham
salt and pepper

1 cup fresh breadcrumbs
½ cup flour
1 egg, beaten
1½ cups fine dried breadcrumbs
oil for deep frying

For the Ratatouille:
⅔ cup olive oil
1 clove garlic, peeled and crushed
1 onion, sliced
2 medium-size tomatoes, peeled, seeded and chopped
1 small sweet green or red pepper, seeded and chopped
1 eggplant, quartered
3 zucchini, sliced
1 tablespoon tomato paste
pinch thyme
1 bay leaf
salt and pepper

1 Cook the cannelloni in boiling salted water for 5 minutes. Drain and place under running cold water.

2 Heat the oil in a skillet and sauté the chopped pepper until soft. Add the mushrooms and sauté for a further 3 minutes.

3 Heat the white sauce and stir in the onion and mushroom mixture and the ham. Season with salt and

Cannelloni Fries are an unusual way of serving stuffed cannelloni with ratatouille and are ideal for lunches

pepper and mix in the fresh breadcrumbs.

4 Dry the cannelloni on absorbent paper and fill the tubes with the sauce. Dredge the stuffed tubes with flour and then coat with the beaten egg and crumbs. Chill for 1 hour.

5 Meanwhile, make the ratatouille. Heat the oil in a pan and sauté the garlic and onion for 5 minutes, then add the tomatoes and green (or red) pepper. Add the eggplant and zucchini. Stir in the tomato paste, thyme and bay leaf and season. Cover the pan and simmer for 30–45 minutes.

6 Heat the oil and deep fry the can-

nelloni until crisp and golden. Drain on absorbent paper. Arrange the cannelloni on top of the ratatouille in a serving dish and serve.

Serves 4

Tip: Other stuffings can be used for both fried and baked cannelloni. Try using a Bolognese sauce or a ricotta cheese and spinach stuffing. If ricotta is not available, use cottage cheese. Just mix together equal quantities of cheese and cooked chopped spinach and season with salt and pepper. Any kind of meat can be used to stuff cannelloni — chicken, ham, veal, pork or ground beef. For different flavors, try using corn, pimentos, parsley or anchovies. Fish stuffings are delicious — try shrimp, tuna or white fish in a creamy sauce.

Pasta Salads

Pasta makes a delicious addition to salads of all types and blends well with acidic salad dressings such as mayonnaise and French dressing.

Here are recipes for making pasta salads mixed with meat and fresh vegetables.

Pasta with Avocado and Lemon Sauce

2 cups large pasta shells
salt and pepper
¼ cup oil and vinegar dressing
1 large ripe avocado
juice and grated rind 1 lemon
1 clove garlic, finely chopped
2 teaspoons sugar
3-4 tablespoons stock or milk
4 scallions, chopped
2 tablespoons chopped parsley

1 Cook the pasta shells in boiling seasoned water until tender. Drain thoroughly and, while still warm, toss lightly in the oil and vinegar dressing.

2 Cut the avocado in half, discard the pit and scoop out the flesh. Mix the avocado flesh with the lemon juice, lemon rind, salt and pepper, garlic, sugar and stock or milk and then blend until smooth either in a blender or by pushing the mixture through a strainer or food mill.

3 Stir in the scallions and parsley, and then stir the avocado and lemon sauce into the pasta. Serve as an appetizer or accompaniment to cold meat.

Serves 4

Oriental Pasta Salad

1¼ cups pasta shapes or short macaroni
salt and pepper
6 ozs. bean sprouts
2 carrots, grated or thinly sliced
½ small cucumber, cut in thin diagonal slices
1 cup canned pineapple chunks, drained (reserve the juice)

Pasta with Avocado and Lemon Sauce is a delightful appetizer or is delicious served with cold ham, chicken or salmon

For the Dressing:
6 tablespoons oil
6 tablespoons orange juice
2 tablespoons reserved pineapple juice
1 tablespoon soy sauce
pinch ground ginger

For the Garnish:
4 scallions

1 Cook the pasta in boiling salted water until just tender. Meanwhile, mix all the dressing ingredients.

2 Drain the pasta and while it is still warm, mix it with the dressing. Cool.

3 Add the bean sprouts, carrot, cucumber and pineapple chunks to the pasta and toss lightly together.

4 Trim the scallions to within 2

inches of the bulbs. Chop the green parts finely and sprinkle over the salad.

5 With a sharp knife, make several cuts in the scallion bulbs from the stem end toward the root end, stopping $\frac{1}{4}$ inch from the bottom. Place the bulbs in ice water until they open out into "water lilies." Use to garnish the salad.

Serves 4–6

Ratatouille Pasta

3 eggplants
salt and pepper
1¼ cups olive oil
2 medium onions, sliced
3 cloves garlic, peeled and crushed

Oriental Pasta Salad brings a touch of the Orient to your dinner table — refreshing, fruity and very exotic

2 medium-size tomatoes, skinned, seeded and chopped
2 sweet red or green peppers, seeded and chopped
6 zucchini, quartered
bouquet garni
1⅔ cups macaroni

For the Dressing:
3 tablespoons oil
1 tablespoon vinegar
1 small onion, chopped

1 Quarter the eggplants, sprinkle them with salt and leave for about 20 minutes. Rinse and dry.

2 Heat half the oil in a pan and sauté the sliced onions for a few minutes until lightly colored, then

add the garlic. Sauté for 5 minutes more then add the tomatoes and peppers.

3 In a separate pan, sauté the eggplant and zucchini for a few minutes in the rest of the oil. Drain and add to the other pan. Season with salt and pepper, add the bouquet garni and simmer for 30 minutes.

4 Meanwhile, cook the macaroni in boiling salted water until tender. Mix the dressing ingredients. Drain the cooked pasta, refresh in cold water and toss in the dressing.

5 When the ratatouille is cooked, remove the bouquet garni and blend the mixture with the pasta. Allow to cool and serve.

Serves 6

Tip: This dish is very versatile: you can serve it hot or cold and vary the pasta — perhaps using pasta shells.

Meat and Pasta

Beef Fritters with Spaghetti Creole Sauce

½ cup flour
2 eggs, beaten
⅓ cup cornflakes, crushed
1 tablespoon chopped almonds
oil for deep frying
1 cup spaghetti
¼ cup butter
½ cup grated Parmesan cheese

For the Fritters:
½ lb. ground beef
¼ lb. ground pork
1 cup chopped mushrooms
½ cup chopped onion
1 egg
1 cup fresh breadcrumbs
1 tablespoon chopped parsley
1 clove garlic, minced
salt and pepper
pinch paprika

For the Sauce:
2 tablespoons oil
1 small onion, chopped
3 tablespoons diced bacon
¼ cup flour
1 dried chili
6 tablespoons tomato paste
2 cups water
1 beef bouillon cube, crumbled
bouquet garni
2 mint leaves

1 Combine all the ingredients for the fritters and divide into 8 balls. Roll them in the flour, then dip in the beaten egg and roll in the cornflakes and almonds. Heat the oil to 375°F. and fry the fritters for 4 minutes.

2 Cook the spaghetti in boiling salted water for 10-12 minutes, then drain, season and add the butter and cheese. Mix well and keep warm.

3 Next, make the sauce. Heat the oil in a pan and sauté the onion and bacon for 5 minutes. Add the flour and cook for 1 minute more.

4 Add the remaining ingredients, bring to a boil and simmer for 15 minutes.

5 Season the sauce and strain. Blend half the sauce with the cooked spaghetti.

6 Arrange the fritters in a circle on a plate and pour the spaghetti into the center. Serve the rest of the sauce separately.

Serves 4

Spaghetti Chinese-style

¼ cup peanut oil
1 onion, shredded
½ lb. cooked lean pork, cut in strips
1 sweet red pepper, cut in strips
1 green pepper, cut in strips
½ lb. bean sprouts
1 tablespoon soy sauce
1 tablespoon vinegar
½ teaspoon sugar
salt and pepper
1½ cups cooked spaghetti

1 Heat the oil in a pan and sauté the onion for 3 minutes. Add the pork, peppers and bean shoots and cook for 6 minutes.

2 Add the soy sauce, vinegar, sugar and seasoning.

3 Add the cooked spaghetti and stir-fry until hot.

Serves 4

Veal Oregano

salt and pepper
3-lb. veal roast
½ cup oil
⅔ cup dry vermouth
1¼ cups water

2 carrots, chopped
2 onions, chopped
1 branch celery, chopped
¾ cup diced bacon
½ cup flour
¼ cup tomato paste
1 clove garlic, crushed
1 tablespoon basil
1 tablespoon oregano
bouquet garni
1 cup spaghetti
¼ cup butter
½ cup grated Gruyère cheese
12 black olives
12 artichokes, boiled and quartered

1 Preheat the oven to 375°F.

2 Season the veal. Brush with ¼ cup oil and roast for 1½ hours. Baste with the vermouth and water frequently. Remove and keep hot.

3 Heat the rest of the oil in a saucepan and gently sauté the chopped vegetables and bacon for 8 minutes on low heat, covered.

4 Sprinkle with flour and make a roux. Stir in the tomato paste. Cook for 2 minutes, add the garlic and juices from the roasting pan to make a thin sauce. Season and add half of the herbs, and the bouquet garni and boil for 20 minutes. Strain and keep hot.

5 Boil the spaghetti for 10 minutes in salted water. Drain and toss in butter, and keep warm.

6 Carve the meat between the ribs into cutlets and arrange on a dish. Surround with the spaghetti, sprinkled with cheese and decorated with 6 black olives, and quarters of cooked artichokes. Pour a little sauce on the meat and sprinkle with basil and oregano. Serve the remainder of the sauce with the olives.

Serves 6

All about Rice

Rice with Mushrooms and Scrambled Egg

Rice is a cereal which grows in the Far East, China, Italy, and the United States. Rice originated in India and China and was later introduced into ancient Egypt and Greece. It gradually became popular in Europe. Rice is versatile and increasingly popular as many people are substituting it for other starchy foods such as potatoes and pasta.

There are several varieties of rice. The best known are the white polished and brown unpolished. Most people in the West eat the white polished varieties but brown rice is much better for you. It is the whole unpolished grain with only the inedible husk and a little bran removed. It has an unusual chewy texture and a slightly nutty flavor. Wild rice is wrongly named since it is not really a cereal but the green seeds of a grass which grows wild in Minnesota. It is usually eaten with game.

Rice comes in different grain sizes — long, medium and short. The long grain is the most familiar. It is used in savory dishes such as curries, risottos, paellas and salads. Medium grain is generally used for stuffings, croquettes and molds and, of course, short grain for sweet puddings and desserts.

Cooking Rice
Rice is very versatile and can be boiled or fried, served plain, colored or mixed with chopped meats, fish or vegetables. Boil in a pan of salted water. Use $2\frac{1}{2}$ cups water for each $\frac{1}{4}$ cup rice. Allow $\frac{1}{4}$ cup uncooked rice per person and remember that rice triples in bulk during cooking. Add the rice to the pan when the water is boiling and boil white rice for 12-15 minutes until soft but firm; brown rice takes longer, about 25 minutes. Turn off the burner and allow rice to steam covered for 5 minutes at the end. This produces fluffy rice. The rice should be dry, not soggy, and slightly fluffy in texture. You can serve the rice immediately but it is better to return it to the empty pan with a pat of butter. Cover the pan with a lid and leave the rice to dry

out for about 5 minutes. The grains should be separate, not sticking together.

Coloring and Flavoring Rice
Cooked rice can be colored, and therefore made more attractive, by adding saffron or turmeric and mixing well with a fork. Turmeric is cheaper than saffron, but take care not to use too much as it has a very distinctive flavor. For a different flavor, try cooking rice in stock instead of water. Use fresh stock or add a bouillon cube to the cooking water.

Rice Salads
Never worry about cooking too much rice — it will never go to waste. Rice can be stored in an air-tight container in a refrigerator for up to a week. It can be reheated or used up as cold leftover rice in a salad. Just toss it with a vinaigrette dressing or some thinned mayonnaise. You can mix in cooked meat such as ham, chicken or bacon; flaked fish such as salmon or tuna; shellfish, shrimp or lobster; or chopped up peppers, scallions and herbs. For a Chinese flavor, fry up the cold rice with onions, mushrooms, corn, peppers, bean sprouts and peas. Add some chicken and shrimp and lay thinly cut strips of cooked omelet across the top.

Famous Rice Dishes
Rice forms the basis of many famous ethnic dishes, the most famous of which are the Italian *risotto*, the eastern *pilau* (or pilaf) and the Spanish *paella*. All these dishes are main meals in themselves. Risotto and pilaf are often confused in many people's minds but really they are quite different. Risotto is more moist and not as highly spiced as pilaf, and it is always served with grated cheese. A paella, unlike risottos and pilafs, is cooked in a skillet and all the ingredients are cooked together.

Soups and Appetizers

Rice need not only be served as an accompaniment to a main course. It can also form the basis of many exciting soups and appetizers. Try mixing it with chopped fruits, salad vegetables and shrimp, pile it into individual dishes and serve as an appetizer. Below are some delicious recipes and ideas.

Curry and Rice Soup

1 lb. onions, chopped
2 tablespoons butter
2 tablespoons oil
1 tablespoon curry powder
2 tablespoons shredded coconut
2 tablespoons flour
6 cups stock
1 branch celery, thinly sliced
$\frac{1}{3}$ cup long grain rice
salt and pepper

1 Sauté the onions in the butter and oil in a heavy saucepan, until soft. Add the curry powder and coconut and cook for a further minute. Add the flour and cook for 1 minute. Pour in the stock and bring to a boil, stirring all the time.

2 Add the celery and rice and season with salt and pepper. Boil gently covered with a lid, for 35 minutes until the rice is tender, then serve.

Serves 6

Tip: Another idea for a soup with rice is to use tomato soup and add cooked rice, pimientos and diced tomatoes. Or why not try a quick bisque? Just add a pinch of paprika, some cooked rice and shrimp to tomato soup.

Curry and Rice Soup is a hot and spicy soup for the start of an Indian meal or ideal for a cold wintry day

Shrimp and Melon Cocktail

2 tomatoes, peeled, seeded and
  chopped
1 green pepper, seeded and
  chopped
$\frac{1}{2}$ fresh honeydew melon, scooped
  into balls
$\frac{1}{2}$ cucumber, chopped
$\frac{1}{2}$ cup raisins
$\frac{1}{2}$ cup stuffed green olives, sliced
6 ozs. peeled, deveined, cooked
  shrimp
3 cups boiled rice
few crisp lettuce leaves, shredded
4 slices cucumber
4 sprigs parsley

For the Dressing:
3 tablespoons vinegar
$\frac{1}{2}$ cup olive oil
$\frac{1}{2}$ teaspoon dry mustard
salt and freshly ground black
  pepper

1 Mix together the tomatoes, green pepper, melon, cucumber, raisins, olives and shrimp. Add the cold, cooked rice.

2 Combine together the ingredients for the dressing and beat well. Toss the vegetable and shrimp mixture lightly in the dressing.

3 Place the shredded lettuce leaves in the bottom of some individual cocktail glasses and top with the rice mixture. Garnish with the cucumber slices and sprigs of parsley.

Serves 4

Tip: If you wish you can serve the shrimp and melon cocktails over crushed ice, either in the bowl or on a plate. To make the cocktails even more attractive, you can garnish them with whole shrimp and wedges of lemon. Try mixing in some lemon juice for a tangy flavor.

Shrimp and Melon Cocktails make a tangy start to any meal, garnished with olives and served on a bed of crushed ice

Risotto Rosso

1 tablespoon olive oil
¼ cup butter
1 large onion, chopped
1 sweet red pepper, seeded and
  chopped
1 cup long grain rice
1 tablespoon tomato paste
salt and pepper
pinch each oregano and basil
2½ cups fish stock or water
¼ lb. peeled deveined shrimp
2 large tomatoes, peeled, seeded
  and chopped
pinch paprika

1 Heat the oil and half of the butter in a large skillet. Gently sauté the onion and red pepper for 4 minutes until soft but not browned.

2 Add the rice and stir while cooking for 3 minutes. Stir in the tomato paste and season with salt and pepper and a pinch of oregano and basil. Pour in the fish stock or water, bring to a boil, and simmer for 10 minutes.

3 Stir in the peeled shrimp and the chopped tomato and continue to simmer gently for 10 minutes or until the rice is tender. Transfer to a warm serving dish, stir in the rest of the butter, and sprinkle with a pinch of paprika before serving.

Serves 4

Curried Fish Risotto

1 cup dried kidney beans, soaked
  overnight
6 scallions, shredded lengthwise
1 tablespoon oil
¼ cup butter
1 large onion, chopped
1 green pepper, split, seeded
  and sliced
1 cup long grain rice

½ teaspoon each turmeric and
  coriander
pinch each mace, ginger, cayenne
  pepper
2½ cups fish stock or water
⅓ cup golden raisins
1 bay leaf
1 lb. cod or other firm white fish,
  filleted and cut in 2-inch chunks

1 Boil beans in salted water until tender. Rinse and drain. Decorate with the scallions.

2 In a heavy skillet heat the oil and ½ the butter. Gently sauté the onion and green pepper 3 minutes until softened. Stir in the rice and cook for 3 minutes.

3 Add the spices, fish stock or water, raisins and bay leaf. Bring to a boil and simmer gently for 10 minutes. Add the fish pieces, cover again and cook for 15 minutes, checking from time to time that the rice is not sticking.

4 When the fish is cooked and the rice tender, check the seasoning and turn into a heated serving dish. Stir in the rest of the butter and serve immediately with a salad of kidney beans and scallions.

Serves 4

Paella Cartagena

¼ cup olive oil
1 large onion, chopped
½ sweet red pepper, seeded and
  diced
1 breast of chicken, skinned,
  boned and diced
1 cup long grain rice
2½ cups chicken stock
salt and pepper
pinch paprika
small pinch saffron
2 cloves garlic, crushed

2 chorizo sausages (spiced smoked
  Spanish sausages)
6 jumbo shrimp, peeled and
  deveined
24 fresh mussels, washed and
  scraped
¾ cup cooked fresh peas
4 tomatoes, skinned, seeded and
  chopped
1 tablespoon chopped parsley

1 Heat the oil in a large, heavy skillet or if possible, a 2-handled paella pan. Sauté the onion and red pepper until soft. Add the diced chicken and sauté, stirring, until just browned.

2 Stir in the rice and cook for 4 minutes until it starts to turn opaque. Add the chicken stock, salt and pepper, paprika, a small pinch of saffron and the garlic. Bring to a boil and simmer over low heat for 15 minutes.

3 Add the sausage (cut into thick slices), shrimp, and mussels. Cover with a lid and cook for 5 minutes. Stir in the peas and tomatoes and cook for another 3 minutes.

4 Check the seasoning, sprinkle with chopped parsley, and serve the paella at once in the paella pan or a large dish.

Serves 6

Tips: The principle of a paella (a dish which originated in Moorish Spain) is that the ingredients are added to the dish according to the time required to cook them, starting with those that take longest.

A paella should contain at least 4 or 5 different meats, including chicken and sausage; shellfish such as mussels, scampi or jumbo shrimp, squid, crayfish; and other meats such as pork or duck.

Paella is characteristically colored and flavored with a small pinch of saffron, but a pinch of turmeric may be used instead to give the golden color required.

*Curried Fish Risotto makes an
unusual alternative to the
traditional dish, served with
kidney beans*

566

Dolmades

8 cabbage leaves
1 lb. ground beef
1 medium onion, chopped
¼ cup oil
½ cup cooked rice
1 teaspoon mixed parsley and mint
salt and pepper
1¼ cups tomato sauce

1 Preheat the oven to 350°F.

2 Boil the cabbage leaves in salted water for 5 minutes. Drain and dry on absorbent paper.

3 Put the beef with the chopped onion in a saucepan and sauté gently in the oil until the meat is brown, about 10 minutes.

4 Add the cooked rice, herbs, and seasoning.

5 Divide the filling between the cabbage leaves, roll up and place close together in a baking dish just big enough to hold them. Pour on the tomato sauce, cover with a lid, and bake for 40 minutes. Serve hot as an appetizer or as a main dish with plain, boiled rice.

Serves 4

Tip: Traditional Greek Dolmades consist of lamb wrapped up in grape leaves, blanched for 5 minutes, and flavored with mint. You may try this with grape leaves to enjoy the authentic taste. Grape leaves are available bottled and sold in the specialty sections of most supermarkets.

Salonika Cutlets

½ lb. ground beef
1½ cups cooked rice
1 egg, beaten
1 onion, chopped
salt and pepper
grated peel 1 lemon
⅓ cup golden raisins
½ cup flour seasoned with salt
¼ cup oil

1 Mix the beef, rice, egg, onion, salt and pepper, grated lemon peel and raisins together and form into four triangular 'cutlets,' ½ inch thick.

2 Dredge with the seasoned flour.

3 Heat the oil in a skillet and fry the 'cutlets' for 8 minutes on each side until golden.

4 Serve with boiled rice and a tomato sauce. Fried squash fritters would go well with this dish.

Serves 4

Keftedhes Kebabs

1 lb. ground beef
1 onion, chopped
½ cup cooked rice
1 cup breadcrumbs
1 egg, beaten
salt and pepper
¼ cup oil

For the Barbecue Sauce:
1 tablespoon sugar
1 tablespoon vinegar
pinch cayenne pepper
1¼ cups tomato sauce

1 Preheat the oven to 400°F.

2 Mix the beef, onion, rice, breadcrumbs, egg and seasoning together.

3 Divide meat mixture into four portions and mold onto short skewers in long, oval shapes.

4 Heat the oil in a skillet and brown the kebabs for 15 minutes covered with a lid.

5 Meanwhile, add the sugar, vinegar and cayenne pepper to the tomato sauce and boil for 5 minutes.

6 Arrange the kebabs in a shallow dish, pour on the sauce and heat through in the oven for 10 minutes.

7 Serve with plain, boiled rice.

Serves 4

Calypso Chicken with Rice

6 tablespoons white wine
1¼ cups white sauce, made with chicken stock
4 chicken parts
1½ tablespoons oregano
1 tablespoon lemon juice

For the Rice:
¾ cup long grain rice
¼ cup chopped onion
1 clove garlic, peeled and chopped
2 tablespoons oil
1 large sweet red or green pepper, chopped
½ cup corn
salt and pepper
2½ tablespoons diced mango chutney

1 Preheat the oven to 375°F.

2 Stir the white wine into the white sauce and simmer for 10 minutes.

3 Place the chicken in an oven-proof dish. Pour on the sauce and sprinkle with oregano. Bake for 1½ hours.

4 Meanwhile, make the rice. Boil the rice in salted water for 20 minutes. Drain and run hot water through the rice in a strainer to remove any trace of starch.

5 Sauté the onion and garlic in the oil for 5 minutes.

6 Stir in the chopped peppers and corn. Cook for 3 minutes.

7 Mix with the rice, season with salt and pepper. Mix in the chutney. Keep warm.

8 When ready to serve, add the lemon juice to the chicken. Put the rice in a dish, and place the chicken on top.

Serves 4

Reading from the top, clockwise: Yogurt and Cucumber Soup, Almond Fritters, Keftedhes Kebabs, Dolmades and Calypso Chicken with Rice. These are all traditional Greek dishes which you could try at home

Rice with Spices

Because of its bland flavor, rice — especially polished white rice — blends very well with spices. Although curry powder is a useful item in any kitchen cupboard, it is worthwhile experimenting with the common spices (listed opposite) and some of the less familiar ones. Do not be afraid to try new spices and combinations, but use them sparingly at first, and keep a note of quantities so that you can repeat your successes. Spices should be added to the fat and sautéed for a few minutes before the cooking liquid is added.

Turkey Rajah

1 small turkey (or large roasting chicken)
⅓ cup oil
1 teaspoon each salt, black pepper, paprika
½ teaspoon ground ginger

For the Rice:
1 cup long grain rice
2½ cups water
⅔ cup crushed pineapple
12 purple grapes, halved and seeded
rind 1 orange, cut in matchstick strips

For the Sauce:
1 onion, chopped
1 clove garlic, crushed
2 tablespoons oil
2 tablespoons flour
1 teaspoon each turmeric and coriander
½ teaspoon each dry mustard and ginger
pinch each cinnamon and cayenne
6 cardamom seeds
2½ cups chicken stock

Turkey Rajah uses the whole bird and makes an impressive dinner party dish

1 tablespoon vinegar
1 tablespoon honey
1 tablespoon tomato paste
juice 1 orange

1 Preheat the oven to 400°F. In a roasting pan brush the turkey with the oil and rub the salt, pepper, paprika and ginger evenly into the skin. Roast for 25 minutes per lb. turning the oven down to 350°F. after the first ½ hour.

2 Cook the rice in the boiling salted water until tender. Rinse and drain.

3 Sauté the onion and garlic in the oil for 4 minutes until soft. Stir in the flour and sauté 1 minute. Add the spices, stir to blend and cook 1 minute. Pour in the rest of the sauce ingredients, bring to a boil and simmer for 20 minutes until the sauce is thickened, stirring frequently.

4 When the turkey is cooked, mix the cooked rice with the pineapple, halved grapes and orange rind. Place the roasted turkey in the middle of a large serving dish and arrange the rice around it. Pour the sauce over the turkey, reserving some in a sauce boat. Serve immediately with curry side dishes — yogurt, poppadums, sliced raw onion and fruit chutney.

Serves 6–8

Tip: The spices in this recipe can be replaced by commercial curry powder, if desired.

All about Spices

Commercial curry powders are so cheap and available that many cooks get into the habit of using them in so-called Indian dishes. In fact the genuine Indian cuisine never uses a prepared curry powder, but different combinations of spices. Buy spices fresh, in small quantities. Store them in glass jars in a dark, dry place.

Cardamom

Tiny dark seeds in a greenish-buff bean-size pod, cardamoms have a delightful mild flavor and are very aromatic. Several seeds, used whole, impart a delicate flavor to meat, vegetables, cakes and sweet dishes. In India the seeds are chewed to sweeten the breath.

Cayenne and Paprika

Cayenne, a bright orange-red pepper, is the dried and powdered form of chili peppers — small red or green pods of *Capsicum frutescens*. Chilies are extremely hot and become even hotter when dried. They are closely related to the red and green bell or sweet peppers, from which the much milder spice paprika is made. Cayenne is widely used in curries, but should be added very sparingly, according to taste; it also provides red coloring. Paprika may be used where color and flavor are required without the scorching pungency of cayenne.

Cinnamon

The dried inner bark of a tree grown mainly in Sri Lanka, cinnamon has a warm, spicy, sweet flavor well suited to sweet dishes, eggs, cream cheese and butter.

Cloves

Cloves are the dried buds of a tree related to the myrtle and grown in the tropics, especially in Zanzibar. Cloves have a warmly pungent, spicy aroma, excellent in a wide variety of dishes from fruit pies to marinades for meat and fish.

Coriander

Coriander consists of the dried seeds of an umbelliferous plant from the Mediterranean. They may be used whole or ground. Coriander is a pleasantly sweet, aromatic spice used in curries and savory dishes, cakes and desserts.

Cumin

A very important spice in Indian, Oriental and African cooking, cumin has a slightly bitter but pleasant flavor and is strongly aromatic. The small brown seeds are used whole (as in pickles, or in some Dutch cheeses) or ground. It goes particularly well with lamb and vegetables such as cabbage.

Ginger

Ground ginger is most frequently used in Indian cookery, while the Chinese make use of the fresh root from which the spice comes. Ginger has a superbly strong, hot, aromatic flavor which is widely used in both savory and sweet dishes throughout the world.

Mace and Nutmeg

Different parts of the same fruit, mace and nutmeg are aromatic spices similar in flavor; mace has a lighter, more orangey taste, while nutmeg is warm and bittersweet. Nutmeg is the seed of the tree *Myristica fragrans*, and mace is the seed covering. Nutmeg can be bought ground but is best if ground from the whole seed as needed. It is used in meat recipes but mostly in sweet and milky dishes. Mace may be used whole, as in pickles, or ground in meat and fish dishes and sauces.

Turmeric

Most characteristic of all spices used in curry, turmeric comes from the root of a plant related to ginger. Turmeric is a very mild-flavored spice, faintly bitter and only slightly aromatic. Its main effect is in coloring food yellow as it contains a strong dye chemical.

Lamb and Nut Korma

¼ cup cashews
3 dried chilies
½ teaspoon cinnamon
pinch ground cardamom
1 teaspoon ginger
pinch cloves
2 cloves garlic, crushed
2 teaspoons coriander
1 teaspoon cumin
⅔ cup water
2 onions, chopped
¼ cup butter
⅔ cup yogurt
1½ lbs. lean lamb, cubed
grated rind ½ lemon
2 teaspoons lemon juice
½ teaspoon turmeric

1 Grind the nuts and chilies in a blender; add water if needed.

2 Mix the cinnamon, cardamom, ginger, cloves, garlic, coriander and cumin. Add the nuts and chilies, and mix with the water to a paste.

3 Sauté the onion gently for 5 minutes in the butter. Add the paste and yogurt and sauté until the oil separates.

4 Add the lamb, lemon rind and juice, and turmeric. Cover and simmer for 1 hour.

Serves 4

Pork Goulash with Sour Cream

1½ lbs. pork, cubed
salt and pepper
¼ cup paprika
2 tablespoons butter
1 large onion, chopped
¼ cup flour
⅔ cup chicken stock
1¼ cups mushrooms
8 tomatoes, chopped
⅔ cup sour cream

1 Toss the pork in the seasoning and half the paprika.

2 Brown the meat in butter in a casserole, and remove.

3 Sauté the onion for 5 minutes and remove.

4 Add the flour and remaining paprika and sauté for 3 minutes.

5 Add the stock, stir and bring to a boil.

6 Return the pork and onion to the casserole, add the mushrooms and tomatoes, cover and simmer for 45 minutes.

7 Add the sour cream.

Serves 4

Chicken Tandoori

grated rind 1 lemon
6 tablespoons lemon juice
2 teaspoon salt
4 chicken quarters
1 teaspoon coriander
½ teaspoon cumin
1 teaspoon ginger
1 clove garlic, crushed
2 teaspoons paprika
pinch cayenne
1¼ cups yogurt
1 tablespoon vinegar
¼ cup butter

1 Mix the lemon rind, 2 tablespoons of the juice, and the salt. Make gashes in the flesh of the chicken and rub in the mixture.

2 Mix the coriander, cumin, ginger, garlic, paprika and cayenne. Blend with the rest of the lemon juice, add the yogurt and vinegar. Spread over the chicken and cover. Marinate overnight in the refrigerator.

3 Preheat the oven to 400°F.

4 Place the chicken on a rack in a roasting pan for 15 minutes. Baste with the remaining marinade and the butter.

5 Reduce the heat to 350°F. and cook for 1 hour, then increase the heat again to 400°F. for 15 minutes to dry the chicken pieces.

Serves 4

Lamb Biriani

1½ lbs. diced lean lamb
4¾ cups water
sprig coriander or parsley
3 chilies, red and green, seeded
¼ cup oil
¼ cup butter
4 onions
2 cups long grain rice
1 teaspoon turmeric
1 tablespoon coriander seeds
pinch cumin
2 cloves garlic, crushed
salt and pepper
8 crushed cardamoms
⅔ cup raisins
4 canned litchis
sprig watercress

1 Scald the lamb in boiling water for 5 minutes. Drain and place in a saucepan with the fresh water, the coriander or parsley, and the chilies. Simmer covered for 1½ hours. Remove the meat, keep the stock.

2 Heat half of the oil and butter and sauté two chopped onions for 5 minutes. Add the rice and cook for 1 minute. Add half the turmeric, coriander, cumin, and garlic. Sauté for 1 minute. Add the stock and season. Cover and simmer for 20 minutes.

3 Heat the remaining oil and butter and brown the meat. Sprinkle with the rest of the spices and raisins and brown for 3 minutes.

4 Preheat oven to 375°F.

5 Slice the remaining onions and sauté separately until golden.

6 Mix the meat and rice in a dish and cover with the onions. Reheat in oven for 15 minutes. Garnish with litchis and watercress.

Serves 4

Reading clockwise: Pork Goulash with Sour Cream, Lamb and Nut Korma with rice, Lamb Biriani and Chicken Tandoori

Sautéed Chicken with Cumin

1 teaspoon cumin
1 teaspoon paprika
1 teaspoon cardamom
1 clove garlic, crushed
pinch dry mustard
salt and pepper
1 chicken, cut in pieces
⅓ cup oil
2 large onions, chopped
1 teaspoon flour
1¼ cups stock
1 tablespoon soy sauce
1 tablespoon tomato paste
¾ cup mango chutney
pinch cayenne
1 cup rice
2 tablespoons butter
1 green pepper, seeded
2 large tomatoes
1 cup shredded coconut
2 bananas
1 tablespoon lemon juice

1 Blend the spices, garlic, mustard, salt and pepper together and rub them all over the chicken pieces.

2 Heat half of the oil and sauté the onions. Sprinkle with any spices left over from the chicken and cook for 1 minute. Add the flour and stir for 1 minute. Add the stock, soy sauce and tomato paste and simmer for 15 minutes. Strain and check the seasoning. Add 1 tablespoon of the mango chutney and a pinch of cayenne.

3 Preheat the oven to 400°F.

4 In a skillet, heat the rest of the oil and fry the chicken until brown for 12 minutes, covered with a lid, turning the pieces over. Place the chicken in a casserole with the sauce.

5 Bake for 20 minutes, basting with the sauce.

6 Meanwhile, cook the rice in salted water for 20 minutes. Drain and wash to remove starch. Stir in the butter and keep warm.

Sautéed Chicken with Cumin is highly spiced and served with boiled rice, sambals and crisp, fried poppadums

7 Prepare the following sambals in separate bowls as accompaniments to the chicken. Dice the pepper, slice the tomatoes, and place the coconut in a bowl (if you wish, toast the coconut in the oven first for extra flavor). Slice the bananas, and sprinkle with lemon juice to prevent them from turning brown. Put the remaining mango chutney in a bowl.

8 When ready to serve, put the chicken in a dish, and place on the table with the rice and sambals.

Serves 4

Sweet and Sour Chicken

¼ cup vinegar
⅓ cup sugar
1 tablespoon tomato paste
2 tablespoons soy sauce
⅔ cup pineapple juice
1¼ cups water

1 onion, quartered
1 green pepper, cut in squares
1 cup crushed pineapple
1 tablespoon cornstarch
4 tomatoes, quartered
salt and pepper
4 chicken pieces, cooked

1 Preheat the oven to 400°F.

2 Mix the vinegar, sugar, tomato paste, soy sauce, pineapple juice and 1 cup of the water in a pan.

3 Add the onion, pepper and pineapple and bring to a boil. Mix the cornstarch with the rest of the water and add to the pan.

4 Boil, stirring for 1 minute to thicken. Add the tomatoes and season.

5 Pour the sauce over the chicken and heat through in the oven for 20 minutes.

Serves 4

Sweet and Sour Chicken and boiled rice bring a taste of the Orient to your dinner table

Papaya Maori

$\frac{1}{4}$ **cup oil**
1 large onion, chopped
1 clove garlic, chopped
$\frac{3}{4}$ **cup long grain rice**
2$\frac{1}{2}$ cups chicken stock
$\frac{2}{3}$ **cup diced, cooked chicken**
$\frac{1}{3}$ **cup pineapple juice**
salt and pepper
$\frac{1}{3}$ **cup crushed pineapple**
4 papayas, split and seeded
lemon wedges

1 Heat the oil and sauté the onion and garlic for 3 minutes.

2 Add the rice and stir for 1 minute until it becomes translucent. Add the stock, chicken, pineapple juice and seasoning. Bring to a boil and simmer for 20 minutes until the rice

is tender. Add the chopped pineapple and heat for 2 minutes.

3 To serve, fill the cavities of the papayas with the hot rice mixture. Garnish with the lemon wedges.

Serves 4

Sweet and Sour Variations
There are many Sweet and Sour Dishes. Try using cubes of lean pork which you first marinate in a mixture of soy sauce, sherry, salt, sugar and pepper. After 20 minutes, the meat is dipped in a batter of flour, egg, water and salt, and deep fried until golden brown. The pieces are then mixed with other vegetables which have been stir-fried. This can also be done using a whole fish. Make gashes in the skin, rub in the marinade and proceed as for the pork.

Wild Rice

Wild rice is not strictly a cereal but a grass which grows wild in northern Minnesota. Unfortunately, it is expensive and classified as a luxury food. However, if you do have the opportunity to try it, it is well worthwhile. Wild rice has a delicate, nutty flavor with a slightly crunchy texture. It is the harvesting process which makes wild rice so prohibitively expensive. It was traditionally harvested by American Indians who took their boats through the marshes and knocked the wild rice plants as they passed. The grains were released and fell into the boat.

Wild rice is usually served with game birds, venison or fowl. It can also form the basis of a tasty risotto. Alternatively, you can make a ring of wild rice and fill the center with mushrooms or chicken livers in a creamy sauce. Always soak wild rice overnight to obtain the best results. You do not need to use much as it expands to four times its normal size when cooked. To make it go further, you can mix it with brown or white rice. Always wash it well before cooking and place in boiling water with a pinch of salt for about 40 minutes, until tender.

Savory Wild Rice Manitoba

¾ cup wild rice
3 cups water
salt and pepper
¼ cup butter
2 onions, chopped
⅔ cup raisins
½ cup sliced almonds
pinch cinnamon

1 Soak the wild rice overnight, drain and wash well.

2 Bring the water to a boil in a saucepan, season and add the wild rice. Boil gently for 40 minutes until tender.

3 Meanwhile, heat the butter in a skillet and sauté the onions until golden. Add the raisins, flaked almonds, cinnamon and season with salt and pepper.

4 Add the strained, cooked wild rice and heat through. Serve with game or fowl.

Serves 4–6

Tip: Wild rice can be mixed with a variety of vegetables such as cooked peas, corn, lentils or beans. Try mixing in some chopped cooked meat or poultry.

Capon and Wild Rice

one 5-lb. capon
salt and pepper
2 tablespoons oil
¼ lb. butter
¾ cup wild rice, soaked overnight
1 onion, chopped
3 cups water

For the Gravy:
neck, gizzard and giblets of the capon
1¼ cups water
1 chicken bouillon cube
bouquet garni

1 Preheat the oven to 400°F.

2 Rub the capon, both inside and out with the salt and pepper. Then rub with the oil and half of the butter. Roast the capon for 1 hour, basting from time to time.

3 Meanwhile, wash the wild rice thoroughly. Heat the remaining butter in a saucepan and gently sauté the onion for about 5 minutes until soft. Add the wild rice, cook for 1 minute, then add the water and season with salt and pepper. Bring to a boil and boil gently for 40 minutes, until tender.

4 Make the gravy by boiling together the capon giblets, neck and gizzard with the water. Crumble in the bouillon cube, add salt and pepper and the bouquet garni and boil for 10 minutes.

5 Serve the wild rice and gravy separately with the capon. Serve with cranberry sauce and garnish the capon with sprigs of watercress. Serve with green vegetables such as sautéed zucchini, broccoli or sprouts.

Serves 6

Wild Rice with Shallots and Green Peppers

1 cup wild rice
4 cups water
1 chicken bouillon cube
pinch salt
¼ cup butter
2 shallots, finely chopped
½ small green pepper, chopped
1 branch celery, chopped
½ cup chopped walnuts
freshly ground black pepper

1 Soak the wild rice in water overnight, drain and wash well.

2 Put the water, bouillon cube and salt in a saucepan, bring to a boil and add the rice. Cook for about 40 minutes until tender.

3 Melt the butter and sauté the shallots, green pepper and celery for 3 minutes.

4 Add the walnuts, pepper and wild rice and serve as a dressing for game or fowl.

Serves 6

Capon and Wild Rice is a special dish for dinner parties, served with cranberry sauce and pear and apple purée

Rice Stuffings

Using rice in stuffings is a good way of adding carbohydrates and nutrients to your meal.

The rice used must always be at least half cooked and some fat should be included in the stuffing ingredients so that the rice remains separate and does not become sticky.

Tomatoes Stuffed with Rice

12 large, firm tomatoes
2 teaspoons sugar
salt and pepper
½ cup oil
2 onions, chopped
1 bunch parsley, chopped
1⅓ cups long grain rice
2 tablespoons currants
2 tablespoons pine nuts
2 tablespoons dried breadcrumbs

1 Preheat the oven to 400°F. Cut a lid from the stalk end of each tomato and scoop out the centers of the tomatoes. Discard the seeds and dice the pulp. Sprinkle the insides of the tomatoes with sugar, salt and pepper.

2 Heat 4 tablespoons of the oil in a pan and cook the onion until softened. Add the parsley and tomato pulp and cook over low heat until most of the moisture has evaporated.

3 Meanwhile, cook the rice in boiling salted water.

4 Add the currants and pine nuts to the rice. Add the onion and tomato mixture.

5 Fill the tomatoes with the rice mixture. Place them in an ovenproof dish and sprinkle with the breadcrumbs and the rest of the oil.

Bake in the oven for 15 minutes. Serve very hot.

Serves 6

Stuffed Papayas

3 firm ripe papayas
¼ cup butter
1 small onion, thinly sliced
1 branch celery, finely chopped
1 tomato, skinned, seeded and chopped
1 tablespoon chopped blanched almonds, skins removed
¾ lb. ground beef
1 teaspoon curry powder
½ cup water
salt and pepper
1¼ cups cooked rice
1 tablespoon dried breadcrumbs

Tomatoes Stuffed with Rice are a delicious appetizer or ideal accompaniment to salads and broiled meats

1 Preheat the oven to 400°F. Peel and halve the papayas and scoop out the seeds.

2 Heat half the butter in a pan and sauté the onion and celery for 1 minute. Add the tomato and chopped almonds and sauté lightly for a few minutes.

3 Add the beef, curry powder, water and seasoning and simmer for 5 minutes. Stir in the cooked rice.

4 Place the papaya halves in an ovenproof dish and fill them with the stuffing mixture. Sprinkle with the breadcrumbs and the rest of the butter, melted. Bake in the preheated oven for 20 minutes.

Serves 6

Spring Rolls with Ginger Rice

½ lb. puff pastry

oil for deep frying

For the Ginger Rice:
1 cup long grain rice
2 cups water
1 teaspoon salt
1½ tablespoons chopped ginger
2 teaspoons chopped onion
1 tablespoon butter

For the Filling:
2 tablespoons oil
⅓ lb. ground beef
1 small onion, chopped
1 teaspoon curry powder
salt and pepper
1 egg
½ cup breadcrumbs

1 Prepare the rice: put the rice, water and salt in a pan and bring to a boil. Stir once and cover. Simmer for 15 minutes or until the rice is tender and the liquid has been absorbed.

2 Meanwhile, prepare the filling. Heat the oil in a pan and cook the beef and onion for 5 minutes. Add the curry powder, salt and pepper and mix. Remove from the heat and cool. Blend in the egg and the breadcrumbs.

3 Roll out the puff pastry to ⅛ inch thickness and cut into oblongs 3 × 4 inches. Place a spoonful of the meat mixture on each oblong of pastry and roll up.

4 Heat the deep fat to 375°F. and fry the rolls for 5 minutes.

5 Meanwhile, sauté the ginger and the onion in the butter for a few minutes.

6 Drain the rice and mix with the ginger and onion. Drain the spring rolls and serve them with the ginger rice.

Serves 6

Spring Rolls with Ginger Rice can be served as a snack or with sweet and sour Chinese dishes

Maltese Rice Mold

1 tablespoon oil
¾ cup short grain rice
½ cup water
pinch salt
3½ cups milk
¼ cup gelatin
¼ cup superfine sugar
5 drops orange extract
2 drops orange food coloring
4 oranges
4 egg yolks
2 tablespoons orange-flavored liqueur
⅔ cup heavy cream, whipped
20 candied cherries

1 Preheat the oven to 350°F. Oil a 2-pint gelatin mold.

2 Place the rice, water and salt in an ovenproof dish and bake for 12 minutes until the water has been absorbed. Add the milk and bake for a further 30 minutes, covered with foil.

3 Meanwhile, mix the gelatin, sugar, orange extract and orange coloring.

4 Remove the rice from the oven and blend in the gelatin mixture. Peel 1 orange thinly and cut the rind into thin strips. Place in a pan, cover with water and boil for 5 minutes. Drain and rinse. Blend into the rice with the egg yolks. Stir the rice over gentle heat, without boiling, for about 4 minutes until thickened. Add the liqueur.

5 Remove from the heat and when completely cold, fold in the whipped cream. Fill the mold and chill for 2 hours until firm.

6 Peel the oranges, removing the white pith, and cut into sections.

7 Turn out the rice mold and decorate with the orange sections and the cherries.

Maltese Rice Mold is a superb blend of oranges, cream and rice, ringed with cherries

Serves 8

1 Boil the milk and sprinkle in the cornmeal. Simmer for 5 minutes and stir until it thickens **2** Remove from the heat, season, and add the egg yolks and butter **3** Stir until the butter melts **4** Pour the hot cornmeal porridge onto a greased baking sheet **5** When cold, turn out on a board and cut into triangles **6** Meanwhile, sauté the onions, peppers and mushrooms. Add the sliced ham and cook **7** Add the baked beans **8** Arrange the vegetables and ham in a dish surrounded by the triangles of cornmeal and reheat in the oven at 400°F. for 10 minutes. Serve hot

Polenta

2 cups milk
¾ cup cornmeal
salt and pepper
pinch mace
2 egg yolks
¼ cup butter
2 tablespoons oil
1 onion, sliced
4 mushrooms, sliced
1 green pepper, seeded and
  chopped
1 chili, seeded and chopped
¼ lb. ham
½ cup baked beans in tomato sauce

1 Boil the milk and sprinkle in the cornmeal and stir. Cook for 5 minutes, simmering until thick and like porridge. Season with salt, pepper and mace.

2 Remove from the heat and add the egg yolks and butter. Stir until the butter has melted.

3 Pour the mixture into a greased shallow dish. Smooth with a spatula and cool.

4 When cold, turn out on a board and cut into triangles.

5 Heat the oil and sauté the onion for 3 minutes, then add the mushrooms, pepper and chili. Cook for 4 minutes. Add the ham, cut in strips, and the baked beans and simmer for 4 minutes. Season.

6 Preheat the oven to 400°F.

7 Place the mixture in a dish with the triangles of cornmeal arranged around the edge. Reheat for 10 minutes, and serve hot.

Serves 4

Tortillas with Avocado Guacamole Dip

¾ cup cornmeal
1 cup + 2 tablespoons all-purpose
  flour

1 teaspooon salt
1 teaspoon baking powder
3 tablespoons lard or vegetable
  shortening
⅓ cup water
1 egg
For the Dip:
2 ripe avocados, chopped
1 tablespoon diced onion
1 tablespoon lemon juice
3 ozs. cream cheese
½ cup celery, chopped
1 teaspoon chili powder
½ teaspoon salt

1 Sift the cornmeal, flour, salt and baking powder. Rub in the lard or shortening until the mixture resembles breadcrumbs.

2 Add some of the water with the egg to form a stiff dough. Knead it for a few minutes and then let it rest for ½ hour.

3 Take pieces the size of a walnut, and roll out to 6-inch circles, ⅛ inch thick.

4 Preheat the oven to 400°F.

5 Heat a heavy cast-iron griddle or skillet, ungreased, until a drop of water sizzles on the surface. Cook each tortilla for 1 minute on each side until brown flecks appear. When cooked, keep warm in the oven, wrapped in foil.

6 To make the dip, mix the avocados, onion and lemon juice in an electric blender until smooth.

7 Beat the cream cheese until light and add to the avocado mixture. Add the celery, chili powder and salt.

8 Serve immediately as a dip for the tortillas.

Serves 4

Tortillas with Avocado Guacamole dip is typically Mexican. The dip is mild and creamy in texture

Old Crusader Frumenty

The word frumenty is derived from the Latin frumentum, meaning corn. The dish is of Turkish origin and was brought to England by the Crusaders in the thirteenth century. The Arabs call this dessert "Azure."

¾ **cup cracked wheat**
5 cups water
2 cups milk
1¼ cups light cream
½ **cup honey**
⅓ **cup golden raisins**
⅓ **cup currants**
2 tablespoons candied peel
grated rind and juice 1 lemon
few drops vanilla extract
few drops orange extract

few drops rose water extract

For the Thickening:
½ **cup + 1 tablespoon cornstarch**
3 egg yolks
⅔ **cup milk**

For the Decoration:
⅔ **cup heavy cream**
1 pomegranate, cut in wedges
1 stick angelica, cut in strips
4 candied cherries
8 walnuts

1 Soak the cracked wheat in the water for 1 hour. Transfer to a saucepan and bring to a boil, then

---

Frumenty is a Turkish dish which was brought to England by the Crusaders in the thirteenth century

reduce the heat and simmer with the lid on for 30 minutes. Add the milk and cream and bring back to a boil.

2 Blend together the cornstarch, egg yolks and milk in a bowl. Then stir into the wheat mixture until it thickens. Bring to a boil and cook for 4 minutes.

3 Remove from the heat and sweeten with the honey. Add the dried fruits, candied peel, lemon rind and juice and extracts. Cool and pour into a glass dish.

4 Whip the cream until stiff and pipe in rosettes around the top of the bowl in a decorative pattern. Decorate with the pomegranate wedges, angelica, candied cherries and walnuts. Chill and serve.

Serves 6

All about Batters, Custards and Rice Desserts

Individual Crème Caramels

Crêpes

It has been the custom to leave crêpe batter to stand for a while before cooking, but experiments have shown that this makes no difference to the final results. Cooked crêpes will keep for a week if wrapped in foil and stored in the refrigerator. Reheat the crêpes in a lightly greased hot pan, turning once.

Basic Crêpes

1 cup + 2 tablespoons flour
½ teaspoon salt
1 egg
1¼ cups milk
oil for frying

1 Sift the flour and salt into a bowl. Add the egg and half of the milk and beat thoroughly until smooth. Mix in the remaining milk and beat until bubbly.

2 Put the oil for frying in a heat-

Basic Crêpes, cooked to perfection and served with spoonfuls of your favorite jam, are a warming breakfast dish

proof pitcher. Pour a little of the oil into a 6-inch skillet over a fairly high heat. Tilt the pan to coat with oil, then pour any excess back into the pitcher.

3 When the pan is hot, pour in a little batter, tilting the pan to thinly coat the base. Cook quickly, shaking the pan and loosening the edge with a spatula, until the underside is golden brown. Toss the crêpe and cook the second side.

4 Slide the cooked crêpe out onto a plate and keep it warm, covered with a second plate. Repeat with the remaining batter, to make 8-10 crêpes.

5 Fold the crêpes into quarters and serve with jam.

Serves 4

Brandy and Orange Crêpes

Basic Crêpe batter
finely grated rind 1 orange
¼ cup sugar
¼ cup butter
juice 2 oranges
6 tablespoons brandy

1 Make up the batter, adding the grated orange rind with the egg, and make the crêpes following the instructions for the Basic Crêpe recipe. Fold the crêpes in quarters.

2 Gently heat the sugar in a skillet, shaking the pan, until the sugar is golden brown. Remove the pan from the heat and add the butter, orange juice and half of the brandy.

3 Place the folded crêpes in the pan and simmer for a few minutes, spooning on the sauce.

4 Warm the remaining brandy, pour it over the crêpes, ignite and serve immediately.

Serves 4

Brandy and Orange Crêpes are a variation of the famous Crêpes Suzette. You can prepare this dish well in advance

Pear Crêpe Cake

1½ recipes Basic Crêpe batter
2 tablespoons butter
¼ cup flour
1¼ cups milk
2 pears, peeled, quartered and
  cored
2 tablespoons pistachios
2 tablespoons sugar
few drops almond extract
⅓ cup apricot jam

1 Make the crêpes following the instructions for the basic recipe (see page 586). Pile the crêpes flat and keep them warm between two plates while making the sauce.

2 Preheat the oven to 375°F. Melt the butter in a pan, stir in the flour and cook over low heat for 2 minutes. Gradually stir in the milk, bring to a boil and simmer for 3 minutes, stirring continuously.

3 Slice the pears thinly. Skin and chop the pistachios. Add the pears and pistachios to the sauce with the sugar and almond extract and warm through.

4 Place a crêpe on a serving dish and spread it evenly with 2 teaspoons of the jam and some of the sauce. Place another crêpe on top and spread with jam and sauce. Continue to layer crêpes in the same way, finishing with a plain crêpe.

5 Place the crêpe cake in the oven for 10 minutes to heat through. Serve hot, cut into wedges.

Serves 8

Pear Crêpe Cake — wafer-thin crêpes layered with sweet apricot jam and a delicious pear and pistachio sauce

put a scoop of ice cream onto each and fold the crêpe in half. Serve immediately with the lemon sauce.

Serves 4

Lemon Surprise Crêpes

⅔ cup sour cream
2 tablespoons sugar
finely grated rind and juice 1
  lemon
Basic Crêpe batter

1 teaspoon ground ginger
8-10 scoops vanilla ice cream

1 Make the lemon sauce by mixing together the sour cream, sugar, lemon rind and juice.

2 Make up the crêpe batter, adding the ginger with the flour. Make the crêpes following the instructions for the Basic Crêpe recipe (see page 586). Pile the crêpes flat and keep them warm between two plates.

3 When all the crêpes are cooked,

Apple-Pear Crêpes

Basic Crêpe batter
1 teaspoon cinnamon
2 red apples

Chocolate Walnut Crêpes

Basic Crêpe batter
⅓ cup raisins
3 tablespoons rum
¼ cup butter
1 cup very finely chopped walnuts
¾ cup sugar
½ teaspoon vanilla extract
3 tablespoons light cream

For the Chocolate Sauce:
4 ozs. milk chocolate
2 teaspoons cornstarch
1 cup milk
2 teaspoons sugar
3 tablespoons light cream
½ teaspoon cinnamon

1 First make the walnut filling: soak the raisins in the rum for 15 minutes. Soften the butter and blend in the walnuts, sugar, vanilla and cream. Mix well, then add the rum and fruit.

2 Make the chocolate sauce: break the chocolate into a small pan and add 3 tablespoons cold water. Stir over gentle heat until melted and smooth. Blend the cornstarch with a little of the milk and stir into the chocolate with the sugar and remaining milk. Gradually bring to a boil and simmer for 5 minutes, stirring. Remove from the heat and stir in the cream and cinnamon.

3 Make the crêpes following the instructions for the Basic Crêpe recipe (see page 586). Put a little of the walnut filling onto each cooked crêpe, roll up the crêpes and transfer to a heated serving dish. Cover and keep warm.

4 Gently reheat the chocolate sauce and pour it over the crêpes. Serve immediately.

Serves 4

---

3 pears
¼ cup sugar
1 tablespoon cornstarch
juice 1 orange
3 tablespoons apricot jam
sugar for sprinkling

1 Make up the batter, adding the cinnamon with the flour. Make the crêpes following the instructions for the Basic Crêpe recipe (see page 586). Pile the crêpes flat and keep them warm between two plates while making the filling.

2 Quarter the apples and pears, remove the cores and cut the fruit into chunks.

3 Place the sugar in a pan with 1¼

Apple-Pear Crêpes are easy to prepare and are sure to become a favorite with your family for winter suppers

---

cups cold water and stir over low heat until dissolved. Blend the cornstarch with the orange juice and stir into the pan with apricot jam. Bring to a boil and simmer for 3 minutes, stirring continuously.

4 Put some of the filling in the middle of each crêpe, roll up the crêpes and transfer to a heated serving dish. Sprinkle with a little sugar and serve.

Serves 4

Custards

Custard is made from a base of milk and egg yolks. It must be cooked gently and stirred frequently to prevent curdling. Once you have perfected the art of making a good custard you can flavor and sweeten it to taste, use it as a filling for pastries and cakes or simply as an accompaniment to your favorite stewed fruit. The following recipes will give you some idea of the many ways you can enhance the simple charm of this underrated dessert.

Crème Brulée

2 tablespoons butter
6 egg yolks
½ cup sugar
2½ cups light cream
3 tablespoons brown sugar

1 Preheat the oven to 300°F. Grease a 3¾-cup shallow ovenproof dish with the butter.

2 In a bowl, cream the egg yolks and sugar. Bring the cream almost to a boil and stir it very gradually into the egg mixture. Strain the custard into the shallow dish. Stand the dish in 1 inch of cold water in a roasting pan and bake in the oven for 1–1½ hours or until the custard has firmly set.

3 Remove the custard from the oven and let it cool. Chill it overnight in the refrigerator.

4 About 1 hour before serving, sprinkle the top with the brown sugar. Brown it very quickly under the broiler, turning the dish occasionally so that the sugar melts evenly. Cool until the sugar topping becomes crisp. Serve with a bowl of whipped cream.

Serves 6

Confectioners' Custard

½ cup flour
4 eggs
⅓ cup sugar
2½ cups milk

1 Sift the flour. Separate the eggs and place the yolks in a bowl — you will not need the whites.

2 Add the sugar to the egg yolks and beat the mixture until it becomes creamy and has increased in bulk. Add the sifted flour all at once and beat in.

3 Bring the milk to a boil in a thick-bottomed saucepan. Gradually whisk the milk into the egg mixture. Return the mixture to the saucepan and bring slowly to a boil, whisking continually. Cook gently until it becomes a smooth cream — the flour will stop it from curdling.

Makes about 3¾ cups

Zuppa Inglese

6 eggs
1⅓ cups sugar
1 tablespoon grated orange rind
⅔ cup flour
⅔ cup cornstarch
1 tablespoon butter
pinch salt

For the Filling:
½ lb. candied fruits
½ cup cherry-flavored liqueur
1¼ cups confectioners' custard

For the Meringue:
3 egg whites
¼ cup sugar
2 tablespoons confectioners' sugar

1 The day before the meal, make the cake. Separate the egg whites from the yolks and place them in separate bowls. Add the sugar to the yolks and beat them until thick and creamy. This should take about 8 minutes of constant beating by hand. Add the orange rind, flour and cornstarch and mix well.

2 Preheat the oven to 325°F. Grease an 8-inch cake pan with the butter.

3 Add a pinch of salt to the egg whites and beat them until they are stiff. Fold the egg whites gently into the cake mixture. Pour the mixture into the cake pan and place it in the oven for 25 minutes. The cake should be just colored when the cooking time is over. Turn the cake out on a rack and cool.

4 On the day of the meal, dice the candied fruits. Place them in a bowl with the liqueur and soak for 2 hours. Drain the fruits, reserving the liquid, and stir them into the confectioners' custard.

5 Cut the cake into 2 layers. Pour half the reserved liquid over each layer. Spread the bottom layer with the confectioners' custard and place the other layer on top.

6 Preheat the oven to 325°F.

7 Prepare the meringue. Beat the egg whites until they start to whiten. Add the sugar and continue beating until stiff. Cover the cake with large swirls of the meringue, using a decorators' bag or large spoon. Sprinkle the meringue with the confectioners' sugar.

8 Place the cake on the top shelf of the oven for 6-8 minutes to lightly brown the meringue. Remove from the oven and allow to cool. Chill in the refrigerator and serve.

Serves 6-8

1 Separate the eggs and place the yolks in a bowl. You will not need the whites **2** Add the sugar to the yolks and whisk until they are creamy **3** Whisk in the sifted flour **4** Bring the milk to a boil, whisking occasionally to stop a skin from forming **5** Gradually whisk it into the egg mixture **6** Return the custard to the saucepan and whisk gently over low heat until it is smooth

Basic Baked Egg Custard

2¼ cups milk
3 eggs
2 tablespoons sugar
1 teaspoon grated nutmeg

1 Preheat the oven to 325°F.

2 Heat the milk gently in a saucepan. Make sure that it does not boil.

3 Meanwhile, beat the eggs and sugar together in a mixing bowl.

4 Pour in the hot milk, stirring continuously. Then pour the custard into a greased ovenproof dish and sprinkle on the grated nutmeg.

5 Place the dish in the preheated oven and bake until set (about 45 minutes).

Serves 4

Pear and Almond Custard

4 pears, peeled, cored and
  quartered
1¼ cups water
⅔ cups sugar
⅓ cup blanched almonds
few drops almond extract
2 egg yolks
3 tablespoons cornstarch
1¼ cups light cream
4 candied cherries
1 tablespoon sliced almonds

1 Place the pears, water and sugar together in a saucepan and bring to a boil. Poach until the pears are tender.

2 Strain off the syrup and purée

Pear and Almond Custard tastes as good as it looks with its fresh juicy pears in a delicately flavored almond custard

with the blanched almonds and almond extract.

3 Blend the egg yolks, cornstarch and 2 tablespoons of the cream together in a bowl. Then stir in the syrup and the rest of the cream.

4 Reheat in a saucepan just to boiling point, then allow to cool.

5 Divide the pears between four attractive glasses and pour in the almond custard.

6 Decorate with candied cherries and sliced almonds. Chill before serving.

Serves 4

Tips: If fresh pears are out of season or unavailable, you can always substitute canned pears.

To blanch almonds, just pour boiling water over them and leave for a few minutes. Remove the skins by squeezing the end of each nut — the almond will pop out.

Baked Custard Tarts

dough for one 9-inch pie crust
butter
1¾ cups milk
½ teaspoon vanilla extract
3 eggs
1 tablespoon sugar
1 teaspoon grated nutmeg

1 Preheat the oven to 400°F.

2 Roll out the dough ⅛ inch thick. Butter some tartlet tins and line with the dough. Prick the bottoms and put aside in a cool place.

3 Place the milk and vanilla extract in a saucepan and heat through.

4 Meanwhile, cream together the eggs and sugar until light and creamy. Pour on the hot milk, stirring well, and then strain. Cool.

5 When cool, pour the custard into the prepared tartlet tins. Leave about ¼ inch at the top of each tin.

6 Sprinkle the tarts with grated nutmeg and bake in the oven for about 20 minutes until cooked and golden. Serve cold with cream.

Serves 4–6

Tips: You can flavor these delicious tarts with a few drops of your favorite liqueur — orange liqueurs are particularly good. Or add some instant coffee granules or cocoa. Another idea is to stir some chestnut purée into the custard mixture.

Also, be careful not to overcook these tarts. As soon as the custard rises and feels firm, the tarts are cooked. It is easy to overcook and allow them to become watery. It helps if you place the tartlet tins on a hot baking sheet in the oven.

Floating Islands with Oranges — egg whites floating on top of a creamy custard which is flavored with oranges

Floating Islands with Oranges

4 eggs, separated
pinch salt
1 cup sugar
2¼ cups milk
2 oranges
¼ cup orange-flavored liqueur

1 Beat the egg whites with a pinch of salt until they form stiff peaks. Beat in ½ cup of the sugar, a little at a time.

2 Bring water to a boil and drop the meringue, a few tablespoonfuls at a time, into the water. Simmer for about 10 minutes until cooked through. Remove, drain and dry on a clean cloth. Repeat until all the meringue is used up.

3 Meanwhile, heat the milk and grate the rind and squeeze the juice of 1 orange. Add the grated rind to the milk.

4 Cream together the egg yolks with the remaining sugar and gradually whisk in the hot milk away from the heat. When all the milk is added, return the mixture to the saucepan and gently reheat, stirring all the time, until the custard is thick and coats the back of a spoon. Cool a little, then stir in the orange juice and liqueur. Pour into a serving dish.

5 With a zesting knife, make vertical grooves at regular intervals around the remaining orange. Then slice it thinly, horizontally. Decorate the top of the custard with the meringues and arrange the slices of orange around the sides of the dish to form an attractive border.

Serves 4

Tip: As a variation on this dish, you can stretch it further by pouring the orange custard onto a layer of sponge cake soaked in sherry, or crushed macaroons sprinkled with an orange-flavored liqueur.

Another way of cooking the whisked egg white meringue is to drop the spoonfuls into the hot milk which you intend to use for the custard.

593

Look 'n Cook Floating Islands

1 and 2 Separate the eggs and place the yolks and whites in different bowls 3 Add half the sugar to the egg yolks and whisk them to a cream 4 and 5 Whisk the egg whites until stiff, add the remaining sugar and continue to whisk until they are very stiff 6 Heat the milk and vanilla extract in a large saucepan. Drop 4 tablespoonfuls of the meringue into the hot (not boiling) milk and poach them for 5 minutes on either side

594

7 Remove and place them to drain on a clean cloth **8** Bring the milk to a boil and gradually whisk it into the egg yolks **9** and **10** Return the custard to the saucepan and cook it gently, stirring continually, until it coats the spoon **11** and **12** Strain it and pour it into 4 individual serving dishes. Let it cool. Place a poached meringue on top, chill and serve

Floating Islands

5 eggs
⅔ cup sugar
3 cups milk
½ teaspoon vanilla extract

1 Break the eggs and place the whites and yolks in separate bowls.

2 Add half the sugar to the yolks and beat them until they are creamy. Beat the egg whites until they are stiff, add the remaining sugar and continue to beat until the meringue is very stiff.

3 Bring the milk and vanilla to a boil, reduce the heat and drop 4 tablespoonfuls of the meringue mixture into the saucepan. Let the meringues poach for 5 minutes on either side. Remove them with a slotted spoon and place them on a clean cloth to dry.

4 Return the milk to a boil and gradually whisk it into the egg yolk mixture. Return this mixture to the saucepan and cook it over low heat, stirring constantly with a wooden spoon until the custard is smooth and coats the spoon.

5 Strain the custard and pour it into 4 individual serving dishes. Allow the custard to cool. Place a poached meringue on top of each dish and chill in the refrigerator for 1 hour before serving.

Serves 4

Almond Coffee Cream

2 eggs
⅔ cup sugar
1 cup heavy cream
¾ cup almonds
¼ cup cold black coffee
¾ cup confectioners' sugar

Almond Coffee Cream is a smooth, rich dessert, topped with almonds and garnished with rich coffee-flavored candies

For the Garnish:
24 coffee-flavored candies

1 Separate the eggs and place the yolks in a bowl. You will not need the whites.

2 Place the bowl containing the egg yolks in a bowl of hot, but not boiling, water. Add the sugar to the yolks and beat the mixture thoroughly for 3 minutes. Gradually pour in ¼ cup of the cream and continue to beat until the mixture is thick and smooth.

3 Preheat the oven to 400°F. Place the almonds in a small saucepan with just enough water to cover them. Bring the water to a boil and remove the saucepan from the heat. Drain and rinse the almonds and peel off their skins. Chop them into fine slivers. Wrap them in aluminum foil and place in the preheated oven for 2 minutes. Allow them to cool in the foil.

4 Reserve 1 tablespoon of the almond slivers and mix the rest into the egg mixture.

5 Whip the remaining cream and stir in the black coffee. Gently fold in the confectioners' sugar. Mix this coffee cream with the egg yolk mixture.

6 Pour the cream into 4 individual serving dishes. Place them in the refrigerator to chill for at least 4 hours. Sprinkle with the reserved almonds, garnish with the coffee-flavored candies and serve.

Serves 4

Cabinet Pudding

one plain 8-inch sponge cake
⅓ cup candied cherries
2 tablespoons angelica
1 tablespoon butter
1 tablespoon sugar

For the Custard:
3 eggs
¼ cup sugar
½ teaspoon vanilla extract
2¼ cups milk

1 Cut the sponge cake into ½-inch cubes and place them in a bowl. Quarter the cherries and cut the angelica into small strips. Carefully

Cabinet Pudding, a traditional British dessert, is a tasty mixture of sponge cake and candied fruits set in an egg custard

mix them both with the cake cubes.

2 Butter the inside of six ⅔-cup molds and sprinkle each with a little sugar. Divide the cake mixture between the 6 molds. Preheat the oven to 400°F.

3 Prepare the custard. In a bowl, cream together the eggs, sugar and vanilla extract. Heat the milk without letting it boil and blend it thoroughly with the egg mixture. Pass the custard through a strainer and divide it between each of the 6 molds. Allow 30 minutes for the custard to soak through the cake.

4 Place the molds in a roasting pan with 1½ inches of water. Bake them in the oven for 30 minutes or until they are set. Turn them out onto a serving dish and serve immediately with a bowl of whipped cream.

Serves 6

Coffee Banana Custard

3 eggs
2 tablespoons sugar
1 tablespoon instant coffee
 granules
2¼ cups milk
2 bananas
grated chocolate to decorate

1 Beat together the eggs, sugar and coffee. Warm the milk and pour into the egg mixture, stirring well.

2 Strain the mixture into a heavy-based pan and stir over gentle heat with a wooden spoon until the custard thinly coats the back of the spoon. Do not allow it to boil. Cool slightly.

3 Slice the bananas thinly and divide between 4 individual glass serving dishes.

4 Pour the warm coffee custard over the bananas and sprinkle the tops with grated chocolate. Serve immediately.

Serves 4

Tip: Orange Strawberry custard can be made following the recipe above. Omit the instant coffee granules and grated chocolate from the ingredients. Put a few strips of thinly pared orange rind in the milk when it is warmed, cover the pan and let it infuse for 10 minutes before pouring into the egg mixture. Slice some fresh strawberries into the serving dishes and decorate the tops with finely grated orange rind.

Whisky Sabayon

6 egg yolks
¾ cup sugar
pinch grated nutmeg
⅓ cup whisky
juice 1 lemon
grated rind and juice 1 orange

1 Beat together the egg yolks, sugar and nutmeg in a large bowl.

2 Add the whisky, place the bowl over a pan of hot water and beat until the mixture is thick.

3 Add the lemon and orange juice and continue to beat over the pan of hot water until the mixture is thick and pale.

4 Remove the bowl from the heat and beat until the mixture is cool. Spoon into 4 individual glass serving dishes, and decorate each with a little grated orange rind. Serve chilled.

Serves 4

Pear Brioche — yeasty, rich brioche stuffed with fresh chopped pears, crisp macaroons and cherry-flavored custard

Pear Brioche

3¾ cups flour
1 teaspoon salt
1½ tablespoons fresh yeast
3 tablespoons sugar
⅓ cup milk
2 eggs, beaten
¼ cup butter

For the Filling:
3 egg yolks
1 whole egg
½ cup flour
⅓ cup sugar
2¼ cups milk
2 tablespoons cherry-flavored
 liqueur

4 ripe pears
6 almond macaroons, crushed
½ cup apricot jam

1 For the brioche: sift the flour and salt into a warm bowl. Blend the yeast with 1 teaspoon of the sugar, and add to the flour with the milk, beaten eggs, and the remaining sugar. Beat well until the dough is smooth and elastic. Work the butter into the dough.

2 Cover the bowl with a damp cloth and let rise in a warm place for 40 minutes. Preheat the oven to 425°F.

3 Stir the dough well and turn into a lightly greased Charlotte mold or cake pan. Cover and leave to rise for 15 minutes.

4 Bake for 50 minutes, until golden brown. Turn out onto a wire rack to cool.

5 For the filling: place the egg yolks, whole egg, flour and sugar in a bowl and mix together well. Heat the milk and pour into the egg mixture, stirring. Return the mixture to the pan and stir continuously over medium heat until the mixture comes to a boil. Remove from the heat immediately, add the liqueur and cool.

6 Peel, core and dice the pears. Stir the pears and crushed macaroons into the cooled custard.

7 Turn the oven to 375°F. Remove a slice from the top of the brioche and scoop out some of the inside, leaving a hole almost large enough to hold the pear custard. Wrap the brioche loosely in aluminum foil and place in the oven for about 15 minutes to warm through.

8 Meanwhile, melt the apricot jam in a pan with 2 tablespoons water. Gently reheat the pear custard.

9 Stand the brioche on a heated serving dish and pour on the melted jam, coating the inside generously, and allowing a little to drizzle down the outside. Fill the brioche with the heated pear custard and serve immediately.

Serves 6

Lemon Sabayon is a smooth and creamy custard dessert made with fresh lemons, orange liqueur, egg yolks, sugar and milk

Lemon Sabayon

4 egg yolks
1 whole egg
¼ cup sugar
finely grated rind and juice 1 lemon
1 tablespoon orange-flavored liqueur
1¼ cups sweet vermouth

1 Place the egg yolks, whole egg and sugar together in a bowl and beat for 5 minutes.

2 Beat in the lemon rind and juice, liqueur and vermouth.

3 Place the bowl over a pan of hot water and continue to beat until the mixture is thick and pale.

4 Remove the bowl from the heat and beat until the mixture is cool. Spoon into 4 individual glass dishes and serve chilled.

Serves 4

Queen of Puddings

2¼ cups milk
¾ cup sugar
4 cups cake crumbs
grated rind 2 lemons
2 eggs, separated
¾ cup apricot jam

1 Preheat the oven to 350°F. Heat the milk and ¼ cup of the sugar gently in a saucepan. Stir in the cake crumbs and lemon rind and remove from the heat. Beat in the egg yolks.

2 Pour half the mixture into a buttered earthenware dish and bake it in the oven for 30 minutes or until set.

3 Heat the apricot jam in a saucepan and spread half over the top of the set custard. Fill up the dish with the remaining egg yolk mixture and return it to the oven for a further 30 minutes or until it is thoroughly set.

4 Cover the top of the pudding with the rest of the jam. Beat the egg whites with ⅓ cup of the remaining sugar until stiff.

5 Raise the oven temperature to 375°F. Spoon the meringue onto the pudding and sprinkle with the remaining sugar. Return to the oven and bake for 5 minutes or until the meringue is golden. Serve immediately.

Serves 6

Crème Caramel

2 tablespoons water
½ cup sugar

Crème Caramel is a classic French dessert which is always a favorite at parties with its creamy texture and caramel topping

4 eggs
¼ cup sugar
½ teaspoon vanilla extract
2¼ cups milk

1 Make the caramel. Bring half of the water and ½ cup sugar to a boil in a heavy-based saucepan. When it begins to caramelize, add the remaining water and reboil until the water and caramel mix.

2 Line the mold as shown on the opposite page.

3 Preheat the oven to 350°F. Cream together the eggs, sugar and vanilla extract. Heat the milk, without letting it boil, and gradually blend it into the egg mixture. Strain this cream and pour it into the mold. Place the mold in a roasting pan, half-filled with water, and bake for 1 hour, or until set.

4 Chill thoroughly before turning out the caramel onto a serving dish. Pour any caramel remaining in the mold around the dish and serve.

Serves 6

1 Hold the rim of the mold with a clean cloth to prevent burning your hands and pour in the caramel **2** and **3** Tip and rotate the mold so the base is covered in caramel **4** and **5** Tip the mold so it is almost on its side and continue to rotate it until all the sides are well coated **6** When the interior of the mold is completely coated, pour off and discard the excess caramel

Rice Desserts

Rice pudding is not a name that conjures visions of exotic culinary delights; for many people it is a reminder of institutional cooking that they prefer to forget. However, rice pudding is not only easy, cheap and nutritious — it can also be delicious and impressive. Even a basic rice pudding can be varied in many ways. Try adding beaten egg, spices, raisins, chopped candied fruits, or cream. Serve it with unusual fruits such as mango, papaya or passion fruit.

Basic Rice Pudding

¼ cup short grain rice
2 tablespoons butter
2 tablespoons sugar
2¼ cups milk
pinch grated nutmeg

1 Preheat the oven to 300°F.

2 Wash the rice in a colander under running water, and drain. Butter an ovenproof dish.

3 Place the rice and sugar in the dish. Pour in the milk and top with the rest of the butter, cut in small pieces. Dust with freshly grated nutmeg.

4 Bake in the oven for 2 hours, stirring the pudding after ½ hour. Serve hot or cold.

Serves 4

Banana Rice Caramel

½ cup short grain rice
3⅔ cups milk
1 cup sugar
1 tablespoon water
4 bananas
½ teaspoon vanilla extract
4 eggs, beaten

1 Place the rice in a pan of cold water and bring it to a boil. Rinse with cold water and drain.

2 Bring the milk to a boil in a pan and add the rice. Cook for about 40 minutes until the rice is very tender and has absorbed the milk.

Banana Rice Caramel is served either hot or cold. Your children will adore the flavor of the bananas and sticky toffee

3 Meanwhile, make the caramel by melting ½ cup sugar in the water, stirring constantly. Boil to 315°F. when it starts to color. Remove the pan from the heat and dip its base at once into cold water to stop the sugar from cooking further.

4 Pour the caramel into a mold. Holding the mold with a cloth, turn it so that the caramel is distributed over the sides. Allow the caramel to cool to a sticky consistency.

5 Preheat the oven to 350°F. Peel and slice 3 bananas. Arrange the slices over the bottom of the mold and in one row around the sides.

6 When the rice is cooked, stir in ½ cup sugar and the vanilla extract. Fold in the beaten eggs. Pour the mixture into the mold lined with caramel and banana.

7 Bake the rice in a pan of water in the oven for 40 minutes. Turn out the mold onto a serving dish. Peel and slice the remaining banana and arrange the slices around the pudding. Serve hot or cold.

Serves 4-6

Mandarin Condé

⅓ cup rice
2¼ cups milk
¼ cup sugar
½ teaspoon vanilla extract
1 tablespoon candied orange peel cut in small strips
1 cup canned mandarin orange sections
½ cup candied cherries

For the Apricot Glaze:
¼ cup apricot jam
2 tablespoons sugar
1¼ cups water

Mandarin Condé is a substantial dessert — the tangy flavor of mandarin oranges provide a contrast to the creamy rice

2 teaspoons cornstarch
1 tablespoon orange-flavored liqueur

1 Place the rice in a pan of cold water. Bring to a boil. Rinse in cold water.

2 Bring the milk to a boil in a pan. Add the rice and cook until it is soft and has absorbed the milk.

3 Stir in the sugar and vanilla extract and add the pieces of candied orange peel. Moisten a mold and pour the rice into it. Press it down level and firmly, and let it cool.

4 To make the apricot glaze, heat the jam, sugar and water gently until they are melted and smooth. Add the cornstarch, dissolved in a little water, and boil for 2 minutes until the glaze clears. Stir in the liqueur.

5 When the rice is cold and set, turn it out onto a serving dish. Arrange the mandarin sections on top of and around, the rice. Place a whole cherry in the middle and halved cherries in the mandarin sections around the rice. Pour the apricot glaze over the middle of the rice so that it flows down the sides. Serve cold.

Serves 4–6

Tip: Many different orange liqueurs may be used to flavor the apricot glaze. Or the liqueur can be replaced by orange extract, but this is much stronger, so use only 2-3 drops.

Look 'n Cook Rice Condé with Apricots

1 Place the rice in a saucepan of cold water and bring it to a boil **2** Rinse the rice in cold water and leave it until it is quite cold **3** Drain the rice through a colander **4** Bring the milk to a boil and pour the rice into it **5** Br-ing the mixture back to a boil, then cover the pan and place it in a preheated oven. Bake for about 40 minutes until the rice is completely cooked **6** Add the vanilla extract and mix well **7** Gently stir in the sugar **8**

Dampen a shallow cake pan. Pour the rice into it and press it down firmly and evenly **9** Allow the rice to cool. Turn it out onto a serving dish **10** Decorate the top with the apricot halves **11** Glaze the top of the fruit with the apricot glaze **12** Decorate the dish with candied cherries and angelica

Rice Condé with Apricots

½ cup short or long grain rice
3 cups milk
½ teaspoon vanilla extract
½ cup sugar
¼ cup apricot jam
2 teaspoons cherry-flavored
  liqueur
12 canned apricot halves
6 candied cherries
1 stick candied angelica

1 Preheat the oven to 325°F.

2 Place the rice in a saucepan of cold water and bring to a boil. Drain, rinse in cold water, and drain again through a colander.

3 In an ovenproof pan or casserole, bring the milk to a boil. Add the rice and bring it back to a boil. Cover the pan or casserole and place it in the oven. Cook for 1 hour or until the rice has absorbed all the milk.

4 Remove the rice from the oven. Gently stir in the vanilla extract (do not add too much) and the sugar with a fork.

5 Moisten a shallow cake pan with cold water and pour the rice into it. Press it down firmly and make an even flat surface. Let cool.

6 Melt the apricot jam in a pan over low heat and stir in the liqueur.

7 Place a serving dish over the rice mold and turn it over so that the rice comes out of the pan in one piece. Arrange the canned apricot halves over the top and pour the melted apricot glaze over them. Decorate with the cherries and the candied angelica, cut in short strips. Serve cold.

Serves 4–6

Tip: Do not add sugar to the milk while it is cooking, as this will prevent the rice from swelling up. You could substitute other fruit for the apricots in this recipe: try using peaches, pears or cherries.

606

Empress Rice Pudding

3 cups milk
⅓ cup short grain rice
½ cup sugar
½ teaspoon vanilla extract
¼ cup unflavored gelatin
¼ cup diced mixed candied fruit
  and peel
⅔ cup all-purpose cream
2 egg whites
9 candied cherries to garnish

1 In a saucepan, bring the milk to a boil. Wash the rice and add it to the

Empress Rice Pudding is a creamy and colorful dessert, and is decorated with delicious diced candied fruits and mixed peel

milk. Simmer until the rice is tender and has absorbed the milk.

2 Stir the sugar gently into the rice. Blend in the vanilla extract.

3 Dissolve the gelatin in a little hot water. Cool and add to the rice. Add the diced candied fruit and peel, and mix well.

4 Cool. Beat the cream lightly and fold it into the rice.

5 Beat the egg whites until stiff. Fold them into the rice. Moisten a ring mold with cold water and pour the rice mixture into it. Place the mold in the refrigerator and chill until the mixture is firmly set.

6 Turn the rice pudding out onto a serving dish. Place the cherries around the top to decorate and serve.

Serves 4–6

All about Cheesecakes, Sponge Desserts and Meringues

Apricot Cheesecake

Cheesecakes

Cheesecakes are becoming increasingly popular and you can easily make your own at home. They can be baked or set with gelatin. They are nearly always served cold. There is a wide range of attractive and delicious cheesecake recipes to choose from. They may be made with cream, cottage or ricotta cheese on a base of rich crust or cookie crumbs.

You can top cheesecakes with whipped cream, fresh or candied fruit, or a fruit glaze. You can sprinkle a layer of fresh fruit, such as raspberries; or dried fruits between the crust and the cheesecake mixture. Cream and cottage cheese have rather a bland flavor, therefore the grated rind and juice of a lemon or orange are often added. In Italy, grated Parmesan cheese is sometimes mixed into the cheesecake for extra flavor.

Cheesecakes freeze particularly well so you can make one in advance, freeze it until you need it, and decorate just before serving with fruit, cream or a glaze.

Pineapple Cheesecake

1¼ cups gingersnap crumbs
¼ lb. butter
4 ozs. cream cheese
½ cup crushed pineapple
¼ cup sugar
1 tablespoon lemon juice
¼ cup water
2 tablespoons unflavored gelatin

⅔ cup heavy cream
4 pineapple rings
6 candied cherries
angelica to decorate

1 Crush the gingersnaps. This is best done by placing them in a paper bag. Secure the end and crush with a heavy rolling pin.

2 Place the crushed cookies in a bowl. Heat the butter in a saucepan and mix well with the melted butter.

3 Spread the cookie mixture over the base of an 8-inch diameter shallow springform pan.

4 Blend together the cream cheese, crushed pineapple and sugar. Stir in the lemon juice.

5 Warm the water and dissolve the gelatin. Stir well until it is dissolved. Cool a little, then add to the cream cheese mixture.

6 Whip the cream until stiff and fold in with a metal spoon. Pour the cheesecake mixture over the crust base and level off the top. Chill in the refrigerator for about 3 hours until firm and set.

7 Remove the cheesecake from the mold and place on an attractive serving plate.

8 Cut the pineapple rings into chunks and slice the cherries in half. Slice the angelica to make two thin 'stems' and four diamond-shaped 'leaves.'

9 Next, make two flowers using the pineapple chunks as 'petals,' the cherries as centers and angelica 'stems' and 'leaves.' Arrange these flowers on the top of the cheesecake. Place the remaining pineapple and cherries alternately around the base to form a decorative border.

Serves 6

Tips: You can use cottage cheese instead of cream cheese in this recipe. To give it a more lemony, sharper flavor, add a little grated lemon rind.

Chocolate Orange Cheesecake

1¼ cups graham cracker crumbs
¼ lb. butter
pinch cinnamon
butter for greasing
¼ cup milk
3 ozs. semisweet chocolate
8 ozs. cream cheese
¼ cup water
4 tablespoons unflavored gelatin
juice and grated rind 1 orange
⅔ cup heavy cream, whipped
3 candied cherries
chocolate wafer candies to decorate

1 Crush the graham crackers as described above. Melt the butter and blend with the crumbs and cinnamon.

2 Butter the bottom of an 8-inch springform pan and line the sides with wax paper.

3 Spread the crumb mixture over the base of the pan.

4 Place the milk and chocolate in a saucepan and heat gently, stirring until the chocolate melts. Mix well with the cream cheese.

5 Heat the water and dissolve the gelatin. Reheat until you have a clear jelly-like substance.

6 Stir the gelatin into the cream cheese and the orange rind and juice. Fold in the whipped cream, and then pour the mixture into the pan.

7 Chill in the refrigerator for 3 hours until set and firm. Remove the cheesecake from the pan and place on a serving plate. Decorate the top with halved cherries and chocolate wafers before serving.

Serves 6–8

Pineapple Cheesecake (top) and Chocolate Orange Cheesecake (below) are good to look at and great to eat

¼ **cup light cream**
2 drops vanilla extract
⅓ **cup raisins**
⅔ **cup all-purpose cream**

1 Preheat the oven to 400°F. Roll the dough on a floured board to ¼ inch thick. Lightly butter a flan ring and line it with the dough. Prick the bottom and bake for 10-15 minutes.

2 Meanwhile, peel, core and thinly slice the apples. Melt the butter in a pan and cook the apple slices over gentle heat for a few minutes until tender. Strain and allow to cool.

3 To make the cheesecake filling, beat the egg with the sugar. Blend in the flour. Add the cream cheese and beat until soft. Gradually beat in the cream and vanilla extract. Finally, fold in the raisins.

4 Remove the crust from the oven and lower the oven temperature to 375°F. Let the crust cool and then

Apple and Raisin Cheesecake is layered with fruit to help make it light and moist, and is garnished with whipped cream

pour in half the cheesecake mixture. Cover it with a layer of apple slices. Pour the rest of the mixture over the top. Bake for 30 minutes.

5 Beat the all-purpose cream until stiff. Remove the cheesecake from the oven and remove the ring. When it is cool, top with whipped cream and serve.

Serves 6

Tip: To give the apple slices a delicious flavor, cook them with 1 teaspoon powdered cinnamon. Other seasonal fruits, such as plums or pears, could be substituted for the apples.

Mock Cheesecake

1½ **cups cookie crumbs**
2 tablespoons sugar
¼ **cup butter, melted**
4 eggs, separated
1¼ **cups sweetened condensed milk
grated rind and juice 2 lemons**

1 Preheat the oven to 375°F. In a mixing bowl blend the cookie crumbs, sugar and melted butter. Line a springform pan with the mixture.

2 Beat the egg yolks. Stir in the condensed milk, lemon rind and juice. Beat the egg whites until stiff. Fold the whites into the mixture and pour it into the crust. Bake for 15-20 minutes in the preheated oven, cool and serve.

Serves 6

Apricot Cheesecake

15 ozs. canned apricots in syrup
1 package orange gelatin
1 lb. cottage cheese
2 tablespoons sugar
⅔ cup heavy cream, whipped
1 cup gingersnap crumbs
2 tablespoons brown sugar
¼ cup butter, melted

For the Decoration:
2 tablespoons apricot jam
15 ozs. canned apricots in syrup
2 tablespoons sliced almonds

1 Make up the syrup from the canned apricots to 1¼ cups with water. Bring to a boil, add the gelatin and stir to dissolve. Cool.

2 Purée the apricots and cheese and stir in the cooled gelatin and sugar. Fold in the cream.

3 Line the base of an 8-inch springform pan with wax paper. Pour in the mixture and chill to set.

4 Combine the crumbs, brown sugar and butter, sprinkle over the set mixture and press down with a spoon.

5 Melt the jam with 1 tablespoon of the apricot syrup, strain and cool. Turn out the cheesecake and decorate with the apricots. Brush with the jam glaze and sprinkle with almonds.

Serves 8

Avocado Orange Cheesecake

1¼ cups cookie crumbs
¼ cup butter, melted
1 avocado

¼ cup lemon juice
3 ozs. cream cheese
⅔ cup sour cream
1 orange
2 tablespoons sugar
1½ teaspoons unflavored gelatin dissolved in 1 tablespoon water
1 egg white

1 Mix the crumbs with the butter, and press the mixture evenly into the base of a lightly greased flan pan. Place in the refrigerator and chill until set.

2 Peel, pit and mash ¾ of the

Avocado Orange Cheesecake has a deliciously unusual flavor, and would be the perfect choice for a summer buffet

avocado. Thinly slice the remaining ¼ and dip the slices in lemon juice; reserve for garnish.

3 Beat the cream cheese, sour cream, and remaining lemon juice into the mashed avocado. Grate the rind of ½ the orange and add. Stir in the sugar.

4 Combine the gelatin with the avocado mixture. Beat the egg white until stiff and fold in.

5 Pour the mixture into the crumb crust and chill until set. Remove the flan from the ring. Peel and slice the rest of the orange, and decorate the top of the cheesecake with orange slices and the reserved avocado slices.

Serves 6

Trifles

The dictionary defines a 'trifle' as a paltry, insignificant thing; and as a dessert. A classic trifle dessert, however, is far from insignificant. At its best it is light but lavish, somewhat alcoholic and highly decorative. The trifle was developed in Great Britain in the eighteenth century, from the Elizabethan dish of syllabub. A trifle should have four layers: the first of sponge cakes soaked in sherry and fruit juice; then a layer of fruit; then one of custard, and a topping of whipped cream. The modern, less rich and filling versions often substitute flavored gelatin for one of these layers, and do not include sherry. Whatever the layers contain, trifles are easy and popular with old and young alike.

Country Trifles

2 ozs. raspberry gelatin
1 cup canned fruit cocktail with
  syrup
½ cup granola
2 tablespoons powdered custard
  mix
2 tablespoons sugar
2 cups milk

For the Topping:
⅔ cup heavy cream
2 tablespoons granola
2 candied cherries

1 In a pan dissolve the gelatin in ⅔ cup boiling water. Stir in the syrup from the can of fruit cocktail. Measure the liquid and make it up to 1¼ cups with cold water.

2 Divide the fruit salad and the granola between four single-serving sundae glasses. Pour the gelatin into the glasses. Leave them in a cool place or in the refrigerator until set.

3 Mix the custard powder with the sugar and ¼ cup of the milk in a bowl, until smooth. Heat the rest of the milk in a pan until almost boiling. Stir in the custard powder mixture and return the pan to the heat, stirring while the custard comes to a boil. Cook for 1 minute, stirring constantly. Remove the pan from the heat. Cover the custard while it cools. Leave until almost cold.

4 When the custard is nearly set, pour it over the gelatin in the sun-

---

Country Trifles — delicious layers of granola, fruit salad, gelatin and custard, topped with rosettes of cream

dae glasses. Spread it level and chill until the custard is firm.

5 Whip the cream until stiff and place it in a decorator's bag. Pipe the cream in rosettes around the edge of the custard. Place the granola for the topping inside the cream border in each glass. Put a candied cherry on top of each trifle and serve cold.

Serves 4

Tip: To vary the trifles, you could arrange mandarin orange sections over the top and perhaps sprinkle a little orange-flavored liqueur over the fruit before adding the gelatin. Allow 1 teaspoon of the liqueur per portion.

Look 'n Cook Tipsy Trifle

1 The ingredients: sponge cake, sherry, brandy, eggs, milk, jam, almond-flavored cookies, candied fruits and almonds **2** Split the sponge cakes and spread with raspberry jam. Sandwich them together and cut into squares **3** Place the cake squares, cookies and sliced almonds in a glass bowl. Mix the sherry, brandy and extracts (optional) and pour over the cake **4** In a bowl combine the egg yolks, cornstarch and a little milk. Pour in the boiling milk and stir. Return to the pan and reheat until thickened **5** Pour the custard over the cakes and leave in a cool place to set **6** Whip the cream until stiff and spread it over the set custard. Make a swirling pattern on it and decorate with candied cherries and strips of candied angelica **7** The finished dish should be served cold. Almonds may also be used to decorate the top

Christmas Cake Trifle

½–¾ lb. leftover Christmas or fruit
   cake
2 tablespoons brandy
1 lb. ripe pears
2¼ cups custard
⅔ cup all-purpose cream

1 Cut or break the cake into chunks. Place them in a glass bowl and sprinkle with brandy. Peel, core and slice the pears. Mix them with the cake.

2 Pour the custard over the cake and fruit and let set. Decorate with whipped cream.

Serves 6–8

Tipsy Trifle

2 plain sponge cakes, 8 inches in
   diameter
⅓ cup raspberry jam
12 almond-flavored cookies
2 tablespoons sliced almonds
⅔ cup sherry
2 tablespoons brandy
2 drops each lemon and orange
   extract (optional)
4 egg yolks
2 teaspoons cornstarch
2 cups milk
¼ cup sugar
⅔ cup all-purpose cream
6 candied cherries
two 4-inch stems candied angelica

1 Split the sponge cakes horizontally and spread them liberally with jam on the inside. Sandwich them together again and cut into squares.

2 Arrange the cake squares, cookies and almonds in the base of a large glass bowl.

3 Measure the sherry into a pitcher and add the brandy and fruit extracts, if wished. Pour it over the cake and let soak.

---

4 In a bowl beat together the egg yolks, cornstarch and 2 tablespoons of the milk. Meanwhile, bring the rest of the milk to a boil in a pan. Gradually pour the hot milk into the bowl, beating all the time. Pour the mixture back into the pan and reheat, without boiling, to thicken.

5 Pour the custard over the cakes and leave in a cool place to set. Whip the cream until stiff and spread it evenly on top of the set custard.

6 Decorate the top with a swirling pattern and arrange the candied cherries and 'leaves' of angelica as decoration. Serve well chilled.

Serves 6–8

Chocolate Orange Trifle

1 chocolate jelly roll cake
2 tablespoons orange-flavored
   liqueur
2 oranges
2¼ cups chocolate custard
⅔ cup all-purpose cream
6 candied cherries, halved
2 ozs. grated semisweet chocolate

1 Cut the jelly roll into slices about ¾ inch thick. Arrange them to line a glass dish as evenly as possible. Sprinkle them with the liqueur.

2 Grate the rind of one of the oranges and reserve. Peel both oranges and cut them in thin slices across the sections, removing any seeds. Cut the slices in half and arrange them over the slices of cake.

3 Pour the custard over the orange and cake slices and chill to set. Beat the cream until thick, then fold in the grated orange rind. Decorate the top of the trifle with whipped cream, halved cherries and grated

---

chocolate. Serve cold.

Serves 6

Apple Trifle

5 cooking apples
juice and grated rind 1 lemon
½ cup sugar
squares from 2 sponge cakes
2 tablespoons sherry (optional)
⅓ cup blackberry jelly
⅔ cup all-purpose cream
8 candied cherries
two 4-inch stems candied angelica

1 Peel and core the apples and cut them in slices. Place them with 1 tablespoon water and the lemon juice and grated rind in a pan, cover and cook gently for 5 minutes until tender. Pass them through a strainer and return the purée to the pan with the sugar. Cook gently, stirring frequently, until the sugar is melted and the mixture thickened. Cool.

2 Place a layer of sponge cake squares on the base and sides of a glass dish. Sprinkle with the sherry, if used. Pour the apple purée into the bowl and chill.

3 Melt the blackberry jelly over low heat, stirring. Pour it over the apple purée. Let set.

4 Beat the cream until stiff and place it in a decorator's bag. Pipe the cream in rosettes around the dish where the sponge cakes meet and in the middle. Cut the cherries in half and the candied angelica in diamond-shaped 'leaves,' and use them to decorate the cream rosettes. Serve immediately or chill until ready to serve.

Serves 8

Apple Trifle contains a lovely mixture of apple, sponge cake and blackberry jelly, and it is topped with cream and fruits

Sponge Cake Desserts

The following delicious sponge cakes filled with flavored creams, soaked in sweet syrups and often covered with exotic fresh fruits, are rich and luxurious. They make impressive desserts for special occasions and are well worth the small extra effort involved in preparing them.

Peach Chantilly

butter
2 large eggs
¼ cup sugar
½ cup flour, sifted
4 large ripe peaches
⅓ cup sugar
2 tablespoons orange-flavored liqueur
1¼ cups heavy cream, whipped
¾ cup strained apricot jam
1 teaspoon cornstarch
½ cup sliced almonds

1 The day before serving, make the cake. Preheat the oven to 375°F. Butter an oblong cake pan and line its base with wax paper.

2 Place the eggs and sugar in a bowl over a saucepan of hot water. Beat until the mixture is pale and thick. Remove the bowl from the heat and continue to beat until the mixture cools. Fold in the flour and pour the cake mixture into the pan. Bake in the oven for 25 minutes and turn the cake out onto a rack to cool overnight.

3 The following day, cut the cake lengthwise into 3 layers. Bring water to a boil and scald the peaches in it for 30 seconds. Drain them and peel off their skins. Halve them and remove their pits.

Peach Chantilly is sandwiched together with layers of fresh peaches, orange liqueur, and stiffly whipped cream

4 Preheat the oven to 375°F. Place the peach halves in a shallow oven-proof dish with ¾ cup water, the sugar and liqueur. Cover and bake in the oven for 20 minutes. Allow the peaches to cool in their syrup.

5 Place ⅔ of the cream in a bowl and the rest in a decorator's bag fitted with a star nozzle. Chill the bag of cream in the refrigerator.

6 Drain the peach halves, straining the syrup into a saucepan. Cut 3 peach halves into thin slices. Blend the slices with the cream in the bowl.

7 Build up the cake in the following way. Spread the bottom and middle layers of the cake with ⅓ of the apricot jam and half the cream and sliced peach mixture. Sandwich them together and finish with the third piece of cake. Arrange the remaining peach halves along the top of the cake.

8 Heat the syrup, stirring in the remaining apricot jam and 2 tablespoons water. Blend the cornstarch with 1 tablespoon water and stir it into the syrup. Boil for 3 minutes.

9 Using a spoon, coat the peaches and cake with the syrup. Press the almonds to the sides of the cake with your hand and pipe the reserved cream along the top rim. Chill the cake for 2 hours and serve.

Serves 6–8

Tipsy Cake

2 eggs
2 egg yolks
1 cup + 3 tablespoons sugar
2 egg whites
grated rind 1 lemon
¾ cup all-purpose flour
3 tablespoons cornstarch
pinch salt
1 cup sweet white wine
1 tablespoon brandy
1¼ cups heavy cream, whipped
1¾ cups raspberries

1 Line the base of a greased 8-inch cake pan with wax paper. Preheat the oven to 350°F.

2 Place the eggs, egg yolks and 1 cup of the sugar in a bowl over a pan of hot water. Beat the mixture until it is thick. Beat the egg whites until stiff and fold them into the egg mixture with the lemon rind.

Strawberry Sponge Ring looks exotic, but is really a simple combination of a sponge cake, cream and juicy strawberries

3 Sift together the flour, cornstarch and salt and fold into the mixture. Pour it into the pan and bake in the oven for ¾–1 hour. Turn the cake onto a rack to cool.

4 Boil the remaining sugar with ¼ cup of water for 1 minute, stirring constantly. Let the syrup cool and add the wine and brandy.

5 When the cake has cooled, cut around the top, using a serrated knife to remove a cone-shaped piece 2 inches deep. Soak the cake with ⅔ of the wine syrup. Fill the cavity with half the cream and half the raspberries. Replace the cone

and baste with the remaining syrup. Decorate with the remaining cream and raspberries.

Serves 6–8

Strawberry Sponge Ring

butter for greasing
¾ cup butter
¾ cup sugar
3 eggs
1⅓ cups self-rising flour, sifted
1¼ cups heavy cream, whipped
2 tablespoons cherry-flavored liqueur
½ cup strained apricot jam
⅓ cup water
2 cups fresh strawberries, hulled

1 Preheat the oven to 325°F. Butter a 7-cup tube pan.

2 Beat together the butter and sugar until light and fluffy. Beat in the eggs, one at a time, adding 1 tablespoon of the flour with each egg. Gently fold in the rest of the flour. Turn into the mold and bake it in the oven for 1¼ hours. Cool the cake on a rack.

3 In a bowl blend the whipped cream and half the liqueur.

4 Place the apricot jam, remaining liqueur and water in a pan. Stirring continually, slowly bring to boil. Brush the cooled cake with the hot syrup.

5 Place the cake on a serving dish. Pile the whipped cream into the center and decorate it with half the strawberries. Arrange the rest around the dish and serve.

Serves 6–8

Look 'n Cook Chantilly Cream

1 and **2** Measure ¼ cup of the cream and the same quantity of milk into a bowl. Blend well **3** Add the rest of the cream and whisk it gently, using a circular movement from the wrist, until it begins to thicken **4** and **5** Add the sugar all at once and then the vanilla extract **6** Rapidly whisk the cream until it is very firm and forms peaks **7, 8** and **9** Decorate the Yellow Plum Cake: spoon half of the cream onto the bottom

layer of the cake and spread it evenly with a knife. Arrange the prepared plums on the bed of cream and sandwich them with the top cake layer. Fill a decorator's bag, fitted with a star nozzle, with the remaining cream. Decorate the top of the cake with swirls of cream **10** and **11** Decorate with a candied cherry and 4 pieces of angelica

Raspberry Torte

¾ **cup butter**
¾ **cup sugar**
3 eggs
1½ **cups self-rising flour, sifted**
finely grated rind 1 orange

For the Filling and Topping:
3 tablespoons cornstarch
3 tablespoons sugar
1¼ **cups milk**
1¼ **cups heavy cream**
2 tablespoons orange-flavored
 liqueur
3 cups raspberries

1 Preheat the oven to 375°F.

2 Cream the butter and sugar together until light and fluffy, then beat in the eggs, one at a time, adding a spoonful of the flour with each to prevent curdling. Fold in the orange rind and remaining flour.

3 Divide the mixture between two buttered and lined 8-inch pans. Bake for 25-30 minutes until well-risen and firm to the touch. Turn out and cool on a wire rack.

4 Prepare the filling: blend the cornstarch and sugar to a smooth paste with a little of the milk. Heat the remaining milk and pour into the cornstarch, stirring well. Return

---

Raspberry Torte is a treat for anyone with a sweet tooth. Its layers of soft sponge cake are interspersed with cream and fruit

to the pan, bring to a boil and simmer for 3 minutes, stirring continuously. Place a piece of wax paper on the custard. Cool completely.

5 Whip the cream until thick. Remove the paper from the cold custard and fold in 3 tablespoons of the cream. Fold half of the liqueur and half of the raspberries into the custard. Fold the remaining liqueur into the cream.

6 Split the cold sponge cakes in half and sandwich them together with the custard mixture, so that there are four layers of sponge and three of filling. Transfer to a serving plate.

7 Spread the cream over the top of the cake, making a thick border, 1½ inches wide, around the edge. Fill the center with the remaining raspberries.

Serves 8

Fruity Layer Cake

ingredients for sponge cake as in
 Raspberry Torte
1¼ **cups heavy cream, whipped**
confectioners' sugar
1 tablespoon rum
3 tablespoons lemon custard
1 lb. assorted canned fruit,
 drained

1 Prepare and cook the sponge cake following the instructions for the Raspberry Torte.

2 Sweeten the cream to taste with confectioners' sugar and add the rum.

3 Split the cold sponge cakes in half and spread 3 with lemon custard. Sandwich and decorate with the cream and fruit.

Serves 8

Fruity Layer Cake looks exotic, but is simple and economical to prepare using canned fruit and cream

Coffee Rum Cake

¾ cup butter
¾ cup sugar
3 eggs
1½ cups self-rising flour
¼ cup sugar
1¼ cups hot, strong coffee
2 tablespoons rum
1¼ cups heavy cream
few drops vanilla extract
2 tablespoons toasted sliced
  almonds

1 Preheat the oven to 375°F.

2 Cream the butter and sugar together until light and fluffy. Beat in the eggs, one at a time, adding a spoonful of the flour with each to prevent curdling. Sift the remaining flour and fold it into the mixture with a metal spoon.

3 Turn the mixture into a tube pan. Bake for 25-30 minutes, until well risen and firm to the touch. Turn out and cool on a wire rack.

4 Dissolve the sugar in the hot coffee, add the rum and cool.

5 When the cake is cold, return it to the clean pan and pour on the coffee. Let stand until all the liquid is absorbed, then turn onto a serving plate.

6 Whip the cream with the vanilla until it is just thick. Cover the cake completely with the cream and sprinkle with the toasted almonds to decorate. Serve chilled.

Serves 6–8

Apricot-Almond Cake is not difficult to make. It is decorated with almond-flavored cookies and then topped with canned apricots

Pear and Chocolate Sponge Cake

¾ cup butter
¾ cup sugar
3 eggs
1½ cups self-rising flour
¼ cup chopped walnuts
6 poached pear halves, drained
7 walnut halves

For the Chocolate Buttercream:
1⅔ cups confectioners' sugar
½ lb. butter
4 teaspoons cocoa
few drops vanilla extract

1 Preheat the oven to 375°F.

2 Cream the butter and sugar until light and fluffy, then beat in the eggs, one at a time, adding a spoonful of the flour with each. Sift the

remaining flour and fold in with a metal spoon.

3 Divide the mixture between two buttered and lined 8-inch pans. Bake for 25-30 minutes. Turn out and cool on a wire rack.

4 Make the chocolate buttercream: sift the confectioners' sugar and cream it with the butter until light and fluffy. Blend the cocoa with a little boiling water, and stir into the butter and sugar with a few drops of vanilla.

5 Split each sponge in half. Spread 3 of them with ½ of the buttercream. Sandwich together with the plain sponge on top.

6 Spread the top and sides of the cake with buttercream. Press the chopped nuts onto the sides. Arrange the pears over the top and decorate with swirls of buttercream and the walnut halves.

Serves 8

Pear and Chocolate Sponge is a delicious cake which you could serve either as a dessert or for a special afternoon tea

Apricot-Almond Cake

¾ **cup butter**
¾ **cup sugar**
3 eggs
1½ cups self-rising flour
½ cup ground almonds
almond-flavored cookies
1 lb. canned apricot halves, drained
2 tablespoons apricot jam

For the Almond Filling:
2½ cups confectioners' sugar
¾ cup butter
2 tablespoons milk
few drops almond extract

1 Preheat the oven to 375°F. Cream the butter and sugar until light, then beat in the eggs, one at a time, adding a spoonful of the flour with each. Add the almonds, then

sift the remaining flour and fold in with a metal spoon.

2 Divide the mixture between two buttered and lined 8-inch pans. Bake for 25-30 minutes. Turn out and cool.

3 Make the almond filling: cream the confectioners' sugar with the butter until light and fluffy. Beat in the milk and almond extract.

4 Sandwich the cold sponge cakes with half the almond filling, and spread the rest over the top and sides.

5 Press crushed cookies into the sides of the cake. Drain the apricot halves, reserving 2 tablespoons of the syrup and arrange the apricot halves, cut side down, over the top of the cake. Melt the jam with the reserved apricot syrup and use to brush over the apricots.

Serves 8

Apple and Hazelnut Cake

¼ lb. butter
½ cup sugar
2 eggs, separated
½ cup ground hazelnuts, toasted
1 cup + 2 tablespoons self-rising flour
pinch salt
1 tablespoon milk

For the Filling:
3 tart apples
2 tablespoons apricot jam
juice and grated rind 1 lemon
3 tablespoons sugar
3 tablespoons brandy
1¼ cups heavy cream

1 Preheat the oven to 375°F. Cream the butter and sugar until light and beat in the egg yolks. Stir in ¾ of the hazelnuts. Fold in the flour and salt with the milk. Beat the egg whites until stiff and fold in with a metal spoon.

2 Turn the mixture into a buttered and floured 8-inch cake pan, and bake for 25 minutes, until the cake has shrunk slightly from the sides of the pan and is firm. Cool on a wire rack.

3 Peel, core and slice the apples, and place in a small pan with the jam, lemon rind and juice. Cover and cook gently until the apples are soft. Cool.

4 Dissolve the sugar in a small pan with 3 tablespoons water, bring to a boil and boil until syrupy. Stir in 2 tablespoons of the brandy and cool.

5 Whip the cream until thick and fold in the remaining brandy.

6 Split the cold cake and sprinkle each half with some of the syrup. Sandwich the sponges with some of the cream and the apples. Moisten the cake with the remaining syrup.

7 Decorate with the remaining cream and reserved hazelnuts.

Serves 6–8

Strawberry Cream Cake

¾ cup flour
½ teaspoon cinnamon
pinch salt
3 eggs
½ cup sugar
finely grated rind ½ lemon
1¼ cups heavy cream
few drops vanilla extract
1 pint strawberries, hulled
6 macaroons, crushed
½ cup red currant jelly
1 tablespoon orange juice

1 Preheat the oven to 350°F. Sift the flour with the cinnamon and salt.

2 Break the eggs into a bowl and gradually beat in the sugar. Stand the bowl over a pan of hot water and beat until thick and pale in color. Remove from the heat and continue to beat until cool.

3 Fold in the flour and the grated lemon rind. Pour the mixture into a buttered and lined 8-inch cake pan. Bake in the preheated oven for 15-20 minutes. Turn out and cool on a wire rack.

4 Whip the cream with a few drops of vanilla and divide between two bowls. Slice one-quarter of the strawberries and mix with one bowl of the cream. Use to sandwich the sponge cakes together.

5 Use the remaining cream to pipe a decorative border around the top of the cake and to spread around the sides. Press the crushed macaroons onto the sides.

6 Heat the red currant jelly with the orange juice until completely dissolved. Allow to cool, without setting. Arrange the remaining strawberries over the top of the cake inside the cream border, and brush with the red currant glaze.

Serves 8

Chocolate Rum Cake

1¼ cups flour
¼ cup cocoa
½ teaspoon salt
½ teaspoon baking powder
⅔ cup soft brown sugar
2 eggs, separated
⅓ cup oil
⅓ cup milk
½ teaspoon vanilla extract
¼ cup rum
⅔ cup light cream
⅔ cup heavy cream
3-4 ozs. grated semisweet chocolate

1 Preheat the oven to 350°F.

2 Sift together the flour, cocoa powder, salt and baking powder and stir in the sugar.

3 Mix together the egg yolks, oil, milk and vanilla and beat with the flour mixture to a smooth batter.

4 Beat the egg whites until stiff and peaking and fold into the batter with a metal spoon.

5 Divide the mixture between two 8-inch buttered and lined pans and bake for about 30 minutes until well-risen and firm to the touch. Turn out and cool on a wire rack.

6 Return the cold cakes to the clean pans and sprinkle with the rum. Let stand until all the rum has been absorbed.

7 Whip the creams together until thick. Use a little less than half to sandwich the sponge cakes together, then transfer the cake to a serving plate. Spread the remaining cream over the top and sides. Press the chocolate onto the sides and sprinkle over the top.

Serves 8

Strawberry Cream Cake and Chocolate Rum Cake are two quite different treats which cannot fail to impress

Meringue Desserts

Meringue desserts are always popular and, although they look impressive, they are really very easy to make. There are three different types of meringue:

Swiss Meringue is the one that most people know about and is used for meringue shells and the topping on most hot meringue puddings.

American Meringue is another topping for meringue pies, but cream of tartar and vinegar are added to the meringue mixture.

Cooked Meringue is made with confectioners' sugar and is hard and powdery. It is suitable for cakes or as a topping for desserts.

Most of our recipes are made with the Swiss meringue mixture. A wire whisk is best if you are to obtain a stiff, shiny meringue — electric and rotary beaters can be used with some success but the results will not be as good. However, they do save you time and arm-ache!

Strawberry Meringue Tart

3 egg whites
¾ cup sugar
1⅓ cups strawberries
1¼ cups heavy cream
2 tablespoons orange-flavored liqueur

1 Preheat the oven to 250°F. or even lower, if possible.

2 Cover a baking sheet with some wax paper. Draw a circle of 8 inches in diameter on the paper.

3 Beat the egg whites until stiff, then beat in half of the sugar. When stiff, fold in the remaining sugar with a metal spoon.

4 Spread some of the meringue over the circle to make the base of the tart. Fill a decorator's bag, fitted with a large star nozzle, with the rest of the meringue and pipe large, attractive rosettes around the base to form the sides of the tart. Bake in the oven until dry and white (about 1½–2 hours). Do not allow the meringue to brown. Cool the meringue shell on a wire rack.

5 Hull and wash the strawberries. Whip the cream until stiff and stir in the liqueur.

6 Place a layer of cream inside the base of the meringue and pile the strawberries on top. Place the rest of the cream in a bowl and serve separately.

Serves 4–6

Tips: You can fill this meringue shell with any fresh fruit. Peaches, raspberries and bananas are all suitable. To make it more attractive, you can pipe rosettes of cream across the top and around the sides of the meringue shell. Another idea is to soak the fruit in brandy or a liqueur before filling the shell. Be careful to drain them thoroughly, though, as the liqueur will make the meringue soggy.

If you prefer, you can make individual meringue shells so that your guests can have one each. This is a good idea for parties and buffets. Just draw smaller circles on the wax paper and pipe the meringue as before.

Flamed Pineapple Meringue

2 whole eggs
6 egg yolks
¾ cup confectioners' sugar
1 cup + 2 tablespoons flour, sifted
1 cup pineapple juice
3 cups milk
1 teaspoon vanilla extract
10 pineapple slices
¼ cup butter, softened
⅔ cup white rum

For the Meringue:
4 egg whites
¾ cup confectioners' sugar

1 In a mixing bowl, blend together the whole eggs, egg yolks and confectioners' sugar. Beat well, then mix in the flour. Stir in the pineapple juice.

2 Heat the milk in a heavy saucepan and, when boiling, pour it over the egg and pineapple mixture, stirring all the time. Add the vanilla and pour back into the saucepan.

3 Return the pan to the heat and boil for several minutes, stirring continuously, until it thickens. Then remove from the heat.

4 Cut 2 of the pineapple slices into cubes and mix into the pastry cream. Then stir in the butter and ¼ cup of the rum.

5 Preheat the oven to 400°F.

6 Beat the egg whites until stiff. Gradually add the sugar, beating all the time until stiff and shiny.

7 Spread the pastry cream over the base of an ovenproof dish. Arrange the remaining pineapple slices on top and then cover with the meringue. Place in the oven and bake until the meringue is cooked and golden.

8 Just before serving, heat the rest of the rum in a small saucepan. Pour it over the meringue, ignite it, and serve the flaming dish to your guests.

Serves 8

Tip: There are a number of variations on this dish which you can try. You can substitute brandy or another spirit for rum and can even use alternative fruits for the filling.

Strawberry Meringue is filled with delicious orange liqueur-flavored cream and then topped with juicy strawberries

Quick Vacherin

⅔ cup heavy cream
few drops vanilla extract
1 meringue shell
12-16 scoops ice cream (raspberry
  or strawberry)
2⅔ cups strawberries, hulled
8 pink oval-shaped meringues
  (see Cream Meringues)
8 brown oval-shaped meringues
  (see Cream Meringues)

1 Whip the cream until thick and stir in the vanilla. Transfer to a decorator's bag fitted with a large star nozzle.

2 Place the meringue base on a serving plate and cover with the ice cream. Pile the strawberries on top, reserving a few for decoration.

3 Stand the pink and brown meringues alternately around the sides, pressing onto the ice cream to secure.

4 Pipe the cream in swirls around the meringues and over the strawberries, and decorate with the reserved strawberries. Serve immediately.

Serves 6–8

Coconut Pyramids

lard for greasing
2 egg whites
⅔ cup sugar
1½ cups shredded coconut

1 Preheat the oven to 275°F. Grease a baking sheet and cover with wax paper.

2 Beat the egg whites until they are stiff and peaking, and fold in the sugar and coconut with a metal spoon.

3 Put the mixture onto the prepared baking sheet in 12 small pyramids and press into a neat shape. Bake in the oven for ¾-1 hour until the pyramids are very

lightly browned. Cool on a wire rack.

Makes 12

Cherry Alaska Tarts

¾ cup butter cookie crumbs
3 tablespoons sugar
1 teaspoon ground ginger
⅓ cup butter

For the Filling:
2 egg whites
⅓ cup sugar
12 ozs. canned cherries, drained
1 tablespoon finely chopped
  preserved gingerroot in syrup
1 tablespoon ginger syrup
6 scoops vanilla ice cream

1 Preheat the oven to 350°F.

2 Crush the cookies finely and stir in the sugar and ground ginger. Melt the butter and mix well with the crumbs. Divide the mixture between six 4-inch fluted flan pans, and, using the back of a teaspoon, press the mixture firmly and evenly over the base and sides.

3 Bake in the preheated oven for 10 minutes. Allow to cool in the pans.

4 Increase the oven temperature to 450°F. Remove the cool cookie crusts from the pans and place on a baking sheet.

5 Make the filling: beat the egg whites until they are softly peaking, add half the sugar and continue to beat until glossy and firm. Gently fold in the remaining sugar with a metal spoon.

6 Divide the cherries among the crusts and sprinkle with the finely chopped gingerroot and the syrup. Put a scoop of ice cream on top and cover the ice cream and fruit com-

pletely with the meringue. Put into the oven for 2-3 minutes until the outside of the meringue begins to brown.

7 Slide each Alaska Tart onto an individual serving plate and serve immediately.

Serves 6

Cream Meringues

2 egg whites
½ cup sugar
⅔ cup heavy cream
optional: a few drops of food
  coloring of choice

1 Preheat the oven to 225°F. Line a baking sheet with aluminum foil or wax paper.

2 Beat the egg whites until they are softly peaking, add half the sugar and continue to beat until the mixture is glossy and firm. Fold in the remaining sugar with a metal spoon.

3 Transfer the mixture to a decorator's bag fitted with a large star nozzle, and pipe 10-12 swirls onto the prepared baking sheet. Alternatively, you can spoon the mixture in neat mounds.

4 Dry the meringues in the coolest part of the oven for 2-3 hours, until the meringues are firm and crisp, but still white. If the meringues begin to brown, prop open the oven door a little.

5 Remove the meringues from the paper and cool on a wire rack.

6 Whip the cream until it is just thick and use to sandwich the meringue shells in pairs.

Makes 5 or 6

Black Currant Meringue Pie

1 cup + 2 tablespoons flour
pinch salt
1 teaspoon cinnamon
¼ cup softened butter
¼ cup sugar
2 eggs, separated
½ teaspoon vanilla extract
12 ozs. canned black currants
1 teaspoon cornstarch
3 tablespoons sugar

For the Topping:
½ cup sugar
½ teaspoon cinnamon

1 Sift the flour, salt and cinnamon onto the table. Make a well in the center and in this, place the butter, sugar, egg yolks and vanilla.

2 With the fingertips of one hand, blend together the butter, sugar and egg yolks until well mixed, then work in the flour. Knead lightly until smooth, then wrap and chill for about 1 hour.

3 Meanwhile, make the filling. Pour off half the juice from the black currants, using a little to blend with the cornstarch. Place the remaining black currants and juice in a pan with the sugar and bring to a boil. Add the blended cornstarch and simmer for 3 minutes, stirring continuously. Cool.

4 Preheat the oven to 375°F. Roll out the pastry and use to line a 7-inch flan ring, set on a baking sheet. Line with wax paper, fill with baking beans and bake in the pre-heated oven for 15 minutes. Remove the paper and beans and bake for a further 5 minutes, or until a pale brown. Cool in the flan ring.

5 Reduce the oven temperature to 300°F. Pour the black currant mixture into the pie shell.

6 Make the topping: beat the egg whites until stiff and peaking. Add 2 teaspoons of the sugar and beat until firm, then fold in the remaining sugar and the cinnamon with a metal spoon. Spoon the meringue on top of the pie to completely cover the filling and bake in the oven for 30 minutes.

7 Serve warm or cold.

Serves 5 or 6

Tip: If black currants are not available, you can replace them with the same weight of pitted black cherries, blackberries or damson plums.

Swiss Peach Meringue, topped with meringue pyramids, has a jelly roll base with peaches, custard and macaroons

Swiss Peach Meringue

1 jelly roll
4 almond macaroons, crushed
2 tablespoons brandy
2 peaches, pitted, skinned and sliced
3 tablespoons custard mix
2½ tablespoons sugar
1¾ cups milk

For the Topping:
2 egg whites
½ cup sugar
1 tablespoon sliced almonds

1 Slice the jelly roll and arrange the slices around the sides and base of an ovenproof serving bowl.

Sprinkle on the macaroons, then moisten with the brandy. Arrange the sliced peaches over the top.

2 Make the custard: blend the custard mix and sugar with a little of the milk. Bring the rest of the milk to a boil and pour onto the custard mixture, stirring. Return to the pan and simmer for 3 minutes, stirring. Cool slightly, then pour gently over the peaches and sponge cake.

3 Beat the egg whites until they are stiff and peaking. Add 2 teaspoons of the sugar and beat until firm. Carefully fold in the remaining sugar with a metal spoon. Transfer the mixture to a decorator's bag fitted with a star-shaped nozzle and cover the custard with peaks of meringue.

4 Stud some of the peaks with the flaked almonds and place under the

Creole Meringue Cake has all the color and exciting flavors of South America and the French Caribbean, where it originated

broiler until golden brown. Serve immediately.

Serves 4 or 5

Créole Meringue Cake

1 cup sugar
4 eggs, separated
¼ cup flour
7½ tablespoons cornstarch
pinch salt
½ cup candied cherries
½ cup cherry-flavored liqueur

¼ cup rum

For the Meringue Topping:
2 egg whites
pinch salt
2 tablespoons confectioners' sugar

1 Preheat the oven to 350°F.

2 Add half of the sugar to the egg yolks and beat together until light and fluffy. Sift the flours together and fold into the egg yolk mixture with a metal spoon.

3 Beat the egg whites and salt in a separate bowl until they are stiff and peaking. Add the remaining sugar, a little at a time, beating well after each addition.

4 Carefully fold the egg whites into the yolk mixture and pour into an 8-inch buttered and floured cake pan. Bake in the preheated oven for 20 minutes. Increase the oven temperature to 375°F., and bake for a further 10 minutes. Do not turn off the oven since it will be needed at a later stage. Turn out the cooked cake onto a cooling rack and cool completely.

5 Cut the cherries into small pieces and place them in a bowl with the liqueur and rum for 15 minutes. When the cake is cold, slice it in half through the middle and sandwich together again with the cherries and their liquid. Place on a flat ovenproof serving dish.

6 Prepare the meringue topping: beat the egg whites with the salt and sugar until thick and firm. Spread the mixture evenly over the top and sides of the cake, and bake in the hot oven for 8-10 minutes until golden brown.

7 Cool the cake completely before serving.

Serves 6

Tip: For a crisper, crunchier topping, sprinkle some crushed toasted peanuts over the meringue before baking. The filling can also be altered — try using cubed pineapple or papaya instead of the cherries.

All about Tarts, Flans and Pies

Apple Bakewell Tart

Tarts and Flans

Tarts and flans are tremendously versatile; whether rich in protein or light and fruity, from practical weekday snacks to sophisticated party desserts, there's something suitable for every occasion. Try some of the more unusual combinations — cottage cheese filling in an almond-flavored crust, rich eggnog in a chocolate-flavored shell, or even a shell of ice cream filled with creamy coffee and honey.

Whole Wheat Yogurt Flan

dough for one 8-inch pie crust
3 fresh peaches
1¼ cups plain yogurt
1⅓ cups cottage cheese
3 tablespoons honey
½ teaspoon vanilla extract

1 Preheat the oven to 400°F.

2 Roll out the dough and use it to line an 8-inch flan ring. Set on a baking sheet. Bake for 20 minutes. Cool.

3 Peel and halve the peaches, remove the pits and slice the fruit neatly.

4 Mix together the yogurt and cottage cheese and pass through a strainer. Stir in the honey and vanilla.

5 Arrange two-thirds of the sliced peaches in the cold flan shell and spoon over the yogurt mixture. Top with the remaining sliced peaches and chill in the refrigerator for several hours.

Serves 6

Crunchy Peanut Tart

dough for one 8-inch pie crust
3 eggs
¼ cup corn syrup
¼ cup butter
½ teaspoon vanilla extract
¼ lb. unsalted peanuts, chopped

1 Preheat the oven to 400°F.

2 Roll out the dough and use it to line an 8-inch flan ring set on a baking sheet. Line with paper and fill with baking beans and bake for 15 minutes. Remove the paper and beans and bake for a further 5 minutes. Remove from the oven and reduce the oven temperature to 325°F.

3 Beat the eggs and syrup together. Melt the butter and add it with the vanilla and peanuts to the egg mixture. Pour into the flan shell.

4 Bake for 30 minutes, cool slightly, then remove the flan ring. Serve warm or cold.

Serves 6

Strawberry Cream Flan

dough for one 8-inch pie crust
2 cups strawberries
⅔ cup heavy cream
⅔ cup light cream
2 tablespoons sugar
2 tablespoons strawberry jam
2 teaspoons water

1 Preheat the oven to 400°F.

2 Roll out the dough and use it to line an 8-inch flan ring, set on a baking sheet. Line with paper, fill with baking beans and bake for 15 minutes. Remove the paper and beans and bake for a further 5 minutes. Cool, then remove the flan ring.

3 Hull the strawberries and slice them. Whip the creams together and fold in the sugar and half of the strawberries. Spoon into the flan shell and decorate with the remaining sliced strawberries.

4 Melt the jam with the water, strain and brush over the strawberries to glaze. Serve chilled.

Serves 6

Tarte Tatin

dough for one 8-inch pie crust
4 tart apples
⅓ cup butter
⅔ cups sugar

1 Preheat the oven to 400°F.

2 Make the filling: peel, quarter and core the apples, then cut them into slices.

3 Grease an 8-inch flan pan with half of the butter and sprinkle with half of the sugar. Arrange the apple slices on it, then sprinkle with the remaining sugar and dot with the remaining butter.

4 Roll out the dough thinly, and cut a neat circle a little larger than the flan pan. Place the circle over the apples, tucking the edge inside the flan pan, and bake in the preheated oven for 25-30 minutes until the dough is cooked and the apples have caramelized.

5 Invert the tart onto a serving plate and serve warm.

Serves 6

Tarte Tatin is baked upside down and then inverted onto the plate to reveal its sticky, golden caramelized filling

Russian Apricot Tart

dough for one 9-inch pie crust
1 lb. fresh apricots
½ cup brown sugar
**1 teaspoon mixed mace and
  allspice**
beaten egg to glaze

1 Preheat the oven to 400°F.

2 Roll out two-thirds of the dough and use it to line a 9-inch flan pan. Prick the base with a fork.

3 Halve the apricots and remove the pits. Arrange them, cut-side down, in the crust, and sprinkle with the sugar and spice.

4 Roll out the remaining dough and cut into strips ½ inch wide, using a ravioli cutter. Place the strips, lattice-fashion, across the tart, sealing the ends of the strips to the tart edge with a little water.

5 Brush the strips with beaten egg to glaze, place the flan pan on a baking sheet and bake in the pre-

Russian Apricot Tart is a very attractive dessert with its lattice pattern of crinkle-cut strips of crisp pastry

heated oven for 25-30 minutes.

Serves 6

Chocolate Eggnog Flan

1¼ cups flour
**3 tablespoons instant chocolate
  drink mix**
¼ cup butter
3 tablespoons lard or shortening
2 tablespoons cold water

For the Filling:
6 tablespoons sugar
2 eggs
¼ cup flour
1¼ cups milk
1 teaspoon vanilla extract

⅔ cup light cream
1 tablespoon rum
grated nutmeg

1 Preheat the oven to 400°F. Sift the flour and chocolate and add the lard or shortening, cut into pieces. Rub in until the mixture resembles fine breadcrumbs. Mix to a firm dough with the water.

2 Knead the dough lightly and roll out to fit an 8-inch flan ring. Bake for 20 minutes.

3 Make the filling: place ¼ cup of the sugar in a bowl with 1 egg and 1 egg yolk. Beat well and mix in the flour. Warm the milk with the vanilla and pour onto the egg mixture, stirring. Return to the pan and stir over gentle heat until thickened. Pour into the crust, cool, then chill.

4 Beat the remaining egg white until stiff and peaking, then beat in the rest of the sugar. Whip the cream with the rum and fold gently into the egg whites. Spread the mixture over the filling and sprinkle with nutmeg.

Serves 6

Lemon Breeze Tart

⅓ cup butter
¾ cup butter cookie crumbs
3 tablespoons sugar
1¼ cups canned sweetened condensed milk
finely grated rind and juice 2 large lemons
⅔ cup light cream

1 Preheat the oven to 350°F.

2 Melt the butter and stir in the crushed cookies and sugar. Using the back of a metal spoon, press the mixture into the base and up the sides of an 8-inch flan ring set on a baking sheet. Bake for 10 minutes,

then cool in the ring.

3 Combine the condensed milk and lemon rind and juice and stir until the mixture thickens. Add the cream, pour into the cooled flan crust and chill for 2 hours.

Serves 6

Blueberry Surprise Tart

dough for one 9-inch pie crust

Blueberry Surprise Tart has a hidden layer of lemon custard which makes a sweet contrast to the blueberries

¼ cup lemon custard
4 cups blueberries
½ cup sugar
3 tablespoons cornstarch
beaten egg to glaze

1 Preheat the oven to 375°F.

2 Roll out two-thirds of the dough and use to line a 9-inch flan pan. Prick the base and spread with the lemon custard.

3 Fill the tart with the blueberries, sprinkling with the sugar and cornstarch.

4 Roll out the remaining dough and cut into strips ½ inch wide. Place the strips, lattice-fashion, across the tart, sealing the ends to the tart edge with water.

5 Brush the strips with beaten egg to glaze, place the flan pan on a baking sheet and bake in the oven for 30-40 minutes.

Serves 6

Mint Chocolate Flan

3 ozs. bitter chocolate
1 tablespoon butter
1⅓ cups gingersnap cookie crumbs
3 egg yolks
½ cup sugar
2 tablespoons crème de menthe
2 teaspoons unflavored gelatin
2 tablespoons water
few drops green food coloring
⅔ cup heavy cream, whipped

1 Melt the chocolate and butter in a pan and blend in the cookie crumbs. Butter an 8-inch flan pan and spread the crumb mixture evenly over the base and sides, pressing it down firmly. Chill in the refrigerator.

2 In a bowl, beat together the egg yolks, sugar and crème de menthe until smooth and thick.

3 Sprinkle the gelatin over the water in a small bowl and stand it in a pan of hot water. Stir until the gelatin has dissolved. Allow it to cool slightly and gradually beat it into the egg mixture. Fold in the food coloring and the whipped cream. When the mixture is about to set, pour it into the flan crust. Chill until set, and serve.

Serves 6

Apricot Marshmallow Tart

1 lb. fresh apricots, pitted
¾ cup sugar
2 tablespoons cornstarch
1 teaspoon each ground cinnamon and nutmeg
dough for one 8-inch pie crust
¼ lb. miniature marshmallows

1 Place the apricots in a pan with a little water and ⅔ of the sugar. Cook

gently over low heat until the fruit is soft.

2 Blend the rest of the sugar, the cornstarch and the spices with a little water. Add this to the fruit and cook until the mixture thickens.

3 Roll out the dough and line a buttered 8-inch flan pan. Preheat the oven to 425°F.

4 Pour the fruit mixture into the uncooked flan. Roll out the leftover trimmings of dough and cut into ¼-inch strips. Arrange these in a lattice pattern over the top of the fruit mixture.

5 Bake the tart in the middle of the oven for 25-30 minutes. Remove it from the oven and place a marshmallow in each square of the lattice pattern. Return to the oven for 5 minutes until the marshmallow is lightly browned. Serve with cream or custard.

Serves 6

Tip: This tart can be made with a variety of other seasonal fruits.

Egg Custard Tart

dough for one 7-inch pie crust
2 eggs
2 tablespoons sugar
1¼ cups milk
1 teaspoon ground nutmeg

1 Roll out the dough on a floured board and line a 7-inch flan pan. Preheat the oven to 425°F.

2 In a bowl, beat the eggs with the sugar. Warm the milk in a pan and pour it into the egg mixture, stirring. Strain the custard into the uncooked flan shell and sprinkle the nutmeg evenly over the top.

3 Bake in the middle of the oven for 10 minutes. Reduce the oven

temperature to 350°F. and cook for 20 minutes more, or until the custard is set. Cool and serve.

Serves 4–6

Tutti Frutti Tart

dough for one 8-inch pie crust
7 large strawberries
1 banana
1 sweet orange
1 peach, or 6 canned peach slices
2 ozs. canned cherries
1 lemon
⅓ cup apricot jam
1 tablespoon water

1 Preheat the oven to 425°F. Roll out the pastry ⅛ inch thick. Butter an 8-inch fluted flan pan and line it with the pastry. Bake for 20 minutes until the flan shell is crisp and golden-brown. Allow to cool.

2 Prepare the fruit: wash and hull the strawberries, peel and slice the banana. Cut the orange into thin slices and remove any seeds; cut the slices in quarters. Peel and slice the peach, if using a fresh one. Drain the canned cherries. Thinly slice the lemon and quarter the slices.

3 In a pan melt the apricot jam with the water. Pass through a strainer.

4 Arrange the fruit in the flan shell as illustrated, filling ⅙ of the flan with each fruit and finishing with a strawberry in the middle. Pour the apricot glaze over the top. Chill and serve with whipped cream.

Serves 6

Tutti Frutti Tart is a genuine Italian showpiece that is simple to make, and can be filled with a variety of fresh fruits

Raspberry Rumba

one 10-inch sponge cake shell
⅓ cup raspberry jam
3 cups fresh raspberries
2 tablespoons cherry-flavored liqueur
⅓ cup all-purpose cream

1 Place the sponge cake on a serving dish. Spread the raspberry jam over the base.

2 Clean the raspberries and remove any crushed or discolored ones. Arrange the rest of them on the cake, from the outer edge toward the middle.

3 Sprinkle the liqueur over the fruit. Whip the cream until thick and put in a decorator's bag. Pipe a rosette of cream in the middle of the flan.

Serves 6

Gooseberry Tart

¼ lb. butter
1⅔ cups butter cookie crumbs
1 teaspoon cinnamon
1 lb. canned gooseberries
1½ teaspoons unflavored gelatin

1 Use a little butter to grease a fluted flan pan. Melt the rest of the butter and mix it with the cookie crumbs and the cinnamon. Press the mixture evenly around the base and sides of the pan. Chill until set.

2 Drain the canned gooseberries, reserving the syrup. Arrange the gooseberries evenly over the crust.

3 Soften the gelatin in the syrup for 5 minutes, then stand the bowl in a pan of hot water and stir until the gelatin is completely dissolved. Measure the liquid and make up to

1¼ cups with cold water, if necessary. Allow to cool until almost set, then pour over the gooseberries to cover. Chill until set.

Serves 6

Apricot Cheese Flan: a colorful combination of canned apricots and strawberries conceals a layer of cream cheese

---

Raspberry Rumba, Blueberry Belle and Gooseberry Tart are three simple tarts which are all made with a different base

Apricot Cheese Flan

2¾ cups flour
pinch salt
1 teaspoon cinnamon
6 tablespoons butter
¼ cup lard or shortening
⅓ cup water
12 ozs. cream cheese
½ cup sugar
1 teaspoon grated orange rind
2 tablespoons orange juice
2 tablespoons heavy cream
2 lbs. canned apricot halves with
  syrup
2 tablespoons strained apricot jam
1 tablespoon cornstarch
1⅓ cups strawberries, hulled

1 Preheat the oven to 400°F.

2 Sift the flour with the salt and cinnamon into a bowl and rub in the butter and lard or shortening until it resembles fine breadcrumbs. Add the water and mix to a firm dough.

3 Knead the dough on a floured board until it is smooth. Roll it out to a thickness of ¼ inch and use it to line a 12 × 8 inch flan dish. Remove the trimmings and roll them into strips long enough to cover the rims of the flan dish. Brush the rims with a little water and arrange the strips on top. Flute the strips with a knife and prick the bottom with a fork, then bake the crust for 20 minutes. Cool in the dish.

4 Meanwhile, blend together the cream cheese, sugar, orange rind, juice and cream.

5 Strain the syrup from the apricots into a saucepan and drain the halved apricots on absorbent paper.

6 Gently heat the syrup and stir in the apricot jam. Mix the cornstarch with a little syrup and stir it back into the saucepan. Boil for 1-2 minutes until the syrup is clear.

7 Spread the cream cheese mixture over the bottom of the crust and arrange the apricot halves in rows, hollow side upward, on top. Spoon on the syrup and garnish with the strawberries. Chill and serve.

Serves 8–10

Banana Cream Flan

dough for one 8-inch pie crust
8-10 sugar lumps
2 large oranges
4-5 ripe bananas
1¼ cups heavy cream

1 Preheat the oven to 400°F.

2 Roll out the dough and use to line an 8-inch flan ring set on a baking sheet. Line with paper, fill with baking beans and bake for 15 minutes. Remove the paper and beans and bake for a further 5 minutes. Remove the flan ring when the flan is cool.

3 Rub the sugar lumps over the orange rind until they are well soaked with the oil. Crush them in a small bowl and add enough orange juice to make a syrup.

4 Slice the bananas, moisten with a little of the orange syrup and spoon into the flan.

5 Whip the cream until it is just thick, and add the remaining orange syrup. Spread the cream thickly over the bananas.

Serves 6

Almond Cheesecake

⅓ cup butter
2 tablespoons lard or shortening
1⅔ cups flour
⅓ cup ground almonds
3 tablespoons sugar
1 egg yolk
1-2 tablespoons water
½ teaspoon vanilla extract

For the Filling:
¼ cup butter
¼ cup sugar
1⅓ cups cottage cheese
2 eggs, beaten

⅓ cup dried currants
finely grated rind ½ orange
2 drops almond extract

1 Preheat the oven to 375°F.

2 Make the pastry: rub the lard or shortening into the flour, add the almonds and sugar and bind with the egg yolk, water and vanilla.

3 Roll out the pastry and use to line an 8-inch flan ring, set on a baking sheet.

4 Prepare the filling: cream together the butter and sugar until light. Strain the cheese and stir into the butter and sugar with the beaten eggs, currants, orange rind and almond extract. Pour into the crust.

5 Bake in the preheated oven for 30 minutes. Cool slightly before removing the flan ring, and serve warm or cold.

Serves 6

Meringue Mincemeat Tart

dough for one 8-inch pie crust
1½ cups mincemeat
1 egg white
¼ cup sugar
candied cherries and angelica

1 Preheat the oven to 400°F.

2 Roll out the dough and use it to line an 8-inch flan ring set on a baking sheet. Bake for 20 minutes. Remove from the oven and reduce the temperature to 375°F.

3 Fill the flan shell with the mincemeat.

4 Beat the egg white until it is softly peaking, add half of the sugar and continue to beat until the mixture is glossy and forms peaks. Gently fold in the remaining sugar and transfer to a decorator's bag fitted with a large star nozzle. Pipe a border of swirls just inside the flan edge and bake in the oven for

15-20 minutes, until set and lightly browned. Decorate with pieces of cherry and angelica.

Serves 6

Mincemeat Party Tarts

dough for one 9-inch pie crust
1½ cups mincemeat

For the Toppings:
¼ cup unsalted butter
¼ cup sugar
1 tablespoon brandy
¼ lb. marzipan

1 Preheat the oven to 375°F.

2 Make the brandy butter: cream the butter thoroughly. Beat in the sugar a little at a time and continue to beat until the mixture is white. Gradually beat in the brandy, then chill until quite firm.

3 Roll out the marzipan about ¼ inch thick and cut 8 or 9 circles with a 2-inch fluted cutter.

4 Roll out the dough thinly and use to line 16-18 tartlet pans. Prick the bases with a fork and bake in the preheated oven for 8 minutes. Put a heaping teaspoonful of mincemeat into each tartlet and bake for a further 6-8 minutes until the mincemeat is hot and the pastry light golden. Cool slightly on a wire rack.

5 Top half of the warm mincemeat pies with a swirl of brandy butter. Cover the other pies with marzipan lids.

Makes 16–18

Meringue Mincemeat Tart (in the background) and Mincemeat Party Tarts taste good at Thanksgiving or at any other time of year

Look 'n Cook Apple Bakewell Tart

1 The ingredients: pie crust dough, apples, flour, sugar, ground almonds, eggs, butter, coffee liqueur **2** Roll out the dough to line a buttered 8-inch flan pan **3** Prick the base of the crust with a fork **4** Peel and core the apples and slice them in rings. Sauté them gently in butter and honey until tender **5** Place the apple slices in the flan shell **6** Beat the butter and sugar. Add the beaten eggs, liqueur, flour and ground almonds to

make a thick paste **7** With a spatula, spread the paste evenly over the layer of apple rings **8** Cut the dough trimmings into narrow strips. Place these in a lattice pattern across the flan **9** Brush the lattice strips with beaten egg. Dust the flan with confectioners' sugar and bake in a moderate oven for 30-40 minutes **10** Cool and serve with custard or cream

Apple Bakewell Tart

dough for one 8-inch pie crust
2 apples
1 tablespoon butter
1 tablespoon honey
¼ lb. butter
½ cup sugar
2 eggs, beaten
2 tablespoons coffee-flavored liqueur
½ cup flour
¾ cup ground almonds
1 tablespoon confectioners' sugar

1 On a floured board, roll out the dough to ¼ inch thick, and line a buttered 8-inch fluted flan pan. Prick the base of the flan with a fork.

2 Peel and core the apples and cut them in rings. Cook them in a skillet with 1 tablespoon butter and honey for 5-10 minutes until tender. Place the apple slices in the base of the crust.

3 Preheat the oven to 375°F.

4 In a mixing bowl, cream together the remaining butter and sugar until fluffy. Reserve 2 teaspoons of the beaten egg and mix the rest of the egg into the butter and sugar. Add the liqueur.

5 Fold in the flour and the ground almonds and mix to a thick, smooth paste. Spread the paste evenly over the layer of apples in the flan.

6 Cut the dough trimmings into strips ½ inch wide and place these in a lattice pattern across the flan. Brush the lattice strips with the reserved beaten egg and sprinkle the flan with the confectioners' sugar. Bake for 30-40 minutes, allow to cool and serve with cream.

Serves 6–8

Tip: The traditional Bakewell Tart does not include fruit, but a layer of jam. The tart may also be iced with a thin layer of white icing instead of the lattice pattern.

You can also add 2 tablespoons of currants to the almond paste.

Mandarin Crisp

1 cup gingersnap cookie crumbs
2 tablespoons butter
2 ozs. bitter chocolate
¼ cup orange-flavored gelatin
⅔ cup hot water
⅔ cup evaporated milk
grated rind ½ orange
4 ozs. canned mandarin orange sections

1 Place the cookie crumbs in a bowl. Melt the butter and chocolate together and mix them into the crumbs. Lightly grease a 9-inch flan pan and spoon the crumb mixture into it, pressing it evenly and tightly around the sides and base. Chill in the refrigerator until set.

2 Melt the gelatin in a pan with the water. In a bowl, beat the evaporated milk until thick. Fold in the grated orange rind and the melted gelatin.

3 When the mixture is nearly set, pour it into the crumb shell. Drain the mandarin segments and arrange them over the top. Chill until set. Serve garnished with whipped cream.

Serves 6–8

Foolish Tart

1 lb. rhubarb
½ cup sugar
2 tablespoons water
pinch ground ginger
½ teaspoon cinnamon
one 10-inch sponge cake shell
⅓ cup apricot jam
⅔ cup heavy cream

1 Wash the rhubarb thoroughly and cut it into 1¼-inch lengths. Put the rhubarb, sugar, water, ginger and cinnamon in a pan, cover and cook over low heat until the fruit is soft and pulpy. Strain off any excess water and mash the fruit pulp to a purée.

2 Place the sponge shell on a serving dish. Spread the base and sides with apricot jam.

3 Beat the cream until stiff. Fold in the rhubarb purée and pour the mixture into the shell. Chill in the refrigerator until the filling is set, and serve.

Serves 6–8

Pineapple Flan

dough for one 9-inch pie crust
8 canned pineapple rings
1¼ cups pastry cream or very thick custard
7 strawberries

1 Preheat the oven to 375°F.

2 Roll out the pie crust on a floured board, and line a 9-inch flan pan.

3 Finely chop one of the pineapple rings, and mix it into the pastry cream. Pour into the crust. Bake for 30-40 minutes until just golden brown. Remove from the pan and allow to cool.

4 Drain the rest of the canned pineapple rings and arrange them in an overlapping circle around the flan. Place a strawberry in the middle of each pineapple ring. Serve with cream or custard.

Serves 6

Pineapple Flan is a golden delight with different textures — crisp pastry, a creamy filling and fresh juicy pineapple

Apricot Cream Tartlets

dough for one 9-inch pie crust
1 egg white
¼ cup sugar
1¼ cups pastry cream or very thick
** custard**
⅓ cup apricot jam

1 Preheat the oven to 375°F. Roll out the pie crust to line 6 small tartlet tins. Bake for 8-10 minutes, then remove from the oven.

2 Meanwhile, beat the egg white until stiff. Gradually fold in the sugar. Place the mixture in a decorator's bag.

3 Fill the base of the tartlets with pastry cream. Spread apricot jam on top of each one. Pipe rosettes of meringue around the edge of each tart. Return to the oven for 5 minutes until the meringue is lightly

Apricot Cream Tartlets are very light and simple— a creamy filling topped with swirls of fluffy meringue

toasted. Cool and serve.

Serves 6

Yellow Plum Tart

dough for one 10-inch pie crust
1 lb. yellow plums
⅔ cup sweet white wine
⅔ cup water
1⅓ cups sugar
5 egg yolks
1 cup + 2 tablespoons flour
1⅞ cups milk
½ teaspoon vanilla extract

1 Preheat the oven to 400°F. Roll out the dough to line a 10-inch flan pan and bake for 15-20 minutes. Remove from the oven and cool.

2 Meanwhile, place the plums, white wine, water, and ¼ cup of the sugar in a pan. Simmer gently over low heat for about 5 minutes until the plums are tender. Cool in the syrup.

3 In a mixing bowl, beat the egg yolks, then gradually add the flour and the rest of the sugar. Pour in the milk, beating all the time to produce a smooth mixture. Add the vanilla and a little of the plum syrup. Place in a pan and heat gently, stirring, until the mixture thickens.

4 Pour the thickened custard into the crust. With a slotted spoon, drain the plums and arrange them on top of the custard mixture. Chill and serve cold.

Serves 6–8

Rice Tart

¼ cup butter
¼ cup lard or shortening
2¼ cups flour
1 tablespoon brandy, sherry or rum
1 tablespoon light cream or sour cream
1 tablespoon water
⅓ cup sugar
pinch salt

For the Filling:
⅔ cup short-grain rice
3 cups milk

2 eggs, separated
pinch salt
¼ cup sugar
½ teaspoon cinnamon
1½ tablespoons finely chopped almonds

1 Rub the butter and lard or shortening into the flour in a mixing bowl. Make a well in the middle and pour in the liquor, cream or sour cream, water, sugar and salt. Blend and knead lightly to a dough. Leave in a cool place for 1 hour.

2 Meanwhile, rinse the rice for the filling and cook it in a pan of boiling water for 3 minutes. Drain and rinse in cold water.

3 Place the milk in a pan and bring it to a boil. Add the rice and cook

Yellow Plum Tart is bubbling with sunny golden plums set in a smooth, creamy base of pastry cream

over very low heat for about 10 minutes. Stir in the egg yolks, salt, sugar, cinnamon and chopped almonds.

4 In a bowl beat the egg whites until stiff. Fold them into the rice mixture.

5 Preheat the oven to 350°F. On a floured board roll out the pie crust dough and use it to line a 9-inch lightly greased flan pan. Pour the rice mixture into the crust. Bake in the oven for about 45 minutes. Serve hot or cold.

Serves 6

Tip: This flan goes well with fresh or canned fruit, such as plums or mandarin oranges. To make an Apple and Rice Flan, halve the quantities for the filling and cover the base of the crust with slices of peeled, cored cooking apples sprinkled with sugar, then top with the rice.

Chocolate Meringue Flan

dough for one 8-inch pie crust
3 tablespoons cornstarch
¼ cup cocoa
⅔ cup sugar
1¾ cups milk
¼ cup butter
3 egg yolks
½ teaspoon vanilla extract

For the Meringue:
3 egg whites
⅓ cup sugar

1 Preheat the oven to 400°F. Prepare an 8-inch flan crust and bake it. Let it cool.

2 In a mixing bowl, blend together the cornstarch, cocoa and sugar. Warm the milk and add it gradually to this mixture. Return it to the pan and cook, stirring, over gentle heat until the mixture thickens.

3 Remove the pan from the heat. Stir in the butter and egg yolks and flavor with a little vanilla. Pour the mixture into the crust.

4 In another bowl beat the egg whites until stiff. Gradually add the sugar. Spoon the meringue over the chocolate filling. Bake for about 15 minutes until the meringue is crisp and golden on top. Cool before serving.

Serves 6

Amandine Tarts, crunchy with almonds and garnished with cherries, can be served either at dinner or at a tea party

Amandine Tarts

dough for one 9-inch pie crust
¼ cup butter
¼ cup sugar
1 egg, beaten
⅓ cup ground almonds
2 tablespoons flour
few drops almond extract
⅓ cup sliced almonds
¼ cup apricot jam
6 candied cherries

1 Preheat the oven to 375°F.

2 On a floured board roll out the dough to ¼ inch thick and line 6 greased and floured tart tins. Bake for 20 minutes, then remove from the oven, leaving the oven on.

3 Meanwhile, cream the butter with the sugar until pale and fluffy. Gradually add the egg. Then beat in

the ground almonds, sifted flour, and flavor with a little almond extract.

4 Fill the half-cooked tart shells with the almond paste. Cover with sliced almonds and return to the oven for 10 minutes or until the dough is cooked.

5 Melt the apricot jam in a pan over low heat, adding a little water if necessary. Top each tart with a cherry and spread with apricot glaze. Cool before serving.

Serves 6

Cherry Meringue Flan

dough for one 10-inch pie crust
1¼ cups pastry cream or very thick custard
2 teaspoons cherry-flavored liqueur

Cherry Meringue Flan is a real party special, with rings of big luscious cherries set in snowy meringue peaks

1 egg white
¼ cup sugar
½ teaspoon vanilla extract
1 lb. canned tart cherries

1 Preheat the oven to 400°F. Roll out the pie crust to ¼ inch thickness and line a buttered 10-inch flan dish. Prick the dough and bake for 20 minutes.

2 Meanwhile, flavor the pastry cream with the liqueur. Spread it over the base of the cooled crust.

3 Beat the egg white until stiff and fold in the sugar. Flavor with vanilla. Put in a decorator's bag and pipe around the flan and in the middle. Arrange the cherries in a double ring on the flan.

4 Return the flan to the oven for 5 minutes so that the meringue is just tinged with gold. Let it cool before serving.

Serves 6–8

Edinburgh Tart

dough for one 8-inch pie crust
¼ cup butter, melted
¼ cup sugar
½ cup chopped candied peel
1 tablespoon raisins
½ cup flour
2 eggs, beaten

1 Preheat the oven to 375°F. Roll out the dough to line an 8-inch flan pan.

2 Mix the butter, sugar, peel, raisins and flour. Stir in the eggs and pour into the pastry shell. Bake for 40 minutes, cool and serve.

Serves 6

651

Pies

Pies are easy to make and can be filled with a variety of fruity fillings. You can use common fruits such as apples, pears and plums, or more exotic tropical fruits such as mangoes and pineapple. Serve a fruit pie with freshly made hot custard or some whipped cream. Pies can be made with either puff or pie crust pastry. For extra special results, try adding some ground almonds or cinnamon to the pie crust mix. The flavor of apple and pear pies is more interesting if you add a pinch of cinnamon and some cloves and serve with Cheddar cheese.

Deep Dish Spicy Apple Pie

4-5 cooking apples
butter
½ teaspoon cinnamon
½ cup brown sugar
4 cloves
grated rind and juice 1 lemon
3 tablespoons water
dough for one 9-inch pie crust
2 teaspoons milk
2 tablespoons sugar

1 Peel, core and thinly slice the apples. Butter a deep pie dish and arrange the apples inside in layers with the cinnamon and brown sugar. Spike some apple slices with the cloves and sprinkle the grated lemon rind and juice over the top. Add the water.

2 Preheat the oven to 400°F. Roll out the dough to the diameter of the pie dish and use to cover the pie. Trim around the edge and seal firmly. Crimp and decorate it if you wish. Make a small incision in the top of the pie with a sharp knife.

3 Brush with milk and sprinkle with sugar. Bake in the oven and reduce the temperature to 350°F. after 10 minutes. Bake for another 20 minutes until the pie is cooked and golden brown. Serve hot or cold, with cream.

Serves 6

Deep Dish Pumpkin Pie

½ lb. pumpkin, peeled and seeded
½ lb. cooking apples, peeled and cored
⅔ cup dried currants
¼ cup chopped mixed peel
1 teaspoon mixed ground clove and cinnamon
butter
¼ cup soft brown sugar
1 tablespoon water
dough for one 9-inch pie crust
1 teaspoon milk
2 tablespoons sugar

1 Cut the pumpkin and apples into cubes and mix with the currants, mixed peel and spice.

2 Butter a deep pie dish and fill with the fruit mixture. Sprinkle on the soft brown sugar and add the water.

3 Preheat the oven to 400°F. Roll out the dough to a large circle, the same diameter as the pie dish. Wet the rim of the dish and cover with the dough. Trim and crimp the edges and make a small hole in the top. Brush with milk and sprinkle with sugar.

4 Bake in the oven for 10 minutes, then reduce the temperature to 350°F. and bake for a further 30 minutes until crisp and golden brown. Serve with whipped cream.

Serves 6

Spiced Date and Pear Pie

¼ lb. butter
1 cup whole wheat flour
½ cup rolled oats
water to mix
butter for greasing
½ cup dates, seeded and chopped
4 dessert pears, peeled, cored and sliced
½ teaspoon cinnamon
grated rind and juice ½ lemon
¼ cup soft brown sugar
1 teaspoon milk
2 tablespoons sugar

1 Rub the butter into the flour and oats with your fingertips. Then mix in enough water to make a stiff pastry dough. Roll out half of the dough on a floured surface and use it to line a 7-inch greased shallow pie dish.

2 Preheat the oven to 425°F.

3 Place the dates, pears, cinnamon, lemon rind, juice and brown sugar inside the pie. Roll out the remaining dough to make a lid. Cover the pie, then trim and crimp the edges. Brush the lid of the pie with milk and sprinkle on the sugar.

4 Bake in the oven for 10 minutes, then reduce the temperature to 375°F. for the remaining 20 minutes. Remove the pie when it is crisp and golden brown. Serve the pie hot with whipped cream or hot custard.

Serves 6

Tips: If fresh pears are not available, you can make this pie using the same weight of drained canned pears. Also, if you prefer plain pastry, you can make it with ordinary white flour instead of whole wheat flour.

Rhubarb Pie

dough for two 9-inch pie crusts
10 sticks rhubarb cut into $\frac{1}{2}$-inch
  pieces
$1\frac{1}{2}$ cups sugar
2 tablespoons butter
grated rind 1 orange
2 tablespoons cornstarch
$\frac{1}{4}$ cup orange juice
$\frac{1}{2}$ teaspoon cinnamon
1 egg yolk
2 tablespoons milk
$\frac{1}{4}$ cup confectioners' sugar

1 Preheat the oven to 400°F. Roll out the dough on a floured board to a thickness of $\frac{1}{4}$ inch. Use half to line the bottom and sides of a 9-inch pie plate.

2 Arrange the rhubarb over the bottom of the dish. Add the sugar, butter and orange rind.

3 Blend the cornstarch with the orange juice and pour it over the other ingredients. Sprinkle with the cinnamon and cover with the second round of dough. Brush the top with the egg yolk mixed with milk and bake the pie in the oven for 30 minutes or until the crust is golden.

4 Dust with the confectioners' sugar and serve.

Serves 6

Rum and Date Pie

$3\frac{1}{3}$ cups flour
$1\frac{1}{4}$ cups butter
$\frac{1}{4}$ cup sugar
1 egg yolk
2 tablespoons cold water
butter
$\frac{1}{2}$ cup chopped dates
$\frac{1}{4}$ cup chopped preserved ginger
2 tablespoons rum

1 Preheat the oven to 400°F. Sift the flour into a bowl. Cut 1 cup of the butter into pieces and rub it into the flour until the mixture resembles fine breadcrumbs. Stir in 2 teaspoons of the sugar. Blend the egg yolk and water together and pour into the flour, mixing quickly to form a firm dough. Turn the dough onto a floured board and knead lightly until it is smooth. Roll out the dough to a thickness of $\frac{1}{4}$ inch.

2 Line a well-buttered pie plate with half the dough and cover it with the dates and ginger.

3 Cream together the remaining butter and sugar and the rum and spread it over the filling.

4 Cover with the remaining dough and bake the pie in the preheated oven for 15 minutes. Reduce the heat to 350°F. and bake for a further 30 minutes.

Serves 6

Orange Raisin Pie

dough for two 8-inch pie crusts
2 cups raisins
2 tablespoons orange juice
2 tablespoons corn syrup
2 tablespoons confectioners' sugar

1 Preheat the oven to 425°F.

2 Roll out the dough on a lightly floured board to a thickness of $\frac{1}{4}$ inch. Use half to line an 8-inch pie plate. Trim the edges.

3 In a bowl blend together the raisins, orange juice and syrup. Spread the mixture evenly over the pie plate. Sprinkle the rims of the plate with a little water and arrange the remaining dough, being careful not to stretch it, over the top. Seal the rims with your fingers and cut off any trimmings.

4 Bake the pie on the middle shelf of the oven for 25-30 minutes. Sprinkle with the confectioner's sugar and serve.

Serves 6

Apple and Blackberry Pie

2-3 cooking apples
$1\frac{1}{2}$ cups blackberries
dough for two 9-inch pie crusts
butter for greasing
$\frac{1}{3}$ cup sugar
1 tablespoon water
beaten egg for glazing

1 Peel, core, quarter and cut the apples into slices. Remove the stalks from the blackberries and wash them thoroughly.

2 Preheat the oven to 400°F.

3 Roll out the dough on a floured board to a thickness of $\frac{1}{4}$ inch. Use half the dough to line a buttered $3\frac{3}{4}$-cup pie dish. Cut off and reserve the trimmings. Cover the base with half the apples and blackberries. Add the sugar and water and then the remaining fruit.

4 Dampen the rim of the pie plate and cover the pie with the remaining dough. Seal and flute the edges. Decorate the top with 5 leaves made from the reserved pastry trimmings and brush it with the beaten egg. Place the dish on a baking sheet and bake it for 10 minutes in the preheated oven. Reduce the heat to 350°F. and cook for a further 30 minutes. If the dough browns too quickly, cover it with foil. Serve hot.

Serves 6–8

Greengage Pie

1⅔ cups flour
pinch salt
3 tablespoons butter
3 tablespoons lard or shortening
2 tablespoons water

For the Filling:
1½ lbs. greengage plums
½ cup sugar
2 tablespoons water
1 teaspoon cinnamon

1 Sift the flour and salt into a bowl. Rub in the butter and lard or shortening until the mixture resembles fine crumbs. Gradually add the water, stirring with a spatula, until the dough starts to stick together. Knead lightly and set aside for 15 minutes.

2 Wash the fruit and remove any pieces of stalk. Arrange them in a large pie dish and sprinkle with the sugar, water and cinnamon.

3 Preheat the oven to 425°F. Roll out the dough to ¼ inch thick, about 1 inch larger in diameter than the pie dish. Cut a strip the width of the dish rim, dampen the rim and stick the strip around. Dampen the strip and lay the rest of the dough across the pie. Cut off any excess and crimp the edges with a fork. Use leftover dough to make leaves to decorate the top.

4 Bake for 15 minutes, then lower the oven heat to 350°F. Bake for 20-30 minutes until the fruit is cooked. Serve hot or cold, with whipped cream.

Serves 6

Greengage Pie would be ideal for Sunday lunch, with its light pastry shell and filling of tender, juicy, hot plums

Exotic Pie

3⅓ cups flour
pinch salt
⅓ cup butter
⅓ cup lard or shortening
1 tablespoon sugar
¼ cup water

For the Filling:
1 cup strawberries
½ lb. litchis
2-lb. pineapple
3 bananas
2 mangoes
juice ½ lemon
¼ cup rum
2 tablespoons brown sugar

1 Sift the flour into a mixing bowl with the salt. Rub in the butter and the lard or shortening to make fine crumbs. Add the sugar. Stir with a knife while adding the water, little by little, until the mixture begins to stick together. Knead lightly to form a smooth dough. Leave it to rest for 15 minutes.

2 Prepare the fruit: wash and hull the strawberries. If using fresh litchis, peel them. Peel the pineapple and remove the dark spots, and cut into cubes. Peel and slice the bananas. Cut the mango flesh into chunks.

3 Preheat the oven to 400°F. Roll out the dough on a floured board to cover a large 9 cup pie dish. Mix the fruits and arrange them in the dish. Sprinkle with the lemon juice, rum and brown sugar. Place the dough over the top, cut off any excess around the sides and crimp the edges. With the point of a sharp knife, cut out a star shape from the middle of the dough. Bake in the oven for 20-25 minutes; serve hot or cold.

Serves 8

Tip: Before serving, pour thick cream through the star-shaped hole into the pie underneath.

Exotic Pie owes its name to the filling of unusual fruits—litchis, pineapple, mango and banana

Raspberry Pie

5 cups raspberries
butter
1 tablespoon cornstarch
¼ cup sugar
pinch nutmeg
few drops almond extract
dough for one 9-inch pie crust
1 teaspoon milk
sugar for dusting

1 Preheat the oven to 400°F. Wash, drain and hull the raspberries. Place them in a deep buttered pie dish and sprinkle the cornstarch between the layers — this will thicken the syrup. Add the sugar, nutmeg and almond extract.

2 Roll out the dough on a floured surface to the diameter of the pie dish. Dampen the edges of the pie dish and cover the top with the dough. Trim and crimp the edges and make a small hole in the top with a sharp knife. Brush with milk.

3 Bake in the oven and, after 10 minutes, reduce the temperature to 350°F. Cook for a further 20 minutes until crisp and golden. Just before serving, dust generously with sugar.

Serves 6

Crusty Plum Pie

butter
1½ lbs. Italian damson plums
½ cup sugar
½ teaspoon cinnamon
1 tablespoon water
dough for one 9-inch pie crust
1 teaspoon milk
sugar for dusting

1 Butter a deep pie dish and preheat the oven to 400°F.

2 Fill the pie dish with the plums, sugar, cinnamon and water.

3 Roll out the pie crust to the diameter of the pie dish. Cover the pie with the dough lid. Trim and crimp the edges, then brush lightly with the milk and dust with sugar.

4 Place in the oven and, after 10 minutes, reduce the temperature to 350°F. Bake for another 20 minutes until crisp and golden. Serve with cream or custard.

Serves 6

Tip: You can always use greengage plums in this pie for an unusual variation — cook them in exactly the same way.

Raspberry Pie is just right for feeding the family — whatever the weather — serve it cold with cream or hot with custard

Index

v